ELDER LAW: READINGS, CASES, AND MATERIALS

THIRD EDITION

ELDER LAW: READINGS, CASES, AND MATERIALS

THIRD EDITION

A. KIMBERLEY DAYTON
Professor of Law
William Mitchell College of Law

MOLLY M. WOOD
Stevens & Brand, L.L.P.
Attorneys at Law
Lawrence, Kansas

JULIA BELIAN
Visiting Associate Professor of Law
University of Missouri-Kansas City
School of Law

Library of Congress Cataloging-in-Publication Data

Dayton, A. Kimberley

Elder law: readings, cases, and materials / A. Kimberley Dayton, Molly M. Wood., Julia Belian —
3rd ed.

    p. cm.

Rev. ed. of: Elder law / A. Kimberley Dayton, Thomas P. Gallanis, Molly M. Wood. 2nd ed. c2003

Includes bibliographical references and index.

ISBN 1-4224-0794-2 (hard cover)

1. Older people — Legal status, laws, etc. — United States. I. Dayton, A. Kimberley. II. Wood,
Molly M. III. Belian, Julia Elder law. IV. Title.

KF390.A4G35 2007

346.7301'3— dc22   2007025902

NOTE TO USERS

**To ensure that you are using the latest materials available in this area,
please be sure to periodically check the LexisNexis Law School web site
for downloadable updates and supplements at www.lexisnexis.com/
lawschool**

Editorial Offices
744 Broad Street, Newark, NJ 07102 (973) 820-2000
201 Mission St., San Francisco, CA 94105-1831 (415) 908-3200
701 East Water Street, Charlottesville, VA 22902-7587 (804) 972-7600
www.lexis.com

(Pub.3532)

DEDICATIONS

For my late grandparents, Dock Ballard, Myrtle Johnson Ballard,
Robert P. Dayton, and Rhoda Yoder Dayton Gross,
Arthur D. and LaVonia B. Dayton
A.K.D.

For my parents, Julia Belle Tucker Wood and Harold Pope Wood, Jr.
M.M.W.

PREFACE TO THE THIRD EDITION

Introduction. This book is designed to serve as the main textbook for courses and seminars on the intersection of law and aging. This area of the law is of rapidly-increasing significance because of the demographic changes affecting the United States and, indeed, the rest of the world. The percentage of Americans aged 65 or older has more than tripled since the beginning of the twentieth century, and this percentage will rise even more as the so-called "Baby Boomers" begin to join the ranks of the elderly. As people age, they often face a bewildering array of legal issues, ranging from age discrimination to retirement planning, from elder abuse to assisted suicide. Legal issues involving the elderly are more and more in the news; in the four years since publication of the second edition Congress has enacted a prescription drug benefit in Medicare and greatly restricted the access of seniors to Medicaid.

Coverage. The chapters in this book explore these topics in a systematic fashion. We begin in Chapters 1 and 2 with a general introduction to the legal and ethical issues facing the elderly and their lawyers. We then turn in Chapter 3 to the problem of age and disability discrimination. Chapter 4 addresses retirement planning and contains material on government programs (such as Social Security and SSI), private pensions, and Individual Retirement Accounts. Some elderly people need help in managing their assets, so Chapter 5 deals with the legal devices designed to assist with property management: powers of attorney, joint ownership, agency accounts, and inter vivos trusts. The second edition's Chapter 6 has been divided into two chapters: Chapter 6 of the third edition addresses guardianship, which can be of the person or of the estate; Chapter 7 concerns elder abuse, which can be physical, emotional, or financial. Chapter 8 then turns to health care, which is a major concern for most older people; the chapter examines the relevant government programs (such as Medicare and Medicaid), the need for Medigap or long-term care insurance, and the use of living wills, powers of attorney, and surrogacy statutes to preserve or delegate medical decisions in the face of incapacity. Chapter 9 then covers issues pertaining to housing, including the regulation of nursing homes and the rise of assisted living facilities. Chapter 10 explores issues surrounding grandparents who are the primary caregivers for their grandchildren. Chapter 11, which we expect will be the last chapter to be covered in the typical semester, addresses end-of-life issues: viatical settlements, anatomical donations, and the right to die. Old Chapter 11, which comprised a summary of estate planning principles, has been deleted.

Division of Responsibility. We have worked largely independently, focusing on our respective areas of expertise. Professor Dayton has supervised the production of the Third Edition and has prepared the introductory chapter and materials on discrimination, guardianship, elder abuse, the end of life, and the new chapter on grandparents as parents (Chapters 1, 3, 6, 7, 10, and 11). Professor Wood has prepared the materials on ethical issues, public benefits, health care, and housing (Chapters 2, 4A, 8A, 8B, and 9). The book's new co-author, Professor Belian, has prepared the materials on pensions and private savings, and property management.

Statutory Supplment. This book of readings is designed to be used with a companion code book, ELDER LAW: STATUTES AND REGULATIONS, Third Edition. Rather than reproduce statutes and regulations in a piecemeal fashion among our readings, we believe that it is better and easier to study legislative materials in a separate volume.

Acknowledgments. First and foremost, we would like to thank Sean Caldwell, Jennifer Beszley, and Don Cambria at LexisNexis for their encouragement and support during the development and execution of this project. For financial support and invaluable library assistance, we would like to thank our respective institutions, the William Mitchell College of Law, the University of Kansas School of Law, and the University of Missouri-Kansas City School of Law. Finally, Professors Dayton and Wood would like to thank all of the students who have been enrolled in the University of Kansas Elder Law Clinic since its inception in Fall 1995; the dedication of these students to their clients has been remarkable.

A. KIMBERLEY DAYTON
Minneapolis, Minnesota
MOLLY M. WOOD
Lawrence, Kansas
JULIA BELIAN
Omaha, Nebraska
July 2007

TABLE OF CONTENTS

Chapter 1

AGING IN AMERICA

> *The senior boom is one of the central challenges of the coming century. . . .*
> *[O]ne of the central worries of my generation is that, as we age, we will*
> *impose unsustainable burdens on our children and undermine their*
> *ability to raise our grandchildren. We must use this time now to do*
> *everything in our power, not only to lift the quality of life and the secu-*
> *rity of the aged and disabled today, and the baby boom aged and dis-*
> *abled, but to make sure that we do not impose that intolerable burden on*
> *our children.*

— President Bill Clinton, January 4, 1999

The phenomenon of "the aging of America" has begun. The first of the post-war "baby boomers" are now in their fifties, and the population of persons over age sixty-five is expected to rise by over 70% between 2010 and 2030. This major demographic shift presents both challenges and opportunities for our society and the legal system. Among the policy challenges suggested by the aging of America are increasing stresses on so-called entitlement programs such as government retirement and health benefit programs, housing and transportation issues stemming from aging-related disabilities that may compromise an older person's ability to remain in a familiar environment without assistance, and a host of ethical problems relating to individual autonomy respecting financial, health care, and end of life issues.

The growth of the senior population has affected profoundly the legal infrastructure. Because of their numbers, older Americans represent a powerful political constituency. The past decade has produced much legislation aimed at addressing the needs of this demographic group. Moreover, the complexity of the socio-legal issues that impact on seniors has spawned an entirely new legal practice specialty known as "elder law." The elder law attorney must be cognizant not simply of such matters as estate planning, wills, and probate, but as well of such varied substantive legal and quasi-legal areas as public benefits (including Social Security, Medicare and Medicaid, and veterans' benefits), employment and retirement law, elder abuse, bioethics, and housing and long-term care. Nor can the elder law attorney expect a practice confined either to state or federal law, for the legal texts that govern this area comprise a complex web of federal, state, and sometimes local regulations.

In this chapter, we offer an overview of the phenomenon of the aging of America and its consequences. Parts A and B include materials that document the "senior boom" about which President Clinton spoke and provide details about its nature, including cultural differences that affect how aging within particular groups of American society is regarded. Part C provides selected examples of social and legal matters that are or will be affected by this boom. Finally, Part D contains readings on the nature and practice of elder law.

A. AGING IN AMERICA: AN OVERVIEW

U.S. Department of Health and Human Services, Administration on Aging
A Profile of Older Americans: 2005
http://aoa.gov/PROF/Statistics/profile/2005/profiles2005.asp

The Older Population

The older population — persons 65 years or older — numbered 36.3 million in 2004 (the most recent year for which data are available). They represented 12.4% of the U.S. population, about one in every eight Americans. The number of older Americans increased by 3.1 million or 9.3% since 1994, compared to an increase of 13.3% for the under-65 population. However, the number of Americans aged 45-64 — who will reach 65 over the next two decades — increased by 39% during this period.

In 2004, there were 21.1 million older women and 15.2 million older men, or a sex ratio of 139 women for every 100 men. The female to male sex ratio increases with age, ranging from 115 for the 65-69 age group to a high of 222 for persons 85 and over.

Since 1900, the percentage of Americans 65+ has tripled (from 4.1% in 1900 to 12.4% in 2004), and the number has increased almost twelve times (from 3.1 million to 36.3 million). The older population itself is getting older. In 2004, the 65-74 age group (18.5 million) was over eight times larger than in 1900, but the 75-84 group (13.0 million) was 17 times larger and the 85+ group (4.9 million) was 39.8 times larger.

In 2003, persons reaching age 65 had an average life expectancy of an additional 18.5 years (19.8 years for females and 16.8 years for males).

A child born in 2003 could expect to live 77.6 years, about 30 years longer than a child born in 1900. Much of this increase occurred because of reduced death rates for children and young adults. However, the period of 1980-2003 also has seen reduced death rates for the population aged 65-84, especially for men — by 32.5% for men aged 65-74 and by 24.8% for men aged 75-84. Life expectancy at age 65 increased by only 2.5 years between 1900 and 1960, but has increased by 4.2 years from 1960 to 2003.

Over 2.0 million persons celebrated their 65th birthday in 2004. In the same year, about 1.8 million persons 65 or older died. Census estimates showed an annual net increase of over 375,000 in the number of persons 65 and over.

There were 64,658 persons aged 100 or more in 2004 (0.18% of the total population). This is a 73% increase from the 1990 figure of 37,306.

Future Growth

The older population will continue to grow significantly in the future (*see* Figure 1). This growth slowed somewhat during the 1990s because of the relatively small number of babies born during the Great Depression of the 1930's. But the older population will burgeon between the years 2010 and 2030 when the "baby boom" generation reaches age 65.

The population 65 and over will increase from 35 million in 2000 to 40 million in 2010 (a 15% increase) and then to 55 million in 2020 (a 36% increase for that decade). By 2030, there will be about 71.5 million older persons, almost twice their number in 2004. People 65+ represented 12.4% of the population in the year 2004 but are expected to grow to be 20% of the population by 2030. The 85+ population is projected to increase from 4.2 million in 2000 to 6.1 million in 2010 (40%) and then to 7.3 million in 2020 (44% for that decade).

Figure 1: Number of Persons 65+, 1900 – 2030 (numbers in millions)

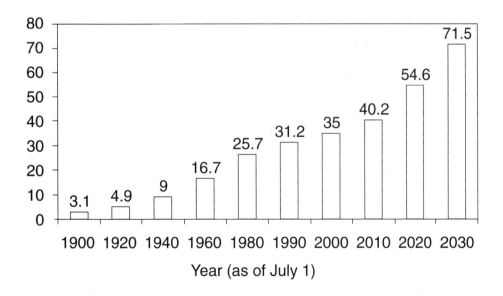

Minority populations are projected to increase from 5.7 million in 2000 (16.4% of the elderly population) to 8.1 million in 2010 (20.1% of the elderly) and then to 12.9 million in 2020 (23.6% of the elderly). Between 2004 and 2030, the white population 65+ is projected to increase by 74% compared with 183% for older minorities, including Hispanics (254%), African-Americans (147%), American Indians, Eskimos, and Aleuts (143%), and Asians and Pacific Islanders (208%).

Marital Status

In 2004, older men were much more likely to be married than older women — 72% of men, 42% of women. Almost half of all older women in 2004 were widows (43%). There were over four times as many widows (8.2 million) as widowers (2.0 million).

Divorced and separated (including married/spouse absent) older persons represented only 10.6% of all older persons in 2004. However, this percentage has increased since 1980, when approximately 5.3% of the older population were divorced or separated/spouse absent.

Living Arrangements

Over half (54.7%) of the older non-institutionalized persons lived with their spouse in 2004. Approximately 10.7 million or 72.4% of older men, and 8.2 million or 41.6% of older women, lived with their spouse. The proportion living with their spouse decreased with age, especially for women. Only 29.2% of women 75+ years old lived with a spouse.

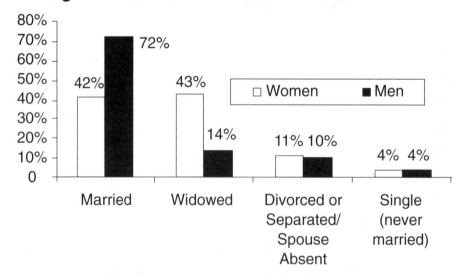

Figure 2: Marital Status of Persons 65+ – 2004

About 30.8% (10.7 million) of all non-institutionalized older persons in 2004 lived alone (7.9 million women, 2.8 million men). They represented 39.7% of older women and 18.8% of older men. The proportion living alone increases with advanced age. Among women aged 75 and over, for example, half (49.9%) lived alone.

About 671,000 grandparents aged 65 or over maintained households in which grandchildren were present in 2004. (Another 231,000 elderly were spouses of such people.) In addition, 618,000 grandparents over 65 years lived in parent-maintained households in which their grandchildren were present. A total of about 1.53 million older people lived in households with a grandchild present in the house. About 415,000 of these grandparents over 65 years old were the persons with primary responsibility for their grandchildren who lived with them.

While a relatively small number (1.56 million) and percentage (4.5%) of the 65+ population lived in nursing homes in 2000, the percentage increases dramatically with age, ranging from 1.1% for persons 65-74 years to 4.7% for persons 75-84 years and 18.2% for persons 85+. In addition, approximately 5% of the elderly lived in self-described senior housing of various types, many of which have supportive services available to their residents.

Racial and Ethnic Composition

In 2004, 18.1% of persons 65+ were minorities — 8.2% were African-Americans. Persons of Hispanic origin (who may be of any race) represented 6.0% of the older population. About 2.9 were Asian or Pacific Islander, and less than 1% were American Indian or Native Alaskan. In addition, 0.6% of persons 65+ identified themselves as being of two or more races.

Only 6.8% of minority race and Hispanic populations were 65+ in 2004 (8.3% of African-Americans, 8.4% of Asians and Pacific Islanders, 7.2% of American Indians and Native Alaskans, 5.2% of Hispanics), compared with 15.0% of whites.

Geographic Distribution

The proportion of the older persons in the population varies considerably by state with some states experiencing much greater growth in their older populations. In 2004, about half (52%) of persons 65+ lived in nine states. California had over 3.8 million; Florida 2.9 million; New York 2.5 million; Texas 2.2 million; and Pennsylvania 1.9 million. Ohio, Illinois, Michigan, and New Jersey each had well over 1 million.

Persons 65+ constituted approximately 14% or more of the total population in 8 states in 2004: Florida (16.8%); West Virginia (15.3%); Pennsylvania (15.3%); North Dakota (14.7%); Iowa (14.7%); Maine (14.4); South Dakota (14.2); and Rhode Island (13.9%). In eight states, the 65+ population increased by 20% or more between 1994 and 2004: Nevada (58.1%); Alaska (47.9%); Arizona (30.9%); New Mexico (26.4%); Colorado (22.2%); Delaware (22.2%); Utah (22.1%); and Idaho (20.9%). The ten jurisdictions with the highest poverty rates for elderly over the period 2002-2004 were Mississippi (17.2%); Arkansas (16.2%); Texas (15.0%); South Carolina (13.9%); the District of Columbia (13.8%); New York (13.6%); Louisiana (13.1%); North Carolina (13.0%); Alabama (12.8%); and New Mexico (12.4%).

Most persons 65+ lived in metropolitan areas in 2003 (77.4%). About 50% of older persons lived in the suburbs, 27.2% lived in central cities, and 22.6% lived in nonmetropolitan areas.

The elderly are less likely to change residence than other age groups. During the year 2004 only 4.4% of older persons moved as opposed to 14.3% of the under 65 population. Most older movers (53.7%) stayed in the same county and 76.0% remained in the same state. Only 24% (of the movers) moved out-of-state. However, five year Census migration data from 1995-2000 show that the 85+ segment of the older population had a higher rate of moving over time. During that five year period, 32.3% of the 85+ population moved (as opposed to 22.8% of the overall 65+ population), 61.1% of them within the same county.

Income

The median income of older persons in 2004 was $21,102 for males and $12,080 for females. Median money income of all households headed by older people rose by 0.3% from 2003 to 2004; however, this difference was not statistically significant. Households containing families headed by persons 65+ reported a median income in 2004 of $35,825 ($37,375 for non-Hispanic Whites, $26,282 for African-Americans, $40,120 for Asians, and $25,179 for Hispanics). About one of every ten (9.9%) family households with an elderly householder had incomes less than $15,000 and 51.5% had incomes of $35,000 or more.

For all older persons reporting income in 2004 (34.2 million), 28.1% reported less than $10,000. Only 27.3% reported $25,000 or more. The median income reported was $15,193.

The major sources of income as reported by older persons in 2003 were Social Security (reported by 90% of older persons), income from assets (reported by 56%), private pensions (reported by 30%), government employee pensions (reported by 14%), and earnings (reported by 23%). In 2003, Social Security benefits accounted for 39% of the aggregate income of the older population. The bulk of the remainder consisted of earnings (25%), asset income (14%), and pensions (19%). For one third of older Americans, Social Security constituted 90% or more of their income.

Poverty

About 3.6 million elderly persons (9.8%) were below the poverty level in 2004. This change in the poverty rate was a statistically significant decrease from the poverty rate in 2003 of 10.2%. The historic lowest level of 9.7% was reached in 1999. Another 2.3 million or 6.7% of the elderly were classified as "near-poor" (income between the poverty level and 125% of this level).

One of every twelve (7.5%) elderly Whites was poor in 2004, compared to 23.9% of elderly African-Americans, 13.6% of Asians, and 18.7% of elderly Hispanics. Higher than average poverty rates in 2003 for older persons were found among those who lived in central cities (13.1%), outside metropolitan areas (i.e. rural areas) (11.0%), and in the South (11.9%).

Older women had a higher poverty rate (12.0%) than older men (7.0%) in 2004. Older persons living alone were much more likely to be poor (17.9%) than were older persons living with families (5.7%). The highest poverty rates (39.9%) were experienced by older Black women and also among Hispanic women who lived alone.

Housing

Of the 21.6 million households headed by older persons in 2003, 80% were owners and 20% were renters. The median family income of older homeowners was $25,353. The median family income of older renters was $13,540. In 2003, 42% of older householders spent more than one-fourth of their income on housing costs — 35% for owners and 76% for renters — .as compared to 41% of all householders.

For homes occupied by older householders in 2003, the median year of construction was 1965 (it was 1971 for all householders) and 5.2% had physical problems. In 2003, the median value of homes owned by older persons was $122,790 (with a median purchase price of $32,905) compared to a median home value of $140,201 for all homeowners. About 72% of older homeowners in 2003 owned their homes free and clear.

Employment

In 2004, 5.0 million (14.4 %) Americans aged 65 and over were in the labor force (working or actively seeking work), including 2.8 million men (19.0%) and 2.2 million women (11.1%). They constituted 3.4% of the U.S. labor force. About 3.6% were unemployed. Labor force participation of men 65+ decreased steadily from 2 of 3 in 1900 to 15.8% in 1985, and has stayed at 16%-18% since then. The participation rate for women 65+ rose slightly from 1 of 12 in 1900 to 10.8% in 1956, fell to 7.3% in 1985, and has been around 8%-10% since 1988.

Education

The educational level of the older population is increasing. Between 1970 and 2004, the percentage who had completed high school rose from 28% to 73%. Almost 19% in 2004 had a bachelor's degree or more. The percentage who had completed high school varied considerably by race and ethnic origin in 2004: 78% of Whites, 65% of Asians and Pacific Islanders, 53% of African-Americans, and 38% of Hispanics. The increase in educational levels is also evident within these groups. In 1970, only 30% of older Whites and 9% of older African-Americans were high school graduates.

Health and Health Care

In 2004, 36.7% of noninstitutionalized older persons assessed their health as excellent or very good (compared to 66.0% for persons aged 18-64). There was little difference between the sexes on this measure, but African-Americans (25.1%), older American Indians/Alaska Natives (28.2%) and older Hispanics (28.6%) were less likely to rate their health as excellent or good than were older Whites (39.6%) or older Asians (34.6%). Most older persons have at least one chronic condition and many have multiple conditions. Among the most frequently occurring conditions of elderly in 2002-2003 were: hypertension (51%), diagnosed arthritis (48%), all types of heart disease (31%), any cancer (21%), diabetes (16.0), and sinusitis (14%).

Almost 65% reported in 2004 that they received an influenza vaccination during the past 12 months and 57% reported that they had ever received a pneumococcal vaccination. About 24% (of persons 60+) report height/weight combinations that place them among the obese. Over 27% of persons aged 65-74 and 16% of persons 75+ report that they engage in regular leisure-time physical activity. Only 9% reported that they are current smokers and only 4% reported excessive alcohol consumption. Only 2.2% reported that they had experienced psychological distress during the past 30 days.

In 2003, over 13.2 million persons aged 65 and older were discharged from short stay hospitals. This is a rate of 3,679 for every 10,000 persons aged 65+ which is more than three times the comparable rate for persons of all ages (which was 1,195 per 10,000). The average length of stay for persons aged 65+ was 5.8 days; the comparable rate for persons of all ages was 4.8 days. The average length of stay for older people has decreased by 5 days since 1980. Older persons averaged more office visits with doctors in 2003 — 5.9 for those aged 65-74 and 7.5 for persons over 75, while persons aged 45-65 averaged only 3.8 office visits during that year. Almost 96% of older persons reported that they did have a usual place to go for medical care and only 2.6% said that they failed to obtain needed medical care during the previous 12 months due to financial barriers.

In 2003, older consumers averaged $3,899 in out-of-pocket health care expenditures, an increase of 46% since 1993. In contrast, the total population spent considerably less, averaging $2,574 in out-of-pocket costs. Older Americans spent 12.5% of their total expenditures on health, more than twice the proportion spent by all consumers (5.9%). Health costs incurred on average by older consumers in 2003 consisted of $2,142 (55%) for insurance, $920 (24%) for drugs, $678 (17%) for medical services, and $158 (4%) for medical supplies.

Health Insurance Coverage

In 2004, almost all (96%) non-institutionalized persons 65+ were covered by Medicare. Medicare covers mostly acute care services and requires beneficiaries to pay part of the cost, leaving about half of health spending to be covered by other sources. About 61% had some type of private health insurance. Over 7% had military-based health insurance and 9% of the non-institutionalized elderly were covered by Medicaid. Less than 1% did not have coverage of some kind. Over 87% of non-institutionalized Medicare beneficiaries in 2002 had some type of supplementary coverage. However, among Medicare beneficiaries residing in nursing homes, almost 58% were covered by Medicaid in 2001.

Disability and Activity Limitations

In 1997, more than half of the older population (54.5%) reported having at least one disability of some type (physical or nonphysical). Some of these disabilities may be relatively minor but others cause people to require assistance to meet important personal needs. Over a third (37.7%) reported at least one severe disability. The percentages with disabilities increase sharply with age. Disability takes a much heavier toll on the very old. Almost three-fourths (73.6%) of those aged 80+ report at least one disability. Over half (57.6%) of those aged 80+ had one or more severe disabilities and 34.9% of the 80+ population reported needing assistance as a result of disability. There is a strong relationship between disability status and reported health status. Among those 65+ with a severe disability, 68.0% reported their health as fair or poor. Among the 65+ persons who reported no disability, only 10.5% reported their health as fair or poor. Presence of a severe disability is also associated with lower income levels and educational attainment.

In another study which focused on the ability to perform specific activities of daily living (ADLs), over 27.3% of community-resident Medicare beneficiaries over age 65 in 1999 had difficulty in performing one or more ADLs and an additional 13.0% reported difficulties with instrumental activities of daily living (IADLs). By contrast, 93.3% of institutionalized Medicare beneficiaries had difficulties with one or more ADLs and 76.3% of them had difficulty with three or more ADLS. [ADLs include bathing, dressing, eating, and getting around the house. IADLs include preparing meals, shopping, managing money, using the telephone, doing housework, and taking medication]. Limitations on activities because of chronic conditions increase with age. . . . a 2003 study shows that the rate of limitations on activities among persons 85 and older are much higher than those for persons 65-74.

It should be noted that (except where noted) the figures above are taken from surveys of the non-institutionalized elderly. Although nursing homes are being increasingly used for short-stay post-acute care, about 1.6 million elderly are in nursing homes (about half are age 85 and over). These individuals often have high needs for care with their ADLs and/or have severe cognitive impairment, due to Alzheimer's disease or other dementias.

Caregiving

About 11% (3.7 million) of older Medicare enrollees received personal care from a paid or unpaid source in 1999. Almost all community resident older persons with chronic disabilities received either informal care (from family or friends) or formal care (from service provider agencies). Over 90% of all these older persons with chronic disabilities received informal care and/or formal care; and about two thirds received only informal care. About 9% of this chronically disabled group received only formal services.

Computer and Internet Access

Among the 23.0 million households where the householder was 65 or older, 8.0 million households (34.7%) had a computer, slightly more than half the figure for the general population (61.8%). Internet access was present in 6.8 million (29.4%) of the elderly households which is 53.7% of the figure for the general population (54.7%). On an individual basis, 13.8 million (40.1%) of the older persons had home computer access and 11.8 million (34.4%) had home Internet access, which is 58.4% of the figure for the general population . . . these figures represent a substantial increase in computer and internet use among older persons in the four years from 2000 to 2003.

Federal Reserve Board
Remarks by Federal Reserve Board
Chairman Alan Greenspan at a Symposium
Sponsored by the Kansas City Federal Reserve Bank
Jackson Hole, Wyoming, August 27, 2004
http://www.federalreserve.gov/BoardDocs/Speeches/2004/
20040827/default.htm

The so-called elderly dependency ratio — the ratio of older adults to younger adults — has been rising in the industrialized world for at least 150 years. The pace of increase slowed greatly with the birth of the baby-boom generation after World War II. But elderly dependency will almost certainly rise more rapidly as that generation reaches retirement age.

The changes projected for the United States are not as dramatic as those projected for other areas — particularly Europe and Japan — but they nonetheless present substantial challenges. The growth rate of the working-age population in the United States is anticipated to slow from about 1 percent per year today to about 1/4 percent per year by 2035. At the same time, the percentage of the population that is over 65 is poised to rise markedly — from about 12 percent today to perhaps 20 percent by 2035.

These anticipated changes in the age structure of the population and work-forces of developed countries are largely a consequence of the decline in fertility that occurred after the birth of the baby-boom generation. The fertility rate in the United States, after peaking in 1957 at about 3-1/2 births over a woman's lifetime, fell to less than 2 by the early 1970s and then rose to about 2.1 by 1990. Since then, the fertility rate has remained close to 2.1, the so-called replacement rate — that is, the level of the fertility rate required to hold the population constant in the absence of immigration or changes in longevity.

Fertility rates in Europe, on the whole, and in Japan have fallen far short of the replacement rate. The decrease in the number of children per family since the end of the baby boom, coupled with increases in life expectancy, has inevitably led to a projected increase in the ratio of elderly to working-age population throughout the developed world.

The populations in most developing countries likewise are expected to have a rising median age but to remain significantly younger and doubtless will grow faster than the populations of the developed countries over the foreseeable future. Eventually, declines in fertility rates and increases in longevity may lead to similar issues with aging populations in what is currently the developing world but likely only well after the demographic transition in the United States and other developed nations.

* * *

The aging of the population in the United States will significantly affect our fiscal situation. Most observers expect Social Security, under existing law, to be in chronic deficit over the long haul; however, the program is largely defined benefit, and so the scale of the necessary adjustments is limited. The shortfalls in the Medicare program, however, will almost surely be much larger and much more difficult to eliminate. Medicare faces financial pressure not only from the changing composition of the population but also from continually increased per recipient demand for medical services. The combination of rapidly advancing medical technologies and our current system of subsidized third-party payments suggests continued rapid growth in demand, though future Medicare costs are admittedly very difficult to forecast.

Although the sustainability of fiscal initiatives is generally evaluated for convenience in financial terms, sustainability rests, at root, on the level of real resources available to an economy. The resources available to fund the sum of future retirement benefits and the real incomes of the employed will depend, of course, on the growth rate of labor employed plus the growth rate of the productivity of that labor.

The growth rate of the U.S. working-age population is expected to decline substantially over the next two decades and to remain low thereafter. But the fraction of that population that is employed will almost surely be affected by changes in the economic returns to working and, especially for older workers, improvements in health.

Americans are not only living longer but also generally living healthier. Rates of disability for those over 65 years of age have been declining even as the average age of the above-65 population is increasing. This decline in disability rates reflects both improvements in health and changes in technology that accommodate the physical impairments associated with aging. In addition, work is becoming less physically strenuous but more demanding intellectually, continuing a century-long trend toward a more-conceptual and less-physical economic output. For example, in 1900, agricultural and manual laborers composed about three-quarters of the workforce. By 1950, those types of workers accounted for one-half of the workforce, and though still critical to a significant part of our economic value-added, today compose only about one-quarter of our workforce.

To date, however, despite the improving feasibility of work at older ages, Americans have been retiring at younger ages. But rising pressures on retirement incomes and a growing scarcity of experienced labor could eventually reverse that trend.

Of course, immigration, if we choose to expand it, could also lessen the decline of labor force growth in the United States. As the influx of foreign workers that occurred in response to the tight labor markets of the 1990s demonstrated, U.S. immigration does respond to evolving economic conditions. But to fully offset the effects of the decline in fertility, immigration would have to be much larger than almost all current projections assume.

QUESTIONS

1. Why is it important to discuss the aging of Americans in terms of "elderly dependency ratios" as well is in terms of absolute increases in that population? To what extent might predictions about the elderly dependency ratio be

affected by (1) an increase in the number of persons 65+ who continue working full or part-time and (2) future immigration patterns?

2. Of what significance is the fact that as age increases, the percentage of women in a particular age group climbs?

3. How might race, gender, and ethnicity affect the development of legal and social remedies for the particular problems faced by seniors?

4. States and the federal government are increasingly delivering information of importance to seniors exclusively on the Web. Given the statistics discussed above, does this practice make sense?

5. By the year 2025, and for the first time in history, more than half of the voting-age population in the United States will be age 50 or older. In what ways might this demographic shift affect the allocation of public and private resources across generations?

B. INTERDISCIPLINARY ASPECTS OF AGING

Excerpts from the Written Testimony of
Robert N. Butler, M.D. Before the U.S. Senate
Special Committee on Aging
Washington D.C., September 4th, 2002
http://frwebgate.access.gpo.gov/cgi-bin/getdoc.cgi?dbname=107_
senate_hearings&docid=f:83476.wais

The term "ageism" was introduced in 1968 and is now a part of the English language. Ageism can be defined as a systematic stereotyping of and discrimination against people simply because they are old, just as racism and sexism accomplish this with skin color and gender. I originally coined the term ageism in 1968 as chairman of the Washington D.C. Advisory Committee on Aging. During an interview with the Washington Post, I used the term to describe the stormy opposition to the purchasing of public housing for older people in Northwest Washington D.C. The causes of the neighborhood's negativism could have been mixed, for many of the future tenants were not only old, but also black and poor. But in this instance, I thought it was more a function of ageism than racism, since similar opposition to housing had arisen on other occasions in which race and socio-economic status were not factors. Indeed, neighbors spoke openly and negatively about old people cluttering the streets and stores. The best way to describe this reaction was ageism. The underlying basis of ageism is the dread and fear of growing older, becoming ill and dependent, and approaching death. This leads to denial and ambivalence. The young dread aging and the old may envy youth. Behind ageism is a corrosive narcissism, the inability to accept our fate. Ageism is manifested in a wide range of phenomena, on both individual and institutional levels — stereotypes and myths, outright disdain and dislike, simple subtle avoidance of contact, discriminatory practices in housing, employment, and services of all kinds, and of course elder abuse.

I understand this hearing is focused in particular on images of aging in media and marketing, in which ageism certainly exists. Older persons are often stereotyped in print and on television as feeble, ineffective, helpless, and irrelevant. They are robbed of dignity by the words and cartoons used to portray them. It is time to change the language and imagery of old age in the media. We must challenge the advertising, news, and entertainment industries to end ageist stereotypes and alter the climate toward older persons in a positive manner. . . . Our society needs to change the erroneous and hurtful images such as "geezer" to truer images of older people who are active, flexible, relevant, culturally involved, and an increasingly important segment of our society. Ageism should be considered a psycho-social disease, one that can be addressed. As we all know, it is increasingly within our power to intervene directly in the physical realm of older persons (*i.e.*, age-related disorders) with prevention, treatment, and rehabilitation.

However, it is *also* within our power to intervene in the social, cultural, economic, and political realms influencing the lives of older persons. If, however, we fail to alter negative imagery, language, stereotypes, myths, and distortions concerning aging and the aged in society, our ability to exercise these new possibilities will remain sharply curtailed. Fortunately, we can treat the psychosocial disease called "ageism" — those ambivalent and negative attitudes and practices that lead to hatred, discrimination, abuse, and even murder of the aged — by working to transform our cultural sensibility and through legislative initiatives. But until we effectively do so, ageism will remain, despite the fact that prejudice against age is basically a prejudice against everyone. We all chance to become its ultimate victims as longevity increases. In order to treat this societal and personal disease, we first need to realize what is really true about older persons: The antidote to ageism is knowledge. One myth is that all old people are senile and debilitated. But senility is not inevitable with age; rather, it is a function of a variety of brain diseases, most notably Alzheimer's disease and multi-infarct or vascular dementia. There is a clear distinction between aging and diseases that occur in old age. Unfortunately, there may always be some residual ageism resulting from discomfort and distaste for age and its disabilities. Some profound and common disorders of old age — mobility problems, dementia, and incontinence — are unattractive and provoke disgust and fear.

There is also the myth that old people are affluent. An examination of income data, however, reveals that our nation's older people are not a particularly wealthy segment of the population. Although there are pockets of wealth, about 70 percent of older households have an annual income below $35,000 and almost 30 percent have an income of between $10,000 and $20,000. In addition, older women and minorities have very high rates of poverty, around 20 percent. It should be noted that the Census Bureau uses a different income threshold to calculate poverty among older people, with the result being that older people must be poorer to be officially counted as poor. This too is ageist, in that it assumes older people can and should get by on less.

If we are to fight ageism, older persons themselves need to be productive and develop a philosophy of responsible aging. For many of us retirement must be marked by a new kind of responsible aging. Through paid and unpaid work, people must continue to contribute to society, and they must be encouraged to do so. A strong enforcement of the laws to ban age discrimination in employment will help in this regard. The simple ability of older people to have some control over their own lives helps dispel myths that the older population is unproductive, depressed, disengaged, inflexible, sexless, and senile. This is also beneficial to their own health and well-being, as highlighted by one of today's other witnesses, Dr. Levy. Of course, given the recent events involving individual retirement accounts, the need to protect and promote older workers is important for reasons of financial security as well.

Another key intervention against ageism follows the recognition that older people themselves are a market, an economic power. Japan has the most rapidly growing population of older persons in the world, as well as the highest life expectancy. As a result, it has created a new industry of goods and services geared towards older persons called the silver industries. There is a lot of "gold in geriatrics," as *The Wall Street Journal* once wrote, when one considers capitalism as a vital connection between producers and consumers. Thus, the so-called high cost of health and social services produces jobs and consumption. Looked at another way, the health care industry is the second largest producer of jobs and makes a significant contribution to the gross domestic product.

A continued heavy investment in biomedical, behavioral, and social research is another important intervention to address the roots of ageism. Through research on the biological processes associated with aging, as well as on diseases commonly associated with older people like Alzheimer's disease, we can gain freedom from senility and enhanced independence, which will combat negative perceptions of aging.

It is also important to address the ageism that is rooted in medical schools and pervades the medical system. In fact, it is there that a medical student may first became conscious of the medical profession's prejudice toward age, where he or she may first hear the term "crock" — originally applied to patients with no apparent organic basis for disease and thought to be hypochondriacal. The epithet is predominantly applied to middle-aged women and older people. Other terms in this cruel lexicon exist as well and may be applied to other unwelcome patients: "gomer" ("get out of my emergency room"); gork ("God only really knows" the basis of this person's many symptoms), "vegetable," and "geek." Worst of all are "dirt ball" and SPOS ("semi-human or sub-human piece of s***"). Medical ageism also includes a not-so-benign neglect, such as declarations by physicians like "what do you expect at your age" or such injunctions as "take it easy" — which is generally bad advice. Between 1955 and 1966, Morris Rocklin, a volunteer in the NIMH Human Aging Study, was studied until he was 101 years of age. Rocklin complained about his painful right knee to his physician who said, "What do you expect at your age?"

To this typical statement by a physician, Rocklin replied indignantly, "So why doesn't my left leg hurt?" These common occurrences can be addressed by ensuring that all medical students receive appropriate education and training in geriatrics, so that they better understand the diverse health needs of older people and how to relate to them. Most difficult of all, our nation must alter our deep-seated fear, our shunned responsibility, and harmful avoidance and denial of age. Our conscience should be burdened by our obligations to those who have gone before us. Strict legislation and enforcement against age discrimination and elder abuse are essential but insufficient. We must change how we think, feel, and behave about late life. We must help people deal with their fears of aging, dependency and death. We must have a sense of the life course as a whole. Our family life, our educational system and our media must help transform our sensibility, and moral values held by each of us must drive this transformation of the culture and experience of aging in America, and beyond. We are in the midst of a wonderful new world of longevity. It is in our power to make it a celebration. Thank you very much. I am happy to answer any questions you may have.

National Institute on Aging
Portfolio for Progress
Behavioral and Social Aspects of Aging (2002)

Personal behavior and lifestyle choices — whether or not we smoke, or exercise, or take prescribed medicines, even our individual personalities — make a major difference in health and well-being in later life. Society's decisions about such things as access to health care or pension and retirement policy also significantly impact how we age. As the power of these influences, along with the effects of education and wealth, are more evident, behavioral and social research has become an energized area of study. From large national surveys of population trends to research delving into how individuals approach their own aging, behavioral and social research provides intriguing and useful insights into ourselves and the world around us. Armed with such knowledge, scientists seek to inform social policy and develop interventions for improved health.

The interplay among health, behavior, and socioeconomic factors is a particular focus of NIA's [National Institute on Aging] nationwide Health and Retirement Study (HRS). In the mid-1980s, Dr. Richard Suzman, now NIA Associate Director, Behavioral and Social Research Program, joined by a small group of other leading experts in health and economics, began to realize that research on retirement and on health essentially treated these two aspects of aging as if they had nothing to do with each other. Dr. Suzman and his colleagues thought of retirement as a process well beyond simply collecting a pension or Social Security. "It was very clear to us that more needed to be known about the dynamics preceding and during retirement, especially the interrelationships of health, disability, economics, work, and family," he says.

After much discussion and careful design, in 1992, the HRS, one of the largest and most innovative surveys ever conducted in the U.S. on health and retirement, began interviewing participants. Today, the study is conducted by the University of Michigan's Institute for Social Research, which every 2 years surveys about 20,000 Americans age 51 and older about work, health status, disability, pensions and retirement, family relationships, community activities, and other selected aspects of aging.

Scientists are now mining the rich fields of data provided by the HRS. The study has helped define the relationship between health and wealth, suggesting that, throughout life, the dynamic appears to cut both ways — wealth influences health, but poor health also affects the accumulation or loss of wealth in later years. Surprisingly, the HRS findings indicate that a significant percentage of older people support their adult children financially and in other ways, such as caring for grandchildren, challenging the common view of a dependent elderly population. The HRS also hints that employers and pension planners might want to rethink the transition into retirement: about half of people nearing retirement say they would prefer to phase out of the workplace, rather than to quit "cold turkey," as is often the case today.

Over the next few years, the HRS is expected to address a number of significant questions. How well, for instance, are the so-called "baby boomers" prepared for retirement? How will changes in Social Security, Medicare, and Medicaid affect older Americans and their families? What impact will the high rate of divorce in recent years have on pensions and, equally important, on care-giving in later life? "I believe the HRS can play a central role in telling the story of the aging baby boom," says Dr. Suzman. He points out that some other developed countries are now using the HRS as a model for studies of their aging populations as well.

The NIA plays a leading role in funding a variety of major demographic studies and in assuring that national surveys related to aging, health, and retirement are technically sound and useful to the public and policy makers. In 1994, NIA established its Centers on the Demography of Aging at research institutions around the country to improve the quality and relevance of demographic research on health, economics, and population aging. In 2001, NIA supported 11 such centers, each characterized by its own focus or specialization.

In the mid-1980s, NIA helped found the Federal Interagency Forum on Aging-Related Statistics. The Forum works closely with the Bureau of the Census, the National Center for Health Statistics, and other Federal statistical agencies on the quality, collection, and confidentiality of data on older people from government-supported studies.

In July 2000, the Forum published its first status report on aging in America, *Older Americans 2000: Key Indicators of Well-Being*. Based on a review of more than a dozen national data sets, it found that while there is good news about gains in health and wealth among older people, a large proportion of the older population, including many racial and ethnic minorities, still face disability, chronic health problems, and economic stress.

NIA's support of behavioral, psychological, and social research casts a very wide net, as it examines everything from personality to populations. This research looks at the spectrum of possible influences on longevity, health, and behavior, including potential biological and genetic factors that may play a role. A few areas of growing interest are highlighted here — the role that personality and attitudes might play in late-life health, including cognition, and how public health might be improved with greater understanding of individual health behaviors and of the changing patterns of health and mortality.

On the most individual level, can personality and outlook affect your risk of disease or death? Studies of personality suggest that it can. Led by Dr. Paul T. Costa, Jr., chief of the NIA's Laboratory of Personality and Cognition, NIA's researchers have developed a model to provide a way to characterize personality, examine its effects, and measure possible personality-specific interventions against disease and disability. This Five-Factor Model is a comprehensive characterization of five key dimensions — neuroticism, extraversion, openness, agreeableness, and conscientiousness. For example, new data from the Five-Factor Model questionnaire identify several dimensions of personality associated with success or failure to achieve adequate compliance with a drug regimen. In a specific case, studies are now underway to measure personality traits that are linked to complying with anti-retroviral therapies for HIV/AIDS. "By identifying individuals whose questionnaire responses show they are prone to experience stress and have poor self-discipline, we can target these patients for special interventions," says Dr. Costa.

It is also important to obtain information on personality from older people unable to respond to questionnaires, such as those with dementia. New tools developed by scientists at the NIA's laboratory open a window for scientists to assess the previously unmeasured impact of dementing disorders on personality. This "observer-rating" form of the Five-Factor Model questionnaire has been used in a number of studies in the U.S. and Europe to look at patients with Alzheimer's disease (AD), Parkinson's disease, and traumatic brain injury. Information from caregivers and family members show that patients with these diseases undergo significant changes in personality. In AD, for example, personality changes reflect diminished capacity for organization, punctuality, dependability, goal-setting, and planning. Ongoing studies will attempt to determine the ordering of these personality changes, whether they occur before the disease becomes evident or whether they follow memory changes. Scientists are also hoping to determine if personality changes might be an early marker for the start of special interventions or treatment for dementia.

It may be that how we look at life can affect how we age. A study of 1,002 disabled women aged 65 and older participating in the NIA-sponsored Women's Health and Aging Study found that "emotional vitality," that is, a sense of personal mastery, being happy, and having low anxiety and depression, is linked with reduced risk of further disability and even death. Recent findings from the Nun Study, a longitudinal survey of older Catholic Sisters, found a strong relationship between positive emotions expressed in early life writings and reduced risk of death in their 80s and 90s. In the study, handwritten biographies written by 180 nuns in their 20s were evaluated for positive emotional content and then were related to survival. This growing body of research suggests that we might press beyond looking at depression and other aspects of emotional dysfunction to study the role that positive emotions may play in health and longevity.

Researchers are also looking at how social and behavioral factors might affect cognition. According to a number of studies, cognitive ability — the process of thinking, learning, and remembering — can decline with age. This is of concern because cognitive skills are critically important in allowing older people to maintain their vitality and independence.

Social and behavioral influences on cognition may be considerable, according to current research. In one study, older adults were exposed, without being directly aware of it, to both positive and negative stereotypes about aging. Researchers created scenarios using words such as "wise" or "senile," for example, and then tested participants immediately on a variety of measures. On both cognitive tests and physiological measurements, older adults exposed to negative stereotypes about aging performed poorly when compared with those exposed to positive stereotypes. Researchers are now looking at ways to further test the study's findings that link negative age stereotypes to measurable health risk. They also suggest that the reverse may be true — positive self-images of aging might be employed to improve health, including cognitive performance. Maintaining close social relationships as we age may also relate to cognition. Studies are beginning to indicate that these relationships may help protect against declines in cognitive and physical function as well as positively affect longevity.

As scientists continue to examine what may threaten cognitive function in later life, NIA supports testing of potential interventions to maintain it. The ACTIVE (Advanced Cognitive Training for Independent and Vital Elderly) initiative is an ongoing multi-site study in which more than 2,800 older adults receive training in skills related to memory, reasoning, and speed-of-processing. Participants will be tested over time to see if the training helps to maintain function or postpone cognitive decline.

* * *

Behavioral medicine deals with how people develop and maintain behaviors affecting health and illness. It examines the choices we make, almost daily, in lifestyle practices, managing ourselves medically, and, when we have to, coping with chronic disease or disability.

Because of their proven positive benefits on health, well-being, and longevity, physical activity and exercise are a major focus of study. An alarming 75 percent of older Americans do not engage in at least 30 minutes of physical activity a day, as national health guidelines suggest, and public health officials and advocates are in search of ways to turn that sedentary trend around. A key question for research: Once a couch potato always a couch potato? The answer is no, according to new studies in this area. Health behaviors can change at any age. In one test, researchers used a behaviorally based approach at an existing community program. Participants explored their reasons for not exercising and then drew up personal plans for increasing physical activity. Personal attention and telephone calls from staff, plus an informational meeting, were found to help motivate the participants to achieve their goals. One year later, physical activity in the group had increased by an average of 487 calories per week with exercises of moderate intensity, the equivalent of adding five brisk 1-mile walks per week. After 2 years, the exercisers were still burning an average of 445 more calories a week compared with levels before the start of the program.

Even disabled people can turn their activity levels around. A clinical trial involving more than 200 sedentary, disabled older people, ages 60 through 94, tested a home-based strength training program. The program started out with a home visit in which exercisers viewed a motivational tape on the benefits of exercise and potential obstacles to exercise, they set goals and received exercise instruction on how to use elastic bands for strength training. A second, reinforcing home visit 3 weeks later was followed up by an average of 7-8 phone calls between the exercise group and health professionals over the 26 weeks of the study. At the end of 6 months, a high proportion of the older people — some 78 percent — stuck with the exercise program. In this group, function greatly improved and overall disability declined by about 18 percent. This study is one of several conducted at the NIA-supported Edward R. Roybal Centers for Research on Applied Gerontology. The Centers are designed to move promising social and behavioral research findings in a number of areas — exercise, computer skills, driving ability, care-giving, nursing home care — out of the laboratory and into programs that can help improve the lives of older people and their families.

One way older people may also be able to exert more control over their own health is through improved communication with physicians and other clinicians. Research by scientists supported by NIA, as well as the pharmaceutical industry, is trying to open a window into what happens in the doctor's office when it comes to discussing medications. One recent study of communications about over-the-counter (OTC) medications followed 414 patients of 27 doctors. Some 58 percent of the patients in the survey said they discussed the use of these types of medications with their physicians. Doctors asked about OTC use in only 37 percent of the patients' visits. Researchers suggest that more might be done on both sides to encourage discussion about OTC medications so that patients can become more active partners in the management of their medicines.

* * *

As research continues to explore the role that individual capabilities and attitudes play in health and age, it is critical to understand population issues as well. Each of us is part of a larger world of public and social institutions — the health care system, Federal, state, and local government, and other private and public agencies — that can have a direct affect on aging, health, and retirement.

As the population ages, the ability to characterize demographic trends and understand what is behind them will become increasingly important. A number of studies are underway that should help inform policy makers and others in addressing the aging of society.

A most basic question, of course, is how long will we live. As biologists and geneticists search for the molecular and cellular secrets of aging, population studies by NIA-supported demographers provide new and compelling evidence that median life span in industrialized countries is increasing, and at an accelerated rate. A recent examination of Swedish national demographic data from 1861 through 1999, provides the longest available series of reliable information on extreme old age in the world. The data show that the maximum age at death during the time studied rose from 101 to 108. Before 1969, the pace of the increase was .44 years per decade; it accelerated to 1.1 years per decade after 1969. According to researchers, reductions in death rates at older ages are responsible for the increase in life span in Sweden and in other industrialized countries over the last few years. These trends, they say, seem likely to continue and may gradually extend the limits of human longevity even further.

While we are living longer, we are also living better. Researchers were surprised by recent studies finding that, at the same time longevity was increasing in the U.S., disability rates among older Americans were declining. Since these analyses of data from the National Long-Term Care Survey were first presented in the early 1990s, the reduction in the rate of disability has accelerated, suggesting that older people in the U.S. are functioning better than they have in more than a decade. This is true even for the most vulnerable among us, people aged 85 and older. In fact, the most recent findings from this research suggest that the reduction in disability may even be keeping older people out of nursing homes. From 1992 through 1999, the study showed a 22 percent drop — some 200,000 people — in the number of people in nursing homes, a finding that has broad implications for how society might address a possible increase in the need for long-term or nursing home care as the baby boom ages. "The challenge now," says Dr. Suzman, "is to find ways to maintain or even improve the trends in disability amid a steep rise in the number and proportion of older people."

Administration on Aging
The Many Faces of Aging:
Serving Our Hispanic American Elders
http://aoa.gov/press/fact/pdf/HISPANIC.pdf

The Hispanic American population is living longer, growing older, and becoming more diverse. The older Hispanic population is one of the fastest growing groups in the nation. In 1990, 5.1 percent of the Hispanic population was 65 or older. Demographers expect that this number will reach 14.1 percent by 2020. These changing demographics have begun to result in an increase in culturally appropriate programs and services responsive to the diverse needs of older Hispanic American adults and their families. The Hispanic elderly population will be the second most rapidly growing segment between 1990 and 2020.

Diversity of Hispanic Elders

Its many distinct ethnic groups exemplify the racial and ethnic diversity of the Hispanic American population. Members of these groups have unique languages, cultures, and religions and are diverse in terms of education levels and socioeconomic status. Among Hispanic elders living in the United States, nearly 49 percent are of Mexican descent, 15 percent are of Cuban descent, 12 percent are of Puerto Rican descent, and 25 percent are of other Hispanic heritage.

Health and Chronic Illnesses

The leading disease-related causes of death for Hispanic Americans include heart disease, cancer, HIV infection, cerebrovascular diseases, pneumonia, influenza, and diabetes. While the Medicare program covers vaccinations to prevent pneumonia, only 15 percent of Hispanic Americans ages 65 or older receive an annual vaccination. AoA [Administration on Aging] is working to end health disparities among older members of racial and ethnic minority populations as part of the Department of Health and Human Services initiative, "Racial and Ethnic Approaches to Community Health 2010." In 2000, AoA awarded a demonstration grant to the Latino Education Project, Inc. of Corpus Christi, Texas, to develop culturally sensitive community-based health promotion and disease prevention programs and to educate older Latinos in the Coastal Bend area of South Texas about the impact and prevention of cardiovascular disease and late onset diabetes. The Latino Education Project also:

- Identifies culturally appropriate prevention activities;
- Encourages the adoption of healthy lifestyles that acknowledge and integrate appropriate cultural practices and diets; and
- Increases access to medical and health interventions.

Hispanic Americans and Family Caregiving

Twenty-seven percent of Hispanic American households provide informal caregiving to a friend or relative. The typical Hispanic caregiver is a 40-year-old female. More than half of all Hispanic caregivers also have a child age 18 or younger living at home.

Older Hispanic Americans and Poverty

Many older Hispanic American adults are immigrants with limited English language skills, who worked in low-paying jobs that did not provide retirement benefits. This contributed to the fact that 24 percent of Hispanic elders live below the poverty level — more than double the rate of older white, non-Hispanic adults who live in poverty.

Education

On average, older Hispanic American adults have less formal education than the older American population overall. Nearly 60 percent of Hispanic elders have less than a ninth grade education compared to 19.4 percent of older adults nationwide. Sixteen percent have a high school diploma compared to almost 34 percent of elders nationwide. Three percent of Hispanic elders have a bachelor's degree compared to almost 9 percent nationwide.

AoA Encourages Hispanic American Communities to Get Involved

Hispanic communities are encouraged to take a lead role and actively participate in developing state and local plans that affect Hispanic elders. Groups that represent Hispanic elders, their families and service providers are invited to voice concerns and needs during the public hearing process. Under Section 297(8) of the Older Americans Act, state agencies must show their effectiveness in reaching older individuals with the greatest economic and social need, paying particular attention to low-income minority individuals. The state agency will ask people and organizations that know of the needs and concerns of low-income minority older individuals to share their concerns and experiences during the public hearing process.

New York State Office for the Aging
Project 2015
The Future of Aging in New York State
Brief: Lesbian and Gay Issues
http://www.aging.state.ny.us/explore/project2015/briefs03.htm[*]

Introduction

Even as we enter the 21st century, Lesbian, Gay, Bisexual and Transgender (LGBT) subjects remain particularly controversial. According to the American Psychoanalytic Association, homophobia is our society's last permissible prejudice. Such societal attitudes must be recognized before aging professionals can appreciate the environment in which lesbian and gay seniors lived most of their lives. Present LGBT seniors were largely rejected by their biological families, called sinners by their religious institutions, unjustly fired from their jobs, criminalized by selective use of archaic laws, and pathologized by mental health professionals. Even though some of such stigmatization is now changing, the result is a severely scarred current generation of elders. They have internalized homophobia and have learned secrecy for survival. For example: a) Would a lesbian participating in her senior center reminiscence group feel free to admit that she dreads the holidays because she always has to choose between spending them with her life partner or her brother and sister who reject her partnered relationship? b) Would a gay man, facing a terminal condition and trying to protect joint property for his partner of 35 years, be open with Legal Services for the Elderly? c) In working with an EISEP aide would an elderly lesbian feel safe from ridicule or ill treatment (even in her own home) if her true identity were discovered? Indeed, training for service professionals in the field of aging includes little, if anything, about the background and problems of the LGBT community.

Based on the 1990 census, a conservative estimate is 150,000 to 300,000 LGBT seniors residing in New York State. Yet, there are only five programs targeted specifically to this population in all of New York State, four in New York City and one just emerging in Syracuse. Four of these, Sage, NYC, Sage/Queens, Griot Circle, and Sage Upstate provide a meeting place for social activities and a variety of social services, while Pride Senior Network focuses on education and advocacy. Demand for all services already exceeds their capacities. Although the FY '99 NY State budget included a groundbreaking $1 million for lesbian and gay health and human services (non-HIV related), no funds were awarded for LGBT senior services. The distribution of the $2 million allocated for FY'00 has not yet been determined.

---

[*] Reprinted with permission of the New York State Office on Aging.

Additional stressors for these seniors include the fact that their lifetime relationships can put them at financial risk. They receive no social security survivorship benefits, private pension survivorship assistance, rarely family health insurance coverage, family leave coverage, tax advantages, or the same inheritance or property and visitation rights automatically assured under espousal or birth family definitions. While isolation is often a problem for seniors in general, 66% of LGBT seniors live alone as compared to 26% in the general senior population. Interestingly, there are few such statistics available since fear of disclosure results in a less than accurate account of older gays and their characteristics.

The Future

The present generation of closeted LGBT seniors who will be living longer and becoming increasingly frail, will require more formal and informal caregiving. Some of the barriers to such support faced by the gay population are apparent in a recently published report by the Brookdale Center on Aging of Hunter College.

Their data indicated that less than one in five elderly LGBT respondents reported living with a life partner whereas nearly half of the general elderly population reported being currently married. It further shows that nearly 90% of gays/lesbians sampled have no children whereas only 20% of the general senior population are without children. Losses from HIV/AIDS have also thinned the ranks of potential caregivers. Clearly the LGBT senior population will be deprived of an adequate informal caregiving structure unless creative interventions can be mounted within the coming decades. In terms of the more formalized caregiving structures such as home care agencies, assisted living facilities and nursing homes, the persistence of negative societal attitudes and uninformed aging service providers would continue to deprive LGBT elderly of safe, meaningful and respectful care.

LGBT Boomers are now beginning to face their own aging process as well as their roles as possible caregivers for partners, parents, friends and families (both biological and chosen). They can be expected to bring to the public arena a generally more self-accepting attitude, with greater expectations for open LGBT affirmative services and programs. While some areas of New York State and particular environments, i.e., certain religions and national cultures, may continue to be repressive for older lesbians and gays, a large percentage of the senior Boomer generation will not tolerate a "don't ask; don't tell" environment and press for more responsive public policy.

Options

As long as sexual orientation and gender identity remain a way of separating people out, of causing isolation, and closing ones eyes to the uniqueness and needs of a particular population, claims to support the diversity of New Yorkers are untrue. To encourage a more inclusive climate and meet the needs of this population, we urge the following:

TRAINING

Lesbian and gay issues to be a required part of training for any state supported programs providing services and oversight for the elderly. Curriculums should include: 1. An awareness of homophobia and its devastating consequences; 2. Factors that have shaped the lives of gay seniors, their needs, their unique family configurations; 3. How to create safe and welcoming service environments for gay clients; 4 . Legal, financial, and sociological barriers in accessing appropriate services; and 5. Information on accessing resources offered by the lesbian and gay community. These have not been included in requirements for diversity and cultural competency, and while organizations like Pride Senior Network offer training for the aging services system, the need is far greater then their present capacities.

FUND LGBT SPECIFIC PROGRAMS AND SERVICES

Considering that there will be a portion of seniors who, still out of fear of disclosing their sexual orientation, will access only gay services and will not be served otherwise, make adequate funds available for the creation and support of programs tailored accordingly. These might include case management, social programs, ombudsman, elder abuse, telephone reassurance, friendly visiting, adult day services, caregiver training, respite, and enriched housing.

ENCOURAGE RESEARCH

Establish research initiatives able to reach and track a more representative sample of older gays, their caregivers and their needs. NYSOFA can partner with major universities and LGBT community based organizations. NYSOFA might also incorporate information on partnering and living situations in their intake and assessment forms. This will give an opportunity to clients to volunteer information such as being "Partnered" as a choice along with "Married," "Single," "Widowed," and "Divorced."

SUPPORT LEGISLATION TO END DISCRIMINATION

- Include sexual orientation in all anti-discrimination policies protecting employment, public housing and the access and delivery of services. The vulnerable gay senior population must be assured protection against ridicule, neglect or harassment in health care facilities, public housing, senior centers, etc., and LGBT staff working in the aging services system should be free to "come out" on the job and offer their special experience in helping LBGT clients.

- Include sexual orientation in hate crime bills to send a clear message that violence against any individual or groups will not be tolerated.

- Provide the same legal and financial safety nets for all New Yorkers by giving legal recognition to gay and lesbian families. This will help assure equality in retirement benefits, insurance coverage, inheritance rights, nursing home regulations, health care decisions, and hospital visitation rights to name a few.

The interdependence of all these issues will profoundly affect the health and welfare of New York's diverse population as it ages through the 21st century.

QUESTIONS

1. Given the nature of the aging process, should lawyers who wish to practice elder law be encouraged or required to educate themselves in such areas as the biology, sociology, and psychology of aging?

2. How can an attorney working with older clients avoid "ageism"?

3. How might different cultural perceptions of aging affect the lawyer-client relationship?

4. Do policymakers regularly take account of social and cultural differences among different sub-groups of elders? Should they?

C. SOCIAL POLICY AND AGING: SELECTED ISSUES

1. Crime and Fraud

U.S. Department of Justice
Office of Justice Programs
Elder Crime and Victimization
http://www.ojp.usdoj.gov/ovc/ncvrw/2005/pg5h.html

During the 2002-2003 period, there was a 22.6 percent decrease in violent crimes against persons aged 65 or older. Victimization rates for violent crime were 2.7 per 1,000 persons aged 65 or older, down from 3.5 per 1,000 persons in the 2000-2001 period.

On average, each year between 1992 to 1997, the elderly were victims of 2.7 million property and violent crimes; 2.5 million household burglaries, motor vehicle thefts, and household thefts; 46,000 purse snatchings and pocket pickings; and 165,000 non-lethal violent crimes including rape, robbery and aggravated and simple assault.

A 50-state survey found that Adult Protective Services received 472,813 reports of elder abuse in domestic and institutional settings in 2000. Eighty-four percent of the reports received were investigated and almost half were substantiated. Adults over 80 were the most frequent victims of abuse excluding self-neglect.

Self-neglect made up 39 percent of allegations investigated; caregiver neglect/abandonment made up 19 percent of cases; financial abuse/exploitation, 13 percent; physical abuse, 11 percent; emotional/verbal abuse, seven percent; and sexual abuse accounted for one percent of cases.

Family members (e.g., spouse, parents, children, grandchildren, siblings, and other family members) accounted for 61.7 percent of perpetrators in substantiated reports. Spouse/intimate partners made up 30.2 percent of the perpetrators and facility and institution staff made up 4.4 percent of the perpetrators.

More than 33,000 people 60 and older were treated for non-fatal assault-related injuries (not including sexual assault) in emergency room departments in 2001. Assaults happened almost equally at home (25.9 percent) and in public places (27.5 percent).

Rates for persons aged 60 to 69 years were more than two times greater than those for the two older age categories (persons aged 70 to 79 and persons aged 80 and older).

Compared with persons aged 20 to 59 years, a greater proportion of older assault victims were women, had fractures, and were hospitalized at the time of diagnosis.

Older consumers — age 60 and over — reported a higher percentage of complaints for telemarketing frauds in 2003. Almost 34 percent of complaints were made by older victims compared to 27 percent in 2002.

Based on complaints to the National Fraud Information Center, older consumers are especially vulnerable to certain kinds of telemarketing fraud. In 2003, 66 percent of the reports of sweepstakes fraud, 59 percent of the lottery club scams, and 52 percent of magazine sales scams were made by individuals 60 or older.

The proportion of individuals losing at least $5,000 in Internet frauds is higher for victims 60 years and older than it is for any other age category.

The National Aging Resource Center on Elder Abuse estimates that 20 percent of elder abuse victims experience financial exploitation.

There were 852 homicides reported in 2002 of people 60 years of age and over.

Although the number of homicides of people aged 65 and older has been decreasing, this age group still has the highest percentage of homicides that occur during the commission of a felony.

In a recent analysis of nursing home inspections and complaint investigations from 1999 to 2000, it was found that more than nine percent — 1,601 homes — were cited for causing actual harm or immediate jeopardy to residents. Over 30 percent (5,283 homes) were cited for an abuse violation that had the potential to cause harm.

Abuse violations cited during annual state inspections of nursing homes have almost tripled since 1996 — 5.9 percent in 1996 to 16 percent in 2000.

Between one and two million Americans aged 65 or older have been injured, exploited, or otherwise mistreated by someone on whom they depended for care or protection.

There was an increase in older victims of lesbian, gay, bisexual, and transgender violence between 2002-2003. Victims over 50 years of age increased 20 percent overall, and victims 60 and over increased 33 percent.

Statement of Dennis M. Lormel
Chief, Financial Crimes Section
Federal Bureau of Investigation
Before the United States Senate Special
Committee on Aging
Washington, D.C.

http://www.fbi.gov/congress/congress01/lormel0910.htm

I am pleased to appear today on behalf of the Federal Bureau of Investigation and share with your Committee the FBI's efforts to address fraudulent schemes which promise everything from improved memory, sexual vitality, curing of terminal illnesses, relief from chronic pain and, the ultimate promise, a longer life. These schemes target those who are most concerned about reversing the effects of aging, the elderly.

Combining resources with other federal and state investigative agencies has been a winning formula for the FBI in this and many other types of investigations. The joint investigative approach not only brings additional resources in terms of manpower and investigative tools, but also gives investigators access to expertise provided by regulatory agencies such as the FDA as well as a larger selection of applicable criminal and civil statutes from both the federal and state levels.

Let me first emphasize that the FBI has identified elder fraud and fraud against those suffering from serious illness as two of the most insidious of all white collar crimes being perpetrated by today's modern and high tech conman. The Internet, high speed dialers, mail drops, and computers are just some of the tools available to the fraudster to separate a victim from his money. Many elderly citizens rely on pensions, social security and life savings to support themselves. The seriously ill and their families are desperate to find some glimmer of hope. The losses inflicted by these unscrupulous con-men and their organizations are both financially and emotionally devastating to these victims.

It has been the experience of the FBI that the elderly are preyed upon by these unscrupulous individuals for several reasons:

(1) Older American citizens are most likely to have a "nest egg," own their home and/or have excellent credit all of which the con-man will try to tap into. Fraudsters are very familiar with the old saying, "you can't get blood from a stone." Like any other businessman, the fraudster will focus his efforts on the segment of the population most likely to be in a financial position to buy whatever he is selling.

(2) Individuals who grew up in the 30's, 40's and 50's were generally raised to be polite and trusting. Two very important and positive personality traits, except when it comes to dealing with a con-man. The con-man will exploit these traits knowing that it is difficult or impossible for these individuals to say "no" or just hang up the phone.

(3) Older Americans are less likely to report a fraud because they either don't know who to report it to or are too ashamed at having been scammed. In some cases, an elderly victim may not report the crime because he or she is concerned that relatives may come to the conclusion that the victim no longer has the mental capacity to take care of his or her own financial affairs.

(4) When an elderly victim does report the crime, they often make poor witnesses. The con-man knows the effects of age on memory and he is counting on the fact that the elderly victim will not be able to supply enough detailed information to investigators such as: how many times did he call? What time of day did he call? Did he provide a call back number or address? Was it always the same person? Did you meet in person? What did he look like? Did he/she have any recognizable accent? Where did you send the money? What did you receive if anything and how was it delivered? What promises were made and when? Did you keep any notes of your conversations? The realization that they have been victimized may take weeks or, more likely, months after contact with the con-man. This extended time frame will test the memory of almost anyone.

(5) Lastly, when it comes to products that promise increased cognitive function, virility, physical conditioning, anti-cancer properties and so on, older Americans make up the segment of the population most concerned about these issues. In a country where new cures and vaccinations for old diseases has given every American hope for a long and fruitful life, it is not so unbelievable that the products offered by these con-men can do what they say they can do.

Those suffering from cancer, heart disease, multiple sclerosis, diabetes, HIV, Parkinson's disease and other serious illnesses are targeted for one simple reason. The con-man knows that many of these individuals are desperate to find some reason to believe that a "miracle cure" exists. These people, many of whom are elderly but some who are not, are willing to pay whatever price is asked and subject themselves to whatever risk is required to gain an advantage over their disease. Regrettably, in most cases, it is the con-man taking advantage of these individuals. In addition to the financial loss, these patients often lose valuable time away from conventional medical treatment which could have resulted in a higher quality of life and/or prolonged life. Although the FBI has identified several instances where dietary and nutritional supplements promising anti-aging effects have been utilized to defraud American citizens, the number of complaints and related dollar losses have not indicated a substantial crime problem falling within the jurisdiction of the FBI. However, the FBI has been involved in several investigations concerning "miracle cures" in which the bureau has joined forces and shared resources with the Food and Drug Administration (FDA), the U.S. Postal Inspection Service (USPIS) and others.

Several examples of previous cases are as follows:

In March 2001, Gregory E. Caplinger, d/b/a, International Institute of Medical Science hospital and clinics, was indicted in the eastern district of Pennsylvania on 39 counts of wire fraud. Caplinger had falsely represented himself to be a British and U.S. trained physician with a doctor of science degree who was board certified in internal medicine, immunology and oncology. Caplinger used these false credentials and other misrepresentations to convince seriously ill patients to travel from the United States and Canada to the Dominican Republic for treatment. He convinced patients to travel to the Dominican Republic to participate in his immunological protocol at his clinic which used a medication called "Immustim." Caplinger claimed that "Immustim" was a medication effective in the treatment of cancer, HIV/AIDS, Epstein-Barr virus, hepatitis, chronic fatigue syndrome, allergies and other immunological dysfunctions. Caplinger received in excess of $500,000 from patients and approximately $2,000,000 from investors he conned into providing him funding for his "clinic."

Caplinger fled the country on the seventh day of his trial and eventually turned himself in to authorities in the Dominican Republic. Investigation in this matter also determined that Caplinger was not a doctor and had been cited for practicing medicine without a license in 1984 in Florida. He also pled guilty to charges of practicing medicine without a license in the state of North Carolina in 1988. In 1993 he pled guilty to theft charges in Florida for taking money from the elderly after promising to treat patients for Alzheimer's disease. Caplinger is awaiting sentencing and could receive 195 years in jail and a fine of $9.75 million.

The FBI is also involved in a number of on-going cases which I am not at liberty to discuss in detail at this time. However, I can provide you with a summary of several cases without identifying the subjects of these investigations.

In September 1999, the Salt Lake City office of the FBI initiated a joint investigation with the FDA. This investigation centered on the activities of an individual treating seriously ill people with an "all natural" product he produced, the ingredients of which he has advised came to him in a "dream." According to the subject of this investigation, this product was effective in treating migraine headaches, cancer, multiple sclerosis, Parkinson's disease, chronic pain, spinal cord injuries and other illnesses. The subject advised patients that his "all natural" product contained botanical extracts, B vitamins and amino acids. Extensive chemical analysis of the product performed by the FDA determined that among other things, it contained procaine and lidocaine. The cost of these treatments, when performed in the subject's clinic, was $10,000 each. Information developed through investigation determined that the subject had contracted with a pharmacist to mix his product and paid the pharmacist $15.00 per vial. The cost to patients was $500.00 per vial. Hundreds of victims sought treatment from this individual with many parents bringing paraplegic children, who had suffered spinal cord injuries, in the hope that treatment by the subject might result in their being able to walk again. Many of the victims didn't have the financial resources to pay for the treatments and resorted to mortgaging their homes and borrowing from relatives. In one case, a church mobilized its parishioners and through fund raising activities, were able to pay the cost of the treatments for one child. Many of the patients learned of this "miracle treatment" through chatrooms on the Internet frequented by those suffering from specific and serious diseases and ailments. Search warrants were executed at the subject's home, one clinic in Salt Lake City as well as the home of the pharmacist who resided in California.

In November 2000, the Richmond office of the FBI initiated a wire fraud investigation against an individual residing in Henrico county, VA, who was representing himself as a doctor and a surgeon. This individual claimed to have found an herbal cure for various terminal cancers. He was selling a medicine "soup" which he created and claimed would cure cancer. The charge for a 45 day supply of this "soup" was $10,000. The subject of this investigation advised prospective clients that he had cured the queen of Thailand of cervical cancer and cured his own wife of stage IV brain cancer. He also claimed to have cured more than 100 others with his "soup." One victim, identified through investigation, paid $85,000 for "soup" and a skin treatment to cure his skin cancer.

Some of the "patients" learned about the "soup" treatments by word of mouth and others via the Internet. Some of the patients were told that their medical diagnosis was wrong and they did not have cancer. He told them they were only suffering from a virus which, not coincidently, his "soup" would cure. In some instances, victims were instructed to discontinue their conventional medical treatment and to rely solely on his soup. To date, investigation has determined that the subject received over $350,000 from the sale of his soup and bogus medical treatments.

The subject was arrested on 2/16/2001 after investigation determined that he had begun to liquidate various bank accounts. Approximately $207,660 and two vehicles were seized at the time of his arrest.

In April 1999, the San Diego office of the FBI initiated an investigation of an individual who advocated a regime of herbal concoctions, the use of an electric device referred to as a "zapper," and the removal of all metal from the patients mouth, to cure cancer. One of this individual's patients had been diagnosed with breast cancer through conventional medical procedures. A malignant tumor, approximately 1.5 centimeters in size, was discovered and the patient's medical doctor recommended surgery to remove it. This patient, convinced that the subject of this investigation could cure her cancer and on his recommendation, had all of her teeth containing fillings removed by a dentist. Following treatments and tests costing several thousand dollars, the subject advised the patient that her cancer was "healing." At the urging of family members, the patient returned to her regular physician and learned that the tumor was not healing and had actually grown to 14 centimeters.

This investigation determined that the subject was already wanted on a state arrest warrant in Nashville, Indiana, for the unlawful practice of medicine. He was arrested on the outstanding warrant and returned to Indiana for prosecution. The FBI is also involved in several other on-going investigations which, due to the sensitive nature of these investigations, can not be discussed at this time. The FBI will continue to identify, investigate and work to prosecute those who would take advantage of the elderly and the seriously ill.

U.S. Department of Health and Human Services Fact Sheet: Reducing Payment Errors and Stopping Fraud in Medicare

(archived May 7, 2002)

http://www.hhs.gov/news/press/2002pres/fraud.html

Overview

The Department of Health and Human Services (HHS) plays a critical role in ensuring that beneficiaries and taxpayers get their money's worth from the Medicare program. Each year Medicare spends more than $220 billion on health care benefits for nearly 40 million senior citizens and other Americans with disabilities. As steward of the Medicare program, the Centers for Medicare and Medicaid Services (formerly the Health Care Financing Administration) (CMS) is responsible for ensuring Medicare pays correctly for covered services. CMS implements the coverage and reimbursement policies that Congress establishes in the law.

To achieve this goal, HHS has expanded efforts to help doctors and health care providers understand and follow Medicare law and regulations. CMS also is working to simplify requirements and modernize its accounting systems to further reduce payment errors. These efforts are showing significant results. Medicare's estimated error rate has fallen by more than half, from 14 percent in fiscal year 1996 to 6.8 percent in fiscal year 2000, according to annual independent reviews conducted by the HHS Office of Inspector General (OIG). The error rate measures payments made by Medicare which are not properly supported by health care providers' documentation or which otherwise do not meet Medicare reimbursement requirements.

In cases where evidence may suggest fraudulent billing practices, the OIG works closely with other law enforcement agencies and CMS to investigate and enforce the laws in order to protect beneficiaries and taxpayers. Health care providers are not subject to civil or criminal penalties for innocent errors, as the laws only cover offenses involving actual knowledge, reckless disregard or deliberate ignorance of the falsity of claims. As a result of law enforcement activities, the federal government recovered $1.2 billion in fines, settlements and judgments during fiscal year 2000.

Background

In 1996, Congress enacted the Health Insurance Portability and Accountability Act of 1996 (HIPAA), which created stable funding to protect Medicare's program integrity. The law dedicated funding for HHS and the Department of Justice to support efforts to reduce payment errors and to combat fraud and abuse in the Medicare program. The law authorized $680 million to CMS for support of its Medicare Integrity Program activities in fiscal year 2001, including efforts to prevent unnecessary payments and to educate providers. The law also authorized $130 million to the OIG to investigate and prevent Medicare and Medicaid fraud and abuse in coordination with the Department of Justice. HHS' strategy to reduce Medicare payment errors and curb fraud includes efforts to modernize Medicare's management and financial controls, to simplify

Medicare requirements to make unintentional errors less likely, to help doctors and health care providers understand Medicare's coverage and billing requirements, and to aggressively pursue evidence of actual fraud.

Modernizing Medicare's Financial System

HHS' efforts to improve Medicare's financial controls and management systems have helped reduce Medicare's estimated payment error rate in half, from 14 percent in fiscal year 1996 to 6.8 percent in fiscal year 2000. Although Medicare pays virtually all claims correctly based on the information submitted, payments are considered "improper" if they lack sufficient documentation, if the service provided is found to have been unnecessary, or if payment is coded improperly by a physician or other health care providers. Medicare's "improper payment" estimate is not a measure of fraud, though it may include fraud. Ongoing efforts to further reduce errors include:

- *Strengthening oversight of private contractors.* By law, Medicare must rely on private insurance companies to process and pay Medicare claims. In 1999, CMS created national review teams to evaluate contractors' fraud and abuse identification efforts and other key functions, using standardized reporting and evaluation protocols. These teams cut across regions and use their specific expertise to assure more effective evaluations of contractor performance. CMS continues to develop additional defined, measurable standards to support consistent reviews of specific areas of contractor performance.

- *Upgrading Medicare's accounting systems.* Medicare's claims-processing contractors do not currently use a uniform financial management system, increasing the risk of administrative and operational errors and misstatements. HHS' proposed fiscal year 2002 budget includes $53 million to continue to develop state-of-the-art accounting systems for Medicare. The funding would help to develop both an Integrated General Ledger Accounting System for CMS to replace the fragmented, outdated systems now in use by CMS's claims-processing contractors, and a new Financial Accounting and Control System to improve internal financial management controls.

- *Targeting program vulnerabilities.* Since 1999, CMS has used special contractors with program integrity experience to target problem areas, such as reviewing claims for therapy services and developing data analysis centers to identify and stop payment errors and possible fraud. These contractors give CMS the flexibility to meet emerging challenges. Expanded activities planned for 2001 include assessing the accuracy of information used to establish nursing home payments and conducting nationwide statistical analysis that identify program vulnerabilities.

- *Developing contractor-specific error rates.* In 2000, CMS began developing error rates for each of the private insurance companies that pay Medicare claims. Over time, these error rates will guide error-prevention efforts, such as education and program integrity efforts, at each contractor in more detail than Medicare's overall report can.

- *National coordination-of-benefits contractor.* In 1999, CMS hired a national contractor to streamline efforts to ensure that Medicare does not pay claims that are the responsibility of private insurance companies. The contract uses private-sector expertise to build on the roughly $3 billion Medicare saves each year by ensuring that private insurers pay their share of beneficiaries' health care bills.

Clarifying Medicare Requirements

Clarifying and streamlining Medicare rules represents another significant way to further reduce Medicare payment errors. HHS is committed to taking steps to make Medicare more understandable and user-friendly to help physicians and other providers avoid unintended errors. These efforts include:

- *The Physicians' Regulatory Issues Team (PRIT).* In 1998, CMS created the PRIT to improve the agency's responsiveness to the daily concerns of practicing physicians as the agency reviews and creates Medicare requirements. The team, which includes physicians working throughout CMS, seeks to make Medicare simpler and more supportive of the doctor-patient relationship. Ongoing PRIT initiatives include consulting physicians about proposed program changes and researching physician concerns to find ways to simplify or eliminate unnecessary requirements.

- *The Practicing Physicians Advisory Council (PPAC).* The council, established by Congress in 1990, advises CMS on proposed changes in Medicare regulations and manual instructions related to physician services. A CMS physician leads the PPAC, and all 15 members are practicing physicians who bill Medicare and represent a wide variety of specialties and both urban and rural areas.

- *Simplifying evaluation and management guidelines.* CMS continues to seek and obtain broad input from practicing physicians on proposals to simplify documentation guidelines for physician office visits under Medicare. CMS continues to refine proposed new guidelines and is preparing to pilot test them in 2001. The goal is to develop guidelines that intuitively make sense to physicians while ensuring accurate payment for their services.

- *Emphasizing appropriate review.* In 2000, CMS issued clear, unambiguous instructions to Medicare's claims-processing contractors about the appropriate approach to reviewing Medicare claims. Contractors are to use medical review primarily as an education tool for doctors and health care providers. When a doctor or provider is placed on medical review, contractors must tell the providers why they were selected, how to prevent the error in the future, and what they need to do to get off review.

Educating Doctors and Providers

In order to reduce the chances of payment errors, HHS conducts extensive educational and outreach activities in order to assist doctors and other health care providers properly file Medicare claims. These efforts include:

- *The Medicare Learning Network.* The network provides timely, accurate and relevant information about Medicare coverage and payment policies. The online network includes computer-based training courses, relevant e-mail updates and satellite broadcasts to share information on important Medicare topics and issues.

- *Promoting voluntary compliance.* With extensive input from health care businesses, the OIG has developed a series of voluntary compliance guidelines for hospitals, medical equipment suppliers, clinical laboratories, home health agencies, third-party billers, Medicare+Choice organizations, and other providers. These guidelines identify reasonable steps to take to improve adherence to Medicare and Medicaid laws, regulations and program directives.

- *Establishing toll-free information lines.* As part of its increased commitment to customer service, in 2000 CMS required Medicare claims-processing contractors to establish toll-free lines for doctors and other health care providers. Each Medicare contractor offers the lines to answer billing and claims questions from physicians, hospitals, home health agencies, and other providers. Each contractor also maintains an Internet site with important Medicare information for doctors and other providers.

- *Improving customer service.* CMS has expanded its efforts to assess and improve the customer service provided by the claims-processing contractors to ensure that they provide accurate, relevant information about Medicare coverage and billing to physicians and health care providers. CMS is now evaluating contractors' customer service efforts related to program integrity activities.

Stopping Fraudulent Activities

The HIPAA legislation enacted in 1996 established the Health Care Fraud and Abuse Control Account, which dedicated money to help finance expanded activities to control Medicare and Medicaid fraud and abuse. HHS and the Department of Justice share these resources, which are used to coordinate federal, state and local health care law enforcement programs, conduct investigations, provide guidance to the health care industry, and support other anti-fraud efforts. In fiscal year 2001, the account totaled $182 million, including $130 million for OIG activities. This funding has helped to bolster HHS efforts to attack fraud and abuse in the Medicare and Medicaid programs.

- *Expanded OIG presence.* HIPAA's guaranteed funding has enabled the OIG to expand its operations nationally by placing personnel in a total of 45 states, up from 26 prior to HIPAA's enactment. This expanded presence makes it easier for the OIG to carry out investigations and enforcement efforts.

- *Prosecutions and recoveries.* During fiscal year 2000, the Department of Justice and the OIG conducted 414 criminal prosecutions involving health care fraud and recovered $1.2 billion in fines, judgments and settlements. In the four years since HIPAA's enactment, the federal government conducted 1,291 criminal prosecutions and recovered a total of $3.4 billion in fines, judgments and settlements.

- *Exclusions.* Individuals and businesses who are convicted of Medicare fraud or patient abuse, or who engage in other specific activities, may be ineligible to receive payments from Medicare, Medicaid and other federal health care programs. During fiscal year 2000, the OIG excluded a total of 3,350 individuals and businesses. A searchable list of currently excluded entities is available at http://oig.hhs.gov.

- *Anti-fraud hotline.* The OIG maintains an anti-fraud hotline to report potential fraud and abuse in the Medicare and Medicaid programs. The hotline, 1-800-HHS-TIPS (1-800-447-8477), provides assistance to callers in English or Spanish. Tips involving potential errors in beneficiaries' Medicare statements are generally referred to the claims-processing contractors for further review, while suspected fraud is referred to appropriate law enforcement agencies for investigation. The hotline received more than 500,000 calls last year and has fielded more than 1.5 million calls since its creation in 1995.

- *Senior Medicare Patrol grantees.* The HHS Administration on Aging (AoA) provides grants to 48 local organizations to help older Americans be better health care consumers and to help identify and prevent fraudulent health care practices. These Senior Medicare Patrol projects teach volunteer retired professionals, such as doctors, nurses, accountants, investigators, law enforcement personnel, attorneys and teachers, to help Medicare and Medicaid beneficiaries to become better health care consumers. Since 1997, these projects and other AoA grants have trained more than 25,000 volunteers, conducted more than 60,000 community education events and counseled more than 1 million beneficiaries.

2. Mobility, Transportation, and Housing

National Aging Information Center, Administration on Aging
Limitations in Activities of Daily Living Among the Elderly: Data Analyses from the 1989 National Long-Term Care Survey (1996)
http://www.aoa.gov/aoa/stats/adllimits/httoc.htm

Introduction

The tables presented in this report are based on the 1989 National Long-Term Care Survey (NLTCS), a national sample of Medicare-enrolled persons 65 years of age and older who were asked to report on any chronic disabilities lasting 3 months or longer. A disability was defined as the inability to perform, or to perform without assistance, an Activity of Daily Living (ADL) or an Instrumental Activity of Daily Living (IADL). ADLs included eating, getting in and out of bed, getting around inside, dressing, bathing, and using the toilet. IADLs included the ability to do heavy housework, laundry, meal preparation, grocery shopping, getting around outside, getting to places outside of walking distance, money management, using the telephone, and taking medications.

The 1989 NLTCS collected data on elderly persons who were functionally impaired or institutionalized and had received a detailed community resident survey in 1982 or 1984, as well as persons who had passed their 65th birthday since the 1984 NLTCS survey. Using a complex sample design of Medicare recipients, elderly from the 1982 and 1984 surveys were selected to provide national prevalence estimates of disability and institutionalization rates. Approximately 22,150 elders were screened in order to identify eligible community residents or institutional residents. Nearly 6,100 people met selection criteria and were chosen for a detailed interview.

* * *

Highlights

• Overall, nearly 84 percent of persons 65 years of age or older had no IADL or ADL limitations lasting 3 months or longer. Even among the oldest category, persons 85 or older, the majority (51 percent) reported they had neither ADL nor IADL limitations, though almost one-half (48.7 percent) had at least one limitation and more than one-third (38.1 percent) had both.

• Men were more likely (88 percent) than women (81 percent) to have neither an IADL nor an ADL limitation.

• Nearly 89 percent of persons 65 years of age and older who lived in the community had no ADL limitations lasting 6 months or longer. In the 65 to 74 age category, 93.8 percent had no ADL limitations.

• By contrast, 97 percent of institutional residents had ADL limitations lasting 6 months or longer, reflecting the admission policies of most institutions, i.e., that only persons with chronic ADL limitations are eligible for admission.

• Among community residents, 6.7 percent of those aged 65 and over had 1 to 2 ADL limitations, and 6.1 percent had 3 to 6 limitations lasting 3 months or longer. At ages 85 and over, 18.4 percent had 1 to 2 and 22 percent had 3 to 6 ADL limitations. In contrast, over 81 percent of those living in institutions over the age of 65 had 3 to 6 ADL limitations.

• The most frequently reported ADL limitations, lasting 3 months or longer, for community residents aged 65+ were bathing (9.4 percent); getting around inside (8.8 percent); and getting in and out of a bed or chair (5.9 percent). Women reported more ADL limitations than men in every age group and ADL category, with their distributions most like men for dressing and eating and least alike for using the bathroom or toilet and getting around inside.

• The most frequently reported ADL limitations, lasting 3 months or longer, among institutional residents aged 65 years or older were bathing (95.6 percent); getting around inside (81.8 percent); and getting in and out of a bed or chair (77.9 percent). There is a relatively small difference across age categories in the distribution by ADL limitations for those in institutions.

• While the percentage with ADL limitations is far higher among institutional residents, the rank order of ADL limitations is the same for both community and institutional residents.

NLTCS findings and comparable numbers published by the U.S. Census Bureau are similar. Data for the Bureau's Special Tabulations on Aging show that in 1990, 88.1 percent of noninstitutionalized people nationwide aged 65 and over had no ADL limitation lasting 6 months or longer. In the age groups 65 to 74, 75 to 84, and 85+, the percentages were 91.6, 85.3, and 72.1 percent, respectively. Estimates from the NLTCS of elderly community residents with no ADL limitations lasting 6 months or longer . . . are several percentage points higher in each age category (91.3 percent community residents, overall; 94.4 percent at ages 65 to 74; 88.2 percent at ages 75 to 84; and 72.7 percent at ages 85+).

U.S. Department of Health and Human Services
Changes in Elderly Disability Rates and the Implications for Health Care Utilization and Cost
(Brenda C. Spillman, Urban Institute, February 3, 2003)
http://aspe.hhs.gov/daltcp/reports/hcutlcst.htm

Recent research has provided promising evidence that aggregate age-adjusted disability among older Americans has decreased. There also is evidence that cognitive impairment and physical limitations, such as lifting 10 pounds, walking short distances, and climbing a flight of stairs, which may be precursors to disability, may have declined in recent years. On the other hand, some studies show increases in chronic disease, increases in the use of paid long term care, and increasing disability levels within the disabled population. This study was undertaken in order to better understand these trends and their potential implications for use of acute and long term care.

Study Questions

Studies to date have primarily examined aggregate age-adjusted trends. In this study aggregate trends are decomposed into trends in underlying aspects of disability. Specific questions addressed are the following:

• How has the prevalence of chronic disability among the elderly changed since the mid-1980s?

• Does the trend in disability differ for specific components of disability, such as disability only in basic activities necessary for independent living or in use of equipment?

• Do declines differ for younger ages and older cohorts?

- Are there particular activities which have declined more than others or which appear to be more amenable to independence with special equipment or other environmental/social factors

- What are the implications for future costs?

Data and Methodology

Data are from four waves of the National Long Term Care Survey (NLTCS) representing three five-year periods between 1984 and 1999. The NLTCS is conducted by the U.S. Census Bureau under the direction of researchers at the Center for Demographic Studies (CDS) at Duke University.

Chronic disability (defined as lasting at least 3 months) was examined in the aggregate and then decomposed along two dimensions. The first distinguishes the use of human help — long term care — from the use of assistive devices to perform basic activities. The second distinguishes disability only in instrumental activities of daily living (IADLs), which are activities such as money management and meal preparation that are associated with the ability to maintain independence at home, from disability in activities of daily living (ADLs), which are basic personal care activities such as dressing and eating that indicate a higher level of disability or frailty.

The relationship between age-adjusted declines in disability and the actual prevalences in a steadily aging elderly population also were examined, as well as trends for individual IADL and ADL activities and for the mean number of disabilities among the disabled elderly in the community and in institutions.

Major Findings

- The aggregate prevalence of chronic disability among the elderly declined significantly over the 15-year period, from 22.1 percent in 1984 to 19.7 percent in 1999.

- The decline was the result of two countervailing factors — a 3.9 percentage point decline in the percent of the elderly receiving help from someone for ADLs or IADLs and a 1.4 percentage point increase in the percent of the elderly who managed chronic ADL disability in the community with assistive devices only.

- More than 80 percent of the 3.9 percentage point decline in the percent of the elderly receiving human help for a chronic disability was due to a decrease (from 7.4% in 1984 to 4.2% in 1999) in the percent of elderly persons receiving human assistance for IADLs only.

- The percent independent with IADL equipment in the community (0.7 percent) for the one IADL for which we could measure independent equipment use was stable and did not contribute to the disability decline.

- The prevalence of institutional residence, the most costly form of long term care, was about 5 percent of the elderly throughout the period.

- Population aging moderated the decline in the prevalence of chronic disability.

- Nearly all individual IADLs declined over the period, but the most dramatic change was a 3.7 percentage point drop in help with money management between 1984 and 1989, when Social Security direct deposit became the norm, raising a question whether IADL declines reflect improvements in health or improvements in the physical environment.

- No individual ADLs declined in prevalence over the period.

- The mean number of IADLs among the disabled in the community declined over the 15-year period, but the mean number of ADLs for which assistance was received increased for the disabled in both the community and institutions.

Conclusions

The disabilities that saw the most improvements over the 15-year study period were not ones that necessarily imply better health and lower health and long term care costs among the elderly. Rather, a substantial part of disability declines may reflect improvements in the external environment that make it easier to perform such activities as managing money, shopping, and telephoning, regardless of physical state. Help with ADLs changed only slightly from the beginning to the end of the study period. For those receiving ADL help in the community, the total number of chronic disabilities, which is correlated with hours of long term care, fell initially but had returned to its 1984 level by 1999. These findings suggest a need to examine directly both Medicare costs and hours of paid and unpaid long term care for different subgroups of the elderly and the elderly disabled in order to understand the cost implications of disability changes since the mid 1980s.

The growth in the percent of persons who manage various ADL activities with only equipment also suggests the need to know more about which types of equipment are being used and whether the equipment substitutes for or supplements hours of human assistance. Only for bathing was the increase in the prevalence of equipment use accompanied by a decline in the prevalence of human help, but it remains to be seen whether those who manage some activities with equipment use fewer hours of long term care.

Better understanding of the real implications of aggregate disability changes is not an academic exercise as policy makers consider changes in Social Security and Medicare to ensure their long-range financial health. Many argue that declines in disability need to be taken into account in projecting future spending. Until there is a better understanding of these trends and their cost implications, however, it is not clear how they should be taken into account.

Excerpts from U.S Government Accountability Office, GAO-04-971: Transportation-Disadvantaged Seniors: Efforts to Enhance Senior Mobility Could Benefit from Additional Guidance and Information
(August 2004)
http://www.gao.gov/new.items/d04971.pdf

Why GAO Did This Study:

The U.S. population is aging, and access to transportation, via automobile or other modes is critical to helping individuals remain independent as they age. Various federal programs provide funding for transportation services for "transportation-disadvantaged" seniors — those who cannot drive or have limited their driving and who have an income constraint, disability, or medical condition that limits their ability to travel. For those transportation-disadvantaged seniors, GAO was asked to identify (1) federal programs that address their mobility issues, (2) the extent to which these programs meet their mobility needs, (3) program practices that enhance their mobility and the cost-effectiveness of service delivery, and (4) obstacles to addressing their mobility needs and strategies for overcoming those obstacles.

What GAO Found:

Five federal departments — including the Department of Health and Human Services (HHS) — administer 15 programs that are key to addressing the mobility issues of transportation-disadvantaged seniors. These programs help make transportation available, affordable, and accessible to seniors, such as by providing transit passes or reimbursement for mileage.

National data indicate that some types of needs are not being met, including those for trips (1) to multiple destinations or for purposes that involve carrying packages; (2) to life-enhancing activities, such as cultural events; and (3) in rural and suburban areas. However, there are limited data available to assess the extent of unmet needs. HHS's Administration on Aging is required by law to provide guidance to states on how to assess seniors' need for services, but officials said the administration has not done so because it has focused on providing other types of guidance. As a result, the local agencies on aging we interviewed — which are ultimately responsible for performing such needs assessments — used inconsistent methods to assess seniors' mobility needs. The Administration on Aging plans to conduct an evaluation of one of its major programs and thus has an opportunity to improve its understanding of seniors' needs and provide guidance to local agencies on performing needs assessments.

Local transportation service providers have implemented a variety of practices — including increasing service efficiency, improving customer service, and leveraging available funds — that enhance mobility and the cost-effective delivery of services. Federal programs provide funding and some technical assistance for these practices, but several service providers we interviewed said that the implementation of such practices was impeded by limited federal guidance and information on successful practices.

Senior mobility experts and stakeholders identified several obstacles to addressing transportation-disadvantaged seniors' mobility needs, potential strategies that federal and other government entities can consider taking to better meet these needs, and trade-offs associated with those strategies.

GAO is recommending that HHS's Administration on Aging take several actions to improve guidance and information on transportation-disadvantaged seniors' mobility, including developing guidance on assessing mobility needs and publicizing available information on alternative transportation services and on practices service providers can implement to enhance senior mobility. HHS agreed with the findings and recommendations in this report.

Results in Brief:

Working with experts on aging and federal agency officials, we identified 15 key federal programs that address mobility issues for transportation-disadvantaged seniors. These programs, which are administered by five federal departments, distribute funds through state agencies or make them available directly to local service providers. For example, some programs — such as DOT's Capital Assistance Program for Elderly Persons and Persons with Disabilities (Section 5310) — allot funds by formula to state agencies, which then distribute the funds to local nonprofit organizations to purchase vehicles, while other programs — such as HHS's Rural Health Care Services Outreach Program — bypass state agencies altogether and go directly to local service providers. The 15 federal programs help make transportation services senior-friendly, mainly by making them more available, accessible, and affordable (e.g., by providing rides to seniors at reduced fares). In addition to administering the 15 programs, federal agencies also address transportation-disadvantaged seniors' mobility less directly. For example, the Department of Justice has published rules governing the design of transportation facilities, such as bus stops, to make them accessible to people with disabilities. Seniors with disabilities can benefit from the implementation of such designs.

Data on the nature of transportation-disadvantaged seniors' mobility needs indicate that federally supported programs are not meeting certain types of needs, but there is little data on the extent of unmet needs. Needs that are less likely to be met include (1) transportation to multiple destinations or for purposes that involve carrying packages, such as shopping, for which the automobile is better suited than other alternatives; (2) life-enhancing trips, such as visits to spouses in nursing homes or cultural events; and (3) trips in nonurban areas, especially for seniors in rural communities, where alternatives to the automobile are less likely to be available and special transportation services are limited. However, federal programs generally do not collect data on the extent to which seniors' mobility needs are being met because there are few federal requirements to assess such needs. HHS's Administration on Aging is required by law to provide guidance to states on how to assess seniors' unmet needs, which could include transportation, but officials told us that the administration has not done so because state and local agencies on aging have indicated a greater desire for guidance on other aspects of providing services for seniors. However, without guidance on assessing unmet needs, local aging agencies have used a variety of methods to collect data, many of which produce information on the nature of needs rather than on the extent to which needs are being met. Officials from the Administration on Aging said that they are developing an evaluation plan to examine, among other things, (1) the extent to which one of the administration's major senior programs* is meeting the needs and preferences of seniors for supportive services — including transportation — and (2) how needs assessments are performed by state and local entities.

According to literature on senior mobility and our own work, transportation service providers have implemented a variety of practices that enhance transportation-disadvantaged seniors' mobility and the cost-effective delivery of these services; however, the providers we interviewed indicated that implementation of such practices was sometimes impeded by multiple reporting requirements and limited federal guidance. We grouped these practices into three categories: (1) increasing service efficiency, (2) improving customer service, and (3) leveraging available funds. For example, one service provider we interviewed plans to improve service efficiency by using Global Positioning System technology to track its vehicles and automatically schedule trips, allowing seniors to obtain same-day service rather than having to reserve rides 48 hours in advance. Another provider addresses customer service by putting its drivers through a sensitivity training program that helps drivers understand seniors' mobility challenges. Several other providers have entered into contracts with public and private entities to leverage available funds and generate additional revenue for senior transportation services. According to these providers, their practices have resulted in more senior-friendly transportation and more cost-effective service delivery. Our review also showed that the 10 local service providers we interviewed were using funds from some of the key federal programs we identified (e.g., DOT's Capital Assistance Program for Elderly Persons and Persons with Disabilities (Section 5310) and HHS's Medicaid Program) to deliver transportation services to seniors, and that the federal program funding supported the implementation of such practices to some extent. For example, some providers said that they received technical assistance while implementing such practices, either directly from federal agencies or indirectly through federally supported professional organizations. However, many of the providers we interviewed said that certain characteristics of federal programs, such as what the providers view as burdensome reporting requirements and limited program guidance, can impede the implementation of practices that enhance senior mobility. For example, one provider told us that it had not received technical guidance from one of the DOT programs indicating how the funding process works and that, as a result, it had to seek such assistance from other local organizations.

Experts, advocacy groups, professional organizations, local officials, and transportation service providers have identified a number of obstacles to addressing transportation-disadvantaged seniors' mobility needs. They also have identified potential strategies that the federal government, and other government levels, as appropriate, can take to better address transportation-disadvantaged seniors' mobility needs and enhance the cost-effectiveness of the

---

* Grants for Supportive Services and Senior Centers (Title III-B).

services delivered. These obstacles and strategies are centered around three major themes, as follows:

- *Planning for alternatives to driving as seniors age.* Several experts have reported that the federal government and other government levels do not do enough to encourage seniors and their caregivers to identify and use multiple transportation modes for their routine trips. As a consequence, seniors may perceive that driving is their only option and may become isolated or drive even when it is unsafe for them to do so. Experts and other stakeholders have suggested that helping seniors plan for alternatives to driving — such as by providing information about the transportation services available in their community — would extend the lifespan of their mobility, and that the federal government could provide a central forum for state and local agencies to provide such information.

- *Accommodating seniors' varied mobility needs.* The growing senior population could benefit from policies that accommodate its varied needs, including differing physical limitations and diverse trip purposes (such as for work, volunteer activities, medical appointments, and recreation), and address the particular challenges that transportation-disadvantaged seniors face in nonurban areas. For example, according to senior mobility experts and others, some federally funded programs are intended for seniors who do not drive and need assistance all the time; yet some seniors need transportation assistance only under certain circumstances, such as in bad weather or when a medical condition worsens. As a result, these seniors do not qualify for these federally funded transportation services. Experts and other stakeholders have suggested that the federal government require or encourage state and local agencies to focus on seniors' immediate and future mobility needs by including seniors in the transportation-planning process. For example, seniors could advocate for safe walking routes to transit stops and for the use of low-floor buses (which are accessible to both wheelchair users and people with other mobility impairments).

- *Addressing federal and other governmental funding constraints.* Experts and other stakeholders suggested that although public funding resources are limited, strategies exist to leverage them, including increasing funding flexibility among programs and improving the coordination of transportation services at all levels of government. For example, federal programs tend to specify that funds from an individual program can be used only to provide transportation to and from that program's services. Additional funding flexibility and coordination among programs could expand seniors' access to transportation services.

Seniors benefit when the obstacles to their mobility are addressed, but trade-offs also result from implementing the identified strategies. For instance, according to experts and local aging officials, helping seniors plan for alternatives to driving could enable more seniors to maintain mobility while refraining from unsafe driving, but increased demand for services would likely stress already stretched transportation programs. Offering additional transportation services or modifying existing public transit also could help seniors meet their varied needs, but such efforts can be expensive, and additional funds would have to come from new revenues or other programs.

Given the expected growth in the senior population, it will be important for seniors and those who support them to have as much information as possible to plan for the future. Accordingly, our report contains four recommendations to the Secretary of Health and Human Services to improve the guidance and information available to seniors about transportation options and to local agencies about assessments of the need for senior transportation services and successful practices for addressing this need. In commenting on a draft of this report, the Departments of Health and Human Services, Transportation, and Veterans Affairs concurred with the findings, and the Department of Health and Human Services concurred with the recommendations. The Department of Transportation also provided technical clarifications, which were incorporated as appropriate to ensure accuracy. The Departments of Education and Labor said that they did not have any comments on the draft.

Excerpts from Testimony of Jane O'Dell Baumgarten Regarding Elderly Housing and Affordability Issues for the 21st Century Before the Housing and Community Opportunity Subcommittee of the House Financial Services Committee
(July 17, 2001)
http://financialservices.house.gov/media/pdf/071701jb.pdf

Powerful Demographic Forces at Work

There are powerful demographic forces at work in our nation that are revealed in the numbers, proportions and age group distributions among older Americans who will be in need of affordable and appropriate housing. Projections by the U.S. Census Bureau estimate that by the year 2020, the number of persons age 65 and older will grow to over 53 million — representing a 55 percent increase from the 34 million estimated for 1998. Changes in the age distribution of the nation's older population are also occurring. Presently, the aging of the older population is driven by large increases in the number of persons age 75 and older. More specifically, in 1998, there were an estimated 4 million persons age 85 and older. The Census Bureau projects this figure to reach approximately 6.5 million by the year 2020. This would represent an increase of 62 percent for the 85-plus age category alone.

Housing is a critical factor in determining the quality of life and sense of security of all Americans. During the 1990s, on average, Americans — including older Americans — improved the quality of their housing. But despite the prosperity of the 1990s, many older Americans continued to experience serious housing problems because of substandard conditions, lack of affordability, or inappropriateness of their homes for "aging in place." There is a deficit in affordable, available, and appropriate housing that is affecting a growing number of older Americans.

The Availability of Affordable Housing for Older Persons

AARP believes that preserving affordable housing for the elderly must mean more than maintenance, rehabilitation, modernization and subsidizing of existing housing — as critical as it is that these needs be addressed. Beyond these, what is required is an increase in the rate of production of appropriate — specifically including supportive — housing in the near term future. Absent this, what will likely be produced is an affordability and availability housing crisis for a growing number of under-housed, under-served older Americans — leading, potentially, to an increase in costly and premature institutionalization. The frail elderly represent the fastest growing segment among older persons in our nation, and among the most at risk of those who are vulnerable to excessive housing cost burdens.

[H]ousing affordability and availability focus on two different but related aspects of the housing question. Housing affordability refers to the financial ability to gain access to housing, as well as the financial ability to remain a resident. Housing availability refers not only to vacancy rates, but also to the appropriateness of the housing. AARP research consistently documents that as Americans pass through midlife, regardless of whether they own or rent their housing, they strongly prefer to remain in their existing place of residence. The adaptability of housing to the processes of aging in place presents difficult challenges for housing facilities that have often not been designed with these life changes in mind.

Housing affordability and availability remain major problems for many older Americans, especially for those who rent. AARP's analysis of the 1999 American Housing Survey indicates that approximately 25 million households were headed by a person age 62 or older. Of these, nearly 5 million (20 percent) were renters. The same survey analysis indicates that 57 percent of these older renter households paid 30 percent or more of their income on housing, compared to 39 percent of younger renter households who paid 30 percent or more of their income on housing. Households are composed of one or more individuals, therefore the actual numbers of older Americans affected by heavy rent burdens are substantially understated.

In summary, according to the 1999 American Housing Survey data, of the 2.85 million households headed by a person age 62 or older that pay 30 percent or more of their income on housing, 1.7 million households (approximately 60 percent) benefited from one or more of the federal rental housing programs. This means that today, those households headed by someone 62 or older and benefiting from federal housing assistance account for roughly one-third of all households receiving such aid.

The Growing Need for Elderly Housing with Supportive Services

However, many older persons — especially those who live alone — eventually will need some supportive services to remain independent in their homes. The availability of these services varies widely due to the residential distribution patterns of older Americans. Again, according to AARP's analysis of the 1999 American Housing Survey data, seventy-two percent (72%) of older persons live outside central cities, and are dispersed across suburbs, small towns, and rural areas. Such dispersion presents formidable challenges to the efficient delivery of services such as transportation, in-home health care, home-delivered meals and other necessary services.

It is especially relevant for the purposes of today's hearing to recognize that as the elderly population increases, the proportion who have difficulty performing one or more basic activities of daily living — such as bathing, dressing, or eating — will also be increasing. An analysis prepared for AARP by the Lewin Group estimated that in 1994 there were over 1.7 million elderly (65 years of age and older) who had difficulty performing two or more such daily activities. The same study estimated that by the year 2020, the number of similarly aged persons with two or more of these impairments would increase to 2.8 million — a 65 percent increase from 1994.

Census data provide a more precise break-out of where these impaired individuals are likely to be concentrated. There are approximately 20,000 federally subsidized housing projects that serve more than 1.4 million older persons whose median age is approximately 75. The Census Bureau's 1995 Survey of Income and Program Participation indicates that approximately 40 percent of persons of age 62 or older, living in these subsidized rental housing units, had at least one Activity of Daily Living (often referred to as ADLs) limitation (such as moving around the room, transferring from a bed or chair, bathing, eating, dressing and using the toilet); or one Instrumental Activity of Daily Living (IADLs) limitation (such as using the telephone, keeping track of bills, preparing meals, taking medicine and getting outside the home), compared with 28 percent of older persons in unsubsidized rental properties and 19 percent of older persons in owned homes.

Trends Within the Section 202 Supportive Housing Program

The experience of the Section 202 supportive housing program for the elderly helps to illuminate the issues, challenges and — most importantly — the need for supportive services, demonstrating the importance of viewing housing as an effective point of service delivery. The 202 program is the only federally-funded, new construction housing program specifically designed to address the physical frailties of elderly residents. I would like to briefly summarize several key findings from a recently released, extensive AARP-sponsored study of the Section 202 supportive housing program for the elderly.

From the perspective of frail older persons, housing and services are often the keys to continued independence and dignity. Comparisons of the 1998 Section 202 survey findings with those from the 1988 survey document that:

- Section 202 units for older persons continue to be in high demand, as suggested by the low vacancy rates (1 percent for one-bedroom units) and long waiting lists (9 applicants waiting for each vacancy that occurs in a given year — up from 8 in 1988);

- Residents are older and frailer than was indicated in the earlier research (Average resident age increased from 72 years in 1983 to 73.6 years in 1988, rising to 75 years in 1999);

- Legislation and regulatory changes have improved the Section 202 program. For example, in 1999, more than a third of all Section 202 facilities (37.4 percent) had service coordinators on staff, a service authorized by legislative changes in 1990 and 1992;

- Facilities built during the past decade are, on average, much smaller than reported by earlier surveys for preceding years; and

- Capital reserves were generally viewed by managers as inadequate for retrofitting projects to meet the changing needs of aging residents, especially among the older projects, where the oldest residents are concentrated.

Conclusions

The essential conclusion to be drawn from this report is that adapting Section 202 housing to the changing needs of its residents can mean — for them — the critical difference between maintaining an apartment in a supportive community surrounded by one's own belongings, or admission to more expensive nursing home care — often involving sharing a room with a stranger. Today, too many older persons with modest means face the stark choice between living in their own homes with minimal access to support services or moving to expensive and restrictive institutional settings.

AARP has made a commitment to work with the Seniors Housing Commission and the Millennial Housing Commission to conduct an extensive review of the issues, challenges and potential strategies for addressing the growing deficit in affordable and appropriate housing for the vulnerable low and moderate-income elderly population. We are particularly concerned over the mismatch of housing stock with the numerical growth and service needs of the frail elderly. In this regard, AARP is encouraged by the progress being made by the two Commissions, with a number of legislative proposals that have been or will be introduced in the House and Senate this year, and several initiatives being proposed by Secretary Martinez at the U.S. Department of Housing and Urban Development. We look forward to reviewing these proposals and initiatives in greater detail. The Association also looks forward to working with this Subcommittee to assess and help perfect these proposals as elements of an effective short-term and long-term affordable housing strategy for vulnerable older Americans.

QUESTIONS

1. How much do we really know about how disability levels are changing in the aging population? Does it matter?

2. Should states or the federal government bear primary financial responsibility for addressing the daily living problems facing the nation's elderly?

3. Ethical Issues

Edward D. Spurgeon, Charles P. Sabatino, Nancy M. Coleman, Stephen R. McConnell & Rebecca C. Morgan
Symposium: Joint Conference on Legal/Ethical Issues in the Progression of Dementia Foreword
35 GA. L. REV. 391 (2001)[*]

I. Introduction

Marie McDonough Larson, born in 1919, grew up helping in her family's green houses along with her five brothers and sisters and, later, worked as a secretary and shoe model. She married Thomas McDonough at age 21 and raised two loving children, Diane and Jim. She worked primarily as a homemaker before taking on part time work on the community newspaper and in real estate sales. Marie's idea of fun was cooking and entertaining, and she was marvelous at both. As her children grew, Marie was a Camp Fire Girls group leader, a Cub Scout den mother, and an enthusiastic thespian in community theater. Then, her husband Tom died in 1962. Eleven years later, in 1973, she married Earnest Larson. Traveling was their greatest pleasure. When they weren't traveling, Marie worked in sales at Lord & Taylor and volunteered regularly at the local hospital and senior center, where she drove other senior citizens to doctors appointments, grocery shopping, and wherever else needed. She also served as bursar of the Milton Women's Club. In 1993, at age 73, Marie was diagnosed with Alzheimer's disease. Seven years later, she died in her home in Athens, Georgia surrounded by family members. Her daughter, Diane McDonough Riley, was the primary caregiver for her mother.

The Joint Conference on Legal/Ethical Issues in the Progression of Dementia grew out of the pressing need to address the very real legal and ethical dilemmas that arise in situations like the one of Marie McDonough Larson and her family. Five groups joined forces to sponsor the Conference: the Borchard Foundation Center on Law and Aging; the Alzheimer's Association; the American Bar Association's Commission on Legal Problems of the Elderly; the National Academy of Elder Law Attorneys; and the University of Georgia School of Law. Held at the Center for Continuing Education at the University of Georgia, the Conference spanned three days — November 29 to December 2, 2000, and produced a set of cutting-edge recommendations and articles that are contained in this volume and were generated by the collective hard work, lively deliberation, and intense analysis of 75 multidisciplinary experts invited to be a part of this unique event.

The Conference proceeded somewhat like the building of a new house. First, a basic framework was constructed in the opening plenary sessions. Dr. Peter Rabins from Johns Hopkins poured a solid foundation with his presentation on the state-of-the-art of diagnosis and treatment of dementia. Then Ms. McDonough Riley hammered in the framing with a presentation of her mother's

---

[*] Copyright © 2001. Reprinted by permission.

story as a case study to which a multi-disciplinary panel responded. The panel consisted of Ms. Riley as caregiver and a range of experts who are called upon to advise and assist a patient and the family in dealing with dementia — a doctor, lawyer, ethicist, nurse, social worker, and advocate.

Next, Dr. Ram Valle assisted the endeavor by installing the windows. He demonstrated, through his presentation and paper, *Ethics, Ethnicity, and Dementia: A "Culture-Fair" Approach to Bioethical Advocacy in Dementing Illness*, how the windows through which we examine care and treatment decisions are, unavoidably, cultural lenses that affect the fundamental nature of the process and the conclusions we reach. Finally, eight working groups each deliberated in a series of four extended meetings to fill in and finish the floor, walls, ceilings, and wiring of eight issue areas, or rooms of the house. The groups addressed, respectively: Legal Planning, including the use of powers of attorney, trusts, guardianships and other surrogate decision making tools.

- Individual Autonomy vs. Public Safety, including issues of driving, cooking, and other behaviors that could cause harm to self or others.

- Research Consent for both biological and behavioral research on dementia, including surrogate consent for research.

- Treatment Choices, including issues of capacity and informed consent.

- End-of-Life Issues, including access to care, capacity, and surrogate decision making.

- Genetic Discrimination by long-term care insurers and related issues.

- Legal Representation, including the roles of and ethical challenges faced by lawyers representing an individual with dementia or the individual's family.

- Dispute Resolution relating to caring for and making decisions for persons with dementia.

Final inspection of the "house" took place in a plenary session with each group presenting policy and practice recommendations drafted during the course of each group's deliberations. The recommendations are intended to advance public policy and improve ethical practices in addressing the care needs and rights of persons suffering from progressive dementia. Each recommendation was voted on by the Conference participants as a whole, and only those approved by a majority are included as the official recommendations of the Conference.

The McDonough story provided a fitting starting point for the groups' deliberations, because it is both unique and universal — unique in the specific circumstances faced by Marie and the individuals involved; universal in the issues and themes that emerge. It ties the articles, the Working Group efforts, and the recommendations together in a tangible and practical way. Therefore, let us consider the nature of the questions at hand through her story.

Prior to her diagnosis, Marie McDonough Larson lived in Boston with her husband, stepfather of Marie's daughter Diane and son Jim. Diane lived in

Georgia, while Jim lived in San Diego, California. In 1994, one year after her mother was diagnosed with Alzheimer's, Diane took time off from work under the Family and Medical Leave Act to go to Boston and help find suitable housing for her mother and stepfather in a facility that could provide a continuum of care. During her stay there, her stepfather died suddenly, thrusting the responsibility for caregiving onto Diane. Diane moved Marie to Georgia where Marie lived with Diane until she entered an assisted living facility in April of 1999.

II. Legal Planning

For some years prior to the diagnosis of Alzheimer's in 1993, Diane and her brother had noticed significant problems with their mother's memory and word recall. Marie was aware of her difficulty and, as a result, increasingly avoided conversations with her children. By the time Marie was diagnosed by a team of medical personnel, it was obvious to everyone, including Marie, that the culprit was Alzheimer's or a related dementia, though this fact remained largely unspoken in her children's conversations with Marie.

Diane had obtained Marie's financial durable power of attorney prior to the diagnosis, but Marie had never gotten around to putting together a living will or advance directive for health care. Diane and her brother did not pursue this with her for a variety of complex reasons, including a feeling that by the time of diagnosis, she was already incapable of making many decisions. The family did not discuss with Marie what her wishes were for her future health care. Diane made decisions for her mother based on what she thought Marie would want, which was based loosely on "knowing my mother for 57 years." Lack of any health care power did not present major problems for Diane or her family, in part because her brother deferred to Diane's judgment, and because the opinions of a sister of Marie (who was in denial about the disease) were eventually excluded from the decision-making mix. However, there were a few cases (see the feeding tube example below) where having the documentation would have made the situation easier for both Diane and her mom.

The experience of the McDonough family in dealing with the onset and diagnosis of Alzheimer's disease raised questions relating to legal planning, specifically with regard to capacity to engage in legal planning, the necessary elements of legal planning, the strengths and weaknesses of state advance directive statutes, and the role of guardianship. The Working Group on Legal Planning developed several recommendations adopted by the conference as a whole, starting with a broad recognition that legal planning for clients with diminished capacity requires "a holistic approach."

This holistic approach is encouraged in the article by Nancy Dubler, *Creating and Supporting the Proxy-Decider: The Lawyer-Proxy Relationship*. Dubler persuasively sets forth the shortcomings of approaching legal planning merely in terms of preparing advance directive documents such as Living Wills and Durable Powers of Attorney for Health Care. Focusing on these advance directives, Dubler highlights the vagaries and deficiencies of typical living will language and the use of boilerplate documents. She also casts doubt on individually crafted, lawyer-created documents as a solution, particularly in light of the changing realities of medical practice where financial issues and a risk management mentality can skew decisionmaking. She concludes with a reaffirmation of the importance of discussion between patients, providers and family and a recommendation for focusing on the appointment and active support of proxy decisionmakers.

In Professor Leslie Francis' paper, *Decisionmaking at the End of Life: Patients with Alzheimer's or Other Dementias*, the use of advance directives raised questions about the conceptual models relied on to justify and guide surrogate decisionmakers seeking to act in the "best interests" of patients — precedent autonomy, experiential interests, and objective interests. The model of precedent autonomy allows a now-capable person to control decisionmaking at a later point in time when she no longer has the capacity to do so. The concept recognizes the freedom of the now-capable individual to make plans for the individual's own future, incorporates any expression of the patient's wishes or values into the concept of best interests, and calls upon us to follow those expressions. Advance directives for health care are the most formal expression of precedent autonomy, although the concept supports respect for any expression by the patient. The Legal Planning Group (as well as the Working Group on End-of-Life Decisions) supported revitalizing the notion of precedent autonomy, mainly through simplifying and eliminating inconsistencies in advance directive laws. The groups supported moving away from thinking of advance planning primarily as executing legal documents and emphasizing more the need for ongoing discussions and communication among patient, family, and care providers.

Building on the scope of Dubler's and Francis' analyses, the Working Group on Legal Planning recommended that in addressing the planning needs of clients with diminished capacity lawyers consider: (a) the realities of dementia progression; (b) the client's varying capacity; (c) all options for delegation of decisionmaking authority; (d) health care management strategies; (e) financial management strategies; (f) care financing options; and finally (g) testamentary planning. Turning to the population who have not done advance planning — still the majority of Americans today — the Legal Planning Group recommended further study of who may appropriately serve as surrogates, their priority of authority, the appropriate standard for decisionmaking, and how to incorporate cultural considerations.

Finally, the group supported review, improvement, and adequate funding of state guardianship laws and procedures, as well as coverage for residential and home and community-based long-term care, since all are essential planning resources. Recommended priorities for further study included the use, misuse, and barriers to the use of legal planning tools as well as educating court-appointed surrogates.

III. Individual Autonomy vs. Public Safety

Soon after Marie's diagnosis, the issue of driving had to be addressed. Marie was exhibiting some problems with erratic driving that were a concern to her family. Efforts were made to dissuade her from driving, but she would have nothing to do with it. Driving was very important to Marie and she was adamantly opposed to anyone's attempt to convince her to stop driving. Eventually she stopped driving but only after a long, emotional struggle with the rest of the family. The family finally got her to stop driving by asking her to submit to an independent evaluation that was conducted by a driving assessment clinic in Boston (where she was living at the time). Marie agreed to go to the clinic, and the clinic found that she was unable to drive safely. Although she stopped driving after receiving the evaluation from the clinic, she was angry with the family because she felt that they had taken away her independence. Her anger was particularly directed at Diane's sister-in-law, who had located the clinic and made the appointment.

As dementia progresses and individuals engage in behaviors entailing risks to their own safety and that of others, how can caregivers, professionals and the state balance personal autonomy and safety in controlling behavior? The Working Group on Autonomy and Safety addressed this core question. The individual with declining capacity wants to continue to act as he or she always has, but is unable to judge appropriately his or her ability to perform tasks. This poses hazards to the individual or others. Tension with caregivers may increase, and individuals and caregivers experience stress, grief over loss, and physical and emotional fatigue. The activities that create the greatest dilemmas include those posing the greatest safety hazards: driving, cooking, handling sharp objects, walking alone in dangerous conditions, smoking, and handling or using firearms.

The members of the Working Group on Autonomy and Safety discussed the balancing of personal autonomy against concerns for the safety of the person, the public and the caregiver. Their formidable tasks were to determine how to define and assess risk and how to gauge acceptable risk under certain circumstances.

Bruce Jennings, in his article *Freedom Fading: On Dementia, Best Interests, and Public Safety*, discusses three theoretical frameworks for balancing autonomy and safety. The first two models, the Public Health Model and the Guardian Model, are principally grounded in a duty of protection. The third model, the Conservator Model, is therapeutic in goal and mission, and aims toward healing, preserving, and relieving suffering to the extent possible given the impairment in question. Throughout their discussions, the Working Groups reflected on the interplay of these frameworks, as they addressed the divergent interests.

Ed Richards, in his article *Public Policy Implications of Liability Regimes for Injuries Caused by Persons with Alzheimer's Disease* explores the tort liability of persons with Alzheimer's disease, their family caregivers, and their health care providers. He discusses the conflict between protecting third parties from injuries, such as automobile accidents caused by demented drivers, and assuring that persons with Alzheimer's disease are not unnecessarily restricted in their day-to-day lives. Richards concludes that current trends in tort liability will potentially complicate the early diagnosis and management of Alzheimer's disease unless there is intervention by the courts and legislatures.

At the outset, the Working Group developed the "guiding principles" from which their specific recommendations follow. There was general agreement that the diagnosis of Alzheimer's disease does not justify blanket restrictions, except under very limited circumstances. Restrictions should not be based solely on the diagnosis of dementia but as a result of an assessment of the individual's functional limitations.

The example of commercial airline pilots was raised repeatedly as an example of when a restriction is appropriate solely as a consequence of diagnosis. In other circumstances, restrictions on personal freedom, such as driving a car, should be proportional to the importance of the behavior in question to the individual and to the severity of the risk. They discussed the importance of certain activities, such as driving, to a person's independence and quality of life. In suburbia, people are dependent on cars to do most everything or to go anywhere. Yet, there are limited viable public transportation alternatives for people with dementia who can no longer drive. Thus, the Working Group agreed that any restrictions to activities should be accompanied by measures that enhance quality of life and existing capacity.

There was extensive discussion regarding state requirements that physicians report the diagnosis of dementia to a state agency. The Working Group discussed the purposes of reporting to the Department of Motor Vehicles and the Department of Health. A majority of the group agreed that states should not require the reporting of the dementia diagnosis to a state agency, if the person is identified by name. Their concerns are germane to all mandatory-reporting statutes. First, as with HIV/AIDS, there is a potential for bias and discrimination against individuals with dementia. Second, there is an added disincentive for physicians to diagnose individuals with dementia if they know that the identities of the individuals must be reported to a state agency. Third, there may not be adequate confidentiality of an individual's identity and condition disclosed to a state agency. The majority of the Working Group agreed that it would be acceptable to report the diagnosis of dementia to state agencies if a numerical identifier but not an individual's name is used. A minority of the Working Group recommended that the dementia diagnosis be reported only to the state health department, subject to the same confidential restrictions as other disease reports.

The Working Group discussed the response of the criminal justice system and the community to violence by individuals with dementia. The criminal justice system does not respond appropriately to violence or aggressiveness by individuals with dementia. Police, court and jail personnel, and attorneys do not have training to recognize or handle individuals with dementia. There are a growing number of incidents when individuals with dementia are arrested, handcuffed and incarcerated for days due to the lack of alternatives to incarceration to address the needs of this population.

Given that a majority of the violence is targeted against caregivers, the targeted Working Group recommended that existing domestic violence programs improve services to three groups. Services should be provided to address the special needs of victims of dementia-related domestic violence, individuals with dementia acting in a violent manner due to the dementia, and individuals with dementia who are victims of domestic violence. The Working Group discussed how the traditional shelter model is not appropriate for domestic violence due to dementia. If the caregiver is the victim, the caregiver is not inclined to go to the shelter and leave the individual with dementia alone. Yet, the caregiver cannot deliver the "batterer" to a shelter either. The caregiver is caught in a "Catch 22" with nowhere to turn for protection or relief.

In a related matter, there needs to be more education of caregivers on indicators and triggers of violence, and how to diffuse it. Of great concern is the use of guns, knives and other household items that can cause harm to the demented individual and the other members of the house. The Working Group discussed concerns about the prevalence of guns in private homes and the importance of educating caregivers and family members about appropriate measures to store or prevent use of guns and other weapons.

On a final note, there was discussion about the over-utilization of psychotropic drugs and other chemical restraints on individuals with dementia. One member expressed concern that chemical restraints are used inappropriately for the safety of the public, to the detriment of the individual patient. Psychotropic drugs are often used to control "bad behavior" for the convenience of nursing facilities and their staff, rather than the good of the patient. This working group did not adopt a recommendation on this issue because they believed that it was being addressed by the treatment options working group.

IV. Research Consent

Shortly after diagnosis, Marie had the opportunity to participate in a clinical trial run by Dr. Marilyn Albert at Mass General. This pharmaceutical trial offered some potential benefit for research subjects. According to Diane, "we put some pressure on Mom to participate," but it was clear to the entire family that their mother was fully capable of refusing to participate if she really didn't want to. There was, however, no discussion about such matters at an earlier time when Marie was more able to express her views, nor was there an advance directive for research. It turned out that Marie was rejected for the study because of some digestive related problems.

A Working Group on Research Issues considered Mrs. McDonough Larson's experience as well as other research scenarios. The Research Working Group was acutely conscious of the importance of dementia research as well as the need to protect individuals with dementia who participate in research. The group quickly agreed that people with progressive dementia should not be excluded from all research, but that they constitute a vulnerable population requiring special sensitivity and safeguards.

The Research Working Group included individuals who had served on, or been consultants to, the National Bioethics Advisory Commission, the Maryland Attorney General's Working Group on Research Involving Decisionally Incapacitated Subjects, and the New York State Advisory Work Group on Human Subjects Research Involving Protected Classes. As a result, the Research Working Group used as a starting point for discussion the recommendations already formulated by those groups, as summarized in the article by Professor Rebecca Dresser, *Dementia Research: Ethics and Policy for the Twenty-First Century*. The Research Working Group was acutely aware that the legislative and regulatory recommendations of those groups have not been enacted. Rather than recommend legislative and regulatory change, the group sought an alternative way to promote positive change by advancing the substantive issues. Professor Dresser's article aided this endeavor by providing a valuable framework for crafting appropriate safeguards for consent and delegation of consent to research both before and after loss of capacity. The Research Working Group's recommendations focus on actions that can and should be taken by funders and Institutional Review Boards.

With this format for their recommendations, the substantive discussion then focused on: possible safeguards, with an eye toward assuring that such safeguards are effective but not unduly burdensome to researchers; the various degrees of risk involved in research studies and the balancing of risks, potential benefits and the value of the research data to be collected; decision making capacity and loss of capacity as research progresses; informed consent and the issue of research advance directives, particularly the ability to make a decision to participate in unknown future studies; and appropriate third-party decisionmakers.

In discussing the effective safeguards, considerable attention was given to explaining various degrees of risk to the research subjects, particularly minimal risk, minor increase over minimal risk, and greater than minimal risk. The Research Working Group concluded that special protections are necessary whenever the research involves a minor increase over minimal risk and that people with progressive dementia should not be research subjects if the research involves greater than minimal risk and offers no potential for direct benefit.

The Research Working Group recommended further study on the subject of research advance directives. There was considerable concern among members of the group about informed consent in the context of decisions to participate in future studies since the nature of those studies would be unknown at the time the consent is given.

V. Treatment Options

Earlier in the disease, the family considered placing Marie in an assisted living facility. This option turned out to be impossible for two reasons: Marie was a smoker and she had a pet. Therefore, Marie remained at home — initially with her husband and then in 1995 in Georgia with Diane — until four years later in 1999, at which time Marie was admitted to an Alzheimer's unit of an assisted living facility. The decision to place her there was made easier by the fact that she was in need of constant supervision and Diane was exhausted from the constant strain of caregiving. Diane had not made promises to her mother, as many families do, that she would not place her in a nursing home or other facility. Nonetheless, Diane felt some guilt that she was no longer able to care for her at home.

In December 1999, eight months after entering the assisted living facility, Marie fell at the facility and broke her hip. At this point, she was in the advanced stages of the disease, although she was still able to walk prior to the hip fracture. Diane had to make a decision about how to treat the broken hip and was given several options — surgery followed by rehab, no treatment (that would leave her mom permanently confined to a wheelchair), and another option somewhere in between the first two. She ultimately chose the surgery followed by rehab because she knew that her mother valued her mobility. Diane didn't think her mom would want to be confined to a wheelchair because she had been able to walk prior to the fall.

The surgery was successful but her mother went into a rapid decline in functioning and, therefore, could not respond to the rehab therapy. Thus, the overall outcome of the surgery did not accomplish what the family had hoped, and worse, it seemed to precipitate a rapid decline. The orthopedic surgeon had been optimistic about her mother's chances for recovery, stating that "people are up and walking within three days of surgery." The anesthesiologist did not advise Diane of any greater risks posed by her mother's dementia.

Diane's experiences illustrate only a few of the countless treatment questions that may arise during the course of dementia. The Working Group on Treatment Options considered treatment in its broadest sense, perhaps better described as care options, including in-home care. It looked at issues arising before the end of life but after decisionmaking capacity has diminished, or at least when capacity is questionable. Some of the main themes of discussion were: goals of care; the role of the physician in decisionmaking; processes for communicating about and deciding among treatment options; treatment of co-morbid conditions; financing of care; improving institutional care; medication; and palliative care.

The article by Dr. Thomas Finucane, *Thinking About Life — Sustaining Treatment Late in the Life of a Demented Person*, provided a provocative starting point for the Working Group's discussion. Finucane critiques what he labels the "Standard Paradigm" of medical decisionmaking. The Paradigm, Finucane argues, dictates four steps: (1) if you want to know what to do for a patient, ask her what she wants, and do what she says; (2) if she is unable to tell you what she wants, seek guidance from advance directives; (3) if the patient is incapacitated and has no advance directive, identify legitimate substitute decisionmakers who can provide information about what the patient would have said; (4) if no plan to the contrary has been established decisively, act to preserve life. Finucane faults the Paradigm for overestimating most patients' desire to control the details of their medical care and for ignoring most patients' primary desire to be taken care of in hard times with dignity and compassion. The physician's role, according to Finucane, is not merely to deliver a menu of treatment options, but rather, to be a proactive guide in making decisions.

There was strong disagreement in the Treatment Options Working Group on who should make care decisions and what process should be used to make those decisions. Some felt strongly that sometimes the physician may appropriately decide not to present a treatment option and should make a compassionate choice on behalf of the patient. Some also believed that all family members should be party to communications and decisionmaking, even if there is only one authorized decisionmaker. Others believed strongly that the legal model exists to protect patients, that the patient's autonomy should be respected, and that a patient who has designated a proxy may not want other relatives or friends involved in the decisionmaking process. The Working Group also fell short of consensus on how the burdens and benefits of treatment can be weighed in the context of dementia. Therefore, they could not propose consensus recommendations on issues involving weighing treatment options, who decides, what decisionmaking procedure is best, and the appropriate role of the physician in decisionmaking.

Group members also disagreed on how nursing home law and regulations impact dementia care. Some believed that nursing homes are "mercilessly over-regulated" and others expressed the view that nursing home regulation is a needed response to past abuses and substandard care.

Despite these areas of lively discussion and disagreement, the Working Group did achieve consensus on a broad preamble statement and four areas of rec-ommendations. The preamble emphasizes avoiding under- and over-treatment, providing care within the changing context of care needs, and supporting con-tinuity of care. Four recommendations address the intersection of Medicare and Alzheimer's Disease. They urge providers to prescribe individualized care, regardless of real or perceived Medicare coverage rules. They urge that Medicare restrictions on coverage not be based solely on a diagnosis of Alzheimer's Disease. They advocate that eligibility for Medicare coverage of home health services should not rely on the patient's need for a skilled service. Finally, they call on Congress to study broadly the issue of how the Medicare program can best address the health care needs of those with progressive dementia.

The Working Group's recommendations address two other important areas. First, they urge providers and others to resist the influence of the pharmaceu-tical industry. Second, they seek two ways to improve long-term care through research on quality measures of dementia care and through improving the quality of direct care staff in every setting.

Finally, like the Legal Planning and End-of-Life groups, the Treatment Options Working Group struggled with the need to improve decisionmaking where there is no advance directive. This group believed that further study is needed on several facets of default surrogacy and endorsed specific areas of study. That recommendation was adopted by the plenary and merged with sim-ilar recommendations of the other groups that addressed this issue.

VI. End-of-Life Issues

While Marie was in the hospital with the broken hip, she actively stopped eat-ing. At first she ate only small amounts of certain foods but eventually refused to eat at all. The family and nurses tried a number of alternative techniques (liquid diets, blending the food, assisted oral feeding, limiting her diet to her favorite foods, etc.), but Marie flatly refused to eat and at times, threw solid foods across the room and at her caregivers. As Marie began to lose weight, the doctors told Diane that a decision would have to be made regarding how to provide nutrition for her mother. Diane believed that her mother's refusal to eat was a deliberate sign and told the doctors the she did not want a feeding tube for her mother. They did briefly try a nasogastric tube but that caused terrible rashes as well as various stomach problems. Although the doctor respected Diane's decision, other professionals in the Catholic hospital, especially the nurses, were more judgmental. Diane was comfortable with her decision, but it would have been easier had she been able to know exactly how her mother felt about this issue and if the non-family members involved had been more supportive.

As her mother declined after the hip surgery, Diane made the decision to elect hospice care. Diane loved the hospice experience and said the caregivers were terrific. They made her mom as comfortable as possible and were very responsive. Diane felt the hospice care was more self-directed than hospital care. Her mom died just two months after the broken hip incident, but she was comfortable, her quality of life had been preserved and she did not have to go through a lot of invasive procedures.

The Working Group on End-of-Life Decisions considered these scenarios and found considerable consensus on the need to expand the availability of Hospice (under Medicare, Medicaid, and private insurance) and of palliative care, a broader concept than hospice. Persons with Alzheimer's or related dementias do not fit well within current eligibility criteria for Hospice because of the terminal diagnosis, six-month life expectancy requirement.

The Working Group's vision of palliative care is reflected in the World Health Organization's definition of the term, contained in this group's recommendations. The Working Group and the Conference as a whole agreed that the availability of good palliative care for those approaching the end of life is the highest priority. Recommendations call for accrediting organizations and government regulators to adopt requirements for assessing and treating pain, such as those adopted by Joint Conference on the Accreditation of Healthcare Organizations. The recommendations further propose the recognition of palliative care as a reimbursable chronic care benefit separate from hospice and untied to a diagnosis of terminal condition. With respect to the Medicare Hospice benefit, the group developed an immediate recommendation (i.e., actions that the Health Care Financing Administration could take to improve access to hospice right now under current law) and a recommendation for regulatory or legislative change to expand the hospice benefit.

The question of tube feeding as posed by Marie McDonough Larson's experience represents one example of many possible treatment decisions with uncertain value. The Working Group on End-of-Life Decisions also considered decisions regarding: medication for cognitive symptoms; medication for behavioral symptoms; nursing home placement; tube feeding; and use of do-not-resuscitate orders.

The paper by Dr. Thomas Finucane presented an empirical "big-picture" of misperceptions associated with two common interventions in nursing homes — attempted cardiopulmonary resuscitation (ACPR) and tube feeding. While most health facilities retain policies requiring that cardiopulmonary resuscitation be attempted unless there is a clear order to the contrary, the success rates of ACPR are extremely low in nursing homes and, in fact, ACPR is a rare event in nursing homes. Likewise, the hard evidence on the use of tube feedings shows that placement of percutaneous endoscopic gastrostomy (PEG) tubes does not reduce the risk of aspiration pneumonia and, indeed, may increase the risk. Nor is there any evidence that a feeding tube reduces morbidity or mortality, or increases comfort and quality of life.

Despite the evidence, inappropriate patterns of practice, perception, and regulation often persist. Accordingly, the Working Group on End-of-Life Decisions emphasized that a continually updated knowledge base is essential to quality of care. Government regulation of care must incorporate new medical knowledge as close in time as possible to the development of new knowledge.

The Working Group on End-of-Life Decisions also addressed certain aspects of advance planning that were simultaneously considered by the Working Group on Legal Planning. Like the Legal Planning Group, the End-of-Life Group recommended uniformity among the states in connection with the laws regarding capacity, decisionmaking, and treatment of demented patients. The group called attention to the task-specific nature of capacity — especially in the context of advance planning and health-care decisionmaking — and underscored the principle that a diagnosis of dementia by itself should not preclude a patient's ability to participate in health care decisions or create an advance directive. Persons with dementia should be encouraged to participate in decisions as late in the progression of dementia as possible. Further, the End-of-Life Decisions group endorsed the Uniform Health-Care Decisions Act and Uniform Guardianship and Protective Proceedings Act as appropriate models for uniformity.

An ancillary advance directive issue that generated considerable discussion in the Working Group on End-of-Life Decisions was the conceptually problematic and common occurrence in state advance directive laws that permits an individual to revoke her advance directive even if she lacks capacity. The group could not agree upon a specific solution to this feature, but instead recommended further study.

Finally, the End-of-Life Working Group considered the topic of surrogate decisionmaking in the absence of advance directives to be of great importance, as did both the Legal Planning and Treatment Options working groups. The analysis in the Leslie Francis article provided a useful backdrop to three questions considered by this working group: (1) who should be recognized as default surrogates?, (2) what scope of decisionmaking authority should they have?, and (3) what decisionmaking standard should they follow? Because the End-of-Life Working Group offered somewhat different answers to these questions than did the other two groups, the Conference as a whole adopted a recommendation urging further study of the questions.

VII. Genetic Discrimination

Diane and her brother live with an awareness and some trepidation that their mother's condition may have been passed along to them. But, Diane says she does not want to know if she has a genetic predisposition for Alzheimer's. She does worry about the implications of having had a family member with the disease and what that might mean someday for purchasing long-term care or other insurance. To date, the family has no experience with purchasing long-term care insurance.

The members of the Working Group on Genetic Discrimination considered a number of issues: the accuracy and predictive value of genetic testing for Alzheimer's Disease; the privacy of medical information; and the appropriate public policy on genetic testing as it affects the sale of long-term care insurance.

Mark A. Rothstein's article, *Predictive Genetic Testing for Alzheimer's Disease in Long-Term Care Insurance*, provides an overview of long-term care and genetic testing for Alzheimer's Disease. While four genes have been identified that are associated with Alzheimer's Disease, three of these cause early-onset disease which accounts for only about five percent of all cases. The fourth gene, associated with late-onset Alzheimer's, is a susceptibility gene and does not by itself determine whether one develops the condition. Rothstein then describes state and federal law on the use of genetic information by insurance companies. Genetic testing as a basis for medical underwriting is generally prohibited by law for health insurance, but life insurance generally has no such restriction. Finally, Rothstein suggests some analyses for determining appropriate public policy on the issue. He raises the following questions: Is long-term care more like health insurance or life insurance? Does respect for autonomy preclude genetic testing as a precondition for purchase of long-term care insurance? Should we promote broader availability of long-term care insurance to support access to long-term care?

The Working Group discussed the state of the art of genetic testing for Alzheimer's Disease and concluded that currently the testing has little utility as a predictor of the likelihood that an individual will develop the disease. To understand the interaction of heredity and other causative factors, we need further research. Also, the testing has technical difficulties and the costs remain high. Furthermore, the Working Group believed that testing is not useful unless prevention, treatment, and better disease management are developed.

The group concluded that genetic counseling must go hand-in-hand with genetic testing for Alzheimer's Disease. Individuals should receive counseling both before testing and at the time test results are revealed. When the efficacy and costs of genetic testing are improved, an effective counseling program should be developed.

Long-term care insurance should be treated like health insurance rather than life insurance in the context of regulating the use of genetic information, the group concluded. Therefore, legislators should prohibit mandatory testing as a prerequisite to the sale of the insurance, as well as the use of voluntary testing results by sellers.

Finally, the group was very concerned about privacy issues. If long-term care insurers have information on genetic testing for Alzheimer's Disease, participants were fearful that the information could be used to discriminate in the sale of life and health insurance, and in employment. Group members analogized the issue to the adverse impact of genetic screening for cancer susceptibility in a variety of settings.

Building on these discussions, the Working Group drafted a set of recommendations to encourage the availability of long-term care for persons with dementia, all of which were adopted at the conference plenary session. The recommendations encourage the adoption of laws prohibiting insurers from considering genetic predisposition to dementia in setting insurance rates or determining insurability, and from requiring prospective insureds to undergo genetic testing or disclosing the results of previous genetic tests. They urge establishment of standardized long-term care insurance policies, and seek to ban exclusion of coverage for reasons of dementia. The recommendations also endorse education and further study on several aspects of genetic testing, other factors that may be predictive of dementia, confidentiality of genetic information, and long-term care financing.

VIII. Issues in Legal Representation

A multitude of professionals, experts, and formal caregivers became intimately involved in Marie McDonough Larson's life as her disease progressed. However, the conference's mission focused upon the special role of the lawyer.

Client incapacity caused by dementia poses special challenges to the legal profession — practical, professional, and ethical. The predominant ethical benchmark for the profession, the Model Rules of Professional Conduct, provides limited guidance, in part because of the Rules' roots in business and adversarial affairs. Lawyers encounter dementia in a variety of client configurations: representation of an existing client whose capacity begins to decline; spousal representation when the capacity of one spouse is impaired; a child of a former, now impaired, client seeking help in handling the affairs of that client; an existing client seeking help in handling the affairs of a parent with impaired capacity; or family members seeking help for the first time in the affairs of a parent with impaired capacity.

In their article, *Lawyers' Ethical Dilemmas: A "Normal" Relationship When Representing Demented Clients and Their Families*, authors Robert Fleming and Professor Rebecca C. Morgan raise a number of questions. Who can or must be the identified client? How is client confidentiality protected? To what extent can/should confidentiality be waived? To what extent may confidentiality be impliedly waived in the face of impaired capacity? How are conflicts of interest avoided or handled if they arise between clients jointly represented or sequentially represented? How does the lawyer maintain a normal relationship with a client whose capacity is declining? What is the lawyer's responsibility to assess capacity? What protective action can or must the lawyer take if the client is unable to make "adequately considered decisions"? How is confidentiality to be respected in the face of incapacity? The Fleming/Morgan article posits three basic models of representation: (1) one client-one lawyer approach; (2) representation of multiple individual clients; or (3) joint representation of a group of family members. The last option includes further variations in representation — as intermediary, as "third party neutral," as "counsel for the situation," or as true "family representation."

The group concluded that the ABA Commission on Evaluation of the Rules of Professional Conduct's (Ethics 2000) proposed revisions to Model Rule 1.14 and its Comments will go far toward resolving the question of how lawyers can assist persons with dementia and their families within the constraints of the rules of professional conduct. Ethics 2000 would provide greater flexibility and guidance to the rule currently in place. It was recommended that the ABA and individual states and jurisdictions adopt the Ethics 2000 revisions as proposed, and immediately undertake an educational effort that will result in lawyers implementing the underlying principles of this rule.[*]

The question of who is the client was much discussed, and several indicators were suggested, including: Who has the legal problem? Who benefits from the proposed course of action? Who needs (special) protection? Who made the appointment? Who communicates with the lawyer, attends the meeting, or makes phone contact? Who thinks they are the client? Who provides substantial information? Who pays the bill? Who is the focus of the proposed action? The group recommended that Conference sponsors study the issue of whether "family" representation (with fallback positions in event of conflicts) would better serve the interests of the person with diminished capacity than the status quo, with emphasis on the person or persons with diminished capacity.

As for capacity itself, after discussion about who determines capacity and under what circumstances, the group recommended that the Conference sponsors develop practice guidelines for lawyers that provide criteria for assessing capacity in different circumstances/situations that encourage the use of available community resources, e.g., geriatric assessments and multi-disciplinary panels to assist in assessing capacity as well as heightened awareness of issues raised by persons with diminished capacity, including assessing capacity, and sensitivity to gender, culture, religion, ethnicity, and socio-economic status.

An important theme of these discussions was the need for education — of consumers, the legal profession, the judiciary and other professionals about the needs and capabilities of persons with diminished capacity; the causes, etiology, and progression of dementia; community resources and best practices for serving the needs of persons with diminished capacity; and the importance and value of preserving personal autonomy for persons with diminished capacity. Legal professional education on these matters should begin in law schools and be infused across the curriculum, as well as be included in programs for lawyers and the judiciary. In addition, consumers should be made aware of the professional and ethical issues that arise in representing persons with diminished capacity.

IX. Dispute Resolution

Marie McDonough Larson was blessed with a family that successfully worked through the challenges related above in a way that kept them connected and pulling together. However, disputes during trying times are common, and family members may find it hard to reach consensus or even to tolerate proposed decisions. Moreover, individuals with dementia may engage in behaviors that threaten safety and force upon families divisive dilemmas, as with Marie's insistence on continuing to drive. Conflicts involving elderly people with cognitive impairments range from everyday struggles for autonomy to sudden and significant life and death decisions. This population becomes involved in disputes arising in elderly housing and other community settings, and in long-term care facilities such as nursing homes or retirement communities; family or guardianship concerns; and bioethical and health-care delivery problems.

The article by Erica Wood, *Dispute Resolution and Dementia: Seeking Solutions*, points out that "such intractable disputes strain the fundamental nature of the dispute resolution process, which assumes that parties in conflict can remember the facts at issue, understand the process for resolution, and abide by the decision reached." Her article examines how the classic mediation model might be adapted and what practical, legal and ethical issues arise.

The Working Group on Dispute Resolution considered both the myriad sources of disputes and the numerous mechanisms potentially available for resolution. The Working Group observed that these mechanisms — including both formal and informal mediation as well as facilitated consensus approaches — are under-utilized and not tailored to the special problems of individuals with dementia. Dispute resolution simply is "not on the radar screen" for those who regularly interact with such individuals. The absence of alternative dispute resolution strategies only increases the likelihood of resort to costly and emotionally trying guardianship proceedings. This need to heighten awareness and education is reflected in the Working Group's specific recommendations. Group members concurred that collaborative problem-solving approaches should be the first option considered in addressing disputes of persons with dementia.

Working Group members also recognized the need for a set of ethical and operational guidelines for mediation involving persons with dementia. Their recommendations take the first steps toward creating such guidelines, focusing on the determination of capacity to mediate; the reporting of any elder abuse revealed during a mediation; the need for training of mediators in elder rights, dementia-related information, and cultural norms; and the monitoring of mediated agreements through practical plans for follow-up.

X. The Recommendations

The recommendations adopted by the full conference follow this introduction. They represent the product or "house" of the future, built through the collaboration of this interdisciplinary group. We hope that the recommendations will provide direction to policy makers, guidance to practitioners and educators, and an impetus to all for further discussion of the needs and interests at stake. Each of the Conference sponsors is committed to disseminating and implementing these recommendations in the venues and in the manner most meaningful to their respective missions. We each envision a hopeful future for the care and support of individuals with dementia and their families.

QUESTIONS

1. Do you think the elderly are more susceptible to crime, fraud, and abuse than the general population, or just more often targeted as victims? Does it make a difference in how the public and private sectors address these problems?

2. Is the federal government better able than the states to protect the older population from crime, fraud, and abuse? Why?

3. How much do we really know about how disability levels are changing in the aging population? Does it matter?

4. What is the importance to national, state, and local transportation planning efforts of the housing and mobility patterns of persons fifty-five and older?

5. Should states or the federal government bear primary financial responsibility for addressing the daily living problems facing the nation's elderly?

6. Should the legal profession develop a separate or supplemental code of ethics for attorneys who practice elder law?

7. What pragmatic effects might the mobility, transportation, and housing needs of the elderly have on the practitioner's ability to serve this client base?

D. THE PRACTICE OF ELDER LAW

Bureau of Labor Statistics
Occupational Outlook Handbook, 2006-07 Edition
http://www.bls.gov/oco/ocos053.htm

Job Outlook: Lawyers. Employment of lawyers is expected to grow about as fast as average for all occupations through 2014, primarily as a result of growth in the population and in the general level of business activities. Job growth among lawyers also will result from increasing demand for legal services in such areas as health care, intellectual property, venture capital, energy, *elder*, antitrust, and environmental law. In addition, the wider availability and affordability of legal clinics should result in increased use of legal services by middle-income people. . . Also, mediation and dispute resolution increasingly are being used as alternatives to litigation.

Amelia E. Pohl
What Is Elder Law Anyway?
19 NOVA L. REV. 459, 459-63 (1995)[*]

Many of us who now consider ourselves "Elder Law" attorneys were practicing elder law long before it had a name. We were a group of attorneys concerned with problems unique to the elderly who worked as their advocates. Through various publications by agencies such as the Center for Social Gerontology, the American Association of Retired Persons, the Center for Public Representation, and the Legal Counsel for the Elderly, we became aware that other attorneys and agencies had similar interests and concerns. Because of the concern for the unique legal problems facing the elderly during the 1970s, the Department of Health, Education and Welfare awarded grant monies to provide direct legal services to the elderly in 1975.

The legal profession's involvement with the elderly began in 1978 when the American Bar Association formed the Commission on Legal Problems of the Elderly ("Commission"). Since 1988, the Commission has published a quarterly newsletter, BIFOCAL, and a bimonthly bulletin to various bar committees on the elderly. Attorney participation in elder law on the national level began with

---

the formation of the National Academy of Elder Law Attorneys ("NAELA"). The initial group of twenty-six founding members decided to form NAELA while they were attending a joint conference on Law and Aging held in Washington, D.C. The term, "Elder Law," was coined by Michael Gilfix, Esquire, one of NAELA's founding members. The NAELA headquarters were established in Tucson, Arizona in 1987. NAELA grew rapidly to 1150 members in forty-eight states and the District of Columbia by 1991.

It is not surprising that the practice of elder law organized on a national level since much of elder law relates to federal programs that benefit the elderly in general, such as the Medicaid program. Many elder law attorneys join NAELA to meet with other attorneys throughout the United States at the various symposia and institutes offered by NAELA, to exchange information and to determine how government benefit programs are administered in different states of the union.

Other benefits were realized by elder law attorneys through their association with NAELA. By 1992, the express mission of NAELA was to "ensure delivery of quality legal services for the elderly and to advocate for their rights." Its stated purpose was to "provide information, education, networking, and assistance to attorneys, Bar organizations, and other individuals or groups advising elderly clients and their families." NAELA also seeks to promote "technical expertise and ethical awareness among attorneys, Bar organizations . . . [and t]o develop awareness of the issues surrounding legal services for the elderly."

The prominence of NAELA has helped to establish and to define the practice of elder law. At the first NAELA annual institute, held in November 1991 in San Antonio, Texas, a survey was taken of the attorneys attending the institute to determine how those attorneys defined elder law. NAELA found the three major categories to be:

(1) Estate planning and administration, including tax questions;

(2) Disability, Medicaid, and other long-term care issues; and

(3) Guardianship, conservatorship, and commitment matters, including fiduciary administration. Other areas cited by NAELA included retirement benefits, Medicare, disability benefits, litigation in the areas of elder abuse, and elder fraud.

. . . One cannot practice elder law for any period of time without understanding that the needs of the clients extend beyond their legal problems. The clients may be frail or ill and require home health care or placement in an institutional facility. The clients may be well but fearful that future illness may deplete financial resources, and thus may need to consider a long-term care insurance policy. If a client is a caretaker and is overwhelmed with the demands of caring for a person who is suffering from some form of dementia, the client may need other support services offered by various religious organizations or nonprofit organizations, such as the Alzheimer's Association. Peter J. Strauss, author of many elder law publications, notes in his book, AGING AND THE LAW, that meeting the needs of the client(s) depends on moving beyond conventional legal work to offering practical assistance. Quite often, the attorney is the right person to provide information about home care, nursing homes, special geriatric health programs, adult day care, and respite care; handling even a few elder-law cases quickly leads to an accumulation of such information and contacts with the right people. . . .

There is no elder law certification in the State of Florida. However, the National Academy of Elder Law Foundation ("NAELF"), an organization created by the Board of Directors of NAELA, is, for the first time, offering, board certification upon meeting of the requirements set by NAELF. One of these requirements is successful completion of an examination covering the following topics:

(1) Health and Personal Care Planning (including advance medical directives and living wills);

(2) Pre-Mortem Legal Planning (wills and trusts);

(3) Fiduciary Representation (including guardianship, trustees and personal representatives);

(4) Legal Capacity Counseling (advising how capacity is determined and the level of capacity required for various legal activities);

(5) Individual Representation (of those who are or who may be the subject of guardianship or conservatorship procedures);

(6) Public Benefits Advice (including Medicaid, Medicare, social security, and veterans' benefits);

(7) Advice on Insurance (including health, life, long-term disability, and burial/funeral policies);

(8) Resident Rights Advocacy (including advising patients of their rights and remedies in matters such as admission, transfer, discharge policies, and quality of care);

(9) Housing Counseling (reviewing options and financing of options such as mortgage alternatives, life care contracts, and home equity conversion);

(10) Employment and Retirement Advice (pensions, retiree health benefits, and unemployment benefits);

(11) Income, Estate, and Gift Tax Advice;

(12) Counseling about Tort Claims Against Nursing Homes;

(13) Age and/or Disability Discrimination Counseling (including employment and housing, and Americans with Disabilities Act); and

(14) Litigation and Administrative Advocacy (including will contests, contested capacity issues, and elder abuse).

Then what is elder law? Is it all of the fourteen areas identified above? Or is it better understood as described in NAELA's brochure, *Elder Law: A Legal Practice Coming of Age*? Rather than being defined by technical distinctions, the brochure defines elder law by the client to be served. . . .

National Academy of Elder Law Attorneys
Questions & Answers When Looking
For an Elder Law Attorney
http://naela.org/public/QA.htm*

Legal problems that affect the elderly are growing in number. Our laws and regulations are becoming more complex. Actions taken by older people with regard to a single matter may have unintended legal effects. It is important for attorneys dealing with the elderly to have a broad understanding of the laws that may have an impact on a given situation, to avoid future problems.

Unfortunately, this job is not made easy by the fact that Elder Law encompasses many different fields of law.

Some of these include:

- Preservation/transfer of assets seeking to avoid spousal impoverishment when a spouse enters a nursing home

- Medicaid

- Medicare claims and appeals

- Social security and disability claims and appeals

- Supplemental and long term health insurance issues.

- Disability planning, including use of durable powers of attorney, living trusts, "living wills," for financial management and health care decisions, and other means of delegating management and decision-making to another in case of incompetency or incapacity.

- Conservatorships and guardianships

- Estate planning, including planning for the management of one's estate during life and its disposition on death through the use of trusts, wills and other planning documents

- Probate

- Administration and management of trusts and estates

- Long-term care placements in nursing home and life care communities

- Nursing home issues including questions of patients' rights and nursing home quality

- Elder abuse and fraud recovery cases

- Housing issues, including discrimination and home equity conversions

- Age discrimination in employment

---

* Reprinted with permission from NAELA.

- Retirement, including public and private retirement benefits, survivor benefits and pension benefits

- Health law

- Mental health law

Most elder law attorneys do not specialize in every one of these areas. So when an attorney says he/she practices Elder Law, find out which of these matters he/she handles. You will want to hire the attorney who regularly handles matters in the area of concern in your particular case and who will know enough about the other fields to question whether the action being taken might be affected by laws in any of the other areas of law on the list. For example, if you are going to rewrite your will and your spouse is ill, the estate planner needs to know enough about Medicaid to know whether it is an issue with regard to your spouse's inheritance.

Attorneys who primarily work with the elderly bring more to their practice than an expertise in the appropriate area of law. They bring to their practice a knowledge of the elderly that allows them and their staff to ignore the myths relating to aging and the competence of the elderly. At the same time, they will take into account and empathize with some of the true physical and mental difficulties that often accompany the aging process. Their understanding of the afflictions of the aged allows them to determine more easily the difference between the physical versus the mental disability of a client. They are more aware of real life problems, health and otherwise, that tend to crop up as persons age. They are tied into a formal or informal system of social workers, psychologists and other elder care professionals who may be of assistance to you. All of these things will hopefully make you more comfortable when dealing with them and ease your way as you try to resolve your legal problem.

Finding an Elder Law Attorney

Your first question may be: How do I find an elder law attorney? Before making the effort, step back a moment and try to determine whether you actually have a legal problem in which an attorney needs to be involved. If you're not sure, ask your clergy, your social worker, your financial advisor, or a trusted friend to help you decide whether this is a legal issue rather than a medical or a social services issue. Legal expertise is expensive and it serves you well to know that you actually need legal assistance before seeking an attorney.

There are many places to find an attorney in your city or state who specializes in problems of the elderly. This Web site includes a searchable directory of attorneys who belong to NAELA. Also, you may check with local agencies to obtain good quality local referrals. Some of the agencies you may want to call include:

- Alzheimer's Association

- American Association of Retired Persons

- Area Agency (or Council) on Aging

- Children of Aging Parents

- Health Insurance Association of America

- National Citizen's Coalition of Nursing Home Reform

- Older Women's League

- Social Security Office

- State Civil Liberties Union

- State Insurance Commissioner

- State or Local Bar Association

- Support Groups for specific diseases

- Hospital or Nursing Home Social Service Department

Most of the above agencies can be found in the yellow pages under the heading "Associations."

If you know any attorneys ask them for a referral to an elder law attorney. An attorney is in a good position to know who handles such issues and whether that person is a good attorney. Such persons are often the best and safest sources of referrals.

Ask Questions First

Ask lots of questions before selecting an elder law attorney. You don't want to end up in the office of an attorney who can't help you. Start with the initial phone call. It is not unusual to speak only to a secretary, receptionist or office manager during an initial call or before actually meeting with the attorney. If so, ask this person your questions.

- How long has the attorney been in practice?

- Does his/her practice emphasize a particular area of law?

- How long has he/she been in this field?

- What percentage of his/her practice is devoted to elder law?

- Is there a fee for the first consultation and if so, how much is it?

- Given the nature of your problem, What information should you bring with you to the initial consultation?

The answers to your questions will assist you in determining whether that particular attorney has those qualifications important to you for a successful attorney/client relationship. If you have a specific legal issue that requires immediate attention, be sure to inform the office of this during the initial telephone conversation.

Once You Have Found an Attorney

When you have found an appropriate attorney, make an appointment to see him/her. During the initial consultation, you will be asked to give the attorney an overview of the reason you are seeking assistance, so be sure to organize and bring all the information pertinent to your situation.

After you have explained your situation, ask:

- What will it take to resolve it?

- Are there any alternative courses of action?

- What are the advantages and disadvantages of each possibility?

- How many attorneys are in the office?

- Who will handle your case?

- Has that attorney handled matters of this kind in the past?

- If a trial may be involved, does he/she do trial work? If not, who does the trial work? If so, how many trials has he/she handled?

- Is that attorney a member of the local bar association, its health advocacy committee, or trust and estates committee?

- Is that attorney a member of the National Academy of Elder Law Attorneys?

- How are fees computed?

- What is his/her estimate of the cost to resolve your problem and how long will it take?

* * *

Get It in Writing

Once you decide to hire the attorney, ask that your arrangement be put in writing. The writing can be a letter or a formal contract. It should spell out what services the attorney will perform for you and what the fee and expense arrangement will be. REMEMBER — even if your agreement remains oral and is not put into writing, you have made a contract and are responsible for all charges for work done by the attorney and his/her staff.

Make It a Good Experience

A positive and open relationship between attorney and client benefits everyone. The key to getting it is communication. The communication starts with asking the kinds of questions contained in this document. Use the answers to the questions as a guide not only to the attorney's qualification, but also as a way of determining whether you can comfortably work with this person. If your concerns are given short shrift, if you don't like the answers to these questions, if you don't like the attorney's reaction to being asked all those questions, or if you simply do not feel relaxed with this particular person, DO NOT HIRE THAT PERSON. Only if you are satisfied with the attorney you have hired from the very start will you trust him or her to do the best job for you. Only if you have established a relationship of open communication will you be able to resolve any difficulties which may arise between the two of you. If you take the time to make sure that you are happy right at the beginning you can make this a productive experience for both you and the attorney. You will thank yourself, and your attorney will thank you.

QUESTIONS

1. What areas of pre-law education would best serve someone interested in practicing elder law?

2. In view of population demographics and the market outlook of practitioners of elder law, should law schools expand their elder law curricula and encourage interdisciplinary education among law students who anticipate a career in this area?

3. What is the role of professional organizations such as the National Academy of Elder Law Attorneys in defining the scope of a legal practice specialty and regulating lawyers who hold themselves out as specialists in that area? Should membership in NAELA and similar organizations require some proof or evidence of competence or excellence in the particular practice specialty these groups represent?

Chapter 2

SPECIAL ETHICAL PROBLEMS
WHEN REPRESENTING THE ELDERLY

Conduct of one's law practice in accordance with the rules of professional ethics is a burden borne by all lawyers regardless of their clientele. This chapter will, therefore, emphasize the particular problems which arise perhaps more frequently when working with the elderly both because of age-related impairments and family dynamics related to the transfer of wealth from one generation to the next.

These materials are not exhaustive nor do they provide definitive answers to the elder law practitioner's most intractable problems. Many of the questions presented would be answered differently, yet fairly, by different lawyers. The following materials are offered for your consideration, in the hope that you will bring your values and life experience to bear on the application of the rules of our profession to your professional life.

A. JOINT OR MULTIPLE REPRESENTATION

Although joint representation is not recommended, it is practiced routinely. The literature on legal ethics is replete with cautionary tales of parties who seemed to have the same interests at the beginning of the representation, but who, when their interests diverged, left the lawyer stranded. The following materials will focus on the common situations which arise when representing senior citizens whose spouses, children, and caregivers get involved.

1. The Spouse

Molly M. Wood
WHO'S THE CLIENT? Competency and the Lawyer-Client Relationship
http://www.keln.org/ethicsmmw.html[*]

I. WHEN SOMEONE OTHER THAN THE SENIOR CITIZEN REQUESTS REPRESENTATION

A. The Spouse

It is common for spouses, particularly in long-lasting marriages, to become accustomed to acting for one another. It comes as a shock, therefore, when one of the marriage partners encounters barriers when attempting to handle legal matters for the other. Although it is important to handle the contacting spouse diplomatically, it is incumbent upon intake personnel and the responsible lawyer to deal directly with the person whose legal problem is prompting the contact, if at all possible.

1. Joint Representation (*See* Rules[1] 1.7 *Conflict of Interest* & 2.2 *Intermediary*)

Joint representation is potentially at odds with the lawyer's duty of loyalty to a client, but a client may consent to representation notwithstanding a potential conflict. Subparts (a)(1) and (b)(1) of Model Rule 1.7 contemplate a two-part test: The lawyer must reasonably believe that the client will not be adversely affected, and the client must consent after consultation. Thus, the lawyer must disclose that multiple representation is sought and must disclose the implications of common representation, including its risks and advantages. When more than one client is involved, the question of conflict must be resolved as to each client. Moreover, there may be circumstances where it is impossible to make the disclosure necessary to obtain consent. (*See* Comment to Model Rule 1.7).

The key issue in joint representation with respect to married people is whether effective representation of one spouse precludes effective, loyal representation of the other. Ideally, both marriage partners should have individual representation. As noted by example earlier, however, in marriages of longstanding the potential conflict of interest is more theoretical than real. In the estate planning context, for example, marriage partners who have never been married to another, share the same children, own all their property jointly, and want their children to share equally in their property after the death of the survivor must be counseled that that survivor could alter his or her disposition of the jointly held property at will. It would be common practice, however, to counsel both parties regardless of the potential conflict after consultation.

---

[*] Copyright © 1996. Reprinted with permission.

[1] All references to "Rules" in this chapter are to the Model Rules of Professional Conduct adopted by the House of Delegates of the American Bar Association on August 2, 1983.

Division of Assets [*See* Chapter 8, Part B — Eds.], counseling also implicates a potential conflict of interest which often turns out to be academic. The
Medicaid applicant, that is, the institutionalized spouse, is likely to be incompetent and unable to consent to joint representation. When the community
spouse is seeking protection against impoverishment and is pursuing Medicaid
assistance for the institutionalized spouse, however, it is proper to characterize
the community spouse as the client. The institutionalized spouse is unrepre-
sented, but is unlikely to be adversely affected by the lawyer's representation
of the well spouse. Moreover, the Division of Assets process is not typically
adversarial. If it becomes so, the lawyer may be forced to withdraw or take other
remedial action.

2. Scope of Representation (*See* Rules 1.2 *Scope of Representation* & 2.1
   Advisor)

If a lawyer perceives that the client expects assistance that would be
improper or illegal for the lawyer to provide, the lawyer has duty to clarify the
limitations on the scope of the lawyer's conduct. Such a duty to inform the
client protects the client and ensures that the client's decisions regarding
whether and how to proceed are knowledgeable.

"A lawyer may limit the objectives of the representation if the client consents
after consultation." Rule 1.2(c). The lawyer should outline the scope of representation on the representation agreement or employment contract in as much
detail as practicable, and provide a signed copy to the client.

QUESTIONS

1. Besides the problem areas suggested above, what other types of legal
issues would be particularly sensitive to conflicts arising out of joint representation?

2. Wouldn't you be afraid of losing both clients if you suggested that one of the
marriage partners should get separate counsel? How could you avoid this problem?

2. Adult Children

Tim Takacs & David L. McGuffey
Excerpts from *Revisiting the Ethics*
of Medicaid Planning
17 NAT'L ACAD. ELDER L. ATT'YS J.
http://www.abanet.org/genpractice/lawyer/complete/sp98burke.html[*]

[Report from a telephone conversation]: "When the agent learned we had
[no company that would provide long term care insurance for a gentleman in his
90s], he thought they could do some Medicaid Planning instead. I gasped and

---

[*] Copyright © 1996. Reprinted with permission.

said, 'Why in the world do that?' . . . 'Here we have an individual who is coming into the final phase of life, who has accumulated over his 90+ years a tidy sum of a half a million dollars. Why wouldn't we want these last years to be the very best for him and his family? I don't believe Medicaid planning will do that for him, but his own money will!'"

Ethical codes regulate the practice of law, and the practice of Elder Law is fraught with ethical pitfalls. This article explores some of those pitfalls in the Medicaid Planning context. In our 2002 law review article, we began a discussion concerning the tension that arises where Medicaid asset protection planning clashes with an individual's responsibility to pay for his own nursing home care. Under the broad view, which could be called macro-ethics, we concluded that Medicaid Planning as practiced by Elder Law Attorneys is ethically justified in the present economic environment. In a free market system in which "health" is not a right but is bought and sold just like any other commodity, no participant in that market has an obligation to pay more than the legal market price for that commodity.

The inquiry does not end there. Tools such as Medicaid Planning are not always used for just ends. We now return to another conclusion we reached in our first article, that our primary goal as Elder Law Attorneys should be to improve the lives of our clients. In this narrower context, what could be called micro-ethics, we now address how Medicaid Planning should be done and under what circumstances it is dedicated to justice.

In this article, we turn our attention to whether Medicaid Planning is ethically justified in the context of family wealth preservation. More to the point, does Medicaid asset protection planning, if its principal purpose is to pass those assets to the next generation, serve the interests of our Client-Elders?

We don't think so — not if the goal of protecting the Elder's assets takes priority over the goal of bettering the Elder's life. Asset protection, alone, abandons the well-being of the living Elder and, thus, is contrary to the purpose of Elder Law. Asset protection, alone, pits the Elder's well-being against the interests of her heirs, creating a conflict. Our conclusion is that Elder Law Attorneys should resolve this conflict in favor of the Elder and that a failure to do so is unethical. A secondary implicit conclusion is that ethics requires foresight and planning, and that it should begin not later than when the client walks in the Elder Law Attorney's door.

Framing the Issue

The attorney-client relationship is a creature of contract and, once formed, the attorney owes her client a duty of loyalty and diligence. Ordinarily, the attorney-client relationship cannot be formed unless both parties are competent to contract. If competent, the Elder may retain the attorney; if not, she cannot retain the attorney's services and the lawyer's duty will be to the person engaging her services. Nonetheless, because the person approaching the attorney is typically concerned with protection of the Elder's assets, the Elder's interests must be considered and the Elder may be deemed the intended beneficiary of the plan. Taken a step further, unless the person approaching the Elder Law Attorney brings with her the power to transfer the Elder's assets, the Elder Law

Attorney cannot transfer those assets without the Elder's consent. Moreover, where consent pre-exists the attorney-client relationship, the attorney must not assist a client in taking action that the lawyer knows is criminal or fraudulent. Diverging interests could create a "conflict" or a Catch-22, precluding all Medicaid Planning transfers.

Common sense tells us, however, that ethical rules which bind lawyers were designed to prevent abuse; they were not designed to prevent attorneys from assisting persons who face the financially devastating consequences of paying privately for long-term care. If the Elder Law Attorney focuses on the Elder's well-being, these conflicts resolve themselves, and the Elder Law Attorney may proceed by undertaking planning in which asset transfers are directed primarily to caring for the Elder, not asset protection. In this elder-focused, as opposed to asset-focused, approach, the plan centers on what benefits the Elder and is not limited to a review of the Elder's Medicaid eligibility and potential transfer strategies.

The Typical Medicaid Plan

To shift the cost of the nursing home to the State Medicaid program, the Elder must "spend down" until her "countable assets" reach a certain threshold (in most states, $ 2000). The Elder's first contact with the Elder Law Attorney is often at this stage of her health care crisis, when her family members meet the Elder Law Attorney for help in developing a Medicaid Plan to "save the money from the nursing home." For the Elder Law Attorney, the ethical dilemma is whether the Plan is to be structured to benefit the Elder or to benefit someone else.

* * *

The Elder Law Attorney purports to represent the Elder. The Elder Law Attorney's work consists of saving $ 50,000 for the Children and assisting the Children with the Medicaid application. After Medicaid starts paying, he closes his file. But whose interests does he serve here? How has Mom benefited from the Medicaid Plan that her Elder Law Attorney developed for her? If the Plan is not structured to address the Elder's long-term care needs, in our view the attorney has ignored the spirit, if not the letter, of Rule 1.14.

Principlism as an Ethical Framework

For attorneys, "ethics" means the Rules of Professional Conduct, or their state specific counterpart, where the attorney practices. In this article we focus on the American Bar Association's Model Rules of Professional Conduct (MRPC). Attorneys engaged in Medicaid Planning typically act as advisors and, therefore, MRPC Rule 2.1, together with MRPC Rule 1.2(a), define the lawyer's duties to her client. Comment 2 to Rule 1.2 indicates that Rule 1.14 is also applicable where the client suffers from diminished capacity. Rule 1.14 indicates that, as far as reasonably possible, the attorney should maintain a "normal" attorney-client relationship with clients who suffer from diminished capacity. Confronting this tangled web, the Elder Law Attorney asks, quite appropriately, "who is the client, who has decision-making authority, and who do I owe a duty to?" As discussed below, where the client lacks capacity, a departure from the normal attorney-client relationship is justified.

We believe "principlism" provides a framework within which Elder Law Attorneys can resolve conflicts between the interests of the Elder and those who claim to speak for the Elder. The principlism approach to analyzing conflicts in clinical medicine has become the dominant theory of bioethics during the last quarter of the twentieth century. As articulated by Beauchamp and Childress, principlism is a weighted approach to health care decision making that takes into account four central principles: (1) autonomy, (2) nonmaleficence, (3) beneficence, and (4) justice. These four principles serve as general guides for the analysis of specific cases.

Autonomy refers to the individual's freedom from controlling interference by others and from personal limitations that prevent meaningful choices, such as diminished mental capacity that affects understanding. Two conditions are essential for autonomy: liberty, which is the independence from controlling influences; and the individual's capacity for intentional action. The health care professional owes his patient the duty to respect the patient's autonomy. The concepts of the "capacity" of the client to contract with the attorney for legal services and "informed consent" invoke the principle of autonomy.

Nonmaleficence asserts an obligation not to inflict harm on the person to whom a duty of care is owed within a special relationship such as attorney-client or physician-patient. This principle sets the minimum standard for the duties owed by the health care professional to his patient. The direct precursor to this principle is set forth in the physician's Hippocratic Oath to "first, do no harm."

The third principle, beneficence, refers to actions performed that contribute to the welfare of the patient.

Justice refers to fair, equitable and appropriate treatment in light of what is due or owed to a person. When considering the principle of justice, it is important to distinguish between three different types of justice: (1) commutative justice, which refers to that which is owed between individuals, for example, the relationship between principal and agent; (2) contributive justice, which refers to what individuals owe to society for the common good, including the rights and responsibilities of citizens to obey and respect the rights of all and the laws devised to protect peace and social order; and (3) distributive justice, which refers to what society owes to its individual members.

We believe principlism is particularly helpful where the Elder's capacity to consent is questionable. Before embarking on an analysis of principlism, we look briefly at *Fickett v. Superior Court*, 558 P.2d 988 (1976). There, the Arizona Court of Appeals employed a balancing test in determining whether there was sufficient privity between a guardian's attorney and a ward to create a duty to the ward. It "involves the balancing of various factors, among which are the extent to which the transaction was intended to affect the plaintiff, the foreseeability of harm to him, the degree of certainty that the plaintiff suffered injury, the closeness of the connection between the defendant's conduct and the injuries suffered, the moral blame attached to the defendant's conduct, and the policy of preventing future harm." *Id.* at 990. This, in our humble opinion, sounds like principlism.

Beneficence: Do Good

Happily, Elder Law is a practice where attorneys can make a difference in the quality of their lives. It is often said that "elder law attorneys can do well by doing good." How does an elder law attorney "do good"?

For the Elder Law Attorney, the attorney-client relationship often begins, as we wrote earlier, amidst a health care crisis. Initially then, the Elder, or more likely, the Elder's surrogate, seeks the advice of the Elder Law Attorney. The Elder has been hospitalized and may already have been moved to a skilled nursing facility. Mom cannot return home, and the family does not know what to do. They need the counsel of an Elder Law Attorney to help them sort out their options and advise them what to do. The attorney should be proactive and should provide sound advice.

Autonomy: Respect for Client Choices

Respect for individuality is a core value in our society. Implicit within any discussion of autonomy is the concept of equality, at least as it relates to human dignity. Autonomy is the natural by-product of that value and is therefore an ideal foundation on which we build an ethical framework. Frequently, the attorney is called on to maximize the client's autonomy.

"Personal autonomy is, at a minimum, self-rule that is free from both controlling interference by others and from limitations, such as inadequate understanding, that prevent meaningful choice." Exercising autonomy depends upon relevant information and implies a capacity to use that information. We refer to the legal corollary of medicine's concept of "informed consent." The principlism approach to dealing with ethical conflicts, whether in medicine or law, begins by educating the client concerning available options and the probable consequences of each option. Unless autonomy is counterbalanced against another principle, the client exercises autonomy by choosing among his options.

The problem inherent with beneficence (discussed below) is that it may lead to paternalism. By their superior training, knowledge and experience, Elder Law Attorneys, like physicians, are better positioned to determine and advocate for the client's best interests. Those qualifications, however, are not a mandate which overrule the Elder's wishes. Failure to respect the Client-Elder's right to make choices can result in paternalism.

We emphasize that it is not the attorney's place to make decisions for the client. The attorney must respect the client's right to make choices. Once these choices are made, autonomy trumps beneficence, and the lawyer must allow the client to direct the scope of representation, but only after the lawyer has discharged his duty to obtain informed consent. In other words, to enable the Client-Elder to make informed decisions about the Medicaid Plan, the Elder must be given adequate information on the risks and the benefits of shifting nursing home costs to the Medicaid program. This is called the "informed consent process." The Elder Law Attorney must educate the Elder about the alternatives to Medicaid-financed nursing home care available to the Elder, the deficiencies in that care, and the risks and benefits of relying on public financing for the Elder's nursing home care. The Elder Law Attorney must obtain the Client-Elder's (now informed) consent before implementing the Plan and keep the Elder informed on the consequences of the Client-Elder's decision. Obtaining informed consent is as essential to elder law practice as it is to the medical profession. The principlism approach is satisfied through the informed consent process, provided the Elder has capacity to exercise her right to autonomy or the Elder's surrogate who exercises autonomy on her behalf does not have a conflict of interest.

As Elder Law Attorneys, we frequently encounter situations where we have reason to question the Elder's mental capacity to understand his options. If we believe that the Elder's mental capacity is insufficient for adequate understanding of his options, true autonomy cannot exist. Instead, autonomy is exercised through a surrogate. Otherwise stated, a recurring problem we face is the identification of our client or, in this case, the moral agent. An ethical dilemma — or conflict of interest — arises when the Elder lacks capacity, the Elder's surrogate has a conflict of interest (that is, the surrogate's interest in protecting the Elder's assets for his own benefit) may diverge from the Elder's interests, and there is no clear guidance from the Elder to enable us to resolve the issue with reasonable certainty. In these circumstances, MRPC Rules 1.14 and 1.7(b) suggest that the principle of autonomy should be weighed against the principles of nonmaleficence, beneficence, and justice.

We believe the principle of autonomy and the conflict of interest rules are interwoven. While surrogate decision making can render the issue problematic, careful application of the conflict rules (guided by the principles of nonmaleficence, beneficence and justice) will unravel the Gordian knot.

In practice, how does this work? First, the Elder Law Attorney should consider who engaged the attorney's services. If it is the Elder, Rule 1.2 provides that the Elder guides the scope of the representation. If it is a surrogate, Rules 1.2(d) and 1.14 require that the lawyer prevent misconduct. Even where the Elder is clearly not the client, Rule 1.7(b) requires that Elder Law Attorneys weigh the interests in favor of the Elder. It is, after all, the Elder's money that is the focus of the typical Medicaid Plan.

Nonmaleficence: Do No Harm

[A Medicaid Plan typically has] the effect of impoverishing Mom so she [can] qualify for Medicaid-financed nursing home care. Until she attains Medicaid eligibility, she has retained only enough money to purchase and receive the basic package of nursing home services. Once Medicaid begins to pay, Mom continues to receive that basic package. Only the source of payment for the basic package has changed (from private pay to Medicaid). This Medicaid Plan is unethical because it violates the principle of nonmaleficence. Although she qualifies for Medicaid, Mom is nonetheless harmed because the Medicaid Plan deprives her of resources that she could use to purchase supplemental long-term care services that are not included in the basic services paid for by Medicaid. Worse, if there is a possibility that the Elder's needs can be met by not relying on Medicaid to pay for long-term care (for example, the Elder leaves the nursing home), the Medicaid Plan violates the principle of nonmaleficence by making that an economic impossibility.

Medicaid provides a limited bundle of benefits. It finances care that must include certain required elements including, among other things, nursing home care for residents in a manner and in an environment that promotes maintenance or enhancement of each resident's quality of life. Each resident must receive, and the facility must provide, the necessary care and services to attain or maintain the resident's highest practicable physical, mental and psychosocial well-being, in accordance with the resident's comprehensive assessment and plan of care.

There is, unfortunately, no compelling reason to assume the elder's needs will be met in a nursing home. The shortcomings in nursing home care are well known. Recent studies indicate that the quality of care in nursing homes remains deficient. Deficiencies in good nursing home care have been laid directly at the doorstep of inadequate staffing. According to a major federal study, more than 90 percent of nursing homes do not have enough workers to take proper care of residents.

Respect for client autonomy does not abrogate or excuse the lawyer's duty to prevent harm to the client. The Elder Law Attorney is ethically justified in advising the Elder or directing the Elder's surrogate to focus the Plan on bettering the Elder's life, with asset protection concerns becoming secondary. Elder Law Attorneys are not only advisors but advocates for their Client-Elders as well. As client choices are made, the attorney's duty shifts to ensuring that someone is (or will be) available to speak for the Client-Elder and that misconduct or harm is addressed, mitigated, or avoided. "The lawyer is then free, except in circumstances where the [personal representative] might be abusing the position, to follow the [personal representative's] instructions. The burden of determining what is in the best interests of the disabled person is then lifted from the lawyer's shoulders, allowing the lawyer to perform more traditional functions in an objective environment."

Justice

The fourth principle is justice. In our 2002 law review article, we implicitly applied the principles of contributive justice and distributive justice in reaching our conclusion that Medicaid planning is justified in a macro-ethics setting. In a free market health care system, distributive justice protects only access to health care — and, even then, largely only for those with the ability to pay. As a consequence, the duty owed by each individual within this health care market is to pay only for one's own health care. In such a system, justice does not require the health care purchaser to pay a higher price if she can obtain a lower price without violating the system's legal or ethical norms (without, for example, concealing assets which is Medicaid fraud).

In the micro-ethics setting, however, we focus instead on the principle of commutative justice. What duty does the Elder's agent or surrogate owe him? One duty we have already alluded to: to avoid doing harm to the Elder. The duty to avoid harm is especially poignant within the principal-agent relationship. The presumption is that the Elder has selected his agent specifically to shield him from harm in the event the Elder loses his autonomy and capacity. Moreover, the principle of justice invokes another related duty: to respect the Elder's human dignity. Within the micro-ethics setting, this duty requires that the Elder's agent not regard his principal, the Elder, solely as a source of economic gain to the agent.

Applying Principlism: An Elder-Centered Approach

The elements of Principlism are meaningless unless we apply them. If we begin with an assessment of the Elder's needs, we believe the Elder Care Plan will take a different view from the one described above.

Every plan should begin by assessing the Elder's needs with a view toward providing quality care in the least restrictive environment possible. That may involve preserving assets, not for the purpose of passing them to heirs, but for the purpose of spending them on home health care or assisted living. As Beauchamp and Chambless argue, we should contribute to our client's welfare.

In problem-solving for clients, Elder Law Attorneys should be mindful of general demographic trends and should make themselves aware of the Elder's client's specific wishes. Generally, when needs must be addressed, most Elders want them satisfied at home. Of those persons over age 70 living in the community and seriously ill, research shows that 29 percent say they would rather die than go to a nursing home. Of equal significance, home care tends to improve overall health. Regarding the specific client, there is no substitute for taking the time to speak with the Elder or, if that is not possible, exploring other means of determining the Elder's wishes.

Absent an understanding of Medicare and Medicaid home health programs, as well as other caregiver resources available in the community, the Elder Law Attorney's planning will focus primarily, if not solely, on asset protection. Elder Law Attorneys who do not familiarize themselves with those programs and resources will be more likely to leap directly to nursing home care. Nursing home care, however, will separate the Elder from a familiar environment, will impose a more rigid schedule on the Elder and, even if family visits are not physically impeded, will make them more clinical. Where the Elder Law Attorney lacks expertise necessary to recommend home health options, utilization of a geriatric care manager may be appropriate.

When the Elder's need for long-term care can no longer be met either inside the home, or without the intervention of paid providers, the Elder enters, as we say, "the long-term care system." The Elder (and the Elder's family) are now embarking on an arduous journey through murky waters. Let them begin their journey with the observation that "the current system in our country for addressing long-term care is hardly systematic, it is a hodgepodge of services that fail to meet the needs of the elderly and disabled in the variety of long term care settings. The long-term care system is economically inefficient and it fails to assure the quality of services which are provided." The "system" does not fund assisted living and provides home health care in an inconsistent fashion. As a consequence, the long-term care financing system is biased in favor of providing long-term care in an institutional setting, which usually means a nursing home, even though it costs less to support individuals in their own homes and communities.

The Elder Care Plan

Let's now consider an alternative Elder Care Plan under the same facts as before, but apply an approach of "weighing and balancing" the four principles. First, the Elder Law Attorney will have fully investigated the Elder's circumstances. Specifically, the Elder Law Attorney will know Mom's health care needs, both what she needs now and what she can reasonably expect to require in the future. The attorney then provides a full explanation to the Children of possible options on how those needs can be met for the Client-Elder. That explanation includes a discussion of moral, economic, social and political factors. Specifically, the Elder Law Attorney will engage in an extensive explanation of the long-term care system, how long-term care is financed, who furnishes it and how, and the shortcomings in the provision and financing of long-term care. The Elder Law Attorney should be able to discuss understaffing and related problems that occur in nursing homes and other long-term care facilities and how the Elder's funds can be used to ameliorate those problems. That is, the Elder Law Attorney must be familiar with the resources available in her community and how much those resources cost.

Mom's Children are the remainder beneficiaries of her estate. Money she does not spend for her own care can be expected (and it is expected, by the Children) to accrue to the benefit of the Children. The Children, one of whom is Mom's attorney-in-fact, acknowledge that they have a conflict of interest. If Mom could speak clearly and loudly in her own voice, what would she want? All of her money to be paid to the nursing home? None of it? Some set aside for supplemental care? Self-serving declarations that "Mom and Dad would never want all of their money to go to the nursing home" do not rise to the level of certainty of choice required to implement a Medicaid Plan that sets aside nothing for Mom's supplemental needs during the remainder of her actual life expectancy.

Under the guidance of the Elder Law Attorney, the Children define the goals of the Plan for Mom. The first priority of the Plan is that Mom gets good care, whether in a nursing home or other residential facility. Second, the Plan presupposes that the Elder Law Attorney will monitor the performance of the Plan during the remainder of Mom's life and help the Children make decisions about her care. Third, Mom does not want to burden her Children with the costs of her burial. Fourth, Mom wants to leave her Children a financial legacy. Preservation of family wealth is an important goal for her, but under the Elder Care Plan, this goal stands fourth in priority, not first.

* * *

Under this Elder Care Plan, Mom's money is devoted first to improving Mom's quality of life. Who can make a plausible argument that our alternative Elder Care Plan will not provide a greater contribution to the improvement of Mom's life than the Medicaid Plan? In our view, the only plausible criticism of this plan comes from third parties who are more interested in acquiring Mom's assets than in caring for Mom.

While asset protection may be the goal of potential heirs, it may not be the Elder's goal. If another, less restrictive care plan can be developed, our goal as elder law attorneys should be to provide a vehicle for meeting the Elder's needs in a way that achieves the Elder's goals.

Making the Transition to an Elder-Centered Practice

Medicaid Planning is a tool in the Elder Law Attorney's toolbox. But like any tool, it can be misused. Misuse occurs when "the transaction" (that is, asset transfers) takes priority over the Elder's well-being. Our goal in addressing this subject is not to define the model plan. Instead, our goal is to ensure that we, as Elder Law Attorneys, keep our eye on the ball (so to speak) by focusing on the Elderly. Fundamentally, the practice of law requires dedication to justice and the common good.

Elder Law Attorneys who choose to make the transition from an asset-focused to elder-centered practice will enjoy an increasing demand for their services. In our experience, families, almost without exception, are concerned foremost about the care and well-being of their loved one. They may present themselves to our office with questions about "saving Mom's money from the government and the nursing home," but they do want our help navigating the long-term care maze and do want Mom to get the best care. They don't know what it is, where to go for good care, or how to get it. Elder-centered Elder Law Attorneys do.

As former NAELA president Cynthia Barrett recently observed:

> Some elder law attorneys developed a transactional practice focused primarily on Medicaid eligibility, and concentrated on the mechanics of practice management to move the many files through the process. Some elder law attorneys used their expertise in responding to health care crises to build a broader practice, assiduously developing the guardianship, probate, trust administration, and estate-planning tools that they were accustomed to using for health-care crises.

The current recession brought on diminished government revenues, which has caused a tightening of eligibility for Medicaid. The elder law attorney with a solely transactional practice, focused on Medicaid, will see a drop in case numbers as the eligibility gateway closes. The elder law attorney who can handle health-care crises will see an increase in the number of such cases, and an increase in demand for good fiduciary management to make the private pay dollars last longer.

Knowing the ever-changing Medicaid eligibility rules does distinguish the elder law practitioner from the traditional estate planner. . . .

The ethics rules are not handcuffs. Instead, they provide a framework within which we can resolve ethical dilemmas. If the legal profession hopes to maintain credibility in the community, they should be interpreted in a manner consistent with accepted notions of justice or morality. Elder Law Attorneys should not be guided by rules of ethics that elevate the principle of autonomy above all others, particularly where capacity is questionable. This can be accomplished by planning, before the representation begins, to create a holistic care and financial plan which ensures the well-being of the Elder. Anything less will contribute to negative impressions of the legal professional already prevalent in society and will impede our ability as professionals to contribute to the overall well-being of our clients.

* * *

QUESTIONS

1. Under what circumstances do you think it comports with the ethics rules governing the legal profession to assist a client to make gifts of her resources so that she can become eligible for welfare assistance?

2. Would your answer be different depending upon the specific facts surrounding the client's situation? What facts might, in your opinion, change the propriety of the legal strategy?

Molly M. Wood
WHO'S THE CLIENT? Competency and the Lawyer-Client Relationship
http://www.keln.org/ethicsmmw.html*

I. WHEN SOMEONE OTHER THAN THE SENIOR CITIZEN REQUESTS REPRESENTATION

* * *

B. Adult Children & Other Relatives

Generally, the child or other relation must have a Durable Power of Attorney which is broad enough to encompass the scope of the representation sought. A child who has been court-appointed Guardian/Conservator, either limited or otherwise, would generally have the authority to engage a lawyer on behalf of the Ward/Conservatee. Particularly in the case of married seniors who have adult children from prior marriages, children and other relatives can have subtle (or not so subtle) conflicts of interest with respect to the proposed client. Absent an appropriate surrogate decisionmaker or the client's informed consent, it is improper for the lawyer to discuss the legal affairs of a client or proposed client with anyone other than the client. (*See* Section III. CONFIDENTIALITY, *supra*).

* * *

III. CONFIDENTIALITY

A. The Attorney-Client Privilege

Unlike Rule 1.6, the Attorney-Client Privilege is a common law evidentiary rule which prevents the client or the lawyer from being compelled to disclose communications between lawyer and client in the course of their professional relationship. The client should be cautioned against conduct which impliedly

---

* Copyright © 1996. Reprinted with permission.

waives the privilege, however, such as allowing others to participate in attorney-client meetings.

B. Rule 1.6 *Confidentiality of Information*

Rule 1.6 encompasses the duty of loyalty to the client and serves to protect the client's privacy interests. The obligation extends to all information about a client acquired in the course of the representation, regardless of whether disclosure would be embarrassing or detrimental. Thus, the obligation of confidentiality encompasses more than the attorney-client privilege since it can include the client's confidences and secrets even if the same information may be discoverable from other sources. The obligations of loyalty and confidentiality continue after the agency relationship has been concluded. (*See also* Rules 1.8 *Conflict of Interest: Prohibited Transactions,* and 1.9 *Conflict of Interest: Former Client.*)

1. Authorized Disclosures

An exception to confidentiality applies to disclosures to which the client has given informed consent. Rule 1.6(a) also recognizes that client consent may be implied as well as express as to disclosures necessary to effect the representation. A common application of this rule is the lawyer who seeks guidance from an appropriate diagnostician about a disabled client's condition. In such a case, the lawyer is disclosing confidential information for the client's own benefit and may do so even without the client's consent. (*See* Rule 1.14 *Client under a Disability.*)

QUESTIONS

1. If the client expresses the desire to have the adult children or others present in the interview, what is the effect, if any, on the lawyer-client relationship?

2. Can you discuss the client's legal matters with the others outside the presence of the client?

Kansas Statutes Annotated § 59-605
Preparation of will or provision of will that gives any devise or bequest to writer or preparer

Any provision in a will, written or prepared for another person, that gives the writer or preparer or the writer's or preparer's parent, children, issue, sibling or spouse any devise or bequest is invalid unless:

(a) The writer or preparer is related to the testator by blood, marriage or adoption and the devise or bequest is not more than the writer or preparer or the writer's or preparer's parent, children, issue, sibling or spouse would receive under the laws of intestate succession, if the property passed in that manner; or

(b) it affirmatively appears that the testator had read or knew the contents of the will and had independent legal advise with reference thereto. . . .

QUESTIONS

1. Would it be proper for you to draft a Testamentary Will for your grandparents? What ethics rules, court rules, or state laws are implicated?

2. What standard procedures beyond the "testamentary formalities" would you implement to protect your client's estate from a Will contest?

3. Caregivers and Other Unrelated Third Parties

Molly M. Wood
WHO'S THE CLIENT? Competency and the Lawyer-Client Relationship
http://www.keln.org/ethicsmmw.html[*]

I. WHEN SOMEONE OTHER THAN THE SENIOR CITIZEN REQUESTS LEGAL ASSISTANCE

* * *

C. Social Workers, Health Care Professionals, and Others

Although the nature of our work implicates collaboration with social workers, health care professionals, and service organizations devoted to meeting the needs of senior citizens, these professionals do not have the authority to enter into the attorney-client relationship or seek any but the most general legal advice on behalf of senior citizens. They should be encouraged to refer potential clients to us directly.

In re Brantley
920 P.2d (Kan. 1996)

Disciplinary proceeding was brought against attorney in connection with his representation of elderly client for whom conservatorship was established. After recommendation of discipline was made by hearing board of Kansas Board for Discipline of Attorneys, the Supreme Court held that attorney's failure to provide competent representation, to abide by client's decisions as to scope of representation, to keep client reasonably informed, or to communicate basis or rate of fee to client, representation of client despite conflict of interest, failure to maintain normal relationship with client believed to be

---

[*] Copyright © 1996. Reprinted with permission.

under disability, and lack of candor toward tribunal warranted published censure and payment of restitution to client in amount of fees paid to attorney.

* * *

FACTS

1. Respondent, Keen K. Brantley, is a licensed Kansas attorney who has engaged in the general practice of law in Scott City, Kansas, since 1970.

2. The complainant is Carla Hendrix, granddaughter of Mary Storm, a ninety-one year old resident of Anchorage, Alaska, who formerly resided in Scott City, Kansas. Following the death of her personal attorney, Charles Fleming, Mary Storm became a client of the Respondent in 1983. During the time in question, Mary Storm had done most of her banking business at the First National Bank of Scott City but had done some business at the Security State Bank in Scott City. At no time has Mary Storm ever been found to be incompetent, incapacitated or disabled by any medical person or court in Kansas or Alaska.

3. In 1977, Mary Storm's husband, R.E. Pfenninger, died leaving his entire estate to her under a joint and mutual will. The estate was valued at some $77,000.00. Under the terms of the will, any property remaining at Mary Storm's death was to be divided equally between the surviving children of Mr. Pfenninger by a previous marriage and Mary Storm's only child, Wayne Hendrix, by a prior marriage.

4. In 1985, Mary's brother, Leo Scott McCormick, died leaving his entire estate to Mary Storm, the only surviving McCormick sibling. The McCormick estate was valued at approximately $193,000.00. The First National Bank of Scott City was the executor and was represented by Respondent Brantley and his firm.

5. In February 1986, Mary Storm wrote a letter to her son, Wayne Hendrix, and his wife Delores stating, among other things, that her brother's estate would be settled soon and that most of the estate would go to Wayne as she did not need it. She further observed that she and Wayne were the only surviving family members.

6. Following the distribution of the McCormick estate, during the period April 1986, through July 1987, Mary Storm, from time to time, deposited sums of money in a savings account that her son and daughter-in-law had opened at Security State Bank in Scott City, Kansas. Mary Storm wrote seven different checks for deposit to their account over the fifteen month period totaling $191,425.00. Mary Storm's name was not on the Hendrix account, and at no time did Wayne or Delores Hendrix transfer any of Mary Storm's money into their account. During this period of time, Mary Storm, with the assistance of Respondent Brantley, caused Wayne Hendrix's name to be added as a joint tenant to several of her certificates of deposit and parcels of inherited real estate. At no time has Wayne or Delores Hendrix attempted to exercise any right of ownership to the certificates of deposit or the several parcels of real estate or the income therefrom.

* * *

7. From October 1986, through January 1988, the Hendrixes authorized wire transfers in the total amount of $85,000.00 from their Scott City account to their credit union account in Alaska, where they then resided.

8. In December 1986, Mary Storm fell and fractured her hip, which injury required a period of hospitalization followed by nursing home care. Prior to such injury Mary Storm had lived in her own home, had driven her own car, and had been self-sufficient.

9. Mary Storm continued to reside in a nursing home, and in July 1989, she was visited by her step-son, Ralph Pfenninger, who resided in Oklahoma. During this visit, Mr. Pfenninger states that he was advised by the nursing home administrator that Mary Storm was giving all of her money away and would soon have nothing to live on. As a matter of fact, Mary Storm had more than $100,000.00 in liquid assets and a comfortable income.

10. Ralph Pfenninger also visited with an officer of the Security State Bank of Scott City [Louise Wendler], who advised him that there had been some large transfers of funds from Mary Storm to her son, Wayne Hendrix.

11. Ralph Pfenninger then met with Respondent Brantley and expressed his concerns relative to the feared dissipation of Mary Storm's assets. Respondent Brantley was informed that the Security State Bank of Scott City had indicated a willingness to serve as conservator, and he thereupon conferred with Louise Wendler, a Vice President of Security State Bank, who further confirmed to him confidential information that Wayne and Delores Hendrix had made transfers from *their* Kansas account to *their* Alaska account totaling $85,000.00. Ms. Wendler further volunteered that, in her opinion, Mary Storm's deposits into the Hendrixs' account could not possibly be gifts due to their large amount. She admitted, however, that she had never consulted Mary Storm about this assumption.

12. Respondent Brantley never met personally with Mary Storm regarding the voluntary conservatorship but recalls that he talked by telephone with her at the nursing home and inquired if she was aware that Wayne Hendrix was in town withdrawing large amounts from her bank accounts. Understandably, Mary Storm replied that she knew nothing about any recent withdrawals from her accounts. Bank records in evidence reflect that she was correct in her reply.

* * *

13. Without further investigating the reported transfers of Mary Storm's assets, and without further personal conversation with Mary Storm, Respondent Brantley caused voluntary conservatorship proceedings to be prepared and sent the same to the nursing home for Mary Storm's signature with an office employee. The Security State Bank was appointed conservator under the voluntary conservatorship proceeding on July 11, 1989. Respondent Brantley candidly admits that, at this time, he was representing the conservatee, Mary Storm; her step-son, Ralph Pfenninger; and the conservator, Security State Bank, all in the same proceeding.

14. The conservatorship operated without event until September 21, 1989, when Respondent Brantley filed a Petition for Sale of Personal Property at

Public Auction. Respondent Brantley prepared such pleadings for his client Security State Bank. The Petition was set for hearing on September 29, 1989, and copy of notice of hearing was reportedly mailed to Mary Storm. On September 22, 1989, Respondent Brantley filed a Petition for Appointment of Guardian ad Litem. The proposed guardian ad litem, William Wright, was not known to Mary Storm. As in the case of the Petition for Sale, Mary Storm was not consulted in connection with the Petition for Appointment of Guardian ad Litem.

15. Prior to the hearing on the Petition to Sell Personal Property and without court authorization or Mary Storm's knowledge, the Security State Bank contacted an auction company in early September and caused Mary Storm's personal property to be boxed and inventoried. Further, auction handbills were caused to be posted in Scott City and advertisements for sale placed in the local newspaper. Without court approval of the sale, the Security State Bank paid the auction company $450.00 out of Mary Storm's conservatorship funds on September 28, 1989, a day before the hearing.

16. The above mentioned Petition for Sale of Personal Property at Public Auction, prepared by Respondent Brantley, contained an allegation, "It is necessary to sell said personal property to pay taxes and expenses of the conservatorship." The allegation, which is untrue, was verified on behalf of the conservator, Security State Bank.

17. Mary Storm's grandson, Richard Hendrix of WaKeeney, Kansas, was alerted by one of Mary Storm's neighbors a week before the proposed auction. He contacted WaKeeney attorney Paul Oller in regard to representing Mary Storm in having the sale halted. Mary Storm subsequently retained Paul Oller to represent her and instructed him to have the sale stopped and the conservatorship terminated.

18. At the September 29, 1989, hearing on Mary Storm's Petition for Termination of Conservatorship, the voluntary conservatorship was terminated and the Petition to Sell Personal Property was denied.

19. Later, on the same day, Respondent Brantley presented to the magistrate judge, ex parte, a Temporary Order restraining the disposition of the estate of the "conservatee" until the "petition" could be heard and further orders issued. No notice was given to Mary Storm or her attorney, Paul Oller. The Temporary Order was filed at 4:20 o'clock p.m. on September 29, 1989.

20. The above noted Temporary Order contained the caption of the previously terminated voluntary conservatorship proceeding. The order contained no explanation or justification for having been filed in a closed case. The Temporary Order was also silent as to the identity of the client being represented by Respondent Brantley in such matter.

21. The Temporary Order stated that there should be no further disposition or depletion of the estate of the conservatee at a time when there was no conservatee and no conservatee estate. The Temporary Order prepared by Respondent Brantley further provided that the Temporary Restraining Order would continue in effect until the petition could be heard and further orders of the

court issued, all at a time when there was no petition on file. In preparing and filing such order, Respondent Brantley was not following the direction of his purported client Mary Storm, and was acting adversely to her.

22. On October 2, 1989, Respondent Brantley filed an Involuntary Petition for Appointment of Conservator, on which petition he shows himself as attorney for the Petitioner, Ralph Pfenninger. At no time did Respondent consult with his purported client Mary Storm, or obtain her consent to his materially adverse representation of her step-son.

23. The Petition for Involuntary Conservatorship, prepared by Respondent Brantley for his client Ralph Pfenninger, stated that Mary Storm was "completely disoriented as to person, place and time as noted in the letter of Daniel R. Dunn, M.D. marked Exhibit A attached hereto and made a part hereof." In fact, there was no Exhibit A attached to the petition, there was not in existence any letter from Dr. Dunn, Respondent Brantley never contacted Dr. Dunn to request such a letter, and Respondent Brantley candidly admitted that he made up the language supposedly "noted in the letter." At no time during any of the conservatorship proceedings did the Respondent ever meet personally with Mary Storm to determine for himself her state of mind or knowledge of her financial affairs, and his false statements contained in said petition have never been corrected.

24. On October 3, 1989, Respondent Brantley obtained Preliminary Orders which he had prepared on behalf of his client Ralph Pfenninger. On October 10, 1989, Mary Storm, through her attorney, Paul Oller, filed Answer of Proposed Conservatee, which answer raised multiple objections to Respondent Brantley's continued representation adverse to Mary Storm and listed numerous violations of the Model Rules of Professional Conduct. The answer further requested an accounting of all funds received by and spent by the conservator and requested disqualification of Respondent Brantley and discharge of the court appointed attorney. Respondent Brantley did not file a response or withdraw from the adverse representation.

25. Purportedly at the request of the court-appointed attorney for Mary Storm, William Wright, the magistrate judge undertook to interview Mary Storm at the nursing home without any notice to interested parties. Later, he undertook to interview Mary Storm a second time in a Garden City hospital where she was recovering from recent cancer surgery. At the hospital visitation, the magistrate was accompanied by a court reporter. Again, the visitation was without notice to Mary Storm's family or her retained attorney of record. On October 12, 1989, the day following her cancer surgery, the magistrate judge dismissed Mary Storm's granddaughter from the hospital room and proceeded to interrogate Mary Storm. While not within the purview of the panel, the panel is shocked that a magistrate judge would undertake to interrogate an elderly person on the day following major surgery.

* * *

26. On October 16, 1989, hearing was had before the magistrate judge on Ralph Pfenninger's Petition for Involuntary Conservatorship and Mary Storm's Motion for Disqualification of Brantley. Apparently based upon his interview

with Mary Storm, the magistrate judge ordered her attorney, Paul Oller, discharged from her representation and the motions filed by Oller were denied. No decision was reached in connection with the Petition for Involuntary Conservatorship, which matter was continued to November 14, 1989.

27. On October 25, 1989, Mary Storm's attorney, Paul R. Oller, filed an Attorney and Client Agreement with the court followed with the filing of a renewed answer on behalf of Mary Storm raising issues earlier asserted. Mary Storm again requested that Respondent Brantley be disqualified because of a conflict of interest, but the Respondent continued his representation of the step-son in the adversarial involuntary conservatorship proceeding.

28. At a court hearing on November 6, 1989, Respondent Brantley; Louise Wendler from the Security State Bank; Mary Storm's attorney, Paul Oller; and court appointed attorney, Bill Wright, appeared and agreed to a partial conservatorship of Mary Storm's assets which would not include her home, any of her personal property and her personal bank account for her own spending. Security State Bank was discharged and a new conservator appointed. No conservatorship bills were presented at the November 6, 1989, hearing when all of the parties were represented. Instead, Respondent Brantley, representing the discharged conservator, prepared an order for the magistrate's approval for the discharged conservator to pay claims of $1,802.41 including $575.00 to Respondent Brantley. Respondent Brantley gave no notice of such order for proceedings thereon. His bill for services was never furnished to Mary Storm or her attorney, Paul Oller. As a result of the order for approval of claims of the conservator, Mary Storm paid for Respondent Brantley's representation of the Security State Bank and the step-son, Ralph Pfenninger, which services included efforts to sell her personal property and place her in an involuntary conservatorship, both against her expressed wishes.

29. In November 1989, Mary Storm was returned to possession of her home where she continued to reside with minimal outside assistance until the Spring of 1993, at which time she moved to Anchorage, Alaska, to live with her son, Wayne Hendrix, and his wife.

30. In July 1993, Mary Storm executed affidavits and powers of attorney empowering her granddaughter, Carla Hendrix, to return to Kansas, gather her assets, terminate the conservatorship and transfer Mary's assets to Alaska. As an alternative the conservatorship could be transferred to Alaska for court supervision.

31. A hearing was had on Mary Storm's request at which hearing Respondent Brantley appeared on behalf of the step-son in opposition to Mary Storm's expressed wishes. Mary Storm's request was denied by the court for the stated reason that she was not represented at the hearing and needed to be represented in order for a full adjudication to be rendered. Later, however, on October 13, 1993, the Mary Storm conservatorship was transferred to Anchorage, Alaska, to be supervised by the probate court in that jurisdiction. Since such transfer both the step-son, Ralph Pfenninger, and the Respondent Brantley have continued to attempt to monitor said proceedings and to obtain confidential information from the Alaska conservatorship.

32. In ex parte meetings with the magistrate judge and in scheduled hearings in the Storm case, Respondent justified the need for a conservatorship for Mary Storm by stating that the evidence would prove that her son, Wayne Hendrix, was an alcoholic, was financially irresponsible, and was guilty of wrongfully misappropriating some $85,000.00 of her funds. In fact, Respondent did not have evidence to support such claims and had not made a reasonable investigation in such regard.

* * *

33. While never medically or judicially determined, Mary Storm's ability to make adequate considered decisions in connection with Respondent's representation was, from time to time, apparently impaired, particularly during her nursing home stay and her post-cancer surgery period.

DISCUSSION

* * *

MRPC 1.1 — Competence

MRPC 1.1 . . . provides: A lawyer shall provide competent representation to a client. Competent representation requires the legal knowledge, skill, thoroughness and preparation reasonably necessary for the representation.

> The Comment provides in part: In determining whether a lawyer employs the requisite knowledge and skill in a particular matter, relevant factors include the relative complexity and specialized nature of the matter, the lawyer's general experience, the lawyer's training and experience in the field in question, the preparation and study the lawyer is able to give the matter and whether it is feasible to refer the matter to, or associate or consult with, a lawyer of established competence in the field in question. . . ."Competent handling of a particular matter includes inquiry into and analysis of the factual and legal elements of the problem, and use of methods and procedures meeting the standards of competent practitioners. It also includes adequate preparation."

Brantley has been practicing law in Scott City since 1970. He was the attorney for the executor of the estate of Scott McCormick, Mary Storm's brother, with Mary Storm being the sole heir of that estate. Brantley prepared a codicil for Mary Storm's will (naming him as her executor) and in 1986, at her request, prepared assignments by which Mary Storm created joint tenancy ownership in three real estate installment contracts with her son, Wayne. Brantley was an experienced attorney well acquainted with Mary Storm and her legal affairs.

(a) Failure to Fully Investigate Claims of Improper Transfers

According to Brantley, the driving force behind this whole unfortunate scenario was Brantley's belief that Wayne Hendrix had misappropriated $85,000 from Mary Storm. After Ralph Pfenninger and Louise Wendler told him of the supposedly suspicious transfers by Wayne Hendrix in 1986 and 1987, Brantley called Mary Storm at the nursing home in July 1989 and asked her if she knew about them. Brantley did not provide sufficient information to Mary Storm for her to respond to his inquiry. She could not have made an informed decision about transactions that occurred some two years earlier, based on the scant information Brantley provided her over the telephone. There is no indication that Brantley ever asked Mary Storm if she wanted him to investigate the bank records on this matter, or that Brantley (with Mary Storm's permission) ever obtained or showed the documentation or specific information on these transfers to Mary Storm to confirm whether she knew or approved of them.

The subject wire transfers were from the Hendrix account at Security State Bank in Scott City to the Hendrix account in Alaska and all occurred from October 1986 (prior to Mary's broken hip) to January 1988. Those transfers, by themselves, should not have aroused suspicion. There were several large deposits into the Hendrix account at Security State Bank from April 1986 to July 1987, totaling $191,425.62. All but $69,862.88 of those deposits took place prior to December 1986, before Mary Storm broke her hip. The panel's finding of incompetence based on Brantley's failure to investigate the circumstances of the supposedly improper transfers is amply supported in the record.

(b) Failure to Interview Mary Storm Before Proposing the Conservatorship

Establishment of a conservatorship, even a voluntary one, is a drastic step. . . . Yet Brantley took this drastic step without even a face-to-face interview with Mary Storm, choosing instead to rely on a brief telephone conversation and the statements of Ralph Pfenninger, her stepson, and Louise Wendler from Security State Bank.

(c) Permitting Sale-related Activities Prior to Court Approval

As Brantley emphasized, there is no evidence in the record that Brantley knew Security State Bank engaged an auction company and incurred advertising expenses before the sale was approved by the court. The bank's actions were improper, but there was no evidence that Brantley permitted those actions. The panel's conclusion that Brantley permitted the Bank's actions does not appear to be supported by the evidence in the record. Other conduct by Brantley, however, established his violations of MRPC 1.1.

(d) Obtaining Ex Parte Order Prior to Filing Petition for Involuntary Conservatorship

The record indicates that after Judge Goering terminated the voluntary conservatorship, Brantley represented to the judge that he had evidence Wayne Hendrix had misappropriated $85,000 of Mary Storm's funds and that Mary Storm's assets were at risk without a conservatorship in place. Not surprisingly, Judge Goering then suggested that an involuntary conservatorship should be filed, issued the temporary restraining order against Mary Storm's assets, and directed William Wright, as guardian ad litem to lock up her house. Judge Goering acted upon Brantley's inaccurate, incomplete, and unsupported representations. Brantley demonstrated incompetence by making those representations to the judge.

(e) Filing Involuntary Petition Containing Allegation as to Non-existent Medical Report

Brantley excuses this mishap because the allegation was taken from a standardized form and left in the petition by mistake. Also, Judge Goering had already stated he would not rely on a doctor's letter and intended a complete evaluation of Mary Storm by Area Mental Health Center. The fact that Judge Goering would not rely on a doctor's letter does not excuse Brantley's incompetence in leaving this untrue allegation in the petition. If Brantley knew at the time the petition was drafted that Judge Goering was not going to rely on a doctor's letter, then why was the allegation included? Even if this allegation was taken from a standardized form, it specifically referred to both Mary Storm and Dr. Dunn. The involuntary petition was a two-page document easy to proofread.

MRPC 1.2 — Scope of Representation

MRPC 1.2 . . . provides:

> (a) A lawyer shall abide by a client's decisions concerning the lawful objectives of representation, subject to paragraphs (c), (d), and (e), and shall consult with the client as to the means which the lawyer shall choose to pursue.

The Comment provides in part:

> The client has ultimate authority to determine the purposes to be served by legal representation, within the limits imposed by law and the lawyer's professional obligations. . . .

> In a case in which the client appears to be suffering mental disability, the lawyer's duty to abide by the client's decisions is to be guided by reference to Rule 1.14.

Failure to Abide by Mary Storm's Decisions Concerning Representation

Brantley never consulted with Mary Storm as to whether she wanted to have her household property auctioned off. Instead, he relied on Louise Wendler's and the guardian ad litem's statements that Mary Storm had agreed to the sale. At the September 29, 1989, court appearance, when he learned that Paul Oller had filed an objection to the sale on behalf of Mary Storm and the conservatorship had been terminated, Brantley represented to Judge Goering that Hendrix was misappropriating Mary Storm's funds and convinced the judge that a temporary restraining order needed to be issued. Brantley followed that representation by filing the petition for involuntary conservatorship signed by Ralph Pfenninger. Brantley's authority to act on behalf of Mary Storm ended when the voluntary conservatorship was terminated.

Brantley contends that the parties' settlement agreement in November 1989 allowing the conservatorship to continue somehow cures this ethical violation. Brantley ignores the fact that before the settlement agreement was reached, Mary Storm had to retain her own attorney to represent her interests and oppose the involuntary conservatorship.

MRPC 1.4 — Communication

MRPC 1.4 . . . states:

   (a) A lawyer shall keep a client reasonably informed about the status of a matter and promptly comply with reasonable requests for information.

   (b) A lawyer shall explain a matter to the extent reasonably necessary to permit the client to make informed decisions regarding the representation.

The Comment provides in part:

> The client should have sufficient information to participate intelligently in decisions concerning the objectives of the representation and the means by which they are to be pursued, to the extent the client is willing and able to do so. . . .

> . . . The guiding principle is that the lawyer should fulfill reasonable client expectations for information consistent with the duty to act in the client's best interests, and the client's overall requirements as to the character of representation.

> Ordinarily, the information to be provided is that appropriate for a client who is a comprehending and responsible adult. However, fully informing the client according to this standard may be impracticable, for example, where the client is a child or suffers from mental disability. *See* Rule 1.14.

Mary Storm has not been determined to be mentally incompetent or disabled, so she should have been entitled to appropriate communication from Brantley. Brantley breached his ethical obligation to Mary Storm when, prior to the conservatorship, he failed to provide her sufficient information (and get her permission to do so) to make an informed decision concerning the purported suspicious fund transfers by Wayne Hendrix. Thereafter, he failed to communicate at all with Mary Storm, though he claims to have done so through the conservator and the guardian ad litem. Mary Storm obviously was not given sufficient information about the proposed sale of her household property to make an informed decision. She voiced to Judge Goering during his ex parte hospital visit her opposition to the sale.

* * *

MRPC 1.7 — Conflict of Interest

MRPC 1.7 . . . provides in part:

   (a) A lawyer shall not represent a client if the representation of that client will be directly adverse to another client, unless:

      (1) the lawyer reasonably believes the representation will not adversely affect the relationship with the other client; and

      (2) each client consents after consultation.

The Comment provides in part:

> Loyalty is an essential element in the lawyer's relationship to a client. An impermissible conflict of interest may exist before representation is undertaken, in which event the representation should be declined. If such a conflict arises after representation has been undertaken, the lawyer should withdraw from the representation.

Brantley faced a conflict of interest from the beginning. Ralph Pfenninger saw Brantley in July 1989 and wanted a conservatorship for Mary Storm after Louise Wendler told Ralph that she had suspicions that Wayne Hendrix was misappropriating Mary's funds. Ralph was named as a residuary legatee under the mutual will of Mary and Ralph's father, R.E. Pfenninger. R.E. Pfenninger died in 1977. The residuary clause of this mutual will, obligated Mary, as survivor, to devise her residue in equal shares to her natural child, Wayne, and her husband R.E. Pfenninger's four natural children (or their issue, if not then living). Ralph may have believed that he would be entitled to a share of Mary's estate upon her death under this residuary clause. If so, Ralph had an obvious incentive to keep Mary Storm's assets intact until her death and restrict her ability to make inter vivos gifts. Brantley had assisted Mary Storm in placing her interests in three real estate installment contracts in joint tenancy with Wayne. Brantley handled Mary's brother's estate (Scott McCormick), which made a substantial distribution to Mary in 1986. It would be no surprise if Ralph Pfenninger harbored some jealousy and resentment toward Mary's son Wayne and would be anxious to stop Mary from giving her property to Wayne. During oral argument, Brantley stated he was unaware that Ralph Pfenninger was a residuary legatee under Mary's will, but indicated he would not have acted any differently if he had known that fact.

After Mary Storm retained Paul Oller to file an objection to the proposed sale of her household goods and obtain termination of 625 the voluntary conservatorship, Brantley should have withdrawn from the case. Even if Brantley was unaware of Ralph's status as a residuary legatee under Mary's will, the adversarial relationship was clear by that point. He never obtained Mary Storm's consent to represent Security State Bank, Ralph Pfenninger, or both in seeking an involuntary conservatorship. Brantley demonstrated mixed loyalties by failing to adequately investigate and relying on unsubstantiated suspicions of Ralph Pfenninger and Louise Wendler that Wayne Hendrix was misappropriating Mary Storm's funds. Brantley's pursuit of the involuntary conservatorship after Mary Storm retained her own attorney to oppose the sale and conservatorship confirmed this, as did his representation of Ralph Pfenninger in opposing Carla Hendrix's request for funds from the conservatorship to pay for moving expenses of Mary Storm's belongings to Alaska in 1993.

Brantley argues that his representation of Security State Bank or Ralph Pfenninger in the conservatorship matter was never adverse to Mary Storm because she ultimately needed a conservatorship. He contends that the fact she retained Paul Oller to oppose the conservatorship should be disregarded, because Judge Goering struck Oller's pleadings after interviewing Mary Storm ex parte at the hospital. Aside from Judge Georing's own conduct, his interview with Mary Storm made one thing very plain: Mary opposed the efforts to sell her household property.

Brantley cites two cases from other jurisdictions, *Hillman v. Stults,* 263 Cal.App.2d 848, 70 Cal.Rptr. 295 (1968), and *American Nat. Bank v. Bradford,* 28 Tenn.App. 239, 188 S.W.2d 971 (1945), to support his argument that his simultaneous representation of Mary Storm, Security State Bank, and Ralph Pfenninger was not adverse to Mary Storm.   Both cases are distinguishable. *Bradford* involved a ward initially adjudged insane. Mary Storm has never been adjudged incompetent or disabled in any sense. In *Hillman,* the court determined the attorneys' and conservators' prior isolated representation of the conservatee's sister did not present any conflicts or involve confidential information, so disqualification for conflict of interest was not appropriate in a proceeding adversarial to the then-deceased sister. . . . Brantley obtained confidential information concerning Mary Storm's and her son's banking transactions and used that information to advance the interests of Mary Storm's stepson, who wanted an involuntary conservatorship for Mary so that her assets could be preserved.

* * *

MRPC 1.14 — Client Under Disability

MRPC 1.14 states:

(a) When a client's ability to make adequately considered decisions in connection with the representation is impaired, whether because of minority, mental disability or for some other reason, the lawyer shall, as far as reasonably possible, maintain a normal client-lawyer relationship with the client.

(b) A lawyer may seek the appointment of a guardian or take other protective action with respect to a client, only when the lawyer reasonably believes that the client cannot adequately act in the client's own interest."

The Comment provides in part:

The normal client-lawyer relationship is based on the assumption that the client, when properly advised and assisted, is capable of making decisions about important matters. When the client . . . suffers from a mental disorder or disability, however, maintaining the ordinary client-lawyer relationship may not be possible in all respects. In particular, an incapacitated person may have no power to make legally binding decisions. Nevertheless, a client lacking legal competence often has the ability to understand, deliberate upon, and reach conclusions about matters affecting the client's own well-being. Furthermore, to an increasing extent the law recognizes intermediate degrees of competence. . . . [I]t is recognized that some persons of advanced age can be quite capable of handling routine financial matters while needing special legal protection concerning major transactions.

The fact that a client suffers a disability does not diminish the lawyer's obligation to treat the client with attention and respect. If the person has no guardian or legal representative, the lawyer often must act as de facto guardian. Even if the person does have a legal representative, the lawyer should as far as possible accord the represented person the status of client, particularly in maintaining communication. If a legal representative has already been appointed for the client, the lawyer should ordinarily look to the representative for decisions on behalf of the client.

The record indicates that Brantley totally disregarded this rule. He had one telephone call with Mary Storm before filing the voluntary conservatorship and failed to provide her with adequate information in that call. Thereafter, he had no direct communication with Mary Storm.

MRPC 3.3 — Candor Toward the Tribunal

MRPC 3.3 (1995 Kan. Ct. R. Annot. 311-12) states:

"(a) A lawyer shall not knowingly: (1) make a false statement of material fact or law to a tribunal. . . .

"(d) In an ex parte proceeding, a lawyer shall inform the tribunal of all material facts known to the lawyer which will enable the tribunal to make an informed decision, whether or not the facts are adverse."

The Comment provides in part:

"An advocate is responsible for pleadings and other documents prepared for litigation, but is usually not required to have personal knowledge of matters asserted therein, for litigation documents ordinarily present assertions by the client, or by someone on the client's behalf, and not assertions by the lawyer. . . . However, an assertion purporting to be on the lawyer's own knowledge, as in an affidavit by the lawyer or in a statement in open court, may properly be made only when the lawyer knows the assertion is true or believes it to be true on the basis of a reasonably diligent inquiry."

The Comment indicates that a lawyer making an assertion in open court without a belief that the assertion is true, based on reasonably diligent inquiry, may violate the rule.

As described in the panel's Findings of Fact Nos. 16 and 23, Brantley made untrue allegations in pleadings filed in the court. Also, in obtaining the ex parte temporary restraining order, Brantley represented to Judge Goering after termination of the voluntary conservatorship that Wayne Hendrix had misappropriated $85,000 of Mary Storm's funds and her assets were at risk. Brantley continued to make this representation to the court at the 1993 hearing when Carla Hendrix sought funds from the conservator to pay for moving Mary Storm's belongings to Alaska, where Mary Storm lived.

Brantley contends that he made no knowingly false statements to the court and his representation that Hendrix had misappropriated $85,000 of Mary Storm's funds had a reasonable basis.

There does not appear to be any evidence in the record that Brantley made knowingly false statements to the court. However, according to the Comment, Brantley's failure to make a reasonable investigation regarding the Hendrix fund transfers before accusing Hendrix in court of misappropriating funds may be considered a violation of the rule. Making such accusations in an ex parte setting violates MRPC 3.3(d). The record does not show that Brantley provided the judge complete information about these transfers, such as the dates of the transfers (the last one well over a year before the conservatorship) and the fact that they involved only Hendrix's own account.

* * *

Conclusion

The panel recommended that Respondent be publicly censured . . . and that costs be assessed against Respondent. We find in the record clear and convincing evidence sustaining the panel's conclusions that Brantley violated MRPC 1.1, 1.2, 1.4, 1.5, 1.7, 1.9, 1.14, 3.3, and 8.4 and that he be sanctioned by published censure. We accept the report of the panel. We concur in the findings, conclusions, and recommendations of the panel with the additional imposition of restitution of attorney fees received by Brantley. Restitution is ordered in the sum of $1,180.

IT IS ORDERED THAT Keen K. Brantley be subject to published censure for his violations of the Model Rules of Professional Conduct.

IT IS FURTHER ORDERED THAT this order be published in the official Kansas Reports and that the costs of the proceeding, including the sum of $1,180 as restitution, be assessed against respondent, to be paid to the office of the Disciplinary Administrator within 60 days from the date of this opinion.

QUESTION

What methods of investigation could the Respondent have properly employed in response to Ralph Pfenninger's concerns?

B. THE DISABLED CLIENT

While meeting an applicant or representing a client, a lawyer may discern that the client's "ability to make adequately considered decisions in connection with the representation is impaired." Rule 1.14(a). The degree and duration of impairment will vary widely, but the lawyer's fundamental ethical problem is that of approach: Should the lawyer act in accordance with the client's expressed wishes, if any (the "advocacy" model)? Or, should the lawyer act in what the lawyer considers the client's best interests (the "best interests" model)? Or, should the lawyer do what the lawyer thinks the client would direct if the client were capable of instructing counsel competently (the "substituted judgment" model)?

For practical assistance, see Tremblay, *On Persuasion and Paternalism: Lawyer Decisionmaking and the Questionably Competent Client*, 1987 UTAH L. REV. 515, 519-20 (1987), describing the range of choices available to the lawyer whose client's competency is in serious doubt as follows:

- withdraw;
- seek a guardian for the client, with the lawyer either serving as the petitioner or recruiting a third party to do so;
- seek unofficial consent from a family member or close friend;
- seek to persuade the client to make different or "better" choices;
- proceed as de facto guardian; or
- continue to presume competence irrebuttably.

The article goes on the suggest "that pursuing guardianship is legitimate in extreme cases, that reliance on family may be appropriate, that noncoercive persuasion is justified in less extreme cases, and that unilateral usurpation of client autonomy is never appropriate except in emergencies." *Id*. at 584.

1. Evaluating Client Competence

It is axiomatic that a person who has reached the age of majority is presumed competent. Moreover, a competent person is always able to make his or her own decisions. But what about when this "black-letter" principle breaks down? As the scrivener and advisor to your clients, when will you begin to doubt the propriety and competence of the legal work you do?

Paul S. Appelbaum
The Medicalization of Judicial Decision-Making
THE ELDER LAW REPORT (February 1999)[*]

The medicalization of judicial decision-making takes two forms. First, some courts sometimes permit moral issues to be transformed into medical issues. Consider the example of the adjudication of decision-making competence. Competence, of course, is a threshold requirement for persons to be able to exercise their decision-making rights, to make medical decisions, to manage their property, and in extreme cases even to marry. Persons found incompetent are deprived of those decision-making rights and someone else is appointed to make those decisions for them. In this process, for obvious reasons, psychiatrists

---

are often called upon to examine the allegedly incompetent persons and to testify as to their capacities. Psychiatrists and other mental health professionals are experts in the diagnosis of pathological states affecting the mind. Psychiatrists can be expected to detect abnormalities that laypersons might not, to determine their extent, and to describe their effects on relevant aspects of mental functioning. Expert testimony in these areas is perfectly appropriate, indeed, and probably essential to the process in many cases. In practice, however, psychiatrists are often asked to take one additional step: to offer an opinion as to whether a person is or is not competent. Why is this a problem? One might in fact say, if a psychiatrist doesn't know who is mentally competent, then who does?

The problem stems from the confusion that is generated between medical or scientific questions that a psychiatrist can legitimately address and legal issues with a moral underpinning that a psychiatrist cannot legitimately address. Examples of medical or scientific question include the degree of a person's impairment in functions as they relate to decision-making. Also, the subject's understanding of the facts of a given situation and appreciation of the implications of these facts and the consequences of a situation are all questions for the medical profession. Finally, the subject's ability to reason rationally, to weigh the risks and benefits, about a situation is clearly a medical issue. But these is a distinction between addressing these functions and addressing legal issues with intrinsic moral underpinnings that flow from this information.

The question of when a person is sufficiently impaired that he or she can fairly be deprived of the power to make decisions for himself or herself is a legal matter, not a medical one. Other examples of legal questions that psychiatrists should not answer are whether a person is competent to stand trial or is criminally responsible. For psychiatrists to assume this function implies the ability on their part to make moral judgments in an expert fashion. In fact, they have no more of that ability than and layperson does. In effect, the judge who asks for or tolerates psychiatric testimony about the ultimate issue in a hearing in which a legal-moral determination lies at the core of what the court must do is acquiescing in the medicalization of a profoundly moral question.

Unfortunately, my experience leads me to believe that the practice is not rare. Some years ago I testified at the competence hearing of a man whose son was petitioning to be appointed guardian of his estate. The son's attorney had called me and asked if I would examine the alleged incompetent to evaluate his competence to manage his financial affairs. On my examination, the indicia of moderate dementia were fairly evident. I noted memory loss, difficulty finding words, and a general sense of confusion, and, specific to the legal issue at hand, functional impairments were fairly evident as well. He could not perform even the simplest calculations. He could not describe to me what his assets were or how much he had. He could not characterize expenditures that might need to be made in order to sustain him, where his money came from for rent or groceries, or how much that cost, nor could he or would he account to me for significant amounts of money that he had withdrawn from the bank.

I prepared a written report detailing all of this information for the court. I testified to my observations, laying them out in detail, focusing on the description of the symptoms and the functional impairments, and carefully avoiding conclusions about the man's competence in the technical sense of the word or the need for a guardian in the case. From my own legal layperson's point of view, I imagined few more straightforward cases for a judge to adjudicate. But, when my testimony was complete, the judge leaned forward, peered at me, and asked, "But doctor, is he competent or not?" In asking me that question, the judge was requesting my collusion with him in turning a legal issue with moral roots, the question of when someone should be denied the right to control his or her assets, into a medical issue, the sort of question one might ask a doctor. That is, I think, the first way in which medicalization begins to permeate the judicial decision-making process — the turning of a moral, legal issue into a medical issue.

QUESTION

How can the lawyer seek professional guidance informing the lawyer's opinion regarding the client's mental status without violating his or her duty of confidentiality?

2. Model Rules of Professional Conduct 1.14
Client with Diminished Capacity

American Bar Association Center for Professional Responsibility
http://www.abanet.org/cpr/mrpc/rule_1_14.html[*]

(a) When a client's capacity to make adequately considered decisions in connection with a representation is diminished, whether because of minority, mental impairment or for some other reason, the lawyer shall, as far as reasonably possible, maintain a normal client-lawyer relationship with the client.

(b) When the lawyer reasonably believes that the client has diminished capacity, is at risk of substantial physical, financial or other harm unless action is taken and cannot adequately act in the client's own interest, the lawyer may take reasonably necessary protective action, including consulting with individuals or entities that have the ability to take action to protect the client and, in appropriate cases, seeking the appointment of a guardian ad litem, conservator or guardian.

(c) Information relating to the representation of a client with diminished capacity is protected by Rule 1.6. When taking protective action pursuant to paragraph (b), the lawyer is impliedly authorized under Rule 1.6(a) to reveal information about the client, but only to the extent reasonably necessary to protect the client's interests.

Comment

[1] The normal client-lawyer relationship is based on the assumption that the client, when properly advised and assisted, is capable of making decisions about important matters. When the client is a minor or suffers from a diminished mental capacity, however, maintaining the ordinary client-lawyer relationship may not be possible in all respects. In particular, a severely incapacitated person may have no power to make legally binding decisions. Nevertheless, a client with diminished capacity often has the ability to understand, deliberate upon, and reach conclusions about matters affecting the client's own well-being. For example, children as young as five or six years of age, and certainly those of ten or twelve, are regarded as having opinions that are entitled to weight in legal proceedings concerning their custody. So also, it is recognized that some persons of advanced age can be quite capable of handling routine financial matters while needing special legal protection concerning major transactions.

[2] The fact that a client suffers a disability does not diminish the lawyer's obligation to treat the client with attention and respect. Even if the person has a legal representative, the lawyer should as far as possible accord the represented person the status of client, particularly in maintaining communication.

[3] The client may wish to have family members or other persons participate in discussions with the lawyer. When necessary to assist in the representation, the presence of such persons generally does not affect the applicability of the attorney-client evidentiary privilege. Nevertheless, the lawyer must keep the client's interests foremost and, except for protective action authorized under paragraph (b), must to look to the client, and not family members, to make decisions on the client's behalf.

[4] If a legal representative has already been appointed for the client, the lawyer should ordinarily look to the representative for decisions on behalf of the client. In matters involving a minor, whether the lawyer should look to the parents as natural guardians may depend on the type of proceeding or matter in which the lawyer is representing the minor. If the lawyer represents the guardian as distinct from the ward, and is aware that the guardian is acting adversely to the ward's interest, the lawyer may have an obligation to prevent or rectify the guardian's misconduct. *See* Rule 1.2(d).

Taking Protective Action

[5] If a lawyer reasonably believes that a client is at risk of substantial physical, financial or other harm unless action is taken, and that a normal client-lawyer relationship cannot be maintained as provided in paragraph (a) because the client lacks sufficient capacity to communicate or to make adequately considered decisions in connection with the representation, then paragraph (b) permits the lawyer to take protective measures deemed necessary. Such measures could include: consulting with family members, using a reconsideration period to permit clarification or improvement of circumstances, using voluntary surrogate decisionmaking tools such as durable powers of attorney or consulting with support groups, professional services, adult-protective agencies or other individuals or entities that have the ability to protect the client. In taking any protective action, the lawyer should be guided by such factors as the

wishes and values of the client to the extent known, the client's best interests and the goals of intruding into the client's decisionmaking autonomy to the least extent feasible, maximizing client capacities and respecting the client's family and social connections.

[6] In determining the extent of the client's diminished capacity, the lawyer should consider and balance such factors as: the client's ability to articulate reasoning leading to a decision, variability of state of mind and ability to appreciate consequences of a decision; the substantive fairness of a decision; and the consistency of a decision with the known long-term commitments and values of the client. In appropriate circumstances, the lawyer may seek guidance from an appropriate diagnostician.

[7] If a legal representative has not been appointed, the lawyer should consider whether appointment of a guardian ad litem, conservator or guardian is necessary to protect the client's interests. Thus, if a client with diminished capacity has substantial property that should be sold for the client's benefit, effective completion of the transaction may require appointment of a legal representative. In addition, rules of procedure in litigation sometimes provide that minors or persons with diminished capacity must be represented by a guardian or next friend if they do not have a general guardian. In many circumstances, however, appointment of a legal representative may be more expensive or traumatic for the client than circumstances in fact require. Evaluation of such circumstances is a matter entrusted to the professional judgment of the lawyer. In considering alternatives, however, the lawyer should be aware of any law that requires the lawyer to advocate the least restrictive action on behalf of the client.

Disclosure of the Client's Condition

[8] Disclosure of the client's diminished capacity could adversely affect the client's interests. For example, raising the question of diminished capacity could, in some circumstances, lead to proceedings for involuntary commitment. Information relating to the representation is protected by Rule 1.6. Therefore, unless authorized to do so, the lawyer may not disclose such information. When taking protective action pursuant to paragraph (b), the lawyer is impliedly authorized to make the necessary disclosures, even when the client directs the lawyer to the contrary. Nevertheless, given the risks of disclosure, paragraph (c) limits what the lawyer may disclose in consulting with other individuals or entities or seeking the appointment of a legal representative. At the very least, the lawyer should determine whether it is likely that the person or entity consulted with will act adversely to the client's interests before discussing matters related to the client. The lawyer's position in such cases is an unavoidably difficult one.

Emergency Legal Assistance

[9] In an emergency where the health, safety or a financial interest of a person with seriously diminished capacity is threatened with imminent and irreparable harm, a lawyer may take legal action on behalf of such a person even though the person is unable to establish a client-lawyer relationship or to make or express considered judgments about the matter, when the person or

another acting in good faith on that person's behalf has consulted with the lawyer. Even in such an emergency, however, the lawyer should not act unless the lawyer reasonably believes that the person has no other lawyer, agent or other representative available. The lawyer should take legal action on behalf of the person only to the extent reasonably necessary to maintain the status quo or otherwise avoid imminent and irreparable harm. A lawyer who undertakes to represent a person in such an exigent situation has the same duties under these Rules as the lawyer would with respect to a client.

[10] A lawyer who acts on behalf of a person with seriously diminished capacity in an emergency should keep the confidences of the person as if dealing with a client, disclosing them only to the extent necessary to accomplish the intended protective action. The lawyer should disclose to any tribunal involved and to any other counsel involved the nature of his or her relationship with the person. The lawyer should take steps to regularize the relationship or implement other protective solutions as soon as possible. Normally, a lawyer would not seek compensation for such emergency actions taken.

Molly M. Wood
WHO'S THE CLIENT? Competency and the Lawyer-Client Relationship
http://keln.org./ethicsmmw.htm/[*]

II. THE IMPAIRED CLIENT (See Rule 1.14 Client with Diminished Capacity)

* * *

A. Duty to Maintain Normal Attorney-Client Relationship (See Rule 2.1 Advisor)

The resolution of a legal problem may involve such nonlegal considerations as social responsibility, morality, and economic, political or emotional consequences. It may be difficult, and often inappropriate, for a lawyer to limit advice to the narrow confines of compliance with procedural and substantive law. Advice that apprises the client of the full implication of a proposed course of action is ordinarily proper and desirable. Of course, a lawyer should not, under the guise of legal service, exploit the role of counselor.

1. Competency (See Rule 1.4 Communication)

Some of the most difficult ethical issues in the practice of law arise in representing marginally competent clients. The threshold question is whether the client has the capacity to retain the attorney. The next question is whether he or she sufficiently understands and can therefore make the decisions required. For estate planning purpose, for example, [most jurisdictions have] a relatively lenient standard — the testator must know the scope of his or her property and "the natural objects of his or her bounty." For most other transactions a higher

---

standard is required. For instance, to sell a house the owner must have a good idea of its market value.

It would be inappropriate to turn away any client exhibiting some mental deficiency, but it would also be inappropriate to move ahead with representation without taking any precautions. Although it would be advisable to require the applicant to produce medical support for a claim that his or her guardianship and conservatorship should be terminated, to send all such clients to a physician or social worker for an evaluation is not practical. Many clients would resist this move. In addition, taking such overt action might violate the attorney's obligation to act in the best interest of the client.

The alternative is for the attorney to document his or her informal assessment of the client's mental capacity. The attorney should take notes to create a record in case the client's capacity to understand the legal action he or she takes is ever challenged. If the result of this informal and nonprofessional evaluation demonstrates a lack of capacity, then the attorney should consider referring the client to appropriate medical and social services for further diagnosis, treatment, and care.

Ethically sensitive problems often arise when the well spouse or adult child of a senior with a degenerative disease, perhaps Alzheimer's or other dementia-type illness, seeks to become the attorney-in-fact of the proposed client or seeks to enter into some type of transaction which requires the proposed client to exert his or her legal authority to act. Although one's impulse may be to be anxious to assist, an incompetent person is unable to undertake to act for himself or delegate his authority under a Durable Power of Attorney. You must, therefore, make contact with the person who presumably wants to delegate that authority to determine that person's wishes and whether he or she is legally competent to undertake the proposed action.

This is a judgment call based upon the lawyer's appraisal of the functionality of the applicant and the complexity of the proposed legal action. For example, in the context of a Durable POA delegating the client's authority to his wife to handle their property and affairs, and all the property of the marriage is jointly owned, it is unnecessary for the client to understand much more than that his wife could sell the family home and, if she would, make off with the proceeds. Does the client believe his wife is trustworthy, that is, will she exercise her grant of authority for his best interests? Does the client understand that his grant of authority will increase his vulnerability to his attorney-in-fact's misdeeds?

3. Section 35 of The Restatement of the Law Governing Lawyers

Sheila Reynolds
Ethical Considerations in Representing an Impaired Client
KANSAS LONG-TERM CARE HANDBOOK (KANSAS BAR ASS'N 2001)[*]

C. The Guidance of Section 35 of The Restatement of the Law Governing Lawyers

The American Law Institute gave final approval to The Restatement of Law Third: Law Governing Lawyers in May of 1998, after a ten year drafting process. Even before this Restatement received final approval, it was used by lawyers to answer or argue ethical questions and by judges to decide ethical issues. The Restatement has become an important source of guidance on ethical issues because it provides more substance and authority than the Model Rules of Profession Conduct.

The Model Rules of Professional Conduct are adopted by state supreme courts to govern the lawyer disciplinary process. The preliminary material found in the scope section of the Model Rules specifically states that "violation of a Rule should not give rise to a cause of action nor should it create any presumption that a legal duty has been breached. The Rules are designed to provide guidance to lawyers and to provide a structure for regulating conduct through disciplinary agencies." In contrast, the Restatement is intended to serve as a guide of the law of lawyering in all contexts, including the inherent power of the court to control litigation, malpractice actions, and the interpretation of lawyer ethics codes.

A section of the Restatement relevant to this discussion is § 35, Client Under Disability. . . . There are several differences between § 35 and [M]RPC 1.14. Overall, § 35 gives more specific guidance to lawyers representing impaired clients and provides more direct authorization for intervention than [M]RPC 1.14.

1. *Act in the Best Interests of the Client*

Subsection (1) parrots the language of [M]RPC 1.14(a) in requiring lawyers to maintain a normal client-lawyer relationship, as far as reasonably possible, with a client whose "ability to make adequately considered decisions in connection with the representation is impaired." This subsection additionally provides that the lawyer must act in the best interests of the client.

2. *Use Substituted Judgment*

Subsection (2) contains a concept not found in the Model Rule, requiring a lawyer representing an impaired client who has no guardian or other legal rep-

---

resentative to use substituted judgment in pursuing a matter within the scope of the representation.

A lawyer representing a client impaired as described in Subsection (1) and for whom no guardian or other representative is available to act, must, with respect to a matter within the scope of the representation, pursue the lawyer's reasonable view of the client's objectives or interests as the client would define them if able to make adequately considered decisions on the matter, even if the client expresses no wishes or gives contrary instructions.

3. *Possible Duty to Act*

The above section seems to create a duty for the lawyer to take over decision making whenever the lawyer determines the client meets the given definition of "impaired." Such a duty does not exist in the Model Rules or other bodies of law. The language in Rule 1.14 is discretionary, providing that the lawyer "may" take protective action. Although the Comment to Rule 1.14 states, "If the person has not guardian or legal representative, the lawyer often must act as *de facto* guardian," the word "must" here does not create a duty, because it is not part of the black-letter rule and because it is modified by "often."

If a lawyer has a duty to use substituted judgment on behalf of an impaired client, then a lawyer who fails to exercise that duty may be liable to the client who is damaged thereby. A saving grace of the Restatement on this issue is found in Comment d, which provides, "It is often difficult to decide whether the conditions of this Section have been met. A lawyer who acts reasonably and in good faith in perplexing circumstances is not subject to professional discipline or malpractice or similar liability." The language in the comment supports the view that the drafters did not intend to create legal liability for a lawyer who chooses not to use substituted judgment in representing a client the lawyer believes is impaired.

4. *Exceptions to Following Directions of the Client's Guardian*

Subsection (3) is also different from the Model Rule in that it addresses the relationship between the lawyer and the client's legal representative, providing that although usually the lawyer must follow the direction of the representative, these are exceptions when (1) the lawyer is representing the client in a matter against the interests of the representative or (2) the representative is violating his or her legal duties towards the client.

5. *When to Take Protective Action*

The last difference is found in subsection (4), which provides that a lawyer may seek the appointment of a guardian for the client or take other protective action when doing so is "practical" and will advance the client's objectives or interests. This language gives some basis for deciding when to take protective action, which is lacking in the Model Rule.

4. Taking Protective Action

Molly M. Wood
WHO'S THE CLIENT? Competency and the Lawyer-Client Relationship
http://keln.org./ethicsmmw.htm[*]

II. THE IMPAIRED CLIENT (*See* Rule 1.14 *Client with Diminished Capacity*)

* * *

2. Protective Action (*See* Rule 1.14(b))

The lawyer's duty as an advisor to exercise "independent professional judgment" in representing a client is particularly compelling when the client may be incompetent. That independent judgment must be informed by the duty to protect a client's rights. If a lawyer finds that the client's condition makes it impossible to continue the representation, the lawyer may take protective action. Rule 1.14(b).

The first problem the lawyer considering protective action faces is that the information which leads the lawyer to question the client's competency is usually privileged under Rule 1.6, Confidentiality. "Protective action" within the meaning of the rule perforce entails the disclosure of "information gained with respect to the representation." So disclosure, to the extent necessary to serve the client's best interest, therefore, may be "impliedly authorized" within the meaning of Rule 1.6. (ABA Comm. on Ethics and Professional Responsibility, Informal Op. 89-1530 (1989)). Thus, the lawyer in this position may properly consult a physician concerning the suspected disability.

The next problem the lawyer faces, if a guardianship is to be sought, is the role the lawyer is to play in the proceedings, because appointment of a guardian is a drastic deprivation of civil rights and fundamentally inconsistent with the lawyer's duty of loyalty to the client. The statutory requirement of appointed counsel for the proposed ward in guardianship proceedings at least partly addresses this problem. . . . It is generally not desirable, therefore, for the lawyer to participate in the imposition of a guardianship upon a person to whom the attorney-client privilege may have attached, except as appointed counsel.

Finally, when the lawyer is acting on behalf of a disabled person through a court-appointed guardian or attorney-in-fact, but believes that the guardian or agent is acting contrary to the ward's best interests, the lawyer's authority to take "protective action" may come into play.

C. Abuse, Neglect and Exploitation (*See* Rule 2.3 *Evaluation for Use by Third Persons*)

A lawyer may only undertake an evaluation for third parties if the lawyer "reasonably believes that making the evaluation is compatible with other aspects of the lawyer's relationship with the client." Rule 2.3 (a)(1). Typically, it is a lawyer's past relationship with a client which casts into question the "compatibility" of an evaluation. The most obvious incompatibility is that created by the tension between a lawyer's duty to maintain the confidentiality of information relating to representation of a client and a lawyer's duty not to provide fraudulent or misleading information to third persons who will be relying on the lawyer's evaluation. (*See* Rules 1.6 *Confidentiality* & 4.1 *Truthfulness in Statements to Others*.)

Client Under a Disability
American Bar Association Formal Ethics Opinion 96-404
(August 2, 1996)[*]

When a client is unable to act adequately in his own interest, a lawyer may take appropriate protective action including seeking the appointment of a guardian. The lawyer may consult with diagnosticians and others, including family members, in assessing the client's capacity and for guidance about the appropriate protective action. The action taken should be the least restrictive of the client's autonomy that will yet adequately protect the client in connection with the representation. Withdrawal from representation of a client who becomes incompetent is disfavored, even if ethically permissible under the circumstances.

The lawyer may recommend or support the appointment of a particular person or other entity as guardian, even if the person or entity will likely hire the lawyer to represent it in the guardianship, provided the lawyer has made reasonable inquiry as to the suggested guardian's fitness, discloses the self-interest in the matter and obtains the court's permission to proceed. In all aspect of the proceeding, the lawyer's duty of candor to the court requires disclosure of pertinent facts, including the client's view of the proceedings.

Mary Alice Jackson, Boyer & Jackson, P.A.
Ethics in Guardianship:
A Discussion for Attorneys and Guardians[**]

I. *Introduction*

Several years ago, in a publication of the New York State Commission on Quality of Care, a writer offered this warning about the dark-side of guardian-

---

ship, ". . . negatively, improperly or illegally conducted guardianship can amount to *tyranny, thievery and harm* to the guardianee's life and health [Issue 40, May-Jun 1989]." The title of this entry (which I found on the internet) was: "Guardianship: Problem or a Solution."

That title probably sums up the feelings of most professionals who work in the guardianship arena. Looking back, there are some guardianships in which I have been involved which never should have happened. Others which I held back on, trying to seek less restrictive alternatives, resulted in greater harm to the Ward. There are no crystal balls for us. But for purposes of this presentation let's presume that guardianship is a viable *solution* in "appropriate" instances, and that one role that our ethical foundation plays lies in helping us understand *when* a situation is or becomes appropriate. In our lives today, unethical behavior has a variety of repercussions. The result of failing unethical behavior in a guardianship can mean devastation to basic individual dignity, for individuals for whom dignity has already been challenged.

Ethics guide our decision making processes. Whether to seek a determination of incapacity and the appointment of a guardian can create enormous ethical dilemmas. Let's consider a case in point. Just like the old picture games, see how many ethical issues you can spot:

> Mrs. B. is a 92 year old woman who has been a musician all of her life. She still writes music and speaks enthusiastically on the subject. Mrs. B. is brought to see you by her daughter, who tells you that Mrs. B. wants to change her trust. You meet with them for a few minutes, then ask to meet with Mrs. B. alone. In the course of your representation, you discover that Mrs. B. has a daughter, and a grandson, both of whom try to exert influence over her. This is the fourth time in two years that she has wanted to changed the terms of her trust. Every time a change is made, either the daughter or grandson takes her to a new lawyer and urges her to alter the terms again so as to be more favorable to that party. Her current assets are in excess of $800,000, and it is clear to you that the daughter and grandson are primarily concerned with their inheritances. There are bitter feelings between these parties and Ms. B. is caught in the middle, helplessly.

> It becomes apparent to you that while she knows both the nature of her assets and the members of her family, Mrs. B. has short term memory loss and neglects her personal care and hygiene. She has poor eyesight. She has refused any offers of assistance and has fired several caregivers who were brought in by her grandson. She is a smoker. She does not eat well. You observe that her home is dirty and in disarray. Mrs. B. will not cooperate in any family efforts to help her. In particular, the grandson is close to Mrs. B (in his own way) and does take her to the doctor. The doctor reports that the grandson, while very pushy, follows his instructions and appears to care for Mrs. B appropriately.

> At Mrs. B's request, you draft a trust amendment which names a corporate successor trustee. The goal is for Mrs. B. to resign and have the successor take over immediately and relieve her of the pressures of

writing the bills and family bickering. Mrs. B. executes the trust amendment, the bank takes over as trustee and the trust takes control of all of Mrs. B's assets, paying her bills and working as her fiduciary.

You remain concerned about Mrs. B's personal situation. You believe that she would meet the criteria for incapacity of her person and that a guardian might be able to improve the quality of her life and provide for her safety. You know that the family will object strenuously. For all their faults, Mrs. B. is attached to her family and hates any kind of conflict. At this point, a number of questions arise:

(a) *As her attorney, can you petition for a determination of incapacity?*

(b) *If so, can you be the petitioner? Can you seek a third party to do so?*

(c) *Even if you believe the guardianship to be warranted and appropriate, is it the best course when you know from your experience with these clients that the proceeding will be contested by her daughter and grandson?*

(d) *Is the guardianship warranted when it is likely to cause tremendous strain for Mrs. B?*

(e) *Is the guardianship warranted when you know that a contested proceeding may cost many thousands of dollars?*

(f) *Is there is a less restrictive alternative for Mrs. B? What if that alternative will not improve the quality of her life as much as the assistance of a guardian might provide?*

(g) *What will the guardian's responsibilities be if Mrs. B wants to maintain close ties with the family, who the guardian may believe to be harmful to her, and whose motives are suspect to the guardian?*

(h) *How will the guardian deal with the family, who in your experience, constantly make a barrage of phone calls and demands?*

Throughout the remainder of this paper, we'll examine the ethical standards which attorney and guardians are charged with observing. Together with our individual belief systems, those standards guide us through the innumerable and sometimes agonizing ethical land mines which we face in the field of adult guardianship.

* * *

There are innumerable questions, some answers are clear and others will never be. Good people may sometimes disagree. *Every situation must be examined anew on its own facts and circumstances.* In the following sections, let's look at some of the most common ethical issues which confront attorneys and guardians. Some are common to both, others are exclusive to one profession. Each profession works under a set of professional standards which are listed below. Although I have tried to be thorough, I'm certain that there are many more issues which we can examine. As in any self-examination, we can ask: Am I doing the right thing? Are there other alternatives? Can I defend my position if called upon to do so?

* * *

III. Ethical Dilemmas for Attorneys

A. *Under what circumstances can an attorney petition for a determination of incapacity regarding a client whom he or she represents?*

The Florida Bar Rules of Professional Conduct, Rule 4-1.14, states that "a lawyer may seek the appointment of a guardian or take other protective action with respect to a client only when the lawyer reasonably believes that the client cannot adequately act in the client's own interest." Before doing so, the attorney must thoroughly investigate to determine whether any less restrictive alternative to guardianship might exist. This investigation may require the attorney to consult family members, physicians or neighbors to learn more information. Such actions should be taken with the consent, and when possible, the release, of the client. Oftentimes, discussions with family physicians, bankers or caregivers will provide essential information for the attorney to use in determining what course of action may be advisable.

Although it cannot be found specifically in the Rules, it is arguable that attorneys will be held to an additional ethical standard based upon §744.702, Fla. Stat., that is, ". . . [t]he Legislature . . . finds that alternatives to guardianship and less intrusive means of assistance shall *always* be explored before an individual's rights are removed through an adjudication of incapacity." This emphasis on a less restrictive alternative recognizes the high personal and financial costs of guardianship and places an affirmative duty on the petitioner and attorney, as well as the court, to ensure that such alternatives are explored.

B. *If the attorney is uncertain as to whether the client is truly incapacitated, can the attorney seek diagnostic assistance?*

Yes. Both the Florida and ABA Rules (4-1.14 and 1.14, respectively) allow for the attorney to seek the assistance of an "appropriate" diagnostician. Depending on the situation, such diagnostician may be a gerontologist, psychologist, social worker or physician, among others. It is apparently the attorney's role to determine the appropriateness of the source. This may be particularly important for older individuals who are suffering from depression, nutritional deficits, urinary tract infection, adverse drug reactions and other conditions which may mask as incapacity. Failure to seek sufficient information may constitute an ethical failure on its face. It's probably not a good idea to rely exclusively on the observations of family or friends unless the attorney knows those individuals and has confidence in their judgment. Because incapacity is a legal definition not based solely upon medical opinion, the attorney should compare the information received with other facts about the client's functional capacity.

C. *If a petition to determine incapacity is warranted, can the attorney who represents the client serve as petitioner?*

Rule 1.14 seems to imply that the attorney may serve as petitioner, although it makes no specific reference to the signing of the petition. Under §744.3201, Fla. Stat. (1997) the petition be executed by an "adult person"; there is no specific exclusion in the statute forbidding the attorney from serving in that capacity. On occasion, when the client has lived in isolation and there is no family, the attorney is the only individual with sufficient knowledge to execute the petition.

An attorney who is not comfortable in doing so, and who believes that the client may be a victim of self-neglect, abuse or exploitation, may want to call the Elder Abuse Hotline (1-800-96ABUSE). Upon investigation, it is possible that the adult protective investigator may be willing to serve as petitioner. Other times, a neighbor or health care provider may be found. There is no liability to the individual executing the petition as long as it is done in good faith and upon personal knowledge of the facts.

> D. *Can an attorney who has initiated in, petitioned for, or become aware of a petition to determine incapacity of a client thereafter serve as attorney for the guardian?*

If you represent a client who faces incapacity, what now? Do you represent that client in the incapacity proceeding? Do you represent the petitioner? What if a conflict arises? Can or should you represent the guardian if one is appointed? These questions often provoke heated debated among practitioners. It has been opined that while the attorney may petition for incapacity, or some other party may do so, it is *not* appropriate for the attorney to represent a third party petitioning for guardianship over the client. Chapter 1, § 1.06[4], *Tax, Estate and Financial Planning for the Elderly*, Regan, Morgan and English, Matthew Bender and Co., Inc. (1997). Two of the basic ethical principles which come into play are (a) confidentiality and (b) conflict of interest.

Rule 4-1.7(a), Rule Reg. Fla. Bar; Conflict of Interest. The lawyer may not represent a client if such representation would be directly adverse to the interests of another client, except when the representation will not adversely affect the lawyer's responsibilities to and relationship with the other client and each client consents after consultation. To remain in compliance with the Rule, the attorney would have to essentially negate the possibility of potential conflicts, and to obtain the consent of the client, who may be incapacitated and unable to consent.

Rule 4-1.6, Rules of Professional Conduct, Confidentiality. This section states that the lawyer may not reveal information relating to the representation of the client unless the client consents after disclosure to the client, except under very limited circumstances. Those circumstances include a time when the lawyer reasonably believes that it is necessary to do so "to serve the client's interest." The attorney will have determine for him or herself whether the facts of any given situation warrant such disclosure when the client is no longer able to consent.

There is a growing segment of attorneys who advocate an ethical concept of "family representation." In these situations, they argue that when a client becomes completely incapacitated as a result of illness or injury and is likely to remain so, and the attorney has a long association with the client, the attorneys may continue to represent the spouse or a family member as guardian. The attorney sees this as a continuation of his or her "family" representation, and many times feel that to bring in outside counsel will be upsetting and unnecessarily expensive for the family. Presumably, the family has previously agreed to this and who waive the rules of confidentiality and conflict of interest.

More difficult is the situation where the client's disability is less clear, or even when clearly disabled, the client is aware of the proceedings and objects to them. In these cases, how can the attorney reconcile the duty of confidentiality to the client and the potential for a conflict of interest?

There is currently no specific guidance to be found in either the statutes or rules. No one rule can adequately cover the innumerable shades of variation found in guardianship practice. As always, each situation must be carefully reviewed by the attorney.

* * *

Because of the potential for ethical violation, it is not advisable for the attorney for an AIP to represent the petitioner or guardian. An attorney who takes on such representation should be prepared to defend that decision in light to the ethical rules if called upon to do so, remembering that doubts will normally be resolved in favor of the client's expectation of confidentiality and protection.

E. *Can the attorney serve as attorney for the alleged incapacitated person when the attorney has an established relationship with the AIP and believes that a guardianship is warranted?*

The rules do not impose an affirmative duty to represent the client in any incapacity proceeding by virtue of their previous relationship, but the attorney may do so if both attorney and client agree. In some circumstances, it may be unwise to do so, especially if the client suffers from delusions or paranoia, and such representation would adversely and unnecessarily adversely affect the existing attorney/client relationship. Other times, the attorney may be inexperienced in guardianship work and feel ill-prepared to adequately represent the client. If the attorney wishes to undertake the representation due to his or her knowledge of and relationship with the alleged incapacitated person, it may have a beneficial effect on the proceedings. The attorney often may have more information than any other party about the client's situation, and may be the client's most effective and zealous advocate, even when incapacity is found.

G. *What is the duty of the attorney for the AIP if he or she is asked by the AIP to launch an expensive, ill-advised defense?*

"[A]dopting the "zealous advocacy" model does not mean [the lawyer] should resist or litigate every guardianship appointment. . . . It should be understood that in a legal sense, being a zealous advocate is not the equivalent of being a zealot." *Guardianship of the Elderly: A Primer for Attorneys,* American Bar Association Commission on Legal Problems of the Elderly (Feb. 1990).

Most court appointed attorneys feel this burden acutely. The client demands a vigorous defense, but has no insight into the reality that his or her capacity has been compromised. The lawyer seeks to present an adequate and advised defense as required by the rules of the profession, but within the realm of practicality and without unnecessary expense.

The statute and rules do not contemplate that the attorney shall serve in an "ad litem" capacity, but should rather conduct his or her representation in as normal a fashion as possible and upon consultation with the Ward.

* * *

H. Are there specific limitations on the amount of fees which may be charged in a guardianship?

Guardianship is the most wonderful example of the old adage: "adding insult to injury." As we all know, the Ward not only loses most civil rights in a guardianship proceeding, but also must pay for the costs of those proceedings, and for the services of the guardian whom he never wanted. The financial impact of the guardianship upon the Ward should be considered by the parties as a factor before the guardianship is initiated. That consideration is not whether a guardian should be appointed when there are insufficient funds for the parties to be paid, but whether the financial impact of the guardianship, when balanced against the benefits anticipated, is warranted. At times, enormously costly proceedings result in very little benefit to the Ward. Those experiences leave a taint on the system and those who participate in it. While it is sometimes impossible to avoid the expense of a guardianship, and both the attorneys and guardians deserve reasonable compensation for their services, all parties should be sensitive to the Ward's financial situation.

The court, which bears the responsibility for awarding fees in a guardianship, is the best and most important protector of the Ward's interests.

* * *

. . . The ABA has recently revised Rule 1.14, and in that revision has made the following statement in its comment: "Emergency Legal Assistance. . . . [7] A lawyer who acts on behalf of a disabled person in an emergency should keep the confidences of the disabled person as if dealing with a client. . . . The lawyer shall take steps to regularize the relationship or implement other protective solutions as soon as possible. *Normally, a lawyer would not seek compensation for such emergency actions taken on behalf of a disabled person.*"

This addition is troubling because it implies that the attorney may commit an ethical violation for seeking payment for services rendered in an emergency temporary guardianship. This provision is not found in the Florida rules, and our statute permits the court to take all factors, including the Ward's assets, into consideration when determining a reasonable fee. The practitioner should be aware of this rule change and its possible implications.

I. If a guardian is appointed, does the attorney who represents the guardian owe a duty of care to the Ward, and if so, how does that duty affect the attorney/client relationship between the attorney and guardian?

* * *

ABA Rule 1.14 does not specifically address this issue, but the comments to that rule do. The comment states:

> If the lawyer represents the guardian as distinct from the ward and is aware of the guardian acting adversely to the ward's interest, the lawyer may have an obligation to prevent or rectify the guardian's misconduct.

Note that the comment says "may" and not "shall." Under what circumstances "may" the attorney do so? In his article, "Ethical Obligations of Counsel in Representing Clients Petitioning to be Appointed as Guardian of Others or of their Estates, or both" 8 NAELA QUARTERLY 13 (Spring 1995), Clifton B. Kruse, discusses this comment and the proposed "Commentaries on [the] Model Rules of Professional Conduct" which were drafted by ACTEC. Kruse speaks about a proposed Commentary to ABA Rule 1.14 which addresses a lawyer's duty to consider the wishes of a disabled person, and suggests that a lawyer may take action if he or she believes that it is in the best interests of the disabled person to have an attorney or ad litem appointed. A lawyer's focus, Kruse points out, "is perhaps inappropriate if it is directly solely on client interest where a person affected by the representation is disabled. It is that person's best interests that are primary in the activity relating to fiduciary appointment and service". *Id.* at 14. He goes on to cite from an ethics opinion issued in Alaska (Opinion 87-2 [9-3-87]) in which the traditional attorney/client relationship, including confidentiality are addressed: "Historic requirements in the lawyer-client relationship, including confidentiality and quiet loyalty to a client engaged in wrongdoing, are rarely virtuous in the context of a client's violation of a fiduciary duty." *Id.*

Kruse reaches the conclusion that the duties imposed under Rule 1.14 requires counsel to "engage in moral conversations with their clients." *Id.* at 15. These ideas are so foreign to the traditional concepts which lawyers learn in classes about professional responsibility and ethics, that advocates such as ACTEC, NAELA and the Real Property and Probate members of the Bar have found it necessary to draft new, broader rules which can guide members who practice in this perilous area. To date, though, no broader rules have been adopted in either the national or state regulations, and each lawyer must continue to pursue the best course possible under each circumstance. The trend of modern courts has been to uphold the rights of the incapacitated persons over the interests in the client/guardian, and attorneys can take direction from that trend.

5. Withdrawal

Molly M. Wood
WHO'S THE CLIENT? Competency and the Lawyer-Client Relationship
http://www.keln.org/ethicsmmw.html[*]

II. THE IMPAIRED CLIENT (*See* Rule 1.14 *Client Under a Disability*)

* * *

D. Withdrawal from Representation (*See* Rule 1.16 *Declining or Terminating Representation*)

A client can discharge a lawyer with or without cause, and no lawyer can continue to represent a client who does not wish to be represented. In the case of a disabled client, however, a client's severe mental impairment may operate to suspend or terminate a pre-existing attorney-client relationship. Because with-

---

drawal from representation, though depending on the degree of impairment and the status of the proceedings may be necessary, is not favored, absent other cause, the client's refusal to accept a lawyer's advice regarding the resolution of a policy question is not sufficient grounds for withdrawal where termination will prejudice the client. (*But see* Rule 3.1 *Meritorious Claims and Contentions.*)

Client Under a Disability
AMERICAN BAR ASSOCIATION FORMAL ETHICS OPINION 96-404
(August 2, 1996)*

In the absence of Rule 1.14, a lawyer whose client becomes incompetent would have no choice but to withdraw, not only because a lawyer who continues the representation would be acting without authority, but also because the lawyer would be unable to carry out his responsibilities to the client under the Rules. *See* Rule 1.16(a)(1) (withdrawal required where "the representation will result in violation of the rules of professional conduct.") While Rule 1.14 permits a lawyer to take protective action in such situations, it does not compel the lawyer to do so, and many lawyers are uncomfortable with the prospect of having to so act. The Committee considers that withdrawal is ethically permissible as long as it can be accomplished "without material adverse effect on the interests of the client." Rule 1.16(b).

On the other hand, while withdrawal in these circumstances solves the lawyer's dilemma, it may leave the impaired client without help at a time when the client needs it most. The particular circumstances may also be such that the lawyer cannot withdraw without prejudice to the client. For instance, the client's incompetence may develop in the middle of a pending matter and substitute counsel may not be able to represent the client effectively due to the inability to discuss the matter with the client. Thus, without concluding that a lawyer with an incompetent client may never withdraw, the Committee believes the better course of action, and the one most likely to be consistent with Rule 1.16(b), will often be for the lawyer to stay with the representation and seek appropriate protective action on behalf of the client.

C. LAWYER'S DUTY TO IMPAIRED THIRD PARTY

ESTATE OF TREADWELL EX REL. NEIL v. WRIGHT
61 P.3d 1214 (Wash. App. 2003).

APPELWICK, J.

A guardian depleted the accounts of an incapacitated ward. The ward's estate sued the attorney hired by the ward's guardian to establish a guardianship for breach of duty. The alleged breach of duty was the attorney's failure to fully comply with the statutes requiring that prior to the inception of the guardian-ship a bond or bond agreements blocking access to unbonded funds absent a court order be in place. The attorney argued that she had no duty to the inca-pacitated ward because the ward was not her client. The trial court granted summary judgment to the attorney, finding no duty to the ward. Reconsidera-tion was sought based on a recent decision in *In re Guardianship of Karan,* 110 Wash. App. 76, 38 P.3d 396 (2002), but was denied. The Estate appeals. We reverse and remand for trial.

FACTS

Kathleen M.S. Wright (Wright) is an attorney licensed to practice law in Washington State. In June 1997, Linda Morrison (Morrison) retained Wright to commence a guardianship proceeding for Morrison's great-aunt, Katherine M. Treadwell (Treadwell). On June 17, 1997, Wright appeared before a court com-missioner and presented a petition for "Appointment of Guardian of Person." The petition asserted that Treadwell: (1) was over 90 years old; (2) was a victim of potential physical and financial abuse; (3) was unable to protect herself; (4) was unable to manage her estate and person; and (5) suffered from memory problems.

Simultaneous with these proceedings, the court appointed attorney Randy Boyer from the court's guardian ad litem register to serve as guardian ad litem for Treadwell. Boyer's findings corroborated the assertions Wright had outlined in her June 17, 1997 verified petition. In his guardian ad litem report, Boyer observed that "Mrs. Treadwell suffers from very impaired recent memory and moderately severe impairment as to orientation of time," and that Treadwell needed "full time assistance with all financial matters and to meet her daily needs." Boyer also estimated that Treadwell had approximately $225,000 in assets. He recommended a $30,000 bond, and that funds in excess of $30,000 be in blocked accounts. Wright was provided with a copy of Boyer's report. On August 26, 1997, a court commissioner signed an order appointing a guardian for Treadwell. The draft of the order that Wright submitted to the court included a provision requiring a $30,000 bond, but not a provision stipulating that assets in excess of $30,000 be maintained in blocked accounts. The court added a pro-vision requiring blocking agreements. The court interlineated on the order that those agreements were set for review in 30 days, but was silent as to whether the letters of guardianship were final before the blocking agreements were in place. The court clerk issued letters of guardianship on September 16, 1997, with a special instruction sheet to Morrison. Wright forwarded the letters of guardianship and instruction sheets to Morrison on September 22, 1997. Wright included a letter outlining Morrison's responsibilities as a guardian and enclosed copies of Washington statutes detailing Morrison's duties. Wright also included a receipt for blocked account form, explaining to Morrison, "I will prepare this for a particular institution once you have determined what the assets are and how they will be held. All funds in excess of $30,000 must be held in a blocked account."

Shortly thereafter, Morrison stopped contacting Wright, and Wright's attempts to contact Morrison were unsuccessful. Wright's last contact with

Morrison was in January 1998. On June 1, 1999, Wright filed a notice of intent to withdraw, effective June 21, 1999.

Treadwell died on November 17, 1999. Treadwell's estate (the Estate) was unable to recover from Morrison, and began legal proceedings against Wright in June 2000. On November 30, 2001, Wright obtained summary judgment dismissing the Estate's claim on the grounds that she owed Treadwell no duty. Shortly after this court's decision in *Karan. . .*, the Estate filed a CR 60(b) motion to vacate the summary dismissal entered in favor of Wright. That motion was denied. The Estate appeals the orders granting Wright summary judgment and denying the Estate's motion to vacate.

ANALYSIS

I. An Attorney's Duty to a Guardianship

Whether Wright owed a duty to Treadwell under RCW 11.88.100 and .105, is a question of law that we review de novo. *Rasmussen v. Bendotti,* 107 Wash. App. 947, 955, 29 P.3d 56 (2001). The relevant test was discussed in *Karan:*

> The general rule is that only an attorney's client may file a claim for legal malpractice. *Trask v. Butler,* 123 Wash.2d 835, 840, 872 P.2d 1080 (1994). But an attorney may owe a nonclient a duty even in the absence of this privity. *Stangland v. Brock,* 109 Wash.2d 675, 680, 747 P.2d 464 (1987). . . .

> To determine whether a lawyer owes a duty to a nonclient which then creates standing to sue for malpractice, Washington applies a six-element test. . . . To establish whether the lawyer owes the plaintiff a duty of care in a particular transaction, the court must determine:

> 1. The extent to which the transaction was intended to benefit the plaintiff;

> 2. The foreseeability of harm to the plaintiff;

> 3. The degree of certainty that the plaintiff suffered injury;

> 4. The closeness of the connection between the defendant's conduct and the injury;

> 5. The policy of preventing future harm; and

> 6. The extent to which the profession would be unduly burdened by a finding of liability.

> * * *

> *Trask* is factually distinguishable. The *Trask* case resolved a dispute between an adult, competent beneficiary of a will who was in an adversarial relationship with another adult beneficiary. The second beneficiary was also both the personal representative of the deceased father's estate and attorney-in-fact for the surviving mother. And the lawsuit against the lawyer was over day-to-day judgment calls in managing the estate.

By contrast, here we have: (1) a legally incompetent infant ward, (2) a non-adversarial relationship, and (3) legal services solely consisting of setting up the guardianship. . . .

1. *Intended Beneficiary.* The primary reason to establish a guardianship is to preserve the ward's property for his or her own use. It is not for the benefit of others. . . .

Karan, 110 Wn. App. At [81-82,] 84-85. . . .

The only factual difference in the case before us as to this factor of the *Trask* test is that Treadwell was an incompetent adult rather than an incompetent minor. We see no basis for this distinction to lead to a different result. Here, as in *Karan*, the incompetence of the ward is the key fact. Treadwell was the intended beneficiary of the guardianship Wright established because she was (1) a legally incompetent ward, (2) in a non-adversarial relationship with Morrison, and (3) because Wright's legal services for Morrison solely consisted of setting up Treadwell's guardianship. The policy analysis of *Trask* factors 5 and 6 applied in *Karan,* applies equally in this case:

5. *Future Harm.* In matters involving the welfare of minors and other legally incompetent individuals, the courts assume a particular duty to protect the interests of the ward. *Durham v. Moe,* 80 Wash. App. 88, 91, 906 P.2d 986 (1995). Policy considerations favor finding a duty in the interests of preventing future harm. *In re Guardianship of Ivarsson*, 60 Wash. 2d 733, 738, 375 P.2d 509 (1962).

* * *

In contrast to *Trask,* the legitimate interests of the guardian here are inseparable from those of the ward. The profession will not be unduly burdened by finding a duty in this case because the applicable law mandates either a bond or a blocked account. The obligation to protect the interests of wards in a circumstance such as this does not put lawyers in an ethical bind.

Karan, 110 Wash. App. at 85-86, 38 P.3d 396.

In *Karan*, the alleged malpractice was failure to provide for a bond or blocked account. Here, the alleged malpractice was failure to provide for adequate bond and/or blocked accounts before issuing the order appointing the guardian. In each case, the guardian's attorney is alleged to have violated the requirements of RCW 11.88.100 and .105. In *Karan,* the allegation is total failure to protect assets. Here, the allegation is partial failure to protect assets. The difference is not one of kind, but one of degree.

The analysis of *Trask* factors 2 and 4 also apply equally here:

2. *Foreseeability of Harm.* It is foreseeable that failure to put in place the statutory safeguards for the protection of the estate will leave the ward vulnerable to the kind of losses Amanda incurred. This is why the Legislature required the safeguards. . . .

* * *

4. *Connection between Lawyer's Conduct and Injury.* If established, the connection between the alleged conduct and the injury is direct. The lawyer bypassed the statutory safeguards that protect a ward from a guardian's squandering the funds.

Karan, 110 Wash. App. at 85, 38 P.3d 396.The last factor in the *Trask* analysis is the certainty that the plaintiff suffered injury. Actual loss was not disputed in *Karan* and is not disputed here.We conclude that a guardian's attorney owes an incompetent ward a duty to establish the guardianship consistent with the requirements of RCW 11.88.100 and .105.

The court in *Karan* declined to create a bright-line rule that an attorney who undertakes to represent the guardian of an incompetent thereby automatically assumes a relationship with the ward. *Karan,* 110 Wash. App. at 83, 38 P.3d 396. Likewise, we do not hold that a guardian's attorney owes a duty to the ward for all purposes or for all transactions during the pendency of the guardianship. Rather, the trial court should apply the *Trask* test and determine whether such a duty exists as each type of transaction is put before it. As to the question before us, the trial court need not undertake a *Trask* analysis. If *Karan* left any doubt, we intend not to. RCW 11.88.100 and .105 impose duties on the attorney for the guardian that are owed to the incompetent ward. The summary judgment finding that Wright owed no duty to Treadwell was error as a matter of law.

* * *

QUESTIONS

1. What action do you think Ms. Wright should have taken once she realized her client, the guardian, was not following through on her obligations to the ward?

2. Do you agree that: "The profession will not be unduly burdened by finding a duty in this case"?

FURTHER READING. Ethical Issues in Representing Older Clients, 62 FORD-HAM L. REV. 961-1583 (1994).

Chapter 3

DISCRIMINATION

During the past quarter century, legislative and judicial activity at both the state and federal levels has resulted in the creation of a broad array of civil rights enforceable against private and public entities. Comprehensive statutory schemes such as the Age Discrimination in Employment Act, the Americans with Disabilities Act, and their state counterparts, contemplate a society in which age or handicap do not limit an individual's ability fully to participate in all spheres of public and private activity. The broadening and strengthening of civil rights laws has, not surprisingly, had significant costs. The number of federal lawsuits involving workplace discrimination doubled during the 1990s; in 2006, age discrimination claims comprised almost 22% of all claims filed with the U.S. Equal Employment Opportunity Commission. Disability-related claims now make up nearly 21% of civil rights claims filed with EEOC. Government and private entities are now required to make public accommodations, broadly defined, accessible to all but the most severely impaired. Although both employment law and disability law each comprise their own practice specialties, it is important for the elder law practitioner to understand some of the basic principles associated with these important substantive areas. In this chapter, we introduce discrimination law as it relates primarily to the senior population.

A. INTRODUCTION

U.S. Equal Opportunity Commission
Federal Laws Prohibiting Job Discrimination
Questions and Answers
http://www.eeoc.gov/facts/qanda.html

Federal Equal Employment Opportunity (EEO) Laws

I. What Are the Federal Laws Prohibiting Job Discrimination?

1.

- Title VII of the Civil Rights Act of 1964 (Title VII), which prohibits employment discrimination based on race, color, religion, sex, or national origin;

- the Equal Pay Act of 1963 (EPA), which protects men and women who perform substantially equal work in the same establishment from sex-based wage discrimination;

- the Age Discrimination in Employment Act of 1967 (ADEA), which protects individuals who are 40 years of age or older;

- Title I and Title V of the Americans with Disabilities Act of 1990 (ADA), which prohibit employment discrimination against qualified individuals with disabilities in the private sector, and in state and local governments;

- Sections 501 and 505 of the Rehabilitation Act of 1973, which prohibit discrimination against qualified individuals with disabilities who work in the federal government; and

- the Civil Rights Act of 1991, which, among other things, provides monetary damages in cases of intentional employment discrimination.

The U.S. Equal Employment Opportunity Commission (EEOC) enforces all of these laws. EEOC also provides oversight and coordination of all federal equal employment opportunity regulations, practices, and policies.

Other federal laws, not enforced by EEOC, also prohibit discrimination and reprisal against federal employees and applicants. The Civil Service Reform Act of 1978 (CSRA) contains a number of prohibitions, known as prohibited personnel practices, which are designed to promote overall fairness in federal personnel actions. 5 U.S.C. § 2302. The CSRA prohibits any employee who has authority to take certain personnel actions from discriminating for or against employees or applicants for employment on the bases of race, color, national origin, religion, sex, age or disability. It also provides that certain personnel actions cannot be based on attributes or conduct that do not adversely affect employee performance, such as marital status and political affiliation. The Office of Personnel Management (OPM) has interpreted the prohibition of discrimination based on conduct to include discrimination based on sexual orientation. The

CSRA also prohibits reprisal against federal employees or applicants for whistle-blowing, or for exercising an appeal, complaint, or grievance right. The CSRA is enforced by both the Office of Special Counsel (OSC) and the Merit Systems Protection Board (MSPB).

Discriminatory Practices

II. What Discriminatory Practices Are Prohibited by These Laws?

Under Title VII, the ADA, and the ADEA, it is illegal to discriminate in any aspect of employment, including:

- hiring and firing;
- compensation, assignment, or classification of employees;
- transfer, promotion, layoff, or recall;
- job advertisements;
- recruitment;
- testing;
- use of company facilities;
- training and apprenticeship programs;
- fringe benefits;
- pay, retirement plans, and disability leave; or
- other terms and conditions of employment.

Discriminatory practices under these laws also include:

- harassment on the basis of race, color, religion, sex, national origin, disability, or age;
- retaliation against an individual for filing a charge of discrimination, participating in an investigation, or opposing discriminatory practices;
- employment decisions based on stereotypes or assumptions about the abilities, traits, or performance of individuals of a certain sex, race, age, religion, or ethnic group, or individuals with disabilities; and
- denying employment opportunities to a person because of marriage to, or association with, an individual of a particular race, religion, national origin, or an individual with a disability. Title VII also prohibits discrimination because of participation in schools or places of worship associated with a particular racial, ethnic, or religious group.

Employers are required to post notices to all employees advising them of their rights under the laws EEOC enforces and their right to be free from retaliation. Such notices must be accessible, as needed, to persons with visual or other disabilities that affect reading.

Note: Many states and municipalities also have enacted protections against discrimination and harassment based on sexual orientation, status as a parent, marital status and political affiliation. For information, please contact the EEOC District Office nearest you.

III. What Other Practices Are Discriminatory Under These Laws?

Title VII

Title VII prohibits not only intentional discrimination, but also practices that have the effect of discriminating against individuals because of their race, color, national origin, religion, or sex.

National Origin Discrimination

- It is illegal to discriminate against an individual because of birthplace, ancestry, culture, or linguistic characteristics common to a specific ethnic group.

- A rule requiring that employees speak only English on the job may violate Title VII unless an employer shows that the requirement is necessary for conducting business. If the employer believes such a rule is necessary, employees must be informed when English is required and the consequences for violating the rule.

The Immigration Reform and Control Act (IRCA) of 1986 requires employers to assure that employees hired are legally authorized to work in the U.S. However, an employer who requests employment verification only for individuals of a particular national origin, or individuals who appear to be or sound foreign, may violate both Title VII and IRCA; verification must be obtained from all applicants and employees. Employers who impose citizenship requirements or give preferences to U.S. citizens in hiring or employment opportunities also may violate IRCA.

Religious Accommodation

- An employer is required to reasonably accommodate the religious belief of an employee or prospective employee, unless doing so would impose an undue hardship.

Sex Discrimination

Title VII's broad prohibitions against sex discrimination specifically cover:

- Sexual Harassment — This includes practices ranging from direct requests for sexual favors to workplace conditions that create a hostile environment for persons of either gender, including same sex harassment. (The "hostile environment" standard also applies to harassment on the bases of race, color, national origin, religion, age, and disability.)

- Pregnancy Based Discrimination — Pregnancy, childbirth, and related medical conditions must be treated in the same way as other temporary illnesses or conditions.

Additional rights are available to parents and others under the Family and Medical Leave Act (FMLA), which is enforced by the U.S. Department of Labor. For information on the FMLA, or to file an FMLA complaint, individuals should contact the nearest office of the Wage and Hour Division, Employment Standards Administration, U.S. Department of Labor. The Wage and Hour Division is listed in most telephone directories under U.S. Government, Department of Labor or at http://www.dol.gov/esa/public/whd_org.htm.

Age Discrimination in Employment Act

The ADEA's broad ban against age discrimination also specifically prohibits:

- statements or specifications in job notices or advertisements of age preference and limitations. An age limit may only be specified in the rare circumstance where age has been proven to be a bona fide occupational qualification (BFOQ);

- discrimination on the basis of age by apprenticeship programs, including joint labor-management apprenticeship programs; and

- denial of benefits to older employees. An employer may reduce benefits based on age only if the cost of providing the reduced benefits to older workers is the same as the cost of providing benefits to younger workers.

Equal Pay Act

The EPA prohibits discrimination on the basis of sex in the payment of wages or benefits, where men and women perform work of similar skill, effort, and responsibility for the same employer under similar working conditions.

Note that:

- Employers may not reduce wages of either sex to equalize pay between men and women.

- A violation of the EPA may occur where a different wage was/is paid to a person who worked in the same job before or after an employee of the opposite sex.

- A violation may also occur where a labor union causes the employer to violate the law.

Titles I and V of the Americans with Disabilities Act

The ADA prohibits discrimination on the basis of disability in all employment practices. It is necessary to understand several important ADA definitions to know who is protected by the law and what constitutes illegal discrimination:

Individual with a Disability

An individual with a disability under the ADA is a person who has a physical or mental impairment that substantially limits one or more major life activities, has a record of such an impairment, or is regarded as having such an impairment. Major life activities are activities that an average person can perform with little or no difficulty such as walking, breathing, seeing, hearing, speaking, learning, and working.

Qualified Individual with a Disability

A qualified employee or applicant with a disability is someone who satisfies skill, experience, education, and other job-related requirements of the position held or desired, and who, with or without reasonable accommodation, can perform the essential functions of that position.

Reasonable Accommodation

Reasonable accommodation may include, but is not limited to, making existing facilities used by employees readily accessible to and usable by persons with disabilities; job restructuring; modification of work schedules; providing additional unpaid leave; reassignment to a vacant position; acquiring or modifying equipment or devices; adjusting or modifying examinations, training materials, or policies; and providing qualified readers or interpreters. Reasonable accommodation may be necessary to apply for a job, to perform job functions, or to enjoy the benefits and privileges of employment that are enjoyed by people without disabilities. An employer is not required to lower production standards to make an accommodation. An employer generally is not obligated to provide personal use items such as eyeglasses or hearing aids.

Undue Hardship

An employer is required to make a reasonable accommodation to a qualified individual with a disability unless doing so would impose an undue hardship on the operation of the employer's business. Undue hardship means an action that requires significant difficulty or expense when considered in relation to factors such as a business' size, financial resources, and the nature and structure of its operation.

Prohibited Inquiries and Examinations

Before making an offer of employment, an employer may not ask job applicants about the existence, nature, or severity of a disability. Applicants may be asked about their ability to perform job functions. A job offer may be conditioned on the results of a medical examination, but only if the examination is required for all entering employees in the same job category. Medical examinations of employees must be job-related and consistent with business necessity.

Drug and Alcohol Use

Employees and applicants currently engaging in the illegal use of drugs are not protected by the ADA when an employer acts on the basis of such use. Tests for illegal use of drugs are not considered medical examinations and, therefore, are not subject to the ADA's restrictions on medical examinations. Employers may hold individuals who are illegally using drugs and individuals with alcoholism to the same standards of performance as other employees.

The Civil Rights Act of 1991

The Civil Rights Act of 1991 made major changes in the federal laws against employment discrimination enforced by EEOC. Enacted in part to reverse several Supreme Court decisions that limited the rights of persons protected by these laws, the Act also provides additional protections. The Act authorizes compensatory and punitive damages in cases of intentional discrimination, and provides for obtaining attorneys' fees and the possibility of jury trials. It also directs the EEOC to expand its technical assistance and outreach activities.

Employers and Other Entities Covered by EEO Laws

IV. Which Employers and Other Entities Are Covered by These Laws?

Title VII and the ADA cover all private employers, state and local governments, and education institutions that employ 15 or more individuals. These laws also cover private and public employment agencies, labor organizations, and joint labor management committees controlling apprenticeship and training.

The ADEA covers all private employers with 20 or more employees, state and local governments (including school districts), employment agencies and labor organizations.

The EPA covers all employers who are covered by the Federal Wage and Hour Law (the Fair Labor Standards Act). Virtually all employers are subject to the provisions of this Act.

Title VII, the ADEA, and the EPA also cover the federal government. In addition, the federal government is covered by Sections 501 and 505 of the Rehabilitation Act of 1973, as amended, which incorporate the requirements of the ADA. However, different procedures are used for processing complaints of federal discrimination. For more information on how to file a complaint of federal discrimination, contact the EEO office of the federal agency where the alleged discrimination occurred.

The CSRA (not enforced by EEOC) covers most federal agency employees except employees of a government corporation, the Federal Bureau of Investigation, the Central Intelligence Agency, the Defense Intelligence Agency, the National Security Agency, and as determined by the President, any executive agency or unit thereof, the principal function of which is the conduct of foreign intelligence or counterintelligence activities, or the General Accounting Office.

The EEOC's Charge Processing Procedures

Federal employees or applicants for employment should see the fact sheet about Federal Sector Equal Employment Opportunity Complaint Processing.

V. Who Can File a Charge of Discrimination?

- Any individual who believes that his or her employment rights have been violated may file a charge of discrimination with EEOC.

- In addition, an individual, organization, or agency may file a charge on behalf of another person in order to protect the aggrieved person's identity.

VI. How Is a Charge of Discrimination Filed?

- A charge may be filed by mail or in person at the nearest EEOC office. Individuals may consult their local telephone directory (U.S. Government listing) or call 1-800-669-4000 (voice) or 1-800-669-6820 (TTY) to contact the nearest EEOC office for more information on specific procedures for filing a charge.

- Individuals who need an accommodation in order to file a charge (e.g., sign language interpreter, print materials in an accessible format) should inform the EEOC field office so appropriate arrangements can be made.

- Federal employees or applicants for employment should see the fact sheet about Federal Sector Equal Employment Opportunity Complaint Processing.

VII. What Information Must Be Provided to File a Charge?

- The complaining party's name, address, and telephone number;

- The name, address, and telephone number of the respondent employer, employment agency, or union that is alleged to have discriminated, and number of employees (or union members), if known;

- A short description of the alleged violation (the event that caused the complaining party to believe that his or her rights were violated); and

- The date(s) of the alleged violation(s).

- Federal employees or applicants for employment should see the fact sheet about Federal Sector Equal Employment Opportunity Complaint Processing.

VIII. What Are the Time Limits for Filing a Charge of Discrimination?

All laws enforced by EEOC, except the Equal Pay Act, require filing a charge with EEOC before a private lawsuit may be filed in court. There are strict time limits within which charges must be filed:

- A charge must be filed with EEOC within 180 days from the date of the alleged violation, in order to protect the charging party's rights.

- This 180-day filing deadline is extended to 300 days if the charge also is covered by a state or local anti-discrimination law. For ADEA charges, only state laws extend the filing limit to 300 days.

- These time limits do not apply to claims under the Equal Pay Act, because under that Act persons do not have to first file a charge with EEOC in order to have the right to go to court. However, since many EPA claims also raise Title VII sex discrimination issues, it may be advisable to file charges under both laws within the time limits indicated.

- To protect legal rights, it is always best to contact EEOC promptly when discrimination is suspected.

- Federal employees or applicants for employment should see the fact sheet about Federal Sector Equal Employment Opportunity Complaint Processing.

IX. What Agency Handles a Charge that is also Covered by State or Local Law?

Many states and localities have anti-discrimination laws and agencies responsible for enforcing those laws. EEOC refers to these agencies as "Fair Employment Practices Agencies (FEPAs)." Through the use of "work sharing agreements," EEOC and the FEPAs avoid duplication of effort while at the same time ensuring that a charging party's rights are protected under both federal and state law.

- If a charge is filed with a FEPA and is also covered by federal law, the FEPA "dual files" the charge with EEOC to protect federal rights. The charge usually will be retained by the FEPA for handling.

- If a charge is filed with EEOC and also is covered by state or local law, EEOC "dual files" the charge with the state or local FEPA, but ordinarily retains the charge for handling.

X. What Happens after a Charge is Filed with EEOC?

The employer is notified that the charge has been filed. From this point there are a number of ways a charge may be handled:

- A charge may be assigned for priority investigation if the initial facts appear to support a violation of law. When the evidence is less strong, the charge may be assigned for follow up investigation to determine whether it is likely that a violation has occurred.

- EEOC can seek to settle a charge at any stage of the investigation if the charging party and the employer express an interest in doing so. If settlement efforts are not successful, the investigation continues.

- In investigating a charge, EEOC may make written requests for information, interview people, review documents, and, as needed, visit the facility where the alleged discrimination occurred. When the investigation is complete, EEOC will discuss the evidence with the charging party or employer, as appropriate.

- The charge may be selected for EEOC's mediation program if both the charging party and the employer express an interest in this option. Mediation is offered as an alternative to a lengthy investigation. Participation in the mediation program is confidential, voluntary, and requires consent from both charging party and employer. If mediation is unsuccessful, the charge is returned for investigation.

- A charge may be dismissed at any point if, in the agency's best judgment, further investigation will not establish a violation of the law. A charge may be dismissed at the time it is filed, if an initial in-depth interview does not produce evidence to support the claim. When a charge is dismissed, a notice is issued in accordance with the law which gives the charging party 90 days in which to file a lawsuit on his or her own behalf.

- Federal employees or applicants for employment should see the fact sheet about Federal Sector Equal Employment Opportunity Complaint Processing.

XI. How Does EEOC Resolve Discrimination Charges?

- If the evidence obtained in an investigation does not establish that discrimination occurred, this will be explained to the charging party. A required notice is then issued, closing the case and giving the charging party 90 days in which to file a lawsuit on his or her own behalf.

- If the evidence establishes that discrimination has occurred, the employer and the charging party will be informed of this in a letter of determination that explains the finding. EEOC will then attempt conciliation with the employer to develop a remedy for the discrimination.

- If the case is successfully conciliated, or if a case has earlier been successfully mediated or settled, neither EEOC nor the charging party may go to court unless the conciliation, mediation, or settlement agreement is not honored.

- If EEOC is unable to successfully conciliate the case, the agency will decide whether to bring suit in federal court. If EEOC decides not to sue, it will issue a notice closing the case and giving the charging party 90 days in which to file a lawsuit on his or her own behalf. In Title VII and ADA cases against state or local governments, the Department of Justice takes these actions.

- Federal employees or applicants for employment should see the fact sheet about Federal Sector Equal Employment Opportunity Complaint Processing.

XII. When Can an Individual File an Employment Discrimination Lawsuit in Court?

A charging party may file a lawsuit within 90 days after receiving a notice of a "right to sue" from EEOC, as stated above. Under Title VII and the ADA, a charging party also can request a notice of "right to sue" from EEOC 180 days after the charge was first filed with the Commission, and may then bring suit within 90 days after receiving this notice. Under the ADEA, a suit may be filed at any time 60 days after filing a charge with EEOC, but not later than 90 days after EEOC gives notice that it has completed action on the charge.

Under the EPA, a lawsuit must be filed within two years (three years for willful violations) of the discriminatory act, which in most cases is payment of a discriminatory lower wage.

Federal employees or applicants for employment should see the fact sheet about Federal Sector Equal Employment Opportunity Complaint Processing.

XIII. What Remedies Are Available When Discrimination Is Found?

The "relief" or remedies available for employment discrimination, whether caused by intentional acts or by practices that have a discriminatory effect, may include:

- back pay,

- hiring,

- promotion,

- reinstatement,

- front pay,

- reasonable accommodation, or

- other actions that will make an individual "whole" (in the condition s/he would have been but for the discrimination).

Remedies also may include payment of:

- attorneys' fees,

- expert witness fees, and

- court costs.

Under most EEOC-enforced laws, compensatory and punitive damages also may be available where intentional discrimination is found. Damages may be available to compensate for actual monetary losses, for future monetary losses, and for mental anguish and inconvenience. Punitive damages also may be available if an employer acted with malice or reckless indifference. Punitive damages are not available against the federal, state or local governments.

In cases concerning reasonable accommodation under the ADA, compensatory or punitive damages may not be awarded to the charging party if an employer can demonstrate that "good faith" efforts were made to provide reasonable accommodation.

An employer may be required to post notices to all employees addressing the violations of a specific charge and advising them of their rights under the laws EEOC enforces and their right to be free from retaliation. Such notices must be accessible, as needed, to persons with visual or other disabilities that affect reading.

The employer also may be required to take corrective or preventive actions to cure the source of the identified discrimination and minimize the chance of its recurrence, as well as discontinue the specific discriminatory practices involved in the case.

The Commission

XIV. What Is EEOC and How Does It Operate?

EEOC is an independent federal agency originally created by Congress in 1964 to enforce Title VII of the Civil Rights Act of 1964. The Commission is composed of five Commissioners and a General Counsel appointed by the President and confirmed by the Senate. Commissioners are appointed for five-year staggered terms; the General Counsel's term is four years. The President designates a Chair and a Vice-Chair. The Chair is the chief executive officer of the Commission. The Commission has authority to establish equal employment policy and to approve litigation. The General Counsel is responsible for conducting litigation.

EEOC carries out its enforcement, education and technical assistance activities through 50 field offices serving every part of the nation.

* * *

QUESTIONS

1. Of the various types of discrimination that might occur in a workplace or other setting, what form(s) would an older worker be most likely to experience?

2. How would you begin to counsel a client whom you believe to have been the victim of unlawful age or disability discrimination? Is it inevitably in such a client's interest to litigate her claim?

B. AGE DISCRIMINATION

1. Federal Law

In connection with the following excerpts, read the Age Discrimination in Employment Act (incorporating the Older Workers Benefit Protection Act) in the statutory supplement.

U.S. Equal Employment Opportunity Commission
Age Discrimination
http://www.eeoc.gov/types/age.html

The Age Discrimination in Employment Act of 1967 (ADEA) protects individuals who are 40 years of age or older from employment discrimination based on age. The ADEA's protections apply to both employees and job applicants. Under the ADEA, it is unlawful to discriminate against a person because of his/her age with respect to any term, condition, or privilege of employment, including hiring, firing, promotion, layoff, compensation, benefits, job assignments, and training.

It is also unlawful to retaliate against an individual for opposing employment practices that discriminate based on age or for filing an age discrimination charge, testifying, or participating in any way in an investigation, proceeding, or litigation under the ADEA.

The ADEA applies to employers with 20 or more employees, including state and local governments. It also applies to employment agencies and labor organizations, as well as to the federal government. ADEA protections include:

- *Apprenticeship Programs.* It is generally unlawful for apprenticeship programs, including joint labor-management apprenticeship programs, to discriminate on the basis of an individual's age. Age limitations in apprenticeship programs are valid only if they fall within certain specific exceptions under the ADEA or if the EEOC grants a specific exemption.

- *Job Notices and Advertisements.* The ADEA generally makes it unlawful to include age preferences, limitations, or specifications in job notices or advertisements. A job notice or advertisement may specify an age limit only in the rare circumstances where age is shown to be a "bona fide occupational qualification" (BFOQ) reasonably necessary to the normal operation of the business.

- *Pre-Employment Inquiries.* The ADEA does not specifically prohibit an employer from asking an applicant's age or date of birth. However, because such inquiries may deter older workers from applying for employment or may otherwise indicate possible intent to discriminate based on age, requests for age information will be closely scrutinized to make sure that the inquiry was made for a lawful purpose, rather than for a purpose prohibited by the ADEA.

- *Benefits.* The Older Workers Benefit Protection Act of 1990 (OWBPA) amended the ADEA to specifically prohibit employers from denying benefits to older employees. Congress recognized that the cost of providing certain benefits to older workers is greater than the cost of providing those same benefits to younger workers, and that those greater costs would create a disincentive to hire older workers. Therefore, in limited circumstances, an employer may be permitted to reduce benefits based on age, as long as the cost of providing the reduced benefits to older workers is the same as the cost of providing benefits to younger workers.

Waivers of ADEA Rights

An employer may ask an employee to waive his/her rights or claims under the ADEA either in the settlement of an ADEA administrative or court claim or in connection with an exit incentive program or other employment termination program. However, the ADEA, as amended by OWBPA, sets out specific minimum standards that must be met in order for a waiver to be considered knowing and voluntary and, therefore, valid. Among other requirements, a valid ADEA waiver must:

1. be in writing and be understandable;

2. specifically refer to ADEA rights or claims;

3. not waive rights or claims that may arise in the future;

4. be in exchange for valuable consideration;

5. advise the individual in writing to consult an attorney before signing the waiver; and

6. provide the individual at least 21 days to consider the agreement and at least seven days to revoke the agreement after signing it.

If an employer requests an ADEA waiver in connection with an exit incentive program or other employment termination program, the minimum requirements for a valid waiver are more extensive.

Statistics

In Fiscal Year 2006, EEOC received 13,569 charges of age discrimination. EEOC resolved 14,146 age discrimination charges in FY 2006 and recovered $51.5 million in monetary benefits for charging parties and other aggrieved individuals (not including monetary benefits obtained through litigation

The U.S. Equal Employment Opportunity Commission Filing a Charge of Employment Discrimination
http://www.eeoc.gov/charge/overview_charge_filing.html

Who can file a charge of [age] discrimination?

Any individual who believes that his or her employment rights have been violated may file a charge of discrimination with EEOC. In addition, an individual, organization, or agency may file a charge on behalf of another person in order to protect the aggrieved person's identity.

How is a charge of discrimination filed?

A charge may be filed by mail or in person at the nearest EEOC office. Individuals who need an accommodation in order to file a charge (e.g., sign language interpreter, print materials in an accessible format) should inform the EEOC field office so appropriate arrangements can be made. Federal employees or applicants for employment should see Federal Sector Equal Employment Opportunity Complaint Processing.

What information must be provided to file a charge?

The complaining party's name, address, and telephone number; the name, address, and telephone number of the respondent employer, employment agency, or union that is alleged to have discriminated, and number of employees (or union members), if known; a short description of the alleged violation (the event that caused the complaining party to believe that his or her rights were violated); and the date(s) of the alleged violation(s). Federal employees or applicants for employment should see Federal Sector Equal Employment Opportunity Complaint Processing.

What are the time limits for filing a charge of discrimination?

All laws enforced by EEOC, except the Equal Pay Act, require filing a charge with EEOC before a private lawsuit may be filed in court. There are strict time limits within which charges must be filed:

- A charge must be filed with EEOC within 180 days from the date of the alleged violation, in order to protect the charging party's rights.

- This 180-day filing deadline is extended to 300 days if the charge also is covered by a state or local anti-discrimination law. For ADEA charges, only state laws extend the filing limit to 300 days.

- These time limits do not apply to claims under the Equal Pay Act, because under that Act persons do not have to first file a charge with EEOC in order to have the right to go to court. However, since many EPA claims also raise Title VII sex discrimination issues, it may be advisable to file charges under both laws within the time limits indicated.

- To protect legal rights, it is always best to contact EEOC promptly when discrimination is suspected.

- Federal employees or applicants for employment should see Federal Sector Equal Employment Opportunity Complaint Processing.

What agency handles a charge that is also covered by state or local law?

Many states and localities have anti-discrimination laws and agencies responsible for enforcing those laws. EEOC refers to these agencies as "Fair Employment Practices Agencies (FEPAs)." Through the use of "work sharing agreements," EEOC and the FEPAs avoid duplication of effort while at the same time ensuring that a charging party's rights are protected under both federal and state law. If a charge is filed with a FEPA and is also covered by federal law, the FEPA "dual files" the charge with EEOC to protect federal rights. The charge usually will be retained by the FEPA for handling. If a charge is filed with EEOC and also is covered by state or local law, EEOC "dual files" the charge with the state or local FEPA, but ordinarily retains the charge for handling.

How is a charge filed for discrimination outside the United States?

U.S.-based companies that employ U.S. citizens outside the United States or its territories are covered under EEO laws, with certain exceptions. An individual alleging an EEO violation outside the U.S. should file a charge with the district office closest to his or her employer's headquarters. However, if you are unsure where to file, you may file a charge with any EEOC office.

QUESTIONS

1. How can an employer protect itself from workplace litigation?

2. Does the prospect of obtaining attorney's fees in civil rights litigation suggest any ethical dilemmas for the elder law attorney?

O'CONNOR v. CONSOLIDATED
COIN CATERERS CORPORATION
517 U.S. 308 (1996)

JUSTICE SCALIA delivered the opinion of the Court.

Petitioner James O'Connor was employed by respondent Consolidated Coin Caterers Corporation from 1978 until August 10, 1990, when, at age 56, he was fired. Claiming that he had been dismissed because of his age in violation of the ADEA, petitioner brought suit in the United States District Court for the Western District of North Carolina. After discovery, the District Court granted respondent's motion for summary judgment, and petitioner appealed. The Court of Appeals for the Fourth Circuit stated that petitioner could establish a prima facie case under *McDonnell Douglas* only if he could prove that (1) he was in the age group protected by the ADEA; (2) he was discharged or demoted; (3) at the time of his discharge or demotion, he was performing his job at a level that met his employer's legitimate expectations; and (4) following his discharge or demotion, he was replaced by someone of comparable qualifications outside the protected class. Since petitioner's replacement was 40 years old, the Court of Appeals concluded that the last element of the prima facie case had not been made out.[1] Finding that petitioner's claim could not survive a motion for summary judgment without benefit of the *McDonnell Douglas* presumption (*i.e.*, "under the ordinary standards of proof used in civil cases"), the Court of Appeals affirmed the judgment of dismissal. We granted O'Connor's petition for certiorari.

In *McDonnell Douglas*, we "established an allocation of the burden of production and an order for the presentation of proof in Title VII discriminatory treatment cases." *St. Mary's Honor Center v. Hicks*, 509 U.S. 502, 506 (1993). We held that a plaintiff alleging racial discrimination in violation of Title VII of the Civil Rights Act of 1964, 42 U.S.C. § 2000e *et seq.*, could establish a prima facie case by showing "(i) that he belongs to a racial minority; (ii) that he applied and was qualified for a job for which the employer was seeking applicants; (iii) that, despite his qualifications, he was rejected; and (iv) that, after his rejection, the position remained open and the employer continued to seek applicants from persons of [the] complainant's qualifications." Once the plaintiff has met this initial burden, the burden of production shifts to the employer "to articulate some legitimate, nondiscriminatory reason for the employee's rejection." If the trier of fact finds that the elements of the prima facie case are supported by a preponderance of the evidence and the employer remains silent, the court must enter judgment for the plaintiff.

In assessing claims of age discrimination brought under the ADEA, the Fourth Circuit, like others,[2] has applied some variant of the basic evidentiary

---

[1] The court also concluded that even under a modified version of the *McDonnell Douglas* prima facie standard which the Fourth Circuit applies to reduction in force cases, see *Mitchell v. Data General Corp.*, 12 F.3d 1310, 1315 (1993), petitioner could not prevail. We limit our review to the Fourth Circuit's treatment of this case as a non reduction in force case.

[2] *See, e.g.*, Roper v. Peabody Coal Co., 47 F.3d 925, 926-27 (7th Cir. 1995); Rinehart v. Independence, 35 F.3d 1263, 1265 (8th Cir. 1994), *cert. denied*, 514 U.S. 1096 (1995); Seman v. Coplay

framework set forth in *McDonnell Douglas*. We have never had occasion to decide whether that application of the Title VII rule to the ADEA context is correct, but since the parties do not contest that point, we shall assume it. On that assumption, the question presented for our determination is what elements must be shown in an ADEA case to establish the prima facie case that triggers the employer's burden of production.

As the very name "prima facie case" suggests, there must be at least a logical connection between each element of the prima facie case and the illegal discrimination for which it establishes a "legally mandatory, rebuttable presumption." The element of replacement by someone under 40 fails this requirement. The discrimination prohibited by the ADEA is discrimination "because of [an] individual's age," 29 U.S.C. § 623(a)(1), though the prohibition is "limited to individuals who are at least 40 years of age," § 631(a). This language does not ban discrimination against employees because they are aged 40 or older; it bans discrimination against employees because of their age, but limits the protected class to those who are 40 or older. The fact that one person in the protected class has lost out to another person in the protected class is thus irrelevant, so long as he has lost out *because of his age*. Or to put the point more concretely, there can be no greater inference of *age* discrimination (as opposed to "40 or over" discrimination) when a 40 year old is replaced by a 39 year old than when a 56 year old is replaced by a 40 year old. Because it lacks probative value, the fact that an ADEA plaintiff was replaced by someone outside the protected class is not a proper element of the *McDonnell Douglas* prima facie case.

Perhaps some courts have been induced to adopt the principle urged by respondent in order to avoid creating a prima facie case on the basis of very thin evidence — for example, the replacement of a 68 year old by a 65 year old. While the respondent's principle theoretically permits such thin evidence (consider the example above of a 40 year old replaced by a 39 year old), as a practical matter it will rarely do so, since the vast majority of age discrimination claims come from older employees. In our view, however, the proper solution to the problem lies not in making an utterly irrelevant factor an element of the prima facie case, but rather in recognizing that the prima facie case requires "evidence *adequate to create an inference that an employment decision was based on a[n] [illegal] discriminatory criterion. . . .*" *Teamsters v. United States*, 431 U.S. 324, 358 (1977) (emphasis added). In the age discrimination context, such an inference can not be drawn from the replacement of one worker with another worker insignificantly younger. Because the ADEA prohibits discrimination on the basis of age and not class membership, the fact that a replacement is substantially younger than the plaintiff is a far more reliable indicator of age discrimination than is the fact that the plaintiff was replaced by someone out-

---

Cement Co., 26 F.3d 428, 432, n.7 (3d Cir. 1994); Roush v. KFC Nat. Mgt. Co., 10 F.3d 392, 396 (6th Cir. 1993), *cert. denied*, 513 U.S. 808 (1994); Lindsey v. Prive Corp., 987 F.2d 324, 326, n.5 (5th Cir. 1993); Goldstein v. Manhattan Industries, Inc., 758 F.2d 1435, 1442 (11th Cir.), *cert. denied*, 474 U.S. 1005 (1985); Haskell v. Kaman Corp., 743 F.2d 113, 119, and n.1 (2d Cir. 1984); Cuddy v. Carmen, 694 F.2d 853, 856-57 (D.C. Cir. 1982); Douglas v. Anderson, 656 F.2d 528, 531-32 (9th Cir. 1981); Loeb v. Textron, Inc., 600 F.2d 1003, 1014-16 (1st Cir. 1979); Schwager v. Sun Oil Co. of Pa., 591 F.2d 58, 60-61 (10th Cir. 1979).

side the protected class. The judgment of the Fourth Circuit is reversed, and the case is remanded for proceedings consistent with this opinion.

It is so ordered.

QUESTIONS

1. Do you agree with the outcome of this case? Why or why not?

2. Does the plain language of the ADEA or its underlying purposes suggest a preference for older to younger workers within the protected age group?

3. Soon after *O'Connor* was decided, the EEOC issued enforcement guidelines interpreting this decision for its investigators and others interested in compliance with the ADEA as interpreted in *O'Connor*. *See* EEOC Notice No. 915.002 (9-18-96), http://www.eeoc.gov/policy/docs/oconnor.html. Review these guidelines. Do you agree with the EEOC's interpretation of *O'Connor*?

SCOTT v. THE GOODYEAR TIRE AND RUBBER CO.
160 F.3d 1121 (6th Cir. 1998)

Nathaniel R. Jones, Circuit Judge. Plaintiff Albert J. Scott appeals the grant of summary judgment in favor of Defendant Goodyear Tire and Rubber Company ("Goodyear") in this age discrimination case brought under the Age Discrimination in Employment Act ("ADEA"), 29 U.S.C. §§ 621 *et seq.* and Ohio's counterpart statute.[3] Specifically, Scott contends that Goodyear constructively discharged him when it eliminated his position following company restructuring and offered him early retirement instead of redeployment[4] to a comparable position within the company. Upon consideration of the record and applicable law, we reverse the grant of summary judgment and remand for proceedings consistent with this opinion.

I.

Albert Scott began his employment with Goodyear on June 6, 1952 and continued working for the company until December 1993 — the date of his decision to retire. During his 41 years of uninterrupted service to Goodyear, Scott held many positions including stockman, gas man, general service man, delivery and sales person of Tires, Batteries and Accessories, credit sales manager, store manager, retail store operations representative, division inventory coordinator and, finally, Operations Manager. Scott received satisfactory reviews throughout his employment with Goodyear.

In his final position as Operations Manager, Scott bore responsibility for administering, implementing, and coordinating policy and procedures dictated by the company to its eastern region district managers and retail stores. Although Goodyear centered its operations managers within its headquarters

---

[3] Although Scott brought his claim under section 4101.17, the Ohio age discrimination statute has since been recodified at Ohio Rev. Code Ann. § 4112.14 (Anderson 1988).

[4] "Redeployment" and its derivatives are the parties' choice terms for "reassignment."

in Akron, Ohio, Scott's duties sometimes required him to travel to store locations to handle administrative matters directly with store managers.

In May of 1993, Goodyear began a comprehensive restructuring of its upper-level management structure, which resulted in the elimination of the five Operations Manager positions maintained by the company, including the position held by Scott[5] The other four positions were held by John Cox (63 years old), Rodney Gwinn (51 years old), Greg Wahrle (35 years old) and Shayon Smith (32 years old). Scott, who was 61 years old when his position was eliminated, was told that he had not been redeployed because others could better meet the experience, skill, educational and other characteristic needs of the company. Redeployed employees, as Gordon Hewitt, a Goodyear executive described it, would need, among other things, a "high energy level."

With the elimination of the operations manager position, Goodyear created the new position of Retail Administrator. Where, according to Goodyear management, the former position had fed the "heavily paperwork oriented system" and bred "inefficiency between Akron and the regions," Goodyear intended the new position to help improve management efficiency and customer relations. Under the new structure, the retail administrator position demanded a familiarity with computer technology, as the prevailing paper-based data recording system had become a major source of inefficiency.

Sometime around early December 1993, Ken Gable and Rob Morris, both subordinates of Goodyear's Manager of Human Resources Paul Evert, were instructed by Evert to travel to Cleveland, Ohio and inform Scott that his position had been eliminated. Evert also requested that Gable cover the options available to Scott in the wake of his job loss. According to Gable's deposition testimony, he inquired into the decision to eliminate Scott's position, but was "advised that the decision had been made and that [informing Scott of the elimination and decision not to redeploy him] was [his] assignment and that [Evert] was not going to discuss how the decision was arrived at [sic]." With Evert having closed off that discussion, Gable and Morris traveled to Cleveland the next day, and informed Scott that his job had been eliminated. Scott questioned Gable about the reasons for the decision, and Gable responded that he was not in a position to tell him because he did not know.

Gable then presented Scott with three options in lieu of continuing on as an operations manager. First, Scott could accept layoff status and receive no benefits at all and no possibility of recall. Second, Scott could accept layoff status, receive supplemental unemployment compensation benefits on a regular basis and remain under consideration for recall to a new position, if such a position became available at a later date.[6] Finally, Scott could opt for retirement and receive a lump sum payment of $114,500.86, as well as monthly retirement checks and continued health benefits into retirement. Scott ultimately chose retirement.

---

[5] The company only maintained five operations manager positions. Each operations manager took responsibility for a particular region of Goodyear's national business.

[6] Under this second option, Scott risked losing medical benefits after 18 months of taking layoff status.

As it turns out, some of the other former operations managers were retained and redeployed within the company. Shayon Smith was redeployed into a newly created retail administrator position based on his ability to "look at the overall process and then to get other people to cooperate with him that were not his peers" and his electronics background, as was Greg Wahrle, because his "programming skills" and his "team player" approach were highly rated among executives. Rodney Gwinn accepted a district manager position in Phoenix. Goodyear officials stated in deposition testimony that Gwinn's previous experience as a district manager made him a natural fit for the Phoenix position. Thus, of the five former operations managers, only Scott and John Cox, the two oldest managers, were not offered definite redeployment opportunities within the company.[7]

After his retirement, Scott brought this age discrimination action under the ADEA and a corresponding Ohio anti-discrimination statute on May 12, 1995, alleging that Goodyear's decision to eliminate his position was impermissibly motivated by age considerations. During the subsequent discovery phase, Scott compiled a number of suspicious facts. First, as noted above, he uncovered the irregular manner with which the decision to eliminate his position was handled. According to the undisputed deposition testimony of Evert and Gable, the latter was instructed to inform Scott of the elimination of his operations manager position without asking further questions. Consequently, Gable entered the discussion with Scott unable to answer questions about why the company had decided not to redeploy him. According to Gable, this occurrence deviated from normal practice, since he, as human resources representative, was generally given latitude to inquire into the basis for a given employment decision and to assess for the adversely-treated worker his or her prospects for future employment with the company. On occasion, in fact, Gable was given permission to find other employment within the company for a dismissed employee.

In addition to the unusually vague response given to Scott, various statements of two of the three managers responsible for the decision to eliminate Scott's position indicated age bias. According to Edward Ercegovich[8] a Goodyear employee at the time of the reorganization, Ed Gallagher, who was then Vice President of the Retail Sales Division, made statements in 1993 such as "this company is run by white haired old men, waiting to retire" and "this must change." Ercegovich similarly attested that he heard Hewitt state in August 1995 in reference to Goodyear's upcoming Budget planning: "Some people will lose their jobs, but in time, we will replace them with young college graduates

---

[7] The operations manager positions were not the only positions eliminated as a result of the corporate reorganization. In all, forty-eight positions were eliminated as part of this restructuring, including regional secretaries, operations staff persons, administrative managers and district administrators.

[8] Ercegovich himself brought a substantively identical age discrimination suit against Goodyear after Goodyear eliminated his position and failed to redeploy him. We reversed the district court's grant of summary judgment to Goodyear because we found that material issues of fact existed as to whether Ercegovich was denied a transfer because of his age. Ercegovich v. Goodyear Tire & Rubber Co., 154 F.3d 344 (6th Cir. 1998).

at less money."[9] Further, Scott presented deposition testimony from two of the three redeployed operations managers, Shayon Smith and Greg Wahrle, indicating that they had not been told that they were being laid off. Finally, Scott presented statistical evidence showing the average age of eliminated employees at 47.35 years old and that of non-eliminated employees at 40.47 years old. In reviewing these statistical findings, Drs. Harvey Rosen and John Burke, both economists, performed a chi-square test[10] to determine whether the age of an employee was a non-factor in determining whether his or her position was eliminated. After conducting further statistical analysis using a chi-square testing model, the economists concluded that the "data marginally *fail to reject* the null hypothesis that employee age is insignificant in explaining whether or not an employee's position was eliminated."

Prior to trial, however, Goodyear submitted a summary judgment motion on May 3, 1996, which the district court granted. Inexplicably, in the face of the economist's conclusions, the district court stated that no evidence supported Scott's contention that Goodyear managers forced him into retirement due to his age and thereby created an actionable instance of discrimination. Further, the

---

[9] The affidavit states in full substantive part:

Edward E. Ercegovich, after being duly sworn, according to law deposes and states that he is of legal age, sound mind, and has personal knowledge of the following:

1. That he was employed by the Goodyear Tire and Rubber Company in its Retail Stores Division from February 7, 1962, until October 28, 1994;

2. That from or about January, 1992, through the end of his employment with Goodyear he served as Quality Systems Coordinator;

3. That while functioning in that position in or about late 1993, he had the opportunity to hear and did hear Edward Gallagher, then Vice President of the Retail Stores Division, substantively state in a meeting on the seventh floor that "This company is being run by white haired old men, waiting to retire," and "This must change"; and

4. That while still functioning in the same position with the Retail Stores Division in or about August 25, 1995, I heard Gordon Hewitt, Director of Finance for the Retail Stores Division, substantively state in his 1995 Budget/Business Plan presentation to the group that "Some people will lose their jobs, but in time, we will replace them with young college graduates at less money."

J.A. at 202. While Ercegovich's affidavit seems in order, we note that Scott, in his brief, also attributes quotes to Hewitt through deposition testimony of Gable to the effect that Goodyear "needs to hire younger men." However, a closer look at the deposition in question suggests that Gable was actually quoting former Goodyear Executive Mel Morrison, not Hewitt. *See* J.A. at 549. Morrison left Goodyear in 1990, several years before the relevant temporal period regarding Goodyear's allegedly discriminatory acts. Hence, we have serious doubts of any probative value that the quotes from the Gable deposition may have in this case.

[10] In *King v. General Electric Co.,* 960 F.2d 617 (7th Cir. 1992), the Seventh Circuit explained:

A chi-square test evaluates the disparity between the expected and observed frequency of a certain outcome. For example, suppose that of the individuals terminated at a given time, a greater percentage of them are within the protected age class. We want to determine whether the disparity in termination rates can be attributed to chance, or whether the disparity is so large, that some factor other than chance probably influence[s] the selection of the individuals terminated. . . . A [c]hi-square test will determine whether the chance or other factors influenced the outcome.

Id. at 626 n.5 (citing Walter Connolly, Jr. et al. *Use of Statistics in Employment Opportunity Litigation* § 10.05[2] (1991)).

district concluded that, even if Scott had raised a genuine factual question regarding a constructive discharge theory, he failed to provide additional evidence to support an inference that age-related bias motivated the adverse redeployment decision. Moreover, the district court determined that Scott failed to establish a prima facie case of age discrimination because he voluntarily accepted early retirement. Scott then filed this timely appeal.

II.

Summary judgment is proper "if the pleadings, depositions, answers to interrogatories, and admissions on file, together with the affidavits, if any, show that there is no genuine issue as to any material fact and that the moving party is entitled to a judgment as a matter of law." Fed. R. Civ. P. 56(c). This court exercises *de novo* review of a grant of summary judgment below.

Under the ADEA, a plaintiff is typically required to proffer evidence of the following to make out a prima facie case of age discrimination: (1) that plaintiff was between 40 and 65 years old; (2) that he was qualified for the particular position; (3) that he was subjected to adverse employment action; and (4) that he was replaced by a younger individual. Once a prima facie case has been established, this court applies the shifting burden framework of *McDonnell Douglas v. Green,* 411 U.S. 792 (1973), to age discrimination cases as well. Thus, upon presentation of a prima facie case, the defendant must submit a legitimate, nondiscriminatory reason motivated the adverse employment action. The plaintiff is then required to demonstrate that the reason proffered by the defendant was pretextual. In the words of the Supreme Court, the pretext inquiry considers whether "the legitimate reasons offered by the defendant were not its true reasons, but were a pretext for discrimination."

The district court found, and parties appear to concede, that the law applicable to work force reduction cases is appropriate here. In such cases, this court takes account of the fact that the employer may not replace the plaintiff with a single worker. "Where, as here, there is a reduction in force, a plaintiff must either show that age was a factor in eliminating his position, or, where some employees are shifted to other positions, that he was qualified for another position, he was not given a new position, and that the decision not to place him in a new position was motivated by plaintiff's age." Consequently, the fourth prong of the prima facie age discrimination showing is supplanted by a requirement that the plaintiff proffer "additional direct, circumstantial, or statistical evidence tending to indicate that the employer singled out [the plaintiff] for discharge for impermissible reasons." For purposes of our review of the summary judgment grant below, this case turns on two issues: whether the actions taken against Scott by Goodyear can be construed as constructive termination and, if so, whether Scott has provided sufficient evidence of discriminatory intent regarding the alleged adverse actions to create a factual question on the pretext issue. We answer in the affirmative as to both issues.

A.

The first two prima facie elements appear to be established on the record. There is no dispute that Scott was 61 years old at the time his position was eliminated. Further, Scott maintained satisfactory marks throughout his 41 years of employment with the company and presented deposition testimony indicating that he took advantage of company-provided career development computer training. Thus, in common with the district court, we find that sufficient evidence exists on record to indicate that Scott was qualified for his position as operations manager.

Turning to the third prong, Scott alleges two theories of adverse treatment by Goodyear. First, Scott claims that he was constructively terminated by Goodyear due to his age. Second, Scott claims that Goodyear management intentionally decided against redeploying him on the basis of his age. We discuss each theory in turn.

The discriminatory termination to which Scott alleges to have fallen victim must overcome a significant hurdle — the menu of options given to him at the time his position was eliminated, all of which involved either accepting lay-off status or retiring, and his ultimate decision to retire. Scott maintains that he was laid off by Goodyear, even though he accepted the retirement option. Given this circumstance, Scott cannot prevail on a theory of actual discharge but must rely on the constructive discharge doctrine. As Scott phrased the issue in his brief in opposition to summary judgment below, he alleges to have been "forced to accept a lay-off without the likelihood of recall at the expense of much-needed medical benefits[.]"

"The law in this circuit is clear that a constructive discharge exists if working conditions are such that a reasonable person in the plaintiff's shoes would feel compelled to resign." *Bruhwiler v. University of Tennessee*, 859 F.2d 419, 421 (6th Cir. 1988) (citing *Henry v. Lennox Industries, Inc.*, 768 F.2d 746, 752 (6th Cir. 1985)). In the typical discriminatory constructive discharge case, the employer does not overtly seek a discontinuation in the employment relationship but the employee claims to be subjected to intolerable working conditions due to discriminatory behavior. *See, e.g., id.* at 420 (research toxicologist hired by University possessing more seniority than her male supervisors and paid much less than her less experienced male supervisors resigned after receiving an "unsatisfactory" evaluation and being given names of possible job contacts by a superior when she did not asked for them); *Henry v. Lennox Industries, Inc.*, 768 F.2d 746, 751-52 (6th Cir. 1985) (constructive discharge occurred where employee was required to train the person who would supervise her, refused an explanation for her demotion, and never was seriously considered for a supervisory position). However, in the instant case, Scott alleges that the offer of layoff with possible recall amounted to a choice between voluntary and involuntary retirement. According to Scott's view, Goodyear had no intention of recalling him had he accepted layoff status.

The district court addressed the constructive discharge issue by analyzing this court's decisions in *Ackerman v. Diamond Shamrock Corp.*, 670 F.2d 66 (6th Cir. 1982), and *Wilson v. Firestone Tire & Rubber Co.*, 932 F.2d 510 (6th Cir. 1991), to find that the constructive discharge doctrine should not apply to this case:

> There is no evidence that Gable coerced Scott into accepting retirement. On the contrary, the record indicates that Gable fully explained Scott's available options. Although Scott contends that the "evidence is

clear" that Goodyear never intended to recall him and that this rendered the layoff option illusory, there is no evidence to substantiate this allegation.

We disagree.

The *Ackerman* court considered an instance in which the plaintiff, Edward Ackerman, at age 59, was informed that his director of communications job was being eliminated in the wake of corporate reorganization. Ackerman was offered an early retirement package which gave him "much more than the benefits to which he would be entitled if he were simply terminated." Although the record conflicted over whether Ackerman consulted an attorney before signing the early retirement agreement, he testified that he signed the agreement "of his own free will, that he understood the terms of the agreement, and that his employer complied with the agreement."

Finding no evidence of discriminatory intent, other than the conclusory allegations of Ackerman that he could "think of no reason for his discharge other than his age," we determined that Ackerman voluntarily signed the early retirement offer and thus was not constructively discharged. The court determined that Ackerman had not upheld his prima facie burden. *Ackerman,* therefore, stands for the proposition that a mere allegation that improper motives led an employer to offer early retirement benefits is insufficient to prove that the employee who accepted those benefits was constructively discharged.

In *Wilson*, this court considered whether the plaintiff in that case presented adequate evidence indicating that age considerations motivated the decision to (1) eliminate his position and (2) offer him a choice of a lesser position or early retirement. The plaintiff in that case, Ival Wilson, had presented circumstantial evidence of illicit motivation on the part of Firestone management in its determination to offer Wilson early retirement benefits, which this court found unpersuasive. Wilson offered the following three facts to support his claim: (1) that management had referred to his 33 years of employment with the company in a memo written by a manager at the time Wilson's severance package was being developed; (2) a conversation with his immediate supervisor a few months prior to the decision to eliminate his position in which his immediate supervisor stated that he hoped that older employees would accept the new company-wide early retirement option so that younger workers would not be displaced and; (3) the personnel documents kept by Firestone that included the birthdates and years of service of its employees. On this record, we concluded that an inference of discriminatory motivation in an adverse employment decision had not been proven.

Additionally, the *Wilson* court determined that the plaintiff did not demonstrate that he was actually or constructively discharged. A key factor in the decision to find against discharge was that Firestone had offered Wilson "legitimate opportunities for continued employment." Since Wilson had, among other choices, the option to replace any of three of his former subordinates or accept early retirement, the court found that he was not forced to resign from the company.

Wilson and *Ackerman*, while similar to the facts of the instant case, both differ by the evidence presented by the plaintiff and, at least with respect to *Wilson*, on the facts surrounding the alleged discharge. In its reliance on these two cases, the district court overlooked some vitally important evidence submitted by Scott at the summary judgment phase indicating that the retirement decision was less than voluntary.

First, we note the odd directives given to Gable, the Goodyear Human Resources executive. Gable was informed by Paul Evert that the position held by Scott would be eliminated and was told to travel to the Cleveland field office to report that fact to Scott. Gable, who testified that he had participated in at least three corporate reorganizations with Goodyear, had informed other Goodyear employees of such job eliminations in the past and many times received instructions to offer such employees lower level positions in lieu of lay-off. However, in this case, it appears that Evert cut off any further discussion regarding the decision to eliminate Scott's position.

Additionally, Scott recalled in deposition testimony that Gable and Morris, the other Goodyear executive present at the meeting with Scott in Cleveland, used the term "laid off" to describe the elimination of his position. Consequently, when Scott attempted to query Gable about the reasons for the elimination of his position and the possibility of future employment, Gable could not provide any answers. While the record does not reflect whether Gable made a formal or informal practice of informing other persons subjected to job elimination of their likelihood of being recalled, his inability to address the reasons for the elimination and decision not to redeploy Scott seem substantial enough reason for Scott to entertain the subjective belief that he would not be recalled if he chose lay-off status. Further, it seems that Wahrle and Smith may not have been told that they were being "laid off," and, more significantly, both were redeployed.

Scott thus chose retirement having no definite prospect of continued employment with the company. Therefore, where ordinary charges of constructive discharge typically entail a decision on the part of the employee to resign in light of an intolerable working environment or some such allegation, Scott decided upon the option best suited to his needs with the understanding that he did not have the option of continued employment. For that reason, we find that the doctrine of constructive discharge applies in this case.

In addition to the constructive termination theory, Scott charges that the decision not to redeploy him serves as an actionable basis for going forward with his case. We note that, while this court has never recognized a right to redeployment under the ADEA, a decision made by an employer to redeploy younger employees while not redeploying older ones is a recognized form of adverse employment action.

Examining the pertinent facts, we first note that the two oldest operations managers, Scott, at age 61, and Cox, at age 63, were not redeployed by the company at the time those positions were eliminated. Further, Scott has presented statistical evidence suggesting that the average age of employees whose positions were eliminated (47.35 years old) was significantly higher than the

average age of employees whose positions remained intact through the corporate restructuring (40.47 years old). The district court took exception to the
probative value of these statistics because 66 employees included in the redeployed comparison group "were never considered for redeployment since their
positions were not in jeopardy [and therefore] the presumption that the sample
was representative of all candidates for redeployment is false." After reviewing
the statistical findings, however, we conclude that the district court hastily
cast them aside for the following reasons.

First, while the statistics were not as probative as they perhaps may have
been, they do reveal some startling age comparisons between persons occupy-
ing positions that were eliminated and those unaffected by the reorganization.
In addition to showing a nearly seven-year age disparity between the two
groups, the statistical evidence, which was compiled by two economists, Drs.
Harvey Rosen and John Burke, pointed to a less than 1% chance that the discrepancy arose due to randomness. Not only does this evidence increase the likelihood that the decisions to eliminate certain positions were based on age but it
also makes more likely the possibility that age played a part in redeployment
decisions.

Second, the district court, borrowing language from *Chappell v. GTE Products
Corp.*, 803 F.2d 261, 268 n.2 (6th Cir. 1986), deemed the seemingly inculpatory
comments attributed to Goodyear managers Gallagher and Hewitt as "too
abstract, in addition to being irrelevant and prejudicial, to support a finding of
age discrimination." However, it would seem that a statement that the company
"is run by white haired old men, waiting to retire," and "[t]his must change,"
both of which are attributed to Gallagher, as well as a statement that those who
lose their jobs through reorganization will be replaced with "young college graduates at less money," which was attributed to Hewitt, read in a light most
favorable to Scott, would be deemed relevant and probative by the district
court. Such statements may have been "abstract, irrelevant and prejudicial" had
they been made well-after the operative events or some other such occurrence.
But these statements appear to have been made in and around the time of the
corporate reorganization. In addition, the statements are consistent with what
took place — Cox and Scott, the two oldest operations managers were not redeployed. We thus agree with the *Ercegovich* panel that "[b]oth remarks on their
face strongly suggest that the speaker harbors a bias against older workers."

B.

Having found Scott to have presented a prima facie case of discrimination, we
turn to the question of whether "the legitimate reasons offered by the defendant
were not its true reasons, but were a pretext for discrimination." We find that
a jury question pertains to this issue, as there is conflicting evidence on the
record. On the one hand, Goodyear has proffered an ostensibly legitimate motive
to reduce its management layers for greater efficiency. On the other hand, however, as has been indicated, statements indicating bias against older workers
have been attributed to Goodyear managers Gallagher and Hewitt. Both managers played a role in the decision to eliminate the position held by Scott. Evert
ordered Gable not to answer routine questions from Scott regarding his position's elimination. The two oldest operations managers, Scott and Cox, were not

redeployed. Further the statistical evidence seems to suggest that age considerations factored into the job elimination decisions and, by consequence, the redeployment determinations.

III.

Because we find that Scott has presented sufficient evidence to support a prima facie case, we find that the district court ruling to the contrary should be reversed. Additionally, we further conclude that the district court had sufficient evidence of pretext to create a jury question on that issue. Accordingly, we reverse the district court's grant of summary judgment to Goodyear and remand this case for proceedings consistent with this opinion.

[Judge Alan E. Norris dissented on the ground that the plaintiff/appellant had failed to come forward with circumstantial or statistical evidence of discriminatory intent.]

QUESTIONS

1. Does the Sixth Circuit's decision in this case "open the door" to a flood of unwarranted age discrimination litigation?

2. Should a company-wide restructuring that results in the retirement or severance of a large number or proportion of older employees be presumed to be motivated by discriminatory intent?

SMITH v. CITY OF JACKSON, MISSISSIPPI
544 U.S. 228 (2005)

Justice Stevens announced the judgment of the Court and delivered the opinion of the Court with respect to Parts I, II, and IV, and an opinion with respect to Part III, in which Justice Souter, Justice Ginsburg, and Justice Breyer join.

Petitioners, police and public safety officers employed by the city of Jackson, Mississippi (hereinafter City), contend that salary increases received in 1999 violated the Age Discrimination in Employment Act of 1967 (ADEA) because they were less generous to officers over the age of 40 than to younger officers. Their suit raises the question whether the "disparate-impact" theory of recovery announced in *Griggs v. Duke Power Co.*, 401 U.S. 424 (1971), for cases brought under Title VII of the Civil Rights Act of 1964, is cognizable under the ADEA. Despite the age of the ADEA, it is a question that we have not yet addressed. See *Hazen Paper Co. v. Biggins*, 507 U.S. 604, 610 (1993); *Markham v. Geller*, 451 U.S. 945 (1981) (Rehnquist, J., dissenting from denial of certiorari).

I

On October 1, 1998, the City adopted a pay plan granting raises to all City employees. The stated purpose of the plan was to "attract and retain qualified people, provide incentive for performance, maintain competitiveness with other public sector agencies and ensure equitable compensation to all employees regardless of age, sex, race and/or disability." On May 1, 1999, a revision of the plan, which was motivated, at least in part, by the City's desire to bring the starting salaries of police officers up to the regional average, granted raises to all police officers and police dispatchers. Those who had less than five years of tenure received proportionately greater raises when compared to their former pay than those with more seniority. Although some officers over the age of 40 had less than five years of service, most of the older officers had more.

Petitioners are a group of older officers who filed suit under the ADEA claiming both that the City deliberately discriminated against them because of their age (the "disparate-treatment" claim) and that they were "adversely affected" by the plan because of their age (the "disparate-impact" claim). The District Court granted summary judgment to the City on both claims. The Court of Appeals held that the ruling on the former claim was premature because petitioners were entitled to further discovery on the issue of intent, but it affirmed the dismissal of the disparate-impact claim. Over one judge's dissent, the majority concluded that disparate-impact claims are categorically unavailable under the ADEA. Both the majority and the dissent assumed that the facts alleged by petitioners would entitle them to relief under the reasoning of *Griggs*.

We granted the officers' petition for certiorari, and now hold that the ADEA does authorize recovery in "disparate-impact" cases comparable to *Griggs*. Because, however, we conclude that petitioners have not set forth a valid disparate-impact claim, we affirm.

II

During the deliberations that preceded the enactment of the Civil Rights Act of 1964, Congress considered and rejected proposed amendments that would have included older workers among the classes protected from employment discrimination. *General Dynamics Land Systems, Inc. v. Cline*, 540 U.S. 581, 587 (2004). Congress did, however, request the Secretary of Labor to "make a full and complete study of the factors which might tend to result in discrimination in employment because of age and of the consequences of such discrimination on the economy and individuals affected." The Secretary's report, submitted in response to Congress' request, noted that there was little discrimination arising from dislike or intolerance of older people, but that "arbitrary" discrimination did result from certain age limits. Report of the Secretary of Labor, The Older American Worker: Age Discrimination in Employment 22 (June 1965), reprinted in U.S. Equal Employment Opportunity Commission, Legislative History of the Age Discrimination in Employment Act (1981) (hereinafter Wirtz Report). Moreover, the report observed that discriminatory effects resulted from "[i]nstitutional arrangements that indirectly restrict the employment of older workers." *Id.*, at 15.

In response to that report Congress directed the Secretary to propose remedial legislation, and then acted favorably on his proposal. As enacted in 1967, § 4(a)(2) of the ADEA, now codified as 29 U.S.C. § 623(a)(2), provided that it shall be unlawful for an employer "to limit, segregate, or classify his employees in any way which would deprive or tend to deprive any individual of employment opportunities or otherwise adversely affect his status as an employee, because of such individual's age. . . ." Except for substitution of the word "age" for the words "race, color, religion, sex, or national origin," the language of that provision in the ADEA is identical to that found in § 703(a)(2) of the Civil Rights Act of 1964 (Title VII). Other provisions of the ADEA also parallel the earlier statute. Unlike Title VII, however, § 4(f)(1) of the ADEA contains language that significantly narrows its coverage by permitting any "otherwise prohibited" action "where the differentiation is based on reasonable factors other than age" (hereinafter RFOA provision).

III

In determining whether the ADEA authorizes disparate-impact claims, we begin with the premise that when Congress uses the same language in two statutes having similar purposes, particularly when one is enacted shortly after the other, it is appropriate to presume that Congress intended that text to have the same meaning in both statutes. *Northcross v. Board of Ed. of Memphis City Schools*, 412 U.S. 427, 428 (1973) (per curiam). We have consistently applied that presumption to language in the ADEA that was "derived *in haec verba* from Title VII." *Lorillard v. Pons*, 434 U.S. 575, 584 (1978). Our unanimous interpretation of § 703(a)(2) of the Title VII in *Griggs* is therefore a precedent of compelling importance.

In *Griggs*, a case decided four years after the enactment of the ADEA, we considered whether § 703 of Title VII prohibited an employer "from requiring a high school education or passing of a standardized general intelligence test as a condition of employment in or transfer to jobs when (a) neither standard is shown to be significantly related to successful job performance, (b) both requirements operate to disqualify Negroes at a substantially higher rate than white applicants, and (c) the jobs in question formerly had been filled only by white employees as part of a longstanding practice of giving preference to whites." 401 U.S., at 425-426. Accepting the Court of Appeals' conclusion that the employer had adopted the diploma and test requirements without any intent to discriminate, we held that good faith "does not redeem employment procedures or testing mechanisms that operate as 'built-in headwinds' for minority groups and are unrelated to measuring job capability." *Id.*, at 432.

We explained that Congress had "directed the thrust of the Act to the consequences of employment practices, not simply the motivation." Ibid. We relied on the fact that history is "filled with examples of men and women who rendered highly effective performance without the conventional badges of accomplishment in terms of certificates, diplomas, or degrees. Diplomas and tests are useful servants, but Congress has mandated the commonsense proposition that they are not to become masters of reality." *Id.*, at 433. And we noted that the Equal Employment Opportunity Commission (EEOC), which had enforcement responsibility, had issued guidelines that accorded with our view. *Id.*, at 433-434. We thus squarely held that § 703(a)(2) of Title VII did not require a showing of discriminatory intent.

While our opinion in *Griggs* relied primarily on the purposes of the Act, buttressed by the fact that the EEOC had endorsed the same view, we have subsequently noted that our holding represented the better reading of the statutory text as well. *See Watson v. Fort Worth Bank & Trust*, 487 U.S. 977, 991 (1988).

Neither § 703(a)(2) nor the comparable language in the ADEA simply prohibits actions that "limit, segregate, or classify" persons; rather the language prohibits such actions that "deprive any individual of employment opportunities or otherwise adversely affect his status as an employee, because of such individual's" race or age. *Ibid.* (explaining that in disparate-impact cases, "the employer's practices may be said to 'adversely affect [an individual's status] as an employee'" (alteration in original) (quoting 42 U.S.C. § 2000e-2(a)(2))). Thus the text focuses on the effects of the action on the employee rather than the motivation for the action of the employer.

Griggs, which interpreted the identical text at issue here, thus strongly suggests that a disparate-impact theory should be cognizable under the ADEA. Indeed, for over two decades after our decision in *Griggs*, the Courts of Appeal uniformly interpreted the ADEA as authorizing recovery on a "disparate-impact" theory in appropriate cases. It was only after our decision in *Hazen Paper Co. v. Biggins*, 507 U.S. 604 (1993), that some of those courts concluded that the ADEA did not authorize a disparate-impact theory of liability. Our opinion in *Hazen Paper*, however, did not address or comment on the issue we decide today. In that case, we held that an employee's allegation that he was discharged shortly before his pension would have vested did not state a cause of action under a disparate-treatment theory. The motivating factor was not, we held, the employee's age, but rather his years of service, a factor that the ADEA did not prohibit an employer from considering when terminating an employee. *Id.*, at 612. While we noted that disparate-treatment "captures the essence of what Congress sought to prohibit in the ADEA," *id.*, at 610, we were careful to explain that we were not deciding "whether a disparate impact theory of liability is available under the ADEA. . . ." In sum, there is nothing in our opinion in *Hazen Paper* that precludes an interpretation of the ADEA that parallels our holding in *Griggs*.

The Court of Appeals' categorical rejection of disparate-impact liability, like Justice O'Connor's, rested primarily on the RFOA provision and the majority's analysis of legislative history. As we have already explained, we think the history of the enactment of the ADEA, with particular reference to the Wirtz Report, supports the pre-*Hazen Paper* consensus concerning disparate-impact liability. And *Hazen Paper* itself contains the response to the concern over the RFOA provision.

The RFOA provision provides that it shall not be unlawful for an employer "to take any action otherwise prohibited under subsectio[n] (a) . . . where the differentiation is based on reasonable factors other than age discrimination. . . ." In most disparate-treatment cases, if an employer in fact acted on a factor other than age, the action would not be prohibited under subsection (a) in the first place. *See Hazen Paper*, 507 U.S., at 609 ("[T]here is no disparate treatment under the ADEA when the factor motivating the employer is some feature other than the employee's age."). In those disparate-treatment cases, such as in *Hazen Paper* itself, the RFOA provision is simply unnecessary to avoid liability under the ADEA, since there was no prohibited action in the first place. The RFOA provision is not, as Justice O'Connor suggests, a "safe harbor from liability,"(emphasis deleted), since there would be no liability under § 4(a). *See Texas Dept. of*

Community Affairs v. Burdine, 450 U.S. 248, 254 (1981) (noting, in a Title VII case, that an employer can defeat liability by showing that the employee was rejected for "a legitimate, nondiscriminatory reason" without reference to an RFOA provision).

In disparate-impact cases, however, the allegedly "otherwise prohibited" activity is not based on age. *Ibid.* (" '[C]laims that stress "disparate impact" [by contrast] involve employment practices that are facially neutral in their treatment of different groups but that in fact fall more harshly on one group than another. . . .' " (quoting *Teamsters v. United States*, 431 U.S. 324, 335-336, n. 15 (1977)). It is, accordingly, in cases involving disparate-impact claims that the RFOA provision plays its principal role by precluding liability if the adverse impact was attributable to a nonage factor that was "reasonable." Rather than support an argument that disparate impact is unavailable under the ADEA, the RFOA provision actually supports the contrary conclusion.

Finally, we note that both the Department of Labor, which initially drafted the legislation, and the EEOC, which is the agency charged by Congress with responsibility for implementing the statute, 29 U.S.C. § 628 have consistently interpreted the ADEA to authorize relief on a disparate-impact theory. The initial regulations, while not mentioning disparate impact by name, nevertheless permitted such claims if the employer relied on a factor that was not related to age. 29 C.F.R. § 860.103(f)(1)(I) (1970) (barring physical fitness requirements that were not "reasonably necessary for the specific work to be performed"). *See also* § 1625.7 (2004) (setting forth the standards for a disparate-impact claim).

The text of the statute, as interpreted in *Griggs*, the RFOA provision, and the EEOC regulations all support petitioners' view. We therefore conclude that it was error for the Court of Appeals to hold that the disparate-impact theory of liability is categorically unavailable under the ADEA.

IV

Two textual differences between the ADEA and Title VII make it clear that even though both statutes authorize recovery on a disparate-impact theory, the scope of disparate-impact liability under ADEA is narrower than under Title VII. The first is the RFOA provision, which we have already identified. The second is the amendment to Title VII contained in the Civil Rights Act of 1991. One of the purposes of that amendment was to modify the Court's holding in *Wards Cove Packing Co. v. Antonio*, 490 U.S. 642 (1989), a case in which we narrowly construed the employer's exposure to liability on a disparate-impact theory. *See* Civil Rights Act of 1991, § 2. While the relevant 1991 amendments expanded the coverage of Title VII, they did not amend the ADEA or speak to the subject of age discrimination. Hence, *Wards Cove*'s pre-1991 interpretation of Title VII's identical language remains applicable to the ADEA.

Congress' decision to limit the coverage of the ADEA by including the RFOA provision is consistent with the fact that age, unlike race or other classifications protected by Title VII, not uncommonly has relevance to an individual's capacity to engage in certain types of employment. To be sure, Congress recognized that this is not always the case, and that society may perceive those differences to be larger or more consequential than they are in fact. However, as Secretary Wirtz noted in his report, "certain circumstances . . . unquestionably affect older workers more strongly, as a group, than they do younger workers." Wirtz Report 28. Thus, it is not surprising that certain employment criteria that are routinely used may be reasonable despite their adverse impact on older workers as a group. Moreover, intentional discrimination on the basis of age has not occurred at the same levels as discrimination against those protected by Title VII. While the ADEA reflects Congress' intent to give older workers employment opportunities whenever possible, the RFOA provision reflects this historical difference.

Turning to the case before us, we initially note that petitioners have done little more than point out that the pay plan at issue is relatively less generous to older workers than to younger workers. They have not identified any specific test, requirement, or practice within the pay plan that has an adverse impact on older workers. As we held in *Wards Cove*, it is not enough to simply allege that there is a disparate impact on workers, or point to a generalized policy that leads to such an impact. Rather, the employee is " 'responsible for isolating and identifying the specific employment practices that are allegedly responsible for any observed statistical disparities.' " 490 U.S., at 656 (emphasis added) (quoting *Watson*, 487 U.S., at 994). Petitioners have failed to do so. Their failure to identify the specific practice being challenged is the sort of omission that could "result in employers being potentially liable for 'the myriad of innocent causes that may lead to statistical imbalances. . . .' " 490 U.S., at 657. In this case not only did petitioners thus err by failing to identify the relevant practice, but it is also clear from the record that the City's plan was based on reasonable factors other than age.

The plan divided each of five basic positions — police officer, master police officer, police sergeant, police lieutenant, and deputy police chief — into a series of steps and half-steps. The wage for each range was based on a survey of comparable communities in the Southeast. Employees were then assigned a step (or half-step) within their position that corresponded to the lowest step that would still give the individual a 2% raise. Most of the officers were in the three lowest ranks; in each of those ranks there were officers under age 40 and officers over 40. In none did their age affect their compensation. The few officers in the two highest ranks are all over 40. Their raises, though higher in dollar amount than the raises given to junior officers, represented a smaller percentage of their salaries, which of course are higher than the salaries paid to their juniors. They are members of the class complaining of the "disparate impact" of the award.

Petitioners' evidence established two principal facts: First, almost two-thirds (66.2%) of the officers under 40 received raises of more than 10% while less than half (45.3%) of those over 40 did. Second, the average percentage increase for the entire class of officers with less than five years of tenure was somewhat higher than the percentage for those with more seniority. Because older officers tended to occupy more senior positions, on average they received smaller increases when measured as a percentage of their salary. The basic explanation for the differential was the City's perceived need to raise the salaries of junior officers to make them competitive with comparable positions in the market.

Thus, the disparate impact is attributable to the City's decision to give raises based on seniority and position. Reliance on seniority and rank is unquestionably reasonable given the City's goal of raising employees' salaries to match those in surrounding communities. In sum, we hold that the City's decision to grant a larger raise to lower echelon employees for the purpose of bringing salaries in line with that of surrounding police forces was a decision based on a "reasonable factor other than age" that responded to the City's legitimate goal of retaining police officers. *Cf. MacPherson v. University of Montevallo*, 922 F.2d 766, 772 (CA11 1991).

While there may have been other reasonable ways for the City to achieve its goals, the one selected was not unreasonable. Unlike the business necessity test, which asks whether there are other ways for the employer to achieve its goals that do not result in a disparate impact on a protected class, the reasonableness inquiry includes no such requirement.

Accordingly, while we do not agree with the Court of Appeals' holding that that the disparate-impact theory of recovery is never available under the ADEA, we affirm its judgment.

It is so ordered.

The Chief Justice took no part in the decision of this case.

[Footnotes and some citations are omitted. The concurring opinions of Justices Scalia and O'Connor are omitted. Ed.]

OUBRÉ v. ENTERGY OPERATIONS, INC.
522 U.S. 422 (1998)

JUSTICE KENNEDY delivered the opinion of the Court.

An employee, as part of a termination agreement, signed a release of all claims against her employer. In consideration, she received severance pay in installments. The release, however, did not comply with specific federal statutory requirements for a release of claims under the Age Discrimination in Employment Act of 1967 (ADEA). After receiving the last payment, the employee brought suit under the ADEA. The employer claims the employee ratified and validated the nonconforming release by retaining the monies paid to secure it. The employer also insists the release bars the action unless, as a precondition to filing suit, the employee tenders back the monies received. We disagree and rule that, as the release did not comply with the statute, it cannot bar the ADEA claim.

Petitioner Dolores Oubré worked as a scheduler at a power plant in Killona, Louisiana, run by her employer, respondent Entergy Operations, Inc. In 1994, she received a poor performance rating. Oubré's supervisor met with her on January 17, 1995, and gave her the option of either improving her performance during the coming year or accepting a voluntary arrangement for her severance. She received a packet of information about the severance agreement and had 14 days to consider her options, during which she consulted with attorneys. On January 31, Oubré decided to accept. She signed a release, in which she "agree[d] to waive, settle, release, and discharge any and all claims, demands, damages, actions, or causes of action . . . that I may have against Entergy. . . ." In exchange, she received six installment payments over the next four months, totaling $6,258.

The Older Workers Benefit Protection Act (OWBPA) imposes specific requirements for releases covering ADEA claims. OWBPA, 29 U.S.C. §§ 626(f)(1)(B), (F), (G). In procuring the release, Entergy did not comply with the OWBPA in at least three respects: (1) Entergy did not give Oubré enough time to consider her options, (2) Entergy did not give Oubré seven days after she signed the release to change her mind, and (3) the release made no specific reference to claims under the ADEA.

Oubré filed a charge of age discrimination with the Equal Employment Opportunity Commission, which dismissed her charge on the merits but issued a right-to-sue letter. She filed this suit against Entergy in the United States District Court for the Eastern District of Louisiana, alleging constructive discharge on the basis of her age in violation of the ADEA and state law. Oubré has not offered or tried to return the $6,258 to Entergy, nor is it clear she has the means to do so. Entergy moved for summary judgment, claiming Oubré had ratified the defective release by failing to return or offer to return the monies she had received. The District Court agreed and entered summary judgment for Entergy. The Court of Appeals affirmed, 112 F.3d 787 (CA5 1996) (per curiam), and we granted certiorari.

II

The employer rests its case upon general principles of state contract jurisprudence. As the employer recites the rule, contracts tainted by mistake, duress, or even fraud are voidable at the option of the innocent party. *See* 1 RESTATEMENT (SECOND) OF CONTRACTS § 7, and Comment b (1979); *e.g., Ellerin v. Fairfax Sav. Assn.,* 78 Md. App. 92, 108-09, 552 A.2d 918, 926-27 (Md. Spec. App.), *cert. denied,* 316 Md. 210, 557 A.2d 1336 (1989). The employer maintains, however, that before the innocent party can elect avoidance, she must first tender back any benefits received under the contract. *See, e.g., Dreiling v. Home State Life Ins. Co.,* 213 Kan. 137, 147-48, 515 P.2d 757, 766-67 (1973). If she fails to do so within a reasonable time after learning of her rights, the employer contends, she ratifies the contract and so makes it binding. RESTATEMENT (SECOND) OF CONTRACTS, *supra,* § 7, Comments d, e; *see, e.g., Jobe v. Texas Util. Elec. Co.,* No. 05-94-01368CV (Tex. App. — Dallas, Aug. 14, 1995) (unpublished). The employer also invokes the doctrine of equitable estoppel. As a rule, equitable estoppel bars a party from shirking the burdens of a voidable transaction for as long as she retains the benefits received under it. *See, e.g., Buffum v. Peter Barceloux Co.,* 289 U.S. 227, 234 (1933) (citing state case law from Indiana and New York). Applying these principles, the employer claims the employee ratified the ineffective release (or faces estoppel) by retaining all the sums paid in consideration of it. The employer, then, relies not upon the execution of the release but upon a later, distinct ratification of its terms.

These general rules may not be as unified as the employer asserts. *See generally* Annot., 76 A.L.R. 344 (1932) (collecting cases supporting and contradicting these rules); Annot., 134 A.L.R. 6 (1941) (same). And in equity, a person suing to rescind a contract, as a rule, is not required to restore the consideration at the very outset of the litigation. *See* 3 RESTATEMENT (SECOND) OF CONTRACTS, *supra,* § 384, and Comment b; RESTATEMENT OF RESTITUTION § 65, Comment d (1936); D. Dobbs, LAW OF REMEDIES § 4.8, p. 294 (1973). Even if the employer's statement of the general rule requiring tender back before one files suit were correct, it would be unavailing. The rule cited is based simply on the course of negotiation of the parties and the alleged later ratification. The authorities cited do not consider the question raised by statutory standards for releases and a statutory declaration making nonconforming releases ineffective. It is the latter question we confront here.

In 1990, Congress amended the ADEA by passing the OWBPA. The OWBPA provides: "An individual may not waive any right or claim under [the ADEA] unless the waiver is knowing and voluntary. . . . [A] waiver may not be considered knowing and voluntary unless at a minimum" it satisfies certain enumerated requirements, including the three listed above. 29 U.S.C. § 626(f)(1).

The statutory command is clear: An employee "may not waive" an ADEA claim unless the waiver or release satisfies the OWBPA's requirements. The policy of the Older Workers Benefit Protection Act is likewise clear from its title: It is designed to protect the rights and benefits of older workers. The OWBPA implements Congress' policy via a strict, unqualified statutory stricture on waivers, and we are bound to take Congress at its word. Congress imposed specific duties on employers who seek releases of certain claims created by statute. Congress delineated these duties with precision and without qualification: An employee "may not waive" an ADEA claim unless the employer complies with the statute. Courts cannot with ease presume ratification of that which Congress forbids. The OWBPA sets up its own regime for assessing the effect of ADEA waivers, separate and apart from contract law. The statute creates a series of prerequisites for knowing and voluntary waivers and imposes affirmative duties of disclosure and waiting periods. The OWBPA governs the effect under federal law of waivers or releases on ADEA claims and incorporates no exceptions or qualifications. The text of the OWBPA forecloses the employer's defense, notwithstanding how general contract principles would apply to non-ADEA claims.

The rule proposed by the employer would frustrate the statute's practical operation as well as its formal command. In many instances a discharged employee likely will have spent the monies received and will lack the means to tender their return. These realities might tempt employers to risk noncompliance with the OWBPA's waiver provisions, knowing it will be difficult to repay the monies and relying on ratification. We ought not to open the door to an evasion of the statute by this device.

Oubré's cause of action arises under the ADEA, and the release can have no effect on her ADEA claim unless it complies with the OWBPA. In this case, both sides concede the release the employee signed did not comply with the requirements of the OWBPA. Since Oubré's release did not comply with the OWBPA's stringent safeguards, it is unenforceable against her insofar as it purports to waive or release her ADEA claim. As a statutory matter, the release cannot bar her ADEA suit, irrespective of the validity of the contract as to other claims.

In further proceedings in this or other cases, courts may need to inquire whether the employer has claims for restitution, recoupment, or setoff against the employee, and these questions may be complex where a release is effective as to some claims but not as to ADEA claims. We need not decide those issues here, however. It suffices to hold that the release cannot bar the ADEA claim because it does not conform to the statute. Nor did the employee's mere retention of monies amount to a ratification equivalent to a valid release of her ADEA claims, since the retention did not comply with the OWBPA any more than the original release did. The statute governs the effect of the release on ADEA claims, and the employer cannot invoke the employee's failure to tender back as a way of excusing its own failure to comply.

We reverse the judgment of the Court of Appeals and remand for further proceedings consistent with this opinion.

It is so ordered.

[The Appendix, which sets out the text of 29 U.S.C. § 626(f), is omitted.]

JUSTICE BREYER, with whom JUSTICE O'CONNOR joins, concurring.

This case focuses upon a worker who received a payment from her employer and in return promised not to bring an age-discrimination suit. Her promise failed the procedural tests of validity set forth in the OWBPA, 29 U.S.C. § 626(f)(1). I agree with the majority that, because of this procedural failing, the worker is free to bring her age-discrimination suit without "tendering-back" her employer's payment as a precondition. As a conceptual matter, a "tender-back" requirement would imply that the worker had ratified her promise by keeping her employer's payment. For that reason, it would bar suit, including suit by a worker (without other assets) who had already spent the money he received for the promise. Yet such an act of ratification could embody some of the same procedural failings that led Congress to find the promise not to sue itself invalid. For these reasons, as the majority points out, a tender-back precondition requirement would run contrary to Congress' statutory command. *Cf.* 1 RESTATEMENT (SECOND) OF CONTRACTS § 85, Comment b (1979) (a promise ratifying a voidable contract "may itself be voidable for the same reason as the original promise, or it may be voidable or unenforceable for some other reason"); D. Dobbs, LAW OF REMEDIES 982 (1973) (hereinafter Dobbs) ("[C]ourts must avoid allowing a recovery that has the effect of substantially enforcing the contract that has been declared unenforceable, since to do so would defeat the policy that led to the . . . rule in the first place.").

I write these additional words because I believe it important to specify that the statute need not, and does not, thereby make the worker's procedurally invalid promise totally void, i.e., without any legal effect, say, like a contract the terms of which themselves are contrary to public policy. *See* 1 RESTATEMENT (SECOND) OF CONTRACTS, §7, Comment a; 2 *id.*, § 178. Rather, the statute makes the contract that the employer and worker tried to create voidable, like a contract made with an infant, or a contract created through fraud, mistake or duress, which contract the worker may elect either to avoid or to ratify. *See* 1 *id.*, § 7 and Comment b .

To determine whether a contract is voidable or void, courts typically ask whether the contract has been made under conditions that would justify giving one of the parties a choice as to validity, making it voidable, *e.g.,* a contract with an infant; or whether enforcement of the contract would violate the law or public policy irrespective of the conditions in which the contract was formed, making it void, *e.g.,* a contract to commit murder. *Compare* 1 *id.,* § 7, Comment b (voidable) with 2 *id.,*§ 178 and Comment d (void). The statute before us reflects concern about the conditions (of knowledge and free choice) surrounding the making of a contract to waive an age-discrimination claim. It does not reflect any relevant concern about enforcing the contract's substantive terms. Nor does this statute, unlike the Federal Employers' Liability Act, 45 U.S.C. § 51 et seq., say that a contract waiving suit and thereby avoiding liability is void. § 55. Rather, as the majority's opinion makes clear, the OWBPA prohibits courts from finding ratification in certain circumstances, such as those presented here, namely, a worker's retention of a employer's payment for an invalid release. That fact may affect ratification, but it need not make the contract void, rather than voidable.

That the contract is voidable rather than void may prove important. For example, an absolutely void contract, it is said, "is void as to everybody whose rights would be affected by it if valid." 17A AM. JUR. 2d, CONTRACTS § 7, p. 31 (1991). Were a former worker's procedurally invalid promise not to sue absolutely void, might it not become legally possible for an employer to decide to cancel its own reciprocal obligation, say, to pay the worker, or to provide ongoing health benefits — whether or not the worker in question ever intended to bring a lawsuit? It seems most unlikely that Congress, enacting a statute meant to protect workers, would have wanted to create — as a result of an employer's failure to follow the law — any such legal threat to all workers, whether or not they intend to bring suit. To find the contract voidable, rather than void, would offer legal protection against such threats.

At the same time, treating the contract as voidable could permit an employer to recover his own reciprocal payment (or to avoid his reciprocal promise) where doing so seems most fair, namely, where that recovery would not bar the worker from bringing suit. Once the worker (who has made the procedurally invalid promise not to sue) brings an age-discrimination suit, he has clearly rejected (avoided) his promise not to sue. As long as there is no "tender-back" precondition, his (invalid) promise will not have barred his suit in conflict with the statute. Once he has sued, however, nothing in the statute prevents his employer from asking for restitution of his reciprocal payment or relief from any ongoing reciprocal obligation. *See* RESTATEMENT OF RESTITUTION § 47, Comment b (1936) ("A person who transfers something to another believing that the other thereby comes under a duty to perform the terms of a contract . . . is ordinarily entitled to restitution for what he has given if the obligation intended does not arise and if the other does not perform"); Dobbs, *supra*, at 994 (restitution is often allowed where benefits are conferred under voidable contract). A number of older state cases indicate, for example, that the amount of consideration paid for an invalid release can be deducted from a successful plaintiff's damages award. *See, e.g., St. Louis-San Francisco R. Co . v. Cox*, 171 Ark. 103, 113-15, 283 S.W. 31, 35 (1926) (amount paid for invalid release may be taken into consideration in setting remedy); *Koshka v. Missouri Pac. R. Co.*, 114 Kan. 126, 129-30, 217 P. 293, 295 (1923) (the sum paid for an invalid release may be treated as an item of credit against damages); *Miller v. Spokane Int'l R. Co.*, 82 Wash. 170, 177-78, 143 P. 981, 984 (1914) (same); *Gilmore v. Western Elec. Co.*, 42 N.D. 206, 211-12, 172 N.W. 111, 113 (1919).

My point is that the statute's provisions are consistent with viewing an invalid release as voidable, rather than void. Apparently, five or more Justices take this view of the matter. As I understand the majority's opinion, it is also consistent with this view, and I consequently concur in its opinion.

[JUSTICE SCALIA dissented on the ground that the OWBPA did not abrogate the common-law doctrines of "tender back" and ratification, and, because no "tender back" was made, the judgment of the lower court should have been affirmed. JUSTICES THOMAS, with whom CHIEF JUSTICE REHNQUIST joined, dissented on the ground that the OWBPA does not clearly and explicitly abrogate the doctrines of ratification and tender back, and the lower court had determined that petitioner had ratified her release.]

QUESTIONS

1. Does the majority's interpretation of the ADEA's waiver provision imply a paternalistic view of older workers?

2. In July 1998, the EEOC promulgated final regulations intended to implement this decision. Read 22 C.F.R. § 1625.22 (1998) in the statutory supplement. Do you think the regulations fairly capture the substance of *Oubré*?

2. State Law

Although many lawyers assume that federal law provides the most effective means of redressing age-related employment discrimination, most states have also enacted laws that provide older workers from workplace discrimination. In many circumstances, state remedies, which may include administrative or informal procedures can sometimes provide more speedy justice and effective relief to the client. In some circumstances, however, resort to such remedies may foreclose a subsequent lawsuit based on federal law. The elder law attorney thus must balance carefully the legal and strategic consequences of pursuing a state remedy for age-based discrimination in lieu of or concurrently with a federal claim.

Memorandum of Understanding Between the National Association of Attorneys General and the Equal Employment Opportunity Commission(Nov. 10, 1997)

http://www.eeoc.gov/policy/docs/naagmem.html

The enforcement of laws against employment discrimination and the eradication of unfair employment practices is a national priority. State and federal officials' strong interest in enforcement and elimination of employment discrimination crosses regional lines as well as particular Administrations. The signatories to this Memorandum of Understanding agree that it is critical to develop effective and lasting mechanisms for communication and cooperation among state Attorneys General and the Equal Employment Opportunity Commission (EEOC) responsible for the enforcement of federal and state employment discrimination laws. It is also agreed that those mechanisms should continue through changes in administration at the national and state levels. Accordingly, the signatories to this Memorandum of Understanding agree to establish the following institutional mechanisms for communication, cooperation and joint work on affirmative enforcement of employment discrimination laws:

1. The EEOC will designate a district office liaison to each state Attorney General office that chooses to participate in the program who will be responsible for ensuring communication and cooperation with the participating state Attorneys General. The EEOC will also designate headquarters liaison(s) to state Attorneys General for amicus requests and for other specified purposes. Each participating state Attorney General will designate an employment discrimination liaison who will be responsible for ensuring communication and cooperation with other state Attorneys General and the EEOC. The co-chairs of the permanent Working Group described in paragraph 6 below will be responsible for circulating a list of liaisons and for notifying the liaisons of any changes in designations that are made. The liaisons' responsibilities will include: sharing information about pending or proposed litigation or projects which are likely to contribute significantly to the development of employment discrimination laws or which involve significant pattern and practice violations; identifying technical assistance and training needs; providing pleadings and briefs to each other; bringing important judicial decisions and other emerging issues to the attention of other liaisons; notifying each other of pending legislation concerning employment laws and practices; making requests for amicus assistance or intervention or other types of legal assistance; and otherwise ensuring the timely and effective dissemination of significant information related to employment discrimination.

2. The EEOC will provide informational reports (limited to information of public record) to the National Association of Attorneys General (NAAG) for circulation to each participating state Attorney General. State Attorneys General offices will submit reports to NAAG for a quarterly report on important employment discrimination developments in their states which will be shared with all signatories to this agreement.

3. Representatives of state Attorneys General and the EEOC will participate in regular conference calls and will meet annually to, as appropriate: discuss

national, regional and state employment discrimination issues; share investigative techniques and information regarding effective methods of enforcement; identify potential joint enforcement efforts; identify and initiate joint litigation and policy enforcement efforts; organize and coordinate training activities; and bring important judicial decisions and emerging issues to the attention of each other. The representatives will also share information about fair employment initiatives and coordinate and combine efforts to address employment discrimination in a manner that most effectively utilizes the expertise and resources of the represented offices. Any sharing of information shall be consistent with applicable confidentiality provisions. NAAG's staff, in consultation with representatives of state Attorneys General, and a representative of the EEOC, will be responsible for coordinating the annual meetings and the conference calls.

4(a). In order to effectively address common concerns, the EEOC and the state Attorneys General intend to develop joint enforcement initiatives in one or more areas of mutual concern. The signing of this Memorandum does not obligate the EEOC or any state Attorney General to participate in any joint initiative. A state Attorney General that desires to participate in a joint initiative with the EEOC will supply a letter of participation to the EEOC.

(b) The signatories direct the establishment of an Employment Task Force to report on the most effective means practicable for carrying out the joint initiatives referenced in paragraph 4(a) and to coordinate the implementation of the joint initiatives. The Task Force will consider, among other things, joint initiatives in which each participating agency commits personnel and resources to policy initiatives and investigation and litigation efforts. The Task Force will make recommendations about which agencies should lead the enforcement efforts in a particular subject area and geographic location, taking into account the relative expertise of the participants, the extent of resources each agency commits to the project, the nature of the remedies or sanctions for the violation of law available in a state or federal forum, and similar criteria. Problems in the implementation of joint initiatives will be brought to the attention of the Working Group described in paragraph 6, below, for resolution.

5. The EEOC and the state Attorneys General will continue to enforce laws independently of one another. EEOC and participating state Attorneys General will notify in writing each other's offices functioning in their jurisdiction of their enforcement efforts whenever an office commences a civil enforcement action in an administrative agency or court, which it believes is likely to contribute significantly to the development of employment discrimination law. Notifications will be made to the relevant liaison(s) designated pursuant to paragraph 1 above within two business days of the event triggering the notification requirement, if possible. Notifications will not be made if any office determines that such notification is inappropriate under the circumstances.

6. The signatories to this Agreement direct the establishment of an Employment Working Group which will continue as a permanent body. It will consist of representatives designated by the EEOC and representatives of state Attorneys General designated by the President of the National Association of Attorneys General. The Working Group will be co-chaired by a representative of the

EEOC and representatives of two state Attorneys General. The Working Group will serve as a clearinghouse for information and complaints about the implementation of this agreement, investigate whether improvements in the mechanisms for communication and cooperation are needed, identify common training requirements and plan training events, assist in the resolution of conflicts arising in joint initiatives or enforcement efforts, and otherwise make recommendations for ways to advance the objective of joint enforcement of employment discrimination laws. Each co-chair of the Employment Working Group will be available to receive information from employment discrimination liaisons about problems in the implementation of this agreement. The Working Group will communicate with each other regularly, but not less than once a year.

QUESTION

Read the Kansas Act Against Discrimination, KSA 44-1001 to 44-11013 (1998), in the statutory supplement. In what ways does the substance of this statute differ from federal age discrimination law? In what ways do procedures for enforcement differ?

POZZOBON v. PARTS FOR PLASTICS, INC.
770 F. Supp. 376 (N.D. Ohio 1991)

SAM H. BELL, United States District Judge.

Currently pending before the court in the above-captioned matter is a motion to dismiss the third and fourth counts of plaintiff Orlando J. Pozzobon's complaint under Fed. R. Civ. P. 12(b)(6) filed by defendant Parts for Plastic, Inc. The underlying complaint, filed on March 5, 1991, alleges age discrimination in violation of the Age Discrimination in Employment Act (ADEA), 29 U.S.C. § 621 *et seq.* (Counts One and Two), and OHIO REVISED CODE § 4112.02(A) (Count Three); wrongful discharge in violation of Ohio public policy (Count Four); and intentional infliction of emotional distress (Count Five). The claim of age discrimination under Ohio law is brought pursuant to O.R.C. §§ 4112.02(N) and 4112.99. Plaintiff seeks a declaration that the policies and practices of defendant are in violation of the ADEA, a permanent injunction, and $500,000 in compensatory and punitive damages.

When considering a motion to dismiss for failure to state a claim pursuant to Federal Rule of Civil Procedure 12(b)(6), the court is constrained to accept as true the allegations of a complaint. The motion to dismiss under 12(b)(6) should be denied unless it can be established beyond a doubt that the plaintiff can prove no set of facts in support of his claim which would entitle him to relief.

The court's analysis begins with a consideration of plaintiff's third count, the allegation of age discrimination under Ohio law. Plaintiff claims a violation of O.R.C. § 4112.02(A), which provides as follows:

It shall be unlawful discriminatory practice:

(A) For any employer, because of the race, color, religion, sex, national origin, handicap, age, or ancestry of any person, to discharge without just cause, to refuse to hire, or otherwise to discriminate against that person with respect to hire, tenure, terms, conditions, or privileges of employment, or any matter directly or indirectly related to employment.

Plaintiff's asserted basis for a private cause of action under this section is twofold, O.R.C. §§ 4112.02(N) and 4112.99. The former section provides as follows:

(N) An aggrieved individual may enforce his rights relative to discrimination on the basis of age as provided for in this section by instituting a civil action, within one hundred eighty days after the alleged unlawful practice occurred, in any court of competent jurisdiction for any legal or equitable relief that will effectuate his rights. A person who files a civil action under this division is, with respect to the practices complained of, thereby barred from instituting a civil action under section 4101.17 of the Revised Code or from filing a charge with the Ohio civil rights commission under section 4112.05 of the Revised Code.

Section 4112.99 provides that "whoever violates this chapter is subject to a civil action for damages, injunctive relief, or any other appropriate relief." Prior to 1987, § 4112.99 only provided for criminal sanctions. In 1987, an amendment was enacted which resulted in the section in its present form.

Defendant argues that O.R.C. § 4112.08 expressly bars plaintiff's claim of age discrimination under Ohio law in this case. This section provides as follows:

The provisions of section 4112.01 to 4112.08 of the REVISED CODE, shall be construed liberally for the accomplishment of the purposes thereof and any law inconsistent with any provision hereof shall not apply. Nothing contained in section 4112.01 to 4112.08 and 4112.99 of the Revised Code, shall be deemed to repeal any of the provisions of any law of this state relating to discrimination because of race, color, religion, sex, national origin, age, or ancestry; *except that any person filing a charge under section 4112.05 of the Revised Code is, with respect to the practices complained of, thereby barred from instituting a civil action under section 4101.17 or division (N) of section 4112.02 of the Revised Code.*

O.R.C. § 4112.08 (emphasis added). Section 4112.05 provides for the filing of a grievance with the Ohio Civil Rights Commission in order to redress alleged unlawful discriminatory practices. § 4112.05(B). The complaint herein states that plaintiff has filed such a grievance, and plaintiff does not controvert this in his brief in opposition to the motion to dismiss. Consequently, according to defendant, plaintiff is precluded from bringing this suit due to the explicit and unambiguous language of § 4112.08.

In response, plaintiff argues that the Code expressly allows the bringing of the instant cause, citing to § 4112.99. According to plaintiff's logic, while the language of § 4112.08 may bar an aggrieved party from bringing a private action under § 4112.02(N) if that person has already filed a claim with the Civil Rights Commission under § 4112.05, it does not also bar one from bringing such an action under § 4112.99, which is not mentioned in § 4112.08. Having filed the instant cause under § 4112.99 as well as § 4112.02(N), plaintiff contends that § 4112.08 thus cannot be utilized to bar his claim.

In support of the proposition that the language of § 4112.99 allows the filing of a private action in the instant cause, plaintiff cites to three cases: *Elek v. Huntington National Bank*, 1989 Ohio App. LEXIS 3299, 50 Fair Empl. Prac. Cas. (BNA) 1396 (Ohio App. Franklin Cty. 1989); *Eyerman v. Mary Kay Cosmetics*, 1990 U.S. Dist. LEXIS 618, 51 Fair Empl. Prac. Cas. (BNA) 1594 (S.D. Ohio 1990); and *Grant v. Monsanto Co.*, 1989 U.S. Dist. LEXIS 16015, 51 Fair Empl. Prac. Cas. (BNA) 1593 (S.D. Ohio 1989). *Elek* and *Grant* stand for the proposition that § 4112.99 provides for a private right of action for any violation of Chapter 4112, notwithstanding the fact that other parts of the chapter create overlapping private causes of action for specific types of discrimination. The *Grant* court specifically held that § 4112.99 creates an entirely new, separate private cause of action, and that an aggrieved person may bring an age discrimination in employment suit under either § 4112.99 or § 4112.02(N). On June 12, 1991, the Ohio Supreme Court affirmed the court of appeals decision in *Elek. See Elek v. Huntington National Bank*, 60 Ohio St. 3d 135, 573 N.E.2d 1056 (1991). The case involved a handicap discrimination claim brought as a private civil action pursuant to § 4112.99. In rejecting the defendant's argument that § 4112.99 does not create a new, independent private right of action, the Supreme Court found, inter alia, that the language of this section is unambiguous and that the legislative history supports such an interpretation. *Id.*, 60 Ohio St. 3d at 137. Due to this recent Supreme Court holding, we are constrained to hold that an age discrimination claimant may utilize either § 4112.02(N), § 4112.99, or both in pursuing an action for age discrimination.

The Supreme Court in *Elek*, however, did not face the more narrow issue before this court, viz., whether § 4112.99 allows a private right of action for age discrimination where the plaintiff-employee has previously filed a claim with the Civil Rights Commission under § 4112.05. This court does not believe that *Elek* could reasonably be read to stand for such a proposition. If the legislature had desired that § 4112.99 would so modify the language of § 4112.08 in cases of age discrimination, we believe that it would have done so in a less ambiguous fashion, either by changing the language of § 4112.08 or by more clearly stating its intent in § 4112.99. In holding as we do, we are guided by the caveat contained in § 4112.08 that "nothing contained in sections 4112.01 to 4112.08 and 4112.99 of the REVISED CODE shall be deemed to repeal any of the provisions of law of this state relating to discrimination. . . ." The court takes this language to mean that the 1987 amendment to § 4112.99 creating an independent private right of action was not intended to and does not alter the final sentence of § 4112.08, nor does it alter the detailed, comprehensive legislative scheme created for age discrimination suits, *see infra.*

The holding of this court, thus, has no bearing upon the efficacy of *Elek*. The court there was not faced with issues regarding the effect of § 4112.99 on § 4112.08 in age discrimination suits. *Elek*, rather, stands for the proposition that both § 4112.99 and § 4112.02(N) create independent private rights of action in age discrimination suits. With this holding we are in complete agreement. The court does not believe, however, that the amendment to § 4112.99 nullifies the effect of § 4112.08 in age discrimination suits. Thus, while an employee is permitted to bring a private action for age discrimination under § 4112.99, he should not be allowed to circumvent Ohio's detailed legislative scheme for bringing age discrimination suits, including the mandate of § 4112.08.

In closing this portion of the opinion, and holding that Count Three of the complaint is barred, the court adopts the following reasoning:

Protection against age discrimination is provided under Ohio law by three statutory sections: (1) O.R.C. § 4101.17(B), which permits a civil action for violation of subsection (A) of that section; (2) O.R.C. § 4112.02(N), which permits a civil action to be brought against those who violate the other subsections of that section; and (3) O.R.C. § 4112.05, which permits a complaint to be brought with the Ohio Civil Rights Commission for violations of §§ 4112.02 and 4112.021.

Each of these statutory remedies is exclusive — the choice of one remedy precludes recourse to other remedies. *See* O.R.C. §§ 4101.17(B), 4112.02(N) and 4112.08. This exclusivity of remedies, however, causes a conflict in the context of the joinder of an Ohio age discrimination suit with one brought under the ADEA. The ADEA requires, in states with administrative procedures for resolution of age discrimination claims, that proceedings under those state procedures be brought at least 60 days before the filing of a claim under federal law. *See* 29 U.S.C. § 633. Thus, in order to fulfill the prerequisite to a suit under the federal law in Ohio, a plaintiff must file a complaint with the OCRC pursuant to O.R.C. § 4112.05, and thus, by the terms of that section, waive his or her right to bring a civil action under either O.R.C. § 4101.17(B) or § 4112.02(N).

However, simply because Ohio's age discrimination law has the effect of requiring a litigant to choose between his or her state and federal remedies does not invalidate the law or require the Court to construe the terms of that law inconsistently with its plain meaning. *Keister v. Delco Products*, 680 F. Supp. 281, 282 (S.D. Ohio 1987). We recognize that this decision, issued prior to the amendment of § 4112.99, did not discuss the effect of that statute. However, we do not deem it reasonable to conclude that the single, broadly worded sentence contained in § 4112.99 could possibly have been intended to eradicate the detailed legislative scheme discussed in *Keister* and still in existence in the Ohio Revised Code.

The fourth count of plaintiff's complaint alleges that defendant's actions, i.e., the alleged wrongful discharge, "violate public policy in that all of the above-named statutes prohibit discipline and/or discharge against plaintiff for unlawful reasons." Complaint at para. 22.

In its motion to dismiss, defendant contends that Ohio does not recognize a tort cause of action for wrongful discharge in violation of public policy. In response, plaintiff relies upon *Greeley v. Miami Valley Maintenance Contractors*,

Inc., 49 Ohio St. 3d. 228, 551 N.E.2d 981 (1990), for the proposition that a tort cause of action for wrongful discharge in violation of public policy is available in Ohio.

In *Greeley*, the court held that public policy warrants an exception to the employment-at-will doctrine where the employee is discharged for a reason which is prohibited by statute. *Id.*, 49 Ohio St. 3d at 234. Due to the fact that the statute at issue, O.R.C. § 3113.213(D), did not itself provide plaintiff with a private cause of action, but rather only imposed a fine upon the employer, the court held that a common law tort action for wrongful discharge in violation of public policy was available to plaintiff.

Plaintiff would have this court read *Greeley* as holding that, where an employer is alleged to be in violation of an Ohio statute, the employee may bring a wrongful discharge tort action even where the statute at issue itself provides for a comprehensive private right of action. *Greeley* does not stand for such a proposition. In *Greeley*, the aggrieved plaintiff had no other recourse, due to the fact that the statute only provided that the employer be fined. The Ohio Supreme Court thus deemed it necessary to create an exception to the employment-at-will doctrine and allow employees a tort wrongful discharge action for violations of § 3113.213(D).

In the case at bar, an exception to the at-will doctrine already exists in the statutes themselves. Victims of age discrimination are entitled to bring civil actions under §§ 4101.17(B), 4112.02(N), 4112.05, or 4112.99, regardless of whether the employer-employee relationship is deemed as one "at-will." There is certainly no reason here to carve out another exception to the employment-at-will doctrine, as was the case in *Greeley*, and permit a tort action.

For the foregoing reasons, the court finds that the third and fourth counts of plaintiff's complaint fail to state claims for which relief can be granted. As such, defendant's motion to dismiss these portions of the complaint is hereby granted pursuant to Fed. R. Civ. P. 12(b)(6).

It is so ordered.

QUESTION

Is the result in *Pozzobon* consistent with the purposes that underlie the ADEA and its state counterparts?

RAYGOR v. REGENTS OF THE UNIVERSITY OF MINNESOTA
534 U.S. 533 (2002)

JUSTICE O'CONNOR delivered the opinion of the Court.

In federal court, petitioners asserted state law claims under the supplemental jurisdiction statute, 28 U.S.C. § 1367, against respondent university, an arm of the State of Minnesota. Those claims were dismissed on Eleventh

Amendment grounds, and petitioners refiled them in state court past the period of limitations. The supplemental jurisdiction statute purports to toll the period of limitations for supplemental claims while they are pending in federal court and for 30 days after they are dismissed. § 1367(d). The Minnesota Supreme Court held that provision unconstitutional when applied to claims against nonconsenting state defendants, such as respondent university, and dismissed petitioners' claims. We affirm the judgment on the alternative ground that the tolling provision does not apply to claims filed in federal court against nonconsenting States.

I

In August 1995, petitioners Lance Raygor and James Goodchild filed charges with the Equal Employment Opportunity Commission (EEOC). The charges alleged that their employer, the University of Minnesota, discriminated against them on the basis of age in December 1994 by attempting to compel them to accept early retirement at the age of 52. After petitioners refused to retire, the university allegedly reclassified petitioners' jobs so as to reduce their salaries.

The EEOC cross-filed petitioners' charges with the Minnesota Department of Human Rights (MDHR) and later issued a right-to-sue letter on June 6, 1996, advising that petitioners could file a lawsuit within 90 days under the Age Discrimination in Employment Act of 1967 (ADEA), 29 U.S.C. § 621 et seq. The MDHR likewise issued right-to-sue letters on July 17, 1996, advising petitioners that they could file suit within 45 days under the Minnesota Human Rights Act (MHRA). 620 N.W.2d 680, 681 (Minn. 2001).

On or about August 29, 1996, each petitioner filed a separate complaint against respondent Board of Regents of the University of Minnesota (hereinafter respondent), in the United States District Court for the District of Minnesota. Each complaint alleged a federal cause of action under the ADEA and a state cause of action under the MHRA. The suits were subsequently consolidated. Respondent filed answers to these complaints in September 1996, setting forth eight affirmative defenses, including that the suits were " 'barred in whole or in part by Defendant's Eleventh Amendment immunity.' " The District Court entered a scheduling plan that the parties agreed upon. According to the plan, discovery would finish by May 30, 1997, and dispositive motions would be filed by July 15, 1997. The parties then engaged in discovery as well as mediation.

In early July 1997, respondent filed its motion to dismiss petitioners' claims pursuant to Federal Rule of Civil Procedure 12(b)(1). The motion argued that the federal and state law claims were barred by the Eleventh Amendment. Petitioners' response acknowledged respondent's " 'potential Eleventh Amendment immunity from state discrimination claims in Federal Court,' " but urged the District Court to exercise supplemental jurisdiction over the state claims if the federal claims were upheld. On July 11, 1997, the District Court granted respondent's Rule 12(b)(1) motion and dismissed all of petitioners' claims. Petitioners appealed, but the appeal was stayed pending this Court's decision in *Kimel v. Florida Bd. of Regents*, 528 U.S. 62 (2000). *Kimel* held that the "ADEA does not validly abrogate the States' sovereign immunity." 528 U.S. at 92. Given that result, petitioners moved to withdraw their appeal, and it was dismissed in January 2000.

In the meantime, approximately three weeks after the Federal District Court had dismissed their state law claims, petitioners refiled their state law claims in Hennepin County District Court. Respondent's answer asserted that "'plaintiff's claims are barred, in whole or in part, by the applicable statute of limitations.'" The state court initially stayed the lawsuit because of the pending federal appeal, but lifted the stay in December 1998 for the purpose of allowing respondent to move for dismissal on statute of limitations grounds. Respondent moved for summary judgment in February 1999, arguing that petitioners' state claims were barred by the applicable 45 day statute of limitations. *See* MINN. STAT. §§ 363.06, subd. 3, 363.14, subd. 1(a)(1) (2000). Respondent also argued that the tolling provision of the federal supplemental jurisdiction statute, 28 U.S.C. § 1367, did not apply to toll the limitations period on the state law claims while they were pending in federal court because the Federal District Court never had subject matter jurisdiction over petitioners' ADEA claims. Petitioners argued that the tolling provision of the supplemental jurisdiction statute applied because their state law claims had been dismissed without prejudice. State District Court treated respondent's motion for summary judgment as a motion to dismiss and granted it, holding that § 1367(d) did "not apply . . . because the federal district court never had 'original jurisdiction' over the controversy" since "both the state and federal claims were dismissed for lack of subject matter jurisdiction."

The Minnesota Court of Appeals reversed. The court first decided that the Federal District Court had original jurisdiction over the case before respondent's Eleventh Amendment defense was "successfully asserted." 604 N.W.2d at 132 (citing *Wisconsin Dept. of Corrections v. Schacht*, 524 U.S. 381 (1998)). The court then held that § 1367(d) applied to toll the statute of limitations for petitioners' state law claims because that provision "allows tolling of any claim dismissed by a federal district court, whether dismissed on Eleventh Amendment grounds or at the discretion of the federal district court under [§ 1367](c))." 604 N.W.2d at 132-133.

The Minnesota Supreme Court reversed. The court noted that respondent was an arm of the State, and found that the federal tolling provision facially applied to petitioners' state law claims. The court concluded, however, "that application of section 1367(d) to toll the statute of limitations applicable to state law claims against an unconsenting state defendant first filed in federal court but then dismissed and brought in state court is an impermissible denigration of [respondent's] Eleventh Amendment immunity." *Id.* at 687. The court thus concluded that § 1367(d) could not constitutionally apply to toll the statute of limitations for petitioners' state law claims, and it dismissed those claims. We granted *certiorari*, 532 U.S. 1065 (2001), on the question whether 28 U.S.C. § 1367(d) is unconstitutional as applied to a state defendant.

II

In *Mine Workers v. Gibbs*, 383 U.S. 715 (1966), this Court held that federal courts deciding claims within their federal-question subject matter jurisdiction, 28 U.S.C. § 1331, may decide state law claims not within their subject matter jurisdiction if the federal and state law claims "derive from a common nucleus of operative fact" and comprise "but one constitutional 'case.'" Juris-

diction over state law claims in such instances was known as "pendent jurisdiction." This Court later made clear that absent authorization from Congress,
a district court could not exercise pendent jurisdiction over claims involving parties who were not already parties to a claim independently within the court's
subject matter jurisdiction. *See Finley v. United States*, 490 U.S. 545 (1989).

In the wake of *Finley*, the Federal Courts Study Committee recommended
that "Congress expressly authorize federal courts to hear any claim arising out
of the same 'transaction or occurrence' as a claim within federal jurisdiction,
including claims, within federal question jurisdiction, that require the joinder
of additional parties." Report of Federal Courts Study Committee 47 (Apr. 2,
1990). Soon thereafter, Congress enacted the supplemental jurisdiction statute,
28 U.S.C. § 1367, as part of the Judicial Improvements Act of 1990. Subsection
(a) of § 1367 states that

> "[e]xcept as provided in subsections (b) and (c) or as expressly provided
> otherwise by Federal statute, in any civil action of which the district
> courts have original jurisdiction, the district courts shall have supple-
> mental jurisdiction over all other claims that are so related to claims in
> the action within such original jurisdiction that they form part of the
> same case or controversy under Article III of the United States Consti-
> tution. Such supplemental jurisdiction shall include claims that involve
> the joinder or intervention of additional parties."

Subsection (b) places limits on supplemental jurisdiction when the district
court's original jurisdiction is based only on diversity of citizenship jurisdiction
under 28 U.S.C. § 1332 (1994 ed. and Supp. V). Subsection (c) allows district
courts to decline to exercise supplemental jurisdiction in certain situations,
such as when a "claim raises a novel or complex issue of State law." § 1367(c)(1)
(1994 ed.).

Petitioners originally sought to have their state law claims heard in federal
court as supplemental claims falling under § 1367(a). Prior to the enactment of
§ 1367, however, this Court held that the Eleventh Amendment bars the adjudication of pendent state law claims against nonconsenting state defendants in
federal court. *See Pennhurst State School and Hospital v. Halderman*, 465 U.S.
89, 120 (1984). In that context, the Eleventh Amendment was found to be an
"explicit limitation on federal jurisdiction." *Id.* at 118. Consequently, an express
grant of jurisdiction over such claims would be an abrogation of the sovereign
immunity guaranteed by the Eleventh Amendment. Before Congress could
attempt to do that, it must make its intention to abrogate " 'unmistakably clear
in the language of the statute.' " *Dellmuth v. Muth*, 491 U.S. 223, 228 (1989)
(quoting *Atascadero State Hospital v. Scanlon*, 473 U.S. 234, 242 (1985)).

The most that can be said about subsection (a), however, is that it is a general
grant of jurisdiction, no more specific to claims against nonconsenting States
than the one at issue in *Blatchford v. Native Village of Noatak*, 501 U.S. 775
(1991). There, we considered whether 28 U.S.C. § 1362 contained a clear statement of an intent to abrogate state sovereign immunity. That grant of jurisdiction provides that

"[t]he district courts shall have original jurisdiction of *all civil actions*, brought by any Indian tribe or band with a governing body duly recognized by the Secretary of the Interior, wherein the matter in controversy arises under the Constitution, laws, or treaties of the United States." (Emphasis added.)

Such a facially broad grant of jurisdiction over "all civil actions" could be read to include claims by Indian tribes against nonconsenting States, but we held that such language was insufficient to constitute a clear statement of an intent to abrogate state sovereign immunity. Likewise, we cannot read § 1367(a) to authorize district courts to exercise jurisdiction over claims against nonconsenting States, even though nothing in the statute expressly excludes such claims. Thus, consistent with *Blatchford*, we hold that § 1367(a)'s grant of jurisdiction does not extend to claims against nonconsenting state defendants.

Even so, there remains the question whether § 1367(d) tolls the statute of limitations for claims against nonconsenting States that are asserted under § 1367(a) but subsequently dismissed on Eleventh Amendment grounds. Subsection (d) of § 1367 provides that

"[t]he period of limitations for any claim asserted under subsection (a), and for any other claim in the same action that is voluntarily dismissed at the same time as or after the dismissal of the claim under subsection (a), shall be tolled while the claim is pending and for a period of 30 days after it is dismissed unless State law provides for a longer tolling period."

On its face, subsection (d) purports to apply to dismissals of "any claim asserted under subsection (a)." Thus, it could be broadly read to apply to any claim technically "asserted" under subsection (a) as long as it was later dismissed, regardless of the reason for dismissal. But reading subsection (d) to apply when state law claims against nonconsenting States are dismissed on Eleventh Amendment grounds raises serious doubts about the constitutionality of the provision given principles of state sovereign immunity. If subsection (d) applied in such circumstances, it would toll the state statute of limitations for 30 days in addition to however long the claim had been pending in federal court. This would require a State to defend against a claim in state court that had never been filed in state court until some indeterminate time after the original limitations period had elapsed.

When the sovereign at issue is the United States, we have recognized that a limitations period may be "a central condition" of the sovereign's waiver of immunity. *United States v. Mottaz,* 476 U.S. 834, 843 (1986); *see also Block v. North Dakota ex rel. Board of Univ. and School Lands*, 461 U.S. 273, 287 (1983) ("When waiver legislation contains a statute of limitations, the limitations provision constitutes a condition on the waiver of sovereign immunity"). In suits against the United States, however, there is a rebuttable presumption that equitable tolling under federal law applies to waivers of the United States' immunity. *See Irwin v. Department of Veterans Affairs*, 498 U.S. 89, 95 (1990). From this, the dissent argues that any broadening of a State's waiver of immunity through tolling under § 1367(d) presumptively does not violate the State's sovereign immunity. But this Court has never held that waivers of a State's immunity presumptively include all federal tolling rules, nor is it obvious that such a presumption would be "a realistic assessment of legislative intent." *Irwin, supra*, at 95.

Moreover, with respect to suits against a state sovereign in its own courts, we have explained that a State "may prescribe the terms and conditions on which it consents to be sued," and that "[o]nly the sovereign's own consent could qualify the absolute character of [its] immunity" from suit in its own courts. Thus, although we have not directly addressed whether federal tolling of a state statute of limitations constitutes an abrogation of state sovereign immunity with respect to claims against state defendants, we can say that the notion at least raises a serious constitutional doubt.

Consequently, we have good reason to rely on a clear statement principle of statutory construction. When "Congress intends to alter the 'usual constitutional balance between the States and the Federal Government,' it must make its intention to do so 'unmistakably clear in the language of the statute.'" *Will v. Michigan Dept. of State Police*, 491 U.S. 58, 65 (1989). This principle applies when Congress "intends to pre-empt the historic powers of the States" or when it legislates in "'traditionally sensitive areas'" that "'affec[t] the federal balance.'" In such cases, the clear statement principle reflects "an acknowledgment that the States retain substantial sovereign powers under our constitutional scheme, powers with which Congress does not readily interfere." *Gregory v. Ashcroft*, 501 U.S. 452, 461, 464 (1991).

Here, allowing federal law to extend the time period in which a state sovereign is amenable to suit in its own courts at least affects the federal balance in an area that has been a historic power of the States, whether or not it constitutes an abrogation of state sovereign immunity. Thus, applying the clear statement principle helps "'assur[e] that the legislature has in fact faced, and intended to bring into issue, the critical matters involved in the judicial decision.'" This is obviously important when the underlying issue raises a serious constitutional doubt or problem. *See Vermont Agency of Natural Resources v. United States ex rel. Stevens*, 529 U.S. 765, 787 (2000) (relying in part on clear statement principle to decide the False Claims Act, 31 U.S.C. § 3729-3733, did not authorize "an action in federal court by a qui tam relator against a State" and avoiding whether such a suit would violate the Eleventh Amendment, an issue raising a serious constitutional doubt); *Gregory, supra*, at 464 (relying on clear statement principle to determine that state judges were excluded from the ADEA in order to "avoid a potential constitutional problem" given the constraints on the Court's "ability to consider the limits that the state-federal balance places on Congress' powers under the Commerce Clause").

The question then is whether § 1367(d) states a clear intent to toll the limitations period for claims against nonconsenting States that are dismissed on Eleventh Amendment grounds. Here the lack of clarity is apparent in two respects. With respect to the claims the tolling provision covers, one could read § 1367(d) to cover any claim "asserted" under subsection (a), but we have previously found similarly general language insufficient to satisfy clear statement requirements. For example, we have held that a statute providing civil remedies for violations committed by "'*any* recipient of Federal assistance'" was "not the kind of unequivocal statutory language sufficient to abrogate the Eleventh Amendment" even when it was undisputed that a State defendant was a recipient of federal aid. *Atascadero*, 473 U.S. at 245-246 (quoting 29 U.S.C. § 794a(a)(2) (1982 ed.) (emphasis in original)). Instead, we held that "[w]hen Congress chooses to subject the States to federal jurisdiction, it must do so specifically." 473 U.S. at 246. Likewise, § 1367(d) reflects no specific or unequivocal intent to toll the statute of limitations for claims asserted against nonconsenting States, especially considering that such claims do not fall within the proper scope of § 1367(a) as explained above.

With respect to the *dismissals* the tolling provision covers, one could read § 1367(d) in isolation to authorize tolling regardless of the reason for dismissal, but § 1367(d) occurs in the context of a statute that specifically contemplates only a few grounds for dismissal. The requirements of § 1367(a) make clear that a claim will be subject to dismissal if it fails to "form part of the same case or controversy" as a claim within the district court's original jurisdiction. Likewise, § 1367(b) entails that certain claims will be subject to dismissal if exercising jurisdiction over them would be "inconsistent" with 28 U.S.C. § 1332. Finally, § 1367(c) lists four specific situations in which a district court may decline to exercise supplemental jurisdiction over a particular claim. Given that particular context, it is unclear if the tolling provision was meant to apply to dismissals for reasons unmentioned by the statute, such as dismissals on Eleventh Amendment grounds. *See Davis v. Michigan Dept. of Treasury*, 489 U.S. 803, 809 (1989) ("It is a fundamental canon of statutory construction that the words of a statute must be read in their context and with a view to their place in the overall statutory scheme"). In sum, although § 1367(d) may not clearly exclude tolling for claims against nonconsenting States dismissed on Eleventh Amendment grounds, we are looking for a clear statement of what the rule includes, not a clear statement of what it excludes. *See Gregory*, 501 U.S. at 467. Section 1367(d) fails this test. As such, we will not read § 1367(d) to apply to dismissals of claims against nonconsenting States dismissed on Eleventh Amendment grounds.

In anticipation of this result, petitioners argue that the tolling provision should be interpreted to apply to their claims because Congress enacted it to prevent due process violations caused by state claim preclusion and anti-claim-splitting laws. In other words, petitioners contend that Congress enacted the tolling provision to enforce the Due Process Clause of the Fourteenth Amendment against perceived state violations. We have previously addressed the argument that if a statute were passed pursuant to Congress' § 5 powers under the Fourteenth Amendment, federalism concerns "might carry less weight." *Gregory*, 501 U.S. at 468. We concluded, however, that "the Fourteenth Amendment does not override all principles of federalism," *id.* at 469, and held that insofar as statutory intent was ambiguous, we would not "not attribute to Congress an intent to intrude on state governmental functions regardless of whether Congress acted pursuant to . . . § 5 of the Fourteenth Amendment." *Id.* at 470. That same rule applies here. As already demonstrated, it is far from clear whether Congress intended tolling to apply when claims against nonconsenting

States were dismissed on Eleventh Amendment grounds. Thus, it is not relevant whether Congress acted pursuant to § 5.

Petitioners also argue that our construction of the statute does not resolve their case because respondent consented to suit in federal court. We have stated that "[a] sovereign's immunity may be waived" and have "held that a State may consent to suit against it in federal court." *Pennhurst*, 465 U.S. at 99. Petitioners claim that respondent consented to suit by not moving to dismiss petitioners' state law claims on Eleventh Amendment grounds until July 1997, some 10 months after the federal lawsuits were filed in August 1996. Yet respondent raised its Eleventh Amendment defense at the earliest possible opportunity by including that defense in its answers that were filed in September 1996. Given that, we cannot say that respondent "unequivocally expressed" a consent to be sued in federal court. *Pennhurst*, *supra*, at 99. The fact that respondent filed its motion in July 1997 is as consistent with adherence to the pretrial schedule as it is with anything else.

Indeed, such circumstances are readily distinguishable from the limited situations where this Court has found a State consented to suit, such as when a State voluntarily invoked federal court jurisdiction or otherwise "ma[de] a 'clear declaration' that it intends to submit itself to our jurisdiction." *College Savings Bank v. Florida Prepaid Postsecondary Ed. Expense Bd.*, 527 U.S. 666, 676 (1999). And even if we were to assume for the sake of argument that consent could be inferred "from the failure to raise the objection at the outset of the proceedings," *Wisconsin Dept. of Corrections v. Schacht*, 524 U.S. at 395 (Kennedy, J., concurring) — a standard this Court has not adopted — consent would still not be found here since respondent raised the issue in its answer. Thus, we find no merit to petitioners' argument that respondent was a consenting state defendant during the federal court proceedings. We express no view on the application or constitutionality of § 1367(d) when a State consents to suit or when a defendant is not a State.

III

We hold that respondent never consented to suit in federal court on petitioners' state law claims and that § 1367(d) does not toll the period of limitations for state law claims asserted against nonconsenting state defendants that are dismissed on Eleventh Amendment grounds. Therefore, § 1367(d) did not operate to toll the period of limitations for petitioners' claims, and we affirm the judgment of the Minnesota Supreme Court dismissing those claims.

It is so ordered.

JUSTICE GINSBURG, concurring in part and concurring in the judgment [Omitted — Eds.].

JUSTICE STEVENS, with whom JUSTICE SOUTER and JUSTICE BREYER join, dissenting.

The federal interest in the fair and efficient administration of justice is both legitimate and important. To vindicate that interest federal rulemakers and judges have occasionally imposed burdens on the States and their judiciaries. Thus, for example, Congress may provide for the adjudication of federal claims in state courts, *Testa v. Katt*, 330 U.S. 386 (1947), and may direct that state lit-igation be stayed during the pendency of bankruptcy proceedings, 11 U.S.C. § 362(a). In appropriate cases federal judges may enjoin the prosecution of state judicial proceedings. By virtue of the Supremacy Clause in Article VI of the Constitution, in all such cases the federal rules prevail "and the Judges in every State shall be bound thereby, any Thing in the Constitution or Laws of any State to the Contrary notwithstanding."

The "supplemental jurisdiction" provisions of the Judicial Improvements Act of 1990, 28 U.S.C. § 1367, impose a lesser burden on the States than each of these examples, and do so only in a relatively narrow category of cases — those in which both federal- and state-law claims are so related "that they form part of the same case or controversy." Adopting a recommendation of the Federal Courts Committee, Congress in § 1367(a) overruled our misguided decision in *Finley v. United States*, 490 U.S. 545 (1989), and expressly authorized federal courts to entertain such cases even when the state-law claim is against a party over whom there is no independent basis for federal jurisdiction.

Subsection (d) of § 1367 responds to the risk that the plaintiff's state-law claim, even though timely when filed as a part of the federal lawsuit, may be dis-missed after the state period of limitations has expired. To avoid the necessity of duplicate filings, it provides that the state statute shall be tolled while the claim is pending in federal court and for 30 days thereafter. The impact of this provision on the defendant is minimal, because the timely filing in federal court provides it with the same notice as if a duplicate complaint had also been filed in state court.

The tolling of statutes of limitations is, of course, an ancient and widespread practice. Some federal tolling statutes apply only to federal limitations periods, but others apply to state statutes as well. All of these statutes are broadly worded and none of them excludes any special category of defendants. The plain text of all these statutes, including § 1367, applies to cases in which a State, or an arm of a State, is named as a defendant. Thus, as the Minnesota Court of Appeals correctly held, "the plain language of subsection (d) allows tolling of any claim dismissed by a federal district court, whether dismissed on Eleventh Amendment grounds or at the discretion of the federal district court under subsection (c)."

The Minnesota Supreme Court reversed, because it considered this Court's holding in *Alden v. Maine*, 527 U.S. 706 (1999), to compel the view that § 1367(d) was an invalid attempt by Congress to make the State of Minnesota subject to suit in state court without its consent. Unlike the State in *Alden*, however, Minnesota has given its consent to be sued in its own courts for alleged viola-tions of the MHRA within 45 days of receipt of a notice letter from the State Department of Human Rights. The question whether that timeliness condi-tion may be tolled during the pendency of an action filed in federal court within the 45-day period is quite different from the question whether Congress can entirely abrogate the State's sovereign immunity defense. For the Court's Eleventh Amendment jurisprudence concerns the question *whether* an uncon-senting sovereign may be sued, rather than *when* a consenting sovereign may be sued.

The Court recognized this crucial distinction in *Irwin v. Department of Veterans Affairs*, 498 U.S. 89 (1990), a case in which the application of equitable tolling to a waiver of federal sovereign immunity was at issue. Although the Court required the Government's assent as to whether it may be sued to be "unequivocally expressed," it presumed the rule of equitable tolling applied once assent was established because tolling would "amoun[t] to little, if any, broadening of the congressional waiver." *Id.* at 95. The Court reached this holding despite the inclusion in the waiver provision of a limitations period shorter than the one for suits against private parties.

The waiver at issue in this case is more unequivocally expressed than the one in *Irwin*. Minnesota has consented to suit under the MHRA by agreeing to be treated in the same manner as a private employer. The 45-day limitations period is thus applicable to any suit under the MHRA, not only those against state entities. In light of such a clear consent to suit, unencumbered by any special limitations period, it is evident that tolling under § 1367(d) similarly "amounts to little, if any, broadening of the [legislature's] waiver." Given the fact that the timely filing in Federal Court served the purposes of the 45-day period, it seems to me quite clear that the application of the tolling rule does not raise a serious constitutional issue.

It is true, of course, that the federal tolling provision, like any other federal statute that pre-empts state law, "affects the federal balance" even though it does not "constitut[e] an abrogation of state sovereign immunity." But that consequence is surely not sufficient to exclude state parties from the coverage of statutes of general applicability like the Bankruptcy Code, the Soldiers' and Sailors' Civil Relief Act of 1940, or any other federal statute whose general language creates a conflict with a pre-existing rule of state law. In my judgment, the specific holding in *Alden v. Maine* represented a serious distortion of the federal balance intended by the Framers of our Constitution. If that case is now to provide the basis for a rule of construction that will exempt state parties from the coverage of federal statutes of general applicability, whether or not abrogation of Eleventh Amendment immunity is at stake, it will foster unintended and unjust consequences and impose serious burdens on an already-overworked Congress. Indeed, that risk provides an additional reason for reexamining that misguided decision at the earliest opportunity.

Accordingly, I respectfully dissent.

QUESTIONS

1. Review the Minnesota Humans Rights Act, set out in the statutory supplement. Given this statute, why would the plaintiffs have chosen to pursue federal remedies for the alleged aged discrimination?

2. *Raygor* is one of several of the Supreme Court's recent "New Federalism" decisions restricting the scope of federal civil rights statutes. What other federal remedies of particular interest to the senior population might *Raygor* conceivably affect? How might the so-called "New Federalism" affect the practitioner's approach to a client's discrimination claims?

C. DISABILITY DISCRIMINATION

Excerpts from Disability Status: 2000
Census 2000 Brief
(March 2003)
http://www.census.gov/prod/2003pubs/c2kbr-17.pdf

Census 2000 showed disability rising with age.

Disability rates rose with age for both sexes, but significant differences existed between men and women. For people under 65 years old, the prevalence of disability among men and boys was higher than among women and girls. In contrast, disability rates were higher for women than men aged 65 and older. Specifically, in 2000, the disability rate was 7.2 percent for boys 5 to15 years old and 4.3 percent for girls the same age. Nearly two thirds of all children with disabilities were boys. Census 2000 found 1.7 million boys this age with one or more disabilities, compared with 949,000 girls this age. Among people aged 16 to 64 in the civilian noninstitutionalized population,19.6 percent of men and 17.6 percent of women reported one or more disabilities. Among people 65 and older, the disability rate was 43.0 percent for women and 40.4 percent for men. In this age group, 59.7 percent of people with disabilities were women. However, 58.2 percent of all people aged 65 and older were women. In the civilian noninstitutionalized population, people 65 and older were much more likely than people of working age (16 to 64) to report a sensory, physical, mental, or selfcare disability, or a disability causing difficulty going outside the home. While only 6.4 percent of working-age adults experienced difficulty going outside the home alone to shop or visit the doctor, 20.4 percent of older adults reported these problems. Physical disabilities affected 6.2 percent of the working-age population and 28.6 percent of older adults. About 3.8 percent of working-age adults reported difficulties in learning, remembering, or concentrating (a mental disability), compared with 10.8 percent of older adults. The prevalence of a selfcare disability was more than 5 times greater among older adults (9.5 percent) than among people of working age (1.8 percent). Also, the occurrence of sensory disabilities was more than 6 times greater among older adults than working age people, 14.2 percent compared with 2.3 percent.

Disability rates varied among the major racial and ethnic groups.

Census 2000 allowed respondents to choose more than one race. With the exception of the two or more races group, all race groups discussed in this report refer to people who indicated *only one* racial identity among the six major categories: White, Black or African American, American Indian and Alaska Native, Asian, Native Hawaiian and Other Pacific Islander, and Some other race. The use of the single-race population in this report does not imply that it is the preferred method of presenting or analyzing data. The Census Bureau uses a variety of approaches.

Interestingly, people who indicated that they were White (and no other race) and were not of Hispanic or Latino origin had a low overall disability rate despite the fact that their median age was higher than for other racial and ethnic groups examined in this brief. In Census 2000, they reported a disability rate of 18.3 percent, compared with 19.3 percent for all noninstitutionalized civilians aged 5 and older, as shown in Table 2.

Among the racial and ethnic groups examined in this report, the highest overall estimated disability rate, 24.3 percent, was shared by two groups — people who reported Black and people who reported American Indian and Alaska Native. The disability rates for these two groups were higher than the rates for non-Hispanic Whites in each of the broad age groups investigated in this report (see Table 2). Among children 5 to 15 years old, the disability rate was 5.7 percent for non-Hispanic Whites, but 7.0 percent for Black children and 7.7 percent for American Indian and Alaska Native children. Although the disability rate was 16.2 percent for non-Hispanic Whites of working age (16 to 64), it was 26.4 percent for Blacks and 27.0 percent for American Indians and Alaska Natives. Among people 65 and older, the rates were 40.4, 52.8, and 57.6 percent, respectively.

Asians who reported only one race had the lowest overall disability rate of any of the racial and ethnic groups examined in this report: 16.6 percent. Their child disability rate, 2.9 percent, was also the lowest. The disability rate for working-age Asians (16.9 percent) was slightly higher than the rate for working-age non-Hispanic Whites, whereas the rates for those 65 and older were not significantly different.

The overall disability rate for single race Pacific Islanders (19.0 percent) and their child disability rate (5.1 percent) were both slightly higher than the corresponding rates for Asians, but not statistically different from the rates for non-Hispanic Whites. However, the rates for Pacific Islander working-age adults (21.0 percent) and older adults (48.5 percent) were higher than the rates for Asians and non- Hispanic Whites in these same age groups.

Even though people reporting two or more races had the lowest median age among the racial or ethnic groups examined in this report, their disability rates were among the highest in 2000 — 21.7 percent overall. Among those reporting two or more races, 7.1 percent of children, 25.1 percent of working-age adults, and 51.8 percent of older adults reported at least one disability.

The overall disability rate was higher for Hispanics (20.9 percent) than for non-Hispanic Whites (18.3 percent). However, their child disability rate was lower — (5.4 percent compared with 5.7 percent). Still, the disability rates for Hispanics of working-age (24.0 percent) and older (48.5 percent) exceeded the rates for non-Hispanic Whites.

Figure 3.

Percentage of the Civilian Noninstitutionalized Population With a Disability by Age and Type of Disability: 2000

(For more information on confidentiality protection, sampling error, nonsampling error, and definitions, see *www.census.gov/prod/cen2000/doc/sf3.pdf*)

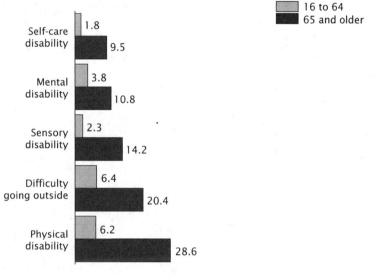

Source: U.S. Census Bureau, Census 2000 Summary File 3.

P41. Age by Types of Disability for the Civilian Noninstitutionalized Population 65 Years and Over With Disabilities for Each State

Disability status of the civilian noninstitutional population - Numbers						See Percentages below
Note: A person may have more than one disability						
Data Set: Census 2000 Summary File 3 (SF 3) - Sample Data						

Geography	Civilian noninstitutional population 65 years and over	Persons with any disability	Persons with a Sensory disability	Persons with a Physical disability	Persons with a Mental disability	Persons with a Self-care disability	Persons with a Go-outside-home disability
	Number	Number	Number	Number	Number	Number	Number
U.S. Total (50 States+DC)	33,346,626	13,978,118	4,738,479	9,545,680	3,592,912	3,183,840	6,795,517
Alabama	555,405	275,044	94,555	197,242	81,229	71,904	139,401
Alaska	34,301	15,849	7,097	11,021	4,224	3,560	6,938
Arizona	653,778	259,521	92,168	178,646	63,448	50,882	113,732
Arkansas	354,606	173,400	62,248	126,694	50,233	43,519	81,117
California	3,469,810	1,465,593	501,450	985,115	423,518	345,113	721,927
Colorado	398,644	159,289	60,149	107,416	38,971	31,743	72,320
Connecticut	439,935	162,931	53,610	103,962	36,947	36,350	82,914
Delaware	97,072	36,606	12,332	25,127	8,285	7,227	16,822
District of Columbia	66,478	28,280	7,382	18,695	7,413	7,413	15,726
Florida	2,720,127	1,075,545	354,848	713,534	260,487	216,868	506,259
Georgia	754,654	358,545	119,668	256,057	107,051	89,319	182,589
Hawaii	157,997	64,144	21,830	39,149	19,361	13,640	34,737
Idaho	140,644	59,704	24,955	40,445	15,007	11,698	24,800
Illinois	1,416,418	573,878	183,010	393,927	134,985	129,097	285,225
Indiana	707,369	301,630	105,274	209,251	70,735	64,661	138,302
Iowa	403,731	152,602	52,875	102,519	30,642	28,386	65,513
Kansas	330,661	137,088	46,485	94,531	29,767	27,096	60,443
Kentucky	476,540	235,049	84,172	170,609	67,805	59,006	113,981
Louisiana	489,574	235,482	80,244	167,803	66,337	60,916	116,107
Maine	174,998	71,901	27,944	49,351	16,895	14,741	30,024
Maryland	572,977	227,895	71,858	153,499	57,568	52,021	116,401
Massachusetts	807,006	305,241	105,118	199,828	71,309	69,091	151,835
Michigan	1,171,080	495,677	165,125	336,818	122,042	110,015	239,215
Minnesota	554,138	204,204	69,703	134,360	43,043	38,812	94,635
Mississippi	325,801	168,410	58,595	124,227	53,016	46,752	83,287
Missouri	711,417	303,279	102,002	212,122	73,373	65,162	141,075
Montana	114,359	45,284	18,740	30,311	10,026	7,844	18,404
Nebraska	216,774	80,401	27,713	52,444	16,026	15,807	36,832
Nevada	214,065	86,816	29,516	61,255	18,510	16,630	37,113
New Hampshire	139,078	53,610	20,204	35,749	11,629	10,108	22,603
New Jersey	1,063,982	411,059	127,389	271,630	97,770	93,994	213,150
New Mexico	205,591	92,015	36,264	64,070	25,829	20,239	43,482
New York	2,333,555	940,680	293,707	625,437	241,264	231,369	499,015
North Carolina	924,128	422,788	141,872	298,213	121,874	104,763	209,578
North Dakota	87,361	33,601	12,048	21,070	6,803	5,633	15,369
Ohio	1,422,071	583,034	192,291	395,543	136,021	128,475	282,607
Oklahoma	429,566	200,612	73,496	146,160	53,377	46,310	91,167
Oregon	423,459	175,929	65,507	122,161	47,254	38,199	76,019
Pennsylvania	1,809,320	712,795	232,348	468,772	163,441	154,460	356,888
Rhode Island	143,565	57,788	19,158	36,846	12,848	11,281	27,844
South Carolina	465,847	213,448	71,628	149,545	62,296	53,890	106,977
South Dakota	100,501	39,728	14,564	26,094	7,628	6,724	17,071
Tennessee	668,071	319,663	110,564	228,973	95,692	80,737	161,007
Texas	1,966,272	879,978	302,787	619,167	238,048	219,321	433,549
Utah	183,813	73,386	28,367	49,274	18,363	14,546	32,868
Vermont	73,355	28,293	10,844	18,925	7,036	5,948	12,266
Virginia	753,882	317,085	103,068	219,291	83,977	76,135	156,053
Washington	639,648	270,456	107,165	184,896	72,244	59,936	120,075
West Virginia	265,759	129,170	46,571	93,758	36,476	32,837	64,499
Wisconsin	662,813	242,237	78,834	159,880	50,183	49,928	117,174
Wyoming	54,630	21,475	9,137	14,268	4,606	3,734	8,582
Puerto Rico	417,218	246,523	106,418	165,562	94,348	66,790	143,423
Total (50 States, DC, PR)	33,763,844	14,224,641	4,844,897	9,711,242	3,687,260	3,250,630	6,938,940

QUESTIONS

1. What might account for the fact that a larger percentage of African-American and Hispanic-origin seniors are disabled as compared to white seniors? That more women than men in the 65+ age group report disabilities?

2. Why would disability rates among the elderly be higher in southern and industrial states than in many midwestern states?

In connection with the following excerpts, read titles I, IIA, and III of the Americans With Disabilities Act in the statutory supplement.

1. Federal Law: The Americans with Disabilities Act

The passage of the Americans with Disabilities Act of 1990 (ADA) marked a major paradigm shift in public policy concerning the treatment of the disabled. For the first time in history, virtually all public and private entites were charged with an obligation to make facilities accessible, provide job accomodations, and otherwise allow those with phyisical and mental impairments full, or nearly full, participation the full range of human activity. The ADA is of special import to the senior population, as persons age 55 and older make up a majority of the severely disabled, and a majority of persons over the age of 65 have at least some kind of disability that interferes with one or more activities of daily living. (*See* below.) Thus, disability discrimination is a major concern for many older clients. In this section, we introduce some basic principles of disability law as it pertains to the aging population.

U.S. Equal Employment Opportunity Commission
Enforcement Guidance: Reasonable Accommodation and Undue Hardship Under the Americans with Disabilities Act
http://www.eeoc.gov/docs/accommodation.html

Reasonable Accommodation

Title I of the Americans with Disabilities Act of 1990 (the "ADA") requires an employer to provide reasonable accommodation to qualified individuals with disabilities who are employees or applicants for employment, unless to do so would cause undue hardship. "In general, an accommodation is any change in the work environment or in the way things are customarily done that enables an individual with a disability to enjoy equal employment opportunities." There are three categories of "reasonable accommodations":

  (i)   modifications or adjustments to a job application process that enable a qualified applicant with a disability to be considered for the position such qualified applicant desires; or

  (ii) modifications or adjustments to the work environment, or to the manner or circumstances under which the position held or desired is customarily performed, that enable a qualified individual with a disability to perform the essential functions of that position; or

(iii) modifications or adjustments that enable a covered entity's employee with a disability to enjoy equal benefits and privileges of employment as are enjoyed by its other similarly situated employees without disabilities.

The duty to provide reasonable accommodation is a fundamental statutory requirement because of the nature of discrimination faced by individuals with disabilities. Although many individuals with disabilities can apply for and perform jobs without any reasonable accommodations, there are workplace barriers that keep others from performing jobs which they could do with some form of accommodation. These barriers may be physical obstacles (such as inaccessible facilities or equipment), or they may be procedures or rules (such as rules concerning when work is performed, when breaks are taken, or how essential or marginal functions are performed). Reasonable accommodation removes workplace barriers for individuals with disabilities.

Reasonable accommodation is available to qualified applicants and employees with disabilities. Reasonable accommodations must be provided to qualified employees regardless of whether they work part-time or full-time, or are considered"probationary." Generally, the individual with a disability must inform the employer that an accommodation is needed.

There are a number of possible reasonable accommodations that an employer may have to provide in connection with modifications to the work environment or adjustments in how and when a job is performed. These include:

• making existing facilities accessible;

• job restructuring;

• part-time or modified work schedules;

• acquiring or modifying equipment;

• changing tests, training materials, or policies;

• providing qualified readers or interpreters; and

• reassignment to a vacant position.

A modification or adjustment is "reasonable" if it "seems reasonable on its face, *i.e.*, ordinarily or in the run of cases"; this means it is "reasonable" if it appears to be "feasible" or "plausible." An accommodation also must be effective in meeting the needs of the individual. In the context of job performance, this means that a reasonable accommodation enables the individual to perform the essential functions of the position. Similarly, a reasonable accommodation enables an applicant with a disability to have an equal opportunity to participate in the application process and to be considered for a job. Finally, a reasonable accommodation allows an employee with a disability an equal opportunity to enjoy the benefits and privileges of employment that employees without disabilities enjoy.

<u>Example A</u>: An employee with a hearing disability must be able to contact the public by telephone. The employee proposes that he use a TTY to call a relay service operator who can then place the telephone call and relay the conversation between the parties. This is "reasonable" because a TTY is a common device used to facilitate communication between hearing and hearing-impaired individuals. Moreover, it would be effective in enabling the employee to perform his job.

<u>Example B</u>: A cashier easily becomes fatigued because of lupus and, as a result, has difficulty making it through her shift. The employee requests a stool because sitting greatly reduces the fatigue. This accommodation is reasonable because it is a common-sense solution to remove a workplace barrier being required to stand when the job can be effectively performed sitting down. This "reasonable" accommodation is effective because it addresses the employee's fatigue and enables her to perform her job.

<u>Example C</u>: A cleaning company rotates its staff to different floors on a monthly basis. One crew member has a psychiatric disability. While his mental illness does not affect his ability to perform the various cleaning functions, it does make it difficult to adjust to alterations in his daily routine. The employee has had significant difficulty adjusting to the monthly changes in floor assignments. He asks for a reasonable accommodation and proposes three options: staying on one floor permanently, staying on one floor for two months and then rotating, or allowing a transition period to adjust to a change in floor assignments. These accommodations are reasonable because they appear to be feasible solutions to this employee's problems dealing with changes to his routine. They also appear to be effective because they would enable him to perform his cleaning duties.

There are several modifications or adjustments that are not considered forms of reasonable accommodation. An employer does not have to eliminate an essential function, *i.e.*, a fundamental duty of the position. This is because a person with a disability who is unable to perform the essential functions, with or without reasonable accommodation, is not a "qualified" individual with a disability within the meaning of the ADA. Nor is an employer required to lower production standards — whether qualitative or quantitative — that are applied uniformly to employees with and without disabilities. However, an employer may have to provide reasonable accommodation to enable an employee with a disability to meet the production standard. While an employer is not required to eliminate an essential function or lower a production standard, it may do so if it wishes.

An employer does not have to provide as reasonable accommodations personal use items needed in accomplishing daily activities both on and off the job. Thus, an employer is not required to provide an employee with a prosthetic limb, a wheelchair, eyeglasses, hearing aids, or similar devices if they are also needed off the job. Furthermore, an employer is not required to provide personal use amenities, such as a hot pot or refrigerator, if those items are not provided to employees without disabilities. However, items that might otherwise be considered personal may be required as reasonable accommodations where they are specifically designed or required to meet job-related rather than personal needs.

Undue Hardship

"Undue hardship" means significant difficulty or expense and focuses on the resources and circumstances of the particular employer in relationship to the cost or difficulty of providing a specific accommodation. Undue hardship refers not only to financial difficulty, but to reasonable accommodations that are unduly extensive, substantial, or disruptive, or those that would fundamentally alter the nature or operation of the business. An employer must assess on a case-by-case basis whether a particular reasonable accommodation would cause undue hardship. The ADA's "undue hardship" standard is different from that applied by courts under Title VII of the Civil Rights Act of 1964 for religious accommodation.

U.S. Department of Justice, Civil Rights Division, Disability Rights Section
A Guide to Disability Rights Laws (May 2002)
http://www.usdoj.gov/crt/ada/cguide.htm

Americans With Disabilities Act (ADA)

The ADA prohibits discrimination on the basis of disability in employment, State and local government, public accommodations, commercial facilities, transportation, and telecommunications. It also applies to the United States Congress.

To be protected by the ADA, one must have a disability or have a relationship or association with an individual with a disability. An individual with a disability is defined by the ADA as a person who has a physical or mental impairment that substantially limits one or more major life activities, a person who has a history or record of such an impairment, or a person who is perceived by others as having such an impairment. The ADA does not specifically name all of the impairments that are covered.

ADA Title I: Employment

Title I requires employers with 15 or more employees to provide qualified individuals with disabilities an equal opportunity to benefit from the full range of employment-related opportunities available to others. For example, it prohibits discrimination in recruitment, hiring, promotions, training, pay, social activities, and other privileges of employment. It restricts questions that can be asked about an applicant's disability before a job offer is made, and it requires that employers make reasonable accommodation to the known physical or mental limitations of otherwise qualified individuals with disabilities, unless it results in undue hardship. Religious entities with 15 or more employees are covered under Title I.

Title I complaints must be filed with the U.S. Equal Employment Opportunity Commission (EEOC) within 180 days of the date of discrimination, or 300 days if the charge is filed with a designated State or local fair employment practice agency. Individuals may file a lawsuit in Federal court only after they receive a "right-to-sue" letter from the EEOC.

Charges of employment discrimination on the basis of disability may be filed at any U.S. Equal Employment Opportunity Commission field office. Field offices are located in 50 cities throughout the U.S. and are listed in most telephone directories under "U.S. Government."

* * *

ADA Title II: State and Local Government Activities

Title II covers all activities of State and local governments regardless of the government entity's size or receipt of Federal funding. Title II requires that State and local governments give people with disabilities an equal opportunity to benefit from all of their programs, services, and activities (e.g. public education, employment, transportation, recreation, health care, social services, courts, voting, and town meetings).

State and local governments are required to follow specific architectural standards in the new construction and alteration of their buildings. They also must relocate programs or otherwise provide access in inaccessible older buildings, and communicate effectively with people who have hearing, vision, or speech disabilities. Public entities are not required to take actions that would result in undue financial and administrative burdens. They are required to make reasonable modifications to policies, practices, and procedures where necessary to avoid discrimination, unless they can demonstrate that doing so would fundamentally alter the nature of the service, program, or activity being provided.

Complaints of Title II violations may be filed with the Department of Justice within 180 days of the date of discrimination. In certain situations, cases may be referred to a mediation program sponsored by the Department. The Department may bring a lawsuit where it has investigated a matter and has been unable to resolve violations.

* * *

Title II may also be enforced through private lawsuits in Federal court. It is not necessary to file a complaint with the Department of Justice (DOJ) or any other Federal agency, or to receive a "right-to-sue" letter, before going to court.

ADA Title II: Public Transportation

The transportation provisions of Title II cover public transportation services, such as city buses and public rail transit (e.g. subways, commuter rails, Amtrak). Public transportation authorities may not discriminate against people with disabilities in the provision of their services. They must comply with requirements for accessibility in newly purchased vehicles, make good faith efforts to purchase or lease accessible used buses, remanufacture buses in an accessible manner, and, unless it would result in an undue burden, provide paratransit where they operate fixed-route bus or rail systems. Paratransit is a service where individuals who are unable to use the regular transit system independently (because of a physical or mental impairment) are picked up and dropped off at their destinations.

ADA Title III: Public Accommodations

Title III covers businesses and nonprofit service providers that are public accommodations, privately operated entities offering certain types of courses and examinations, privately operated transportation, and commercial facilities. Public accommodations are private entities who own, lease, lease to, or operate facilities such as restaurants, retail stores, hotels, movie theaters, private schools, convention centers, doctors' offices, homeless shelters, transportation depots, zoos, funeral homes, day care centers, and recreation facilities including sports stadiums and fitness clubs. Transportation services provided by private entities are also covered by Title III.

Public accommodations must comply with basic nondiscrimination requirements that prohibit exclusion, segregation, and unequal treatment. They also must comply with specific requirements related to architectural standards for new and altered buildings; reasonable modifications to policies, practices, and procedures; effective communication with people with hearing, vision, or speech disabilities; and other access requirements. Additionally, public accommodations must remove barriers in existing buildings where it is easy to do so without much difficulty or expense, given the public accommodation's resources.

Courses and examinations related to professional, educational, or trade-related applications, licensing, certifications, or credentialing must be provided in a place and manner accessible to people with disabilities, or alternative accessible arrangements must be offered.

Commercial facilities, such as factories and warehouses, must comply with the ADA's architectural standards for new construction and alterations.

Complaints of Title III violations may be filed with the Department of Justice. In certain situations, cases may be referred to a mediation program sponsored by the Department. The Department is authorized to bring a lawsuit where there is a pattern or practice of discrimination in violation of Title III, or where an act of discrimination raises an issue of general public importance. Title III may also be enforced through private lawsuits. It is not necessary to file a complaint with the Department of Justice (or any Federal agency), or to receive a "right-to-sue" letter, before going to court.

ADA Title IV: Telecommunications

Title IV addresses telephone and television access for people with hearing and speech disabilities. It requires common carriers (telephone companies) to establish interstate and intrastate telecommunications relay services (TRS) 24 hours a day, 7 days a week. TRS enables callers with hearing and speech disabilities who use telecommunications devices for the deaf (TDDs), which are also known as teletypewriters (TTYs), and callers who use voice telephones, to communicate with each other through a third party communications assistant. The Federal Communications Commission (FCC) has set minimum standards for TRS services. Title IV also requires closed captioning of Federally funded public service announcements.

QUESTIONS

1. What fundamental changes in workplaces, public spaces, and educational institutions do you think the ADA requires?

2. Does the ADA create too much potential liability for employers who wish to terminate the employment of incompetent older workers?

3. Some older persons suffer from psychiatric disabilities, for example, Alzheimer's disease, that may severely compromise their ability to act "normally." How can such persons be accommodated under the ADA — or can they be?

4. In *Board of Trustees of University of Alabama v. Garrett*, 531 U.S. 356 (2001), the Supreme Court held that the ADA did not reflect Congress' clear intent to override the states' Eleventh Amendment immunity. Thus, as with the ADEA, successful ADA claimants against state entities may not obtain money damages, but injunctive relief only. Review again the Minnesota Human Rights Act in the statutory supplement. Might state law fill this gap in the remedial provisions of the federal ADA?

Settlement Agreement Between the United States of America and Moon River Enterprises, Inc., Branson, Missouri

re: Moon River Theater, Branson, Missouri
(removal of architectural barriers in a live performance theater)
(June 2, 1998)
http://www.usdoj.gov/crt/ada/moonrivr.htm

Background

1. This matter was initiated by a complaint filed with the United States Department of Justice ("the Department") against Moon River Enterprises, Inc., the owner and operator of Andy Williams' Moon River Theatre ("Respondent"). The complaint was investigated by the Department under the authority granted by Section 308(b) of the Americans with Disabilities Act of 1990 ("ADA"), 42 U.S.C. § 12188.

The Parties

2. The parties to this Settlement Agreement ("Agreement") are the United States of America and Moon River Enterprises, Inc.

3. Andy Williams' Moon River Theatre is a theater located at 2500 W. Highway 76, Branson, Missouri 65616.

4. Respondent, the owner and operator of Andy Williams' Moon River Theatre, is a public accommodation as defined by Title III of the ADA because respondent is the owner or operator of a "theater . . . or other place of exhibition or entertainment." 42 U.S.C. § 12181; 28 C.F.R. § 36.104(3).

5. The subject of this Agreement is readily achievable barrier removal at the Andy Williams' Moon River Theatre.

6. The Department conducted a site visit of the Moon River Theatre that identified a number of architectural barriers to access in and around the theater. The Department believes that the failure to remove barriers violates Title III of the ADA.

Accordingly, it is hereby agreed that:

7. Moon River Enterprises, Inc. is a private entity that owns and operates the Andy Williams' Moon River Theatre, a place of public accommodation as defined by title III of the ADA, 42 U.S.C. § 12181, and 28 C.F.R. § 36.104. The theater is subject to the "readily achievable" barrier removal provisions of the ADA at 42 U.S.C. § 12184 and 28 C.F.R. § 36.304 because it is a place of public accommodation as defined in § 36.104.

8. This Agreement is final and binding on all parties to this action, including all principals, agents, and successors in interest of Andy Williams' Moon River Theatre and the United States Department of Justice.

9. Respondent has cooperated fully towards the removal of barriers to access where readily achievable to do so since it was first notified of the complaint filed with the Department. This Agreement does not constitute an admission of a violation of the ADA on the part of Moon River.

Actions to be taken by Moon River Enterprises, Inc.

10. In the time since Respondent was first notified of violations at the theater and the date of this Agreement, Respondent has corrected many of the problems identified in the Department's site survey, paragraph 6 above, including adding additional signage, making the public telephones accessible, installing visual alarms in the mens' and womens' rooms, and improving accessibility in the restrooms. In order to fully resolve this matter, Respondent agrees to take the following additional steps to remove barriers to access by April 15, 1998:

    (a) Provide a designated area adjacent to an accessible route where persons with disabilities may be dropped off and picked up if all designated accessible parking spaces are filled;

    (b) Install additional vertical signage at the accessible parking spaces closest to the main entrance of the theater that complies with the ADA Accessibility Guidelines for Buildings and Facilities ("Standards") §§ 4.1.2(5), 4.6.4;

    (c) Ensure that the accessible route from the designated accessible parking spaces to the designated accessible entrance has no change in level at the walkway joints, Standards §§ 4.1.2(1), 4.3.8, 4.5.2, and is regularly inspected;

    (d) Convert the existing designated accessible stall into an alternate toilet stall in the mens' and womens' room in the upper and lower lobbies; the stall is to be 36 inches wide with parallel grab bars complying with Figures 30(b) and (d) and Standards §§ 4.1.3(11), 4.17.3, 4.26, and 4.22.4.

(e) Provide grab bars in all alternate stalls (see paragraph 10(d) above) that are mounted in the required location and at the required height in accordance with Standards §§ 4.1.3(11), 4.17.6, 4.22.4, and Figure 30(d).

(f) Ensure that the centerline of the toilet is exactly 18 inches in all mens' and women's room alternate stalls. Standards §§ 4.1.3(11), 4.17.3, 4.22.4.

(g) Relocate the toilet paper dispenser so that it does not obstruct the grab bar in both the mens' and women's room alternate stalls. Standard §§ 4.1.3(11), 4.16.6, 4.22.4.

(h) Provide the required number of accessible wheelchair locations in the theater area. Standards §§ 4.1.3(19)(a), 4.33.1.

11. Nothing herein shall require Respondent to invalidate, refuse to honor, modify and/or exchange any tickets already sold for the 1998 holiday season as of the date of this Agreement which are for seats that ultimately will become designated as accessible wheelchair locations pursuant to paragraph 10(h) herein.

12. Prior to commencement of work, but no later than March 29, 1998, Respondent shall provide the United States with a detailed dimensioned sketch or drawing of the proposed barrier removal work. The United States shall have 15 days from receipt of Respondent's list to notify Respondent in writing of its approval of the plans or of its objections.

Implementation and Enforcement of the Settlement Agreement

13. The Attorney General is authorized, pursuant to 42 U.S.C. § 12188(b)(1)(B), to bring a civil action under Title III, enforcing the ADA in any situation where a pattern or practice of discrimination is believed to exist or a matter of general public importance is raised. In consideration of the terms of this Agreement, the Attorney General agrees to refrain from filing civil suit under Title III in this matter regarding the specific issues discussed herein, so long as Respondent complies with the terms of this Agreement.

14. The Department may review compliance with this agreement at any time. If the Department believes that this agreement or any requirement thereof has been violated, it agrees to notify Respondent in writing of the specific violation(s) alleged. Respondent shall have forty-five (45) days from its receipt of the notice to cure the violation(s) and provide written certification, and photographs if appropriate, to the Department. If Respondent fails to cure the violation(s) or provide written certification within the forty-five (45) day period, the Department may institute a civil action for relief in Federal district court, and the Department is authorized to seek civil penalties for any violation of this agreement, pursuant to 42 U.S.C.§ 12188(b)(2)(C).

15. A violation of this Agreement that is not cured pursuant to paragraph 14 above shall be deemed a subsequent violation of the ADA. 42 U.S.C. § 12188(b)(3) and 28 C.F.R. § 36.504(b).

16. By April 30, 1998 the Respondent shall certify to the Department, in writing, that they have fulfilled all of their obligations under this Agreement. The certification shall describe the steps that have been taken to fulfill those obligations and shall be accompanied by photographs depicting the completed barrier removal work. The parties expressly agree that providing such certification is essential to the enforcement of this agreement, and that a failure to provide the certification required by this paragraph constitutes a breach of this agreement sufficient to warrant the penalties set out in paragraph 14.

17. The United States agrees that Respondent's completion of the steps set forth in this Agreement has fully resolved the complaint submitted to the United States and the issues detailed in paragraphs 6 and 10, above. The United States further agrees that the complaint and the investigation in this matter shall be administratively closed upon completion of the steps set forth in this Agreement.

18. This Agreement is a public document. A copy of this document or any information contained in it, may be made available to any person. Respondent or the United States shall provide a copy of this Agreement to any person on request.

19. The effective date of this Agreement is the date of the last signature below. This Agreement shall be binding on Respondent and its successors in interest, and Respondent has a duty to so notify all such successors in interest.

20. Failure by the Department of Justice to enforce this entire Agreement or any provision thereof with regard to any deadline or any other provision herein shall not be construed as a waiver of its right to do so with regard to other deadlines and provisions of this Agreement.

21. This Agreement constitutes the entire agreement between the parties on the matters raised herein, and no other statement, promise, or agreement, either written or oral, made by either party or agents of either party, that is not contained in this written Agreement, shall be enforceable. This Agreement is limited to the facts set forth herein and it does not purport to remedy any other potential violations of the Americans with Disabilities Act, including violations of the alterations or new construction provisions of the Act, or any other Federal law. This Agreement does not affect the continuing responsibility of Respondent to comply with all aspects of the Americans with Disabilities Act, including readily achievable barrier removal.

22. A signor of this document in a representative capacity for a partnership, corporation, or other such entity, represents that he or she is authorized to bind such partnership, corporation or other entity to this Agreement.

QUESTIONS

Does the Moon River consent agreement adequately protect the interests of persons with physical disabilities? Is it likely that persons who attend performances at the Moon River Theatre have other disabilities that this agreement does not address?

U.S. Department of Justice, Civil Rights Division, Disability Rights Section
How to File a Title III Complaint
http://www.usdoj.gov/crt/ada/t3compfm.htm

This is in response to your request for information on how to file a complaint under Title III of the Americans with Disabilities Act.

Title III prohibits discrimination based on disability in public accommodations. Private entities covered by Title III include places of lodging, establishments serving food and drink, places of exhibition or entertainment, places of public gathering, sales or rental establishments, service establishments, stations used for specified public transportation, places of public display or collection, places of recreation, places of education, social service center establishments, and places of exercise or recreation. Title III also covers commercial facilities (such as warehouses, factories, and office buildings), private transportation services, and licensing and testing practices.

If you feel you or another person have been discriminated against by an entity covered by Title III, send a letter to the Department of Justice, at the address below, including the following information:

- Your full name, address, and telephone number, and the name of the party discriminated against;

- The name of the business, organization, or institution that you believe has discriminated;

- A description of the act or acts of discrimination, the date or dates of the discriminatory acts, and the name or names of the individuals who you believe discriminated; and

- Other information that you believe necessary to support your complaint. Please send copies of relevant documents. Do *not* send original documents. (Retain them.)

Sign and send the letter to [this address]: Disability Rights Section, Civil Rights Division, U.S. Department of Justice, Post Office Box 66738, Washington, D.C. 20035-6738.

The Disability Rights Section will consider your complaint and inform you of its action. The office will investigate the complaint and determine whether to begin litigation. We will not necessarily make a determination on each complaint about whether or not there is an ADA violation. If we believe there is a pattern or practice of discrimination, or the complaint raises an issue of general public importance, we may attempt to negotiate a settlement of the matter or we may bring an action in U.S. District Court. Any such action would be taken on behalf of the Unites States. We do not act as an attorney for, or representative of, the complainant. You also have the option of filing your own case in U.S. District Court.

Depending on the nature of your complaint, other information would also be helpful to our investigation:

1. Small businesses have limited protection from lawsuits. Except with respect to new construction and alterations, no lawsuit can be filed concerning acts or omissions that occur before —

> 1) July 26, 1992, by businesses with 25 or fewer employees and gross receipts of $1,000,000 or less.

> 2) January 26, 1993, by businesses with 10 or fewer employees and gross receipts of $500,000 or less.

2. The name or names of the individuals or entities who have an ownership and/or managerial interest in each facility or business that is the subject of your complaint, with phone numbers and addresses, including zip codes, if you have them.

3. Information specifying whether the facility is owned and/or operated by a private entity or a state or local government.

4. The nature of the activity or service provided by the business.

5. If you are alleging failure to remove architectural barriers, a description, including as much detail as possible, of the barriers. If possible, please provide pictures, videotapes, diagrams, or other illustrations that accurately set forth the alleged violation.

6. Any suggestions for remedying the alleged violations of the ADA.

7. Information about whether you have filed a related complaint with a U.S. Attorneys Office, or any other Federal, State, or local agency, or any court, or whether you intend to file such a complaint.

Privacy Act Statement

The authority for collecting this information is contained in 42 U.S.C. § 12188(b). We need this information in order to investigate your complaint. The personal information will be used primarily for authorized civil rights compliance and enforcement activities conducted by the Department of Justice. The Department will not disclose the name of, or other identifying information about, an individual unless it is necessary for enforcement activities against an entity alleged to have violated federal law, or unless such information is required to be disclosed under the Freedom of Information Act, 5 U.S.C. § 552, or as is allowed through the publication of a routine use in accordance with the Privacy Act of 1974, 5 U.S.C. § 552a. To further the Department's enforcement activities, information we have about you may be given to appropriate Federal, State, or local agencies. Additional disclosures of information may be made: to Members of Congress or staff; to volunteer student workers within the Department of Justice so that they may perform their duties; to the news media when release is made consistent with the Freedom of Information Act and 28 C.F.R. § 40.2; and to the National Archives and Records Administration and General

Services Administration to perform records management inspection functions in accordance with their statutory responsibilities. Furnishing of the requested information is voluntary except that the failure to provide such information may result in our being unable to process your complaint.

QUESTION

The Department of Justice document above is intended to guide the layperson on how to proceed pro se in connection with a claim under Title III of the ADA. Do you believe it accomplishes its purpose? Do you think that the attorney has a role to play even at the administrative level?

2. State Law

QUESTION

Reread the Kansas Act Against Discrimination in the statutory supplement. In what ways does the protection against disability discrimination available under this law differ from that guaranteed by the ADA?

CITY OF MOORPARK v. SUPERIOR COURT
959 P.2d 752 (Cal. 1996)

Labor Code section 132a (section 132a) prohibits employers from discriminating against employees "who are injured in the course and scope of their employment." When an injury of this kind results in disability, we have held that section 132a prohibits discrimination based on the disability. In addition, the California Fair Employment and Housing Act (Gov. Code, § 12900 et seq. (FEHA)) prohibits various types of employment discrimination, including discrimination based on a disability. (Gov. Code, § 12921.) Finally, we have recognized a common law protection against certain types of discriminatory or retaliatory termination of employment. This common law remedy for wrongful discharge arguably extends to disability discrimination, though we have not addressed the issue.

Several Court of Appeal decisions have held that section 132a provides the exclusive remedy for discrimination based on a work-related disability, precluding FEHA or common law wrongful discharge claims. More recent decisions have reached this conclusion despite a 1993 amendment to the FEHA that plaintiff argues repealed section 132a, at least in part. Before the 1993 amendment, the FEHA provided: "Nothing contained in [the FEHA] shall be deemed to repeal any of the provisions of . . . any . . . law of this state relating to discrimination because of . . . physical disability [or] mental disability. . . ." (Gov. Code, former § 12993, subd. (a); Stats. 1992, ch. 913, § 25, p. 4325.) The 1993 amendment added the phrase: "unless those provisions provide less protection to the enumerated classes of persons covered under this part." (Gov. Code, § 12993, subd. (a).)

In this case, we consider whether FEHA and common law wrongful discharge remedies are available to an employee who has suffered discrimination based on a work-related disability, meaning, for present purposes, a disability resulting from an injury "arising out of and in the course of the employment" that gave rise to the discrimination. (Lab. Code, § 3600.) We conclude that section 132a does not provide the exclusive remedy for this type of discrimination and that FEHA and common law remedies are available.

Factual and Procedural Background

Theresa L. Dillon's complaint alleges that the City of Moorpark employed her as an administrative secretary from May 1990 until February 28, 1994. After she recovered from knee surgery and her doctor released her to return to work, City Manager Steve Kueny terminated her employment, informing her that her residual disability prevented her from performing her essential job functions. Dillon told Assistant City Manager Richard Hare that she could perform her job and that she wanted to return to work, but Hare told her she could not have her job back. Dillon also objected in writing to Kueny, again to no avail. Dillon then filed a charge of disability discrimination with the California Department of Fair Employment and Housing and received notice of a right to sue under Government Code section 12965, subdivision (b). On February 22, 1995, Dillon sued the City of Moorpark, Kueny, and Hare, alleging causes of action for discrimination in violation of the FEHA, wrongful termination in violation of public policy (common law wrongful discharge), breach of contract, and intentional and/or negligent infliction of emotional distress. She sought both compensatory and punitive damages.

Defendants demurred to all causes of action, arguing in part that, because Dillon's disability was work related, section 132a provided her exclusive remedy. Defendants asked the court to take judicial notice of Dillon's section 132a petition, which alleged essentially the same disability discrimination as part of a workers' compensation proceeding. The superior court disagreed that section 132a provided Dillon's exclusive remedy and overruled the demurrers to the FEHA and common law wrongful discharge causes of action. The court sustained the demurrers to the breach of contract and emotional distress causes of action on grounds not relevant here. Dillon then amended her complaint, dropping the breach of contract cause of action and restating the emotional distress cause of action.

On July 7, 1995, defendants petitioned the Court of Appeal for a writ of mandate, again arguing that section 132a provided Dillon's exclusive remedy and that the trial court therefore had erred in overruling the demurrers to Dillon's first two causes of action. The Court of Appeal denied the petition, citing the 1993 amendment to the FEHA, which it found to be "clear and intelligible." According to the Court of Appeal, the 1993 amendment meant "simply this: should any provision of state law offer less protection than does the FEHA, then such provision is inoperable and effectively preempted by the FEHA." The court concluded that section 132a offered "less protection" than the FEHA to victims of disability discrimination because it did not offer as many remedial options, did not provide a right to a jury trial or a right to appeal, and resulted in smaller overall awards. Because section 132a offered "less protection," the court concluded that the FEHA implicitly repealed section 132a. Without explanation, however, the court held that the FEHA only repealed the exclusivity aspect of section 132a. The court stated that section 132a remained an "alternative mechanism[ ]" for resolving disability discrimination claims.

We granted review in order to consider the interrelationship between section 132a and other statutory and common law remedies for disability discrimination in the workplace.

Discussion

1. Exclusivity of section 132a remedy.

Section 132a provides: "It is the declared policy of this state that there should not be discrimination against workers who are injured in the course and scope of their employment. (1) Any employer who discharges, or threatens to discharge, or in any manner discriminates against any employee because he or she has filed or made known his or her intention to file a claim for compensation with his or her employer or an application for adjudication, or because the employee has received a rating, award, or settlement, is guilty of a misdemeanor and the employee's compensation shall be increased by one-half, but in no event more than ten thousand dollars. . . , together with costs and expenses not in excess of two hundred fifty dollars. . . . Any such employee shall also be entitled to reinstatement and reimbursement for lost wages and work benefits caused by the acts of the employer."

On its face, section 132a's remedies apply only when employers retaliate against employees for pursuing their rights under the workers' compensation law. In *Judson Steel Corp. v. Workers' Comp. Appeals Bd.*, 586 P.2d 564 (1978), however, we focused on the first sentence of section 132a, which declares a general policy barring discrimination against injured employees. We concluded that section 132a's remedies are available whenever an employee suffers "discrimination incurred as the result of his injury," including discrimination based on disability.

In *Portillo v. G.T. Price Products, Inc.*, 131 Cal. App. 3d 285 (1982), the court held that, in cases where section 132a applied, it provided an employee's exclusive remedy. The plaintiff in *Portillo* brought a common law wrongful discharge action, alleging her employer discharged her in retaliation for filing a workers' compensation claim. Defendant demurred, arguing that section 132a provided the plaintiff's exclusive remedy, and the trial court sustained the demurrer.

The Court of Appeal affirmed. Noting that the Workers' Compensation Appeals Board had "'full . . . jurisdiction'" to resolve section 132a claims, the court found applicable the exclusive remedy provisions that apply to other workers' compensation remedies. The court emphasized the legislative compromise underlying the workers' compensation law:

"The Workers' Compensation Act is designed to afford workers quick determination of their claims for injury without regard to the common law questions of liability, negligence or fault on the part of and other common law defenses available to the employer. *The Legislature has balanced this imposition or burden on the employer by limiting the employee to seek redress in a single forum, the Workers' Compensation Appeals Board.* On balance, the fact that the *exclusivity of remedy* before the Workers' Compensation Appeals Board is for the benefit of workers generally outweighs any occasional disadvantage that could be argued."

The court also quoted Labor Code section 5300, which provides that proceedings "[f]or the recovery of compensation, or concerning any right or liability arising out of or incidental thereto" "shall be instituted before the [Workers' Compensation] [A]ppeals [B]oard *and not elsewhere. . . .*" Finally, the court emphasized that section 132a addressed the precise wrong that the plaintiff alleged and that courts should not, by enforcing a common law remedy, "say that a different rule for the particular facts should have been written by the Legislature" (*id.* at p. 290). Accordingly, the court held that section 132a provided the plaintiff's exclusive remedy and affirmed the judgment of dismissal.

In *Pickrel v. General Telephone Co.*, 205 Cal. App. 3d 1058 (1988), the court extended *Portillo* to a case specifically involving disability discrimination. The plaintiff in *Pickrel* brought a FEHA cause of action alleging termination of her employment based on a "physical handicap." The trial court sustained a demurrer, and the Court of Appeal affirmed. Citing and following much of its reasoning, the court held that section 132a provided the exclusive remedy for an employee claiming discrimination based on a work-related disability. The court stated that the result in *Portillo* was "consonant with the trend of recent decisions '. . . to narrow the range of exceptions to exclusivity, [thus] benefit[ing] both employers and employees within the system, by . . . preserving the low cost, efficiency and certainty of recovery which characterizes workers' compensation.'"

After the *Pickrel* decision, we addressed the scope of workers' compensation exclusivity in *Shoemaker v. Myers*, 801 P.2d 1054 (1990) and *Gantt v. Sentry Insurance*, 824 P.2d 680 (Cal. 1992). Both cases considered what remedies are available to an employee who suffers a physical or psychological injury as a result of wrongful termination of employment, but neither case involved termination based on a work-related injury or disability. Therefore, neither case implicated section 132a directly.

In *Shoemaker*, the employee alleged wrongful termination and related causes of action, including termination in violation of a "whistleblower" protection statute (Gov. Code, former § 19683). We concluded "that disabling injuries, whether physical or mental, arising from termination of employment are generally within the coverage of workers' compensation and subject to the exclusive remedy provisions, unless the discharge comes within an express or implied statutory exception or the discharge results from risks reasonably deemed not to be within the compensation bargain." By referring to the "compensation bargain," we recognized the same legislative compromise that the *Portillo* court cited: "[T]he employer assumes liability for industrial personal injury or death without regard to fault in exchange for limitations on the amount of that liability. The employee is afforded relatively swift and certain payment of benefits to cure or relieve the effects of industrial injury without having to prove fault, but, in exchange, gives up the wider range of damages potentially available in tort."

Though we stated that most injuries arising from termination of employment fall within the compensation bargain, we noted that "the exclusive remedy provisions are not applicable [to injuries arising from] 'conduct where the employer or insurer stepped out of their proper roles' [citations]. . . ." Therefore, we concluded that an injury resulting from a wrongful termination in violation of a whistleblower statute "lies well outside the compensation bargain," and the exclusive remedy provisions do not apply. We reasoned that, by enacting the whistleblower statute, "[t]he Legislature clearly intended to afford an *additional* remedy to those already granted under other provisions of the law; otherwise [the whistleblower statute] would be rendered meaningless."

The decision in *Shoemaker* turned in part on the fact that the whistleblower statute constituted a specific declaration of the Legislature's intent to create a new, additional remedy. The same could not be said about common law remedies, and we expressly did not decide in *Shoemaker* whether, in addition to a claim under the whistleblower statute, the plaintiff could also pursue a common law wrongful discharge claim. We addressed that unresolved question in *Gantt*, concluding that "the . . . 'compensation bargain' cannot encompass conduct, such as sexual or racial discrimination, 'obnoxious to the interests of the state and contrary to public policy and sound morality.' " Accordingly, we held that workers' compensation exclusivity did not preclude a common law wrongful discharge claim: "we decline the invitation to retreat from our long-held view that employees discharged in violation of fundamental public policy may bring an action against their employers sounding in tort."

In *Angell v. Peterson Tractor, Inc.*, 21 Cal. App. 4th 981 (1994), the court considered whether *Pickrel*'s holding remained valid in light of *Shoemaker* and *Gantt*; that is, whether wrongful termination in violation of section 132a "could be considered 'a risk reasonably encompassed within the compensation bargain'" for which workers' compensation is the exclusive remedy. The court seemed to accept without discussion that disability discrimination could form the basis of a common law wrongful discharge claim. The court also acknowledged our holding in *Gantt* that these claims do not fall within the compensation bargain. Nevertheless, the court concluded that, by enacting section 132a, ". . . the Legislature specifically placed this type of discriminatory termination within the scope of the compensation bargain." Accordingly, the court held that section 132a provided an employee's exclusive remedy for discrimination based on a work-related disability, precluding claims under both the FEHA and the common law.

In rejecting the conclusion of *Portillo, Pickrel, Angell*, and related cases, the Court of Appeal in this case focused on the 1993 amendment to the FEHA, reading it as repealing by implication all antidiscrimination laws that provide "less protection" than the FEHA, including section 132a. Notably, the Court of Appeal did not find an outright repeal of section 132a, but merely a repeal of its exclusivity, thus permitting employees to pursue FEHA and common law remedies in addition to section 132a remedies. We agree with the Court of Appeal that section 132a does not preclude Dillon's FEHA and common law causes of action, but, unlike the Court of Appeal, we reach this conclusion without relying on the 1993 amendment to the FEHA. Accordingly, we do not decide what effect, if any, the 1993 FEHA amendment had on section 132a.

Though the Court of Appeal decided *Portillo* 16 years ago, and though other Court of Appeal decisions have affirmed its holding, we have never addressed its validity. We do so now.

As noted, the *Portillo* court held that, when section 132a applies, it provides an employee's exclusive remedy. In reaching this conclusion, the court applied the exclusive remedy provisions that apply to other workers' compensation remedies. (*See* Lab. Code, §§ 3600, 3602, subd. (a).) But section 132a is quite different from other workers' compensation remedies. Most workers' compensation remedies compensate an employee for a medical injury. Section 132a, however, addresses a breach of an employee's civil rights and applies regardless of whether that breach causes a medical injury. Because of this distinction, we see no compelling reason to treat section 132a like other workers' compensation remedies.

Moreover, the existence of a workers' compensation remedy does not by itself establish that the remedy is exclusive. Rather, the scope of workers' compensation exclusivity depends on the terms of the exclusive remedy provisions. Section 132a does not itself contain an exclusive remedy clause, and, as explained below, the general exclusive remedy provisions of the workers' compensation law expressly do not apply to section 132a.

Labor Code section 3600, subdivision (a), provides: "Liability for the compensation provided *by this division*, in lieu of any other liability whatsoever . . . , shall . . . exist against an employer for any injury sustained by his or her employees arising out of and in the course of the employment. . . ." (Italics added.) When section 3600 refers to "this division," it refers to division 4 of the Labor Code. Section 132a, on the other hand, is in division 1 of the Labor Code. Similarly, Labor Code section 3602, subdivision (a), provides: "Where the conditions *of compensation* set forth in Section 3600 concur, the right to recover *such compensation* is . . . the sole and exclusive remedy of the employee. . . ." (Italics added.) Labor Code section 3207 defines "'[c]ompensation'" as "compensation under Division 4 . . . includ[ing] every benefit or payment conferred by Division 4 upon an injured employee. . . ." Again, section 132a is in division 1 of the Labor Code, not division 4. Thus, the plain language of the exclusive remedy provisions of the workers' compensation law apparently limits those provisions to division 4 remedies. Remedies that the Legislature placed in other divisions of the Labor Code are simply not subject to the workers' compensation exclusive remedy provisions.

The *Portillo* court also relied on the "compensation bargain" underlying the workers' compensation law, whereby "[t]he Workers' Compensation Act . . . afford[s] workers quick determination of their claims" but "limit[s] the employee to . . . a single forum, the Workers' Compensation Appeals Board." The court reasoned that this same "compensation bargain" applied implicitly to section 132a. In other words, section 132a affords workers an inexpensive and quick remedy for discrimination based on a work-related disability, but that remedy is exclusive.

Again, the *Portillo* court erred. Though the compensation bargain, and in particular the exclusive remedy principle, applies to most workers' compensation proceedings, we recognized in *Shoemaker* and *Gantt* that certain employer conduct falls outside the compensation bargain. Specifically, we held in *Shoemaker* that an injury resulting from a wrongful termination in violation of a whistle-blower protection statute "lies well outside the compensation bargain," and the exclusive remedy provisions do not apply. In *Gantt*, we reaffirmed *Shoemaker* and extended its holding to a case involving a common law wrongful discharge cause of action. We concluded that "the . . . 'compensation bargain' cannot encompass conduct, such as sexual or racial discrimination, 'obnoxious to the interests of the state and contrary to public policy and sound morality.'" Termination in violation of section 132a is just as "'obnoxious to the interests of the state and contrary to public policy and sound morality'" as sexual or racial discrimination. Therefore, a section 132a violation, like sexual and racial discrimination, falls outside the compensation bargain, and workers' compensation is not the exclusive remedy.

In addition, the *Portillo* court relied in part on Labor Code section 5300, which provides that proceedings "[f]or the recovery of compensation, or concerning any right or liability arising out of or incidental thereto" "shall be instituted before the [Workers' Compensation] [A]ppeals [B]oard *and not elsewhere. . . .*" (Lab. Code,§ 5300, subd, (a), italics added.) But, even assuming an employee's rights under section 132a are "right[s] . . . incidental" to "the recovery of compensation," Labor Code section 5300 merely establishes the Workers' Compensation Appeals Board as the exclusive *forum* for pursuing a section 132a claim; it does not establish that the section 132a claim is the employee's exclusive remedy. Therefore, Labor Code section 5300 provides weak support for the *Portillo* court's conclusion.

Finally, the *Portillo* court emphasized that section 132a addressed the precise wrong that the plaintiff alleged (*Portillo, supra*, 131 Cal. App. 3d at pp. 288-89) and that courts should not "say that a different rule for the particular facts should have been written by the Legislature." This argument, however, fails to recognize that the Legislature sometimes enacts a new remedy, intending to *supplement* other remedies. When courts enforce a common law remedy despite the existence of a statutory remedy, they are not "say[ing] that a different rule for the particular facts should have been written by the Legislature." They are simply saying that the common law "rule" coexists with the statutory "rule."

Accordingly, we find *Portillo*'s reasoning unpersuasive. Moreover, the Court of Appeal cases that followed *Portillo* do not persuade us that section 132a is exclusive. In *Pickrel*, the court simply cited *Portillo* and followed much of its reasoning. The court noted that the result in *Portillo* was "consonant with the trend of recent decisions," but of course we do not decide cases based on trends. In *Angell*, as in *Portillo,* the court failed to recognize that the Legislature sometimes intends statutory remedies to supplement, not supplant, common law remedies.

The provisions of the FEHA and our decisions interpreting it further support our conclusion that section 132a is not exclusive. The FEHA broadly announces "the public policy of this state that it is necessary to protect and safeguard the right and opportunity of all persons to seek, obtain, and hold employment without discrimination or abridgment on account of . . . physical disability [or] mental disability. . . ." (Gov. Code, § 12920.) The FEHA further provides that "[i]t shall be an unlawful employment practice . . . [f]or an employer, because of the . . . physical disability [or] mental disability . . . of any person, to . . . discriminate against the person. . . ." (Gov. Code, § 12940, subd. (a).) Nothing in these provisions suggests that the FEHA only applies to physical or mental disabilities that are unrelated to work. Moreover, the FEHA declares that its "provisions . . . shall be construed liberally for the accomplishment of the purposes thereof." (Gov. Code, § 12993, subd. (a).) A construction of section 12940, subdivision (a), that narrows the term "disability" to disabilities unrelated to work seems inconsistent with the principle of liberal construction.

Furthermore, our decisions have consistently emphasized the breadth of the FEHA. In *State Personnel Bd. v. Fair Employment & Housing Com.* (1985) 39 Cal. 3d 422, we considered whether the FEHA covered state civil service employees despite similar antidiscrimination provisions in the Civil Service Act. (*See* Gov. Code, § 19702, subd. (a).) We concluded that "[t]he FEHA was meant to supplement, *not. . . be supplanted by*, existing antidiscrimination remedies, in order to give employees the maximum opportunity to vindicate their civil rights against discrimination.. . . ." (*State Personnel Bd. v. Fair Employment & Housing Com., supra,* 39 Cal. 3d at p. 431, italics added.) Similarly, in *Rojo*, we considered whether victims of sex discrimination could bring common law wrongful discharge claims in addition to FEHA claims. We concluded that the Legislature intended the FEHA "to amplify" (*Rojo, supra,* 52 Cal. 3d at p. 75) other remedies and "to expand" (*id.* at p. 80) the rights of persons who are victims of employment discrimination. (*See also Jennings v. Marralle* (1994) 8 Cal. 4th 121, 135 [The Legislature intended "to create new rights within the FEHA statutory scheme while leaving existing rights intact. . . ."].) None of these cases suggests that non-FEHA remedies circumscribe the scope of the FEHA.

Finally, the public education provisions of the workers' compensation law support our conclusion that section 132a is not exclusive. Labor Code section 139.6 provides: "(a) The administrative director shall establish and effect within the Division of Workers' Compensation a continuing program to provide information and assistance concerning the rights, benefits, and obligations of the workers' compensation law to employees and employers subject thereto. The program shall include, but not be limited to, the following: . . . (2) The preparation, publishing, and as necessary, updating, of a pamphlet advising injured workers of their basic rights under workers' compensation law, *and informing them of rights under . . . the provisions of the Fair Employment and Housing Act relating to individuals with a disability*." (Italics added.) This legislative mandate to inform "injured workers" of their FEHA rights would make little sense if section 132a provided an injured worker's exclusive remedy for disability discrimination.

In conclusion, we hold that section 132a does not provide an exclusive remedy and does not preclude an employee from pursuing FEHA and common law wrongful discharge remedies. We disapprove any cases that suggest otherwise. Nevertheless, we emphasize that not every instance of disability discrimination in violation of section 132a gives rise to a valid FEHA claim. The term "disability" has a specific meaning in the context of the workers' compensation law that it has in no other context. On the other hand, the FEHA includes detailed definitions of "'Physical disability'" and "'Mental disability'" that make no reference to the workers' compensation law. (Gov. Code, § 12926, subds. (i), (k).) Because the standards for establishing disability discrimination may well be different under the FEHA than under section 132a, a decision in an employee's favor on a section 132a petition would not establish a FEHA violation. Moreover, to the extent section 132a and the FEHA overlap, equitable principles preclude double recovery for employees. For example, employees who settle their claims for lost wages and work benefits as part of a section 132a proceeding could not recover these damages as part of a subsequent FEHA proceeding.

2. Dillon's common law wrongful discharge cause of action.

In the case of Dillon's common law wrongful discharge cause of action, our conclusion that section 132a does not provide an exclusive remedy is only half the analysis. We must also decide whether disability discrimination can form the basis of a common law action of this type.

In *Tameny*, we reaffirmed "that when an employer's discharge of an employee violates fundamental principles of public policy, the discharged employee may maintain a tort action. . . ." (*Tameny, supra*, 27 Cal. 3d at p. 170.) In that case, the plaintiff alleged that his employer terminated him because he refused to participate in an illegal scheme to fix gasoline prices. (*Id.* at p. 169.) The trial court sustained the defendants' demurrer to the plaintiff's tort cause of action for wrongful discharge, and the plaintiff appealed. (*Id.* at p. 171.) We reversed, noting the long-standing rule "that a wrongful act committed in the course of a contractual relationship may afford both tort and contractual relief. . . ." (*Id.* at pp. 174-175.) We reasoned that "an employer's obligation to refrain from discharging an employee who refuses to commit a criminal act . . . reflects a duty imposed by law upon all employers in order to implement the fundamental public policies embodied in the state's penal statutes. As such, a wrongful discharge suit exhibits the classic elements of a tort cause of action." (*Id.* at p. 176.) In subsequent cases applying *Tameny*, we recognized tort causes of action for wrongful discharge based on sex (*Rojo, supra*, 52 Cal. 3d at pp. 90-91), age (*Stevenson, supra*, 16 Cal. 4th at pp. 897, 909), and retaliation for testifying truthfully (*Gantt, supra*, 1 Cal. 4th at pp. 1086-1087). We have not, however, addressed whether disability discrimination, like sex and age discrimination, can form the basis of a common law wrongful discharge claim.

In *Stevenson*, we articulated a four-part test for determining whether a particular policy can support a common law wrongful discharge claim. The policy "must be: (1) delineated in either constitutional or statutory provisions; (2) 'public' in the sense that it 'inures to the benefit of the public' rather than serving merely the interests of the individual; (3) well established at the time of the discharge; and (4) substantial and fundamental." (*Stevenson, supra*, 16 Cal. 4th at p. 894; *see also Jennings v. Marralle, supra*, 8 Cal. 4th at p. 130; *Gantt, supra*, 1 Cal. 4th at pp. 1090, 1095; *Rojo, supra*, 52 Cal. 3d at pp. 89-90.) "'[P]ublic policy' as a concept is notoriously resistant to precise definition, and . . . courts should venture into this area, if at all, with great care. . . ." (*Gantt*, *supra*, 1 Cal. 4th at p. 1095.) Therefore, when the constitutional provision or statute articulating a public policy also includes certain substantive limitations in scope or remedy, these limitations also circumscribe the common law wrongful discharge cause of action. Stated another way, the common law cause of action cannot be broader than the constitutional provision or statute on which it depends, and therefore it "presents no impediment to employers that operate within the bounds of law." (*Ibid.*) For example, in *Jennings*, we noted that the FEHA does not apply to employers of fewer than five employees (Gov. Code, § 12926, subd. (d)), and therefore we found no fundamental public policy against age discrimination by these employers. (*Jennings v. Marralle, supra*, 8 Cal. 4th at pp. 135-136; *see also Reno v. Baird* (1998) 18 Cal. 4th 640, 663-664.)

As in *Stevenson*, "[t]hree of the[ ] four requirements [of a policy that can support a common law wrongful discharge claim] are not reasonably subject to dispute in this case." (*Stevenson, supra*, 16 Cal. 4th at p. 894.) First, the FEHA clearly delineates a policy against disability discrimination in employment — at least in the case of employers of five or more employees. (Gov. Code, §§ 12940, subd. (a), 12926, subd. (d).) Moreover, the FEHA is just one expression of a much broader policy against disability discrimination that appears in a variety of legislative enactments. (*See, e.g.*, Civ. Code, §§ 51, 54 [barring disability discrimination in public accommodations]; Gov. Code, §§ 11135 [barring disability discrimination in state-funded programs], 19230, subd. (a) [declaring state policy to encourage disabled persons to participate in the social and economic life of the state], 19230, subds. (b), (c), 19702 [barring disability discrimination in state civil service employment].) Second, the policy "'inures to the benefit of the public'" (*Stevenson, supra,* 16 Cal. 4th at p. 894) because (1) any member of the public may develop a disability and become the victim of disability discrimination, (2) the public at large benefits from the productivity of disabled employees, and (3) any type of invidious discrimination "'foments. . . strife and unrest.'" (*Id.* at p. 895.) Third, the policy against disability discrimination has been included in the FEHA since July 1, 1974, and therefore is well established. (Stats. 1973, ch. 1189, §§ 6, 9, pp. 2501-2502.)

Accordingly, we turn to whether the policy against disability discrimination is "substantial and fundamental." Disability discrimination is indistinguishable in many ways from race and sex discrimination. Specifically, it can "attack[] the individual's sense of self-worth in much the same fashion as race or sex discrimination." (*Stevenson, supra*, 16 Cal. 4th at p. 896.) Nevertheless, an employer may have valid reasons to treat disabled employees differently than nondisabled employees, and the FEHA recognizes this fact by expressly providing that it does not "subject an employer to any legal liability resulting from the refusal to employ or the discharge of an employee with a physical or mental disability, where the employee, because of his or her physical or mental disability, is unable to perform his or her essential duties even with reasonable accommodations. . . ." (Gov. Code, § 12940, subd. (a)(1).)

But this caveat does not lead us to conclude that the policy against disability discrimination is not "substantial and fundamental." Even in the case of race, sex, and age discrimination, the FEHA does not prohibit discrimination that is "based upon a bona fide occupational qualification." (Gov. Code, § 12940.) Similarly, our opinions articulating "substantial and fundamental" policies against sex and age discrimination use the term "discrimination" only in the pejorative sense to refer to arbitrary judgments about individuals based on group stereotypes. (*Stevenson, supra*, 16 Cal. 4th at p. 896.)

Disability sometimes impacts a person's ability to perform a particular job, in which case the employer may treat a disabled employee differently than a nondisabled employee. Nevertheless, if disabled employees can prove that they can perform the job duties as effectively as nondisabled employees, taking into consideration the possibility, if any, that their condition will change, as well as the employer's short and long-term needs, then we think discrimination based on disability, like sex and age discrimination, violates a "substantial and fundamental" public policy and can form the basis of a common law wrongful discharge claim. Nevertheless, this remedy must be "carefully tethered to fundamental policies that are delineated" in the FEHA on which it is based. (*Gantt, supra*, 1 Cal. 4th at p. 1095.) Accordingly, just as disability discrimination in violation of section 132a does not alone establish a valid FEHA claim, it also does not alone establish a valid common law wrongful discharge claim. Furthermore, to the extent section 132a, the FEHA, and the common law remedies overlap, equitable principles preclude multiple recoveries for the same injury.

We conclude that disability discrimination can form the basis of a common law wrongful discharge claim. Because section 132a does not provide the exclusive remedy for discrimination based on a work-related disability, the trial court was correct to overrule the demurrer to Dillon's common law wrongful discharge cause of action.

3. Dillon's intentional infliction of emotional distress cause of action.

We held in *Cole v. Fair Oaks Fire Protection Dist.* (1987) 43 Cal. 3d 148, 160, that the exclusive remedy provisions of the workers' compensation law preclude a civil claim for intentional infliction of emotional distress if the employer's actions giving rise to the claim were "a normal part of the employment relationship." The Court of Appeal did not decide whether *Cole* applies here, and defendants did not raise this issue in their petition for review. Accordingly, we also do not reach the issue.

Conclusion

Section 132a does not provide an exclusive remedy precluding FEHA and common law wrongful discharge claims. In addition, disability discrimination can form the basis of a common law wrongful discharge claim. Accordingly, the trial court was correct to overrule defendants' demurrer to Dillon's FEHA and common law wrongful discharge claims, and the Court of Appeal was correct to deny defendants' petition for a writ of mandate. We affirm the judgment of the Court of Appeal.

[The concurring and dissenting opinions have been omitted. — Eds.]

QUESTIONS

1. The premise of workers' compensation is that it provides protection for employers from multiple claims for workplace related injuries. Is *City of Moorpark* consistent with that premise?

2. The Equal Employment Opportunity Commission has said that employers may ask job applicants about any state workers' compensation claims that they may have filed in the past. What would be the purpose of such a question? Doesn't the ADA cover disabilities that are due to workplace injuries?

FURTHER READING. Ruth Colker & Bonnie Poitras Tucker, THE LAW OF DISABILITY DISCRIMINATION (2d. ed. 1998); Peter J. Strauss & Nancy M. Lederman, THE ELDER LAW HANDBOOK CH. 16 (1996); Peter J. Strauss et al., AGING AND THE LAW, ch. 6 (1996).

Chapter 4

PLANNING FOR RETIREMENT

The aging — and retirement — of the Baby Boomers has been characterized by some as nothing short of apocalyptic. Will the Social Security system remain financially viable as fewer workers contribute to support the retirement of the elderly population bulge? Will the predicted shortfall be made up in personal savings (which the Boomers have notoriously neglected)? Will we continue to protect low income elderly with Supplemental Security Income? Some current retirees have pensions, but few current workers have that option. (In fact, about 22% of current beneficiaries get *all* their income from Social Security.) Will the gap created by the lack of conventional pensions be filled adequately by voluntary contributions to retirement savings vehicles?

This chapter will provide a brief outline of the current sources of retirement income for the elderly as well as stimulate the reader's interest and concern over the financial security of future generations of workers.

Government programs have been the bulwark protecting the elderly from poverty since the depression. Part A surveys the mechanics of Social Security benefits, Old Age, Survivors, and Disability Insurance and its companion welfare program, Supplemental Security Income. It also explores some of the problems and possibilities of this most popular of social safety nets. The disability, medical, and retirement programs available to veterans of U.S. military service deserve a mention in the context of retirement planning because such a significant number of Americans and their dependents are affected.

Part B examines the employer-based pension plan: its history and its modern operation.

Among the topics considered are the growth of pensions in the 20th century, the different types of plans, the tax treatment of contributions and distributions, and the use of rollovers from one plan to another or from a pension plan to an individual retirement account.

Part C concerns private savings. Savings take many forms, ranging from checking accounts to real estate investments; instead of canvassing them all, this chapter concentrates on one form of savings that is particularly keyed to retirement: the individual retirement account, or IRA. IRAs now come in three varieties — traditional, Roth, and Education — and the chapter examines their characteristics, purposes, and relative merits.

A. GOVERNMENT PROGRAMS

1. Old Age, Survivor's, and Disability Insurance (OASDI)

The Social Security Act was signed into law by President Roosevelt on August 14, 1935.

In addition to several provisions for general welfare, the new Act created a social insurance program designed to pay retired workers age 65 or older a continuing income after retirement.

> *"We can never insure one hundred percent of the population against one hundred percent of the hazards and vicissitudes of life, but we have tried to frame a law which will give some measure of protection to the average citizen and to his family against the loss of a job and against poverty-ridden old age."*
>
> *— President Roosevelt upon signing the Social Security Act.*

a. Origins

Since Social Security became law in 1935, millions of American families have depended on this far reaching, complex social insurance program to take the sharp financial edge off disability, retirement, and the loss of the family bread-winner. In 1997, one out of every six Americans received some assistance from one or more of the many benefits available from Social Security Administration (SSA) programs. No group of citizens has more contact with SSA than the elderly. In 2005, persons 65 and over accounted for 72% of all OASDI benefits recipients.

Social Security Administration
Pre-Social Security History
http://www.ssa.gov/history/briefhistory3.html

The "Miracle" of the Market

In the heady days of the Roaring Twenties another idea arose for providing economic security to average Americans — the presumed ever-upward march of the stock market.

From 1927 to 1929 the volume of shares traded on the stock market doubled, with much of it bought on "margin" where investors actually had to pay as little as 10% of the full price of a stock. By late 1929 the amount of stock debt outstanding was nearly three times larger than the total federal budget for that year. And in the 1920s it was not just the prosperous who invested their futures and fortunes in the stock market, many small investors bet their meager incomes on dreams of future riches.

In the spirit of the times people believed that the stock market could only go up. A week before the stock market crash a Yale University economist would say that the stock market had reached "what looks like a permanently high plateau." A major Wall Street financier published an article in the Ladies Home Journal entitled "Everybody Ought to Be Rich" in which he told the Journal's readers that they could be worth $80,000 in ten years by investing only $15 a week in the stock market (this was at a time when the average worker's take-home pay was $1,300 per year). As one historian described the resulting era: ". . . such figures were extraordinary, magical, intoxicating. What was more, any number could play, and as many as a million did. They were, most of them, amateurs. . . . On their lunch hours, they crowded into the customer's rooms of the brokerage houses to watch their money, 'feverish young men and heated elders, eyes intent upon the ticker tape.' "

Despite all the promises of unlimited wealth, all the expectations of an endless upward spiral in national income, and despite all those eyes intently watching the ticker tapes, the stock market would crash, and with it the "roaring twenties" would come to a screeching halt, and the economic security of millions of Americans would disappear overnight.

The Stock Market Crash & The Great Depression

When the New York Stock Exchange opened on the morning of Thursday, October 24, 1929, nervous traders sensed something ominous in the trading patterns. By 11:00 a.m. the market had started to plunge. Shortly after noon a group of powerful bankers met secretly at J.P. Morgan & Co. next door to the Exchange and pledged to spend $240 million of their own funds to stabilize the market. This strategy worked for a few days, but the panic broke out again the following Tuesday, when the market crashed again, and nothing could be done to stop it.

Before three months had passed, the Stock Market lost 40% of its value; $26 billion of wealth disappeared. Great American corporations suffered huge financial losses. AT&T lost one-third of its value, General Electric lost half of its, and RCA's stock fell by three-fourths within a matter of months.

As America slipped into economic depression, unemployment exceeded 25%; nine thousand banks failed; the Gross National Product declined from $105 billion in 1929 to only $55 billion in 1932. Compared to pre-Depression levels, net new business investment was a minus $5.8 billion in 1932. Wages paid to workers declined from $50 billion in 1929 to only $30 billion in 1932.

Radical Calls to Action

The decade of the 1930s found America facing the worst economic crisis in its modern history. Millions of people were unemployed, two million adult men ("hobos") wandered aimlessly around the country, banks and businesses failed and the majority of the elderly in America lived in poverty. These circumstances led to many calls for change.

* * *

The Establishment Response

If America was to avoid the siren songs of the "radical calls to action," responsible political leaders would need to offer some persuasive alternatives. As the Depression grew, three general approaches emerged: do nothing; rely on voluntary charity; and expand welfare benefits for those hardest hit by the Depression.

The Do Nothing Response

It seemed to many politicians and leading public figures that the Depression was just another dip in the economic cycle and that it would right itself soon enough. These voices counseled a restrained response, or no response at all. In the early aftermath of the stock market crash such views were especially common. On New Year's Day 1930, Secretary of the Treasury Andrew Mellon stoically observed: "I can see nothing in the situation which warrants pessimism." President Herbert Hoover defiantly stated: "Any lack of confidence in the economic future or the basic strength of business in the United States is foolish." And publisher Arthur Brisbane confidently predicted that "All the really important millionaires are planning to continue prosperity."

This view that nothing very much was wrong, and nothing very much needed to be done, began to fade quickly as the Depression deepened. Even so, it held considerable sway in the early years after The Crash. President Hoover's own innate optimism would also cause him to make several statements about the economic crisis that seemed at considerable variance with the day-to-day experience of most Americans, which undermined the persuasiveness of this viewpoint.

Expand Welfare

Even before the Depression hit, the States had been forced to deal with the problems of economic security in a wage-based, industrial economy. Workers Compensation programs were established at the state level before Social Security, and there were state welfare programs for the elderly in place before Social Security. Prior to Social Security, the main strategy for providing economic security to the elderly, in the face of the demographic changes discussed above, was to provide various forms of old-age "pensions." These were welfare programs, eligibility for which was based on proof of financial need. By 1934, most states had such "pension" plans. Even at the state level, however, these plans were inadequate. Some had restrictive eligibility criteria which resulted in many of the elderly being unable to qualify. The most generous plan paid a maximum of $1 per day.

In the Congress, the consensus of conventional wisdom was for more old-age assistance like that available in the states. This was an attitude widely shared in both major political parties. Conservatives preferred this approach because it restricted government aid to the smallest possible number of people (the truly needy) thus restricting the role of government in the provision of economic security. And because it fit with the idea that the Depression was a temporary problem that would soon go away, and when it went away the old-age pensions could go away too — again, reducing the role of government. This became the conservative viewpoint on economic security for the elderly. . . .

The problem with this strategy was that the Depression didn't go away, and the underlying challenges to the traditional approaches to economic security were being driven by factors much larger and more permanent than the economic crisis of the 1930s. That is, this approach was based on the belief that nothing fundamental had changed about America and that the old tried and true approaches would continue to work. . . .

The "New" Alternative

With the coming to office of President Roosevelt in 1932, and the introduction of his economic security proposal based on social insurance rather than welfare assistance, the debate changed. It was no longer a choice between radical changes and old approaches that no longer worked. The "new" idea of social insurance, which was already widespread in Europe, would become an innovative alternative.

Social insurance, as conceived by President Roosevelt, would address the permanent problem of economic security for the elderly by creating a work-related, contributory system in which workers would provide for their own future economic security through taxes paid while employed. Thus it was an alternative both to reliance on welfare and to radical changes in our capitalist system. In the context of its time, it can be seen as a conservative, yet activist, response to the challenges of the Depression.

The Social Insurance Movement

The Social Security program that would eventually be adopted in late 1935 relied for its core principles on the concept of "social insurance." Social insurance was a respectable and serious intellectual tradition that began in Europe in the 19th century and was an expression of a European social welfare tradition. It was first adopted in Germany in 1889 at the urging of the famous Chancellor, Otto von Bismarck. Indeed, by the time America adopted social insurance in 1935, there were 34 European nations already operating some form of social insurance program. . . .

Although the definition of social insurance can vary considerably in its particulars, its basic features are: the insurance principle under which a group of persons are "insured" in some way against a defined risk, and a social element which usually means that the program is shaped in part by broader social objectives, rather than being shaped solely by the self-interest of the individual participants.

* * *

One of the earliest American advocates of a plan that could be recognized as modern social insurance was Theodore Roosevelt. In 1912, Roosevelt addressed the convention of the Progressive Party and made a strong statement on behalf of social insurance: "We must protect the crushable elements at the base of our present industrial structure . . . it is abnormal for any industry to throw back upon the community the human wreckage due to its wear and tear, and the hazards of sickness, accident, invalidism, involuntary unemployment, and old age should be provided for through insurance." TR would succeed in having a plank adopted in the Progressive Party platform that stated: "We pledge ourselves to work unceasingly in state and nation for: . . .The protection of home life against the hazards of sickness, irregular employment, and old age through the adoption of a system of social insurance adapted to American use."

b. Mechanics

Richard L. Kaplan
Top Ten Myths of Social Security
3 ELDER L.J. 191, 196-98 (Fall 1995)*

One of the myths that makes the Social Security program so politically untouchable is the belief that current retirees are simply recovering their own contributions. If this were true, one would indeed be hard pressed to suggest reducing Social Security benefits. If people do not recover their own investments, after all, Social Security might be seen as just another tax-like government imposition. Social Security, in fact, is partially a program of social insurance and partially a program of ensuring retirement income. Yet many, if not most, retirees seem to believe that its retirement income function is its overwhelmingly predominant, if not sole, characteristic. Accordingly, they view the monthly payments that they receive as a return of the taxes that they paid to the system during their working lives.

During much of Social Security's existence, its taxes were imposed at much lower rates and on a much lower wage base than is currently the case. For example, from 1937 through 1949, the Social Security tax rate was only 2% rather than the present 12.4%, which continues to be split between the employer and employee. Rates were increased after that date, but on an irregular sched-

---

ule — sometimes once every four years, sometimes every year. But the total tax rate was only half of the current rate as recently as 1962, and did not reach 10% until 1978. Similarly, the wage base on which this tax was imposed was only $3,000 through 1950, and was then raised on an irregular schedule until it reached $7,800 in 1968. The wage base was then raised again in 1972 and every year thereafter. Even so, it did not rise above $30,000 until 1982. Due to these low rates and low wage base during many of the years in which current retirees were working, their maximum Social Security tax — including their employer's portion — was only $60. As recently as 1972, in fact, the maximum amount paid in was only $828. And of course, during those years, persons who did not earn the maximum wage cap paid in even smaller amounts. Consequently, when current retirees relate their payments of Social Security taxes — both their own and their employer's share — to current benefits, a low-wage earner retiring in 1995 at age sixty-five recovers all of the Social Security taxes paid in forty months. Even a maximum-wage earner who paid tax on whatever wage cap was in effect, recovers the cumulative investment in less than seven years. In other words, after four and one-half years of receiving Social Security benefits, an average-wage-earning retiree is collecting welfare. That is, *all* of that worker's money has been repaid, including the employer's portion paid on the worker's behalf. Even if one includes interest earned during that interval, at some point most current retirees are receiving funds in excess of what they had put into the system.

On the other hand, the relationship between payments to, and benefits received from, Social Security is changing over time. As noted above, the Social Security tax rate has increased dramatically in the past twenty years or so. The wage base on which those Social Security taxes are collected, moreover, has risen dramatically since 1972, and has more than tripled since 1978. As a result, people who retire in the future may not, in fact, recover all of their investments in the form of retirement benefits. Some computations involving unmarried men earning maximum earnings and having average life expectancies indicate that they may not recover all of the Social Security taxes when they retire. Another way of describing this phenomenon is that the number of year needed to recover the much-greater Social Security taxes paid into the system in recent years may exceed the person's anticipated life expectancy upon attaining retirement age. On the other hand, huge categories of beneficiaries will not face this predicament for many years — namely, married men (whose spouses receive additional Social Security benefits and who have longer life expectancies generally), women (who have longer life expectancies generally), and workers who earned less than the wage cap (whose taxes paid into the system were necessarily lower).

To summarize, in the future, some retirees will be simply recovering their own funds. But *at the present time*, and for many years to come, almost all retirees will have long since recovered their tax payments into the Social Security program, often many times over.

QUESTION

Is it accurate for Professor Kaplan to characterize some retirees' receipt of benefits as "welfare"?

Social Security Administration
History: Frequently Asked Questions
http://www.ssa.gov/history/hfaq.html

Q4:   Is it true that Social Security was originally just a retirement program?

A: Yes. Under the 1935 law, Social Security only paid retirement benefits to the primary worker. A 1939 change in the law added survivors benefits and benefits for the retiree's spouse and children. In 1956 disability benefits were added.

* * *

Q7:   Is it true that life expectancy was less than 65 back in 1935, so the Social Security program was designed in such a way that people would not live long enough to collect benefits?

A: Not really. Life expectancy at birth was less than 65, but this is a misleading measure. A more appropriate measure is life expectancy after attainment of adulthood, which shows that most Americans could expect to live to age 65 once they survived childhood.

Q8:   When did COLAs (cost-of-living allowances) start?

A: COLAs were first paid in 1975 as a result of a 1972 law. Prior to this, benefits were increased irregularly by special acts of Congress.

* * *

Q23:   Has Social Security ever been financed by general tax revenues?

A: Not to any significant extent.

(See detailed explanation at http://www.ssa.gov/history/genrev.html.)

Q24:   How much has Social Security paid out since it started?

A: From 1937 (when the first payments were made) through 2005 the Social Security program has expended more than $8.9 trillion.

Q25:   How much has Social Security taken in taxes and other income since it started?

A: From 1937 (when taxes were first collected) through 2005 the Social Security program has received more than $10.7 trillion in income.

Q26:   Has Social Security always taken in more money each year than it needed to pay benefits?

A: No. So far there have been 11 years [1959, 1961, 1962, 1965, 1975-81 — Eds.] in which the Social Security program did not take enough in FICA taxes to pay the current year's benefits. During these years, Trust Fund bonds in the amount of about $24 billion made up the difference.

Q27: Do the Social Security Trust Funds earn interest?

A: Yes they do. By law, the assets of the Social Security program must be invested in securities guaranteed as to both principal and interest. The Trust Funds hold a mix of short-term and long-term government bonds. The Trust Funds can hold both regular Treasury securities and "special obligation" securities issued only to federal trust funds. In practice, most of the securities in the Social Security Trust Funds are of the "special obligation" type. The Trust Funds earn interest which is set at the average market yield on long-term Treasury securities. Interest earnings on the invested assets of the combined OASI and DI Trust Funds were $55.5 billion in calendar year 1999. This represented an effective annual interest rate of 6.9 percent. The Trust Funds have earned interest in every year since the program began.

QUESTION

What attributes of an insurance program does the Old Age, Survivors, and Disability Insurance program have?

c. Eligibility

Patrick H. Donahue
Social Security
KANSAS LONG-TERM CARE HANDBOOK 8-9
(KANSAS BAR ASS'N 2001)[*]

1. *Insured status.*

To be eligible for Social Security retirement benefits, an individual must meet the requirements for "fully insured" status. Insured status requires the accumulation of a lifetime minimum number of OASDI quarters of coverage. Individuals born in 1929 or later need 40 quarters of coverage. Fewer quarters of coverage are needed for persons born prior to 1929. An individual earns one quarter of coverage for earning a specified amount of taxable income — in [2007] one quarter of coverage is earned for each [$1,000] of earnings. A maximum of four quarters of coverage can be earned each year. Individuals who have not earned the required number of credits may return to work and do so.

2. *Retirement age.*

Full retirement age is the age at which individuals receive full retirement benefits. Because of longer life expectancies, Social Security is increasing the retirement age in gradual steps. The present retirement age is 65. This applies

---

to persons born in 1937 or earlier. The following chart shows how the increase to age 67 in full retirement age has been phased-in:

Birth Year	Full Retirement Age
1938	65 and 2 months
1939	65 and 4 months
1940	65 and 6 months
1941	65 and 8 months
1942	65 and 10 months
1943-54	66
1955	66 and 2 months
1956	66 and 4 months
1957	66 and 6 months
1958	66 and 8 months
1959	66 and 10 months
1960 and later	67

Persons can retire as early as 62, but the permanent reduction in benefits for retiring at 62 is between 20% and 30%, depending upon one's "full retirement age." Individuals retiring before full retirement age will have their benefits reduced by 5/9ths of one percent for the first 36 months and 5/12ths of one percent for each additional month. *Early retirement is contrasted by delayed retirement.* There is no requirement that an individual receive retirement benefits at full retirement age. In fact, SSA encourages delayed retirement. Individuals gain approximately 8% more benefits for each year of retirement delay after full retirement age up to age 70.

3. Bona fide *retirement.*

With self-employed or partially self-employed individuals it is often unclear when work stops and retirement really begins. Social Security has a procedure for investigating questionable retirement cases. Individuals who continue to carry on work-like activity may be disqualified from receiving retirement benefits. To determine whether retirement is *bona fide*, SSA uses the "substantial services test." Work-like activity more than 45 hours per month is presumed to be substantial services. This defeats retirement. The presumption, however, is rebuttable. On the other hand, work-like activity totaling less than 15 hours per month is presumed *not* to be a substantial service. Again, the presumption is rebuttable. SSA will challenge "sham" retirements. *Bona fide* retirement cases usually arise in the context of small, closely held businesses in which the principal wants to maintain some control over day-to-day operations. Similarly situated persons who often carry on some work-like activity after retirement, including lawyers, ministers, farmers, insurance agents and consultants, may also be the subject of questionable retirement reviews.

QUESTIONS

1. Is increasing "full retirement age" a fair approach to solvency of the Social Security system? Why or why not?

2. Why would it be necessary for SSA to monitor a beneficiary's *bona fides* with respect to retirement status?

d. Retirement Planning

David M. English
What Estate Planners and Their Clients Should Know About Social Security
ESTATE PLANNING 90 (February 1998)*

How are a worker's contributions calculated? Social Security is funded principally by FICA withholding on wages and by taxes on self-employment income. Almost all workers are subject to FICA withholding. The employer pays 7.65%, and an additional 7.65% is withheld from the worker's paycheck. From this 15.3% total, 12.4% is allocated to Social Security and 2.9% for Part A Medicare hospital benefits. The 15.3% maximum applies to the first [$97,500] of wages or self-employment income (in [2007]). Only the 2.9% Medicare tax is assessed on the excess above [$97,500].

The computations become more complicated for workers holding more than one job during the year. For such workers, each employer must withhold FICA on the first [$97,500] in wages paid by that employer. If this results in withholding on more than [$97,500] in wage income, the excess withheld on the worker's, but not the employer's, portion of the tax may be claimed as a credit on the worker's income tax return for the year.

Self-employed individuals must pay both portions of the tax: a 15.3% levy on the first [$97,500] in self-employment income subject to the tax, and a tax of 2.9% on the excess. To place self-employed persons on an equal footing with those who are employed, the tax is assessed on only 92.35% (100% − 7.65%) of the taxpayer's self-employment income, and the self-employed individual may deduct half of the tax payable as an adjustment to gross income. In addition, for self-employed persons who also hold regular jobs, the maximum tax rate applies to only the first [$97,500] of combined wage and self-employment income. Self-employment tax is computed on Schedule SE to the Form 1040.

What happens if a recipient takes a part-time job? With the exception of persons receiving disability benefits, who are covered by separate work rules,

---

Social Security recipients are subject to what is know as the "earnings test." The Social Security benefits of a worker or beneficiary under full retirement age are reduced $1 for each $2 of earned income above a minimum floor. A worker under full retirement age may earn up to [$12,960 in 2007] without reduction of benefits, a figure adjusted annually for cost of living increases. The earnings limit does not apply to Social Security recipients at full retirement age and older, who may earn unlimited amounts without a reduction of benefits.

To what extent are Social Security benefits subject to income tax? Code Section 86 subjects up to 85% of a recipient's Social Security benefits to income tax. As originally enacted, Section 86 taxed no more than 50% of Social Security benefits, and the benefits of lower income individuals retained their former exemption. In 1993, Congress, in need of yet additional revenue for the Trust Fund (to which the tax on Social Security benefits is allocated), increased the maximum to 85%, but only for those with higher income. The result is a three-tier system: recipients with lower incomes whose benefits are exempt, a middle group for whom no more than 50% of benefits are subject to tax, and a higher income group for whom up to 85% of benefits may be included in gross income.

The starting point in computing the benefits includable in gross income is to determine the taxpayer's "modified adjusted gross income" (MAGI). MAGI equals the taxpayer's adjusted gross income (AGI) increased by the amount of tax-exempt interest received or accrued. The next step is to add to MAGI one-half of the Social Security benefits received during the year. Then, the total of MAGI and half the Social Security benefits received is compared to a "base amount" determined by the taxpayer's filing status: $32,000 for taxpayers filing a joint return, and $25,000 for taxpayers filing as single individuals or heads of households. A severe penalty is exacted against married taxpayers filing separately. Their base amount is zero. Because of their zero base amount, they may sidestep much of the computational process. A minimum of 42½% (1/2 of 85%) of their Social Security benefits are includable in gross income.

For taxpayers whose MAGIs plus half the Social Security benefits received exceed the respective $25,000 and $32,000 base amounts, a portion of their Social Security benefits are included in gross income. To determine how much, the next step is to compare the sum of MAGI plus half the benefits received to yet another figure, the "adjusted base amount." The adjusted base amount is $44,000 for taxpayers filing a joint return, $34,000 for taxpayers filing as single taxpayers and heads of household, and once again an unfavorable zero for married taxpayers filing separately.

What results from completion of this next step are the second and third tiers. For joint filers whose MAGI plus half the benefits received is between $32,000 and $44,000, up to 50% of benefits are included in gross income. For those above $44,000, the maximum possible percentage is 85%. For single taxpayers and heads of households, the 50% maximum applies to persons whose MAGIs plus half the benefits received are between $25,000 and $34,000; up to 85% of benefits are included in gross income for those above $34,000.

The final step is to actually compute the portion of benefits includable in gross income. The computation is relatively straight-forward for those in the second or middle tier. For those in the second tier, the Social Security benefits includable in gross income equal the lesser of (1) one-half of the benefits received or (2) one-half of the amount by which the MAGI plus half the Social Security benefits received exceeds the base amount.

The computation is more complicated for those in the third or highest tier. For higher earners, the amount of benefits includable in gross income is the lesser of two figures. The first of these figures is 85% of the benefits received. The second figure equals one-half of the second tier spread (1/2 times $44,000 less $32,000, or $6,000 for joint filer; 1/2 times $34,000 less $25,000, or $4,500 for single taxpayers and heads of households) plus 85% of the excess by which the taxpayer's MAGI plus half the benefits received exceeds the adjusted base amount ($44,000 for joint filers, $34,000 for single taxpayers and heads of households). For taxpayers with the highest incomes, this computation will always result in 85% of the Social Security benefits being included in gross income.

✳ *What planning can be done to reduce this tax bite?* For individuals with very low or very high incomes, planning to reduce or avoid the tax on Social Security benefits is either unnecessary or unrealistic. Either none or 85% of benefits will be includable in gross income. Planning is more beneficial for those in the large middle group — those in the second tier and those not too far into the third tier. The key to planning is <u>income</u> deferral, not necessarily income avoidance. Purchasing tax-exempt securities does nothing to avoid the tax on Social Security benefits because tax-exempt interest is added to AGI for purposes of calculating MAGI. But income that is deferred is excluded from consideration.

Popular methods for creating deferred income include the purchase of Series EE bonds, on which the interest income need be reported only when the bonds are redeemed, and the purchase of single-premium annuities, on which tax is avoided until withdrawals begin. A decision to take a qualified plan benefit in the form of an immediate lump sum can be advantageous at least as far as the taxation of Social Security benefits is concerned. Lump-sum distributions eligible for capital gains treatment or five- or ten-year averaging are excluded from AGI and hence do not make their way into MAGI.

Given the earnings test and tax on benefits, what is the true cost of taking a part-time job? When the possible loss of benefits due to taking part-time work is combined with the income tax that will be assessed on the additional income earned plus the possibility that the extra earned income will result in a greater percentage of the remaining Social Security being included in gross income, a decision to return to work can result in what is in effect a marginal tax rate of close to 100%. Consider the following example.

Example. A single individual, age 63, receives in 1998 a $10,000 pension, $10,000 in Social Security, and $10,000 from a part-time job; she does not itemize her deductions. Her base income for purposes of computing the tax on Social Security benefits is $25,000 (i.e., the sum of MAGI plus half her Social Security benefits, which equals $20,000 from the pensions and part-time job plus one-half her Social Security benefits). Her taxable income is $13,050 ($10,000 pension plus $10,000 part-time job less $4,250 standard deduction and $2,700 personal exemption), and her tax bill is $1,958. None of her Social Security benefits are includable in gross income. She decides to take a second part-time job that will pay her an additional $10,000.

This decision will cost her at least $7,666 in reduced benefits and additional taxes, or what amounts to an effective tax rate of 77%. Her Social Security benefits will be reduced by $5,000 — that is, by half of her additional earned income. Her taxable income will increase by $12,500, consisting of the $10,000 in additional earnings plus $2,500 or 50% of the remaining $5,000 in Social Security benefits. This will increase her taxable income to $25,550, on which she will pay a tax of $3,859 or an increase of $1,901. Finally, her second employer will withhold a total of 7.65% or $765 in FICA taxes. Should the $10,000 in extra income be derived from self-employment, the results will be even worse. Instead of FICA withholding of $765, she would have to pay self-employment tax of $1,530.

e. Alienation of Benefits

PHILPOTT v. ESSEX COUNTY WELFARE BOARD
409 U.S. 413, 34 L. Ed. 2d 608, 93 S. Ct. 590 (1973)

The Essex County Welfare Board sued its welfare recipient and his trustee in the Essex County Court, New Jersey, to reach a bank account in which the recipient's trustee had deposited a check for six months' retroactive disability benefits paid to the recipient under the Social Security Act.

On certiorari, the United States Supreme Court reversed. In an opinion by Douglas, J., expressing the unanimous view of the court, it was held that all claimants, including a state, are subject to the provision of 42 U.S.C. § 407 exempting social security payments from all legal process.

MARENGO v. FIRST MASSACHUSETTS BANK, N.A.
152 F. Supp. 2d 92 (D. Mass. 2001)

This case arises out of the setoff by defendant of plaintiffs' bank account. Pending before this Court is defendant's motion to dismiss for failure to state a claim upon which relief can be granted.

I. BACKGROUND

Plaintiffs, Ralph and Vona Marengo ("the Marengos"), are elderly, disabled individuals. In the 1970s, Mr. Marengo opened a checking account and an unsecured line of credit with Shawmut Bank. When Shawmut Bank was acquired by Fleet Bank, defendant, First Massachusetts Bank ("FMB"), assumed operations of the former Shawmut Bank branch where the Marengos had their account and became the holder by assignment of the obligation on the unsecured line of credit. At some point, Mr. Marengo became delinquent on the unsecured line of credit and, in February 1998, FMB exercised a setoff of the Marengo's NOW checking account in the amount of $343.80 to collect at least part of that debt. At the time of the setoff, the only funds contained in the NOW checking account consisted of the Marengo's Social Security and Supplemental Security Income benefits.

The Marengos complain that they were not given advance notice of the setoff or an opportunity to dispute FMB's right to setoff the deposited funds. They also contend that the setoff caused them to bounce five checks totaling $232.80 and to have suffered humiliation and emotional distress as a result thereof.

On June 22, 2000, the Marengos sent FMB a demand letter seeking relief under the Massachusetts Consumer Protection Act, M.G.L. c. 93A. More than 30 days passed without a response and the Marengos then filed the instant suit in Worcester Superior Court on September 11, 2000, seeking damages and declaratory relief. The complaint alleges: 1) improper taking of exempted Social Security and Supplemental Security Income benefits in violation of the Social Security Act, 42 U.S.C. §§ 407(a) and 1382(d)(1), 2) unfair or deceptive acts or practices in violation of M.G.L. c. 93A, §§ 2 and 9, and 3) intentional infliction of emotional distress. On October 30, 2000, FMB removed the case to this Court claiming federal question jurisdiction on the basis of plaintiffs claims for violation of the Social Security Act.

II. STANDARD FOR MOTION TO DISMISS

A motion to dismiss for failure to state a claim may be granted only if it appears, beyond doubt, that the plaintiffs can prove no facts in support of their claim that entitle them to relief. [Citations omitted.]

III. ANALYSIS

Under the Social Security Act's anti-assignment provision, social security benefit payments are not transferable or assignable and are not "subject to execution, levy, attachment, garnishment, or other legal process. . . ." 42 U.S.C. § 407(a). The purpose of § 407 is to protect social security beneficiaries from creditors' claims, *Dionne v. Bouley*, 757 F .2d 1344, 1355 (1st Cir. 1985), and "it imposes a broad bar against the use of any legal process to reach all social security benefits." *Philpott v. Essex County Welfare Bd.*, 409 U.S. 413, 417, 93 S. Ct. 590, 34 L. Ed. 2d 608 (1973). Section 407 also applies to Supplemental Security Income benefits. 42 U.S.C. § 1383(d)(1)(incorporating § 407 by reference).

The parties agree that FMB's exercise of its right of setoff does not constitute an execution, levy, attachment or garnishment under § 407. They dispute, however, whether the phrase "other legal process" encompasses and therefore prohibits setoffs. FMB contends that "legal process" requires court action and thus does not include extra-judicial self-help remedies such as setoffs. It argues, accordingly, that the federal claims must be dismissed and that this Court should decline to exercise supplemental jurisdiction over the remaining state law claims. The Marengos respond that the phrase "other legal process" should be construed broadly to include non-judicial remedies such as setoffs.

FMB relies principally on two cases which hold that a bank's right of setoff is not "legal process" because it involves neither the courts nor the government. *See Frazier v. Marine Midland Bank, N.A.*, 702 F. Supp. 1000, 1002-04 (W.D.N.Y. 1988); *In re Gillespie*, 41 B.R. 810, 812 (Bankr. D. Colo. 1984). As an initial matter, this Court notes that *In re Gillespie* has been substantially eviscerated, if not overruled, by *Tom v. First American Credit Union,* 151 F.3d 1289 (10th Cir. 1998) which holds that an attempt to setoff an account containing Social Security benefit payments violates § 407. *Id.* at 1291-93. Moreover, the instant case is distinguishable from *Frazier* in which the plaintiff had signed an agreement stating that the defendant bank could use the monies in her account to setoff any indebtedness she might have to the bank. *Frazier,* 702 F. Supp. at 1001. By contrast, there is as yet no evidence that Mr. Marengo signed such an agreement when he opened the checking account and line of credit with FMB's predecessor.

In any event, this Court is not persuaded by the reasoning in either *Frazier* or *In re Gillespie.* Federal benefits statutes "should be liberally construed. . . . to protect funds granted by Congress for the maintenance and support of the beneficiaries thereof. . . ." *Porter v. Aetna Cas. & Sur. Co.,* 370 U.S. 159, 162, 82 S. Ct. 1231, 8 L. Ed. 2d 407 (1962) (interpreting exempt status of benefits paid out by the United States Veterans' Administration) (citations omitted); *see also Philpott,* 409 U.S. at 416, 93 S. Ct. 590 (analogizing the protection given by § 407 to the veterans' benefits exemptions reviewed in *Porter*); *In re Capps,* 251 B.R. 73, 75 (Bankr. D. Neb. 2000) (construing § 407 liberally in light of *Porter*). As noted by the Tenth Circuit Court of Appeals, there is no reason why Congress would, on the one hand, choose to protect Social Security beneficiaries from creditors who utilized the judicial system, a system that is built upon the fairness and protection of the rights of litigants, yet, on the other hand, leave such beneficiaries exposed to creditors who devised their own extra-judicial methods of collecting debts. Such a construction of §§ 407 would run contrary to both logic and the spirit underlying the Social Security Act. *Tom,* 151 F.3d at 1292 (citations omitted); *see also Crawford v. Gould,* 56 F.3d 1162, 1166 (9th "[Section 407] was not designed to preclude use of only the judicial process to obtain Social Security benefits."). Moreover, extra-judicial attempts to reach Social Security benefits may violate § 407 where the procedure used is unduly coercive. *See Crawford,* 56 F.3d at 1165-68 (Section 407 bars state from deducting Social Security benefits in order to pay for the care of institutionalized psychiatric patients without patients' voluntary consent.); *cf. Fetterusso v. New York,* 898 F.2d 322, 328 (2d Cir. 1990) (finding no § 407 violation in absence of evidence that mentally ill, committed persons did not voluntarily agree to use of their Social Security benefits to pay for the costs of their care and treatment).

Although clearly less restricted than an institutionalized individual, the Marengos were nonetheless at FMB's mercy to the extent that the bank had immediate access to their account and could, without notice, exercise its right of offset. As FMB points out, the Marengos could simply have closed their checking account and walked away, but there is something inherently coercive in FMB's actions which this Court finds that § 407 was designed to prevent. Accordingly, this Court reads the phrase "other legal process" to include both judicial and extra-judicial self-help remedies, including setoffs. *See Tom,* 151 F.3d at 1293 ("setoff constitutes 'other legal process' under § 407"); *In re Capps,* 251 B.R. at 75-76 (same). The motion to dismiss will, therefore, be denied.

LOCKHART v. U.S.
126 S. Ct. 699 (2005)

Justice O'CONNOR delivered the opinion of the Court. We consider whether the United States may offset Social Security benefits to collect a student loan debt that has been outstanding for over 10 years.

I.

A. Petitioner James Lockhart failed to repay federally reinsured student loans that he had incurred between 1984 and 1989 under the Guaranteed Student Loan Program. These loans were eventually reassigned to the Department of Education, which certified the debt to the Department of the Treasury through the Treasury Offset Program. In 2002, the Government began withholding a portion of petitioner's Social Security payments to offset his debt, some of which was more than 10 years delinquent.

Petitioner sued in Federal District Court, alleging that under the Debt Collection Act's 10-year statute of limitations, the offset was time barred. The District Court dismissed the complaint, and the Court of Appeals for the Ninth Circuit affirmed. 376 F.3d 1027 (2004). We granted certiorari, 544 U.S. 998, 125 S. Ct. 1928, 161 L. Ed. 2d 772 (2005), to resolve the conflict between the Ninth Circuit and the Eighth Circuit, see *Lee v. Paige,* 376 F.3d 1179 (C.A. 8 2004), and now affirm.

B. The Debt Collection Act of 1982, as amended, provides that, after pursuing the debt collection channels set out in 31 U.S.C. § 3711(a), an agency head can collect an outstanding debt "by administrative offset." § 3716(a). The availability of offsets against Social Security benefits is limited, as the Social Security Act, 49 Stat. 620, as amended, makes Social Security benefits, in general, not "subject to execution, levy, attachment, garnishment, or other legal process." 42 U.S.C. § 407(a). The Social Security Act purports to protect this anti-attachment rule with an express-reference provision: "No other provision of law, enacted before, on, or after April 20, 1983, may be construed to limit, supersede, or otherwise modify the provisions of this section except to the extent that it does so by express reference to this section."§ 407(b).

Moreover, the Debt Collection Act's offset provisions generally do not authorize the collection of claims which, like petitioner's debts at issue here, are over 10 years old. 31 U.S.C. § 3716(e)(1). In 1991, however, the Higher Education Technical Amendments, 105 Stat. 123, sweepingly eliminated time limitations as to certain loans: "Notwithstanding any other provision of statute no limitation shall terminate the period within which suit may be filed, a judgment may be enforced, or an offset, garnishment, or other action initiated or taken," 20 U.S.C. § 1091a(a)(2), for the repayment of various student loans, including the loans at issue here, § 1091a(a)(2)(D).

The Higher Education Technical Amendments, by their terms, did not make Social Security benefits subject to offset; these were still protected by the Social Security Act's anti-attachment rule. Only in 1996 did the Debt Collection Improvement Act-in amending and recodifying the Debt Collection Act-provide that, "[n]otwithstanding any other provision of law (including [§ 407])," with a limited exception not relevant here, "all payment due an individual under the Social Security Act shall be subject to offset under this section." 31 U.S.C. § 3716(c)(3)(A)(I).

II.

The Government does not contend that the "notwithstanding" clauses in both the Higher Education Technical Amendments and the Debt Collection Improvement Act trump the Social Security Act's express-reference provision. *Cf. Marcello v. Bonds*, 349 U.S. 302, 310, 75 S. Ct. 757, 99 L. Ed. 1107 (1955) ("Exemptions from the terms of the Act are not lightly to be presumed in view of the statement that modifications must be express [.] But [u]nless we are to require the Congress to employ magical passwords in order to effectuate an exemption from the Act, we must hold that the present statute expressly supersedes the provisions of that Act" (citation omitted)); *Great Northern R. Co. v. United States*, 208 U.S. 452, 465, 28 S. Ct. 313, 52 L. Ed. 567 (1908).

We need not decide the effect of express-reference provisions such as § 407(b) to resolve this case. Because the Debt Collection Improvement Act clearly makes Social Security benefits subject to offset, it provides exactly the sort of express reference that the Social Security Act says is necessary to supersede the anti-attachment provision.

It is clear that the Higher Education Technical Amendments remove the 10-year limit that would otherwise bar offsetting petitioner's Social Security benefits to pay off his student loan debt. Petitioner argues that Congress could not have intended in 1991 to repeal the Debt Collection Act's statute of limitations as to offsets against Social Security benefits — since debt collection by Social Security offset was not authorized until five years later. Therefore, petitioner continues, the Higher Education Technical Amendments' abrogation of time limits in 1991 only applies to then-valid means of debt collection. We disagree. "The fact that Congress may not have foreseen all of the consequences of a statutory enactment is not a sufficient reason for refusing to give effect to its plain meaning." *Union Bank v. Wolas*, 502 U.S. 151, 158, 112 S. Ct. 527, 116 L. Ed. 2d 514 (1991).

Petitioner points out that the Higher Education Technical Amendments, unlike the Debt Collection Improvement Act, do not explicitly mention § 407. But § 407(b) only requires an express reference to authorize attachment in the first place — which the Debt Collection Improvement Act has already provided.

III.

Nor does the Debt Collection Improvement Act's 1996 recodification of the Debt Collection Act help petitioner. The Debt Collection Improvement Act, in addition to adding offset authority against Social Security benefits, retained the Debt Collection Act's general 10-year bar on offset authority. But the mere retention of this previously enacted time bar does not make the time bar apply in all contexts — a result that would extend far beyond Social Security benefits, since it would imply that the Higher Education Technical Amendments' abrogation of time limits was now a dead letter as to any kind of administrative offset. Rather, the Higher Education Technical Amendments retain their effect as a limited exception to the Debt Collection Act time bar in the student loan context.

Finally, we decline to read any meaning into the failed 2004 effort to amend the Debt Collection Act to explicitly authorize offset of debts over 10 years old. *See* H.R. 5025, 108th Cong., 2d Sess., § 642 (Sept. 8, 2004); S. 2806, 108th Cong., 2d Sess., § 642 (Sept. 15, 2004). "[F]ailed legislative proposals are 'a particularly dangerous ground on which to rest an interpretation of a prior statute.'" *United States v. Craft*, 535 U.S. 274, 287, 122 S. Ct. 1414, 152 L. Ed. 2d 437 (2002) (quoting *Pension Benefit Guaranty Corporation v. LTV Corp.*, 496 U.S. 633, 650, 110 S. Ct. 2668, 110 L. Ed. 2d 579 (1990)). In any event, it is unclear what meaning we could read into this effort even if we were inclined to do so, as the failed amendment — which was not limited to offsets against Social Security benefits — would have had a different effect than the interpretation we advance today. Therefore, we affirm the judgment of the Ninth Circuit.

f. Spousal and Survivor Benefits

Franklin D. Roosevelt
Presidential Statement on Signing Some Amendments to the Social Security Act
August 11, 1939

IT WILL be exactly four years ago on the fourteenth day of this month that I signed the original Social Security Act. As I indicated at that time and on various occasions since that time, we must expect a great program of social legislation, such as is represented in the Social Security Act, to be improved and strengthened in the light of additional experience and understanding. These amendments to the Act represent another tremendous step forward in providing greater security for the people of this country. This is especially true in the case of the federal old age insurance system which has now been converted into a system of old age and survivors' insurance providing life-time family security instead of only individual old age security to the workers in insured occupations. In addition to the worker himself, millions of widows and orphans will now be afforded some degree of protection in the event of his death whether before or after his retirement.

Richard L. Kaplan
Top Ten Myths of Social Security
3 ELDER L.J. 191, 204-05 (Fall 1995)[*]

Social Security is often described as a program that rewards the "traditional" marital relationship, sometimes called "Ozzie and Harriet" after a popular

---

[*] Copyright © 1995. Reprinted by permission. Copyright to the *Elder Law Journal* is held by the Board of Trustees of the University of Illinois.

1950's television program, of a working man married his entire adult life to a woman who does not work in the compensated work force. Indeed, . . . married couples receive greater benefits when only one spouse is employed than when both spouses produce the equivalent earnings. Nevertheless, it is not true that Social Security favors lifelong marital partners.

Social Security provides a derivative benefit not only to the spouse of a worker who has retired, but also to the ex-spouse of a worker, if that ex-spouse was married at least ten years to the worker and has not remarried. In certain circumstances, subsequent remarriages are ignored — namely, when the remarriage occurs after reaching age sixty. But in any case, a person who is a divorced spouse can collect benefits based on the worker's work history without affecting benefits that are paid to that worker, to that worker's current spouse, or to any other recipients (for example, children) who may be, however, collecting derivative benefits from that worker's account. Their marriage, however, must have lasted at least ten years. So if, for example, Hank was married to Alice for eleven years, then to Betty for twelve years, and then to Carol for ten years, all three of this ex-wives could collect benefits equal to one-half of his worker's retirement benefit. Once a person has been married at least ten years, in other words, that person's spouse has become vested in that person's Social Security record, and further years of marriage do not increase the amount of that spouse's Social Security benefit. In effect, Social Security provides no incentive to stay married once a marriage has lasted ten years.

For example, assume that Ozzie and Hank both qualify for a worker's retirement benefit of $1,000. Ozzie and Harriet (Ozzie's wife) will receive Social Security benefits of $1,500 per month — assuming that Harriet would not receive more than $500 based upon her own work record, and assuming that both Ozzie and Harriet have reached "full retirement age." Using the same assumptions about spousal work records and age, Hank would receive his $1,000 per month, and his former wives (Alice, Betty, and Carol) would each receive $500, as would his current spouse, Deborah — a grand total of $3,000 per month, compared to Ozzie and Harriet's $1,500.

Moreover, when a retired worker dies, his or her surviving spouse succeeds to the retired worker's *entire* benefit. Therefore, if Ozzie dies, Harriet's benefit would rise from $500 to $1,000 per month, ignoring intervening cost-of-living adjustments. This stepped-up benefit rule, however, also applies to surviving former spouses — once again, assuming that the marriage lasted at least ten years, and that the spouse's own work record does not provide a greater benefit. As a result, Hank's three surviving ex-wives and his surviving spouse will each receive $1,000 after Hank dies, producing a grand total of $4,000 from Hank's account compared to $1,000 for Harriet from Ozzie's account.

QUESTIONS

1. Why shouldn't former spouses share equally in one benefit amount rather than having the total amount paid from one worker's account limited only by the number of marriages lasting 10 years?

2. What impact does the provision of dependent benefits to families of workers have on the solvency of the Social Security system?

g. The future of Social Security

Robert Eisner
Don't Sock the Elderly, Help Them:
Old Age Is Hard Enough
5 ELDER L.J. 181, 189-93 (No. 1, Spring 1997)[*]

. . . the intermediate projection of the Social Security trustees would have the Old Age and Survivors and Disability trust funds short of funds in thirty-three years. Some would cut benefits or raise payroll taxes or both to keep the funds fully solvent for at least seventy-five years. Others would combine this with "privatization," risking some of the guaranteed benefits of Social Security in the stock market. And some, embracing various elements of these prescriptions, focus on encouraging private saving.

Kenneth S. Apfel
Framing the Social Security Debate: Values,
Politics & Economics
National Academy of Social Insurance 10th Annual Conf., Washington, D.C. (January 1998)[**]

Social Security has been the central factor in reducing poverty among elderly persons over the last two decades. Social Security is more than a retirement program. As an insurance program, it provides disability, survivors, and dependents benefits if the wage-earner is impaired or dies.

The basic financial underpinning of the program is intergenerational. Current workers pay for current retirees.

While Social Security has reduced poverty, it was never intended to provide all retirement income.

The changing demographics of the population drive the need to change the Social Security financing system. While the number of older persons is increasing, the number of younger workers is decreasing.

---

[*] Copyright © 1997. Reprinted with permission. Copyright to the *Elder Law Journal* is held by the Board of Trustees of the University of Illinois.

[**] Copyright © 1998. Reprinted with permission.

President's Commission to Strengthen
Social Security (October 2002)

http://www.csss.gov/index.html

The Commission was asked to make recommendations to modernize and restore fiscal soundness to Social Security, using six guiding principles:

- Modernization must not change Social Security benefits for retirees or near-retirees.

- The entire Social Security surplus must be dedicated only to Social Security.

- Social Security payroll taxes must not be increased.

- The government must not invest Social Security funds in the stock market.

- Modernization must preserve Social Security`s disability and survivors insurance programs.

- Modernization must include individually controlled, voluntary personal retirement accounts, which will augment Social Security.

Social Security Board of Trustees
A Summary of the 2006 Reports

May 2, 2006

http://www.ssa.gov/OACT/TRSUM/trsummary.html

The fundamentals of the financial status of Social Security and Medicare remain problematic under the intermediate economic and demographic assumptions. Social Security's current annual surpluses of tax income over expenditures will soon begin to decline, and will be followed by deficits that begin to grow rapidly toward the end of the next decade as the baby-boom generation retires. Expenditures of Medicare's Hospital Insurance (HI) Trust Fund that pays hospital benefits are projected to exceed taxes and other dedicated revenues in 2006, with annual cash flow deficits expected to continue and to grow rapidly after 2010 as baby boomers begin to retire. The projected growing deficits in both programs will exhaust HI trust fund reserves in 2018 and Social Security reserves in 2040, under current financing arrangements. In addition, the Medicare Supplementary Medical Insurance (SMI) Trust Fund that pays for physician services and the new prescription drug benefit will require substantial increases over time in both general revenue financing and beneficiary premium charges. As Social Security and HI reserves are drawn down and SMI general revenue financing requirements continue to grow, pressure on the Federal budget will intensify. We do not believe the currently projected long-run growth rates of Social Security or Medicare are sustainable under current financing arrangements.

Social Security

The annual cost of Social Security benefits represents 4.2 percent of gross domestic product (GDP) in 2005 and is projected to rise to 6.2 percent of GDP in 2030, and then slightly to 6.3 percent of GDP in 2080. The projected 75-year actuarial deficit in the combined Old-Age and Survivors Insurance (OASI) and Disability Insurance (DI) Trust Funds is 2.02 percent of taxable payroll, up from 1.92 percent in last year's report. This increase is due primarily to advancing the projection period, the availability of recent data that led to revisions in key assumptions, and to changes in methods. Although the program passes our short-range test of financial adequacy, it continues to fail our long-range test of close actuarial balance by a wide margin. Projected OASDI tax income will begin to fall short of outlays in 2017, and will be sufficient to finance only 74 percent of scheduled annual benefits in 2040, when the combined OASDI trust fund is projected to be exhausted.

Social Security could be brought into actuarial balance over the next 75 years in various ways, including an immediate increase of 16 percent in payroll tax revenues or an immediate reduction in benefits of 13 percent (or some combination of the two). To the extent that changes are delayed or phased in gradually, greater adjustments in scheduled benefits and revenues would be required. Ensuring that the system is solvent on a sustainable basis over the next 75 years and beyond would also require larger changes.

* * *

Conclusion

Though highly challenging, the financial difficulties facing Social Security and Medicare are not insurmountable. We must, however, take action to address them in a timely manner. The sooner these challenges are addressed, the more varied and less disruptive their solutions can be. With informed public discussion and creative thinking that relates the principles underlying these programs to the economic and demographic realities, and to the changing needs and preferences of working and retired households, Social Security and Medicare can continue to play a critical role in the lives of all Americans.

Social Security Administration Memorandum
Estimated Financial Effects of a Comprehensive Social Security Reform Proposal Including Progressive Price Indexing
http://www.ssa.gov/OACT/solvency/index.html

[Robert Pozen is an economist, a Democrat, and a former member of the President's 2001 Commission to Strengthen Social Security who is a proponent of "progressive indexing" — the application of a formula which would slow the increase in benefits to all but those who had been low-wage workers. — Eds.]

Date: February 10, 2005
To: Bob Pozen
From: Stephen C. Goss, Chief Actuary

Under the plan specification described below the Social Security program (OASDI) would be expected to be solvent and to meet its benefit obligations throughout the long-range period 2004 through 2078. Moreover, because the combined OASDI Trust Funds are projected to be rising as a percentage of the annual cost of the program at the end of 75 years, the plan would be expected to restore *sustainable solvency* for the program, that is, the program would be expected to be financially solvent for the foreseeable future. . . .

The plan provides for a modification of the basic benefit formula except for the lowest 30 percent of career-average earners whose basic benefits would be unchanged under the plan. It would provide reductions beginning in 2012 for higher paid workers. The reductions would be smaller for workers at medium career earnings levels and larger for workers at higher career earnings levels, reaching the equivalent of full CPI indexing of the benefit for the very highest earners. Individuals becoming eligible for benefits before 2012 would not be affected by this change in the basic benefit formula.

This plan would establish voluntary, progressive individual accounts starting in 2007 for workers who were under age 55 on January 1, 2005 and would provide for an offset against Social Security retirement and aged survivor benefits for those who participate. In addition, for those who die before receiving benefits and have no surviving spouses, their estates would receive the balance in their IAs (individual accounts) at death minus an offset that would be paid to the Trust funds to compensate for their earlier allocation of a portion of the payroll taxes to their IAs.

IA assets would be invested through a central administrative authority (CAA) with a required allocation of 60 percent in broad indexed equity funds, 24 percent in broad indexed corporate bond funds, and 16 percent in a long-term Treasury bond fund. CPI-indexed life annuities would be available for purchase the CAA with IA accumulations at the time of retirement. IA contributions would be redirected from the OASDI Trust Fund. The ability of the Social Security Trust funds to meet benefit obligations would be maintained through transfers from the General fund of the Treasury when needed; such transfers are expected to be needed for years 2030 through 2072.

Plan Specifications

Basic Benefit Provision: Progressive CPI-Indexing

The primary insurance amount (PIA) formula used for the computation of all monthly benefits under the OASDI program would be changed starting for those becoming eligible for benefits in 2012. . . .

This proposal would replicate benefit reductions for the very highest career-average earners who that are provided under a CPI-indexed benefit formula. Benefit levels would be reduced to a lesser extent for workers with lower career-average earnings [A 32-year-old worker earning $47,000 in 2012 would be eligible for annual benefits of $16,417 under this proposal rather than $19,544 as the system now stands. — Eds.], with no reduction for those at or below the 30th percentile of career-average earnings. The career average annual indexed earnings level used for Social Security benefit purposes is estimated to be about $25,000 at the 30th percentile for retirees becoming eligible for benefits in 2012.

Individual Accounts

Starting in 2007, all workers who were under 55 on January 1, 2005 will have the option to enroll in the individual account plan. Enrollees with earnings in OASDI covered employment will have a portion of the payroll tax contribution (12.4 percent of taxable earnings in total) redirected from the OASDI Trust Fund to an individual account. The percentage of taxable earnings to be redirected in 2007 will be 2 percent of the worker's OASDI taxable earnings, up to a maximum IA contribution of $3,000.

Under the plan, IA assets, once allocated on an individual basis, would be automatically invested in the required portfolio through a central administrative authority that would maintain all records of individual transactions and balances. . . . The central administrative authority would group the assets of all participating individuals for the purpose of transactions with private investment firms.

Social Security Administration Memorandum
Estimated OASDI Financial Effects for a Proposal with Six Provisions that would Improve Social Security Financing
http://www.ssa.gov/OACT/solvency/index.html

Date: April 14, 2005
To: Robert M. Ball, Commissioner of Social Security from April 1962 to March 1973
From: Stephen C. Goss, Chief Actuary

* * *

The combined effect of the six provisions is expected to eliminate the 75-year long-range actuarial deficit for the OASDI program and leave a significant positive actuarial balance of about 0.65 percent of taxable payroll using the expected equity yield. The ratio of trust fund assets to annual program cost (TFR) is projected to rise consistently throughout the 75-year period. However, the growth in the TFR slows toward the end of the period and annual deficits are gradually increasing, so that some additional "maintenance" of the provisions would eventually be needed after the 75-year period to maintain sustainable solvency. The proposal in fact recommends such further changes in the form of the balancing tax rate. Even in the absence of such maintenance, the Social Security program would be expected to be solvent for several decades beyond the end of the 75-year period.

With the low-yield assumption for equities, the OASDI program would still be projected to be solvent for the 75-year long-range period, but would require larger balancing tax rate increases to achieve sustainable solvency.

Descriptions of Six Provisions

1. Increase the OASDI contribution and benefit base by an additional 2 percent (beyond wage indexing) for years 2006 through 2043. This change is projected to result in 90 percent of OASDI covered earnings being taxable for 2043 and later. About 6 percent of covered workers have earnings above the current-law taxable maximum each year, and would thus be affected by this provision. This provision alone would reduce the OASDI actuarial deficit by an estimated 0.61 percent of payroll.

2. Require that a federal tax be imposed on the value of all estates with assets in excess of $3.5 million for deaths in 2010 and later. The tax would be 45 percent of any assets in excess of $3.5 million, and the tax revenue would be credited entirely to the OASI and DI trust funds. The $3.5 million dollar exemption would be fixed (not indexed) for years after 2010. The levels of the estate tax rate and exemption are equal to those provided in current law for 2009. Under current law, the estate tax would be repealed for 2010, but would be restored with a lower exemption and a higher rate than in effect for 2009. Thus, this provision would effectively redirect a substantial portion of the revenue from the estate tax for years 2011 and later from the general fund of the Treasury to the Social Security trust funds. This provision is projected to reduce the long-range actuarial deficit of the OASDI program by an estimated 0.51 percent of taxable payroll.

3. Gradually invest 20 percent of the OASDI program trust fund assets in equities. In 2006, invest 1 percent of trust fund assets in a broad based indexed fund representing all equities for corporations based in the United States, such as the Wilshire 5000. In each subsequent year, the percentage of trust fund assets invested in equities would be increased by 1 percentage point, until 20 percent of assets are invested in equities, by the end of 2025. This percentage would be maintained thereafter by periodic rebalancing of assets between equities and special obligations of the Treasury. In no case, however, would the trust funds be allowed to hold more than 15 percent of the total value of all equities represented in the broad index.

Subtotal for Provisions 1 through 3 — The combined effect of provisions 1 through 3 would reduce the long-range OASDI actuarial deficit from 1.89 percent of payroll by 1.47 percent to a deficit of 0.41 percent of payroll. The resulting actuarial deficit would be less than 5 percent of the long-range summarized cost rate and so the program would meet the test of long-range close actuarial balance with just these provisions.

4. Effective December 2006, base the OASDI COLA on a new CPI-W series that would reflect a superlative formula, of the type currently used for the new "chained" CCPI-U. This provision is assumed to reduce the OASDI annual COLA by an average of 0.22 percentage point. This provision alone would reduce the OASDI actuarial deficit by an estimated 0.35 percent of payroll.

5. Cover under the OASDI program the earnings of all State and local government employees hired in 2009 and later. This provision alone would reduce the OASDI actuarial deficit by an estimated 0.19 percent of payroll.

Subtotal for Provisions 1 through 5 — The combined effect of provisions 1 through 5 would improve the long-range OASDI actuarial balance by 1.94 percent of payroll resulting in an estimated positive actuarial balance of 0.05 percent of payroll.

6. Provide for a "balancing tax rate" increase to be effective starting in the first year for which the OASDI combined trust fund ratio (TFR) would otherwise begin to decline under projections reflecting the 5 provisions above, based in the intermediate assumptions of the 2004 Trustees Report. The size of the balancing tax rate increase would be set sufficient to provide for an increasing TFR throughout the 75-year projection period ending with 2078. As shown in table 1, a balancing tax rate increase of 0.5 percent for employers and employees, each, (1 percent for self-employment earnings) would be applied starting in 2023 based on this specification. The incremental effect of this provision on the long-range actuarial balance is projected to be an increase of 0.60 percent of payroll. The proposal would also include a recommendation to future Congresses to adjust the balancing tax rate increase in subsequent years, if needed to continue to maintain a stable or rising TFR.

Total for Provisions 1 through 6 — The combined effect of all 6 provisions would be to improve the long-range actuarial balance of the OASDI program by 2.54 percent of payroll to a positive actuarial balance of about 0.65 percent of taxable payroll with expected returns on equities. With a low-yield assumption for equities, equivalent to a risk-adjusted return equal to that assumed for long-term Treasury bonds, the long-range actuarial balance would be expected to be improved by 2.23 percent of payroll to a positive balance of 0.35 percent of payroll.

Conclusion

The six-provision proposal is expected to restore solvency for the Social Security program through the next 75 years and for decades thereafter. With the expected equity yields and the specified balancing tax rate increase, trust fund ratios are projected to rise throughout the 75-year period. However, to maintain sustainable solvency, and thus solvency for the foreseeable future, some maintenance of the balancing tax rate is expected to be needed after the end of the 75-year projection period, as recommended in the proposal.

QUESTIONS

1. Of the possible solutions to "fixing" Social Security — reducing benefits to workers or their dependents, increasing full retirement age, increasing maximum taxable wages, increasing the percentage contributed by workers and employers, creating individual investment accounts for each worker, investing

the Social Security trust fund partially or wholly in the stock market — or some combination, what approach would you support? Why?

2. What is "progressive" about the proposal outlined in the Pozen memo? Does it represent a benefit cut? A tax increase?

3. Should individual accounts have statutory anti-alienation protection?

2. Supplemental Security Income

SSI is a federal welfare program that provides monthly cash payments to needy aged, blind, and disabled persons in accordance with uniform, nationwide eligibility requirements. One of the largest cash assistance programs for low income individuals, SSI is a means-tested, federally administered program that was established in October of 1972 and began making payments in January of 1974. The SSI program provides "flat grants" based on a uniform federal income support level. In addition to the federal SSI payment, both a mandatory and an optional state supplementation were authorized for SSI.

Social Security benefits are the single highest source of income for SSI recipients. The SSI program was envisioned as a guaranteed minimum income for the aged, blind, and disabled which would supplement the Social Security Program. An income-related program, SSI provides for those who were not covered under Social Security or who had earned only minimal entitlement under the program. In other words, the program was intended to build on the Social Security program as a basic national income maintenance system for the aged, blind and disabled.

Two-thirds of the SSI recipients over age 62 also receive Social Security benefits. The SSI program is funded by general revenues of the U.S. Treasury, while Social Security benefits are funded by the Social Security taxes paid by workers, employers, and self-employed persons. The federal SSI benefits are indexed to the Consumer Price Index (CPI) and by the same percentage as Social Security benefits.

Basic SSI Eligibility Requirements

Eligibility requirements for SSI benefits are stringent. To be eligible, an individual must be at least age 65, blind or disabled, a United States citizen or an eligible noncitizen, and reside in the United States. An individual also must meet income and resource limits. These statutory limits ensure that SSI benefits are targeted toward the neediest among the aged, blind, and disabled.

Social Security Administration field office employees determine whether an individual (aged, blind, or disabled) meets the SSI nonmedical eligibility requirements. An individual cannot be eligible for federal SSI benefits if he or she had countable income of more than the [2007 federal benefits rate of $623 a month ($934 for a couple)]. The monthly benefit rate is reduced dollar for dollar by the amount of the individual's countable income. SSI law defines two kinds of countable income: earned and unearned. Earned income is generally wages, net income from self-employment, and remuneration for work in a sheltered workshop. All other income, such as Social Security benefits, workers' compensation, or income received in kind (that is, food, clothing, or shelter-related items), is defined as "unearned."

The countable resources of an individual cannot exceed $2,000 or, in the case of an individual and spouse, $3,000. SSI regulations define a resource as cash or other liquid assets or any real or personal property that an individual (or spouse) owns and could convert to cash to be used for his or her basic needs.

The amount of a person's income is used to determine both eligibility for, and the amount of, that person's benefit. In certain situations, other people (for example, parents of minor children or spouses) are expected to share financial responsibility for the individual in determining the person's eligibility and payment amount.

Individuals' monthly SSI benefit amounts are also affected by their living arrangements. For example, when individuals move into nursing homes and their expected stay is for more than 3 full months, their benefits are generally reduced to not more than $30 per month. Generally, benefits also are reduced when individuals live in the household of another person and that person provides food, shelter, or both.

Eligibility for SSI benefits based on disability requires that an individual be unable to engage in substantial gainful activity because of an impairment that is expected to last at least 12 months or to result in death. After an individual becomes eligible for disability benefits, SSA periodically conducts continuing disability reviews to determine whether a beneficiary has medically improved and is, therefore, no longer eligible for benefits. While nonmedical eligibility and payment amount determinations are made at the time an initial application is filed, SSA field office staff also conduct periodic reviews, called redeterminations, to determine whether the beneficiary remains eligible and whether the benefit amount is correct.

Social Security Administration
Social Security Program Rules
20 C.F.R. Part 416 [Regulation No. 16]
March 9, 2005

Determining Income and Resources under the Supplemental Security Income (SSI) Program

* * *

Background

The basic purpose of the SSI program (title XVI of the Social Security Act (the Act)) is to ensure a minimum level of income to people who are age 65 or older, or blind or disabled, and who have limited income and resources. The law provides that payments can be made only to people who have income and resources below specified amounts. Therefore, the amount of income and resources a person has is a major factor in deciding whether the person can receive SSI benefits and in computing the amount of the benefits.

The Government Accountability Office (GAO) has reported that annual costs to the Federal Government for administering means-tested Federal programs are significant and that eligibility determination activities make up a substantial portion of these costs. In particular, the GAO cited the variations and complexity of Federal financial eligibility rules as contributing to processes that are often duplicative and cumbersome for staff workers (including state and local caseworkers) and for those who apply for assistance. In order to streamline our eligibility determination process, as well as make our financial eligibility rules more consistent with those of other means-tested Federal programs, we are making the following changes to our rules on determining income and resources under the SSI program.

Explanation of Changes

A. Elimination of Clothing from the Definitions of Income and In-Kind Support and Maintenance.

Section 1612 of the Act defines income as both earned income and unearned income, including support and maintenance furnished in cash or in kind. Under our current rules, income may include anything you receive in cash or in kind that you can use to meet your needs for food, clothing, and shelter. Both earned income and unearned income can include items received in kind. Generally, we value in-kind items at their current market value. However, we have special rules for valuing food, clothing, or shelter that is received as unearned income.

In-kind support and maintenance is unearned income in the form of food, clothing, or shelter that is given to a person or that the person receives because someone else pays for it. Section 1612(a)(2)(A) of the Act provides that if an eligible individual receives in-kind support and maintenance, his or her SSI payment may be reduced by up to one-third of the monthly Federal benefit rate. To determine whether the one-third reduction applies, we must ask claimants and beneficiaries a lengthy series of questions about their living arrangements and household expenses. We also must obtain similar information from the homeowner or head of the household, who often is not a claimant or recipient.

The complexity of the rules for valuing in-kind support and maintenance results in reporting requirements that are difficult for the public to understand and follow. We are, therefore, simplifying the SSI program by eliminating clothing from the definition of income and from the definition of in-kind support and maintenance. Clothing is one of the basic sustenance needs, along with food and shelter. However, unlike food and shelter, clothing generally is not received every month. Items of clothing are more likely to be received infrequently and sporadically, and they generally have no substantial financial value. In addition, our attempts to discover and assign a value to gifts of clothing are not only administratively burdensome, but have been viewed as harsh and demeaning and as providing a disincentive for family members to help needy relatives.

After 30 years of administering the SSI program, our experience shows that clothing received as in-kind support and maintenance rarely affects an individual's eligibility for SSI or the amount of benefits. Thus, questioning individuals about items as personal as basic clothing may be seen as intrusive without achieving any substantial program goal or enhancing program integrity.

We are making this change to simplify our rules and improve our work efficiency. This change will make our rules less intrusive and more protective of the dignity and privacy of claimants and beneficiaries, and will not significantly increase SSI program costs. . . . Counting gifts of clothing puts a negative face on the SSI program without advancing any substantial program goal and incurs administrative costs.

B. Exclusion of Household Goods and Personal Effects.

Section 1613(a)(2)(A) of the Act provides that in determining the resources of an individual (and eligible spouse, if any), SSA will exclude household goods and personal effects to the extent that their total value does not exceed an amount that the Commissioner decides is reasonable. In interpreting "reasonable" value of household goods and personal effects, Sec. 416.1216(b) of our regulations provides for an exclusion of up to $2,000 of the total equity value. The amount in excess of $2,000 is counted against the resource limit, currently $2,000 for an individual and $3,000 for an individual and spouse.

Section 416.1216(a) defines household goods as including household furniture, furnishings, and equipment that are commonly found in or about a house and used in connection with the operation, maintenance, and occupancy of the home. Also included are furniture, furnishings, and equipment used in the functions and activities of home and family life as well as those items that are for comfort and accommodation. This section specifically defines personal effects as including clothing, jewelry, items of personal care, and individual educational and recreational items. In addition, Sec. 416.1216(c) provides specific exclusions for a wedding ring, an engagement ring, and equipment required because of a person's physical condition.

To determine the equity value of household goods and personal effects, we ask the person for a list of household and personal items, the value of each, and what the individual owes on each. This process can be complex, difficult for the public to understand, and unduly intrusive into personal affairs.

We are amending these rules as part of our efforts to simplify the SSI program. We are amending our regulations for household goods and personal effects by eliminating the dollar value limit and by excluding from countable resources all:

> Household goods if they are items of personal property, found in or near a home, that are used on a regular basis, or items needed by the householder for maintenance, use and occupancy of the premises as a home; and Personal effects if they are items of personal property that ordinarily are worn or carried by the individual, or are articles that otherwise have an intimate relation to the individual. Thus, we will interpret the word "reasonable" in section 1613(a)(2)(A) of the Act in terms other than a specific dollar limit. The reasonable value will instead be based on the uses and characteristics of the item. Our current rules on household goods and personal effects reflect our view that it is reasonable to totally exclude certain items of personal property because they are rarely of significant value or are intimately related to the individual and his or her particular needs. Accordingly, we have

determined that requiring conversion of such items for subsistence needs is unreasonable.

Currently, Sec. 416.1216(c) provides for totally excluding a wedding ring and an engagement ring, and household goods and personal effects required because of a person's physical condition. We are expanding this approach generally to household goods and personal effects so that they may be totally excluded from resources because our experience in 30 years of administering the SSI program shows that these items almost never have any substantial value, particularly once they are used.

These rules amend Sec. 416.1216 to define and identify household goods and personal effects that we will not count as resources. Included in the list of excluded personal effects are items of cultural or religious significance since these items have an intimate relationship to an individual. The list of exclusions also includes items required due to an individual's impairment. This will allow for exclusion of items required because of any impairment, not just physical impairments. For example, our experience has shown that children and adults with learning disabilities use personal computers to assist them with schoolwork and other daily activities. This change will allow us to exclude items such as personal computers from countable resources.

We are also amending Sec. 416.1210(b) by referring to Sec. 416.1216 for the definition of household goods and personal effects that we will not count as resources.

While simplifying the SSI program, our changes continue to recognize that individuals applying for SSI may own items for investment purposes which may be quite valuable. Such items as gems, jewelry that is not worn or held for family significance, and collectibles will still be considered countable resources and subject to the limits in Sec. 416.1205. Thus, the exclusion for household goods and personal effects will not apply to such items that have investment value. Our experience in administering the SSI program suggests that the change we are making will affect the eligibility of only a few applicants and recipients. However, this change will simplify our rules and improve our work efficiency without significantly increasing program costs. It will make our rules less intrusive and more protective of the dignity of applicants and recipients. This intrusion into the privacy of a person's home unnecessarily puts a negative face on the SSI program without achieving any corresponding gain in program integrity or payment accuracy. It also will more accurately reflect the reality that all SSI applicants and recipients need household goods and personal effects to perform activities of daily living and maintain quality of life. Accordingly, we believe it would be unreasonable to require applicants and recipients to convert these items to cash in order to meet their subsistence needs. The resale value of typical household items is minimal after the item has been used. Although it could be expensive to replace certain household items, these items would be worth very little if the individual tried to resell them to get cash for subsistence needs.

C. Exclusion of an Automobile From Resources.

Section 1613(a)(2)(A) of the Act provides that, in determining the resources of an individual (and eligible spouse, if any) for SSI purposes, SSA will exclude an automobile to the extent that its value does not exceed an amount that the Commissioner of Social Security decides is reasonable. Current regulations at Sec. 416.1218 define an "automobile" as a passenger car or other vehicle used to provide necessary transportation.

In interpreting "reasonable" value, Sec. 416.1218(b)(1) provides that an automobile is totally excluded regardless of value if it meets any of the four following criteria:

- It is necessary for employment;

- It is necessary for the medical treatment of a specific or regular medical problem; it is modified for a handicapped person; or

- It is necessary because of certain factors to perform essential daily activities.

- If no automobile can be excluded based on its use, one automobile is excluded to the extent its current market value does not exceed $4,500.

See Sec. 416.1218(b)(2). Additional automobiles are counted as non-liquid resources to the extent of their equity value. *See* Sec. 416.1218(b)(3).

We are amending our rules to exclude one automobile from resources regardless of its value if it is used for transportation for the individual or a member of the individual's household. We are doing so because our data establish that the vast majority of "first" automobiles owned by SSI recipients are currently excluded based on one of the four transportation criteria set out in Sec. 416.1218(b)(1). In addition, there is no indication that the automobiles which are not covered by the special circumstances represent significant resources. Based on quality assurance data for 1998, in approximately 98 percent of those SSI cases involving automobile ownership, the value of one car was completely excluded. . . .

The change will have a negligible effect on program costs and will simplify administration of the exclusion. It will eliminate the need for SSA claims representatives to ask the SSI recipient if his/her vehicle meets one of the four specific exclusion criteria or otherwise determine the value of the vehicle.

3. Veterans Compensation and Pension

The Department of Veterans Affairs (VA) administers billions of dollars annually in federal benefits for military veterans and their dependents. When eligible dependents and survivors are included, about one-third of the nation is eligible for benefits and services from VA. Annual Compensation and Pension payments for 2005 topped $32 billion and are expected to peak at about $67 billion in 2035.

Department of Veterans Affairs
Annual Benefits Report, Fiscal 2004
(June 2005)
http://www.vba.va.gov/bln/dmo/reports/fy2004/2004_abr.pdf

Compensation Based Upon Service-Connected Disability or Death

Disability Compensation is a monetary benefit paid to veterans with service-connected disabilities. "Service-connected" means that the disability was the result of a disease or injury incurred or aggravated during active military service. To be eligible for disability compensation, the veteran must have been discharged under conditions other than dishonorable and the disability must not have resulted from the veteran's misconduct. Only veterans (not dependents, survivors, or others) are eligible to receive VA disability compensation.

Disability compensation is graduated according to the degree of the veteran's disability on a scale from 0 percent disabling to 100 percent disabling, in increments of 10 percent. (38 CFR, Part 4) Benefits in addition to the 100 percent disability rate are payable to veterans with extremely severe disabilities. For example, the Rating Schedule provides four possible evaluations for the disabling effect of a disfiguring scar or the head, face, or neck: 0, 10, 30, or 50 percent, according to the extent of the disfigurement. Active pulmonary tuberculosis, on the other hand, is always rated 100 percent disabling. Multiple disabilities will result in a combined degree of disability for purposes of compensation payments.

Dependency and Indemnity Compensation (DIC) is a monetary benefit for survivors of certain deceased veterans or service members. The benefit is payable to surviving spouses, children, and/or dependent parents of:

Service members who die during military service of causes that are not due to the person's willful misconduct

Veterans who die of a service-connected disease or injury;

Veterans who die from a nonservice-connected disability but who were continuously rated 100 percent disabled for service-connected disabilities for at least 10 years immediately preceding death (or at least five years from the date of discharge to the date of death); and

Veterans who are former POWs who die after September 30, 1999, and were continuously rated 100 percent for service-connected disabilities for a period of not less than one year immediately preceding death.

Pension Based Upon Non Service-Connected Disability or Death and Financial Need

VA pension programs provide a minimum level of economic security to non service-connected disabled wartime veterans, as well as survivors or wartime veterans. These programs are means tested and serve veterans and survivors who are experiencing financial hardship. The total family income from sources other than VA determines the amount of pension payable to the beneficiary. Law established income limits and benefits rates for these programs.

a. Eligibility

Department of Veterans Affairs
Federal Benefits for Veterans and Dependents (1996)

Veterans may be eligible for support if they have limited income when they have 90 days or more of active military service, at least one day of which was during a period of war. Their discharge from active duty must have been under conditions other than dishonorable. They must be permanently and totally disabled for reasons traceable neither to military service nor to willful misconduct. Payments are made to qualified veterans to bring their total income, including other retirement or Social Security income, to an established support level [$1,003/mo. without dependents in 2006 — Eds]. Countable income may be reduced by unreimbursed medical expenses. Pension is not payable to those who have assets that can be used to provide adequate maintenance. . . .

b. Dependent benefits

Surviving spouses and unmarried children of deceased veterans with wartime service may be eligible for a nonservice-connected pension based on need. Children must be under age 18, or up to age 23 if attending a VA-approved school. Pension is not payable to those with estates large enough to provide maintenance. The veteran must have been discharged under conditions other than dishonorable and must have had 90 days or more of active military service, at least on day of which was during a period of war, or a service-connected disability justifying discharge for disability. If the veteran died in service not in line of duty, benefits may be payable if the veteran had completed at least two years of honorable service. Children who became incapable of self-support because of a disability before age 18 may be eligible for a pension as long as the condition exists, unless the child marries or the child's income exceeds the applicable limit. A surviving spouse who is a patient in a nursing home, is in need of regular aid and attendance of another person or is permanently housebound may be entitled to higher income limitations or additional benefits.

QUESTIONS

1. What is the difference between Veteran's Administration "compensation" and a VA "pension"?

2. What features distinguish the VA pension system from Social Security's OASDI benefits? In what ways is the VA pension system more like SSI?

B. EMPLOYER-BASED PENSION PLANS

1. A Brief History of Pensions and Pension Regulation

Patricia E. Dilley
The Evolution of Entitlement: Retirement Income and the Problem of Integrating Private Pensions and Social Security
30 LOYOLA L.A. L. REV. 1063, 1085, 1087-88, 1112, 1113-19, 1137 (1997)[*]

Retirement — the extended period of leisure after the end of a working life expected by most workers in the late twentieth century — is a recent phenomenon. While every human culture has some experience of supporting older members who live past the age of productive labor, it was not until widespread industrialization and the development of industrial-laboring and middle classes in Europe and the United States in the twentieth century that retirement became a relatively common occurrence. . . .

The notion of retirement necessarily rests on the ability of an economy to produce enough surplus wealth to support older nonworkers. In agrarian societies generally up until the mid-to-late nineteenth century, advancing age was not automatically associated with cessation of work, which occurred only if and when actual physical incapacity set in. The pattern of frequent famine and plagues that characterized Europe from the thirteenth through eighteenth centuries probably ensured that few of the poor survived to great ages; life past age sixty was largely reserved for the well-off bourgeoisie and the nobility who guaranteed comfort in old age through continued control of their wealth and families. In the absence of such accumulated wealth, the incapacity brought on by advancing age necessitated dependency on family, church, or local organized poor relief.

* * *

Private pensions have never been the principal or even major source of income in old age for United States workers. Nonetheless, limited pension and profit sharing plans existed in the United States long before the federal retirement program [known as Social Security] was pushed through the New Deal Congress in 1935. Employer-sponsored group savings plans, and eventually pension plans, seem to have been an outgrowth of the "private social welfare" efforts begun in the late-nineteenth century by American businesses as employers began to perceive the advantages of pension trusts and stock purchase plans, first as a source of capital and later as a way of easing their older and more highly paid employees off the payroll. . . .

Private employers in the United States began establishing annuity pension plans for their employees late in the nineteenth century, years before the enact-

---

[*] Copyright © 1997. Reprinted with permission.

ment of the federal income tax and the possibility of sheltering income from tax through deferring compensation. The first United States pension plan appears to have been established by the American Express Company in 1875 when American Express was principally associated with the railroad industry. The plan was not a true retirement plan, but rather paid benefits to disabled employees who had twenty years of service with the company, had reached age sixty, and were recommended for the pension by company management.

This type of plan was put into place by many United States and Canadian railroads in the years following 1875, but those plans seem to have been more a response to the occupational hazards presented by railroad employment than an anticipation of retirement pensions. However, most developed into straight retirement plans during the 1900 to 1930 period when the greatest number of industrial pension plans were established. The most widely accepted estimate of pension plans and participation is that between 1875 and 1929 around 400 industrial pension plans were established, with about that number still in operation on the eve of the Depression.

The companies establishing these plans employed about 10% of the industrial labor force — a force substantially less than the entire work force including agricultural and casual labor. It is not clear, however, how many of those employees were eligible to participate in the plan or would eventually qualify for benefits. According to a recent estimate, although industrial pensions were not uncommon by 1935, no more than 4% of male workers and 3% of female workers met the requirements for receipt of pensions at that time. . . .

Most early pension plans were noncontributory. That is, the plans were financed completely by the employer who generally interpreted the obligation to pay benefits as voluntary. Perhaps the earliest case exploring the nature of the promise made to the employee in an industrial pension plan was *McNevin v. Solvay Process Company* [1898, *affirmed* 1901] in which the court analyzed pensions on the theory that they were a gift from employer to employee. In that case the ruling turned on the authority of the company's directors to refuse to pay a pension claim under the plan. Since the pension payment itself was viewed as a gratuity, there was no automatic obligation to pay even though an amount was "credited" under the employee's name in the bookkeeping for the plan.

The "gratuity" theory of pensions matched employers' views of their obligations under pension plans at least until after the inception of the income tax — the plans were written to be strictly discretionary, with payments made out of current income and usually no advance funding for future obligations. Another early case decided a year or two after *Solvay Process* reinforced the gratuity theory by holding that the employer had created no implication of employee vesting in amounts credited under employee names and that upon the bankruptcy of the employer, the employees had no rights as creditors. Even though these cases found no legal entitlement and no employee vesting in the absence of a plan provision specifically providing for it, employers nevertheless stopped the practice of crediting amounts to employee bookkeeping accounts for fear of creating any possible admission of liability under the pension plan.

While the gratuity theory was cited by the courts well into the 1950s, in the 1920s some courts apparently began to uphold employee claims on noncontributory funds on the grounds that the pension was part of a contractual agreement between employer and employee, not simply a gift. Perhaps as a result, employers began to cut back on noncontributory plans: "After 1923, new pension plans were overwhelmingly contributory and insured, and many employers pared back their programs or simply stopped notifying workers or their dependents of pension eligibility.". . . .

The modest expansion of employer-sponsored pension plans from 1900 into the 1920s coincided with increasing use of labor management practices designed to limit employee turnover and fend off union organization. Unions in general opposed establishment of employer-provided plans. They viewed the plans as an interference with bargaining rights although they occasionally set up their own benefit plans, frequently covering sickness, disability, and unemployment, and less frequently old age, payable only if sufficient funds were available.

Employers saw pension plans as a means to an end: workers would trade a pay increase or right to strike for the promise of a pension. Moreover, pensions could be used to "purge the payroll" of older workers who were probably more highly paid and had begun to be perceived as less productive. Since the pension promise itself was so tenuous and required no current funding or payment of benefits except to those who retired immediately after a plan was established with benefits substantially lower than their salaries had been, current employment costs theoretically could be reduced along with turnover of valued employees. . . . .

The very modest use of employer-provided pensions coincided with other labor management practices such as seniority, a fact that both aided and impeded older workers. Workers who "caught on" with a company when they were relatively young could benefit from seniority practices that gave preference in salary and job protection to longer-service workers. Henry Ford's innovation of the wage ladder, an artificial hierarchy of pay based on length of service that encouraged workers to stay with the company, was just one example of the many kinds of employee benefits, including pensions, that were increasingly tied to longevity after 1900. The seniority system probably worked to the disadvantage of those older workers attempting to find new employment in middle age, since they could not offer a long period of service and high youthful productivity, characteristics that seniority and benefit plans were developed to encourage.

The concept of mandatory retirement took hold in American business during this period as well, particularly in industries such as the railroads, which had already established employer-provided pensions and organized their compensation and benefits around longevity of employment. In 1900 the Pennsylvania Railroad established a maximum hiring age of thirty-five and retirement age of seventy, with a company pension, as a way of controlling the costs of expensive older workers while at the same time reducing employee turnover.

Of course, pension promises that appear quite inexpensive when made often turn out to be much more expensive when they actually have to be fulfilled.

While employers limited the likelihood of eligibility for pensions with long service requirements and requirements that the worker be employed at the time of disability or retirement, pension liabilities still became a major cost issue for employers in the late 1920s. . . .

Many employers in the 1920s attempted to mitigate the impact of these rising costs by insuring their pension liabilities, but even the insurers began to be alarmed by the size of future costs. . . .

Thus, even before the advent of the deep economic crisis in the 1930s, companies were attempting to retrench on retirement commitments they had already made. Some larger employers, perhaps recognizing the link between [sic] seniority, employee management, and retirement income, began to support calls for federalization of retirement programs. Most businesses, however, resisted any suggestion of federal intervention and instead continued to cut back on plan promises.

This brief history reveals the limited aspirations of employer-sponsored private pension plans in the pre-World War II era. The goal of most employers was control of their labor forces, not retirement income security. Funded plans were seen as vehicles for capital formation, not income replacement in old age. The continuing pressure from workers for pension plans, and their willingness to accept an extremely insecure pension promise as a tradeoff for current wages, reflects the general insecurity created by industrialization and dislocation of traditional trade occupations. Nonetheless, private pension plans, which were almost always unfunded and benefited almost exclusively long-term — thirty years or more in many cases — high-wage workers, could not be expected to, and did not, underwrite mass retirement. . . .

* * *

Of particular importance to the coordination of Social Security with private pensions is the rejection in 1935 and later of suggestions that workers covered by a private pension should be excluded from Social Security. The original proposal was to cover all manual and non-manual laborers earning less than $250 per month, with the exception of government and railroad employees who had fairly complete retirement plans already in place. Private employer-provided pensions were not viewed as the equivalent of federal civil service or railroad pensions, and with good reason. Both of the latter systems had more or less government-guaranteed sources of financing, and workers with long service were virtually assured of receiving their pensions. Private plans, on the other hand, were few in number, and many, if not most, had failed or gone bankrupt during the economic collapse earlier in the decade; private plans could not be considered any sort of alternative to a government-sponsored plan.

W. Greenough & F. King
PENSION PLANS AND PUBLIC POLICY 38-44, 59-63, 66-67
(1976)[*]

As noted earlier, the railroads were among the first of the industrial employers to establish pension plans, starting with the B&O and the Pennsylvania. This was consistent with the fact that the early pension plans tended to appear in the more prosperous industries and the larger concerns, among which were the railroads — new, growing, and able to attract massive amounts of capital. . . .

The later decline of the railroads illustrates the problems pension plans encounter if they have not made sound financial arrangements to back up their pension promises. Until the late 1920s the railroads continued to flourish and to represent attractive employment opportunities. Beginning with the Great Depression, railroad revenues declined sharply and at the same time the number of railroad workers expecting to be retired because of age or years of service was increasing. . . .

With virtually no pension reserves established to meet pension liabilities, and with many of the roads operating in the red in the late 1920s and early '30s, companies resorted to various expediencies to ease the financial pressures. . . .

These emergency measures were not enough. Without sufficient pension reserves, with a declining capacity to sustain a pay-as-you-go retirement system amidst the economic shambles of the Great Depression, and with growing competition from the trucking industry, the railroads' benevolent and optimistic pension promises were turning into a financial monster. . . .

There was little prospect that the troubled railroads could make good on their pension promises for the quarter-million older employees due to retire within three or four years. Strong pressure developed for some kind of legislative action to bail the railroads out. . . .

The federal government responded with a plan to take over and administer the pension promises of the railroads. The government approach was to inject substantial federal appropriations to cover immediate obligations, and for the future to develop a plan incorporating employee and employer contributions under a federally run plan. . . . The system now operates something along the lines of Social Security and functions as a substitute Social Security system for railroad employees. . . .

. . . .Unfortunately, the catastrophic failure of the railroads' pension plans did not at the time lead to any movement for pension reform.

* * *

While the larger industrial employers were establishing their pension plans in the early years of the 20th century, the trade unions, independently of employers, were attempting their own programs of member benefits. . . .

The first union plan to provide for periodic old-age payments, as distinct from lump-sum or periodic benefits for permanent disability, was established by the Patternmakers in 1900. The plan was not funded and depended on the union treasury. The first plan with a degree of funding for old-age payments was established in 1905 by the Granitecutters. . . .

The first union plan offering old-age benefits as a matter of right rather than as gratuities was established by the Brotherhood of Locomotive Engineers in 1912. . . .

By 1928, it was estimated that about 40 percent of trade union membership belonged to national unions offering one form or another of old age and permanent and total disability benefits. But the funds for the benefits necessarily had to be derived from assessments on union members. As the numbers of older union members increased, the assessments on all members had to be increased. . . . To increase union dues became more difficult, and within a few years after the Great Depression began almost all of the union welfare plans had collapsed. . . .

The Great Depression seriously shook American confidence in the virtues of individual thrift and in personal savings as a way to prepare for old age. With 13 million people out of work, savings erased, and long-standing traditions of self-reliance undermined, the 1930s were becalmed years for both union welfare plans and employer-sponsored pension plans. In this atmosphere the passage of the Social Security Act of 1935, America's first national social insurance legislation, was virtually inevitable. This was to be the main pension development until after World War II.

* * *

At the close of the 1940s the stage was set for a renewal of union interest in pension plans, not in mutual assistance or fraternal benefits, but in the negotiation of pension plans with employers through collective bargaining. Conditions were ready for the next phase of union welfare activity. The Internal Revenue Act of 1942 had placed the tax treatment of pension plans in a clearer light. . . . Combined with the sharp increases in corporate and excess-profits tax rates of the 1940s, the special tax treatment that was accorded pension plans under the 1942 act enhanced employer receptiveness to union pension demands. . . .

The first struggle of a large union for a negotiated pension plan was that of John L. Lewis and the United Mine Workers of America [in 1945-46]. Although the plan that came out of this struggle had spectacular weaknesses, it focused attention on the question of pensions for union members. . . .

* * *

[Greenough and King then go on to discuss demands for pensions in the steel and automotive industries. It is worth noting that, while the preceding excerpts have focused on the development of pensions in the unionized workplace, pensions also developed over the course of the 20th century in other sectors: for example, for public employees (federal, state, and municipal) and for nonprofit employees, such as professors at private universities. For more details, see Greenough & King at 49-59. — Eds.]

* * *

Federal regulation of private pension plans dates from the early 1920s in an amalgam of taxation principles and social principles. The Internal Revenue Code and Treasury regulations have had a considerable influence on private pension plans in the United States, and the evolution of the code as applied to pensions and profit-sharing plans is a significant part of the history of American pension plans.

The 1920s. The first industrial pension plans were usually paid out of current company earnings as a current business expense — a pay-as-you-go basis — but it was not too long before it became evident that at there were advantages in establishing at least some reserves and separate trust or insurance arrangements. By the early 1920s many of the pay-as-you-go plans had been transformed into trusts, although by no means fully funded, and new plans were being initially established as trusts.

Almost immediately a question arose as to the taxability of the income of such trusts and of the status of employer contributions under the relatively new U.S. income tax laws. In 1926, pension trusts created by employers for the exclusive benefit of some or all employees were made exempt from federal income tax. It was also provided that employer contributions to such trusts, and the income therefrom, would not be taxable to the beneficiaries until actually distributed. . . .

The 1942 Revisions. By 1942 it had become apparent that the existing laws and regulations were too simple and needed refinement. Under the earlier legislation, pension trusts on behalf of "some or all employees" . . . had been utilized to develop trusts that included as participants only small groups of officers and favored key employees in the higher income brackets, apparently as a means of tax avoidance (or deferment) for persons in a position to create a trust in the first place. . . .

The new tax code of 1942 brought further into view and placed in statutory form the public policy principle that federal tax laws could and should be used as a means of requirement employers to meet certain expressed standards in voluntarily established private pension plans

. . . . To qualify for the statutory tax treatment of employer contributions . . . under the new code, a plan was required to be: (1) for the exclusive benefit of the employer's employees or their beneficiaries; (2) for the purpose of distributing the corpus and income to the employees; (3) impossible for the employer to use or divert the fund before satisfying the plans' liabilities to the employees and their beneficiaries; and (4) nondiscriminatory as to extent of coverage — a large percentage of regular employees must be eligible to participate, and neither contributions nor benefits were to discriminate in favor of officers, stockholders, or highly compensated employees or supervisory employees.

Amendments to the pension sections of the code between 1942 and 1974 were not fundamental in nature. . . .

The Employee Retirement Income Security Act of 1974. Little significant change took place in U.S. legislation regarding private pension plans in the three decades following the 1942 changes in the Internal Revenue Code. But by the mid-1960s a change in atmosphere could be detected. In 1964, heavy losses in pension expectations were occasioned by a widely publicized shutdown of the South Bend, Indiana, Studebaker Corporation plant. In the same year, Professor Merton C. Bernstein published a comprehensive and influential analysis of private pension plans and their possible future directions. . . . In 1965 a pension policy study group appointed by President Kennedy issued a report . . . offer[ing] numerous recommendations for legislation. . . .

The 1974 Pension Reform Act [known as ERISA] established basic new requirements in virtually every area of pension administration and funding, including rules of participation and eligibility, minimum vesting standards, reporting and disclosure to government and to plan participants, funding standards, actuarial standards, fiduciary conduct, and past service liability amortization rules. It established a Pension Benefit Guaranty Corporation within the Labor Department to protect plan participants through insurance in the event of plan termination. The act's standards are applied to private plans, except for church or church-related plans, but not to public employee plans.

J. Langbein & B. Wolk
PENSION AND EMPLOYEE BENEFIT LAW 92-96 (3d ed. 2000)*

ERISA has been considerably modified since the statute came into force in 1974, and pension taxation has experienced annual legislative tinkering. Following is a list of major post-1974 legislation, with thumbnail sketches of the substance of the changes. . . .

1. *Revenue Act of 1978.* The Act created the SEP-IRA as a pension alternative for small employers. The Act added IRC § 401(k) . . . making employee contributions to employer-sponsored thrift plans tax deferred. . . .

3. *Economic Recovery Tax Act of 1981 (ERTA).* ERTA emphasized tax deferral incentives to promote saving. It increased the contribution ceiling on Keogh plans . . . [and] on IRA accounts . . . and allowed employees already covered by other pension plans to establish IRAs. . . .

6. *Retirement Equity Act of 1984 (REA or REAct).* REAct was meant to address a variety of issues thought to be of special concern to women. ERISA originally allowed a plan to set a minimum age of 25 for plan participation; REAct lowered the age to 21. REAct made the rules for reckoning a break in service more benign, including a protected period for maternity or paternity leave. . . . REAct made express provision for enforcing certain state domestic relations decrees touching pension assets [called qualified domestic relations orders (QDROs)]

. . . REAct introduced mandatory spousal rights in pension plans [known as qualified joint and survivor annuities (QJSAs) and qualified preretirement survivor annuities (QPSAs)].

7. *Consolidated Omnibus Budget Amendment Act of 1985 (COBRA).* COBRA added ERISA Title I, Part 6, requiring that the sponsor of a group health plan make continuation coverage available to certain employees, spouses, ex-spouses, dependents, and others for periods up to three years after coverage might otherwise cease. . . .

8. *Tax Reform Act of 1986 (TRAC).* TRAC reduced the top-bracket rates of personal income taxation from 50 percent to as low as 28 percent, but the 1993 Clinton tax package restored a top bracket of 39 percent. Lower tax brackets reduce the incentive to defer taxation, whether through qualified pension plans or otherwise. TRAC largely repealed the provision of ERTA that allowed persons covered by another pension plan to make tax-deductible contributions to an IRA account. . . .

10. *Age Discrimination in Employment Amendments of 1986.* In 1986, Congress amended the Age Discrimination in Employment Act of 1967 (ADEA) to remove entirely the maximum age limitation applicable to employees protected under the Act. Congress also made it unlawful for employers who maintain defined benefit pension plans to cease an employee's benefit accrual or reducing the rate of such a benefit accrual because of age. Consistent with these, ERISA § 204(b)(1)(H)(i) prohibits a defined benefit pension plan from ceasing benefit accruals because of the attainment of any age. . . .

12. *Americans with Disabilities Act (ADA).* The ADA prevents discrimination against disabled persons in the provision of pension or health insurance benefits.

17. *Small Business Job Protection Act of 1996.* The Act created the savings incentive match plan for employee (SIMPLE), a new type of retirement plan available to small businesses and their employees. . . .

19. *Health Insurance Portability and Accountability Act of 1996 (HIPAA).* HIPAA added ERISA Title I, Part 7, and amended ERISA Title I, Part 6, to impose certain portability requirements upon employer-provided and other health insurance. The legislation limits the application of preexisting condition exclusions to individuals who change jobs.

20. *Mental Health Parity Act of 1996 (MHPA).* Codified as ERISA § 712, the MHPA requires health plans to offer the same annual and lifetime sums for mental health cover that pertain to medical and surgical health benefits.

21. *Defense of Marriage Act of 1996 (DOMA).* For purposes of federal law DOMA defines "marriage" as "a legal union between one man and one woman as husband and wife"; it defines "spouse" as "a person of the opposite sex who is a husband or a wife." After DOMA, pension rights under ERISA that are contingent upon marriage or spousal status are unavailable to same-sex domestic partners unless the plan instrument provides otherwise.

23. *Taxpayer Relief Act of 1997.* The Act created two new types of IRA accounts, education savings accounts and Roth IRAs.[1] Contributions to these accounts are nondeductible. Principal and interest can be withdrawn tax-free from education savings accounts to pay for a child's college or graduate education. Principal and interest can be withdrawn tax-free from a Roth IRA if the account has been open for five years and the taxpayer is age 59½, disabled or deceased, or withdrawing the funds for a first-time home purchase.

Note on More Recent Legislation Affecting Retirement Assets

Among the laws to be added to the previous list are the following:

1. *The Internal Revenue Service Restructuring and Reform Act of 1998.* This Act clarified some of the rules governing IRAs.

2. *The Economic Growth and Tax Relief Reconciliation Act of 2001 (EGTRRA).* Among other things, this Act increased the contributions that can be made to defined-contribution plans and 401(k) plans, increased the benefits that can be paid under defined-benefit plans, increased the contributions that can be made into IRAs, changed the rules governing rollovers, and changed the rules governing the taxation of benefits. It also included a provision that permits employers to add a Roth program to a 401(k) or 403(b) plan.

3. *The Bankruptcy Abuse Prevention and Consumer Protection Act of 2005 (BAPCPA).* Although this law has generally made it more difficult for bankruptcy filers to shield any personal assets, it actually provides enhanced protection for assets held in IRAs.

4. *The Tax Increase Prevention and Reconciliation Act of 2005 (TIPRA).* Starting in 2010, this Act eliminates income limitations on certain IRA conversions.

5. *The Pension Protection Act of 2006 (PPA).* This sprawling bill tightened the rules regarding funding of pension plans in an effort to reduce the incidence of plans going bankrupt. In addition, the Act increased the maximum deduction available to employers and made permanent many of the tax benefits introduced in the EGTRRA. It also permits charitable deductions for distributions from qualified plans directly to eligible charities during 2006 and 2007.

QUESTIONS

1. Why did pensions develop when they did, and not earlier?

2. The history of pensions and pension regulation can be divided into four stages: 19th century origins, slow growth in the early decades of the 20th century, rapid growth in the years after World War II, and the post-1974 "age of ERISA." What characterizes and explains each of these stages?

3. Why are pensions employment-based?

---

[1] Note to students: IRAs will be discussed later in this chapter.

2. Types of Pension Plans

Department of Labor
Types of Retirement Plans
http://www.dol.gov/dol/topic/retirement/typesofplans.htm
(Posted July 22, 2002)

The Employee Retirement Income Security Act (ERISA) covers two types of pension plans: defined benefit plans and defined contribution plans.

A defined benefit plan promises a specified monthly benefit at retirement. The plan may state this promised benefit as an exact dollar amount, such as $100 per month at retirement. Or, more commonly, it may calculate a benefit through a plan formula that considers such factors as salary and service — for example, 1 percent of average salary for the last 5 years of employment for every year of service with an employer. The benefits in most traditional defined benefit plans are protected, within certain limitations, by federal insurance provided through the Pension Benefit Guaranty Corporation (PBGC).

A defined contribution plan, on the other hand, does not promise a specific amount of benefits at retirement. In these plans, the employee or the employer (or both) contribute to the employee's individual account under the plan, sometimes at a set rate, such as 5 percent of earnings annually. These contributions generally are invested on the employee's behalf. The employee will ultimately receive the balance in their account, which is based on contributions plus or minus investment gains or losses. The value of the account will fluctuate due to the changes in the value of the investments. Examples of defined contribution plans include 401(k) plans, 403(b) plans, employee stock ownership plans, and profit-sharing plans.

A Simplified Employee Pension Plan (SEP) is a relatively uncomplicated retirement savings vehicles. A SEP allows employees to make contributions on a tax-favored basis to individual retirement accounts (IRAs) owned by the employees. SEPs are subject to minimal reporting and disclosure requirements. Under a SEP, an employee must set up an IRA to accept the employer's contributions. Employers may no longer set up Salary Reduction SEPs. However, employers are permitted to establish SIMPLE IRA plans with salary reduction contributions. If an employer had a salary reduction SEP, the employer may continue to allow salary reduction contributions to the plan.

A Profit Sharing Plan or Stock Bonus Plan is a defined contribution plan under which the plan may provide, or the employer may determine, annually, how much will be contributed to the plan (out of profits or otherwise). The plan contains a formula for allocating to each participant a portion of each annual contribution. A profit sharing plan or stock bonus plan include a 401(k) plan.

A 401(k) Plan is a defined contribution plan that is a cash or deferred arrangement. Employees can elect to defer receiving a portion of their salary which is instead contributed on their behalf, before taxes, to the 401(k) plan. Sometimes the employer may match these contributions. There are special rules governing the operation of a 401(k) plan. For example, there is a dollar limit on the amount an employee may elect to defer each year. An employer must advise employees of any limits that may apply. Employees who participate in 401(k) plans assume responsibility for their retirement income by contributing part of their salary and, in many instances, by directing their own investments. [Note: section 401(k) applies only to private sector employees. Employees of nonprofit organizations, such as universities, can set up similar plans under section 403(b). — Eds.]

An Employee Stock Ownership Plan (ESOP) is a form of defined contribution plan in which the investments are primarily in employer stock.

A Money Purchase Pension Plan is a plan that requires fixed annual contributions from the employer to the employee's individual account. Because a money purchase pension plan requires these regular contributions, the plan is subject to certain funding and other rules.

A Cash Balance Plan is a defined benefit plan that defines the benefit in terms that are more characteristic of a defined contribution plan. In other words, a cash balance plan defines the promised benefit in terms of a stated account balance. In a typical cash balance plan, a participant's account is credited each year with a "pay credit" (such as 5 percent of compensation from his or her employer) and an "interest credit" (either a fixed rate or a variable rate that is linked to an index such as the one-year treasury bill rate). Increases and decreases in the value of the plan's investments do not directly affect the benefit amounts promised to participants. Thus, the investment risks and rewards on plan assets are borne solely by the employer. When a participant becomes entitled to receive benefits under a cash balance plan, the benefits that are received are defined in terms of an account balance. The benefits in most cash balance plans, as in most traditional defined benefit plans, are protected, within certain limitations, by federal insurance provided through the Pension Benefit Guaranty Corporation (PBGC).

Internal Revenue Service
Retirement Plans FAQs Regarding Designated Roth Accounts
http://www.irs.gov/retirement/article/0,,id=152956,00.html#general

What is a Roth 401(k) or Roth 403(b)? Is it a new type of plan?

No, it is not a new type of plan. Designated Roth contributions are a new type of contribution that can be accepted by new or existing 401(k) or 403(b) plans. This feature is permitted under a Code section added by the **Economic Growth and Tax Relief Reconciliation Act of 2001 (EGTRRA)**, effective for years beginning on or after January 1, 2006. If a plan adopts this feature, employees can designate some or all of their elective contributions as designated Roth contributions, (which are included in gross income) rather than traditional, pre-tax elective contributions. So, starting in 2006, elective contributions come in two types: traditional, pre-tax elective contributions (elective contributions are also referred to as elective deferrals) and designated Roth contributions.

. . .

What is a designated Roth contribution?

A designated Roth contribution is an elective deferral to a section 401(k) or 403(b) plan that has been designated irrevocably by an employee as not excludable from the employee's gross income and to be deposited into a designated Roth account under the plan. Thus, the contribution is treated by the employer as includible in the employee's gross income at the time the employee would have received the amount in cash if the employee had not made the election (hence subject to all applicable wage withholding requirements). Designated Roth contributions are allowed in 401(k) plans and 403(b) plans but not in SARSEPs or SIMPLE IRA plans.

Can I make both pre-tax elective and designated Roth contributions in the same year?

Yes, you can make contributions to both a designated Roth account and a traditional, pre-tax account in the same year in any proportion you choose. However, the combined amount contributed in any one year is limited by the 402(g) limit — $15,000 for 2006 ($15,500 in 2007 plus an additional $5,000 in catch-up contributions if age 50 or older).

Are there any limits as to how much I may contribute to my designated Roth account?

Yes, the combined amount contributed to all designated Roth accounts and traditional, pre-tax accounts in any one year for any individual is limited by the 402(g) limit — $15,000 for 2006 ($15,500 in 2007 plus an additional $5,000 in catch-up contributions if age 50 or older).

. . . .

Must I make the election to make designated Roth contributions at the beginning of the year?

The rules regarding frequency of elections apply in the same manner to both pre-tax elective contributions and designated Roth contributions and must be specified under the plan. Thus, an employee must have an effective opportunity to make (or change) an election to make designated Roth contributions at least once during each plan year. A Roth election must be in place before any money can be placed in a designated Roth account.

Do the same income restrictions that apply to Roth IRAs apply to designated Roth contributions?

No, there are no limits on income in determining if designated Roth contributions can be made. Of course, you have to have salary from which to make any 401(k) or 403(b) deferrals.

Can my employer make matching contributions on my designated Roth contributions? Can the matching contributions be allocated to my designated Roth account?

The employer can make matching contributions on designated Roth contributions. However, only an employee's designated Roth contributions can be allo-

cated to designated Roth accounts. The matching contributions made on accou
of designated Roth contributions must be allocated to a pre-tax account, just
matching contributions on traditional, pre-tax elective contributions are.

John E. Buckley, Bureau of Labor Statistics
Another Retirement Savings Option: Roth 401(k) Plan
http://www.bls.gov/opub/cwc/cm20060221ar01p1.htm
(posted February 22, 2006)

*Comparisons of Roth 401(k), Roth IRA, and traditional
401(k) retirement plans*

Roth 401(k) plan	Roth IRA	Traditional 401(k) plan
Employee contributions are made with *after-tax* dollars.	Same as Roth 401(k) plan.	Employee contributions are made with *before-tax* dollars.
Investment growth accumulates without any tax consequences.	Same as Roth 401(k) plan.	Investment growth is not subject to Federal and most State income taxes until funds are withdrawn.
No income limitation to participate.	Income limits: married couples, $160,000, singles, $110,000 adjusted gross income.	Same as Roth 401(k) plan. No income limitation to participate.
Contribution limited to $15,000 in 2006 ($20,000 for employees 50 or over).	Contribution limited to $4,000 in 2006 ($5,000 for employees 50 or over).	Same as Roth 401(k) plan.
Withdrawals of contributions and investment growth are *not* taxed provided recipient is at least age 59½ and the account is held for at least five years.	Same as Roth 401(k) plan.	Withdrawals of contributions and investment growth *are* subject to Federal and most State income taxes.
Distributions must begin no later than age 70½. (This may change.)	No requirement to start taking distributions.	Same as Roth 401(k) plan.

* * *

[Note: before 1962, self-employed individuals could not participate in qualified pension plans.]

Since 1962, federal policy has encouraged the provision of pensions for the self-employed . . . through the Self-Employed Individuals Tax Retirement Act.

This law created Keogh plans, named for U.S. Rep. Eugene J. Keogh of New York, who sponsored the original legislation. . . .

Keogh plans may be classified as either defined contribution or defined benefit plans.

QUESTIONS

1. Compare the defined-benefit plan offered by the State Teachers Retirement System of Ohio ("STRS") (described at www.strsoh.org/pdfs/arpchart.pdf) with the defined-contribution plan offered by TIAA-CREF (described at http://www.tiaa-cref.org/product_profiles/ras.html). How are benefits calculated under the DB plan of STRS? How are benefits calculated under the DC plan of TIAA-CREF?

2. What are the advantages of defined-benefit plans? What are the advantages of defined-contribution plans?

3. The Changing Balance Between Defined-Benefit and Defined-Contribution Plans

Pension Benefit Guaranty Corporation
An Analysis of Frozen Defined Benefit Plans
http://www.pbgc.gov/docs/frozen_plans_1205.pdf
(December 21, 2005)

Traditional defined benefit pension plans, based on years of service and either final salary or a flat-dollar benefit formula, provide a stable source of retirement income to supplement Social Security. The number of private-sector defined benefit plans reached a peak of 112,000 in the mid-1980s. At that time, about one-third of American workers were covered by defined benefit plans. The number of plans now stands at about 30,000.

In recent years, many employers have chosen not to adopt defined benefit plans, and others have chosen to terminate their existing defined benefit plans. From 1986 to 2004, 101,000 single-employer plans with about 7.5 million participants were terminated. In about 99,000 of these terminations, the plans had enough assets to purchase annuities in the private sector to cover all benefits earned by workers and retirees (a "standard termination"). In the remaining 2,000 cases, companies with underfunded plans shifted their pension liabilities to the PBGC [Pension Benefit Guaranty Corporation].

In contrast to the dramatic reduction in the total number of plans, the total number of participants in PBGC-insured single-employer plans has increased. In 1980, there were about 28 million covered participants; by 2004 this number had increased to about 35 million. However, these numbers mask the downward trend in the defined benefit system because they include not only active workers but also retirees, surviving spouses and separated vested participants. The latter three categories reflect past coverage patterns in defined benefit plans. A better forward-looking measure is the trend in the number of active participants, who continue to accrue benefits. That number is moving downward. In 1985, there were about 22 million active participants in single-employer defined benefit plans. By 2002, the number had declined to 17 million. At the same time, the number of inactive participants has been growing. In 1985, inactive participants accounted for only 28 percent of total participants in single-employer defined benefit plans, a number that has grown to about 50 percent today.

Bureau of Labor Statistics
Employee Benefits in Private Industry
http://www.bls.gov/ncs/ebs/sp/ebsm0002.pdf
(released November 2004)
http://www.bls.gov/ncs/ebs/sp/ebsm0003.pdf
(March 2005)

Percent of workers participating in selected benefits, by worker and establishment characteristics, private industry, [compiled from the] National Compensation Survey, 2004, 2005

Characteristics	All Plans		Defined Benefit		Defined Contribution	
	2004	2005	2004	2005	2004	2005
All workers	50	60	21	22	42	53
Worker characteristics						
White-collar occupations	61	70	24	25	53	64
Blue-collar occupations	50	60	25	26	38	50
Service occupations	22	32	6	7	18	28
Full time	60	69	24	25	50	62
Part time	20	27	9	10	14	23
Union	81	88	69	73	42	49
Nonunion	47	56	15	16	42	54
Average wage less than $15 per hour	36	46	11	12	30	41
Average wage $15 per hour or higher	71	78	35	35	59	69
Establishment characteristics						
Goods producing	63	71	31	33	49	61
Service producing	47	56	18	19	40	51
1 to 99 workers	37	44	9	10	32	40
100 workers or more	67	78	34	37	53	69

Note: Because of rounding, sums of individual items may not equal totals.

Patricia E. Dilley
Hope We Die Before We Get Old: The Attack on Retirement
12 ELDER L.J. 245, 254-259 (2004)[*]

The change from defined benefit pension plans to various types of defined contribution, or essentially employee savings plans, has been underway for decades, but has probably greatly accelerated in the last twenty years. Some of the possible causes for the transition are discussed below, but first it is necessary to see what the change has actually been, and what the effects of the turn away from traditional pension plans are on actual worker pensions. . . . The inequality of total pension wealth increased sharply between 1983 and 2001. This trend is traceable to the switchover from DB plans to DC accounts. . . . [W]hile traditional defined benefit plans had an equalizing effect on overall household wealth, the switch to defined contribution plans has had the opposite effect. . . . [T]his occurred even as the switch was taking place during a historically long and vigorous bull market, when one might have expected that the proliferation of 401(k) plans for middle-income workers would have allowed them to participate more fully in the market's gains. . . .

Indeed, the devolution of the traditional pension system of the 1980s and 1990s has left many families unprepared to meet [the] challenges of retirement. Despite the hype, the switchover from DB to DC has <u>not benefited</u> the <u>average family</u> — it has hurt the average family instead. The shift from DB to DC plans is part of the general unraveling of the "worker safety net." . . .

. . . The private system is based on a set of tax inducements which give a deduction to employers for current contributions to pension plans, and exclusion of those contributions from income for the employees participating in those plans until they actually receive their benefits in retirement. Given the progressive income tax structure still in place, the higher an individual's income is, the more valuable that tax deferral is for them. For low-income workers, the deferral is of little value; most low-income workers would rather have that deferred income now to pay for current needs. As a result of this skewed distribution of the benefit of pension plans, lower-income retirees have far less pension income than workers at higher income levels do. As of now, however, the private retirement system has failed the lower earners. In reality, at any one time, at best no more than fifty percent of the workforce is participating in employer-based plans. Importantly, for those who end up in the bottom forty percent of the income distribution after retirement, employer-based plans are largely irrelevant. For those over age sixty-five in 1996, pensions accounted for only three percent of the retirement income of the lowest quintile, and seven percent of the income of the second-lowest quintile. . . .

Clearly, the decline of traditional pension plans is real, and the growth in defined contribution plans — essentially employer-provided employee savings plans — has not compensated for the decline for workers below the median income level. While higher income workers have probably benefited to some extent from the ability to invest their deferred wages in the stock market dur-

---

ing its boom years, that advantage has apparently not trickled down to the average or low income worker.

QUESTIONS

1. Why did pension coverage increase so rapidly between the 1940s and the 1970s?

2. Why has pension coverage stabilized in the years after the mid-1970s?

3. What explains the growth in defined-contribution plans?

4. Who is likely to be covered by a pension? Who is *not* likely to be covered?

4. Protection of Pension Investments: The Pension Benefit Guaranty Corporation

Who We Are (About the PBGC)
http://www.pbgc.gov/about/about.html
http://www.pbgc.gov/about/operation.html
http://www.pbgc.gov/about/termination.html

Mission Statement

The Pension Benefit Guaranty Corporation (PBGC) protects the retirement incomes of nearly 44 million American workers in 30,330 private-sector defined benefit pension plans. A defined benefit plan provides a specified monthly benefit at retirement, often based on a combination of salary and years of service.

PBGC was created by the Employee Retirement Income Security Act of 1974 to encourage the continuation and maintenance of private-sector defined benefit pension plans, provide timely and uninterrupted payment of pension benefits, and keep pension insurance premiums at a minimum. Defined benefit pension plans promise to pay a specified monthly benefit at retirement, commonly based on salary and years on the job.

PBGC is not funded by general tax revenues. PBGC collects insurance premiums from employers that sponsor insured pension plans, earns money from investments and receives funds from pension plans it takes over.

PBGC pays monthly retirement benefits, up to a guaranteed maximum, to about 612,000 retirees in 3,683 pension plans that ended. Including those who have not yet retired and participants in multiemployer plans receiving financial assistance, PBGC is responsible for the current and future pensions of about 1,271,000 people.

The maximum pension benefit guaranteed by PBGC is set by law and adjusted yearly. For plans ended in 2006, workers who retire at age 65 can receive up to $3,971.59 a month ($47,659.08 a year). The guarantee is lower for those who retire early or when there is a benefit for a survivor. The guarantee is increased for those who retire after age 65. . . .

How PBGC Operates . . .

- The **single-employer program** protects more than 34 million workers and retirees in about 28,800 pension plans.

- The **multiemployer program** protects 9.9 million workers and retirees in about 1,540 pension plans. Multiemployer plans are set up by collectively bargained agreements involving more than one unrelated employer, generally in one industry. . . .

How Pension Plans End

Employers can end a pension plan through a process called "plan termination." There are two ways an employer can terminate its pension plan.

The employer can end the plan in a **standard termination** but only after showing PBGC that the plan has enough money to pay all benefits owed to participants. The plan must either purchase an annuity from an insurance company (which will provide you with lifetime benefits when you retire) or, if your plan allows, issue one lump-sum payment that covers your entire benefit. Before purchasing your annuity, your plan administrator must give you an advance notice that identifies the insurance company (or companies) that your employer may select to provide the annuity. PBGC's guarantee ends when your employer purchases your annuity or gives you the lump-sum payment.

If the plan is not fully funded, the employer may apply for a **distress termination** if the employer is in financial distress. To do so, however, the employer must prove to a bankruptcy court or to PBGC that the employer cannot remain in business unless the plan is terminated. If the application is granted, PBGC will take over the plan as trustee and pay plan benefits, up to the legal limits, using plan assets and PBGC guarantee funds. . . .

Under certain circumstances, PBGC may take action on its own to end a pension plan. Most terminations initiated by PBGC occur when PBGC determines that plan termination is needed to protect the interests of plan participants or of the PBGC insurance program. PBGC can do so if, for example, a plan does not have enough money to pay benefits currently due.

5. The Taxation of Pension Investments When Made

Peter M. Van Zante
Rollover of Retirement Plan Distributions: A Proposal to Eliminate the Dual Rollover Structure
86 KY. L.J. 31, 42-43 (1997-1998)[*]

In contrast [to most forms of savings], retirement savings are <u>not included in</u> the taxpayer's income tax base for so long as the savings are held as identifiable

---

[*] Copyright © 1998. Reprinted with permission.

retirement savings, that is, held in a tax-qualified retirement plan. The exclusion from the income tax base for retirement savings is implemented by a trilogy of Code provisions. The employer, which pays the contribution to its retirement trust, is allowed an income tax deduction for the contribution [citing IRC § 404]. A participating employee need not include in her gross income any amount attributable to the employer's contribution nor to any increase in the value of the participant's vested accrued benefit [citing IRC § 402(a)]. And the retirement trust is exempt from income tax, so the investment earnings on the contributions are accumulated tax-free [citing IRC § 501]. This exclusion of retirement savings from the income tax base continues as long as the savings are held as identifiable retirement savings.

Internal Revenue Code § 402(a)

§ 402. Taxability of beneficiary of employees' trust.

(a) Taxability of beneficiary of exempt trust. — Except as otherwise provided in this section, any amount actually distributed to any distributee by any employees' trust described in section 401(a) which is exempt from tax under section 501(a) shall be taxable to the distributee, in the taxable year of the distributee in which distributed, under section 72 (relating to annuities).

QUESTION

What are the tax advantages offered by pension plans?

6. Pension Distributions: Mechanics and Taxation

a. The Basic Distinction Between Annuity Distributions and Lump-Sum Distributions

There are three forms of distributions from qualified pension plans: (1) annuity distributions, (2) lump-sum distributions, and (3) rollovers. Rollovers are considered later in this chapter.

Annuity Distributions. Under an annuity distribution, the pension benefit is paid out in a stream of regular payments, usually monthly and usually over the life of the participant (or lives of the participant and spouse) but sometimes over some other specified period. As a general rule, all annuity distributions are fully taxable as ordinary income. The rationale for this approach is straightforward: the contributions to the plan were not subject to tax when made, so they should be subject to tax when distributed. An exception to the general rule occurs in the uncommon case where some of the plan assets consist of contributions made by the employee with after-tax dollars. Those dollars were already taxed once (by definition, as they are after-tax), so it would unfair to tax the same dollars again upon distribution. In such cases, the Internal Revenue

Code contains complicated provisions (not discussed in this book but located in IRC § 72) designed to enable the annuity recipient to recover those contributions without paying tax on them a second time. Described in a nutshell, the provisions enable the annuity recipient to exclude from tax a fraction of each monthly payment until the after-tax contribution is fully recovered.

Lump-Sum Distributions. A lump-sum distribution occurs when the pension benefit is paid out within one taxable year. There may be more than one payment within that year; thus, the technical definition of a lump-sum distribution is not necessarily the same as the popular understanding of a single "lump sum." As with annuity distributions, the general rule is that lump-sum distributions are fully taxable as ordinary income in the year in which the distribution is made. (There are special rules from an earlier tax regime that still apply to employees born before 1936, but those rules are not covered in this book.) The principal exception to the general rule, as with annuity distributions, concerns plan assets that consist partly of after-tax contributions. The Internal Revenue Code contains provisions in § 72(e), not discussed in detail in this book, designed to exclude from tax the portion of the lump-sum distribution that corresponds to the after-tax contributions.

b. Penalties for Early Distributions

The Internal Revenue Code imposes a 10% excise (read: additional) tax on distributions made before the plan participant is age 59. IRC §§ 72(t)(1), 72(t)(2)(A)(i). The tax applies only to the portion of the distribution that is includible in gross income. IRC § 72(t)(1).

Among the many exceptions to the general rule, seven are worth noting here. The excise tax does not apply if:

1. The plan participant has died before the age of 59. IRC § 72(t)(2)(A)(ii).

2. The plan participant is "disabled" within the meaning of IRC § 72(m)(7). IRC § 72(t)(2)(A)(iii).

3. The distribution is in the form of an annuity for the lifetime of the participant or the participant and a beneficiary. IRC § 72(t)(2)(A)(iv).

4. The participant is at least 55 years old and has stopped working for his or her employer. IRC § 72(t)(2)(A)(v).

5. The distribution is for amounts paid for medical care and does not exceed the allowable medical-expense deduction (currently 7% of adjusted gross income). IRC § 72(t)(2)(B). Note that it does not matter whether the taxpayer actually itemizes his or her deductions, or takes the standard deduction.

6. The recipient is receiving the payment pursuant to a qualified domestic relations order (QDRO), which is a court order relating to a divorce decree. IRC § 72(t)(2)(C).

7. The distribution is rolled over into another qualified plan or IRA. IRC § 72(t)(1).

c. Penalties for Delayed Distributions

On April 17, 2002, the IRS issued new regulations concerning the required distributions from qualified pension plans and IRAs. 67 Fed. Reg. 18,988. These regulations are complex. The following material focuses on pension plans and provides only the briefest summary.

General Principle. IRC § 401(a)(9) requires that a plan participant (or if the participant has died, the participant's beneficiary) must begin receiving plan benefits no later than the "required beginning date." Failure to do so results in a 50% excise tax under IRC § 4974 on the following amount: (1) the "minimum required distribution" minus (2) the actual distribution.

Before-Death Distributions. If the participant is alive, then the required beginning date is defined in Treas. Reg. § 1.401(a)(9)-2(A-2) as follows: April 1 of the calendar year following the later of: (a) the calendar year in which the participant reaches age 70/ or (b) the calendar year in which the participant retires. (If the participant owns more than 5% of the sponsoring employer, then only option (a) is available.) The minimum required distribution is calculated according to a formula. Treas. Reg. § 1.401(a)(9)-5(A-4)(a). The formula is designed to exhaust the retirement account over an "applicable distribution period." In most cases, the applicable distribution period is drawn from the following table:

Uniform Lifetime Table [from Treas. Reg. § 1.401(a)(9)-9(A-2)]

Age of employee	Distribution period	Age of employee	Distribution period
70	27.4	92	10.2
71	26.5	93	9.6
72	25.6	94	9.1
73	24.7	95	8.6
74	23.8	96	8.1
75	22.9	97	7.6
76	22.0	98	7.1
77	21.2	99	6.7
78	20.3	100	6.3
79	19.5	101	5.9
80	18.7	102	5.5
81	17.9	103	5.2
82	17.1	104	4.9
83	16.3	105	4.5
84	15.5	106	4.2
85	14.8	107	3.9
86	14.1	108	3.7
87	13.4	109	3.4

88	12.7	110	3.1
89	12.0	111	2.9
90	11.4	112	2.6
91	10.8	113	2.4
92	10.2	114	2.1
93	9.6	115+	1.9

However, if the sole designated beneficiary of the pension plan is the participant's spouse *and* the spouse is more than 10 years younger than the participant, then the applicable distribution period is calculated using either the Uniform Lifetime Table or a separate table based on their joint life expectancies, whichever produces the longer period. Treas. Reg. § 1.401(a)(9)-5(A-4)(b). In any event, the amount of the required minimum distribution is redetermined each year and is based on the age of the participant (or the ages of the participant and the spouse) for that year. Treas. Reg. § 1.401(a)(9)-5(A-4).

After-Death Distributions When the Participant Has Died Before the Required Beginning Date. The general rule is that minimum required distributions to the designated beneficiary or beneficiaries must begin no later than the year after the year of the participant's death. The distribution period is based on the beneficiary's life expectancy as predicted by IRS tables. If the participant's spouse is the sole beneficiary, however, then two special rules apply. First, the life expectancy is redetermined each year by using the tables, whereas in other cases the life expectancy is simply reduced by 1 each year. Treas. Reg. § 1.401(a)(9)-5(A-5)(b) and (c). Second, distributions are not required until the year in which the participant would have reached the age of 70. Treas. Reg. § 1.401(a)(9)-3(A-3)(b).

The principal exception to the general rule is known as the five-year rule. Under the five-year rule, the entire account must be distributed within five years after the participant's death but no distribution is required in any year before that fifth year. IRC § 401(a)(9)(B)(ii). The five-year rule applies automatically if the participant did not designate a beneficiary. It also applies where the pension plan permits the participant or beneficiary to elect it and the participant or beneficiary has done so. Treas. Reg. § 1.401(a)(9)-3(A-4).

After-Death Distributions When the Participant Has Died After the Required Beginning Date. The rules here are largely the same as above, except that the distribution period based upon life expectancy is calculated using *the longer of* the life expectancy of the participant and the life expectancy of the beneficiary. Treas. Reg. § 1.401(a)(9)-5(A-5)(a).

d. Rollovers

A rollover is a distribution of assets from a qualified plan that is reinvested into another qualified plan. There are two types of rollovers: *direct rollovers* and *rollover distributions*. A direct rollover occurs when the assets are transferred directly from one plan to another plan. A rollover distribution occurs when the assets are transferred to the plan participant, who subsequently transfers them into the second plan.

Note that rollovers into IRAs are not subject to the IRA contribution limits discussed later in this chapter. IRC § 219(f)(6)(B)(ii).

Distributions Ineligible for Rollover. Not all distributions from a pension plan can be rolled over. Two such ineligible distributions are noted here. First, a distribution that is required under the minimum required distribution rules cannot be rolled over. IRC § 402(c)(4)(B). Second, pension plan distributions cannot be rolled over if they are in the form of an annuity for the lifetime of the individual, the joint lives of the individual and spouse, or for a period of 10 years or more. IRC § 402(c)(4)(A).

Rollover Distributions. To qualify for tax-free treatment, the rollover of the rollover distribution must be completed within 60 days.[2] IRC § 402(c)(3). Yet all rollover distributions from pension plans, even those rolled over within the 60 days, are subject to income tax withholding at the rate of 20%.[3] The amount withheld is treated as a refundable credit on the taxpayer's return for that year, meaning that the taxpayer will not be able to get back the withheld amount until after the end of the year. IRC § 3405(c). (Note that the taxpayer will have to come up with funds from another source to replace, temporarily, the 20% withheld.[4])

The words "tax-free treatment" in the preceding paragraph mean that the distribution will not be included in the individual's gross income and will not be subject to the 10% premature distribution tax discussed earlier in this chapter.

Direct Rollovers. ERISA requires pension plans to permit eligible distributions to be made directly to any "eligible retirement plan," a term defined in IRC § 401(a)(31)(D) but essentially meaning defined-contribution plans and traditional IRAs. The statute does not require plans to *accept* direct rollovers, and some do not. With a direct rollover, no withholding is required.

Amounts That Can Be Rolled Over. Under pre-EGTRRA law, the only part of a distribution from a pension plan that could be rolled over was the part attributable to employer contributions or pre-tax employee contributions. Amounts attributable to after-tax employee contributions could not be rolled over. EGTRRA changed that. Effective January 1, 2002, these after-tax amounts can

---

[2] The IRS has the ability to waive the 60-day rule in cases of casualty, disaster, or other events beyond reasonable control. IRC § 402(c)(3)(B).

[3] No withholding is necessary if all of the eligible rollover distributions received by the taxpayer during a given year total less than $200. Treas. Reg. § 31.3405(c)-1(A-14). Also note that distributions ineligible for rollover, such as minimum required distributions or distributions to the employee's children, are not subject to withholding.

[4] By way of explanation, consider the following hypothetical. A plan participant receives an eligible rollover distribution of $10,000, which she intends to roll over into a traditional IRA. The plan must withhold $2,000, thus giving the participant only $8,000. She must come up with $2,000 from another source to deposit into the IRA. The original $2,000 that was withheld will be returned to her as a credit on her tax return. In contrast, if the participant had elected a direct rollover, nothing would be withheld and the $10,000 would be paid directly from the plan to the IRA.

be rolled over into a defined-contribution plan by direct rollover or into a traditional IRA by direct rollover or rollover distribution. IRC § 402(c)(2).

Who May Roll Over? The general rule is that only distributions to the employee may be rolled over. However, this rule has exceptions, one of which is noted here. Distributions paid after the employee's death to the employee's spouse may be rolled over by the spouse into a traditional IRA. IRC § 402(c)(9).

Rollovers to Roth IRAs. Distributions from pension plans cannot be rolled over into a Roth IRA. However, they can be rolled over into a traditional IRA which can then be rolled over into a Roth IRA (*see* below).

C. PRIVATE SAVINGS: THE INDIVIDUAL RETIREMENT ACCOUNT

An individual retirement account ("IRA") is a savings vehicle that allows an individual to make contributions to an account that he or she manages. There are many types of IRAs. This section of the chapter will focus on the two most common: traditional IRAs and Roth IRAs.

1. Traditional IRAs

General Contribution and Deduction Limits. Each year, an individual who has received or earned taxable compensation during the year (such as wages, salaries, tips, etc., but *excluding* pension payments, Social Security payments, and unemployment compensation) can contribute to a traditional IRA.

Individuals who are under age 70 1/2 and are *not* active participants in a qualified pension plan can contribute to a traditional IRA and deduct from their income the lesser of: (1) the amount listed in the chart below under "General Limit" and (2) their taxable compensation. IRC §§ 219(b)(1), (b)(5)(A), (d)(1). In addition, traditional IRA participants who are at least 50 but under 70 1/2 in the relevant year can contribute and deduct the additional amount listed below under "Catch-up Limit," as long as their taxable compensation for the year is at least that high. IRC § 219(b)(5)(B).

Calendar Year	General Limit	Catch-Up Limit
2002	$3,000	$500
2003	$3,000	$500
2004	$3,000	$500
2005	$4,000	$500
2006	$4,000	$1,000
2007	$4,000	$1,000
2008 (and thereafter)	$5,000	$1,000

If the individual *does* participate in a qualified pension plan, then the amount that can be contributed and deducted will be reduced ("phased-out") based on the individual's filing status (e.g., single, married filing jointly, married filing separately) and income (including the spouse's income, if they file jointly). The rules governing this phase-out can be found in IRC § 219(g)(2) and are not reproduced here; merely by way of example, in 2003 a single individual who participates in a qualified plan and has adjusted gross income between $40,000 and $49,999 would be able to make a deductible contribution of a reduced amount, and with income of $50,000 or greater would be ineligible to make a deductible contribution at all.[5]

If an individual maintains more than one traditional IRA, the limit applies to the total contributions to all of them. IRC §§ 219(a), (b)(1).

Contributions for a given year must be made either during the applicable year or by the due date for filing that year's individual income tax return (for most people, April 15 of the following year). IRC § 219(f)(3).

Contribution Rules Governing Spouses Who Make Their Own Contributions. Where married taxpayers both have compensation, each spouse can set up a traditional IRA. The contribution limit for each spouse is determined separately. Spouses cannot establish joint IRAs.

If both spouses have compensation but only one participates in a qualified pension plan, the phase-out for the participant spouse is determined as described above, but separate phase-out rules (not discussed in this book but set forth in IRC § 219(g)(7)) apply to the nonparticipant spouse.

Contributions to Spousal Traditional IRAs. A spousal traditional IRA involves contributions made to a traditional IRA by one spouse on behalf of the other who has less or no taxable compensation. The limits on these contributions are governed by special rules set forth in IRC § 219(c) but not discussed in this book.

Distributions from Traditional IRAs. Unless rolled over, distributions from a traditional IRA are taxable under the same Internal Revenue Code section that governs distributions from pension plans (IRC § 72). IRC § 408(d)(1). Thus, the basic rules are the same. If the distribution consists of no after-tax contributions, then the distribution is fully taxable as ordinary income. However, if some of the distribution consists of contributions that have already been subject to tax, then a formula is used to prevent double-taxation of those contributions.

Like pension plans, traditional IRAs are subject to the 10% penalty tax on premature distributions. By and large, the same rules and exceptions apply, but you should note the following additional exceptions that apply to traditional IRAs but not to pension plans: no excise tax will be imposed if distributions are used to pay (1) medical insurance if the individual is unemployed, (2) higher

---

[5] Nondeductible contributions to a traditional IRA can be made, but most financial advisors encourage investors to avoid them. Nondeductible contributions trigger complex recordkeeping requirements and are still subject to the general contribution limits. Instead, financial advisors encourage investors to seek out other investments, such as commercial annuities. *See* Sidney Kess & Barbara Weltman, CCH RETIREMENT PLANNING GUIDE 111 (2d ed. 2002).

education expenses of the individual, spouse, or dependent, or (3) up to $10,000 in first-time home-buying expenses of the individual, the spouse, an ancestor, or a descendant. IRC §§ 72(t)(2)(D), (E) and (F).

Traditional IRAs are also subject to the minimum required distribution rules and the 50% penalty tax for failure to comply. The rules governing these required distributions are largely the same as those governing the required distributions from qualified pension plans. Treas. Reg. § 1.408-8(A-1). The one exception noted here is that, for traditional IRAs, the required beginning date is April 1 of the year after the IRA owner reaches age 70½ *whether or not* the IRA owner is still working. Treas. Reg. § 1.408-8(A-3).

2. Roth IRAs

Jolie Howard
The Roth IRA: A Viable Savings Vehicle for Americans?
35 Hous. L. Rev. 1269, 1279-81, 1283-84 (1998)[*]

The 1997 [Taxpayer Relief] Act created a new IRA vehicle named for the Senator who introduced it. The Roth IRA differs from the traditional IRA in that contributions made to it are nondeductible. However, income generated in the Roth IRA will build up tax-free similar to the traditional IRA, but unlike the traditional IRA, distributions from the Roth IRA are tax-exempt.

Qualified individuals may make a maximum annual contribution of $2,000 [$4,000 in 2006, or $5,000 for individuals at least age 50 — Eds.] to a Roth IRA. The amount of the contribution allowed is reduced by any deductible contributions made to other types of IRAs for the applicable tax year. Although the taxpayer may not take a deduction for the contribution, the incentive for contributing to this type of IRA is two-fold. First, the earnings in the account can accumulate tax-free; second, any qualified distributions will not be included in the taxpayer's income. A husband and wife can each contribute up to $2,000 [raised in 2006 to $4,000 or $5,000 if at least age 50 — Eds.] to a Roth IRA [meaning separate IRAs, as joint IRAs are not permitted — Eds.] provided that the combined compensation of the couple is equal to at least the total contributed amount. An individual may continue to make contributions to a Roth IRA account even after he or she reaches age 70 1/2.

Like the traditional IRA, the ability to make contributions to a Roth IRA is subject to limitations based on one's AGI [adjusted gross income]. However, the income phase-out levels are much higher for the Roth IRA than for the traditional IRA. The available contribution limit for the Roth IRA begins to phase-out ratably for single taxpayers with an AGI of $95,000 and for married taxpayers filing jointly with an AGI of $150,000.

Qualified distributions from Roth IRA accounts are not includible in gross income, nor subject to the ten percent penalty on early withdrawals. To reach

---

[*] Copyright © 1998. Reprinted with permission.

qualified status, however, an individual may not take a distribution within the first five years of the account's creation. A qualified distribution is one made: after the taxpayer reaches age 59 1/2; at the death of the individual; due to the individual's disability; or for a qualified special purpose [such as to assist in first-time homebuying expenses, up to the lifetime limit of $10,000 — Eds.]. All other distributions are includible in income to the extent the distribution is attributable to earnings in the account and, therefore, are subject to the ten percent early withdrawal penalty. . . . [Note that distributions attributable to contributions, rather than earnings, are not taxable and hence not subject to the 10% penalty. Moreover, distributions are presumed to come from contributions before earnings. Treas. Reg. § 1.408A-6(A-8). Thus, until the total of distributions exceeds the total of contributions, no portion of the distribution is taxable. — Eds.]

* * *

The main difference between the two IRAs is the timing of the tax benefit to the individual. With a traditional IRA, the taxpayer receives the benefit up-front with a tax deduction for the contribution, accumulates income tax-free, and pays taxes on the distributions when taken at retirement. In contrast, with the Roth IRA, the taxpayer does not receive a tax deduction when the contribution is made, but still accumulates tax-free income, and does not pay taxes when distributions are taken.

One important distinction between the two IRAs is that although Congress raised the level of income eligibility for individuals with respect to the traditional IRA, the income ceilings for the Roth IRA are much higher. For higher income individuals, therefore, "the new Roth IRA wins hands down." Another important distinction between the two IRAs is that the Roth IRA, unlike the traditional IRA, has no required beginning date for distributions. An individual can open a Roth IRA even after he reaches age 70½ and can leave the money in the account, untouched, until he dies. [Note that minimum required distribution rules do apply to the Roth IRA after the individual's death; Treas. Reg. § 1.408A-6(A-14). — Eds.]

* * *

An individual also must consider the amount of the taxpayer's contributions, the return on IRA investment, and his or her current and future tax status. With the Roth IRA, a taxpayer effectively locks in his or her tax rate, meaning that he or she knows the amount of taxes to be paid in the year in which the contribution is made. With the traditional IRA, the individual is betting that the tax rate will be lower after retirement so that he or she receives a benefit by taking the deduction up-front and paying taxes in the future. If the taxpayer's rate increases at the time of retirement, he or she will, in effect, pay more taxes with the traditional IRA because he or she pays the tax when distributions are taken during retirement.

Note on Spousal Roth IRAs

Contributions to a Roth IRA can be made for one's spouse under regulations not discussed in this chapter. The amount contributed reduces the amount that can be contributed for that year to other spousal IRAs. IRC § 219(c)(1)(B)(ii).

Note on
ROUSEY v. JACOWAY
125 S. Ct. 1561 (2005)

In *Rousey v. Jacoway*, the U.S. Supreme Court held that IRAs are exempted from the bankruptcy estate pursuant to 11 U.S.C. § 522(d)(10)(E). This section provides that a debtor may withdraw from the bankruptcy estate his right to receive "a payment under a stock bonus, pension, profitsharing, annuity, or similar plan or contract on account of illness, disability, death, *age*, or length of service, to the extent reasonably necessary for the support of the debtor and any dependent of the debtor. . . ." (emphasis supplied). The Court held that IRAs are exempted because they meet both of the necessary requirements: (1) they are "similar plans or contracts" to those enumerated in the section, and (2) the right to the balance of the IRA is a right to payment "on account of age," because the 10 percent penalty on withdrawals is removed when the account holder reaches age 59½.

Note on
The Bankruptcy Abuse Prevention and Consumer Protection Act of 2005
Pub. L. No. 109-8, 119 Stat. 23 (2005)

The Bankruptcy Abuse Prevention and Consumer Protection Act of 2005 was signed into law on April 20, 2005. Under § 224 of the Act, Congress provided rules for which retirement and IRA assets are protected from creditors during bankruptcy. Specifically, the following assets are shielded from creditors during bankruptcy:

1. Assets within qualified retirement plans, such as pension plans, employer-sponsored 401(k) plans, and profitsharing plans;

2. Rollovers from qualified retirement plans; and

3. An aggregate of $ 1 million in IRAs or Roth IRAs (in addition to amounts representing rollovers from qualified retirement plans).

3. Distributions, Rollovers, and Conversions

a. Distributions

Like pension plans, traditional IRAs are subject to the rules governing minimum required distributions. Treas. Reg. § 1.401(a)(9). Those rules do not apply, however, to Roth IRAs while the owner is alive. Roth IRA owners are not required to take distributions from your Roth IRA at any age. However, after the death of a Roth IRA owner, certain of the minimum distribution rules that apply to traditional IRAs also apply to Roth IRAs as explained. Treas. Reg. § 1.408A-6.

Distributions from traditional IRAs are generally taxable in the year they are received. Treas. Reg. § 1.408(a)(6). Distributions from a Roth IRA are not taxable if they are *qualified distributions* – i.e., if they are a return of regular contributions. Portions of other distributions may be taxable in the year they are made. A distribution is a *qualified distribution* if it is made more than five years after the year in which the first contribution was made to it; and if it is made on or after the date the account owner reaches age 59 1/2; is made because the account owner is disabled; is made to a beneficiary after the account owner dies; or is made to buy, build, or rebuild a first home (up to a lifetime limit of $10,000). IRS regulations set forth specific rules for how to order distributions from Roth IRAs to determine whether they are taxable. Treas. Reg. § 1.408A-6.

b. Rollovers

Distributions Ineligible for Rollover. Distributions from traditional IRAs that are minimum required distributions cannot be rolled over. Treas. Reg. § 1.408-8(A-4). Any distribution from a Roth IRA can be rolled over.

Traditional IRA to Traditional IRA. All or part of an eligible distribution from a traditional IRA can be rolled over into another traditional IRA, as long as the rollover is completed within 60 days. IRC § 408(d)(3)(A). No withholding is involved. The IRS permits an unlimited number of direct rollovers but permits only one rollover distribution per year from each IRA.[6]

Roth IRA to Roth IRA. Distributions from one Roth IRA can be rolled over into another Roth IRA, as long as the rollover is completed within 60 days. No withholding is involved. The IRS permits an unlimited number of direct rollovers but permits only one rollover distribution per year from each IRA. IRC § 408A(a).

Traditional IRA to Pension Plan. The law permits eligible distributions from a traditional IRA to be rolled over into a defined-contribution pension plan, within 60 days, but only if all of the funds in the IRA are attributable to rollovers from a pension plan. IRC §§ 408(d)(3)(A)(ii), (D)(i). These IRAs are known as "conduit IRAs." They are typically used when an employee has left an employer, received a lump-sum distribution upon departure, and wishes to preserve the right to elect a grandfathered tax treatment (known as "lump-sum averaging") that is not covered in this book.

Traditional IRA to Roth IRA. A traditional IRA can be rolled over ("converted") into a Roth IRA, but only if (1) the taxpayer's adjusted gross income does not exceed $100,000 and (2) the taxpayer is not married filing separately.

---

6 *See* Dennis R. Lassila & Bob G. Kilpatrick, CCH U.S. MASTER COMPENSATION TAX GUIDE 531 (3d ed. 2001) (describing the IRS's interpretation of IRC § 408(d)(3)(B)).

IRC § 408A(c)(3)(B). The rollover is treated as a distribution of the assets and is taxable under the standard rules for the taxation of IRA distributions, except that the 10% excise tax on early withdrawals does not apply. IRC § 408A(d)(3).

c. Conversions

Internal Revenue Service
Pub. 590: Individual Retirement Arrangements
http://www.irs.gov/pub/irs-pdf/p590.pdf
(Published for 2005)

You can convert a traditional IRA to a Roth IRA. The conversion is treated as a rollover, regardless of the conversion method used. Most of the rules for rollovers, described in Chapter 1 under *Rollover From One IRA Into Another*, apply to these rollovers. However, the 1-year waiting period does not apply.

Conversion methods. You can convert amounts from a traditional IRA to a Roth IRA in any of the following three ways.

- Rollover. You can receive a distribution from a traditional IRA and roll it over (contribute it) to a Roth IRA within 60 days after the distribution.

- Trustee-to-trustee transfer. You can direct the trustee of the traditional IRA to transfer an amount from the traditional IRA to the trustee of the Roth IRA.

- Same trustee transfer. If the trustee of the traditional IRA also maintains the Roth IRA, you can direct the trustee to transfer an amount from the traditional IRA to the Roth IRA.

Failed Conversions. If the converted amount is not recharacterized the contribution will be treated as a regular contribution to the Roth IRA and subject to the following tax consequences.

- A 6% excise tax per year will apply to any excess contribution not withdrawn from the Roth IRA.

- The distributions from the traditional IRA must be included in your gross income.

- The 10% additional tax on early distributions may apply to any distribution.

How to avoid. You must move the amount converted (including all earnings from the date of conversion) into a traditional IRA by the due date (including extensions) for your tax return for the year during which you made the conversion to the Roth IRA. You do not have to include this distribution (withdrawal) in income.

FURTHER READING. A. Kimberley Dayton, et al., ADVISING THE ELDERLY CLIENT, chs. 15– 20 (2006); Lawrence A. Frolik & Richard L. Kaplan, ELDER LAW IN A NUTSHELL (3 ed.), chs.11–14 (2003); Lawrence A. Frolik & Melissa C. Brown, ADVISING THE ELDERLY OR DISABLED CLIENT ch. 11 (2d ed. 2000 & Supp. 2002); Joan M. Krauskopf et al., ELDERLAW: ADVOCACY FOR THE AGING ch. 23 (2d ed. 1993 & Supp. 2002); Louis A. Mezzullo, AN ESTATE PLANNER'S GUIDE TO QUALI-FIED RETIREMENT PLAN BENEFITS (2d ed. 1998); Louis A. Mezzullo, AN ESTATE PLANNER'S GUIDE TO QUALIFIED RETIREMENT PLAN BENEFITS AND IRAS (3d ed. 2001); Peter J. Strauss & Nancy M. Lederman, THE ELDER LAW HANDBOOK ch. 17 (1996); Peter J. Strauss et al., AGING AND THE LAW, ch. 7 (1996).

Chapter 5

PROPERTY MANAGEMENT

This chapter examines the principal mechanisms — short of guardianship, which is discussed in Chapter 6 — for managing the property of persons who are either unwilling or unable to handle their affairs entirely on their own. It is common to think immediately of a guardianship for an older person who seems to need some help managing their finances and other property, but guardianship proceedings can be costly, both in terms of the attorney and court fees and in terms of the strain it almost inevitably imposes on family relationships. There are many less onerous possibilities available to the practitioner willing to think both creatively and specifically in order to craft a solution tailored to the situation at hand.

The range of mechanisms discussed in this chapter reflects the variety of needs to be met. In some cases, the property owner is simply uninterested in the details of management and happy to appoint or hire someone to do that for them. In other cases, the older person may not need to relinquish all ownership rights, but prefers or requires some outside help in handling the property. For example, an older person may be perfectly capable of handling daily expenses but need someone else to manage investments; conversely, an individual may own little in the way of complex assets, but need assistance balancing a checkbook each month. Others, more dependent still, may need someone else to manage some or all of their property entirely, but nevertheless may not need the strictures of a full-blown guardianship. Property owners have the option of retaining full and sole ownership while appointing agents or attorneys-in-fact to act for them; sharing ownership with another by way of joint title; or transferring legal title entirely to another as trustee or custodian, who then must manage the property for the benefit of the transferor. The exact degree of power and responsibility retained by the older person can often be chosen with great precision, thereby permitting the least intrusive intervention that will enable the older person to remain as independent as possible

The mechanisms by which these goals can be accomplished are, in order of presentation: durable powers of attorney; joint ownership; methods specific to financial accounts; and trusts, including custodial trusts under the Uniform Custodial Trust Act. Each of these arrangements accomplishes slightly different goals and therefore has its relative advantages and disadvantages for particular clients. As you read the material in each section, try to imagine the circumstances for which the technique under discussion would be best suited.

A. DURABLE POWERS OF ATTORNEY FOR PROPERTY

1. Background

Carolyn L. Dessin
***Acting as Agent Under a Financial Durable Power
of Attorney: An Unscripted Role***
75 NEB. L. REV. 574, 576-581 (1996)[*]

A power of attorney is an instrument by which a principal empowers an agent to act on the principal's behalf. At common law, a power of attorney was revoked by the incompetency or incapacity of the principal. Thus, having a power of attorney provided no protection from the difficulties of becoming incompetent or incapacitated because the power of attorney would cease to be effective at the exact moment that the principal needed it most.

The notion of durability had its genesis in this deficiency of a common-law power of attorney. Two approaches to durability are possible: 1) a power of attorney can be immediately effective and survive the incapacity of the principal (the "immediately effective" power) or 2) the power of attorney can become effective only when the principal becomes incapacitated (the "springing" power).

In 1954, Virginia enacted the first statute that allowed an agent to continue to act as empowered by a power of attorney even after the principal became disabled, incompetent, or incapacitated. Ten years later, the National Conference of Commissioners on Uniform State Laws promulgated the Model Special Power of Attorney for Small Property Interests Act ("the 1964 Act"). The 1964 Act was designed to be a less expensive alternative to guardianship or conservatorship proceedings. Designed to be used only in situations involving limited assets, the act was fairly comprehensive, and included a number of safeguards. For example, the Act required that powers executed under it had to be approved by a judge of a court of record to be valid. Interestingly, the 1964 Act offered three standards relating to the liability of the agent. Alternative one made the agent liable only in the case of "intentional wrongdoing, [gross negligence], or fraud." The second alternative held the uncompensated agent liable only for "intentional wrongdoing, gross negligence, or fraud" but held the compensated agent to the standard applied to other fiduciaries. Alternative three held all agents to the standard applied to other fiduciaries. The three alternatives were the result of a divergence of opinion among the Commissioners on Uniform State Laws. Originally, the drafting committee suggested the lowest standard, alternative one, because they thought that small amounts of assets would be involved and relatives or close friends would be serving as agents "without compensation and as a labor of love." The 1964 Act received limited acceptance, although a number of states may have borrowed provisions from it to use in enactments of the later Uniform Probate Code or Uniform Durable Power of Attorney Act.

When the National Conference of Commissioners on Uniform State Laws approved and promulgated the Uniform Probate Code ("U.P.C.") in 1969, it included sections 5-501 and 5-502. These sections provided that the authority of an agent to act under a power of attorney could continue beyond the incompetence of the principal. In addition to the idea of durability, the U.P.C. altered the common-law rule that the death of the principal ended the authority of an agent under a durable power of attorney and voided any acts performed by the agent after the death. After the promulgation of the U.P.C., the durable power of attorney gained rapid acceptance.

In 1979, the National Conference amended and expanded the sections of the U.P.C. dealing with durable powers of attorney and approved the Uniform Durable Power of Attorney Act ("U.D.P.A.A."), a free-standing act paralleling the language of and designed to act as an alternative to sections 5-501 to 5-505 of the U.P.C. All fifty states and the District of Columbia have enacted statutes authorizing durability of powers. Thus, the financial durable power of attorney is an available planning tool throughout the United States. . . .

In most states, the principal must express the intention that the power be durable. It is possible, however, that even an instrument that does not contain an express durability provision can be interpreted to create a durable power of attorney.

QUESTION

Examine, below, the Illinois short form power of attorney (755 ILCS 45/3-3). What makes this a *durable* power? *[handwritten: for any incompleteness]*

755 Illinois Consolidated Statutes 45/3-3

§ 3-3. Statutory short form power of attorney for property.

The following form may be known as "statutory property power" and may be used to grant an agent powers with respect to property and financial matters. When a power of attorney in substantially the following form is used, including the "notice" paragraph at the beginning in capital letters and the notarized form of acknowledgment at the end, it shall have the meaning and effect prescribed in this Act. The validity of a power of attorney as meeting the requirements of a statutory property power shall not be affected by the fact that one or more of the categories of optional powers listed in the form are struck out or the form includes specific limitations on or additions to the agent's powers, as permitted by the form. Nothing in this Article shall invalidate or bar use by the principal of any other or different form of power of attorney for property.

Nonstatutory property powers must be executed by the principal and designate the agent and the agent's powers, but they need not be acknowledged or conform in any other respect to the statutory property power.

ILLINOIS STATUTORY SHORT FORM POWER OF ATTORNEY FOR PROPERTY (NOTICE: THE PURPOSE OF THIS POWER OF ATTORNEY IS TO GIVE THE PERSON YOU DESIGNATE (YOUR "AGENT") BROAD POWERS TO HANDLE YOUR PROPERTY, WHICH MAY INCLUDE POWERS TO PLEDGE, SELL OR OTHERWISE DISPOSE OF ANY REAL OR PERSONAL PROPERTY WITHOUT ADVANCE NOTICE TO YOU OR APPROVAL BY YOU. THIS FORM DOES NOT IMPOSE A DUTY ON YOUR AGENT TO EXERCISE GRANTED POWERS; BUT WHEN POWERS ARE EXERCISED, YOUR AGENT WILL HAVE TO USE DUE CARE TO ACT FOR YOUR BENEFIT AND IN ACCORDANCE WITH THIS FORM AND KEEP A RECORD OF RECEIPTS, DISBURSEMENTS AND SIGNIFICANT ACTIONS TAKEN AS AGENT. A COURT CAN TAKE AWAY THE POWERS OF YOUR AGENT IF IT FINDS THE AGENT IS NOT ACTING PROPERLY. YOU MAY NAME SUCCESSOR AGENTS UNDER THIS FORM BUT NOT CO-AGENTS. UNLESS YOU EXPRESSLY LIMIT THE DURATION OF THIS POWER IN THE MANNER PROVIDED BELOW, UNTIL YOU REVOKE THIS POWER OR A COURT ACTING ON YOUR BEHALF TERMINATES IT, YOUR AGENT MAY EXERCISE THE POWERS GIVEN HERE THROUGHOUT YOUR LIFETIME, EVEN AFTER YOU BECOME DISABLED. THE POWERS YOU GIVE YOUR AGENT ARE EXPLAINED MORE FULLY IN SECTION 3-4 OF THE ILLINOIS "STATUTORY SHORT FORM POWER OF ATTORNEY FOR PROPERTY LAW" OF WHICH THIS FORM IS A PART (SEE THE BACK OF THIS FORM). THAT LAW EXPRESSLY PERMITS THE USE OF ANY DIFFERENT FORM

OF POWER OF ATTORNEY YOU MAY DESIRE. IF THERE IS ANYTHING ABOUT THIS FORM THAT YOU DO NOT

UNDERSTAND, YOU SHOULD ASK A LAWYER TO EXPLAIN IT TO YOU.)

POWER OF ATTORNEY made this. . . . .day of . . . . (month) . . . . . . (year)

1. I,. . . . ., (insert name and address of principal) hereby appoint:
. . . . (insert name and address of agent)
as my attorney-in-fact (my "agent") to act for me and in my name (in any way I could act in person) with respect to the following powers, as defined in Section 3-4 of the "Statutory Short Form Power of Attorney for Property Law" (including all amendments), but subject to any limitations on or additions to the specified powers inserted in paragraph 2 or 3 below:

(YOU MUST STRIKE OUT ANY ONE OR MORE OF THE FOLLOWING CATEGORIES OF POWERS YOU DO NOT WANT YOUR AGENT TO HAVE. FAILURE TO STRIKE THE TITLE OF ANY CATEGORY WILL CAUSE THE POWERS DESCRIBED IN THAT CATEGORY TO BE GRANTED TO THE AGENT. TO STRIKE OUT A CATEGORY YOU MUST DRAW A LINE THROUGH THE TITLE OF THAT CATEGORY.)

  (a)   Real estate transactions.

  (b)   Financial institution transactions.

  (c)   Stock and bond transactions.

  (d)   Tangible personal property transactions.

  (e)   Safe deposit box transactions.

  (f)   Insurance and annuity transactions.

  (g)   Retirement plan transactions.

  (h)   Social Security, employment and military service benefits.

  (i)   Tax matters.

  (j)   Claims and litigation.

  (k)   Commodity and option transactions.

  (l)   Business operations.

  (m) Borrowing transactions.

  (n)   Estate transactions.

  (o)   All other property powers and transactions.

(LIMITATIONS ON AND ADDITIONS TO THE AGENT'S POWERS MAY BE INCLUDED IN THIS POWER OF ATTORNEY IF THEY ARE SPECIFICALLY DESCRIBED BELOW.)

2. The powers granted above shall not include the following powers or shall be modified or limited in the following particulars (here you may include any specific limitations you deem appropriate, such as a prohibition or conditions on the

sale of particular stock or real estate or special rules on borrowing by the agent):

. . . .
. . . .
. . . .
. . . .

3. In addition to the powers granted above, I grant my agent the following powers (here you may add any other delegable powers including, without limitation, power to make gifts, exercise powers of appointment, name or change beneficiaries or joint tenants or revoke or amend any trust specifically referred to below):

. . . .
. . . .
. . . .
. . . .

(YOUR AGENT WILL HAVE AUTHORITY TO EMPLOY OTHER PERSONS AS NECESSARY TO ENABLE THE AGENT TO PROPERLY EXERCISE THE POWERS GRANTED IN THIS FORM, BUT YOUR AGENT WILL HAVE TO MAKE ALL DISCRETIONARY DECISIONS. IF YOU WANT TO GIVE YOUR AGENT THE RIGHT TO DELEGATE DISCRETIONARY DECISION-MAKING POWERS TO OTHERS, YOU SHOULD KEEP THE NEXT SENTENCE, OTHERWISE IT SHOULD BE STRUCK OUT.)

4. My agent shall have the right by written instrument to delegate any or all of the foregoing powers involving discretionary decision-making to any person or persons whom my agent may select, but such delegation may be amended or revoked by any agent (including any successor) named by me who is acting under this power of attorney at the time of reference.

(YOUR AGENT WILL BE ENTITLED TO REIMBURSEMENT FOR ALL REASONABLE EXPENSES INCURRED IN ACTING UNDER THIS POWER OF ATTORNEY. STRIKE OUT THE NEXT SENTENCE IF YOU DO NOT WANT YOUR AGENT TO ALSO BE ENTITLED TO REASONABLE COMPENSATION FOR SERVICES AS AGENT.)

5. My agent shall be entitled to reasonable compensation for services rendered as agent under this power of attorney.

(THIS POWER OF ATTORNEY MAY BE AMENDED OR REVOKED BY YOU AT ANY TIME AND IN ANY MANNER. ABSENT AMENDMENT OR REVOCATION, THE AUTHORITY GRANTED IN THIS POWER OF ATTORNEY WILL BECOME EFFECTIVE AT THE TIME THIS POWER IS SIGNED AND WILL CONTINUE UNTIL YOUR DEATH UNLESS A LIMITATION ON THE BEGINNING DATE OR DURATION IS MADE BY INITIALING AND COMPLETING EITHER (OR BOTH) OF THE FOLLOWING:)

6. ( ) This power of attorney shall become effective on ....

....

.... (insert a future date or event during your lifetime, such as court determination of your disability, when you want this power to first take effect)

7. ( ) This power of attorney shall terminate on ....

....

(insert a future date or event, such as court determination of your disability, when you want this power to terminate prior to your death)

(IF YOU WISH TO NAME SUCCESSOR AGENTS, INSERT THE NAME(S) AND ADDRESS(ES) OF SUCH SUCCESSOR(S) IN THE FOLLOWING PARA-GRAPH.)

8. If any agent named by me shall die, become incompetent, resign or refuse to accept the office of agent, I name the following (each to act alone and successively, in the order named) as successor(s) to such agent:

....

....

....

....

For purposes of this paragraph 8, a person shall be considered to be incompetent if and while the person is a minor or an adjudicated incompetent or disabled person or the person is unable to give prompt and intelligent consideration to business matters, as certified by a licensed physician.

(IF YOU WISH TO NAME YOUR AGENT AS GUARDIAN OF YOUR ESTATE, IN THE EVENT A COURT DECIDES THAT ONE SHOULD BE APPOINTED, YOU MAY, BUT ARE NOT REQUIRED TO, DO SO BY RETAINING THE FOLLOWING PARAGRAPH. THE COURT WILL APPOINT YOUR AGENT IF THE COURT FINDS THAT SUCH APPOINTMENT WILL SERVE YOUR BEST INTERESTS AND WELFARE. STRIKE OUT PARAGRAPH 9 IF YOU DO NOT WANT YOUR AGENT TO ACT AS GUARDIAN.)

9. If a guardian of my estate (my property) is to be appointed, I nominate the agent acting under this power of attorney as such guardian, to serve without bond or security.

10. I am fully informed as to all the contents of this form and understand the full import of this grant of powers to my agent.

Signed ....
          (principal)

(YOU MAY, BUT ARE NOT REQUIRED TO, REQUEST YOUR AGENT AND SUCCESSOR AGENTS TO PROVIDE SPECIMEN SIGNATURES BELOW. IF YOU INCLUDE SPECIMEN SIGNATURES IN THIS POWER OF ATTOR-NEY, YOU MUST COMPLETE THE CERTIFICATION OPPOSITE THE SIG-NATURES OF THE AGENTS.)

Specimen signatures of agent (and I certify that the signatures of my agent successors) (and successors) are correct.

. . . .

   (agent)   (principal)

. . . .

   (successor agent)   (principal)

. . . .

   (successor agent)   (principal)

(THIS POWER OF ATTORNEY WILL NOT BE EFFECTIVE UNLESS IT IS NOTARIZED, USING THE FORM BELOW.)

State of . . . .)

) SS.

County of . . . .)

The undersigned, a notary public in and for the above county and state, certifies that. . . . .,

known to me to be the same person whose name is subscribed as principal to the foregoing power of attorney, appeared before me in person and acknowledged signing and delivering the instrument as the free and voluntary act of the principal, for the uses and purposes therein set forth (, and certified to the correctness of the signature(s) of the agent(s)).

Dated: . . . . (SEAL)

. . . .

Notary Public

My commission expires . . . .

The undersigned witness certifies that . . . ., known to me to be the same person whose name is subscribed as principal to the foregoing power of attorney, appeared before me and the notary public and acknowledged signing and delivering the instrument as the free and voluntary act of the principal, for the uses and purposes therein set forth. I believe him or her to be of sound mind and memory.

Dated: . . . . (SEAL)

. . . .

Witness

(THE NAME AND ADDRESS OF THE PERSON PREPARING THIS FORM SHOULD BE INSERTED IF THE AGENT WILL HAVE POWER TO CONVEY ANY INTEREST IN REAL ESTATE.)

This document was prepared by:

. . . .

. . . .

2. Preparing the Power: The Use of Statutory Forms

Many states have a statutory power-of-attorney form. This means that state's legislature has set forth the form as part of the state's laws. Such forms, if they have been adopted, usually can be found in either the portion of the state's code dealing with probate issues, or in the sections dealing with property matters more generally. It is advisable to consult the code index when researching and preparing powers of attorney. Lawyers drafting powers of attorney in these states must be attentive to whether the statutory form is presented merely as a model, or whether substantially the same language must be used.

QUESTION

Review the code sections reproduced below and compare them to the language that introduces the Illinois statutory form above. With regard to each state, including Illinois:

1. What does it mean when the statute says that forms that "comply substantially" with the statutory form are "legally sufficient"?

2. What would be the result if a power-of-attorney document did not "comply substantially" with the wording of the statute? Would such a document be prohibited? Void? Voidable? Legally effective but lacking some other benefit?

3. How would you determine whether the wording of a document "complies substantially" with the wording of the statutory form? In each state, how much leeway does a drafter have to modify the statutory language to meet the particular needs of her client?

4. What should an attorney do if the statutory model does not seem appropriate?

Okla. Stat. 15 §§ 1003(A)-(B) & 1019

§ 1003. Statutory form [for power of attorney]

A. The following statutory form of power of attorney is legally sufficient:

[form omitted]

B. A statutory power of attorney is legally sufficient under this act, if the wording of the form complies substantially with subsection A of this section, the form is properly completed, and the signature of the principal is acknowledged.

§ 1019. Existing and foreign interests.

The powers described in Sections 5 through 18 of this act are exercisable equally with respect to an interest the principal has when the power of attorney is executed or acquires later, whether or not the property is located in this state, and whether or not the powers are exercised or the power of attorney is executed in this state.

N.M. Stat. §§ 45-5-602(A)-(B) & 45-5-617

45-5-602. Statutory form of power of attorney.

A. The following statutory form of power of attorney is legally sufficient:

[form omitted]

B. A statutory power of attorney is legally sufficient under the Uniform Statutory Form Power of Attorney Act, if the wording of the form complies substantially with Subsection A of this section, the form is properly completed, and the signature of the principal is acknowledged in any form permitted by law.

45-5-617. Existing interests; foreign interest; other powers of attorney.

The powers described in Sections 45-5-601 through 45-5-616 NMSA 1978 are exercisable equally with respect to an interest the principal has when the power of attorney is executed or acquires later, whether or not the property is located in New Mexico, and whether or not the powers are exercised or the power of attorney is executed in New Mexico. Existing statutory form powers of attorney, valid under existing New Mexico law, remain valid. Nothing in the Uniform Statutory Form Power of Attorney Act [45-5-601 to 45-5-617 NMSA 1978] prohibits the use of any other form for a power of attorney. A power of attorney executed in another jurisdiction, which is in compliance with the law of that jurisdiction or with the law of New Mexico, is valid in New Mexico to the extent the document is not inconsistent with the public policy of New Mexico.

Minn. Stat. § 523.23, Subd. 1 and 3

523.23 Statutory short form of general power of attorney; formal requirements; joint agents.

Subdivision 1. **Form.** The following form may be used to create a power of attorney, and, when used, it must be construed in accordance with sections 523.23 and 523.24:

[form omitted]

* * *

Subdivision 3. **Requirements.** To constitute a "statutory short form power of attorney," as this phrase is used in this chapter the wording and content of the form in subdivision 1 must be duplicated exactly and with no modifications, parts First, Second, and Third must be properly completed, and the signature of the principal must be acknowledged.

3. Capacity to Execute or Revoke

Carolyn L. Dessin
Acting as Agent Under a Financial Durable Power of Attorney: An Unscripted Role
75 NEB. L. REV. 574, 581 (1996)[*]

Although the durable power of attorney is designed to survive the incompetency of the principal, the principal must, of course, be competent when he executes the durable power of attorney for the power to be valid. Further, if a person loses competency, he or she cannot revoke a durable power of attorney while incompetent.

In re GUARDIANSHIP OF RAY
1991 LEXIS 4308, *4 (Ohio App. 4 Dist.)

The creation of a power of attorney requires that the principal be mentally competent at the time the power is executed. Derived from contracts law, the test to be used to determine mental capacity is the ability of the principal to understand the nature, scope and the extent of the business she is about to transact.

IN THE MATTER OF RICK
1994 LEXIS 49, *4 (Del. Ch.)

On the question of [the principal's] capacity to execute the 1993 power of attorney, the parties refer to the legal standards for evaluating a claim of lack of testamentary capacity. . . . The standard is that one who makes a will must, at the time of execution, be capable of exercising thought, reflection and judgment, and must know what he or she is doing and how he or she is disposing of his or her property. The person must also possess sufficient memory and understanding to comprehend the nature and character of the act.

HILBERT v. BENSON
917 P.2d 1152, 1156 (Wyo. 1996)

In comparing the governing standards of testamentary capacity for executing wills and of contractual capacity for executing inter vivos conveyances, we agree . . . that a higher degree of mental capacity is required to execute an inter vivos conveyance or contract or to transact business generally, than is required in executing a will.

---

[*] Copyright © 1996. Reprinted with permission.

RESTATEMENT (2d) OF PROPERTY (DONATIVE TRANSFERS) § 34.5(1)-(5) & comment a

§ 34.5 Donor Mentally Incompetent

(1) A mentally incompetent person cannot make a valid will or a valid inter vivos donative transfer.

(2) The legal guardian of a mentally incompetent person may make valid inter vivos donative transfers of the incompetent's property only to the extent authorized by a court.

(3) A person before becoming mentally incompetent may give another person a power of attorney to act for him or her during any incompetency, including the power to make inter vivos donative transfers.

(4) A person before becoming mentally incompetent may transfer property to a trustee to hold in trust with an authorization to the trustee to make valid inter vivos donative transfers of the trust property in the event of the incompetency of the creator of the trust. Such authorized donative transfers cannot be prevented by a legal guardian or any other representative of the mentally incompetent person.

(5) A trustee to whom property is transferred by another for the benefit of a person who is or becomes mentally incompetent may be authorized by the trust instrument to make inter vivos donative transfers of the trust property to others. Such authorized donative transfers cannot be prevented by a legal guardian or any other representative of the mentally incompetent person.

Comment on Subsection (1):

a. *Who is mentally incompetent.* A person is mentally incompetent to make a donative transfer if such person is unable to understand fully the significance of such transfer in relation to such person's own situation. Stated another way, to be mentally competent a person must know and understand the extent of his or her property, comprehend to whom he or she is giving his or her property, and know the natural objects of his or her bounty. A slightly different statement of what constitutes mental capacity is that the person must understand the nature and extent of his or her property, know and recall the natural objects of his or her property, and be able to determine and understand how he or she wishes to dispose of his or her property.

A person who is mentally incompetent part of the time but who has lucid intervals during which he or she comprehends fully the significance of a donative transfer can, in the absence of an adjudication or statute that has contrary effect, make a valid will or a valid inter vivos donative transfer, provided such will or transfer is made during a lucid interval.

RESTATEMENT (3d) OF PROPERTY (WILLS AND OTHER DONATIVE TRANSFERS) § 8.1(a)-(c) & comments c and d

§ 8.1 Requirement of Mental Capacity

(a) A person must have mental capacity in order to make or revoke a donative transfer.

(b) If the donative transfer is in the form of a will, a revocable will substitute, or a revocable gift, the testator or donor must be capable of knowing and understanding in a general way the nature and extent of his or her property, the natural objects of his or her bounty, and the disposition that he or she is making of that property, and must also be capable of relating these elements to one another and forming an orderly desire regarding the disposition of the property.

(c) If the donative transfer is in the form of an irrevocable gift, the donor must have the mental capacity necessary to make or revoke a will and must also be capable of understanding the effect that the gift may have on the future financial security of the donor and of anyone who may be dependent on the donor.

Comments:

c. *Standard for mental capacity to make or revoke a will.* To have mental capacity to make a will, the law requires the testator to be "of sound mind." To be "of sound mind," the testator must, when executing a will, be capable of knowing and understanding in a general way the nature and extent of his or her property, the natural objects of his or her bounty, and the disposition that he or she is making of that property, and must also be capable of relating these elements to one another and forming an orderly desire regarding the disposition of the property.

The natural objects of a testator's bounty include the testator's closest family members, who are not limited to blood or adoptive relatives or to those who would take by intestacy. For example, a testator's stepchildren are natural objects of the testator's bounty, even though stepchildren do not ordinarily take by intestacy (*see* § 2.5, Comment *j*). Relatives by affinity do not take by intestacy but could be counted as natural objects of a testator's bounty in the case in which the testator was close to them. To have testamentary capacity, the testator need not know the identity or location of remote relatives who are beyond his or her immediate family circle.

. . . .

Although many statutes of wills do not expressly say that a testator must be "of sound mind" to revoke a will, the same requirement of mental capacity applies. To revoke a will by revocatory act, the testator must have intent to revoke. . . . An intent to revoke is only recognized if the testator has mental capacity when performing the revocatory act. To revoke a will by subsequent will, the testator must have capacity to make a will when executing the will that revokes the prior will.

A purported will or revocation of a will by a person who lacks the mental capacity to make a will is void. (*See* § 3.1, Comment *a*, for the definition of the term "will.") Because a testamentary power of appointment can only be exercised in a valid will, a person who lacks the mental capacity to make a will lacks the capacity to exercise a testamentary power of appointment.

d. Standard for mental capacity to make an irrevocable gift. Because an irrevocable gift depletes financial resources that the donor may yet need, the standard for mental capacity to make an irrevocable gift is higher than that for making a will. To have mental capacity to make an irrevocable inter vivos gift, the donor must have the mental capacity necessary to make or revoke a will and must also be capable of understanding the effect that the gift may have on the future financial security of the donor and of anyone who may be dependent on the donor. *See* Restatement Third, Trusts § 11, Comment *c*.

For purposes of this section and Comment, the term "gift" includes an inter vivos donative transfer of any kind, in trust or not, and also includes an exercise of a presently exercisable power of appointment.

QUESTIONS

1. Is the required level of capacity for executing a durable power of attorney the same as for executing a contract? For executing a will?

2. What level(s) of capacity *should* be required for these actions?

4. Formalities of Execution

Carolyn L. Dessin
Acting as Agent Under a Financial Durable Power of Attorney: An Unscripted Role
75 Neb. L. Rev. 574, 581-582 (1996)[*]

With respect to execution formalities, durable powers of attorney are generally easier to execute than wills. Typically, the only execution requirements are that the power be in writing and signed by the principal. A few states impose additional execution requirements, none of which are particularly oppressive.

---

[*] Copyright © 1996. Reprinted with permission.

William M. McGovern, Jr.
Trusts, Custodianships, and Durable Powers of Attorney
27 REAL PROP., PROB. & TR. J. 21 (1992)[*]

UPC section 5-501 requires only that durable powers be "in writing," meaning that even an unsigned writing will suffice. However, some states require durable powers to be signed and witnessed like a will, and others require the same formalities as for a deed.

In California, a printed form durable power sold "for use by a person who does not have the advice of legal counsel" must contain a warning that states: "This is an important legal document. . . . If there is anything about this form that you do not understand, you should ask a lawyer to explain it to you."

QUESTIONS

1. Examine the Illinois short form power of attorney. What formalities are required for its execution?

2. How should we understand the relationship between capacity and formalities of execution? What correlation do you find between (a) the level of capacity and (b) the level of formalities required to validly execute durable powers of attorney as opposed to wills? Does this correlation make sense?

5. Taking Effect: The Special Case of the Springing Power

Marc S. Beckerman
Practice Considerations in Estate and Disability Planning
PROB. & PROP. 62, 63 (May/June 1998)[*]

If the power does not take effect immediately, it is a "springing" power, and the client and the drafting lawyer must determine what events will make the power effective. Local law may propose or require language to establish this effectiveness. In New York, for instance, the statutory form of springing power of attorney allows the client to define the event that activates the power and allows the client to name specific persons to certify that such an event has occurred. Similarly, California law provides that a person executing a springing power of attorney "may designate one or more persons who, by a written declaration under penalty of perjury, have the power to determine conclusively that the specified event or contingency has occurred."

Ramona C. Rains
Planning Tools Available to the Elderly Client
19 AM. J. TRIAL ADVOCACY 599, 604-605 (1996)[*]

Another problem associated with the springing durable power of attorney is the difficulty inherent in determining when a person has become incapacitated. If it becomes necessary to have a court determine the mental capacity of the principal, part of the benefit of the durable power of attorney over conservatorship proceedings will be defeated. Some commentators suggest designating an attorney or relative to decide whether the individual has become incapacitated, thus triggering the springing durable power of attorney. Another technique is to state in the durable power of attorney that the agent's affidavit will serve as conclusive proof that the springing durable power of attorney has been triggered. If the client is concerned that the agent will abuse the durable power of attorney, the attorney may want to advise his client to choose another agent. Not all states recognize the springing durable power of attorney [here, the author cites the law of South Carolina — Eds.], thus, the attorney should be aware of the current law in the jurisdiction in which he practices.

QUESTIONS

Using the Illinois short form as a starting point, draft language to create a springing durable power of attorney.

1. What events might be used to trigger the power, and what language would you use to describe these events?

2. Who will determine whether the triggering events have occurred, and what options (if any) will other interested persons have to challenge that determination?

Now evaluate your proposed language.

3. How likely is it that what you have drafted will lead to litigation?

4. How vulnerable is your document to abuse?

---

6. Scope of the Power

Carolyn L. Dessin
Acting as Agent Under a Financial Durable Power of Attorney: An Unscripted Role
75 NEB. L. REV. 574, 582-583 (1996)[*]

With respect to breadth of powers, there are a few restrictions on the acts that can be delegated to agents under durable powers of attorney. The restrictions may come from statutes, common law, public policy limitations, or contract provisions that curtail the delegation of duties or assignment of rights. Although few courts have considered the limits of delegability, the existing decisions suggest that the range of non-delegable acts is fairly narrow. Even if a restriction exists, its validity might be subject to challenge. Thus, the breadth of a durable power is virtually limitless.

Additionally, a court has fairly limited supervisory power over an agent under a durable power of attorney. Court approval for the agent's acts is generally not required.

Daniel S. Brennan
Durable Power of Attorney: An Ethical Option When Planning for Elderly Clients
3 GEO. J. LEGAL ETHICS 751, 755 (1990)[**]

The scope of the durable power of attorney is restricted only by the intent of the principal. The document may be broad and sweeping, or it may confer limited powers. To avoid potential disputes regarding the breadth of the durable power of attorney, it may be advisable to include specific grants of authority in the document. Among the powers that should be considered are: power of access to safe deposit boxes, ability to sign tax returns, the power to settle tax disputes, the power to deal with retirement plans, the power to fund inter-vivos trusts, the power to deal with life insurance, the power to borrow money, and the power to settle or pursue litigation on behalf of the principal. Because the durable power of attorney may potentially encompass many powers, the lawyer drafting the document should take special care to explain to the elderly client the exact duties that are being conferred. The lawyer should be especially aware of the fears and concerns of the elderly client who may be particularly suspicious about the loss of control.

MALLORY v. MALLORY
450 N.Y.S.2d 272, 273-274 (1982)

The plaintiff and the defendant were married on August 16, 1959. On February 29, 1980, a default judgment of divorce was granted against the defendant [Elizabeth Mallory] and in favor of the plaintiff [Shelton Mallory]. Thereafter, by order dated April 7, 1981, the default judgment was vacated upon the consent of the attorneys for both parties. It is this order, vacating the default, which Ethel Aikens, the movant, seeks to vacate. In support of this motion, Ms. Aikens attaches a copy of a general statutory short form power of attorney executed by the plaintiff on March 8, 1980, naming her as plaintiff's attorney in fact. . . .

A careful examination of the affidavits in support of the motion makes it clear that the relief requested could not ultimately be granted to the movant under any circumstances. In making its determination, the court is convinced that Ethel Aikens lacks standing to bring this application. The fact that the movant possesses a power of attorney is of no assistance to her. It appears that on this motion Ethel Aikens is relying on the portion of the power which gives the donee the power to act in "all other matters." This, however, does not give the donee carte blanche. . . .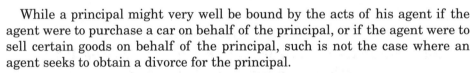

While a principal might very well be bound by the acts of his agent if the agent were to purchase a car on behalf of the principal, or if the agent were to sell certain goods on behalf of the principal, such is not the case where an agent seeks to obtain a divorce for the principal.

QUESTIONS

1. What powers are given to agents under the Illinois short form power of attorney? How does this compare to powers given in other states? How would you find out?

2. If an Illinois resident wanted to create a power of attorney that was more restrictive, how would he or she accomplish this?

3. Why are agents prevented from exercising powers of the kind described in *Mallory*? What does this tell you about the nature of "all other matters" covered by powers of attorney? Specifically, what kinds of rights and/or powers are these instruments designed to delegate?

7. Gift-Giving: A Potential Tax Trap

Excerpts from the Internal Revenue Code

§ 2501. Imposition of [Gift] Tax.

(a) Taxable transfers.

> (1) General rule. A tax . . . is hereby imposed for each calendar year on the transfer of property by gift during such calendar year by any individual, resident or nonresident.

§ 2511. Transfers in general.

(a) Scope. Subject to the limitations contained in this chapter, the tax imposed by section 2501 shall apply whether the transfer is in trust or otherwise, whether the gift is direct or indirect, and whether the property is real or personal, tangible or intangible. . . .

§ 2503. Taxable gifts.

. . . .

(b) Exclusion from gifts.

> (1) In general. In the case of gifts (other than gifts of future interests in property) made to any person by the donor during the calendar year, the first $10,000 of such gifts to such person shall not, for purposes of subsection (a), be included in the total amount of gifts made during such year. . . .

> (2) Inflation adjustment. In the case of gifts made in a calendar year after 1998, the $10,000 amount contained in paragraph (1) shall be increased by an amount equal to —

>> (A) $10,000, multiplied by

>> (B) the cost-of-living adjustment determined under section 1(f)(3) for such calendar year. . . . If any amount as adjusted under the preceding sentence is not a multiple of $1,000, such amount shall be rounded to the next lowest multiple of $1,000.

§ 2001. Imposition and Rate of [Estate] Tax

(a) Imposition. A tax is hereby imposed on the transfer of the taxable estate of every decedent who is a citizen or resident of the United States.

§ 2038. Revocable transfers.

(a) In general. The value of the gross estate [for purposes of the federal estate tax] shall include the value of all property —

> (1) . . . To the extent of any interest therein of which the decedent has at any time made a transfer (except in case of a bona fide sale for an adequate and full consideration in money or money's worth), by

trust or otherwise, where the enjoyment thereof was subject at the date of his death to any change through the exercise of a power (in whatever capacity exercisable) by the decedent alone or by the decedent in conjunction with any other person (without regard to when or from what source the decedent acquired such power), to alter, amend, revoke, or terminate, or where any such power is relinquished during the 3-year period ending on the date of the decedent's death.

§ 2041. Powers of Appointment

(a) In general. The value of the gross estate [for purposes of the estate tax] shall include the value of all property

. . .

(2) . . . with respect to which the decedent has at the time of his death a general power of appointment created after October 21, 1942 . . .

Hans A. Lapping
License to Steal: Implied Gift-Giving Authority and Powers of Attorney
4 ELDER L.J. 143, 143-146 (1996)[*]

As America ages, more people are realizing that they may some day need assistance with their financial affairs should they become incapacitated. Consequently, attorneys are increasingly being called upon by their clients to draft powers of attorney as part of the elderly person's estate plans. Often these general powers authorize the attorney-in-fact to do everything the principal could do if personally present and capable of acting.

In addition to the implementation of a power-of-attorney, prudent estate planning frequently involves a program of estate reduction by making gifts within the limit of the annual $10,000 per donee gift tax exclusion. [Under IRC § 2.503(b)(2), the annual exclusion amount in increased to $12,000 per year in 2006 — Eds.] This gift-giving technique used in estate planning is common and is contemplated by the Internal Revenue Code (Code).

Because these two approaches to estate planning often intersect, it becomes advisable for an attorney-in-fact to make gifts of the principal's assets by taking advantage of the annual gift tax exclusion. Despite the fact that a general grant of power-of-attorney would seemingly include the ability to make gifts, the Internal Revenue Service (IRS or Service) has consistently challenged the authority of those attorneys-in-fact who attempt to make gifts by arguing that the agents are acting ultra vires. According to the IRS, because the attorney-in-fact is acting without authority, the gifts are actually "revocable transfers" and, consequently, are includable in the decedent's estate. Although most courts

---

[*] Copyright © 1996. Reprinted with permission. Copyright to the *Elder Law Journal* is held by the Board of Trustees of the University of Illinois.

have agreed with the IRS's position, several recent Tax Court and court of appeals decisions have interpreted broad grants of power to include the authority to make gifts. Furthermore, both Alabama and Virginia[*] have enacted legislation that specifically recognizes that a general grant of power to an attorney-in-fact includes implied authority to make gifts, thereby denying the IRS the ability to challenge powers-of-attorney on this ground in these two states.

ESTATE OF ROSA B. NEFF v. COMMISSIONER OF INTERNAL REVENUE
73 T.C.M. (CCH) 2606 (1997)

VASQUEZ, Judge:

Respondent determined a deficiency in petitioner's Federal estate tax in the amount of $61,381. . . . The sole issue for decision is whether transfers of decedent's property shortly before her death were incomplete gifts, the value of which should be included in her estate. . . .

FINDINGS OF FACT

Rosa B. Neff (decedent) died on September 13, 1992, at the age of 97. Decedent was a resident of Keyes, Oklahoma, most of her adult life and at the time of her death. Decedent executed her last will and testament on January 18, 1980.

A Federal estate tax return was filed on behalf of petitioner on June 9, 1993. The Federal estate tax return was signed by Chris Hunt, the estate's executor. On May 1, 1993, a Federal gift tax return for the 1992 tax year was filed on behalf of the estate by Chris Hunt.

The 1992 Federal gift tax return showed gifts to 19 relatives of decedent made on August 27 or 28 or September 12, 1992. These gifts included 19 separate annuities, 3 Series E bonds, and $4,000 in cash, with a total reported value of $293,249. The estate claimed nineteen $10,000 exclusions under section 2503(b), in the total amount of $190,000, resulting in a net taxable gift of $103,249. After the gifts in issue were made, the total gross estate, as reported on the estate tax return, exceeded $973,000.

---

* [Enacted in 1992, VA. CODE 11-9.5(A) provides: "If any power of attorney or other writing (i) authorizes an attorney-in-fact or other agent to do, execute, or perform any act that the principal might or could do or (ii) evidences the principal's intent to give the attorney-in-fact or agent full power to handle the principal's affairs or deal with the principal's property, the attorney-in-fact or agent shall have the power and authority to make gifts in any amount of any of the principal's property to any individuals or to organizations described in §§ 170(c) and 2522(a) of the Internal Revenue Code [i.e., gifts qualifying for the income tax charitable deduction or the gift tax charitable deduction] or corresponding future provisions of federal tax law, or both, in accordance with the principal's personal history of making or joining in the making of lifetime gifts." Mississippi, North Carolina, North Dakota, and Tennessee have all enacted similar laws since this article was published. In addition, the Texas statutory power of attorney form permits the principal to specifically authorize the agent to make gifts up to the amount covered by the gift tax annual exclusion amount. TEX. PROB. CODE § 490. —Eds.]

Rosa Neff purchased the 19 separate annuities in 1987 from Delta Life and Annuity Co. (Delta Life). The 19 annuitants were decedent's nephews and nieces, a sister-in-law, and a former brother-in-law (Chris Hunt). On each of the annuities, decedent was listed as the owner, and the annuitant was listed as the contingent owner. The contingent owner would become the owner at the death of decedent. Jess Murphy was the selling agent on behalf of Delta Life with respect to the 19 annuities. The 19 annuities were transferred to their respective "annuitants" on or about August 27, 1992, according to the schedules attached to the Federal estate and gift tax returns. The three Series E bonds were transferred on August 28, 1992. The $4,000 in cash was transferred on September 12, 1992.

These gifts of annuities, bonds, and cash were executed by Chris Hunt, Melvin Hammontree, and Mildred Williams, who at the time jointly held a durable power of attorney on behalf of decedent. Mr. Hunt, Mr. Hammontree, and Ms. Williams were each recipients of one of the annuities in issue. The durable power of attorney contained broad grants of authority which stated, inter alia:

My attorneys-in-fact shall have all of the powers, discretions, elections, and authorities granted by statute, common law, and under any rule of court.

* * *

My attorneys-in-fact may sell, convey, lease, exchange, mortgage, pledge, release, hypothecate, or otherwise deal with, dispose of, exchange, or encumber any of my property, either real or personal.

* * *

My attorneys-in-fact may act in all matters with respect to all powers described herein as freely, fully, and effectively as I could or might do personally if present and of sound and disposing mind.

The power of attorney did not, however, contain an explicit grant of gift-giving authority. Decedent executed the durable power of attorney by her own hand on July 17, 1992, and her signature was notarized. Prior to initiating the transfer of the 19 annuities, Mr. Murphy consulted the attorney who had drafted the durable power of attorney regarding whether the attorneys in fact had the power to make the transfers under the durable power of attorney. Mr. Murphy was told that the attorneys in fact did have the power to make such transfers.

The Rosa Neff Living Trust (the trust), a revocable trust, was created on August 27, 1992, by Mr. Hunt, Mr. Hammontree, and Ms. Williams, acting as decedent's attorneys in fact. Decedent did not personally sign the trust documents; they were executed by her attorneys in fact on August 27, 1992. Decedent's property was distributed according to the provisions of the trust rather than the provisions of decedent's will.

During the period August 16 through September 1, 1992, decedent was hospitalized due to a fall which resulted in a broken hip. On September 1, 1992, decedent returned to her home, where she was under the care of home health care nurses and family members until her death on September 13, 1992. Decedent died of acute heart failure as a result of chronic cardiovascular hypertensive disease and bronchitis from which she had suffered for approximately 10 years. Decedent's death was not unexpected.

Rosa Neff did not file any Federal gift tax returns during the 10-year period preceding her death in 1992. The only gifts made by Rosa Neff to relatives during this 10-year period which can be shown by documents bearing her signature are checks of small amounts, with respect to which gift tax returns were not required to be filed. Decedent also made several gifts of bonds and certificates of deposit during the 10-year period preceding her death, the amounts of which did not require the filing of Federal gift tax returns. Decedent was mentally competent to manage her affairs at all times.

Decedent was concerned about retaining control of her property at the time that she was considering executing a power of attorney. Decedent was present when the power of attorney was discussed with the attorney who drafted the document. Decedent was capable of signing her name in spite of failing eyesight if directed where to sign.

Prior to her injury and hospitalization, decedent informed several individuals that she was considering making a gift of the 19 annuities. Sometime during the summer of 1992, decedent told Betty Aaron, her accountant, that she was considering giving the annuities to the respective annuitants presently rather than after her death. Decedent also talked to Mr. Murphy about the possibility of giving the annuities to the annuitants. Prior to meeting with the attorney regarding the drafting of a durable power of attorney, decedent indicated to Chris Hunt that she wanted to give the 19 annuities to the annuitants.

Prior to her last illness, decedent cashed in two Delta Life annuities whose contingent owners had died. These annuities are not included in the 19 in issue. At the time that decedent cashed in the two annuities, she told Mr. Murphy that she intended to pay the taxes resulting from the transaction and give a portion of the proceeds of the annuities, in the amount of the principal or face amount of $10,000 each, to the heirs of the deceased annuitants/contingent owners.

ULTIMATE FINDING OF FACT

Decedent intended to make a present inter vivos gift of the 19 annuities in issue to the respective recipients.

OPINION

Section 2038(a)(1) provides that a decedent's gross estate includes any interest in property transferred by the decedent for less than full consideration if, at the time of the decedent's death, the transferred interest was subject to the decedent's power to revoke, alter, amend, or terminate. Section 2033 provides that the gross estate includes the value of all property to the extent that the decedent had an interest in it at the time of her death. State law determines the extent of a decedent's interest in property. We will follow the decisions of the highest State court, but in the absence of a decision by that court, we may look to the State's lower courts' rulings and holdings.

Respondent contends that because the durable power of attorney did not specifically grant the attorneys in fact the authority to make gifts of decedent's property, such gifts were incomplete, invalid, or revocable by decedent and thus includable in decedent's gross estate. We disagree.

The elements of a completed gift under Oklahoma law are: (1) intention to give, (2) complete delivery, and (3) acceptance by the donee. In order to establish an inter vivos gift after the death of the alleged donor, "the evidence must be clear, explicit, and convincing in support of every element necessary to constitute a gift." There does not seem to be any dispute that the annuities were delivered and accepted by the donees. Thus, if petitioner can prove donative intent, the transfers will be considered to be completed gifts which are not includable in decedent's gross estate. Respondent claims that the required donative intent cannot be supplied by a written durable power of attorney absent an express written gift authorization. Petitioner contends that the required donative intent is present because decedent authorized her attorneys in fact to make the gifts, because decedent ratified the gifts after the transfers, and because a written durable power of attorney, even absent an express gift authorization, is adequate to allow decedent's attorneys in fact to make effective inter vivos gifts. In order to determine whether the requisite donative intent existed, we must first look to the record as a whole to determine whether decedent possessed the requisite intent, taking into account the authority granted to decedent's attorneys in fact.

Decedent's Intent To Make Gifts

The transfers of property which are in issue in this case were executed shortly before decedent's death by decedent's attorneys in fact. Chris Hunt testified that in the summer of 1992 decedent specifically instructed him and Melvin Hammontree to transfer the annuities in question to the respective annuitants. We found Mr. Hunt's testimony to be credible and supported by the record as a whole. Shortly before the gifts were made, some of decedent's nephews became sick, and they needed money. At that time, decedent decided to give all of the annuities to the annuitants. Mr. Hunt testified that after he completed the transfers and so informed decedent, she was "well pleased" that the transfers were taken care of.

The record provides additional reasons to believe Mr. Hunt's testimony. The annuities were transferred to the annuitants who had been chosen by decedent when she originally purchased the annuities. These 19 annuitants would have become the owners of their respective annuities upon the death of decedent.

Jess Murphy testified that when contingent owners of two annuities not in issue predeceased decedent, it was decedent's desire that a portion of the funds from the annuities go to the heirs of the contingent owners. Mr. Murphy described decedent as "generous in giving." Additionally, Betty Aaron, decedent's accountant since approximately 1984, testified that decedent had talked to her in the summer of 1992 about transferring the annuities in question to the annuitants at that time rather than waiting until her death. Mr. Murphy and

Ms. Aaron were not contingent owners of any of the annuities. Lastly, even after the transfers in question, decedent was left with over $973,000 in assets.

We are cognizant that some States have a flat prohibition against attorneys in fact making gifts to themselves or to third parties absent express written authorization. Oklahoma, however, has not adopted such a rule. We believe that if the Oklahoma Supreme Court were to rule on this issue, it would look for "clear, explicit, and convincing" evidence of intent. . . .

Given the facts and circumstances of this case, we conclude that under Oklahoma law, the transfers in question would be valid gifts. . . .

The power of attorney which decedent executed does not restrict the attorneys in fact from making gifts. The power of attorney which decedent executed authorized her attorneys in fact to "convey . . . any of my property, either real or personal." The power of attorney authorizes the attorneys in fact to "act in all matters . . . as freely, fully, and effectively as I could or might do personally if present." This language evidences an intent to permit the attorneys in fact to make gifts of decedent's property.

Respondent argues that this Court should not allow decedent's intent to make a gift or decedent's ratification of a gift to be proved by the oral testimony of interested parties; namely Mr. Hunt. Respondent points to various factors which she contends show that decedent did not intend to make present inter vivos gifts at the time of the transfers. We disagree. As we have already found, petitioner's witnesses were credible, and their testimony was supported by the record. . . . Based on the record as a whole, we conclude that decedent, acting through her attorneys in fact, made completed inter vivos gifts of the annuities in question. Therefore, the value of the gifts is not includable in decedent's gross estate.

QUESTIONS

1. What does the Illinois short form power of attorney say about an agent's authority to give gifts?

2. How would you draft a power of attorney to avoid the gift-giving tax traps?

8. Durable Powers and Ademption by Extinction

LAYNE v. BOGGS
30 Va. Cir. 275, 1993 Va. Cir. LEXIS 53 (1993)

PAUL M. PEATROSS, Judge.

Ruth Boggs died on November 30, 1991, leaving a will dated November 3, 1980, which was admitted to probate before the Clerk of the Circuit Court on December 16, 1991. The will made specific bequests of $102,500.00 and various personal property, and contained the following paragraph:

Fifth: I direct that my Executor offer to sell to S. C. Sloan, if he survives me, my home at 1325 Kenwood Lane, Charlottesville, Virginia for the sum of $70,500.00 in cash, or at the price of the last fair market value appraisal for real estate tax purposes, whichever is lower. Said S. C. Sloan shall have thirty (30) days from the date of the qualification of my Executor to accept said offer and thirty (30) days after acceptance to close the transaction.

The will further provided that any residuary estate be divided among nieces and nephews. At the date of her death, Ruth Boggs' Estate was valued at $141,441.00.

The Complainant, Julian D. Layne, was named attorney-in-fact for Mrs. Boggs pursuant to a durable power of attorney dated April 19, 1984. He was appointed Guardian of Mrs. Boggs' Estate by Decree of this Court entered March 28, 1985. The will named Mr. Layne, who is Mrs. Boggs' nephew, as the Executor, as well.

On October 31, 1991, about one month before Mrs. Boggs died, Mr. Layne sold the Kenwood Lane property on her behalf, signing the deed as her attorney-in-fact. The net sales price of the property was $118,075.33. On December 16, 1991, Mr. Layne admitted Mrs. Boggs' will into probate and qualified as executor of her estate. He has brought this suit for aid and guidance to determine the effect of the sale of Mrs. Boggs' residence on the option granted to Mr. Sloan in the fifth article of the will. Respondent S.C. Sloan has claimed that he is entitled to at least the difference between the net sales price and the $70,500.00 for which the home was to be offered to Respondent Sloan.

DISCUSSION

The first issue to consider is the nature of the gift contained in the fifth Article of the decedent's will. As noted above, this section of the will directed the Executor of Mrs. Boggs' estate to offer her residence, located at 1325 Kenwood Lane, for sale to S.C. Sloan. The property to be offered was positively identified, and was distinguished from any other property which might have been held in Mrs. Boggs' estate. Clearly, the gift described in Section Five of the will could not be satisfied out of the general assets of the estate, and so must be described as a "specific legacy." In addition, the language of the bequest makes it clear that the Executor, Mr. Layne, was to be given no discretion regarding the sale of the property, so long as Mr. Sloan survived Mrs. Boggs. Rather, Mr. Layne was directed by the will to offer the residence to Mr. Sloan for the price of $70,500, or fair market value, whichever was lower. In turn, Mr. Sloan was given the option to purchase the property, but was not obligated to do so. Because the duty to sell and the duty to buy arising under the will were not reciprocal obligations, the Court concludes that the gift to Mr. Sloan was an option to purchase specific property, and not a right of first refusal.

A testator may, in her will, grant to another an option to purchase property of the estate, whether at its appraised value or at some other named price. However, for such an option to be effective, the specific property subject to the option must be property of the estate. Under Virginia law, this condition must be met at the time of the testator's death, unless a contrary intention plainly appears in the will. If the underlying property is not in the estate at the time of the testator's death, then any bequest purporting to convey an option to purchase that property will ultimately fail. *Conversion*: The critical issue in the case at bar, then, is whether the sale of the residential property by Mr. Layne during Mrs. Boggs' incapacity converted it from real to personal property, thereby removing it from the estate and rendering the option ineffective. The leading authority on this issue appears to be *Bryson v. Turnbull*, 194 Va. 528 (1953), in which the court looked at the judicially-approved sale of land by the conservator of an incompetent testator. There, the court held that where land is sold by order of the court for any purpose, the character of the property should be changed only so far as may be necessary to accomplish the particular purpose. Where an incompetent's real property is sold through compulsory proceedings, the court adopted the rule that the money proceeds paid into court will continue to be considered as real property until its nature is changed voluntarily by the owner, who has a right to elect to treat it as money. Applying this rule in *Bryson*, then, the court held that the proceeds of a guardian's sale of real property would pass under the incompetent testator's will as real estate, to those to whom she had devised those lands. The general holding in *Bryson* has been codified in VA. CODE § 64.1-62.3, which provides that:

> [a] bequest or devise of specific property shall, in addition to such property as is part of the estate of the testator, be deemed to be a legacy of a pecuniary amount if such specific property shall, during the life of the testator and while he is under a disability, be sold by the conservator, guardian, or committee for the testator. . .

By its terms, this language applies only to sales by judicially-appointed representatives of an incompetent testator, and will be effective only where the sale was in the agent's capacity as a representative of the court. The parties have presented no case law or statutory provision which would extend this proposition to sales executed by attorneys-in-fact acting pursuant to a durable power of attorney. In fact, the legislative history of Senate Bill No. 727, which amended and reenacted VA. CODE § 64.1-62.3 in the 1991 Session of the General Assembly, indicates to the Court that the Legislature has actually considered and rejected just such an extension.

Thus, the Court finds that the holding in *Bryson* does not apply to the sale of real estate executed by Mr. Layne in the case at bar. Although Mr. Layne served both as guardian and as attorney-in-fact for Mrs. Boggs, he sold Mrs. Boggs' residence solely in his capacity as attorney-in-fact. He did not seek court approval for the sale, but chose instead to exercise his authority under the durable power of attorney. Consequently, the court must conclude that the sale of Mrs. Boggs' residence converted the real property into personal property, and removed the residence from Mrs. Boggs' estate.

Intent: This result is in accord with VA. CODE § 11-9.1, which permits a principal to vest his agent with powers that survive the principal's disability through a durable power of attorney. Specifically, this section states that:

> All acts done by the attorney-in-fact or agent, pursuant to such power or authority, during the period of any such disability, incompetence or incapacity, shall have in all respects the same effect . . . and bind the

principal as fully as if the principle were not subject to such disability, incompetence or incapacity.

Thus, the statute directs the Court to analyze the transaction in question as though Mrs. Boggs had not been incompetent at the time of the sale. The traditional rule is that a competent principal will be bound by the acts of her agent, within the scope of the agent's ostensible or apparent authority. This rule applies where the agent has been vested with the authority to sell or dispose of real property.

An examination of the durable power of attorney executed by Mrs. Boggs reveals that the actual extent of the authority granted to Mr. Layne was considerable. Mrs. Boggs specified that "[t]his power of attorney shall not terminate upon my disability," and she ratified and confirmed, in advance, all actions which might subsequently be taken by her attorney-in-fact. Of particular relevance to the case at bar, the fifth section of the document authorizes Mr. Layne, in his capacity as attorney-in-fact, to:

> enter upon and take possession of any lands, buildings or other improvements or appurtenances to lands belonging to me now or in the future . . . and to sell or lease such property or any part of or interest in any such property, and make, execute and deliver any deed, mortgage or lease, with or without covenants and warranties, with respect to such property.

It is thus apparent to the Court that Mr. Layne was acting within his authority as Mrs. Boggs' attorney-in-fact when he sold the property at 1325 Kenwood Lane. Had she been competent at the time, Mrs. Boggs would clearly have been bound by that sale, under the ordinary rules of agency. Even though she appears to have been incompetent at the time of the sale, however, 11-9.1 instructs the court to ignore that disability in determining the effect of her agent's actions. Accordingly, the Court finds that Mrs. Boggs is bound by Mr. Layne's actions during her disability. The subsequent ratification and confirmation by Mrs. Boggs of her agent's actions is sufficient to impute to her the intent to sell the property, thereby removing it from her estate.

CONCLUSION

By the language of her will, Mrs. Boggs granted an option to Mr. Sloan to purchase her residence at 1325 Kenwood Lane. In order for that testamentary gift to be valid, however, the property must have been property of the estate at the time of her death. To be sure, the sale by Mr. Layne prior to Mrs. Boggs' death removed the physical property itself from her estate. The question then becomes whether the act of Mr. Layne, as Mrs. Boggs' attorney-in-fact, was sufficient to convert the proceeds of the sale from real to personal property, thereby defeating the testamentary gift. Reviewing the authorities discussed above, the Court can find no reason to treat the cash proceeds of the sale as though they remained real property. In the first instance, the reasoning of the *Bryson* court is inapplicable to this case, primarily because no judicial involvement was involved in the sale. Section 64.1-62.3 is also inapplicable, for much the same reason. Additionally, the scope of the durable power of attorney was broad enough to allow the Court to impute Mrs. Boggs the intent to remove the property from the estate by the sale. Accordingly, the Court finds that the real property subject to the option, the residence at 1325 Kenwood Lane, is no longer property of the estate, and that the testamentary gift of the option must therefore fail. Ms. Smith is directed to prepare an decree consistent with this opinion, circulate it to other counsel for endorsement, and present it to the Court for entry.

QUESTIONS

1. If you had been a member of the Virginia circuit court, how would you have decided this case? Why?

2. Consider VA. CODE § 64.1-62.3(B), below, which was added to the statute in 1995. Would this change the outcome in a case like *Layne v. Boggs*? Why do you think the statute was amended?

Va. Code § 64.1-62.3(B)

Unless a contrary intention appears in a testator's will or durable power of attorney, a bequest or devise of specific property shall, in addition to such property as is part of the estate of the testator, be deemed to be a legacy of a pecuniary amount if such specific property shall, during the life of the testator and while he is incapacitated, be sold by an agent acting within the authority of a durable power of attorney for the testator, or if proceeds of fire or casualty insurance as to such property are paid to the agent. For purposes of this subdivision, (i) the pecuniary amount shall be the net sale price or insurance proceeds, reduced by the sums received under subdivision 2 [concerning condemnation awards], (ii) no adjudication of testator's incapacity before death is necessary, (iii) the acts of an agent within the authority of a durable power of attorney are rebuttably presumed to be for an incapacitated testator, and (iv) an "incapacitated" person is one who is impaired by reason of mental illness, mental deficiency, physical illness or disability, chronic use of drugs, chronic intoxication, or other cause to the extent of lacking sufficient understanding or capacity to make or communicate responsible decisions. This subdivision shall not apply (i) if the agent's sale of the specific property or receipt of the insurance proceeds is thereafter ratified by the testator or (ii) to a power of attorney limited to one or more specific purposes.

9. Lawyers as Agents

ABA Model Code of Professional Responsibility
Canons 5 and 9, and Ethical Consideration 5-6[*]

Canon 5

A Lawyer Should Exercise Independent Professional Judgment on Behalf of a Client

Canon 9

A Lawyer Should Avoid Even the Appearance of Professional Impropriety

EC 5-6 Interests of a Lawyer That May Affect His Judgment

A lawyer should not consciously influence a client to name him as executor, trustee, or lawyer in an instrument. In those cases where a client wishes to name his lawyer as such, care should be taken by the lawyer to avoid even the appearance of impropriety.

Linda J. Whitton
Durable Powers as a Hedge Against Guardianship: Should the Attorney-at-Law Accept Appointment as Attorney-in-Fact?
2 ELDER L.J. 39, 42, 62-65 (1994)[**]

When a client desires the benefits of a durable power of attorney but does not have a trusted family member or friend to serve as attorney-in-fact, the drafting lawyer is faced with the dilemma of how to assist the client with obtaining an appropriate agent. Authors of a comprehensive durable powers practice manual have suggested that one solution is to appoint the attorney-at-law as the client's attorney-in-fact. Likewise, a note writer has recommended advance delegation of durable powers to a client's lawyer as a means of avoiding the problems which could arise if a client loses competency during the course of legal representation. Despite these suggestions, the ethical propriety of a lawyer serving in the dual role of attorney-at-law and attorney-in-fact under a durable powers delegation has heretofore remained unexamined. . . .

Assuming arguendo that a lawyer agrees to accept delegation of durable powers as an accommodation to a client, two questions must be examined. First, would this arrangement pose ethical and practical difficulties for the lawyer when drafting the durable power of attorney? Second, would this

---

[*] Reprinted by permission. Copies of the ABA Model Code of Professional Responsibility (1981) are available from Member Services, American Bar Association, 750 North Lake Shore Drive, Chicago, Illinois 60611, 312-944-5522.

[**] Copyright © 1994. Reprinted with permission. Copyright to the *Elder Law Journal* is held by the Board of Trustees of the University of Illinois.

arrangement compromise the attorney-client relationship or the services provided to the principal after the advent of incompetency?

To answer the first question, it is necessary . . . [to consider three] drafting considerations — scope of authority, time of commencement, and conditions on the agent's performance. Of the three, scope of authority would appear to be least affected by the dual attorney-at-law/attorney-in-fact role. If the goal of the durable power of attorney is to prevent guardianship, the scope of authority will need to be comprehensive regardless of the identity of the agent. Likewise, any specialized powers included within this scope will be dictated by the principal's unique circumstances rather than those of the agent. The same is not true, however, for the remaining drafting considerations.

Choice of when a durable power of attorney is to commence, a matter of client preference, becomes particularly problematic when the attorney-at-law will also serve as attorney-in-fact. If the client prefers a springing power, should the attorney recommend an agent affidavit as proof of the client's incompetency, thereby accepting full responsibility for determining when the client has become incompetent? Or should the attorney recommend physician certification, which requires more effort to obtain, but which will probably better protect the attorney's exposure to liability?

Neither of the foregoing alternatives is totally satisfactory for the attorney or the client. In the first, the attorney breaches, at the very least, client loyalty by becoming the sole judge of the client's competency. In the second, the attorney must not only breach loyalty by questioning the client's competency, but must also breach confidentiality by divulging information about the client's condition in order to obtain the physician's certification of incompetence. The client, on the other hand, risks the attorney assuming control prematurely under the first alternative but faces certain invasion of privacy under the second.

Even more problematic is the issue of conditions on the agent's performance. How can the lawyer maintain independent professional judgment in advising the principal on negotiation of the agent's compensation when it is the lawyer who will be compensated as agent? . . .

[T]he problems associated with accepting delegation of a client's durable powers go beyond the issue of compensation. Limitation of liability, the other primary inducement for agent performance, also raises a dilemma for the drafting attorney. One could argue that a lawyer who agrees to serve as attorney-in-fact is entitled to the same extent of liability limitation and indemnification from the principal as would be recommended if a nonlawyer were appointed. However, wearing both the hat of the draftsperson and the agent places the lawyer in a conflict of interest posture that precludes independent professional judgment about the proper extent of liability limitation. . . .

Furthermore, objective advice with respect to placing limitations in the durable power of attorney for the purpose of monitoring the agent's activities is also impossible when the drafting attorney is the agent. . . .

As the foregoing ethical problems demonstrate, the dual attorney-at-law/attorney-in-fact role would seriously impede the lawyer's independent professional judgment when advising the client with respect to the majority of durable power drafting considerations, thereby compromising the attorney-client relationship. In addition, consideration of the typical issues occasioned by the advent of client incompetency will demonstrate how dual representation would further erode the attorney-client relationship upon the advent of client incompetency, as well as negatively impact the services provided to the incompetent principal.

Upon the onset of client incompetency, the lawyer faces a dilemma similar to that faced by the attorney who institutes guardianship proceedings for a client. . . . First, the lawyer must breach client loyalty by questioning the client's competency and then client confidentiality either by stating, via affidavit, that the client is incompetent, or by revealing the client's condition to a physician to obtain a certification of incompetence. The disintegration of the attorney-client relationship, however, would not stop with breach of loyalty and confidentiality.

At the point when a client loses competency and the attorney-at-law becomes vested with the client's durable powers, the lawyer, in effect, loses a client. The lawyer can no longer communicate with the client about material aspects of the representation, and the client can no longer make the substantive decisions governing the representation. In reality the lawyer, as attorney-in-fact, also becomes the client. There is no longer accountability for any actions taken by the lawyer as attorney-at-law because there is no longer a competent principal to ask questions, make decisions, or file a complaint for malpractice or disciplinary action. This fusion of roles obliterates all of the essential characteristics of the attorney-client relationship: undivided loyalty, confidentiality, client-centered decision making, independent professional judgment, and accountability.

QUESTIONS

1. Do you agree with Professor Whitton that lawyers should always avoid being named as their clients' attorneys-in-fact? Do you reach the same conclusion under the Model Rule 1.14 (*see* excerpt in Chapter 2) as you would under the Model Code?

2. If a client wanted to name you as his or her agent, what steps might you take to minimize any conflicts of interest or appearance of impropriety?

B. JOINT OWNERSHIP AND FINANCIAL ACCOUNTS

1. Joint Ownership Generally: Forms and Issues

Edwin G. Fee, Jr.
New Disclaimer Regs. and Other Rules Affecting Jointly Owned Property
25 EST. PLAN. 117, 117 (March/April 1998)[*]

The most common forms of ownership in which two or more persons may own property are joint tenancy, tenancy in common, and tenancy by the entirety. State law determines which type of ownership exists with respect to particular property. Because the definitions of these categories vary from state to state, the following discussion describes the most common features of these types of ownership.

Joint tenancy. Joint tenancy is a form of ownership by two or more persons pursuant to which each joint tenant owns an undivided interest in the entire property and has a right of survivorship. Depending on applicable state law, a joint tenant may transfer his joint interest to a third person, thus converting the joint tenancy into a tenancy in common (discussed below). A joint tenant might accomplish the same result by transferring his joint interest to himself as a tenant in common. A joint tenant also may seek judicial partition of the property, pursuant to which he would receive a proportionate part of the property.

When a joint tenant dies, his interest automatically passes in equal shares to the remaining joint tenant(s). Because an interest in a joint tenancy does not pass under a deceased owner's will, joint tenancy is a method of avoiding probate.

Tenancy in common. A tenancy in common is not subject to a right of survivorship. Instead, each tenant in common owns an undivided interest in a portion of the property. When one of the owners dies, his interest passes to his named beneficiaries (if the owner has a valid will) or heirs (if the owner dies without a will) according to state probate law. Furthermore, each tenant in common can sell his interest freely. Because tenancy in common is not really a form of joint ownership, this article focuses primarily on joint tenancy and a related form of ownership, tenancy by the entirety.

Tenancy by the entirety. Tenancy by the entirety is a form of joint ownership between spouses that is recognized by approximately half the states. Similar to joint tenancy, in tenancy by the entirety each spouse has a right of survivorship. Thus, tenancy by the entirety can be used to avoid probate on the death of the first spouse to die. Unlike joint tenancy, though, one spouse acting alone generally cannot partition or transfer his interest.

Mary A. Donovan
Pitfalls of Joint Ownership with Children
10 KOLEY JESSEN CLIENT ADVISER, Issue 4, *available at*
http://www.koleyjessen.com/html/resources.cfm?SUBCAT=
4&ArticleID=248 (published 2005)[*]

Under a joint tenancy with rights of survivorship ("JTWROS") titling arrangement, co-tenants own the property in equal shares, and upon the death of one or more co-tenant(s), the interest formerly held by the deceased co-tenant passes automatically to the surviving co-tenant(s) without subjecting the property to probate. In addition, the co-tenants as co-owners have the ability to act with respect to the asset. . . .

JTWROS titling in real estate and other assets creates a present, irrevocable interest in the property among all co-tenants. This may not sound too problematic; however, if at some point a co-tenant fails to pay taxes, defaults on a loan, is sued for inappropriate contact at a holiday party and has a judgment entered against him/her, the creditors of that co-tenant will be able to reach his/her interest in the property in satisfaction of the debt owed. Any judgment or tax lien suffered by a co-tenant will also be a lien against the property held under JTWROS. With respect to real estate and other assets. . . , it is inconsequential that the co-tenant may not have contributed any money toward the purchase of the property; creditors can still reach the interest held by the co-tenant. . . .

Another reason to avoid JTWROS titling with children is that JTWROS titling is often inconsistent with the terms of the parent's estate plan. . . . Even though the surviving children may plan to share the assets. . . , questions and issues inevitably arise. . . .

Additional problems may develop if a parent should ever desire to sell the property while all the co-tenants are still living. As previously mentioned, each co-tenant has a present, irrevocable interest in the property. Thus, each co-tenant must consent to any sale of the property and is entitled to a share of the proceeds. Depending upon intra-family relations, this could pose a significant obstacle to the sale of any property titled as JTWROS. On a related note, each co-tenant may force a division of the property by going to a court and requesting that it be partitioned. If possible, and economically feasible, the court could physically partition the property and award each co-tenant equal shares (an example where this could work would be farm acreage). However, if the property in question is a home or other structure that cannot be feasibly divided, the court would likely order a sale and divide the proceeds among the co-tenants.

2. Joint Bank Accounts

a. Rights During Lifetime: Theory Versus Practice

Uniform Probate Code § 6-211(b)

During the lifetime of all parties, [a joint] account belongs to the parties in proportion to the net contribution of each to the sums on deposit, unless there is clear and convincing evidence of a different intent. As between parties married to each other, in the absence of proof otherwise, the net contribution of each is presumed to be an equal amount.

QUESTION

What happens when one owner of a joint bank account wishes to withdraw all the funds on deposit?

b. Rights at Death: Presumptions and Their Rebuttal

Uniform Probate Code § 6-212(a)

Except as otherwise provided in this part, on death of a party sums on deposit in a multiple-party account belong to the surviving party or parties. If two or more parties survive and one is the surviving spouse of the decedent, the amount to which the decedent, immediately before death, was beneficially entitled . . . belongs to the surviving spouse. If two or more parties survive and none is the surviving spouse of the decedent, the amount to which the decedent, immediately before death, was beneficially entitled . . . belongs to the surviving parties in equal shares . . . and the right of survivorship continues between the surviving parties.

QUESTION

If your client wished to set up a bank account with a survivorship feature, what steps might you take to avoid future litigation about survivorship?

Ronald R. Volkmer
Problems Resulting from Joint Tenancies
21 Est. Plan. 375, 377 (November/December 1994)[*]

The most nettlesome problem in the law of joint tenancy bank accounts involves whether to allow extrinsic evidence to rebut the presumption of survivorship contained in the standard form for a joint tenancy account. The most

---

[*] Copyright © 1994. Reprinted with permission.

widely accepted approach . . . is that there is a presumption that the surviving joint tenants to a joint tenancy are entitled to the balance upon the death of one of the joint tenants. This presumption, however, may be rebutted by evidence of a contrary intent, showing that the depositor did not intend to have survivorship rights attach even though the account is placed in survivorship form. Opening the door to such evidence allows for proof of so-called convenience accounts — as for example, where the grandmother placed the granddaughter's name on the joint account for the limited purpose of making withdrawals.

Allowing extrinsic evidence to be admitted is hazardous because the person whose intent is questioned is now deceased and the written language of the account (providing for survivorship) is being overridden. Almost every state has had to muddle through this difficult issue, with legislatures in some states taking the lead in establishing clear rules. More often than not, though, it is the state appellate courts that have had the unenviable task of sorting all this out. To say there has been much confusion in the law is an understatement.

c. The Reach of Third Parties: Creditors

Edwin G. Fee, Jr.
New Disclaimer Regs. and Other Rules
Affecting Jointly Owned Property
25 EST. PLAN. 117, 117-118 (March/April 1998)*

[The rule that tenancy by the entirety cannot be unilaterally partitioned by one spouse] creates an advantage in some instances, because creditors of only one spouse generally cannot force partition and sale of the property to satisfy the spouse's individual debt. In contrast, creditors often can satisfy an individual debt with an interest held as a joint tenant or a tenant in common. Creditors of both spouses usually can seek satisfaction of the joint debt from property held in any of the forms described above.

QUESTION

How serious is the problem raised by the ability of creditors to reach property held in joint tenancy or tenancy in common?

d. The Reach of Third Parties: Gift Taxes

Excerpts from the Gift Tax Treasury Regulations

§ 25.2511-1. Transfers in general.

(a) The gift tax applies to a transfer by way of gift whether the transfer is in trust or otherwise, whether the gift is direct or indirect, and whether the prop-

---

* Copyright © 1998. Reprinted with permission.

erty is real or personal, tangible or intangible. For example, a taxable transfer may be effected by the creation of a trust, the forgiving of a debt, the assignment of a judgment, the assignment of the benefits of an insurance policy, or the transfer of cash, certificates of deposit, or Federal, State or municipal bonds. Statutory provisions which exempt bonds, notes, bills and certificates of indebtedness of the Federal Government or its agencies and the interest thereon from taxation are not applicable to the gift tax, since the gift tax is an excise tax on the transfer, and is not a tax on the subject of the gift.

§ 25.2511-2. Cessation of donor's dominion and control.

. . . .

(b) As to any property, or part thereof or interest therein, of which the donor has so parted with dominion and control as to leave in him no power to change its disposition, whether for his own benefit or for the benefit of another, the gift is complete. But if upon a transfer of property (whether in trust or otherwise) the donor reserves any power over its disposition, the gift may be wholly incomplete, or may be partially complete and partially incomplete, depending upon all the facts in the particular case. . . .

QUESTIONS

If the governing state law were the Uniform Probate Code, would the transfer of funds into a joint account constitute a taxable gift? If not, at what point would a taxable gift occur?

e. The Reach of Third Parties: Estate Taxes

Excerpts from the Internal Revenue Code

§ 2033. Property in which the decedent had an interest.

The value of the gross estate shall include the value of all property to the extent of the interest therein of the decedent at the time of his death.

§ 2040. Joint interests.

(a) General rule. The value of the gross estate shall include the value of all property to the extent of the interest therein held as joint tenants with right of survivorship by the decedent and any other person, or as tenants by the entirety by the decedent and spouse, or deposited, with any person carrying on the banking business, in their joint names and payable to either or the survivor, except such part thereof as may be shown to have originally belonged to such other person and never to have been received or acquired by the latter from the decedent for less than an adequate and full consideration in money or money's worth: Provided, That where such property or any part thereof, or part of the consideration with which such property was acquired, is shown to have been at any time acquired by such other person from the decedent for less than an adequate and full consideration in money or money's worth, there shall be excepted only such part of the value of such property as is proportionate to the consideration furnished by such other person: Provided further, That where any property has been acquired by gift, bequest, devise, or inheritance, as a tenancy by the entirety by the decedent and spouse, then to the extent of one-half of the value thereof, or, where so acquired by the decedent and any other person as joint tenants with right of survivorship and their interests are not otherwise specified or fixed by law, then to the extent of the value of a fractional part to be determined by dividing the value of the property by the number of joint tenants with right of survivorship.

(b) Certain joint interests of husband and wife. —

(1) Interests of spouse excluded from gross estate. — Notwithstanding subsection (a), in the case of any qualified joint interest, the value included in the gross estate with respect to such interest by reason of this section is one-half of the value of such qualified joint interest.

(2) Qualified joint interest defined. — For purposes of paragraph (1), the term "qualified joint interest" means any interest in property held by the decedent and the decedent's spouse as —

(A) tenants by the entirety, or

(B) joint tenants with right of survivorship, but only if the decedent and the spouse of the decedent are the only joint tenants.

Edwin G. Fee, Jr.
New Disclaimer Regs. and Other Rules Affecting Jointly Owned Property
25 EST. PLAN. 117, 120 (March/April 1998)[*]

Section 2040(a) generally provides that the gross estate includes the entire value of (1) a joint tenancy with right of survivorship; (2) a tenancy by the entirety; or (3) a deposit of money, bond, or other instrument in the name of the decedent and any other person and payable to either or the survivor. Nevertheless, there are several exceptions . . that specifically address (1) property for which the decedent did not furnish all the consideration; (2) property acquired by gift, bequest, or inheritance; and (3) property held by spouses. The rules concerning joint interests do not apply to an interest held as a tenant in common (which is included in the gross estate under Section 2033). In addition, Section 2040(a) should not require inclusion in the decedent's estate of any property in which the decedent had only a nominal, rather than beneficial, joint interest.

QUESTION

What are the estate tax consequences of the typical joint bank account?

---

[*] Copyright © 1998. Reprinted with permission.

f. Joint Accounts: An Evaluation

Richard V. Wellman
New Types of Joint Bank Accounts Resolve Many Problems
22 EST. PLAN. 232, 232 (July/August 1995)[*]

Use of joint checking and savings accounts is perilous for others than happily married couples. Married persons often accept the risk that whatever one of them puts in the account may be lost due to the other's whim or bad luck. Married couples probably intend the survivor of them to enjoy the entire account on the death of the other. They view the joint account as an easily arranged, costless device for achieving mutual money management goals, including having funds accessible to either or to the survivor. The implicit risk that the entire account may be lost to creditors of either coincides with the expectations of married couples with or without joint accounts. As a result, joint accounts are very popular.

The problem is that the advantages of a joint account make it attractive to unmarried persons, many of whom undoubtedly select this form of account without knowing the risks that attend it when used by others than spouses. For example, an account funded by one person as a means of passing to a surviving party any balance remaining at the depositor's death may cause the depositor to be treated as having made an immediate gift of a fraction of the deposited funds to others named as joint parties. This means that the depositor may have to account to the other person for part of a later withdrawal of more than his or her share. In addition, there is a risk that creditors or a spouse of the other party may have a right to reach some or all of the funds. Moreover, litigation over whether the survivor was intended to receive a gift of the balance on hand at death is a distinct possibility.

QUESTIONS

1. What are the advantages and disadvantages of joint bank accounts?

2. If a client with three children wanted to set up a joint account with one of those children, how would you advise that client?

3. How would you evaluate the use of joint bank accounts? Is Professor Wellman's critique accurate or is it overstated?

Alternatives to Joint Accounts: Agency Accounts and P.O.D. Accounts

Excerpts from the Uniform Probate Code

§ 6-201. Definitions.

In this part:

(1) "Account" means a contract of deposit between a depositor and a financial institution, and includes a checking account, savings account, certificate of deposit, and share account.

(2) "Agent" means a person authorized to make account transactions for a party.

. . .

(6) "Party" means a person who, by the terms of an account, has a present right, subject to request, to payment from the account other than as a beneficiary or agent.

§ 6-203. Types of Account; . . .

(a) An account may be for a single party or multiple parties. A multiple-party account may be with or without a right of survivorship between the parties. Subject to Section 6-212(c) [dealing with ownership rights at the death of a party], either a single-party account or a multiple-party account may have a P.O.D. designation, an agency designation, or both.

§ 6-205. Designation of Agent.

(a) By a writing signed by all parties, the parties may designate as agent of all parties on an account a person other than a party.

(b) Unless the terms of an agency designation provide that the authority of the agent terminates on disability or incapacity of a party, the agent's authority survives disability and incapacity. The agent may act for a disabled or incapacitated party until the authority of the agent is terminated.

(c) Death of the sole party or last surviving party terminates the authority of an agent.

§ 6-211. Ownership During Lifetime.

. . .

(d) An agent in an account with an agency designation has no beneficial right to sums on deposit.

§ 6-224. Payment to Designated Agent.

A financial institution, on request of an agent under an agency designation for an account, may pay to the agent sums on deposit in the account, whether or not a party is disabled, incapacitated, or deceased when the request is made or received, and whether or not the authority of the agent terminates on the disability or incapacity of a party.

§ 6-226. Discharge.

(a) Payment made pursuant to this part in accordance with the terms of the account discharges the financial institution from all claims for amounts so paid, whether or not the payment is consistent with the beneficial ownership of the account as between parties, beneficiaries, or their successors. Payment may be made whether or not a party, beneficiary, or agent is disabled, incapacitated, or deceased when payment is requested, received, or made.

(b) Protection under this section does not extend to payments made after a financial institution has received written notice from a party, or from the personal representative, surviving spouse, or heir or devisee of a deceased party, to the effect that payments in accordance with the terms of the account, including one having an agency designation, should not be permitted, and the financial institution has had a reasonable opportunity to act on it when the payment is made. Unless the notice is withdrawn by the person giving it, the successor of any deceased party must concur in a request for payment if the financial institution is to be protected under this section. Unless a financial institution has been served with process in an action or proceeding, no other notice or other information shown to have been available to the financial institution affects its right to protection under this section. . . .

Richard V. Wellman
Joint Accounts: Dangers and Alternatives
The ACTEC Foundation[*]

Unfortunately, useful information about **JOINT ACCOUNTS** and other multiple-name account forms is scarce. Banking companies typically respond to customer questions about these accounts by use of computer menus or other lists of choices, and by offering complex contract forms for customer inspection. New Accounts personnel are often warned against giving advice to customers about their account choices or responding to questions about ownership between persons named on these accounts. This probably is wise bank policy because bank personnel may lack the training and experience needed to advise customers about the complex legal relationships that accompany accounts bearing more than one person's name. . . .

Given the uncertainties and risks implicit in **JOINT ACCOUNTS**, persons should be interested in alternative account forms that offer **JOINT ACCOUNT** advantages but avoid **JOINT ACCOUNT** risks.

JOINT ACCOUNTS serve to (1) assure access to funds in spite of a depositor's loss of capacity; (2) transfer the account balance at death via the survivorship right avoiding probate; and (3) permit full commingling of funds by persons in close relationships who trust each other. Years ago, persons who

---

wanted only some of these features had to choose between all or none because the **JOINT ACCOUNT** was the only multiple-name account offered.

The good news is that most banking institutions now offer alternatives to the **JOINT ACCOUNT** that meet the needs of most persons interested in less than all features of a conventional **JOINT ACCOUNT**. One is an account describing the depositor's selection of a beneficiary who is entitled only to balances in the account at the depositor's death. The other is a single owner account that designates a second person to be recognized by the bank as the depositor's agent having authority to withdraw for the depositor who is not intended to have a personal beneficial interest in account balances immediately or at the depositor's death.

DEATH BENEFICIARY ONLY ACCOUNT

Two account forms enable a depositor to retain sole ownership and control of an account that designates another to receive the account by a nonprobate transfer at the depositor's death. One is known as a "pay on death" (P.O.D.) account. The other, called a trust account or "Totten" trust, takes the form of an account in the name of the depositor who is described as "trustee" for, or as holding "in trust for," the person named as beneficiary. For example, a P.O.D. account title would appear as "John A. Owens, P.O.D. Nancy Owens." A trust account title would appear as "John A. Owens, trustee for Nancy Owens."

Both forms create what we call a **DEATH BENEFICIARY ONLY ACCOUNT**, having the following characteristics:

- the owner [John A. Owens] has sole ownership and control of the account;

- Nancy Owens [whether named as "P.O.D. Nancy Owens" or as beneficiary in a trust account] becomes the new owner of the account upon surviving the owner [John];

- Nancy usually will not have to sign the bank form establishing the account, and may or may not be aware of the account;

- the owner [John] can close the account by withdrawing all money from it, and the beneficiary's consent [Nancy's] is not needed;

- the bank should **not** be counted on to notify a beneficiary of this death benefit, meaning that the owner should tell the beneficiary about the arrangement, or leave information about it in a writing to be read after death such as a Will, so as to enable the beneficiary to apply to the bank for the proceeds.

A DEATH BENEFICIARY ONLY ACCOUNT serves like a Will to give the death beneficiary whatever is in the account at the death of the owner but differs from a Will in that it need not be probated. Also, though Will-like in function, it generally cannot be revoked by a later Will and can be nullified only by closing the account or by signing another [new] account agreement.

Note, too, that in most states, divorce alone revokes a Will's gifts to the former spouse by operation of law, meaning automatically and whether or not that result is intended by the persons involved. This revocation by divorce rule generally does <u>not</u> serve to revoke a former spouse's right as death beneficiary of a **DEATH BENEFICIARY ONLY** account, but some court decisions recognize that the trust account form (but not the P.O.D. form) may be affected by the Will, and a few recent statutes recognize explicit language in a Will as effective to alter any account death benefit.

Despite these possible uncertainties, a **DEATH BENEFICIARY ONLY ACCOUNT** is preferred to a **JOINT ACCOUNT** as a method of transferring money at death without probate. Unlike the **JOINT ACCOUNT**, the **DEATH BENEFICIARY ONLY ACCOUNT** can serve no other purpose but to make a transfer at death; there can be no confusion about the owner's purpose as was suggested in our Aunt Mary-Amanda case described earlier. A claim against a **DEATH BENEFICIARY ONLY ACCOUNT** by heirs of the deceased owner should fail unless the deceased lacked capacity to understand the deposit transaction or was wrongfully misled or coerced in selecting the death benefit form.

A death beneficiary designation can be added to a joint account with survivorship. For example, a married couple might want a joint and survivor account and also want to provide that at the death of the survivor of the couple the account should go to their children. As in the example of John and Nancy Owens, the account could be set up in this fashion:

> payable to John A. Owens and Nancy Owens, and the survivor of them, and upon the death of the survivor, P.O.D. their children, Mary Owens and Mickey Owens, surviving them in equal shares [or in whatever proportion John and Nancy prefer].

The wording may change with particular banks, and even may be in the form of a trust, payable to John A. Owens and Nancy Owens, and the survivor, in trust for Mary Owens and Mickey Owens. Either way, the death beneficiary takes nothing until both John and Nancy die without expending or changing the account. (The survivor of the two original owners is the sole owner following the first death and is free to change the death benefit.)

CONVENIENCE OR AGENCY ACCOUNT

Some persons may want a single or joint owner account with access by another person who is not an owner but is authorized to act as the owner's agent or assistant. This type of account offers the convenience of dual access but avoids the risk of loss to creditors of the assistant <u>and</u> avoids any survivorship benefit for the assistant.

One form serving this purpose is a single or multiple-person account that designates an "additional authorized signatory" who may sign withdrawals on behalf of the owner-depositor. Another form serving the same purpose describes the assistant as the owner's "agent," or as authorized by the owner's "power of attorney." Some banks refer to accounts in either of these forms as "Convenience Accounts." We refer to all of these forms as **AGENCY ACCOUNTS**.

On occasion a bank may insist on receiving an accompanying "durable power of attorney" document incident to opening an **AGENCY ACCOUNT**. More commonly, power of attorney language will be included in account paperwork signed when the account is opened or simply implied from describing the assistant as an agent or otherwise authorized to act on behalf of the account owner.

Authority to access an owner's account as the owner's agent or additional authorized signatory ends when the bank receives written notice of revocation of the agency, or of the depositor's death.

Don't count on the bank to enforce an account agent's responsibility to the owner. Banks accept these arrangements only because they are protected by the account contract in recognizing the agent's withdrawal power as unconditional.

Most banks will recognize that the same person may be designated as the depositor's agent and as a death beneficiary. For example, an account might be entitled:

> Payable to Randolph Jones. Additional authorized signatory: Randolph Jones, II; P.O.D. Richard and Randolph Jones, II.

This form offers the advantage of dual access by one son without risk of loss to the son's creditors during the father's life, and a nonprobate transfer at the father's death to two sons, there being no need to favor the one who was his father's agent to handle account business.

QUESTION

If a new client told you that he had a "joint bank account" with his daughter, which kind of account would you take that to mean? How likely would you think it would be that he understood the difference between a joint account, a P.O.D. account, and a convenience account?

David M. English
The UPC and the New Durable Powers
27 REAL PROP., PROB. & TR. J. 333, 354-358 (1992)[*]

A joint tenancy bank account can be one of the probate lawyer's biggest nightmares. The signature card states that the survivor takes the entire account, but following the depositor's death the attorney may discover that the depositor did not intend to create a true joint tenancy. Instead, the depositor created the account for purposes of "convenience." The other joint tenant was supposed to have authority to pay the depositor's bills but was not to receive the funds at the depositor's death. Litigation then ensues to determine whether the evidence of that intent is sufficient to rebut the presumption that the signature card controls.

This problem has persisted for decades despite continued calls for clarifying legislation and pleas to bankers to exercise care in handing out joint tenancy signature cards. The durable power is an excellent alternative for bankers to consider. A depositor may grant an agent authority to pay bills without granting the

---

[*] Copyright © 1992 by the American Bar Association. Reprinted with permission.

agent an ownership interest, and the agency may survive into incapacity, when it is most needed. The durable power option has yet to take hold, however. Perhaps that is because of a lack of readily available account forms and because banks fear potential liability for making payments after the principal's death, a concern that does not apply if a joint account is substituted.

Although durable power bank accounts are rarely used, that failure is not due to a lack of legislative attention. Wisconsin has authorized the device since 1974 and Washington since 1981. However, since 1988, the durable power bank account has come into its own, with the UPC and four additional states joining the list of enacting jurisdictions. . . .

The most significant recent development in bank powers of attorney is the 1989 revision of Article VI of the UPC. . . . The UPC now authorizes a depositor to create an agency account that may survive incapacity. . . . The UPC provides an omnibus form that covers not only the creation of agency accounts, but also joint accounts, Totten trusts, and payable-on-death accounts, which are referred to by different terms. The form is complex, confusing, and, for all practical purposes, mandatory. The new UPC provisions do, however, respond to bankers' concerns about liability by providing that the bank cannot be held liable until it has (1) received written notice to stop payments and (2) had a reasonable opportunity to act upon the notice.

Richard V. Wellman
New Types of Joint Bank Accounts Resolve Many Problems
22 Est. Plan. 232, 236-237 (July/August 1995)[*]

Finally, and most importantly, the revised UPC form offers an agency account feature. It is triggered if the account form labels a person who is to have withdrawal authority as "agent" for another described as the owner. The label identifies an individual who has authority to make withdrawals but who cannot benefit personally from the position and is accountable to the account owner or the owner's estate for sums withdrawn. This arrangement is called a "convenience account" in at least two states [Florida and Texas], an "agency designation" in states that have enacted the 1989 revision of the UPC as well as in other states, and an account with an "additional authorized signatory" in Tennessee. The concept implicit in this form might be used (1) in a single-owner account without a death beneficiary, (2) in a P.O.D. account naming an owner and one or more death beneficiaries plus an agent for the owner, or (3) in a joint account in which an agent is added to serve for all the parties. Under the best of this legislation, depository protection for payouts on the order of the agent continues until the depository receives written notice of the principal's death or other revocation of the agency. This last provision assures protection of the depository for payouts to the "agent" even though the owner for whom the agent was designated to act may have died, causing termination of the agency for all purposes other than protection of the bank. Without this provision, depositories would continue to have reason to avoid offering agency accounts.

The agency account feature improves the choice of accounts available to the elderly single parent. . . . This person usually chooses a child living nearby to have signature power merely for the parent's convenience, while other children living at a distance, together with the child nearby, are intended to be death beneficiaries of the account. Now, rather than making all the children parties with the parent on a joint account, the parent can designate the nearby child his agent on an account that names the parent as sole owner, and all the children, including the agent-child, as P.O.D. beneficiaries. On the parent's death, the agent will have the power, assuming no written notice terminating the apparent authority has been given to the bank, to withdraw the money and will become legally accountable to divide it as intended. The advantage of this arrangement over the old joint account naming all the children as parties is the absence of risk of loss during the parent's lifetime to creditors of any of the children, because an account agent has no beneficial interest in an account balance.

QUESTION

What are the advantages and disadvantages of an agency account compared to the more traditional joint account?

C. TRUSTS

1. Parties to the Trust Arrangement

Henry Hansmann & Ugo Mattei
The Functions of Trust Law: A Comparative Legal and Economic Analysis
73 N.Y.U. L. Rev. 434, 438 (1998)

In a prototypical Anglo-American trust, three parties are involved: the "settlor" transfers property to the "trustee," who is charged with the duty to administer the property for the benefit of the "beneficiary." Any of these three roles may be played by more than one person. Also, the same person may play more than one of the three roles. In particular, the settlor and the beneficiary may be the same person, in which case the trust involves a simple delegation of responsibility for managing property from the settlor/beneficiary to the trustee.

QUESTIONS

1. What happens if the settlor and the trustee are the same person?

2. What happens if the trustee and the beneficiary are the same person?

3. What happens if the settlor and the trustee and the beneficiary are the same person?

2. Trust Creation

RESTATEMENT (3d) TRUSTS, Introductory Note to Part 2, Chapter 3

There are numerous methods of disposing of property during life and at death. . . . The creation of a trust is another method — a particularly flexible and useful method — of making property dispositions, either inter vivos or by will. As appears from the rules and commentary in this Chapter, the requirements for the creation of a trust are quite simple, even if they sometimes give rise to difficult issues.

In order to create a trust, there must be a proper manifestation of the intention to do so, either by the settlor or in communications between the settlor and the intended trustee; and the settlor ordinarily must make an effective inter vivos or testamentary transfer of the trust property to the trustee, just as other means of disposition ordinarily require that the property owner make an effective transfer to create property interests in others. An important exception to the transfer requirement is that trust dispositions also may be accomplished by the property owner's declaration that certain of the declarant's own property is now held by the declarant in trust for one or more others or for both the declarant and others. In addition, trusts are occasionally created by contract even before the promised transfer occurs, or by transfers eventually made pursuant to promises or pursuant to insurance or retirement plan beneficiary designations, even after the settlor's death.

No consideration is required for the creation of a trust. In fact, most trusts are created by gratuitous transfer. Ordinarily, however, if the property owner does not manifest an intention immediately to create a trust, but only the intention to create a trust in the future, no trust is created. Nor is the property owner bound later to create the trust in such a case, unless the requirements for the formation of a contract are complied with. The result is the same (that is, no trust and no obligation later to create one) where, in the absence of consideration (although language of present transfer is used) the would-be settlor does not at the time own the property purportedly transferred in trust.

Thus, a trust is normally created by an effective disposition of property, either during life or at death, and not by a mere attempt or undertaking to make a disposition in the future. Although a settlor can gratuitously and effectively make a present disposition of property in trust by declaration, an attempt to make a present, outright gift inter vivos that is ineffective (for lack of delivery, for example) will not be treated as a declaration of trust. Similarly, an undertaking to make a disposition at some future date that is not binding as a contract will not be salvaged by treating it as a declaration of trust.

If the trust property is an interest in land, statutes of frauds in nearly all states require that the creation of an enforceable trust be manifested and proved by written instrument. If the trust is to be a testamentary trust, it is ordinarily necessary to satisfy the requirements of the state's statute of wills.

Excerpts from the Uniform Trust Code

§ 401. Methods of Creating Trust.

A trust may be created by:

(1) transfer of property to another person as trustee during the settlor's lifetime or by will or other disposition taking effect upon the settlor's death;

(2) declaration by the owner of property that the owner holds identifiable property as trustee; or

(3) exercise of a power of appointment in favor of a trustee.

§ 407. Evidence of Oral Trust.

Except as required by a statute other than this [Code], a trust need not be evidenced by trust instruments, but the creation of an oral trust and its terms may be established only by clear and convincing evidence.

QUESTIONS

1. What formalities are required to create a trust of which the settlor is also the trustee?

2. What formalities are required to create a trust in which the settlor is not the trustee?

3. Of the mechanisms examined in this chapter, which require a transfer of property? Which do not? With regard to those that do not require a transfer of property, how would you characterize the legal transaction that takes place?

3. Revocability

ESTATE AND TRUST OF PILAFAS
836 P.2d 420 (Ariz. 1992)

McGREGOR, Judge.

The remainder beneficiaries (appellants) under an inter vivos trust agreement appeal the trial court's determination that Steve J. Pilafas (decedent) revoked his inter vivos trust and will and died intestate. Appellants raise two issues on appeal. The first is whether appellees presented sufficient evidence that decedent revoked his will. We find the evidence sufficient and affirm that part of the trial court's judgment. The second issue is whether the trial court erred in determining that decedent effectively revoked his inter vivos trust. We hold that the court did err and reverse.

I.

On August 30, 1982, decedent executed a trust agreement appointing himself trustee of certain described properties for the benefit of himself and other specified beneficiaries. Decedent immediately funded the trust by executing and recording a deed and an assignment that transferred a Phoenix residence and his interest in a note and deed of trust on a mobile home park to himself as trustee under the trust agreement. The trust corpus also included other real property, an agreement of sale, and, eventually, a promissory note payable to the trustee and secured by a deed of trust on real property that decedent acquired on June 2, 1988.

The trust agreement directed the trustee to pay decedent the trust income and any principal amounts that decedent requested in writing. The agreement directed that, upon decedent's death, a portion of the trust estate be distributed to the eight nonprofit organizations that are appellants in this case. The remaining portion was to be held in various trusts for decedent's wife, Geraldine P. Pilafas; brother, appellant Theodore J. Pilafas; sons, Steve J. Pilafas, Jr., and John S. Pilafas; and granddaughter, appellant Stephanie J. Pilafas. Decedent explicitly "omitted any provision for his children NICHOLAS S. PILAFAS, IRENE PILAFAS PAPPAS, and JAMES S. PILAFAS. . . ."

Article X of the trust agreement, entitled "Revocation," provided:

> The Settlor may at any time or times during the Settlor's lifetime by instrument in writing delivered to the Trustee amend or revoke this Agreement in whole or in part. . . . This power is personal to the Settlor and may not be exercised by the Settlor's Personal Representative or others.

In accord with the revocation provision, decedent twice amended the trust agreement by instrument in writing. On September 16, 1982, decedent executed a "First Amendment to Trust Agreement" that substituted a new article VIII regarding trustee succession and added a new article XI regarding the sale of trust property. On January 19, 1987, after his divorce, decedent executed a "Second Amendment to Trust Agreement" that revoked article XI and added an amended article III, thereby deleting his former wife as a trust beneficiary and increasing the share to be distributed to the eight nonprofit beneficiary organizations.

Decedent simultaneously executed a will and the second trust amendment. The will explicitly excluded decedent's former wife, disposed of certain personal property, and directed that other personal property be distributed in accordance with a separate written statement. The will gave the residue of decedent's estate to the trust.

After executing the second amendment to his trust agreement and his new will, decedent apparently improved his relationships with appellees Irene Pappas, James S. Pilafas and Nicholas Pilafas. In communications with his attorney and his family during the last month of his life, decedent indicated an intention to revise his estate plan to include all his children.

Decedent's attorney prepared the trust agreement, the two amendments, and the will, and assisted decedent in executing them. The attorney did not retain decedent's original documents and, to the best of his knowledge, gave decedent the signed originals of the trust agreement, the amendments and the will immediately after they were executed.

Decedent died on September 28, 1988. Subsequently, decedent's son, appellee James S. Pilafas, unsuccessfully searched decedent's house and belongings for the original will and trust documents. No information of record indicates their possible whereabouts.

According to appellees James S. Pilafas and Nicholas S. Pilafas, decedent fastidiously saved important records and was unlikely to have lost his original will and trust. At his death, decedent had a room filled with important documents, including photographs, old divorce papers, his selective service card from 1945, and letters from his children. Appellees also testified that decedent was a man of direct action who sometimes acted impulsively, and who had been known to tear or discard papers that offended him.

On December 2, 1988, appellee James S. Pilafas commenced these proceedings by filing a petition for formal appointment of special administrator and special trustee. On March 8, 1989, he filed a petition for adjudication of intestacy, determination of heirs, determination of revocation of trust, and appointment of personal representative. The petition sought a determination that decedent had revoked his trust agreement and will and died intestate, leaving his five adult children as his lawful heirs. The petition asked the court to authorize James S. Pilafas to transfer all the trust assets to decedent's estate.

Appellants objected to the petition, seeking a determination that decedent had revoked neither his will nor his trust agreement, and asking that the will be admitted to probate. Appellees filed a response and motion for summary judgment that the trial court granted by its order of December 18, 1989. The court determined decedent revoked his trust agreement and his will and died intestate, leaving his five adult children as heirs. The court authorized James S. Pilafas, as special trustee, to transfer all trust assets to the decedent's estate. Appellants timely appealed. . . .

III.

Appellees ask us to extend to revocable inter vivos trusts the common law presumption that a will last seen in the testator's possession that cannot be found after his death has been revoked. Appellees' reliance on this common law presumption is misplaced, however, if decedent's trust agreement was not susceptible to revocation by physical destruction.

Unlike the execution of a will, the creation of a trust involves the present transfer of property interests in the trust corpus to the beneficiaries. Even a revocable trust vests the trust beneficiary with a legal right to enforce the terms of the trust. The terms of the trust also limit the powers of the settlor and trustee over the trust corpus, even when the settlor declares himself trustee for the benefit of himself and others.

The terms of decedent's trust agreement governing revocation provide:

> The Settlor may at any time or times during the Settlor's lifetime by instrument in writing delivered to the Trustee amend or revoke this Agreement in whole or in part. . . .

Appellants argue that under this provision decedent could exercise his power to revoke the trust only through an "instrument in writing delivered to the Trustee. . . ." We agree.

This court, when not bound by previous decisions or legislative enactments, follows the Restatement of the Law. Restatement (Second) of Trusts §330 (1959) provides:

> (1) The settlor has power to revoke the trust if and to the extent that by the terms of the trust he reserved such a power.

> (2) Except as stated in §§ 332 and 333, the settlor cannot revoke the trust if by the terms of the trust he did not reserve a power of revocation.

Restatement § 330(2) makes it clear that, with two narrow exceptions, a trust is revocable only if the settlor expressly reserves a power to revoke, and the terms of the trust strictly define and limit the reserved power of revocation.

These general principles necessarily entail the more specific rule that when the settlor reserves a power to revoke his trust in a particular manner or under particular circumstances, he can revoke it only in that manner or under those circumstances. . . .

Because appellees presented no evidence showing that decedent complied with the required method of revocation, the inter vivos trust was not revoked and remained valid.

IV.

For the foregoing reasons, we affirm the trial court's ruling that decedent revoked his will and died intestate, reverse the court's ruling that decedent revoked his trust agreement and the amendments thereto, and remand for proceedings consistent with this opinion.

GERBER, P.J., and MELVYN T. SHELLEY, Retired Judge, concur.

Uniform Trust Code § 602

(a) Unless the terms of a trust expressly provide that the trust is irrevocable, the settlor may revoke or amend the trust. This subsection does not apply to a trust created under an instrument executed before [the effective date of this [Code]].

. . . .

(c) The settlor may revoke or amend a revocable trust:

    (1) by substantial compliance with a method provided in the terms of a trust; or

    (2) if the terms of the trust do not provide a method or the method provided in the terms is not expressly made exclusive, by:

        (A) a later will or codicil that expressly refers to the trust or specifically devises property that would otherwise have passed according to the terms of the trust; or

        (B) by any other method manifesting clear and convincing evidence of the settlor's intent.

. . . .

QUESTIONS

1. Do you agree with the outcome of *Pilafas*? Why or why not?

2. If you had been Mr. Pilafas's lawyer, how might you have drafted the trust differently in order to avoid litigation?

3. Is a revocable trust more like a durable power of attorney or more like a joint bank account? Is an irrevocable trust more like a joint bank account, an agency account, or a p.o.d. account? Try sketching a table listing the essential characteristics of each technique, and then compare and contrast their qualities.

4. When would a revocable trust be the best solution for an older person needing help managing property? When would an irrevocable trust be better? Can you think of a way to combine the qualities of both in one instrument?

4. The Tax Treatment of Revocable Trusts

Howard B. Soloman
Revocable Trusts: A Contrarian's Viewpoint
68 N.Y. St. B. J. 34, 35 (February 1996)[*]

Revocable trusts (also known as "living trusts") have gained enormous popularity in recent years, often being advertised in seminars and literature as the cure-all for estate and estate tax planning ills. While the technique has its virtues and place in the estate planner's arsenal of techniques, it is not always necessary. . . .

---

[*] Reprinted with permission from the *New York State Bar Journal*, February 1996, published by the New York State Bar Association, One Elk Street, Albany, New York 12207.

(3) Perception: Revocable trusts save income taxes.

Reality: These trusts are "grantor trusts" under IRC Sections 671 *et seq.* and, as such, both items of ordinary income and capital gain are fully reportable on the Grantor's individual income tax return.

(4) Perception: Revocable trusts save estate taxes.

Reality: IRC Section 2038 provides that if the creator of a trust at the time of his or her death has the power to alter, amend or revoke the trust, the principal of the trust is fully includable in his or her estate. Thus, in and of itself, the revocable trust saves no estate taxes. Indeed, if the perception were the reality, everyone, including William Gates, Warren Buffett, and Ross Perot would create one for no purpose other than the avoidance of estate taxes, and the estate tax would be a nullity.

Darin N. Digby
What Powers Can a Donor Retain Over Transferred Property?
24 EST. PLAN. 318, 318-319 (August/September 1997)[*]

Is the transfer a completed gift?

In order for a gratuitous transfer of property to be a completed gift for gift tax purposes, the donor must part with all dominion and control over the property so ". . . as to leave in him no power to change its disposition, whether for his own benefit or for the benefit of another. . . ."

Estate tax effects. . . .

Assuming that the donor successfully completes the gift, the next hurdle is to ensure that the property transferred to the trust is excluded from the donor's gross estate for estate tax purposes. There are many traps for the unwary that, if not avoided, will cause an otherwise effective transfer of property to be included in the donor's estate. Most of these pitfalls can be traced to Sections 2036 and 2038. The grantor's use, possession, right to income, or other enjoyment of the transferred property, whether direct or indirect, is generally treated as if the grantor had retained the property under Section 2036(a)(1). . . .

QUESTION

Are there any tax benefits to a revocable trust?

---

5. Revocable Trusts and the Reach of Creditors

a. During the Settlor's Lifetime

Clifton B. Kruse, Jr.
Revocable Trusts: Creditors' Rights After the Settlor-Debtor's Death
PROB. & PROP. 40, 40 (November/December 1993)[*]

The RESTATEMENT (SECOND) OF TRUSTS § 156 (1959) succinctly states the widespread, if not universal, rule that "where a person creates for his [or her] own benefit a trust with a provision restraining the voluntary or involuntary transfer of his [or her] interest, . . . creditors can reach [the trust estate]." This policy apparently has not been well understood because . . . many revocable trust settlors have tried to avoid their creditors during their lifetimes by transferring their personal wealth into revocable trusts.

Leach v. Anderson, 535 P.2d 1241, 1243 (Utah 1975), typifies the public policy favoring creditors of revocable trust settlors. A person may not use a trust as a device [to avoid creditors] and enjoy substantially all of the advantages of ownership [while] at the same time [placing the assets] beyond the legitimate [reach] of . . . creditors." *Leach* affirms that this rule applies to both the creditors with claims at the time the revocable trust is created and to creditors whose claims arise later. Whether the transferor-settlor intended to avoid or defraud his or her creditors is immaterial. . . .

Whatever objectives a revocable trust might accomplish for its settlor, avoiding the legitimate claims of the settlor's creditors during the settlor's life is not one of them.

Uniform Trust Code § 505

(a) Whether or not the terms of a trust contain a spendthrift provision, the following rules apply:

    (1) During the lifetime of the settlor, the property of a revocable trust is subject to claims of the settlor's creditors.

. . . .

(b) For purposes of this section:

    (1) during the period the power may be exercised, the holder of a power of withdrawal is treated in the same manner as the settlor of a revocable trust to the extent of the property subject to the power; and

    (2) upon the lapse, release, or waiver of the power, the holder is treated as the settlor of the trust only to the extent the value of

the property affected by the lapse, release, or waiver exceeds the greater of the amount specified in Section 2041(b)(2) or 2514(e) of the Internal Revenue Code of 1986, or Section 2503(b) of the Internal Revenue Code of 1986, in each case as in effect on [the effective date of this [Code]] [, or as later amended].

(3) After the death of a settlor, and subject to the settlor's right to direct the source from which liabilities will be paid, the property of a trust that was revocable at the settlor's death is subject to claims of the settlor's creditors, costs of administration of the settlor's estate, the expenses of the settlor's funeral and disposal of remains, and [statutory allowances] to a surviving spouse and children to the extent the settlor's probate estate is inadequate to satisfy those claims, costs, expenses, and [allowances].

Alan Newman
The Rights of Creditors of Beneficiaries Under the Uniform Trust Code: An Examination of the Compromise
69 Tenn. L. Rev. 771, 817-20 (2002)[*]

Under the U.T.C., all of the assets of a revocable trust are subject to the claims of creditors of the settlor during the settlor's lifetime. This simple, bright-line rule is not dependent on whether the settlor directly retained a beneficial interest in the income or principal of the trust-the power to revoke is enough. By contrast, at common law, a settlor's creditor could not reach a power of revocation reserved by a settlor and thus could not compel the settlor to revoke the trust. Because a power of revocation gives the settlor the ability, exercisable unilaterally, to obtain unrestricted ownership of the trust's assets simply by revoking the trust, the U.T.C.'s rule allowing creditors of the settlor to reach assets in a trust that the settlor may revoke is a sensible one.

. . . .

Until the late 1990s, the prohibition on self-settled spendthrift trusts reflected in section 505(a)(2) was the law in most, if not all, jurisdictions. In an effort to attract trust business, Alaska and Delaware in 1997 and Nevada and Rhode Island in 1999 enacted statutes designed to, among other things, allow the settlor of a trust to transfer assets to the trust that would be protected from the claims of most of the settlor's creditors even while retaining a beneficial interest in the trust and its assets. From a policy perspective, several commentators have questioned the wisdom of allowing such self-settled spendthrift trusts and also the ability of such statutes to succeed in preventing creditors of the settlor from reaching the trust assets. In rejecting the approach taken in Alaska, Delaware, Nevada, and Rhode Island, the U.T.C. drafters "concluded that it was undesirable as a matter of policy to allow a settlor to create a trust, retain a beneficial interest, but yet deny the settlor's creditors the right to reach the trust."

---

[*] Copyright © 2002. Reprinted with permission.

Professor Boxx has categorized the policy objections to self-settled spend-thrift trusts as moral and economic. As to the former, "[t]he moral argument is simple and intuitive: You should keep your promises and pay your debts because it is the right thing to do. . . . [T]here is something disturbing about a country that would allow debtors to leave their debts unpaid and still enjoy an extrav-agant lifestyle." With respect to the latter, Professor Boxx notes the warning of Professor LoPucki "that the increasing ability to avoid liability threatens the system of civil enforcement of obligations, both tort and contract." Other eco-nomic objections to allowing self-settled spendthrift trusts include their ten-dency to increase hazardous conduct by settlors who are also beneficiaries of the trusts they create, their negation of the limits of exempt property statutes, the opportunity they provide to mislead voluntary creditors, and the adverse effect they may have on the practices of creditors in setting terms for the exten-sion of credit. While state legislation authorizing self-settled spendthrift trusts may have short-term positive economic effects on the enacting state in attract-ing trust business, to the extent such trusts are effective, externalities will be borne by other states. Thus, the U.T.C. drafters' decision to reject self-settled spendthrift trusts is commendable.

b. After the Settlor's Death

Clifton B. Kruse, Jr.
Revocable Trusts: Creditors' Rights After the Settlor-Debtor's Death
PROB. & PROP. 40, 40-42 (November/December 1993)[*]

[The author notes that older cases tend to favor the settlor's heirs. — Eds.] A decision in 1939 by the Supreme Court of Ohio held that a deceased settlor's creditors cannot invalidate the trust without proof that the conveyance into the trust was in violation of the state's fraudulent transfer laws. *Schofield v. Cleve-land Trust Co.*, 21 N.E.2d 119 (Ohio 1939). . . . A 1942 decision is no more gen-erous to creditors. *Greenwich Trust Co. v. Tyson*, 27 A.2d 166, 173-174 (Conn. 1942). Although a settlor reserves the right to the trust's income for life, the set-tlor's creditors cannot attach the settlor's expired interest. The ownership of the trust estate passes to others at the settlor's death, and therefore the trust cor-pus is not available to satisfy the unpaid obligations of the deceased settlor. . . .

More recent cases do not support the *Schofield* and *Greenwich* decisions and suggest a change in public policy. . . . A 1979 Massachusetts intermediate appel-late court decision is [one of the newer cases] to [this] effect: *State Street Bank and Trust Co. v. Reiser*, 389 N.E.2d 768 (Mass. App. 1979). In *State Street*, a debtor left at his death a trust that he created during his life, funded with most of his wealth. A bank creditor sought to satisfy a debt owing to it by the settlor from the trust. "We conclude," the court wrote, "that the [creditor] can do so." The court recognized that the settlor's death terminated his retained power

---

to amend or revoke the trust and further acknowledged that on the settlor's death, equitable title to the trust assets is vested in the trust's remainder beneficiaries. Notwithstanding these facts, the court observed that the possession of a general power of appointment over trust assets is similar to a right to revoke and noted that the holder can appoint the property to himself or herself or to his or her executors. "[T]he property could have been devoted to the payment of [the power holder's] debts and, therefore, [the person's] creditors have an equitable right to reach that property. . . . [T]he same analysis and policy should . . . apply to trust property over which the settlor retains dominion. . . . [It is] at least as great as a power of appointment" and should, therefore, be subject to the same result. "It is excessive obeisance to the form in which the property is held to prevent creditors from reaching property placed in trust . . . [following the settlor's death]." *State Street, supra,* at 771. . . .

Several states have enacted legislation addressing creditors' rights following the death of a settlor of a fully funded revocable trust. [The author mentions statutes in Missouri, California, Massachusetts, and Michigan, as well as reform efforts underway in Florida and Washington state. — Eds.] The legislation permits creditors to reach the trusts.

Uniform Trust Code § 505

(a) Whether or not the terms of a trust contain a spendthrift provision, the following rules apply:

. . . .

   (3) After the death of a settlor, and subject to the settlor's right to direct the source from which liabilities will be paid, the property of a trust that was revocable at the settlor's death is subject to claims of the settlor's creditors, costs of administration of the settlor's estate, the expenses of the settlor's funeral and disposal of remains, and [statutory allowances] to a surviving spouse and children to the extent the settlor's probate estate is inadequate to satisfy those claims, costs, expenses, and [allowances]. . . .

Alan Newman
The Rights of Creditors of Beneficiaries Under the Uniform Trust Code: An Examination of the Compromise
69 TENN. L. REV. 771, 817-20 (2002)*

In decades past, in at least some jurisdictions, the creditors of a settlor of a revocable trust that became irrevocable upon the settlor's death could not reach assets in the trust after the settlor's death. Under the U.T.C., the assets of such a trust may be reached not only by the deceased settlor's creditors, as is the case under current law in most jurisdictions, but also by those asserting claims for the costs of administering the settlor's estate, the costs of the settlor's

---

funeral, and statutory allowances for the settlor's spouse and children. In each case, recovery may be had against the trust assets only if and to the extent that there are not sufficient assets in the settlor's probate estate to satisfy them. Furthermore, the right of such a claimant to reach the trust's assets is "subject to the settlor's right to direct the source from which liabilities will be paid. . . ." These provisions accommodate the common revocable trust, pourover will plan under which a settlor may shift liabilities his or her estate otherwise would have to the revocable trust.

QUESTION

With respect to the avoidance of creditors, what advantages, if any, do revocable trusts possess?

6. Revocable Trusts and Medicaid

This topic will be covered in greater depth in Chapter 7. However, the following readings are presented by way of introduction to the use of trusts in Medicaid planning.

a. Using Revocable Trusts to Shield Assets During the Lifetime of the Medicaid Recipient

Hal Fliegelman & Debora C. Fliegelman
Giving Guardians the Power to Do Medicaid Planning
32 Wake Forest L. Rev. 341, 362-363 (1997)[*]

In the case of a transfer of assets to a revocable trust, the corpus of the trust is considered a resource available to the individual for determining Medicaid eligibility; thus, the divestiture is not an effective strategy for sheltering the assets transferred. Similarly, that portion of the corpus of an irrevocable trust that could generate income payable to or for the benefit of the individual is also considered to be a resource available to the individual, which also defeats a sheltering strategy. . . . [A]ny portion of the corpus of an irrevocable trust that could not be used to generate income payable to or for the individual will be considered to be a transfer for less than fair market value, [and thus] subject to the transfer rules discussed [earlier in the article].

Clifton B. Kruse, Jr.
Critical Differences in Estate Planning Strategies Between Revocable Trusts and Wills
23 ACTEC NOTES 145, 146 (1997)[*]

Transfer of otherwise exempt assets into revocable trusts may result in loss of their Medicaid exempt status. . . .

Homesteads, otherwise treated as exempt resources of homeowners applying for or receiving Medicaid, may lose their exempt status, however, when transferred into their owners' revocable trusts. . . .

b. Governmental Claims on the Assets of the Medicaid Recipient After the Recipient's Death: The Case of Assets in a Revocable Trust

Jon M. Zieger
The State Giveth and the State Taketh Away: In Pursuit of a Practical Approach to Medicaid Estate Recovery
5 ELDER L.J. 359, 360, 366-367 (1997)[**]

As the cost of providing medical assistance to Medicaid recipients has continued to increase dramatically in the decades since that program's inception, states have sought various methods of reducing Medicaid expenditures. Estate recovery programs, designed to recoup Medicaid assistance from a recipient's estate, represent one method states have implemented to reduce Medicaid costs. Under these programs, the cost of medical assistance provided to a recipient becomes a debt of the recipient's estate or the estate of the recipient's surviving spouse

. . . .

Because estate recovery programs are largely creatures of state law and vary from state to state, a single definition of an estate recovery program is implausible. However, certain common elements can be adduced. . . . Because certain classes of assets are exempted when determining eligibility for Medicaid, a deceased Medicaid recipient may have been sufficiently needy to qualify for Medicaid and yet still leave a substantial estate. An estate recovery program focuses on recovering the amount expended on the recipient's behalf from these exempt assets after the recipient's death.

Clifton B. Kruse, Jr.
Critical Differences in Estate Planning Strategies Between Revocable Trusts and Wills
23 ACTEC NOTES 145, 145 and n.2 (1997)[*]

Revocable trusts do not protect a Medicaid beneficiary's assets held in such a trust from estate recovery laws and regulations. Use of a revocable trust does not insulate assets . . . (including those [assets] that are exempt during a Medicaid beneficiary's life) from recovery by the states who have furnished Medicaid benefits to the settlor. [The author notes, however, that assets exempt during the life of a Medicaid beneficiary may remain exempt "for the life of the Medicaid recipient's spouse, until the beneficiary has no surviving child under age 21, or so long as the recipient's child is blind or disabled as defined in 42 U.S.C. 1382c(a)(3)(A)."]

QUESTION

With respect to the receipt of Medicaid benefits during life and the avoidance of estate recovery after death, what advantages, if any, do revocable trusts possess?

7. The Revocable Trust as an Alternative to Guardianship

William M. McGovern, Jr.
Trusts, Custodianships, and Durable Powers of Attorney
27 REAL PROP., PROB. & TR. J. 1, 3-5 (1992)[**]

Imposing a guardianship on incompetent adults is possible, but it requires burdensome court proceedings, which can be extremely expensive. . . . These proceedings also impose significant emotional costs on family members who are forced to produce evidence of a loved one's incapacity.

A trust, on the other hand, can eliminate most of the emotional and financial costs of a guardianship. For example, parents who think that their adult children can not handle property can put the property into a trust without having the children adjudicated incompetent. A trust can also provide for the settlor's own property without a judicial determination that the settlor has become incompetent.

---

[*] Copyright © 1997. Reprinted with permission.

[**] Copyright © 1992 by the American Bar Association. Reprinted with permission.

QUESTIONS

For the management of property, what advantages do trusts have over guardianships? Are there any advantages that guardianships have over trusts?

8. The Revocable Trust as an Alternative to the Durable Power of Attorney

Carolyn L. Dessin
Acting as Agent Under a Financial Durable Power of Attorney: An Unscripted Role
75 NEB. L. REV. 574, 584, 602, 619 (1996)[*]

Estate planners view the durable power of attorney as an important planning tool, and its use is widely recommended. It can be broad, and it is easy to execute. The cost of executing a durable power of attorney will probably be less than the cost of creating an *inter vivos* trust or instituting a guardianship. A person may not even need to consult an attorney to obtain a durable power of attorney because a state statute may provide a form durable power of attorney. Additionally, powers of attorney in printed form are widely available in stationery and office supply stores. In sum, a durable power of attorney is an inexpensive, popular tool that creates a much more flexible arrangement than either a guardianship or a trust. With flexibility, however, comes the possibility for abuse. . . .

In light of the popularity of the durable power of attorney as a planning tool, it is critically important that the role of the agent be better defined. This is particularly true because estate planning attorneys often market the durable power of attorney to clients as an alternative to a trust or guardianship. Without a clearly defined role, the agent may not perform the way the principal expects, and the principal may suffer financially by choosing to execute the durable power of attorney rather than to create a trust. . . .

Aside from enhanced protection of incompetent principals, another salutary effect of a better-defined standard of behavior for agents under durable powers of attorney would be a likely increase in the willingness of third parties to deal with agents. Many have noted that third parties sometimes refuse to deal with agents under durable powers. Without a reasonable assurance that third parties will deal with the agent, the durable power of attorney is not an acceptable alternative to either the trust or a guardianship in the event of disability.

QUESTIONS

What advantages do durable powers of attorney have over trusts? What advantages do trusts have over durable powers?

9. The Revocable Trust as a Will Substitute

John H. Langbein
The Nonprobate Revolution and the Future of the Law of Succession
97 HARV. L. REV. 1108, 1109, 1113 (1984)[*]

Four main will substitutes constitute the core of the nonprobate system: life insurance, pension accounts, joint accounts, and revocable trusts. When properly created, each is functionally indistinguishable from a will each reserves to the owner complete lifetime dominion, including the power to name and to change beneficiaries until death. . . .

Either by declaration of trust or by transfer to a third-party trustee, the appropriate trust terms can replicate the incidents of a will. The owner who retains both the equitable life interest and the power to alter and revoke the beneficiary designation has used the trust form to achieve the effect of testation. Only nomenclature distinguishes the remainder interest created by such a trust from the mere expectancy arising under a will. Under either the trust or the will, the interest of the beneficiaries is both revocable and ambulatory.

Jay D. Waxenberg & Henry J. Leibowitz
Comparing the Advantages of Estates and Revocable Trusts
22 EST. PLAN. 265, 265-269 (September/October 1995)[**]

Advocates of living trusts frequently contend that using them as will substitutes offers a number of advantages, including saving estate taxes and probate fees, minimizing legal and accounting fees, eliminating delays, and insuring privacy. Many of these claims are untrue or overrated but there are some situations in which a living trust may be useful. An examination of the pros and cons will help you decide whether this device is right for clients.

To be effective, a living trust must be funded during the settlor's lifetime. This involves the re-registration of all the client's assets in the name of the trust. The practitioner must prepare deeds and other transfer documents and beneficiary designations, as well as correspond with banks, transfer agents, brokers, and

---

title companies. The client must pay any transfer or recording fees that may apply. In many cases, this process can be time-consuming and expensive. . . .

Despite the claims (express or implied) of many advocates of living trusts, no estate tax savings can be achieved with a living trust that cannot as easily be accomplished with a traditional will. There are estate tax saving opportunities available through the use of irrevocable trusts created during life but such trusts are vastly different from the revocable living trust, and using them may involve incurring gift tax.

Living trusts do not save income tax either. Indeed, estates governed by traditional wills have available some income tax planning opportunities that are not available to estates governed by living trusts. Perhaps the most important of these is the fact that an estate under a will can select a fiscal year for income tax purposes but a trust must report on a calendar year basis. By choosing a fiscal year, the estate may be able to defer recognition of post-death income for as much as 11 months, almost always enabling the beneficiaries to postpone their tax payments on that income for an entire year. . . .

Because property transferred to a living trust during the settlor's lifetime is not part of the probate estate, the costs directly associated with probating a will may be avoided through the use of a living trust. Nevertheless, since it is often necessary to have a pour-over will where there is a living trust, some probate fees may be unavoidable.

The probate fee structure is different in every jurisdiction, but the fees charged by most courts are modest and are deductible on the estate's tax return. . . .

Except for the legal work involved in the probate proceeding itself, which usually is not significant, the legal and accounting services for an estate governed by a living trust are roughly the same as those for an estate governed by a traditional will. Moreover, the attorney's fees for preparing a living trust agreement, a pour-over will, and all the necessary transfer documents are frequently greater than the fee for preparing a traditional will. . . .

Claims by supporters of living trusts that these entities avoid delays in distributing assets are often grossly exaggerated. Of course, the trustee of a living trust can continue to administer the assets without interruption by the settlor's death, but in most states, including Florida, a will can be admitted to probate after only a minimal delayusually no more than a week or two. Even in New York, where the wait for probate can be longer, an executor acting under a traditional will can apply for preliminary letters testamentary and usually receive authority to perform all essential duties within a few days after death. . . .

Advocates of living trusts often argue that such trusts afford greater privacy as to the disposition of assets than does a traditional will. Although a living trust may never need to be filed in court, in actual practice, many banks and brokerage firms require that a copy of the trust agreement be submitted to them for review before they will open an account, so that the contents of the agreement may never be entirely confidential. . . .

The fact that a living trust is not filed in court does not prevent a challenge to the client's estate plan or to the validity of the governing instrument. A living trust can be contested for the same reasons as can a will (e.g., undue influence, incompetence, or fraud). . . .

A living trust may be an excellent option to consider if the client owns real estate located in more than one state. In an estate governed by a traditional will, additional probate documents must be filed with each of the local probate courts. If the property is held in a living trust, the costs associated with these ancillary probate filings can be avoided. . . .

QUESTIONS

Do you agree with Messrs. Waxenberg and Leibowitz? How would you evaluate the merits of a revocable trust as a substitute will?

10. Custodial Trusts and the Uniform Custodial Trust Act

Prefatory Note to the Uniform Custodial Trust Act

This Uniform Act provides for the creation of a statutory custodial trust for adults to be governed by the provisions of the Act whenever property is delivered to another "as custodial trustee under the (Enacting state) Uniform Custodial Trust Act." The provisions of this Act are based on trust analogies to concepts developed and used in establishing custodianships for minors under the Uniform Transfers to Minors Act (UTMA). The Custodial Trust Act is designed to provide a statutory standby *inter vivos* trust for individuals who typically are not very affluent or sophisticated, and possibly represented by attorneys engaged in general rather than specialized estate practice. The most frequent use of this trust would be in response to the commonly occurring need of elderly individuals to provide for the future management of assets in the event of incapacity. The statute will also be available for accomplishing distribution of funds by judgment debtors and others to incapacitated persons for whom a conservator has not been appointed. Since this Act allows any person, competent to transfer property, to create custodial trusts for the benefit of themselves or others, with the beneficial interest in custodial trust property in the beneficiary and not in the custodial trustee, its potential for use is extensive. Although the most frequent use probably will be by elderly persons, it is also available for a parent to establish a custodial trust for an adult child who may be incapacitated; for adult persons in the military, or those leaving the country temporarily, to place their property with another for management without relinquishing beneficial ownership of their property; or for young people who have received property under the Uniform Transfers to Minors Act to continue a custodial trust as adults in order to obtain the benefit and convenience of management services performed by the custodial trustee.

This Act follows the approach taken by the Uniform Transfers to Minors Act and allows any kind of property, real or personal, tangible or intangible, to be made the subject of a transfer to a custodial trustee for the benefit of a beneficiary. However, the most typical transaction envisioned would involve a person who would transfer intangible property, such as securities or bank accounts, to a custodial trustee but with retention by the transferor of direction over the property. Later, this direction could be relinquished, or it could be lost upon incapacity. The objective of the statute is to provide a simple trust that is uncomplicated in its creation, administration, and termination. The potential for tax problems is minimized by permitting the beneficiary in most instances to retain control while the beneficiary has capacity to manage the assets effectively. The statute contains an asset specific transfer provision that it is believed will be simple to use and will gain the acceptance of the securities and financial industry. A simple transfer document, examples of which are set forth in the Act, and a receipt from the custodian, also in the Act, would provide for identification of beneficiaries or distributees upon death of the beneficiary. Protection is extended to third parties dealing with the custodian. Although the Act is patterned on the Uniform Transfers to Minors Act and meshes into the Uniform Probate Code, it is appropriate for enactment as well in states which have not adopted either UTMA or the UPC.

An adult beneficiary, who is not incapacitated, may: (1) terminate the custodial trust on demand (Section 2(e)); (2) receive so much of the income or custodial property as he or she may request from time to time (Section 9(a)); and (3) give the custodial trustee binding instructions for investment or management (Section 7(b)). In the absence of direction by the beneficiary, who is not incapacitated, the custodial trustee manages the property subject to the standard of care that would be observed by a prudent person dealing with the property of another and is not limited by other statutory restrictions on investments by fiduciaries. (Section 7).

A principal feature of the Custodial Trust under this Act is designed to protect the beneficiary and his or her dependents against the perils of the beneficiary's possible future incapacity without the necessity of a conservatorship. Under Section 10, the incapacity of the beneficiary does not terminate (1) the custodial trust, (2) the designation of a successor custodial trustee, (3) any power or authority of the custodial trustee, or (4) the immunities of third persons relying on actions of the custodial trustee. The custodial trustee continues to manage the property as a discretionary trust under the prudent person standard for the benefit of the incapacitated beneficiary.

Means of monitoring and enforcing the custodial trust include provisions requiring the custodial trustee to keep the beneficiary informed, requiring accounting by the custodial trustee (Section 15), providing for removal of the custodial trustee (Section 13), and the distribution of the assets on termination of the custodial trust (Section 17). The custodial trustee is protected in Section 16 by the statutes of limitation on proceedings against the custodial trustee.

Transactions with the custodial trustee should be executed readily and quickly by third parties because their rights and protections are determined by the Act and a third party acting in good faith has no need to determine the custodial trustee's authority to bind the beneficiary with respect to property and investment matters. (Section 11). The Act generally limits the claims of third parties to recourse against the custodial property, with the beneficiary insulated against personal liability unless he or she is personally at fault and the custodial trustee is similarly insulated unless the custodial trustee is personally at fault or failed to disclose the custodial capacity when entering into a contract (Section 12).

As a consequence of the mobility of our population, particularly the mature persons who are most likely to utilize this Act, uniformity of the laws governing custodial trusts is highly desirable, and the Act is designed to avoid conflict of laws problems. A custodial trust created under this Act remains subject to this Act despite a subsequent change in the residence of the transferor, the beneficiary, or the custodial trustee or the removal of the custodial trust property from the state of original location. (Section 19).

Gerry W. Beyer
Simplification of Inter Vivos Trust Instruments: From Incorporation by Reference to the Uniform Custodial Trust Act and Beyond
32 S. Tex. L. Rev. 203, 213-214, 217-224, 229-230 (1991)[*]

The National Conference of Commissioners on Uniform State Laws began drafting the Uniform Custodial Trust Act in 1984. After three years of work, the Commissioners approved the UCTA at their 1987 conference. The ABA then approved it in February 1988. [So far, the UCTA has been adopted in the District of Columbia and 17 states: Alaska, Arizona, Arkansas, Colorado, Hawai'i, Idaho, Indiana, Louisiana, Massachusetts, Minnesota, Missouri, Nebraska, New Mexico, North Carolina, Rhode Island, Virginia, and Wisconsin. — Eds.]

The UCTA authorizes the creation of a statutory custodial trust by delivering property to another person with a clear indication that the property is to be governed by the provisions of the UCTA. Using trust analogies, the drafters modeled the UCTA after the Uniform Transfers to Minors Act because "of its widespread use and the familiarity of third party financial institutions with the registration concept." . . .

The UCTA was "designed to provide a statutory standby inter vivos trust for individuals who typically are not very affluent or sophisticated, and possibly represented by attorneys engaged in general rather than specialized estate practice." The drafters anticipated that the primary users of the UCTA would be elderly individuals seeking to make arrangements for the future management of their property in the event they were to become incapacitated. Other users would include individuals needing to distribute funds to incapacitated persons without guardians or conservators, parents wishing to make gifts to adult children, military personnel and others temporarily residing outside of the United States, and those persons who have received property under the Uniform

---

Gifts/Transfers to Minors Act and desire to continue the custodial trust arrangement into their adult years. . . .

The UCTA provides a person with several methods with which to create a custodial trust. The methods make it relatively simple to effectuate one of the UCTA's goals of making the creation of custodial trusts an easy process that may be accomplished without legal advice. . . .

The drafters expect the transfer in trust to be the most commonly used method for creating a custodial trust. The property owner simply makes a written transfer directing the transferee to hold the property as a custodial trustee under the UCTA. The transfer must designate a beneficiary, and the transferor is authorized to name himself or herself as the beneficiary. . . .

A property owner may also create a custodial trust by executing a written declaration that describes the property, names a beneficiary, and indicates that the declarant holds the property as a custodial trustee under the UCTA. The property owner, however, cannot be the sole beneficiary of a self-declaration of trust. . . .

The person with the right to designate the recipient of property contingent upon a future event may create a custodial trust effective upon the occurrence of that future event. The designation must be in writing, and it must clearly indicate that the property is to be held in a custodial trust for the named beneficiary. . . .

The . . . methods discussed above are not exclusive; if other methods satisfying UCTA requirements are used to create a custodial trust, they will be equally effective. For example, "[a] custodial trust could be created by the exercise of a valid power of attorney or power of appointment given by the owner of property." The UCTA was not designed to displace or restrict other methods of trust creation. Thus, if a trust fails to meet the requirements of the UCTA — for example where a non-beneficiary transferor reserves the power to revoke the transfer — the trust may still be enforceable under the state's normal trust law. . . .

Acceptance of the custodial trust property triggers the trustee's duties under the UCTA.

. . . .

The beneficiary of a custodial trust has only the beneficial interest in the property; legal title to the property is in the trustee. . . .

The UCTA does not authorize successive interests in a trust. The only situation where the trust may continue beyond the original beneficiary's lifetime is when the at-death distributee is incapacitated. In such a case, the trust continues for the use and benefit of the distributee, but only until the distributee's incapacity is removed or the trust terminates. . . .

As long as the beneficiary is not incapacitated, the trustee must follow the beneficiary's directions concerning the management, control, investment, and retention of trust property. . . .

The trustee need not follow the directions of someone exercising a durable power of attorney given by a beneficiary who has become incapacitated. Accordingly, the incapacitated beneficiary's agent may neither terminate the trust nor direct the administration or distribution of custodial trust property. . . .

A trustee is provided with very broad powers under the UCTA. The trustee has "all the rights and powers over custodial trust property which an unmarried adult owner has over individually owned property, but a custodial trustee may exercise those rights and powers in a fiduciary capacity only." Alternatively, a state could choose to substitute language which refers to its statutes supplying fiduciary powers. . . .

If the beneficiary is not incapacitated, the trustee must follow the beneficiary's distribution instructions. In this situation, the trustee acts more like an agent than a traditional trustee. . . .

The trustee's duties with respect to the distribution of trust property are considerably different if the beneficiary is or becomes incapacitated or if the transferor directs that the trust be administered as if the beneficiary were incapacitated. In this situation, the trustee is authorized to use trust property as the trustee considers reasonably prudent for the use and benefit of the beneficiary, as well as for individuals whom the beneficiary supported when the beneficiary became incapacitated or who are legally entitled to the beneficiary's support, even if such individuals have not been receiving any support (e.g., beneficiary failed to make child support payments). It is significant that the UCTA permits distributions for the benefit of the beneficiary without regard to whether the distributions are needed for the beneficiary's support, maintenance, education, or health care. . . .

QUESTIONS

How do custodial trusts under the UCTA work? What are their advantages and weaknesses, in general and in comparison with the other methods of property management discussed in this chapter?

D. A WORD ABOUT ESTATE PLANNING

Any reader who has already taken a basic course in estates and trusts will no doubt have realized by now that most of the issues and strategies covered in this chapter touch on many of the same topics as should be covered in most estate-planning classes. This raises several points that require a brief mention.

First, there is no doubt that Elder Law is, in some sense, "Everything Law." The issues that face older Americans are really not substantially different from the issues that face every American of every age — issues of income, discrimination, health care, housing, and the inescapable danger of disability and dependence. While some exceptional practitioners may be well-versed and competent in every subcategory of Elder Law, the rest of us must always be mindful that the first demand of professional responsibility is knowing very clearly the limits of our competence.

Second, estate planning has nearly always been a highly specialized practice, and never more so than in the United States in the past century. The federal wealth transfer taxes (estate, gift, and generation-skipping), and the various state taxes that also might pertain at death, made estate planning an extremely challenging area of law, often requiring a decade or more of experience before one could hope to claim any expertise. Although almost any licensed attorney should be able to draft a simple will, the tricky part always has been knowing whether a simple will was, in fact, the best available technique for any particular client. This level of difficulty made it especially prudent for elder lawyers to seek out competent estate planners to whom clients in need of such specialized services could be referred.

Recent changes in the laws regarding the federal estate tax have intensified these problems. A practice area already challenging has evolved into a veritable moving target, with either repeal or additional significant changes looming. Either outcome will have significant effects on all areas of individual tax planning as well as on such government programs as Medicaid. It is simply beyond the scope of this text to give appropriate treatment to all the possible estate and tax issues that an elder client might need to consider.

Those considering elder law as a practice area cannot escape the need to remain informed and up-to-date on the rapid changes taking place in estate planning. Many elder lawyers will find their practice involves more sophisticated issues and techniques than this text could competently cover; but at a minimum, every elder lawyer will find it essential to develop a basic familiarity with the property management mechanisms discussed above.

FURTHER READING. Lawrence A. Frolik & Melissa C. Brown, ADVISING THE ELDERLY OR DISABLED CLIENT chs. 21, 27 (2d ed. 2000 & Supp. 2002); Joan M. Krauskopf et al., ELDERLAW: ADVOCACY FOR THE AGING ch. 8 (2d ed. 1993 & Supp. 2005); Peter J. Strauss & Nancy M. Lederman, THE ELDER LAW HANDBOOK ch. 11 (1996).

Chapter 6

GUARDIANSHIP AND CONSERVATORSHIP

This chapter explores that law of adult protection — state statutory schemes that may be invoked when an elderly person appears to be unable to make financial or personal decisions due to incapacity. A person found by a court to be in need of a guardianship or conservatorship loses some or all autonomy, and protective proceedings should be initiated only if no alternatives are available. As you read the materials in this chapter, consider whether the premises that structure the guardianship system — that protective proceedings are non-adversarial in nature — remain viable.

A. BACKGROUND

1. Terminology

Mark D. Andrews
*The Elderly in Guardianship: A Crisis
of Constitutional Proportions*
5 ELDER L.J. 75, 79-80 (1997)[*]

Guardianship arises under the state power of *parens patriae*, a power "inherited from English law where the Crown assumed the 'care of those who, by reason of their imbecility and want of understanding, are incapable of taking care of themselves.'" As early as 1890, the U.S. Supreme Court recognized the doctrine as it was inherited from England, holding that the American Revolution gave the state the power previously vested in the British Parliament and king. The Court concluded that it is "indispensable that there should be a power in the legislature to authorize a sale of the estates of infants, idiots, insane persons and persons not known, or not in being, who cannot act for themselves." To care for persons unable to care for themselves, the state can appoint a guardian, often a relative. If no suitable guardian is available, the state itself becomes the guardian of the elderly ward.

Guardianship begins when a person asks the court to make a determination whether another person is able to handle her affairs. When this motion is filed, the court often will appoint a guardian ad litem to advise the court of the person in question's ability to manage her affairs or estate. If the guardian ad litem finds that the elderly person is not competent to handle her affairs, the guardian ad litem will recommend to the court how the alleged incompetent's affairs should be handled. If the person is judged incompetent, a court may appoint either a conservator to care for the incompetent's property or a guardian to care for the ward's person and property. The incompetent person is the ward of the guardian or conservator. The terms incompetency and incapacity are most often used to describe the condition that warrants appointment of a guardian. Current trends gravitate toward using incapacity, because it carries a less pejorative stigma and focuses more on the capacity to manage one's affairs, rather than the more blanket term incompetency, which suggests a stigmatizing mental deficiency.

Danielle Priola
Case Note, *Disability Law — Burden of Proof* . . .
In Re M.R., 135 N.J. 155, 638 A.2d 1274 (1994)
26 SETON HALL L. REV. 407, 408 n. 4 (1995)[*]

[G]uardianship arrangements can be classified into four categories: plenary guardianship, guardianship of the person, guardianship of the estate, and limited guardianship. A plenary guardianship arrangement vests the guardian with the authority to make decisions on behalf of the ward at an incompetency adjudication. A guardianship of the estate appointment concerns the financial and property rights of the incompetent while a guardianship of the person arrangement encompasses the remaining rights involved with personal decision-making. The last arrangement, a limited guardianship, particularizes the decision making dynamics to the individual needs of the ward.

Jamie L. Leary
A Review of Two Recently Reformed Guardianship Statutes: Balancing the Need to Protect Individuals Who Cannot Protect Themselves Against the Need to Guard Individual Autonomy
5 VA. J. SOC. POL'Y & L. 245, 264 (1997)[**]

In cases where a guardianship is necessary, some state statutes now mandate that a limited guardianship be used unless it can be shown that a plenary guardianship is necessary. This allows the ward to maintain control over every area that she can until she no longer is able to do so. Such a change requires increased court involvement, however, because guardians have to seek a new court order whenever the ward's abilities change.

QUESTIONS

1. What is the distinction between guardianship and conservatorship? (Note that this book often uses "guardianship" to cover both terms.)

2. What is the distinction between plenary and limited guardianship?

---

[*] Copyright © 1995. Reprinted with permission.
[**] Copyright © 1997. Reprinted with permission.

2. Statistics on Guardianship

Paula L. Hannaford & Thomas L. Hafemeister
The National Probate Court Standards: The Role of the Courts in Guardianship and Conservatorship Proceedings
2 ELDER L.J. 147, 154-56 (1994)[*]

A pervasive problem for organizations examining the use of guardianship for the elderly has been the lack of accurate or reliable information concerning the number of persons actually under the protection of a guardian in the United States. Much of the criticism of guardianship proceedings [in the late 1980s stemmed] from a few highly publicized, notorious, and particularly heinous examples of guardians' abuse and neglect of wards. Whether these examples constitute the exceptions or the rule of how guardianships actually function was unknown, however. To begin to address this problem, staff members from the National Probate Court Standards Project compiled statistical information about the number of guardianship cases filed in thirty-five states and the District of Columbia from 1990 through 1992.

The number of guardianship cases filed varies widely among the states, both in terms of absolute numbers and relative to the state's population. The total number of filings was 86,622 for twenty-two states and the District of Columbia in 1990; 114,882 for thirty-two states and the District of Columbia in 1991; and 133,005 for thirty-four states and the District of Columbia in 1992. Taking into account only those states reporting filings for all three years (twenty-one states and the District of Columbia), the number of filings increased twenty-five percent between 1990 and 1992. Seventeen states and the District of Columbia showed an increase in the number of filings during this period, with Alaska showing the largest percentage increase. The range of the average number of filings for the three-year period varies between a low of 122 in the District of Columbia to a high of 22,675 in Michigan. When adjusted for population, the average number of guardianship filings per 100,000 ranged from a low of 10.9 filings in Virginia to a high of 241.8 in Michigan. Based on the 1992 figures provided by the state courts, the total number of guardianship cases filed in state courts exceeds 300,000 annually, with an average per capita filing estimated at 121.3 per 100,000 of U.S. population.

Guardianship cases appear to be highly concentrated in particular states. The filings in Florida, Indiana, Michigan, New York, and Ohio — the five states with the largest guardianship caseloads — account for more than sixty-four percent of the total for 1990, more than fifty-four percent in 1991, and more than sixty-eight percent in 1992. However, all five are among the ten most populous states in the country. When adjusted for population, the five states with the highest average filing rates per 100,000 were: Michigan (241.8), Vermont (175.4), Connecticut (142.8), Arkansas (119.3), and Indiana (115.2). The five states with

---

[*] Copyright © 1994. Reprinted with permission. Copyright to the *Elder Law Journal* is held by the Board of Trustees of the University of Illinois.

the lowest average filing rates, when adjusted for population, were: Virginia (10.9), the District of Columbia (20.5), Colorado (36.6), Washington (49.7), and Hawaii (54.6). These results may be partially explained by the fact that the states with the highest per capita number of guardianship filings also had an above-average proportion of persons over age eighty-five. Similarly, with the exception of the District of Columbia, the states with the lowest guardianship filing rates had a below-average proportion of persons over age eighty-five. In other words, not surprisingly, states with a comparatively large proportion of elderly persons in their population have higher numbers of guardianship cases filed.

United States Senate Special Committee On Aging Forum On Guardianship
July 22, 2004
Excerpts from Written Comments of A. Frank Johns, JD, CELA, R-G

WRITTEN TESTIMONY

Ingo Keiltz, previously associated with the National Center of State Courts, commenting at the 1992 round table of this committee, raised the need for a national database on guardianship. He commented that Associated Press reporters were astonished to find that there was no data on state guardianship, and nothing existed on a nationwide basis. Keiltz made the obvious point that neither the federal government, nor each state knows how many individuals are subject to guardianship proceedings annually, what guardianship case loads correlate with population, whether or not they correlate with an elderly population and how they compare when adjusted for the population in different states, different jurisdictions and according to different administrative structures. Keiltz also asserted, as was found by professor Windsor Schmidt and other researchers, that there is insufficient research on social, economic, legal and systemic factors affecting the rates at which guardianship files are created in the courts.

A database for each state and the federal government would provide empirical data by which caseloads could be more carefully forecasted and processed. If the number of wards is known, then necessary funding would provide for sufficient staff, and the cost of training and enforcement. A national database could provide consistency and uniformity in the data entry and retrieval forms of the courts, requiring the same kinds of facts and circumstances that would be gathered across the country. After more than a decade since the first guardianship roundtable, I believe funding of such a database may only be realized through a federal effort because so many states continue to struggle near bankruptcy while still in the dark when it comes to statistics regarding guardianship.

Construction of a national database of guardianship was an important concern of the delegates at Wingspan. Two Wingspan recommendations specifically addressed a lack of data, and the need for a uniform system of guardianship data collection:

4. A uniform system of data collection within all areas of the guardian-
    ship process be developed and funded.

Comment: Although significant legislative revisions have been adopted, little data exists on the effectiveness of guardianship within each state or across
the states, and less information is available about how the system actually
affects the individuals involved. States maintain adequate data systems to
assure that required plans and reports are timely filed, and establish an electronic database to house these data while preserving privacy. It is left to the federal agencies to determine whether or not data could be collected on a national
level and integrated with the states. However, individual states have to be
more involved and committed to beginning some form of data collection on the
guardianships that are already in place.

QUESTION

A full decade after the Hannaford and Hafmeister article was published, A.
Frank Johns, one of the nation's leading experts on guardianship, testified as
above regarding the need for statistics on guardianship and conservatorship in
the United States. Without such information, how can the many problems that
beset the country's guardianship system be remedied?

3. The Standard of Incapacity

In connection with the following excerpt, read § 5-103(7) of the 1990 U.P.C.
and § 102(5) of the 1997 Uniform Guardianship and Protective Proceedings
Act ("U.G.P.P.A.") in the statutory supplement.

Phillip B. Tor & Bruce D. Sales
A Social Science Perspective on the Law
of Guardianship: Directions for Improving the
Process and Practice
18 LAW & PSYCHOL. REV. 1, 4-10 (1994)[*]

The chief purpose of a guardianship hearing is to make a legal determination
about a subject's competency. Since determination of incompetency is a legal
conclusion, each state spells out in its guardianship statute the legal requirements for making such a finding. The statutory standards can be categorized
into three groups: the causal link approach, the Uniform Probate Code (U.P.C.)
approach, and the functional approach.

A. *Causal Link Approach*

The causal link approach refers to the traditional standards of incompetency
where mental or physical conditions are linked to a generalized incapacity for
self care. Under these statutes, the court could declare a person incompetent on

---

[*] Copyright © 1994. Reprinted with permission.

the basis of a diagnostic label, such as aged or mentally retarded, if there is testimony that the subject is inadequately caring for himself or herself or his or her property. For example, a discontinued version of the Minnesota guardianship statute included the categories of "old age," "imperfection or deterioration of mentality," and "incompetent to manage his person." This type of statute is based on classifications. Incompetence and the general inability to care for one's self or manage one's responsibilities are viewed as inevitable consequences of that classification. If the petitioner (the party who initiates the guardianship action) can convince the court that the proposed ward has a disabling condition and is not taking proper care of himself or herself or his or her assets, the court could legally approve the guardianship.

* * *

Because causal link statutes offer only vague standards for incompetency, they give the judge wide discretion in deciding what evidence is admissible. In turn, broad judicial discretion gives rise to the likelihood of different outcomes of incompetency determinations for persons with similar disabilities who are adjudicated in the same jurisdiction. It also increases the likelihood of discrepant decisions by the same judge when hearing cases for defendants with similar conditions. Moreover, a person who fits into a statutory category but is capable of some degree of self-maintenance may still be forced to surrender to a plenary guardianship.

B. *Uniform Probate Code Approach*

In an effort to escape the stigmatic labels of the traditional causal link statutes, the Uniform Probate Code (U.P.C.) approach defines "incapacity" as an impairment of cognitive and communicative abilities resulting from one of a number of mental or physical conditions. The operative wording for incapacity in U.P.C. statutes is the lack of "sufficient understanding or capacity to make or communicate responsible decisions concerning his person." Most state legislatures have made changes to their guardianship statutes by incorporating this language.

* * *

This legislative desire to measure incompetency by the impairment of cognitive processes does not alleviate many of the problems with the causal link approach. U.P.C. statutes perpetuate the use of causal categories and give the court too much discretion because the key cognitive processes upon which they focus (i.e., understanding or capacity to make or communicate responsible decisions) remain vague. In addition, although the U.P.C. emphasizes the defendant's ability to make decisions, it allows the court to discount that ability if the decisions are not deemed responsible. This standard of incompetency fails to distinguish the capacity to make a decision, albeit a foolish one, from the capacity to make a socially or morally responsible decision. Thus, the court's finding of incapacity continues to turn on its own values, rather than on functional deficiencies. Finally, courts in U.P.C. jurisdictions may seldom have sufficient information about the proposed ward's conduct to make an objective determination about the proposed ward's decision making abilities. For these reasons, judicial inconsistencies may continue to plague guardianship proceedings.

* * *

C. *Functional Approach*

The functional approach represents the most recent innovation in guardianship standards. It requires that the court look at objective behavioral evidence of functional limitations in the person's daily activities when determining an individual's need for assistance. These statutes list specific activities, such as securing food, clothing, and health care for oneself. Courts will thereby have useful guidelines for determining when and how much assistance is needed to protect the individual from that person's incapacity, without imposing unnecessary restrictions on the individual's autonomy.

The functional approach is familiar and useful to mental health professionals because it focuses on behavioral objectives in the care and treatment of people with mental and physical disabilities. [It has been] argued that the functional approach can aid judicial decision making by referring to the very same objective criteria used by geriatric nurses, social workers, psychologists, physicians, and related health workers to evaluate patients with mental, physical, and social disabilities. This information is expected to help the court in deciding when and to what degree intervention is called for.

A growing number of states have adopted the functional approach. The New Hampshire code, for example, defines "functional limitations" as:

> . . . behavior or conditions . . . which impair (one's) ability to participate in and perform minimal activities of daily living that secure and maintain proper food, clothing, shelter, health care or safety for himself or herself. . . .

> "Incapacity" means a legal, not a medical, disability and shall be measured by functional limitations. . . . Inability to provide for personal needs or to manage property shall be evidenced by acts or occurrences, or statements which strongly indicate imminent acts or occurrences.

The statute also discusses the minimum frequency and duration of the observed limitations which evidence the need for guardianship.

* * *

It has been argued that legislatures should write statutes that not only mandate evidence of functional deficits, but also require prehearing standardized functional evaluations. . . . Both requirements would serve to screen out petitions that do not present a prima facie case worthy of judicial consideration, bring consistency to the determinations of legal incapacity, and create a more accurate and fair adjudicatory process.

Indeed, such evaluations are logically compelled because the functional approach requires that guardianship petitions include information about the prospective ward that only professional health care workers could provide.

* * *

Despite the compelling logic for applying the functional approach, the impact that changes in the statutory definitions of incompetency have had on the guardianship system needs to be empirically examined.

QUESTIONS

Into which of the categories described by Messrs. Tor and Sales would you put 1997 U.G.P.P.A. § 102(5)? How does this section differ from 1990 U.P.C. § 5-103(7)?

B. GUARDIANSHIP PROCEEDINGS

1. The Process of Petitioning for Guardianship

Guardianship procedures vary considerably from state to state. In this section, we examine the procedures contained in two uniform laws: (a) Article V of the U.P.C., which was promulgated in 1969 and revised in 1982, and (b) the U.G.P.P.A., which was promulgated in 1982 and revised in 1997. We begin, however, with some background.

a. Background on U.P.C. Article V and on the U.G.P.P.A.

A. Frank Johns & Vicki Joiner Bowers
Guardianship Folly: The Misgovernment of Parens Patriae and the Forecast of Its Crumbling Linkage to Unprotected Older Americans in the Twenty-First Century — A March of Folly? Or Just a Mask of Virtual Reality?
27 STETSON L. REV. 1, 34-37, 40, 45 (1997)[*]

The Uniform Probate Code (U.P.C.) is a creation of the National Conference of Commissioners on Uniform State Laws. Promulgated in 1969, the U.P.C. resulted from a continuing review and study of probate laws.

* * *

Consistency and continuity of language is the hallmark of any uniform legislation or code. The U.P.C. endeavored to remedy arcane and inconsistent language in guardianship statutes from state to state. U.P.C. Article V applied the then-current language to the guardianship concept, thus eliminating the arcane and embarrassing terms brought into modern American jurisprudence from . . . previous ages.

* * *

---

[*] Copyright © 1997. Reprinted with permission.

Article V covers guardianships for both minors and adults, and protective proceedings for property. It provides terminology continuity in "typical" guardianship legislation, and addresses and incorporates many recommendations of concurrent empirical research and studies.

* * *

During the 1970s, the U.P.C., with its Article V on guardianship and conservatorship, gained acceptance.

* * *

During the mid-1970s, the ABA's Committee on the Mentally Disabled began an effort that promoted revision of the Uniform Probate Code Article V to include "limited guardianship" to avoid an asserted "overkill" implicit in standard guardianship proceedings. U.P.C. spokespersons and the National Conference of Commissioners objected and temporarily barred recommended U.P.C. revisions, contending "typical" guardianship legislation was sufficient.

However, many of the U.P.C. states began amending statutes to include some form of limited guardianship, but the states utilized inconsistent language. . . . To not be left behind, the National Conference of Commissioners changed course, and developed what was to be the Uniform Guardianship and Protective Proceedings Act.

* * *

In 1982, the Commissioners produced a stand alone act entitled The Uniform Guardianship and Protective Proceedings Act (U.G.P.P.A.). The U.G.P.P.A. restructured U.P.C. Article V to include explicit language relative to the concept of limited guardianship, and incorporated the limited guardianship philosophy into all other parts to provide internal consistency and accommodate the limited guardianship concept. Alternatively, with the modifications to Article V, it was offered as a component part to the U.P.C.

Jamie L. Leary
A Review of Two Recently Reformed Guardianship Statutes: Balancing the Need to Protect Individuals Who Cannot Protect Themselves Against the Need to Guard Individual Autonomy
5 VA. J. SOC. POL'Y & L. 245, 269-70 (1997)[*]

In the mid-1970s, the ABA Commission on the Mentally Disabled began reform work to expand Article V of the Uniform Probate Code to include limited guardianships. This effort culminated in the drafting of a "free-standing" act in 1982: the Uniform Guardianship and Protective Proceedings Act ("U.G.P.P.A." or "the Act"). The 1982 U.G.P.P.A. focused on the concept of limited guardianship "so that the authority of the protector would intrude only to the degree necessary on the liberties and prerogatives of the protected person." The National

---

Conference of Commissioners worked to incorporate the concept of the limited guardianship throughout the statute "to provide internal consistency."

The 1997 U.G.P.P.A. makes an important change in the concept of limited guardianships, but has also been expanded to include other important procedural reforms. It ensures due process by providing for adequate representation for the respondent and requiring the respondent's presence at the hearing. It defines incapacity using a functional approach so that an individual who simply needs technological assistance can retain control over other areas of her life. Finally, it requires the court to monitor guardians.

b. The Procedures for Petitioning for Guardianship Under Article V of the 1990 U.P.C. and Under the 1997 U.G.P.P.A.

Answers to the following questions, and to subsequent questions posed in this unit on guardianship, will be found in the 1990 U.P.C., Article V, Part 3, and the 1997 U.G.P.P.A., Article 3, both of which deal with guardianship of the person.

QUESTIONS

Compare the answers to the following questions under Article V of the 1990 U.P.C. and under the 1997 U.G.P.P.A. Which approach is better, and might a third approach be better than either?

1. *Procedural Matters Before the Hearing.* Who may file the guardianship petition? What information must the petition contain? What notice must be provided to the person alleged to be incapacitated?

2. *Procedural Matters at the Hearing.* Who is required or permitted to be present at the hearing? To what extent are lawyers and health-care professionals involved? What form does the hearing take, and what types of evidence may be presented? Who is the ultimate decision-maker? What standard of proof is required before a guardian may be appointed?

3. *Emergencies.* What happens in an emergency?

4. *Selecting the Guardian.* Who may be appointed as guardian? Must the guardian be a person, or may an entity or organization serve as guardian?

2. The Use of Alternative Dispute Resolution ("ADR")

Susan N. Gary
Mediation and the Elderly: Using Mediation to Resolve
Probate DisputesOver Guardianship and Inheritance
32 WAKE FOREST L. REV. 397, 414-15, 424-31, 434 (1997)[*]

Disputes over guardianship can arise either before the guardian is named or after the appointment. One type of dispute occurs when the person who is alleged to be incapacitated does not want to have a guardian appointed. Susan Hartman, the Directing Attorney for the Center for Social Gerontology's Guardianship Mediation Program, has written that, despite law reforms, guardianship proceedings are still handled in a routine manner, with little attention given to the capacity issues and little exploration of alternatives to guardianship. The adult for whom the guardianship is sought may feel betrayed and demeaned by the process. An adversarial legal proceeding may exacerbate these feelings.

Another type of conflict may develop when two adult children each want to be appointed guardian of their mother or father. The conflict may have roots in differing views of appropriate care for the parent, it may hide concern over protecting an inheritance, or it may simply reflect a long-standing sibling rivalry.

Different opinions about decisions that have been made or that need to be made on behalf of the older adult may also lead to conflict before the appoint-ment of a guardian. Family members may disagree about medical or financial decisions. They may disagree about where the older person should live and what type of living arrangement is appropriate. Although the older person may not be incapacitated, if the person is of somewhat limited capacity, failure to resolve a dispute about any of these issues may result in a guardianship pro-ceeding as a last resort. Mediation may be useful as a means of resolving the dis-pute and eliminating the need for a guardianship proceeding.

After a court appoints a guardian, disputes may occur if other family mem-bers disagree with actions taken by the guardian. The conflict may be over the appropriateness of decisions and quality of care, or it may focus on whether the guardian is breaching his fiduciary duties and misusing the protected person's funds. Although the guardian may be acting under legal authority, family dis-agreements may escalate into adversarial battles that lead to continued fight-ing within the family.

In addition to conflicts among family members, conflicts may develop between the older person or family members and hospitals, nursing homes, or service agencies. In some situations, one of these care providers may bring a guardian-ship proceeding as a convenient — albeit inappropriate from the standpoint of the protected person — resolution of the problem.

---

* * *

In discussing the advantages of mediation, this article compares mediation with litigation, the form of legal dispute resolution most widely used to resolve probate disputes. Mediation's beneficial characteristics include the opportunity for privacy and confidentiality, the promotion of therapeutic effects for the parties, the expanded possibility that an ongoing relationship between parties can be maintained, the potential for creating solutions uniquely suited to the problem at hand, and the possible reduction of financial costs as compared with those incurred in litigation. Each of these characteristics makes mediation an appropriate form of dispute resolution for parties to a probate dispute to consider.

* * *

A. *Privacy and Confidentiality*

* * *

Privacy benefits probate disputants in two ways: first, by avoiding public discussion of a family's "dirty laundry," and second, by encouraging disputants to speak freely in an attempt to reach a resolution that deals with the messy relationship problems, as well as the legal property problems.

* * *

B. *Emotional Benefits*

* * *

In a guardianship proceeding, the older adult faces a potential loss of dignity, as well as the loss of legal and civil rights. The appointment of a guardian may assist the older adult with practical or financial needs, but by ignoring the emotional aspect of the proceeding, may leave the protected person confused, angry, or bitter. A mediation proceeding gives the older adult a voice. The process allows him to speak about his concerns and gives the family members a chance to explain the need for the guardianship. Regardless of whether the resolution is a less restrictive solution or a request that the court appoint a guardian, the older adult will benefit from the chance to hear and to be heard.

* * *

In addition to the potential emotional benefits of mediation, parties using mediation to resolve their dispute may avoid some of the emotional costs of litigation. The litigation process itself can be traumatic.

* * *

C. *Ongoing Relationships*

* * *

First, in the course of understanding each other's views of the problem, the process increases communication between the parties. Second, by participating in the process of problem solving, the parties may be better able to work with each other to solve future problems. Both of these aspects of mediation can contribute to a better long-term relationship between the parties.

Mediation may also further an ongoing relationship between the parties by what it does not do. Litigation, in contrast with mediation, encourages parties to become entrenched in their positions and to view a successful outcome as a win for one party and a loss for the other.

* * *

D. *Unique Solutions*

* * *

In a guardianship proceeding, the court will either appoint a guardian, usually significantly depriving the protected person of rights, or decide that a guardian is not necessary, leaving the older person to fend for herself. Mediation allows the older adult and the family members to work together to reach a solution, perhaps arranging for some assistance for the older person without the need to have a guardian appointed.

* * *

E. *Financial Costs*

* * *

Much has been written about the high financial cost of litigation. Although mediation is not necessarily less expensive than litigation, research in family law has shown that mediation costs less than litigation in resolving divorce cases. In addition to potential savings for the parties, a goal of mediation is to reduce societal costs by reducing the burden on the court system.

* * *

V. *Current Attempts to Encourage or Mandate Mediation in Probate*

Mediation in the probate context is still in its infancy; but increasingly legislatures, the judiciary, and attorneys are turning to mediation as an appropriate dispute resolution process for handling probate issues. No data exists on the extent to which probate courts are currently using mediation.

QUESTIONS

1. How would you evaluate the advantages of ADR? Does it have any disadvantages compared to the procedures used in the U.P.C. and U.G.P.P.A.?

2. Should parties be required to try some form of ADR before filing a formal guardianship petition?

3. The Guardian's Powers and Duties: The Statutory Language

QUESTIONS

1. *Authority.* What powers does the guardian have?

2. *Responsibility.* What duties must the guardian perform?

3. *Delegation.* To what extent may a guardian delegate his powers or duties to others?

4. The Guardian's Powers and Duties: The Standard of Decisionmaking

Hal Fliegelman & Debora C. Fliegelman
Giving Guardians the Power to Do Medicaid Planning
32 WAKE FOREST L. REV. 341, 349-352 (1997)[*]

The standards by which courts decide whether a guardian may have certain powers and take certain actions have always been guided by one main principle: avoiding abuse and protecting the ward. What is best for the ward, however, is not always easy to ascertain. Interested parties may disagree over what is best. Judges may feel constrained by statute or common law. Wards may have left incomplete or incoherent instructions, or none at all. In the effort to give guardians the authority to do what is "best" for the ward while also guarding against potential abuse, courts have developed various standards, including the "continuing pattern" theory, "best interests of the ward," and "substituted judgment." In addition, courts have relied on constitutional concepts such as equal protection to permit guardians to take such actions as giving gifts and making transfers from the guardianship estate.

1. *Continuing pattern*

The continuing pattern theory is generally criticized. It requires a determination of what the incompetent would do, based on what he or she has already done. Evidence of the incompetent's prior intent . . . is the only factor given any weight. It is considered a purely subjective test. The subjective test, however, is not always appropriate. As [one] court . . . explained, the subjective test, "however meaningful," is entirely inapplicable in the case of a congenital incompetent:

> To so conclude [that subjective intent "must always stand as an indispensable prerequisite to relief"] would offer an individual as Brennan [a profoundly disabled child — Eds.] less opportunity in the law than persons who have come to know a disability in later life. Brennan has not had the opportunity to consider or formulate a lifetime or testamentary

---

[*] Copyright © 1997. Reprinted with permission.

plan. He has been deprived of the opportunity to know and convey his personal feelings for those who stand as the natural objects of his bounty. He has not had the opportunity to confer with business or legal advisors and reflect upon what meaning the imposition of inheritance taxes may have upon the plans he would make relative to the succession of his property. Brennan is deprived of these opportunities not by his own choice or inaction but rather by reason of multiple physical and mental disabilities brought upon him by the very event of his birth. In this day and these circumstances, it would be inappropriate to cling in dogmatic fashion to rules which are incapable of satisfaction. Rather, the court in pursuit of its equitable powers is called upon to do justice.

Many courts have abandoned subjective intent as the sole standard. . . . Some jurisdictions now combine the subjective test with other, more objective standards.

2. *Best interests of the ward*

The best interests doctrine allows the court to proceed based on what it believes would be most beneficial to the ward. The best interests model has been likened to a parent-child relationship. Like a parent, a "best interests" guardian is expected to intervene where a ward lacks the ability to act according to his own best interests, or lacks the appreciation of the consequences of his actions. "The intervention is not condoned because it suits the parent or the guardian, or because the intervention by guardianship serves some third party or societal interest, but only because the interests of the child or ward are thereby best served." The requirement that the court determine what is in the ward's best interest is "intended to substitute a judicial determination for the guardian's personal discretion in order to provide additional protection to the ward." Determination of a ward's best interests should involve some consideration of the ward's wishes, where they are ascertainable.

"Best interests" statutes usually enumerate factors for the court to consider in determining what is best for the ward.

* * *

The problem with the "best interests" standard is that "the interests of the individual depend upon who is defining them." The definition of "best" is vague and uncertain, even with statutory guidelines.

* * *

3. *Substituted judgment*

The substituted judgment doctrine [involves]. . . . essentially an objective, "reasonably prudent person" standard. . . . "The controlling principle is that the court will act with reference to the incompetent and for his benefit as he would probably have acted if [capable]." [Under this standard,] [a] guardian may not act contrary to the settled intention of the ward.

QUESTIONS

1. What are the advantages and disadvantages of the three approaches described by the authors of the above article?

2. Which of the three approaches has been adopted by the 1990 U.P.C.? By the 1997 U.G.P.P.A.?

5. The Guardian's Powers and Duties: The Rise of Limited Guardianship

Sally Balch Hurme
Current Trends in Guardianship Reform
7 Md. J. Contemp. Legal Issues 143, 160-64, 168, 170-71 (1995-1996)*

Because a grant of full or plenary powers to a guardian results in a drastic loss of legal rights, legislatures have paid substantial attention to the appropriateness of limiting the powers granted to the guardian. As one author has commented, "use of guardians who are limited in their powers would promote the values of autonomy, self-determination, and individual dignity, and discourage the overreach of societal interference and manipulation." Logic makes a compelling case for limiting the deprivation of rights through a tailored guardianship order that matches the particular disabilities of the individual rather than the wholesale removal of rights through plenary orders.

1. *Historical Call for Tailored Orders* — Advocates have called for limited guardianship for more than a decade. As early as 1979, the ABA Commission on the Mentally Disabled recommended that state laws be changed to avoid an asserted "overkill" implicit in standard guardianship proceedings.

A key reason the National Conference of Commissioners on Uniform State Laws adopted the Uniform Guardianship and Protective Proceedings Act (U.G.P.P.A.) in 1982 to amend the Article V guardianship provisions of the Uniform Probate Code (U.P.C.) was to include the concept of limited guardianships. Following the ABA Commission's recommendation, the U.G.P.P.A. recognized the need for more sensitive procedures and for appointments fashioned so that the authority of the protector would intrude only to the degree necessary on the liberties and prerogatives of the protected person. In short, rather than permitting an all-or-none status, there should be an intermediate status available to the courts through which the protected person will have personal liberties and prerogatives restricted only to the extent necessary under the circumstances. The court should be admonished to look for a least-restrictive protection approach.

Seven years later the National Guardianship Symposium called for limited guardianship orders that are "as specific as possible with respect to the guardian's powers and duties." The symposium reformers predicted that such specificity would help the courts limit guardianship and tailor orders to the incapacitated person's circumstances.

The newly issued National Probate Court Standards joins in directing probate judges to "detail the duties and powers of the guardian, including limitations to the duties and powers, and the rights retained by the respondent." The commentary to this standard notes that:

> [b]ecause the preferred practice is to limit the powers and duties of the guardian to those necessary to meet the needs of the respondent, the court should specifically enumerate in its order the assigned duties and powers of the guardian. . . . By listing the powers and duties of the guardian, the court's order can serve as an educational road map to which the guardian can refer and use to help answer questions about what the guardian can or cannot do in carrying out the guardian's assigned responsibilities.

2. *Legislative Efforts* — Most state legislatures have taken major strides in recognizing the need for and appropriateness of limited orders. Limited orders, as used in this context, means more than just differentiating between a guardian of the person and a guardian (or conservator) of the estate. Every state that has implemented major guardianship reform in the past few years has incorporated provisions for limited orders or has mandated the issuance of limited orders enumerating the specific personal and financial powers given to the guardian and assigning the guardian only those duties and powers that the person is incapable of exercising. For example, Florida's comprehensive 1989 revision of its guardianship provisions requires that the order enumerate the guardian's specific powers and duties and state that "the guardian may exercise only those delegable rights which have been removed from the incapacitated person." Further, the order "must be consistent with the incapacitated person's welfare and safety, must be the least restrictive appropriate alternative, and must reserve to the incapacitated person the right to make decisions in all matters commensurate with his ability to do so."

The statute resulting from New York's massive revision requires that guardians have only those powers necessary to assist the incapacitated person to compensate for any limitations. The guardianship is to be "tailored to the individual needs of [an incapacitated] person, which takes into account the personal wishes, preferences and desires of the person, and which affords the person the greatest amount of independence and self-determination and participation in all the decisions affecting such person's life." This conception of limited guardianship is considered the cornerstone of both the Florida and New York statutory schemes.

Other states have followed the trend to provide for limited guardianship by stating a preference for limited guardianship, mandating specific findings of incapacity and providing the choice of the least restrictive intervention.

* * *

3. *Appellate Court Endorsement* — A review of reported decisions finds appellate courts approving the use of tailored orders and enforcing the legislative

mandates to limit the powers delegated to a guardian because of the serious deprivation of civil rights resulting from full guardianship.

* * *

4. *Self-Autonomy* — The overarching public policy to maintain the incapacitated person's self-autonomy to the highest degree possible in the new guardianship practices requires a combined emphasis on less restricted alternatives, functional assessment, and tailored orders. New York's guardianship laws clearly reflect an awareness of, and attention to, these interests. The statute states that guardianships should be "tailored to the individual needs of [an incapacitated] person, which takes into account the personal wishes, preferences and desires of the person, and which affords the person the greatest amount of independence and self-determination and participation in all the decisions affecting such person's life."

QUESTIONS

1. What explains the burgeoning interest in limited guardianship?

2. To what extent has the principle of limited guardianship been embodied in the provisions of the 1990 U.P.C.? In the provisions of the 1997 U.G.P.P.A.?

3. Are there any disadvantages to limited guardianship?

6. The Guardian's Powers and Duties: Monitoring by the Court

Sally Balch Hurme
Current Trends in Guardianship Reform
7 MD. J. CONTEMP. LEGAL ISSUES 143, 182-88 (1995-1996)[*]

The court practices following the guardian's appointment are widely divergent. Some states may require that guardians periodically report on the personal and financial well-being of the incapacitated person and routinely review the need to continue the guardianship. Other states may do little to provide ongoing oversight of the guardian's actions, reviewing the guardianship only if someone formally petitions the court.

The sources of this monitoring diversity are not clear, but a possible cause for a "hands off" policy is the philosophy behind the Uniform Probate Code (U.P.C.). Its underlying premise is that the courts should not be involved in the day-to-day administration of a decedent's estate. The court's role is to be "wholly passive until some interested person invokes its power to secure resolution of a matter." For historical reasons guardianship was included in the probate code. Thus, under the original U.P.C., the guardian, like the probate administrator, received little supervision until filing the final accounting.

Unlike the administration of a decedent's estate, guardianship is for a living person whose needs can change over time. Not only should the court tailor the initial guardianship order to the immediate needs of the incapacitated person, but it should also establish routine procedures to supervise the guardian, to revise the guardianship order, and to resolve problems when the circumstances of the incapacitated person or the guardian change.

A 1991 study of guardianship monitoring by the American Bar Association's Commissions on Legal Problems of the Elderly and Mental and Physical Disability Law revealed that legislatures and courts are becoming more receptive of the need to monitor guardianship cases. The overwhelming legislative trend in the past decade has been to require guardians to report periodically on the incapacitated person's financial and personal status. To this end, all fifty states and the District of Columbia authorize courts to order financial accountings. In 1991, forty-three jurisdictions required guardians of the person to report on the incapacitated person's personal status and ten states require guardians of the property to report on both financial and personal status. All of the new statutes, with the exception of Delaware's, require the guardians of the person and of the estate to file annual financial and personal status reports.

Some states also require initial care reports or property management plans to be filed along with the more traditional inventories.

The South Dakota periodic report is typical of the type of information guardians must provide to the court. The report must state the current mental, physical, and social condition of the protected persons; their living arrangements; medical, educational, vocational, and other professional service provided to the protected persons; the guardian's opinion as to the adequacy of care; a summary of the guardian's visits with and activities on the protected person's behalf; whether the guardian agrees with the current treatment or habilitation plan if the protected person is institutionalized; and a recommendation as to the need to continue or change the guardianship's scope. Texas law requires guardians to file personal reports which include information such as when they most recently saw the incapacitated person and how frequently they see the incapacitated person. Additionally, the guardian must indicate whether the incapacitated person's mental and physical health has improved, deteriorated, or remained unchanged. The guardians also must evaluate whether the incapacitated person is content or unhappy with his or her living arrangements.

It must be emphasized that effective supervision of a guardian should include more than just receiving a periodic report. The court must establish procedures for reviewing and verifying the reports and for reconsidering the need to continue or modify the guardianship. Such procedures would promote more uniform review for all cases and provide up-to-date information on the location and status of the incapacitated person.

Based on the premise that a report is pointless if no one reviews it or acts on it, some legislatures have been fairly specific about the procedures a court must follow once such reports are filed. New York requires a court examiner to review the reports within thirty days of filing and authorizes various sanctions for failure to file. It also establishes specific hours of training for guardians, court evaluators, and court examiners.

Texas has gone further than New York by creating a monitoring system to keep the court abreast of its guardianship cases. The court is directed to use reasonable diligence to determine whether a guardian is performing all required duties. The court is also required to examine the well-being of each incapacitated person, as well as the bond's sufficiency. Finally, the court must review each guardianship annually to see if it should be continued, modified, or terminated. Texas letters of appointment expire one year and 120 days after issuance. The letter can be renewed only if the accounting has been filed and approved. Additionally, the incapacitated person, or any other person, can request modification or termination of the guardianship through the submission of an informal letter.

Rhode Island requires the probate court to monitor each guardianship file and impose sanctions where necessary. In the case of a guardian over property, if the guardian fails to file an annual accounting, the guardian is accountable for the full value of the estate and can receive no compensation. Texas judges have the authority to imprison guardians for up to three days for any one offense, while New York judges can deny or reduce the compensation of the guardian or remove the guardian. Courts have become increasingly willing to impose various sanctions on guardians who have breached their fiduciary duty and misused funds. Guardians have been convicted of embezzlement, had judgments imposed against them, as well as having their gifts and sales set aside. The courts have held guardians liable for failure to segregate funds, denied their commissions, and have even removed guardians in certain situations. In addition, attorneys for guardians have been held liable for failing to discover and disclose their client's misappropriation of funds.

QUESTIONS

1. To what extent do the 1990 U.P.C. and 1997 U.G.P.P.A. provide for the monitoring of guardians?

2. What behavior(s) are these provisions attempting to prevent?

7. Terminating the Guardian(ship)

QUESTIONS

1. *Removal.* Under what circumstances may a court remove a previously-appointed guardian?

2. *Termination.* Under what circumstances may a guardianship be terminated?

C. ETHICAL ISSUES: WHO IS THE CLIENT?

FICKETT v. SUPERIOR COURT OF PIMA COUNTY
558 P.2d 988 (Ariz. Ct. App. 1976)

HOWARD, Chief Judge.

Petitioners are defendants in a pending superior court action filed by the present conservator (formerly guardian) of an incompetent's estate against the former guardian and petitioners, attorneys for the former guardian. The gravamen of the complaint was that petitioner Fickett, as attorney for the former guardian, was negligent in failing to discover that the guardian had embarked upon a scheme to liquidate the guardianship estate by misappropriation and conversion of the funds to his own use and making improper investments for his personal benefit.

Petitioners filed a motion for summary judgment contending that, as a matter of law, since there was no fraud or collusion between the guardian and his attorney, the attorney was not liable for the guardian's misappropriation of the assets of the guardianship estate. In opposing the motion for summary judgment, the present conservator conceded that no fraud or collusion existed. His position, however, was that one could not say as a matter of law that the guardian's attorney owed no duty to the ward. The respondent court denied the motion for summary judgment and petitioners challenge this ruling by special action.

The general rule for many years has been that an attorney could not be liable to one other than his client in an action arising out of his professional duties, in the absence of fraud or collusion. In denying liability of the attorney to one not in privity of contract for the consequences of professional negligence, the courts have relied principally on two arguments: (1) That to allow such liability would deprive the parties to the contract of control of their own agreement; and (2) that a duty to the general public would impose a huge potential burden of liability on the contracting parties.

* * *

We cannot agree with petitioners that they owed no duty to the ward and that her conservator could not maintain an action because of lack of privity of contract. We are of the opinion that the better view is that the determination of whether, in a specific case, the attorney will be held liable to a third person not in privity is a matter of policy and involves the balancing of various factors, among which are the extent to which the transaction was intended to affect the plaintiff, the foreseeability of harm to him, the degree of certainty that the plaintiff suffered injury, the closeness of the connection between the defendant's conduct and the injuries suffered, the moral blame attached to the defendant's conduct, and the policy of preventing future harm.

We believe that the public policy of this state permits the imposition of a duty under the circumstances presented here.

* * *

We are of the opinion that when an attorney undertakes to represent the guardian of an incompetent, he assumes a relationship not only with the guardian but also with the ward. If, as is contended here, petitioners knew or should have known that the guardian was acting adversely to his ward's interests, the possibility of frustrating the whole purpose of the guardianship became foreseeable as did the possibility of injury to the ward. In fact, we conceive that the ward's interests overshadow those of the guardian. We believe the following statement in *Heyer v. Flaig* . . . as to an attorney's duty to an intended testamentary beneficiary is equally appropriate here:

> The duty thus recognized in *Lucas* stems from the attorney's undertaking to perform legal services for the client but reaches out to protect the intended beneficiary. We impose this duty because of the relationship between the attorney and the intended beneficiary; public policy requires that the attorney exercise his position of trust and superior knowledge responsibly so as not to affect adversely persons whose rights and interests are certain and foreseeable.

> Although the duty accrues directly in favor of the intended testamentary beneficiary, the scope of the duty is determined by reference to the attorney-client context. Out of the agreement to provide legal services to a client, the prospective testator, arises the duty to act with due care as to the interests of the intended beneficiary. We do not mean to say that the attorney-client contract for legal services serves as the fundamental touchstone to fix the scope of this direct tort duty to the third party. The actual circumstances under which the attorney undertakes to perform his legal services, however, will bear on a judicial assessment of the care with which he performs his services.

We, therefore, uphold the respondent court's denial of petitioners' motion for summary judgment since they failed to establish the absence of a legal relationship and concomitant duty to the ward.

* * *

HATHAWAY, J., and JACK G. MARKS, Superior Court Judge, concur.

American College of Trust and Estate Counsel
Commentaries on the Model Rules of Professional Conduct
ACTEC Commentary on MRPC 1.14[*]

* * *

Lawyer Retained by Guardian or Conservator for Disabled Person. The lawyer retained by a fiduciary for a disabled person, including a guardian, conservator, or attorney-in-fact, stands in a lawyer-client relationship with respect to the

---

[*] Reprinted with permission.

fiduciary. A lawyer who is retained by a fiduciary for a disabled person, but who did not previously represent the disabled person, represents only the fiduciary. Nevertheless, in such a case the lawyer for the fiduciary owes some duties to the disabled person. *See* ACTEC Commentary on MRPC 1.2 (Scope of Representation). This approach is reflected in the Comment to MRPC 1.14: "If the lawyer represents the guardian as distinct from the ward and is aware of the guardian acting adversely to the ward's interest, the lawyer may have an obligation to prevent or rectify the guardian's misconduct. *See* Rule 1.2(d)."

Disabled Person Was Client Prior to Disability. A lawyer who represented a now disabled person as a client prior to the appointment of a fiduciary may be considered to continue to represent the disabled person. Although incapacity may prevent a disabled person from entering into a contract or other legal relationship, the lawyer who represented the disabled person prior to incapacity may appropriately continue to meet with and counsel him or her. Whether the disabled person is characterized as a client or a former client, the lawyer for the fiduciary owes some continuing duties to him or her. *See* Ill. Advisory Opinion 91-24 (1991) (summarized in the Annotations following the ACTEC Commentary on MRPC 1.6 (Confidentiality of Information)).

Wishes of Disabled Person. A conflict of interest may arise if the lawyer for the fiduciary is asked by the fiduciary to take action that is contrary either to the previously expressed wishes of the disabled person or to the best interests of the disabled person, as the lawyer believes those interests to be. The lawyer should give appropriate consideration to the currently or previously expressed wishes of a disabled person.

Lawyer May Take Action in Best Interests of Disabled Person. If the lawyer believes that the best interests of the disabled person requires representation by an independent party, the lawyer may suggest to family members or to an appropriate tribunal that a guardian ad litem or another lawyer be appointed for the disabled person.

* * *

QUESTIONS

1. Did the court in *Fickett* reach the right result? Why or why not? Consider this question in light of the ACTEC Commentaries on MRPC1.14.

2. Are there any disadvantages to the imposition of attorney liability in such cases?

A. BACKGROUND

1. What is "Elder Abuse"?

Joann Blair
***"Honor Thy Father and Thy Mother" — But For
How Long? — Adult Children's Duty to Care for
and Protect Elderly Parents***
35 U. Louisville J. Fam. L. 765, 765 (1996-1997)[*]

Neglect of the elderly is a prevalent problem facing Americans that has only recently gained widespread attention. Child abuse and spousal abuse were addressed in the 1960s and 1970s, respectively, but in the past decade elder abuse has acquired a place in the spotlight of American politics. . . . In the

---

[*] Copyright © 1997. Reprinted with permission.

United States, the House of Representatives Select Committee on Aging conducted the first major investigation of the elder abuse problem in 1981.

QUESTION

Why did it take so long to discover the problem of elder abuse and bring it to the nation's attention?

National Center on Elder Abuse
NCEA — What Is Elder Abuse?
http://www.elderabusecenter.org/default.cfm?p=mistreatment.cfm[*]

Federal definitions of elder abuse, neglect, and exploitation appeared for the first time in the 1987 Amendments to the Older Americans Act. These definitions were provided in the law only as guidelines for identifying the problems and not for enforcement purposes.

Currently, elder abuse is defined by state laws, and state definitions vary considerably from one jurisdiction to another in terms of what constitutes the abuse, neglect, or exploitation of the elderly. In addition, researchers have used many different definitions to study the problem.

Broadly defined, however, there are three basic categories of elder abuse: (1) domestic elder abuse; (2) institutional elder abuse; and (3) self-neglect or self-abuse. In most cases, state statutes addressing elder abuse provide the definitions of these different categories of elder abuse, with varying degrees of specificity.

The National Committee for the Prevention of Elder Abuse and The National Adult Protective Services Association Abuse of Adults Age 60+: The 2004 Survey of Adult Protective Services
February 2006
http://www.apsnetwork.org/Resources/docs/AbuseAdults60.pdf[**]

Rosa is a 79-year-old widow who lives with Michael, her 52-year-old son. Michael moved in with her after experiencing a divorce in which he lost custody of his two children and ownership of his home. Within months of Michael's move, he assumed responsibility of Rosa's Social Security checks and meager pension. Now, he does not allow her to see visitors and has begun to lock Rosa in her room when he leaves the house. When she has medical appointments, Michael insists on accompanying Rosa throughout all aspects of the examinations. Rosa's long-time neighbors, concerned that they never see their friend, suspect abuse but are unsure of where to turn. Finally, one neighbor dialed the APS hotline.

[*] Reprinted with permission.

[**] Copyright © 2006. Reprinted with permission.

Eddie is 76 years old and a former high school history teacher. A year ago, his wife of 53 years died suddenly due to a massive stroke. Since that time, he has begun to show signs of memory loss. Eddie, who has always liked to "hold onto things," has begun to hoard newspapers. He claims they are a defense against future September 11th terrorists. His three underfed dogs bark incessantly, and the siding is falling off his home. He rarely bathes and leaves the house around 2:00 a.m. to buy groceries once a month. Recently, there was a small fire in his kitchen because he forgot to turn off the stove. His two children, who live out of state, are very worried, but Eddie insists that there is nothing wrong with him. A concerned check-out clerk at the grocery store that Eddie frequents made a report to APS.

Cynthia, a 93-year-old woman with diabetes, has lived in the same home for 60 years. Recently, her granddaughter Carol and her boyfriend Kyle moved in with her to provide caregiving assistance in exchange for rent-free housing. Carol convinced Cynthia to add her to her checking account to help her pay bills. Carol is also trying to convince Cynthia to sign over the deed to the house in order to allow Carol to make house payments and generally "run things more smoothly." Neither Carol nor her boyfriend has worked since moving in with Cynthia. Recently, Carol became physically abusive when she was intoxicated and pushed Cynthia down a short flight of stairs. Cynthia will not contact the authorities because she is embarrassed by the situation. She does not want to have her granddaughter arrested. A teller at Cynthia's bank noticed the irregular account activity and made a report to APS.

* * *

Although states differ in their statutory and regulatory definitions, general definitions are helpful in understanding this report. For example, for the purposes of this study, a committee of key NAPSA members defined *abuse* as the infliction of physical or psychological harm or the knowing deprivation of goods or services necessary to meet essential needs or to avoid physical or psychological harm.

Neglect is defined as the refusal or failure to fulfill any part of a person's obligations or duties to an elder. Neglect may also include failure of a person who has fiduciary responsibilities to provide care for an elder (e.g., pay for necessary home care services) or the failure on the part of an in-home service provider to provide necessary care. Neglect typically means the refusal or failure to provide an elderly person/vulnerable adult with such life necessities as food, water, clothing, shelter, personal hygiene, medicine, comfort, personal safety, and other essentials included in an implied or agreed-upon responsibility to an elder.

Financial or Material Abuse/Exploitation is defined as the illegal or improper use of an older person's or vulnerable adult's funds, property, or assets. Examples include, but are not limited to, cashing an older/vulnerable person's checks without authorization or permission; forging an older person's signature; misusing or stealing an older person's money or possessions; coercing or deceiving an older person into signing any document (e.g., contracts or will); and the improper use of conservatorship, guardianship, or power of attorney.

Self-Neglect is regarded as an adult's inability, due to physical or mental impairment or diminished capacity, to perform essential self-care tasks including (a) obtaining essential food, clothing, shelter, and medical care; (b) obtaining goods and services necessary to maintain physical health, mental health, or general safety; and/or (c) managing one's own financial affairs. Choice of lifestyle or living arrangement is not, in itself, evidence of self-neglect.

Finally, a *vulnerable adult* is defined as a person who is either being mistreated or in danger of mistreatment and who, due to age and/or disability, is unable to protect himself or herself.

Office of the Clark County (Indiana) Prosecuting Attorney Adult Protective Services
What Is Elder Abuse? Is It Really a Crime?
http://www.clarkprosecutor.org/html/aps/apswhat.htm

Often it is a crime. In many cases abusers break the law and can be charged with a criminal offense. People who commit the crime of elder abuse are often related to or responsible for the older man or woman they harm. Victims of elder abuse know their abusers. Most victims of elder abuse depend on the people who hurt them, sometimes for food, shelter, personal care, or companionship.

There are many kinds of elder abuse. Physical abuse includes any kind of physical battery, such as slapping, pushing, kicking, punching, or injuring with an object or weapon. It also includes deliberate exposure to severe weather, inappropriate use of medication and unnecessary physical restraint. Sexual abuse includes any forced sexual activity. All are crimes under Indiana law.

Elder abuse also includes mental cruelty and psychological abuse. If someone humiliates, insults, frightens, threatens, ignores or treats an older person like a child, this is mental cruelty. Threatening to put an older person in a nursing home can be a form of psychological abuse. Removal of decision making power when the elderly person is still competent to make his/her own decisions is also considered to be psychological abuse. Under some circumstances, psychological abuse and other forms of mental cruelty are crimes under Indiana law.

Neglect is any lack of action required to meet the needs of an elderly person. It includes inadequate provision of food, clothing, shelter, required medication or other kinds of health and personal care, as well as social companionship. Passive neglect is the unintentional failure to fulfill a caretaking obligation; infliction of distress without conscious or willful intent. Active neglect includes the intentional failure to fulfill caregiving obligations, infliction of physical or emotional stress or injury, abandonment, denial of food, medication, or personal hygiene. Sometimes neglect is the result of criminal recklessness. Other times it is a deliberate failure to provide necessities. In either case, the neglect is a crime under Indiana law.

Elder abuse also includes financial exploitation, or misuse of property by fraud, trickery, duress, or force. If someone close to an older person forces him or her to sell personal property, or steals money, pension checks, or possessions, this is elder abuse. Theft, fraud, forgery, extortion, and the wrongful use of Power of Attorney can also be elder abuse, and are likewise crimes under Indiana law.

Because there are few federal laws relating to these issues, applicable state laws are of paramount importance. Keep in mind that rules and protections may vary from state to state.

QUESTIONS

1. Having read through these definitions, do you have a better appreciation for the "many faces" of elder abuse?

2. Read the definition of "abuse" contained in FLA. STAT. § 415.102(1) set out in the statutory supplement. In what respects does this definition differ from that used by the authors of the 2004 APS Survey?

3. Do you know anyone who has experienced elder abuse as defined above — even if you did not previously think of it as abuse?

2. Signs, Symptoms, and Causes of Elder Abuse

National Center on Elder Abuse
Elder Abuse Information: The Basics; Risk Factors for Elder Abuse
http://www.elderabusecenter.org/default.cfm?p=basics.cfm *and*
http://www.elderabusecenter.org/default.cfm?p=riskfactors.cfm[*]

Major Types of Elder Abuse

Physical Abuse

Physical abuse is defined as the use of physical force that may result in bodily injury, physical pain, or impairment. Physical abuse may include but is not limited to such acts of violence as striking (with or without an object), hitting, beating, pushing, shoving, shaking, slapping, kicking, pinching, and burning. In addition, inappropriate use of drugs and physical restraints, force-feeding, and physical punishment of any kind also are examples of physical abuse.

Signs and symptoms of physical abuse include but are not limited to:

- bruises, black eyes, welts, lacerations, and rope marks;

- bone fractures, broken bones, and skull fractures;

- open wounds, cuts, punctures, untreated injuries in various stages of healing;

---

[*] Reprinted with permission.

- sprains, dislocations, and internal injuries/bleeding;

- broken eyeglasses/frames, physical signs of being subjected to punishment, and signs of being restrained;

- laboratory findings of medication overdose or under utilization of prescribed drugs;

- an elder's report of being hit, slapped, kicked, or mistreated;

- an elder's sudden change in behavior; and

- the caregiver's refusal to allow visitors to see an elder alone.

Sexual Abuse

Sexual abuse is defined as non-consensual sexual contact of any kind with an elderly person. Sexual contact with any person incapable of giving consent is also considered sexual abuse. It includes, but is not limited to, unwanted touching, all types of sexual assault or battery, such as rape, sodomy, coerced nudity, and sexually explicit photographing.

Signs and symptoms of sexual abuse include but are not limited to:

- bruises around the breasts or genital area;

- unexplained venereal disease or genital infections;

- unexplained vaginal or anal bleeding;

- torn, stained, or bloody underclothing; and

- an elder's report of being sexually assaulted or raped.

Emotional or Psychological Abuse

Emotional or psychological abuse is defined as the infliction of anguish, pain, or distress through verbal or nonverbal acts. Emotional/psychological abuse includes but is not limited to verbal assaults, insults, threats, intimidation, humiliation, and harassment. In addition, treating an older person like an infant; isolating an elderly person from his/her family, friends, or regular activities; giving an older person the "silent treatment;" and enforced social isolation are examples of emotional/psychological abuse.

Signs and symptoms of emotional/psychological abuse include but are not limited to:

- being emotionally upset or agitated;

- being extremely withdrawn and non communicative or non responsive;

- unusual behavior usually attributed to dementia (*e.g.*, sucking, biting, rocking); and

- an elder's report of being verbally or emotionally mistreated.

Neglect

Neglect is defined as the refusal or failure to fulfill any part of a person's obligations or duties to an elder. Neglect may also include failure of a person who has fiduciary responsibilities to provide care for an elder (*e.g.*, pay for necessary home care services) or the failure on the part of an in-home service provider to provide necessary care.

Neglect typically means the refusal or failure to provide an elderly person with such life necessities as food, water, clothing, shelter, personal hygiene, medicine, comfort, personal safety, and other essentials included in an implied or agreed-upon responsibility to an elder.

Signs and symptoms of neglect include but are not limited to:

- dehydration, malnutrition, untreated bed sores, and poor personal hygiene;

- unattended or untreated health problems;

- hazardous or unsafe living condition/arrangements (*e.g.*, improper wiring, no heat, or no running water);

- unsanitary and unclean living conditions (*e.g.*, dirt, fleas, lice on person, soiled bedding, fecal/urine smell, inadequate clothing); and

- an elder's report of being mistreated.

Abandonment

Abandonment is defined as the desertion of an elderly person by an individual who has assumed responsibility for providing care for an elder, or by a person with physical custody of an elder.

Signs and symptoms of abandonment include but are not limited to:

- the desertion of an elder at a hospital, a nursing facility, or other similar institution;

- the desertion of an elder at a shopping center or other public location; and

- an elder's own report of being abandoned.

Financial or Material Exploitation

Financial or material exploitation is defined as the illegal or improper use of an elder's funds, property, or assets. Examples include, but are not limited to, cashing an elderly person's checks without authorization or permission; forging an older person's signature; misusing or stealing an older person's money or possessions; coercing or deceiving an older person into signing any document (*e.g.*, contracts or will); and the improper use of conservatorship, guardianship, or power of attorney.

Signs and symptoms of financial or material exploitation include but are not limited to:

- sudden changes in bank account or banking practice, including an unexplained withdrawal of large sums of money by a person accompanying the elder;

- the inclusion of additional names on an elder's bank signature card;

- unauthorized withdrawal of the elder's funds using the elder's ATM card;

- abrupt changes in a will or other financial documents;

- unexplained disappearance of funds or valuable possessions;

- substandard care being provided or bills unpaid despite the availability of adequate financial resources;

- discovery of an elder's signature being forged for financial transactions or for the titles of his/her possessions;

- sudden appearance of previously uninvolved relatives claiming their rights to an elder's affairs and possessions;

- unexplained sudden transfer of assets to a family member or someone outside the family;

- the provision of services that are not necessary; and

- an elder's report of financial exploitation.

Self-neglect

Self-neglect is characterized as the behavior of an elderly person that threatens his/her own health or safety. Self-neglect generally manifests itself in an older person as a refusal or failure to provide himself/herself with adequate food, water, clothing, shelter, personal hygiene, medication (when indicated), and safety precautions.

The definition of self-neglect excludes a situation in which a mentally competent older person, who understands the consequences of his/her decisions, makes a conscious and voluntary decision to engage in acts that threaten his/her health or safety as a matter of personal choice.

Signs and symptoms of self-neglect include but are not limited to:

- dehydration, malnutrition, untreated or improperly attended medical conditions, and poor personal hygiene;

- hazardous or unsafe living conditions/arrangements (*e.g.*, improper wiring, no indoor plumbing, no heat, no running water);

- unsanitary or unclean living quarters (*e.g.*, animal/insect infestation, no functioning toilet, fecal/urine smell);

- inappropriate and/or inadequate clothing, lack of the necessary medical aids (*e.g.*, eyeglasses, hearing aids, dentures); and

- grossly inadequate housing or homelessness.

Risk Factors for Elder Abuse

Elder abuse, like other types of domestic violence, is extremely complex. Generally a combination of psychological, social, and economic factors, along with the mental and physical conditions of the victim and the perpetrator, contribute to the occurrence of elder maltreatment.

Although the factors listed below cannot explain all types of elder maltreatment, because it is likely that different types (as well as each single incident) involve different casual factors, they are some of the risk factors researchers say seem to be related to elder abuse.

Domestic Violence Grown Old

It is important to acknowledge that spouses make up a large percentage of elder abusers, and that a substantial proportion of these cases are domestic violence grown old: partnerships in which one member of a couple has traditionally tried to exert power and control over the other through emotional abuse, physical violence and threats, isolation, and other tactics.

Personal Problems of Abusers

Particularly in the case of adult children, abusers often are dependent on their victims for financial assistance, housing, and other forms of support. Oftentimes they need this support because of personal problems, such as mental illness, alcohol or drug abuse, or other dysfunctional personality characteristics.

The risk of elder abuse seems to be particularly high when these adult children live with the elder.

Living with Others and Isolation

Both living with someone else and being socially isolated have been associated with higher elder abuse rates. These seemingly contradictory findings may turn out to be related in that abusers who live with the elder have more opportunity to abuse and yet may be isolated from the larger community themselves or may seek to isolate the elders from others so that the abuse is not discovered. Further research needs to be done to explore the relationship between these factors.

Other Theories

Many other theories about elder abuse have been developed. Few, unfortunately, have been tested adequately enough to definitively say whether they raise the risk of elder abuse or not. It is possible each of the following theories will ultimately be shown to account for a small percentage of elder abuse cases.

- Caregiver stress. This commonly-stated theory holds that well-intentioned caregivers are so overwhelmed by the burden of caring for dependent elders that they end up losing it and striking out, neglecting, or otherwise harming the elder. Much of the small amount of research that has been done has shown that few cases fit this model.

- Personal characteristics of the elder. Theories that fall under this umbrella hold that dementia, disruptive behaviors, problematic personality traits, and significant needs for assistance may all raise an elder's risk of being abused. Research on these possibilities has produced contradictory or unclear conclusions.

- Cycle of violence. Some theorists hold that domestic violence is a learned problem-solving behavior transmitted from one generation to the next. This theory seems well established in cases of domestic violence and child abuse, but no research to date has shown that it is a cause of elder abuse.

National Institute of Justice, U.S. Department of Justice
Elder Justice: Medical Forensic Issues Concerning Abuse and Neglect
(Draft Report, December 2000)
http://web.archive.org/web/20021222024449/
http://www.ojp.usdoj.gov/nij/elderjust/elder_02.html

Executive Summary

On October 18, 2000, Attorney General Janet Reno convened a group of preeminent experts for a groundbreaking roundtable discussion of medical forensic aspects of elder abuse and neglect. The roundtable discussion — entitled Elder Justice: Medical Forensic Issues Relating to Elder Abuse and Neglect — was, according to the Attorney General, a "profound step toward successfully addressing elder abuse."

The panel of 27 experts represented a variety of professions and areas of expertise, including geriatrics, forensic pathology, family medicine, psychiatry, pediatrics, gerontology, nursing, social work, psychology, emergency medicine, adult protective services (APS), and Federal, State, and local law enforcement. Prior to the discussion, participants submitted brief papers. The papers are included in this report as appendix E; a transcript of the discussion is included as appendix F [not reproduced here — Eds.].

The discussion focused on four distinct but overlapping subjects relating to elder abuse and neglect: (1) detection and diagnosis, (2) application of forensic science, (3) education and training, and (4) research. At the conclusion of the discussion, participants briefed the Attorney General on the status of each area, described what they would "take home" from the discussion, and offered recommendations for the future. Participants agreed that it was imperative for detection and diagnosis to identify indicators of abuse and neglect and to develop an instrument to screen for elder abuse and neglect.

A general consensus emerged among the participants: Elder abuse and neglect is a national issue that has been overlooked, underreported, and understudied. As a result, we miss too many cases of elder abuse and neglect, victims too often do not receive adequate treatment and remain at risk, and even when indicated, referrals to forensic experts and reports to APS or law enforcement are rare.

Indeed, the experts were of the view that the state of medical and forensic science relating to elder abuse and neglect in the year 2000 is about the equivalent of where child abuse was 30 years ago. Given the lack of the most basic scientific research on all aspects of elder abuse and neglect, the experts pleaded for a national multidisciplinary research agenda to ascertain the real scope of the problem and whether interventions and treatments are working. The experts also described the frequent inability of frontline responders and others to detect or diagnose elder abuse and neglect; the paucity of adequate education and training on these issues; inadequate efforts among the healthcare, social service, and law enforcement professionals to collaborate in responding to elder abuse and neglect; and no comprehensive effort to address the issue nationwide. These factors have made it extremely difficult for professionals to effectively prevent, detect, diagnose, treat, intervene in, or, where necessary, prosecute elder abuse and neglect.

Detection and Diagnosis

The expert panel concluded that elder abuse and neglect is an underdiagnosed and underreported phenomenon based on several factors, including the following:

1. No established signs of elder abuse and neglect. There is a paucity of research identifying what types of bruising, fractures, pressure sores, malnutrition, and dehydration are evidence of potential abuse or neglect. This impedes detection and complicates training. Some forensic indicators, however, are known. For example, certain types of fractures or pressure sores almost always require further investigation, whereas others may not require investigation if adequate care was provided and documented.

2. No validated screening tool. There is no standardized validated screening or diagnostic tool for elder abuse and neglect. Such a tool could greatly assist in the detection and diagnosis of elder abuse and neglect and would serve to educate, and, where appropriate, to trigger suspicion, additional inquiry, and/or reporting to APS or law enforcement. Research is needed to create and validate such a tool.

3. Difficulty in distinguishing between abuse and neglect versus other conditions. Older people often suffer from multiple chronic illnesses. Distinguishing conditions caused by abuse or neglect from conditions caused by other factors can be complex. Often the signs of abuse and neglect resemble — OR ARE MASKED BY — those of chronic illness. Elder abuse and neglect is very heterogeneous; medical indicators should be viewed in the context of home, family, care providers, decisionmaking capacity, and institutional environments.

4. Ageism and reluctance to report. Ageism results in the devaluation of the worth and capacity of older people. This insidious factor may result in a less vigorous inquiry into the death or suspicious illness

of an older person as compared with someone younger. Such ageism may impede and result in inadequate detection and diagnosis, particularly where combined with physicians' disinclination to report or become involved in the legal process,

5. Few experts in forensic geriatrics. In the case of child abuse, doctors who suspect abuse or neglect have the alternative of calling a pediatric forensic expert who will see the child, do the forensic evaluation, do the documentation, and, if necessary, do the reporting and go to court. This eliminates the responsibility of primary care physicians to follow up and relieves them of the burden of becoming involved in the legal process. It increases reporting because the frontline providers feel like they have medical expertise backing them up. Training geriatric forensic specialists to serve an analogous role should similarly promote detection, diagnosis, and reporting, and increase the expertise in the field.

6. Patterns of problems. In the institutional setting, data indicating a pattern of problems also may facilitate detection. For example, the minimum data set (MDS) information for a single facility or for a nursing home chain may indicate an unacceptably high rate of malnourishment, that — absent an explicit terminal prognosis — should trigger additional inquiry. Similarly, a survey may cite a facility for putting its residents in "immediate jeopardy" as a result of providing poor care. Or emergency room staff may identify a pattern of problems from a particular facility. In these examples, the data itself may be a useful tool in facilitating detection of abuse and neglect. This type of information is accessible not only to healthcare providers but also to others.

Application of Forensic Science

This topic was discussed in two parts: Participants first discussed "what lawyers need to prove a case of elder abuse or neglect," and then they discussed multidisciplinary teams (MDTs).

Elder abuse and neglect has been prosecuted civilly and criminally. Medical testimony is critical to ensuring the successful outcome of these cases. For example, physician testimony is critical to determine whether a particular condition is evidence of abuse or neglect, or the result of some other condition. Unfortunately, the paucity of geriatric forensic experts and rigorous research data on elder abuse and neglect makes prosecutions more difficult than they otherwise would be. The forensic pathologists pointed out that their involvement could be useful in cases involving living as well as deceased victims. A wide variety of actions can take on legal relevance in an elder abuse or neglect prosecution. For example, if a hospital emergency room consistently returns residents to a nursing home known to have problems, that fact subsequently might be used defensively by the nursing home to argue "if the facility was so bad, why were the residents returned there?"

There was general consensus that the use of MDTs can be extremely effective in investigating and addressing elder abuse and neglect. Despite diverse views about who should be included on any particular team, the panelists agreed that a team should include at least medical practitioners, social workers, and law enforcement personnel. Other potential team members include forensic pathologists, financial analysts, and members of the clergy. Different types of MDTs have been formed in communities across the country with varying functions. In a few locations, MDTs not only respond to individual cases of suspected elder abuse and neglect but also attempt to determine and address systemic problems giving rise to those individual cases.

There was general consensus that MDTs with any sort of investigative focus also should include forensic specialists and pathologists who have extensive experience in investigating suspected wrongdoing and determining whether a particular condition was caused by abuse or neglect versus other causes.

Participants also discussed another type of multidisciplinary endeavor — medical forensic centers (similar to those for child and sexual abuse). Such centers could analyze whether elder abuse or neglect had occurred and provide supporting documentation, expert opinions, and testimony, if necessary. Three different models for forensic centers were discussed: national, regional, and local/mobile. A national forensic center potentially could be broadly accessible to medical professionals via telemedicine consultations and e-mail record review. This would provide centralized national accessibility to much-needed expertise without duplicating the local infrastructure costs of creating a separate facility in various locales. Participants also discussed creating regional forensic centers, similar to forensic centers for child abuse and neglect, serving a more localized region. Finally, there was a recommendation for mobile medical forensic units that could visit homebound and isolated older people whose plight otherwise might go unnoticed.

The group also discussed the benefits of creating a national database or network of medical forensic experts (from various disciplines) and resources, and of building relationships with university medical centers and similar institutions to promote attention to elder abuse and neglect.

Education and Training

Participants decried the lack of training in elder abuse and neglect, even for those who encounter victims most frequently, such as geriatricians, police officers, social workers, and even APS workers. Some believed that there was a low level of interest in training except to learn about State mandatory reporting laws. The scarcity of research was cited as an impediment to the design of training programs. It was generally acknowledged that determining whether abuse or neglect has occurred can be a complex inquiry given the highly heterogeneous nature of elder mistreatment. Thus, experts agreed that it was important to provide interdisciplinary training to those who come in contact with older people on the systemic and contextual factors that contribute to abuse and neglect.

The types of training recommended by participants fall into two broad categories: discipline specific and multidisciplinary. Training also should be appropriate for the level of expertise of those being trained, and training/education programs should be evaluated as to their effectiveness.

Law enforcement has moved more quickly than other professions in developing training efforts, ranging from basic training in police academies to legal training for attorneys. Although training for prosecutors is not mandated yet in any State, prosecutors in some States are voluntarily learning how to investigate and prosecute elder abuse and neglect.

Research

The participants cited a desperate need for research and for the development of a national research agenda in the area of elder abuse and neglect. Even the most basic question — "How frequently does elder abuse occur?" — cannot be answered. The experts agreed that incidence and prevalence studies relating to elder abuse and neglect are imperative. They also agreed that because of the scarcity of data on this topic, it would be helpful to pursue a few specific contained, less complex research projects (for example, to establish what types of long bone fractures are evidence of possible abuse, or what types of pressure sores are evidence of possible neglect). Broad-based research also needs to be done on what types of bruising, malnutrition, dehydration, falls, fractures, and pressure sores are indicators of potential abuse and neglect.

Research is needed in assessing all types of remedial efforts as well. And although those on the frontlines strive to protect older people, there is little or no rigorous research to verify which efforts to prevent, intervene, treat, or prosecute are effective, and to what degree.

Therefore, participants strongly recommended including a validated evaluation component in all ongoing and future programs to increase scientific rigor, legitimize outcomes, and stimulate further research spending. These efforts will enhance the body of knowledge in this area.

Participants generally were of the view that with increased grant dollars, research on elder abuse and neglect would become more "prestigious" and, in turn, attract more researchers and practitioners to the field. The experts opined that the current demographic trend toward an older population could result in heightened awareness of the issue by medical and legal professionals. In addition, the current National Academy of Sciences study, sponsored by the National Institute on Aging, should expand the knowledge base and stimulate development of additional research proposals and funding in this area.

In sum, the experts called for increased training, coordination, funding, and rigorous research on all aspects of elder abuse and neglect. They also urged identification of a list of indicators to help all practitioners determine when fractures, bruising, pressure sores, malnutrition, or dehydration are evidence of abuse or neglect in elders. Moreover, several participants encouraged exciting and productive "next steps" and spoke of implementing what they learned during the roundtable in their respective institutions or practices.

QUESTIONS

1. Lawyers engaged in an elder law practice are in a special position to detect the abuse of a client. Does the law school curriculum adequately prepare them for this role?

2. Only a handful of states presently allow multidisciplinary practice (MDP). Given the nature of the elder law specialty, wouldn't MDP provide a measure of protection to potentially abused clients? What might be the arguments against MDP in the elder law context?

3. Some states require attorneys to report suspected elder abuse of a client to the appropriate state authority. How can such a duty be reconciled with the duty of confidentiality owed to a client under the Model Rules of Professional Conduct? Suppose an attorney suspects her *client* of abuse. What then?

3. Institutional Abuse

Minority Staff, Special Investigations Division Committee on Government Reform, U.S. House of Representatives
Abuse of Residents Is a Major Problem in U.S. Nursing Homes
July 30, 2001
http://www.oversight.house.gov/Documents/20040830113750-34049.pdf

EXECUTIVE SUMMARY

This report, which was prepared at the request of Rep. Henry A. Waxman, investigates the incidence of physical, sexual, and verbal abuse in nursing homes in the United States. It finds that 5,283 nursing homes — almost one out of every three U.S. nursing homes — were cited for an abuse violation in the two-year period from January 1, 1999, through January 1, 2001. All of these violations had at least the potential to harm nursing home residents. In over 1,600 of these nursing homes, the abuse violations were serious enough to cause actual harm to residents or to place the residents in immediate jeopardy of death or serious injury.

Federal health and safety standards protect the vulnerable residents of nursing homes from physical, sexual, and verbal abuse. To enforce these standards, the U.S. Department of Health and Human Services contracts with the states to conduct annual inspections of nursing homes. These inspections assess whether nursing homes are meeting federal standards of care, including the prohibitions on abuse of residents. In addition, when an individual files an abuse complaint, state inspectors are required to investigate these allegations and assess whether federal standards of care were violated by the nursing home.

This report is the first investigation to assess the incidence of abuse in nursing homes by comprehensively evaluating the results of these state inspections. It is based on an analysis of the results of all annual nursing home inspections or complaint investigations conducted in the two year period from January 1, 1999, through January 1, 2001. The report also reviews a sample of state inspection reports and citations to assess the severity of the abuse violations.

The report does not estimate the number of nursing home residents who have been victims of abuse. In some of the abuse violations reviewed for this report, only one resident in the nursing home was victimized; in other instances, a single abuse violation affected numerous residents. It is likely, however, that the findings in this analysis underestimate the incidence of abuse in nursing homes since researchers have reported that abuse cases are especially likely to go undetected or unreported.

Major Findings

Thousands of nursing homes have been cited for abuse violations. Over thirty percent of the nursing homes in the United States — 5,283 nursing homes — were cited for an abuse violation that had the potential to cause harm between January 1999 and January 2001. These nursing homes were cited for almost 9,000 abuse violations during this two-year period.

Many of these abuse violations caused harm to residents. Over 2,500 of the abuse violations in the last two years were serious enough to cause actual harm to residents or to place residents in immediate jeopardy of death or serious injury. In total, nearly 10% of the nursing homes in the United States — 1,601 nursing homes — were cited for abuse violations that caused actual harm to residents or worse.

Many of these abuse violations are discovered only after the filing of a formal complaint. State inspectors can find evidence of abuse either during annual inspections or during an inspection after a formal complaint is filed. The data indicate that over 40% of the abuse violations — over 3,800 in the two-year period — were discovered only after the filing of a formal complaint. In over one-third of these cases, the violation was determined to have caused actual harm to the resident.

The percentage of nursing homes with abuse violations is increasing. The percentage of nursing homes cited for abuse violations has increased every year since 1996. In 2000, over twice as many nursing homes were cited for abuse violations during annual inspections than were cited in 1996. The reasons for this increase are unclear.

The state inspection reports and citations reviewed in this investigation describe many instances of appalling physical, sexual, and verbal abuse of residents. In some cases, the nursing homes were cited because a member of the nursing staff committed acts of physical or sexual abuse against the residents under his or her care. In other cases, nursing homes were cited because they failed to protect vulnerable residents from violent residents who beat or sexually assaulted them. Examples of incidents reviewed in this report include:

- Numerous instances of physical abuse, such as the case where a nursing home attendant walked into a female resident's room, shouted "I'm tired of your ass," hit the resident in the face, and broke her nose. In another case, nursing home attendants used cigarettes to bribe a brain-damaged resident to attack another resident, then watched as the two residents fought each other.

- The failure of many nursing homes to adequately protect residents from other abusive residents. In one case, a resident with a history of over 50 instances of abusive behavior killed another resident when he picked her up and slammed her into a wall.

- Many instances of sexual abuse, including a case where a male nurse aide molested two elderly residents, putting his finger in their vaginas while bathing them, and a case where a male aide was found attacking a resident with senile dementia. The aide was found on top of the resident with his pants down and the resident's legs spread.

- Cases where nursing homes ignored signs of serious abuse. In one instance, state inspectors asked about a female resident who appeared to have been sexually abused. The director of nursing replied, "maybe she fell on a broomstick."

- Numerous instances of verbal abuse, including cases where staff told residents, "If you hadn't sh*t all over yourself, I wouldn't have to clean your ass" and "I . . . am sorry you were born," and called residents "a blob," "stupid," and "bitch."

United States General Accounting Office
GAO Testimony Before the Special Committee
on Aging, U.S. Senate
Statement of Leslie G. Aronovitz,
Director, Health Care — Program
Administration and Integrity Issues
NURSING HOMES: Many Shortcomings Exist in Efforts
to Protect Residents from Abuse
(March 4, 2002)

GAO-02-448T

http://www.gao.gov/new.items/d02448t.pdf

I am pleased to be here today as you discuss the issue of abuse in nursing homes. The 1.5 million elderly and disabled individuals residing in U.S. nursing homes constitute a population that is highly vulnerable because of their physical and cognitive impairments. Residents typically require extensive assistance in the basic activities of daily living, such as dressing, feeding, and bathing, and many require skilled nursing or rehabilitative care. Residents with dementia may be irrational and combative. This combination of impairments heightens the residents' vulnerability to abuse and impedes efforts to substantiate allegations and build cases for prosecution.

Our work for this committee on nursing home care quality has found that oversight by federal and state authorities has increased in recent years. During these years, however, the number of homes cited for deficiencies involving actual harm to residents or placing them at risk of death or serious injury remained unacceptably high — 30 percent of the nation's 17,000 nursing homes. Concerns exist that too many nursing home residents are subjected to abuse — such as pushing, slapping, beating, and sexual assault — by the individuals entrusted with their care. You therefore asked us to examine efforts by nursing home oversight authorities to protect residents against physical and sexual abuse. My remarks today will focus on (1) inherent difficulties in measuring the extent of the abuse problem, (2) gaps in efforts to prevent and deter resident abuse, and (3) the limited role of law enforcement in abuse investigations. My comments reflect the findings of a report we are issuing today. The report is based on our visits to three states with relatively large nursing home populations and discussions with officials at the Centers for Medicare and Medicaid Services (CMS) — the federal agency charged with oversight of states' compliance with federal nursing home standards.

In brief, the ambiguous and hidden nature of abuse in nursing homes makes the prevalence of this offense difficult to determine. CMS defines abuse in its nursing home regulations and the states we visited maintain definitions consistent with the CMS definition. However, the states vary in their interpretation and application of the definitions. For example, nurse aides in two of the states we visited who struck residents were not considered abusive by state survey agency officials under certain circumstances, whereas the third state's nurse aides under similar circumstances were consistently cited for this offense. Incidents of abuse often remain hidden, moreover, because victims, witnesses, and others, including family members, are unable to file complaints or are reluctant for several reasons, including fear of reprisal. When complaints and incidents are reported, they are often not reported immediately, thus harming efforts to investigate cases and obtain necessary evidence.

Despite certain measures in place at various levels to prevent or deter resident abuse, certain gaps undermine these protections. For instance, states use a registry to keep records on nurse aides within the state, but these state registries do not include information about offenses committed by nurse aides in other states. Unlicensed or uncertified personnel, such as laundry aides and maintenance workers, are not listed with a registry or with a licensing or certification body, allowing those with a history of abuse to be employed without detection, unless they have an established criminal record. In addition, in the states we visited, nursing homes often did not notify state authorities immediately of abuse allegations.

Moreover, states' efforts to inform consumers about available protections appeared limited, as the government agency pages in telephone books of several major cities we visited lacked explicitly designated phone numbers for filing nursing home complaints with the state.

Local and state enforcement authorities have played a limited role in addressing incidents of abuse. Several local police departments we interviewed had little knowledge of the state survey agencies' investigation activities at nursing homes in their communities. Some noted that, by the time the police are called, others may have begun investigations, hampering police efforts to collect evidence. Even the involvement of Medicaid Fraud Control Units (MFCU) — the state law enforcement agencies with explicit responsibility for investigating allegations of patient neglect and abuse in nursing homes — is not automatic. MFCUs get involved in resident abuse cases through referrals from state survey agencies. However, as demonstrated in the states we visited, the extent to which a state's MFCU investigates cases varies according to the referral policies at each state's survey agency. Our review of alleged abuse cases suggests that the early involvement of the state MFCU can be productive in obtaining criminal convictions.

Background

In its federal oversight role, CMS could do more to ensure that nursing home residents are protected from abuse. Requirements for screening and hiring prospective employees, involving local law enforcement promptly when incidents of abuse are alleged, and ensuring the public's access to designated telephone numbers are among the protections that CMS could strengthen. Our report makes recommendations addressing these requirements.

To help ensure that nursing homes provide proper care to their residents, a combination of federal, state, and local oversight agencies and requirements is in place. At the heart of nursing home oversight activities are state survey agencies, which, under contract with the federal government, perform detailed inspections of nursing homes participating in the Medicare and Medicaid programs. The purpose of the inspections is to ensure that nursing homes comply with Medicare and Medicaid standards. CMS, in the Department of Health and Human Services (HHS), is the federal agency with which the states contract and is responsible for oversight of states' facility inspections and other nursing-home-related activities. By law, CMS sets the standards for nursing homes' participation in Medicare and Medicaid.

State survey agencies also investigate complaints of inadequate care, including allegations of physical or sexual abuse. Once aware of an abuse allegation, nursing homes are required by CMS to notify the state survey agency immediately. They must also conduct their own investigations and submit their findings in written reports to the state survey agency, which determines whether to investigate further.

Certain federal and state requirements focus on the screening of prospective nursing home employees. CMS requires nursing homes to establish policies prohibiting employment of individuals convicted of abusing nursing home residents. Although this requirement does not include offenses committed outside the nursing home, the three states we visited — Georgia, Illinois, and Pennsylvania — do not limit offenses to those committed in the nursing home setting and have broadened the list of disqualifying offenses to include kidnaping, murder, assault, battery, or forgery.

As another protective measure, federal law requires states to maintain a registry of nurse aides — specifically, all individuals who have satisfactorily completed an approved nurse aide training and competency evaluation program. This requirement is consistent with the fact that nurse aides are the primary caregivers in these facilities. Before employing an aide, nursing homes are required to check the registry to verify that the aide has passed a competency evaluation. Aides whose names are not included in a state's registry may work at a nursing home for up to 4 months to complete their training and pass a state-administered competency evaluation. . . .

The inclusion of such a finding on a nurse aide's record constitutes a lifetime ban on nursing home employment, as CMS regulations prohibit homes from hiring individuals with these offenses. As a matter of due process, nurse aides have a right to request a hearing to rebut the allegations against them, be represented by an attorney, and appeal an unfavorable outcome. Other nursing home professionals who are suspected of abuse and who are licensed by the state, such as registered nurses, are referred to their respective state licensing boards for review and possible disciplinary action.

Among the local and state law enforcement agencies that may investigate nursing home abuse cases are the MFCUs. MFCUs are state agencies charged with conducting criminal investigations related to Medicare and Medicaid. Generally, MFCUs are located in the state attorney general's office, although they can be located in another state agency, such as the state police. Part of their mission is to investigate patient abuse in nursing homes. MFCUs typically receive abuse cases from referrals by state survey agencies. If criminal charges are brought, prosecuting attorneys within the MFCU or attorneys representing the locality take charge of the case.

Homes receive quarterly bulletins listing all disqualified aides in their state. In addition, they may obtain this information from the survey agency's website or by calling the survey agency.

Ambiguous and Hidden Nature of Nursing Home Abuse Makes Extent of Problem Difficult to Measure

The problem of nursing home abuse is difficult to quantify and is likely understated for several reasons. First, states differ in what they consider abuse, with the result that some states do not count incidents that CMS or other states would count as abuse. Second, powerful incentives exist for victims, their families, and witnesses to keep silent or delay the reporting of abuse allegations. Third, some research focuses on citations of nursing homes for abuse-related violations, which are maintained in a CMS database, but these data reflect only the extent to which facilities fail to comply with federal or state regulations. Abuse incidents that nursing homes handle properly are not counted, because no violation has been committed that warrants a citation.

States Do Not Share Common View of Resident Abuse

Some states may not be citing nurse aides for incidents that other states would consider abuse. Based on the definition of abuse in the Older Americans

Act of 1965, CMS defines abuse as "the willful infliction of injury, unreasonable confinement, intimidation, or punishment with resulting physical harm, pain or mental anguish." States maintain their own definitions that are consistent with the CMS definition. Our review of case files showed that states interpret and apply these definitions differently. For example, on the basis of the abuse cases reviewed, we noted that Georgia survey agency officials were less likely to determine that an aide had been abusive if the aide's behavior appeared to be spontaneous or the result of a "reflex" response. The Georgia officials told us that, to cite an aide for abuse, they must find that the individual's actions were intentional. They said they would view an instance in which an aide struck a combative resident in retaliation after being slapped by the resident as an unfortunate reflex response rather than an act of abuse. Among the Georgia case files we reviewed, we found five cases in which the aides struck back after residents hit them or otherwise made physical contact. In all five cases, Georgia officials had determined that the aides' behavior was not abusive because the residents were combative and the aides did not intend to hurt the residents.

In Pennsylvania, officials emphasized other factors to determine a finding of abuse. They said that establishing intention was important, but they would be unlikely to cite an aide for abuse unless the aide caused serious injury or obvious pain. Our review of Pennsylvania files indicated that most of the aides that were found to have been abusive had, in fact, clearly injured residents or caused them obvious pain. In several cases reviewed in which residents were bumped or slapped and reported being in pain as the result of aides' actions, the survey agency officials decided not to take action against the aides because, in their view, the residents had no apparent physical injuries.

In contrast, the Illinois survey agency considers any non-accidental injury to be abuse. Thus, incidents not considered abusive in Georgia and Pennsylvania — reflex actions and incidents not involving serious injury or obvious pain — could be considered abusive in Illinois. In the 17 Illinois case files we reviewed involving either combative residents or residents who did not suffer serious injury, officials found that aides had been abusive. When Illinois handled a case similar to a Georgia case in which a nursing home employee witnessed a nurse aide strike a combative resident, the state not only included this information in the individual's nurse aide registry file, it also referred the matter to the state's MFCU, resulting in a criminal conviction.

CMS officials indicated that states may use different definitions of abuse, as long as the definitions are at least as inclusive as the CMS definition. The officials agreed that intent is a key factor in assessing whether an aide abused a resident but argued that intent can be formed in an instant. In their view, an aide who slaps a resident, regardless of whether it was a reflexive response, should be considered abusive. In light of these different perspectives, we have recommended that CMS clarify the definition of abuse to ensure that states cite abuse consistently and appropriately.

People May Be Unable or Reluctant to Report Abuse Allegations

The physical and mental impairments typical of the nursing home population handicap residents' ability to respond to abuse. Some residents lack the ability to communicate or even realize that they have been abused, while others are reluctant to report abuse because they fear reprisal. For these reasons, elder abuse in nursing homes is likely underreported or often not reported immediately. In some cases, residents are unable to complain about what was done to them. In other cases, family members may hesitate to report their suspicions because they fear retribution or that, if reported, the resident will be asked to leave the home. In still other cases, facility staff fear losing their jobs or recrimination from coworkers, while facility management may not want to risk adverse publicity or sanctions from the state. In our file reviews, we saw evidence that family members, staff, and management did not immediately report allegations of abuse.

Examples of Allegations Not Immediately Reported

- A resident reported to a licensed practical nurse that she had been raped. Although the nurse recorded this information in the resident's chart, she did not notify the facility's management. The nurse also allegedly discouraged the resident from telling anyone else. About 2 months later, the resident was admitted to the hospital for unrelated reasons and told hospital officials she had been raped. Once hospital officials notified the police, an investigation was conducted and revealed that the resident had also informed her daughter of the incident, but the daughter dismissed it. The resident later told police that she did not report the incident to other staff because she did not want to cause trouble. The case was closed because the resident could not describe the alleged perpetrator. However, the nurse was counseled about the need to immediately report such incidents.

- An aide, angry with a resident for soiling his bed, threw a pitcher of cold water on him and refused to clean him. Another aide witnessed the incident. Instead of informing management, the witness confided in a third employee, who reported the incident to the nursing home administrator 5 days after the abuse took place. The aide who threw the water on the resident was fired and was cited for resident abuse in the state's nurse aide registry.

- Nursing home management failed to promptly notify the state survey agency of an incident in which an aide slapped a resident and visibly bruised the victim's face. Although the home investigated the situation and took appropriate action by quickly suspending and ultimately firing the aide, it did not notify the state survey agency until 11 days after the abuse took place.

Data on States' Nursing Home Citations Provide Little Information About Resident Abuse

Data from states' annual inspections of nursing homes, while a source of information about facility compliance with nursing home standards, provide little precision about the extent of care problems, of which resident abuse-related problems are a subset. Abuse-related violations committed by nursing homes include failure to protect residents from sexual, physical, or verbal abuse; failure to properly investigate allegations of resident abuse or to ensure that nursing home staff have been properly screened before employment; and failure to develop and implement written policies prohibiting abuse.

In 2000, we reported on the wide variation across states in surveyors' identification and classification of serious deficiencies — conditions under which residents were harmed or were in immediate jeopardy of harm or death. The extent to which abuse-related violations are counted as serious deficiencies depends on how the surveyor classifies the severity of the deficiency identified. In our analysis, the problem of "interrater reliability" — that is, individual differences among surveyors in citing homes for serious deficiencies — was one of several factors contributing to the difference of roughly 48 percentage points across states in the proportion of homes cited in 1999 and 2000 for serious deficiencies. The variation ranged from about 1 in 10 homes cited in one state to more than 1 in 2 homes cited in another.

We also found that one state's tally of nursing homes with serious deficiencies would have been highly misleading as an indicator of serious care problems. Of the homes the state surveyed during the 1999-2000 period, it found 84 to be "deficiency free." However, when we cross-checked the annual inspection results for these homes with the homes' history of complaint allegations, we found that these deficiency-free homes had received 605 complaints and that significant numbers of these complaints were substantiated when investigated. This discrepancy illustrates the difficulty of estimating the extent of resident abuse using nursing home inspection data. Nursing home residents' inability to protect themselves accentuates the need for strong preventive measures to be in place in both nursing homes and the agencies overseeing them. Although certain measures are in place, we found them to be, in some cases, incomplete or insufficient. In the states we visited, efforts to screen employees and achieve prompt reporting fell short of creating a net sufficiently tight to protect residents from potential offenders.

Gaps Exist in Efforts to Prevent or Deter Resident Abuse

Nursing homes have available three main tools to screen prospective employees: criminal background checks conducted by local law or enforcement agencies, criminal background checks conducted by the Federal Bureau of Investigation (FBI), and state registries listing information on nursing home aides, including any findings of abuse committed in the state's facilities. The information included in these sources, however, is often not complete or up to date.

State and local law enforcement officials in the three states we visited conduct background checks on prospective nursing home employees, but these checks are made only state wide. Consequently, individuals who have committed disqualifying crimes — including kidnaping, murder, assault, battery, and forgery — may be able to pass muster for employment by crossing state lines. On request, the FBI will conduct background checks outside the prospective employee's state of residence, but in some states these requests are rarely made, according to an FBI official.

Some states allow individuals to begin working before facilities complete their background checks. Pennsylvania permits new employees to work for 30 days and Illinois, for 3 months, before criminal background checks are completed. In contrast, Georgia requires that background checks be completed within 3 days of the request and interprets this requirement to mean that the checks must be completed before prospective employees may assume their duties.

Of the three states we visited, only Illinois requires that the results of criminal background checks on prospective nurse aides be reported to the state survey agency, which enters the information in the registry. A 1998 survey conducted by HHS' Office of Inspector General reported that Illinois was the only state with this requirement. Nursing homes in Illinois checking the state registry are able to determine if an aide has a disqualifying conviction well before an offer of employment is made and a criminal background check is initiated. Alternatively, the survey agencies in states without this requirement do not have the information necessary to warn their respective nursing home communities about inappropriate individuals seeking employment.

Nurse aide registries, designed to maintain background information on nursing home aides, also contain information gaps that can undermine screening efforts. To cite an individual in the state's registry for a finding of abuse, authorities must first establish a finding, notify the individual of the intent to "annotate" the registry, and if the individual requests, hold a hearing to consider whether the finding is warranted. Specifically, the individual must be notified in writing of the state's intent to annotate the registry and be given 30 days from the date of the state's notice to make a written request for a hearing. Because the hearing may not be completed for several months after it is requested and decisions may not be rendered immediately, additional time may elapse. As with background checks, state registries do not track an aide's offenses committed at nursing homes in other states.

Our analysis of nurse aide records from 1999 indicated that hearings to reconsider an abuse finding added, on average, 5 to 7 months to the process of annotating an individual's record in the state registry. During this time, residents of other nursing homes were at risk because, even if an aide was terminated from one home, the individual could find new employment in other homes before the state's registry included information on the individual's offense. Thus, because of the amount of time that can elapse between the date a finding is established and the date it is published, the use of nurse aide registries as a screening tool alone is inadequate.

Facilities can screen licensed personnel, such as nurses and therapists, by checking the records of licensing boards for disciplinary actions, but screening other facility employees, such as laundry aides, security guards, and maintenance workers, is limited to criminal background checks. Unless such employees are convicted of an offense, problems with their prior behavior will not be detected. No centralized source contains a record of substantiated abuse allegations involving these individuals. Even when abuse violations identified through nursing home inspections are cited, they result in sanctions against the homes and not the employees.

We identified 10 uncertified and unlicensed employees in the 158 cases we reviewed who allegedly committed abuse. One of the 10 pled guilty in court, thus establishing a criminal record. However, the disposition of five of these cases left no way to track the individuals through routine screening channels. Three of the nine — all of whom were dismissed from their positions — were investigated by law enforcement but were not prosecuted. Two others were also terminated by their nursing home employers but were not the subject of criminal investigations. (In these cases, physical abuse was alleged but the residents did not sustain apparent injuries.) The remaining four cases involved instances in which the allegations proved unfounded or the evidence was inconsistent; the individuals were thus not tracked, as appropriate.

In 1998, the HHS Office of the Inspector General recommended developing a national abuse registry and expanding state registries to include not only aides but all other nursing home employees cited for abuse offenses. . . .

Efforts to Alert Authorities of Abuse Incidents and Allegations Lack Sufficient Rigor

Enlisting the help of the facilities and the public to report incidents and allegations of abuse can supplement other efforts to protect nursing home residents. However, in the states we visited, nursing homes' performance in notifying the survey agencies promptly was well below par. In addition, access to information on phone numbers the public could use for filing complaints was limited.

In the three states we visited, nursing homes are required to notify their state survey agencies of abuse allegations immediately, which the agencies define as the day the facility becomes aware of the incident or the next day. Using this standard, we examined 111 abuse allegations filed by the three states' nursing homes. We found that, for these allegations, the homes in Pennsylvania notified the state late 60 percent of the time; in Illinois, late almost half of the time; and in Georgia, late about 40 percent of the time. Each state had several cases for which homes notified the state a week or more late and in each state at least one home notified the state more than 2 weeks late. Such time lags delay efforts by the survey agencies to conduct their own prompt investigations and ensure that nursing homes are taking appropriate steps to protect residents. In these situations, residents remain vulnerable to additional abuse until corrective action is taken.

As a nursing home resident's family and friends are another essential resource for reporting abuse to the state authorities, increasing public awareness of the state's phone number for filing complaints should be a high priority. CMS requires nursing homes to post phone numbers for making complaints to the state. However, in major cities of the states we visited, phone numbers specifically for lodging complaints to the state survey agency were not listed in the telephone book. This was the case in Chicago and Peoria, Illinois; in Athens and Augusta, Georgia; and in Philadelphia and Pittsburgh, Pennsylvania. At the same time, the telephone books we examined listed numbers in the government agency pages for organizations that appeared to be appropriate for reporting abuse allegations but did not have authority to take action. In the telephone books of selected cities in the three states we visited, we identified listings for 42 such entities that were not affiliated with the state survey agencies. Of these, six entities said they were capable of accepting and acting on abuse allegations. These included long-term care ombudsmen and adult protective services offices. The other 36 either could not be reached or could not accept complaints, despite having listings such as the "Senior Helpline" or the "Fraud and Abuse Line." Sometimes these entities attempted to refer us to an appropriate organization to report abuse, with mixed success. For example, calls we made in Georgia resulted in four correct referrals to the state survey agency's designated complaint intake line but also led to five incorrect referrals. Five entities offered us no referrals.

Law Enforcement's Involvement in Protecting Residents Is Limited

The involvement of law enforcement in protecting nursing home residents has generally been limited. Owing to the nature of the nursing home population, developing adequate evidence to investigate and prosecute abuse cases and achieve convictions is difficult. The states we visited had different policies for referring cases to law enforcement agencies.

Residents' Impairments Weaken Law Enforcement's Efforts to Develop Cases

Critical evidence is often missing in elder abuse cases, precluding prosecution. Our review of states' case files included instances in which residents sustained black eyes, lacerations, and fractures but were unable or unwilling to describe what had happened. However, despite what appeared to be signs of abuse, investigators could neither rule out accidental injuries nor identify a perpetrator. The cases that are prosecuted are often weakened by the time lapse between the incident and the trial. Law enforcement officials and prosecutors indicated that the amount of time that elapses between an incident and a trial can ruin an otherwise successful case, because witnesses cannot always retain essential details of the incident. For example, in one case we reviewed, a victim's roommate witnessed an incident of abuse and positively identified the abuser during the investigation. By the time of the trial nearly 5 months later, however, the witness could no longer identify the suspect in the courtroom, prompting the judge to dismiss the charges. Law enforcement officials told us that, without testimony from either a victim or witness, conviction is unlikely. Similarly, resident victims may not survive long enough to participate in a trial. A recent study of 20 sexually abused nursing home residents revealed that 11 died within 1 year of the abuse.

Local Law Enforcement Authorities in States Visited Not Frequently Involved With Nursing Home Abuse Incidents

In the states we visited, local law enforcement authorities did not have much involvement in nursing home abuse cases. Our discussions with officials from 19 local law enforcement agencies indicate that police are rarely summoned to nursing homes to investigate allegations of abuse. Of those 19 agencies, 15 indicated that they had little or no contact with their state's survey agency regarding abuse of nursing home residents in the past year. In fact, several police departments we interviewed were unaware of the role state survey agencies play in investigating instances of resident abuse. Several of the police officials we met with noted that, even when the police are called, other entities may have begun investigating, hampering further evidence collection.

Involving law enforcement authorities does not appear to be common for abuse incidents occurring in nursing homes. Facility residents and family members may report allegations directly to the facility. There is no federal requirement compelling nursing homes that receive such complaints to contact local law enforcement, although some states, including Pennsylvania, have instituted such requirements.

MFCUs Not as Involved as Their Mission Would Suggest

The involvement of MFCUs — the state law enforcement agencies whose mission is to, among other things, investigate allegations of patient neglect and abuse in nursing homes — is not automatic. MFCUs get involved in resident abuse cases through referrals from state survey agencies. Each of the states we visited had a different referral policy. In Pennsylvania, by agreement, the state's MFCU typically investigates nursing home neglect matters, while local law enforcement agencies investigate nursing home abuse. In contrast, the survey agencies in Illinois and Georgia both refer allegations of resident abuse to their states' MFCUs, but these two states' referral policies also differ from one another.

Of the cases we reviewed in Illinois, the survey agency consistently referred all reports of physical and sexual abuse to the state's MFCU, regardless of whether the source of the report was an individual or a nursing facility. The Illinois MFCU, in turn, determined whether the cases warranted opening an investigation. The Georgia survey agency, on the other hand, screened its allegations before referring cases to the state's MFCU, basing its assessment of a case's merit on the severity of the harm done and the potential for the MFCU to obtain a criminal conviction.

Our review of case files from Illinois and Georgia suggests that the more the state's MFCU is involved in resident abuse investigations, the greater the potential to convict offenders. (This case file review consisted of only those cases that were opened in 1999 and closed at the time of our review.) The Illinois MFCU obtained 18 convictions from 50 unscreened referrals. In Georgia, however, where the survey agency tried to avoid referring weak cases to the state's MFCU, 14 of 52 cases were referred and 3 resulted in convictions. The state's small number of convictions from the cases opened in 1999 was not consistent with the expectation that prescreened cases would have greater potential for successful prosecution.

In 2000, the Georgia survey agency substantially changed its MFCU referral policy, leading to a four-fold increase in the state's total number of referrals from the previous year. The policy change followed a meeting between survey agency and MFCU officials, at which the MFCU indicated a willingness to investigate instances that the survey agency had previously assumed the MFCU would have dismissed — such as incidents involving nursing home employees slapping residents. The timeliness of referrals made to the MFCU may also play a role in achieving favorable results. Of the 64 cases referred in the two states, we determined that the Illinois survey agency referred its cases to the MFCU earlier than did Georgia's. Illinois referred its cases, on average, within 3 days after receiving a report of abuse, whereas Georgia referred its cases, on average, 15 days after learning about an allegation.

Concluding Observations

The problem of resident abuse in nursing homes is serious but of unknown magnitude, with certain limitations in the adequacy of protections in the states we visited. Nurse aide registries provide information on only one type of employee, are difficult to keep current, and do not capture offenses committed in other states. At the same time, local law enforcement authorities are seldom involved in nursing home abuse cases and therefore are not in a position to help protect this at-risk population. MFCUs, which are likely to have expertise in investigating nursing home abuse cases, must rely on the state survey agencies to refer such cases.

When a state's referral policy is overly restrictive, the MFCU is precluded from capitalizing on its potential to bring offenders to justice. Several opportunities exist for CMS to establish new safeguards and strengthen those now in place. Our report includes recommendations for CMS to, among other things, clarify what is included in CMS' definition of abuse and increase the involvement of MFCUs in examining abuse allegations. Without such improvements, vulnerable nursing home residents remain considerably ill-protected. Mr. Chairman, this concludes my prepared remarks. I will be pleased to answer any questions you or the committee members may have.

United States Government Accountability Office
Excerpts from Report to Congressional Requesters:
Nursing Homes: Despite Increased Oversight, Challenges Remain in Ensuring High-Quality Care and Resident Safety
December 2005
GAO-06-117
http://www.gao.gov/new.items/d06117.pdf

Why GAO Did This Study:

Since 1998, GAO has issued numerous reports on nursing home quality and safety that identified significant weaknesses in federal and state oversight. Under contract with the Centers for Medicare & Medicaid Services (CMS), states conduct annual nursing home inspections, known as surveys, to assess compliance with federal quality and safety requirements. States also investigate complaints filed by family members or others in between annual surveys. When state surveys find serious deficiencies, CMS may impose sanctions to encourage compliance with federal requirements.

GAO was asked to assess CMS's progress since 1998 in addressing oversight weaknesses. GAO (1) reviewed the trends in nursing home quality from 1999 through January 2005, (2) evaluated the extent to which CMS's initiatives have addressed survey and oversight problems identified by GAO and CMS, and (3) identified key challenges to continued progress in ensuring resident health and safety.

GAO reviewed federal data on the results of state nursing home surveys and federal surveys assessing state performance; conducted additional analyses in five states with large numbers of nursing homes; reviewed the status of its prior recommendations; and identified key workforce and workload issues confronting CMS and states.

What GAO Found:

Nursing home survey data show a significant decline in the proportion of nursing homes with serious quality problems since 1999, but this trend masks two important and continuing issues: inconsistency in how states conduct surveys and understatement of serious quality problems. Inconsistency in states' surveys is demonstrated by wide interstate variability in the proportion of homes found to have serious deficiencies — for example, about 6 percent in one state and about 54 percent in another. Continued understatement of serious deficiencies is shown by the increase in discrepancies between federal and state surveys of the same homes from 2002 through 2004, despite an overall decline in such discrepancies from October 1998 through December 2004. In five large states that had a significant decline in serious deficiencies, federal surveyors concluded that from 8 percent to 33 percent of the comparative surveys identified serious deficiencies that state surveyors had missed. This finding is consistent with earlier GAO work showing that state surveyors missed serious care problems. These two issues underscore the importance of CMS initiatives to improve the consistency and rigor of nursing home surveys.

CMS has addressed many survey and oversight shortcomings, but it is still developing or has not yet implemented several key initiatives, particularly those intended to improve the consistency of the survey process. Key steps CMS has taken include (1) revising the survey methodology, (2) issuing states additional guidance to strengthen complaint investigations, (3) implementing immediate sanctions for homes cited for repeat serious violations, and (4) strengthening oversight by conducting assessments of state survey activities. Some CMS initiatives, however, either have shortcomings impairing their effectiveness or have not effectively targeted problems GAO and CMS identified. For example, CMS has not fully addressed issues with the accuracy and reliability of the data underlying consumer information published on its Web site.

The key challenges CMS, states, and nursing homes face in their efforts to further improve nursing home quality and safety include (1) the cost to older homes to be retrofit with automatic sprinklers to help reduce the loss of life in the event of a fire, (2) continuing problems with hiring and retaining qualified surveyors, and (3) an expanded workload due to increased oversight, identification of additional initiatives that compete for staff and financial resources, and growth in the number of Medicare and Medicaid providers. Despite CMS's increased nursing home oversight, its continued attention and commitment are warranted in order to maintain the momentum of its efforts to date and to better ensure high-quality care and safety for nursing home residents.

CMS generally concurred with the report's findings. CMS noted several areas of progress in nursing home quality and identified remaining challenges to conducting nursing home survey and oversight activities.

Numerous congressional hearings since July 1998 have focused attention on the need to improve the care and safety of the nation's 1.5 million nursing home residents, a highly vulnerable population of elderly and disabled individuals for whom remaining at home is no longer feasible. Many nursing home residents require help with feeding, toileting, grooming, or other routine activities of daily living; are cognitively impaired; or have chronic health care conditions such as heart disease. Some individuals with chronic conditions are long-term residents of nursing homes, while others enter nursing homes for a short period, such as after a hospitalization. With the aging of the baby boom generation, the number of individuals needing nursing home care is expected to increase in size dramatically. Combined Medicare and Medicaid payments for nursing home services were about $65 billion in 2003, including a federal share of about $43 billion.

In a series of reports, we have identified significant weaknesses in federal and state activities designed to detect and correct quality and safety problems at nursing homes. Our key findings included the following:

- A small but unacceptable proportion of nursing homes repeatedly caused actual harm to residents, such as worsening pressure sores or untreated weight loss, or placed residents at risk of death or serious injury.

- The results of state inspections, known as surveys, understated the extent of serious quality-of-care and fire safety problems, reflecting weaknesses in the surveymethodology and an inconsistent application of federal standards.

- Serious complaints by residents, family members, or staff alleging harm to residents remained uninvestigated for weeks or months, and delays in the reporting of abuse allegations compromised the quality of available evidence, hindering investigations.

- When serious deficiencies were identified, federal and state enforcement policies did not ensure that the deficiencies were addressed and remained corrected.

- Federal mechanisms for overseeing state monitoring of nursing home quality and safety were limited in their scope and effectiveness.

The Centers for Medicare & Medicaid Services (CMS) — the federal agency responsible for managing the Medicare and Medicaid programs, as well as overseeing compliance with federal nursing home standards — announced a set of initiatives intended to address many of the weaknesses we identified in July 1998 as well as needed improvements CMS identified in its own self-assessment. Over time, CMS has refined and expanded these initiatives, including launching a Web site — Nursing Home Compare — that has progressively increased the data available to the public about the care provided by nursing homes. [The Congress] asked us to review the progress made by CMS since 1998 in addressing quality and safety problems in the nation's nursing homes. In response to your request, we (1) reviewed the trends in nursing home quality by analyzing nursing home survey results, (2) evaluated the extent to which initiatives have addressed survey and oversight shortcomings identified by us and CMS, and (3) identified key remaining challenges to continued progress in ensuring resident health and safety.

* * *

Results in Brief:

Nursing home survey data show a significant decrease in the proportion of nursing homes with serious quality problems, from about 29 percent in 1999 to about 16 percent by January 2005, but this trend masks two important and continuing issues: inconsistency among state surveyors in conducting surveys and understatement by state surveyors of serious deficiencies. Inconsistency in states' surveys is demonstrated by CMS data that reveal continued wide interstate variability in the proportion of homes found to have serious deficiencies. For example, in the most recent time period, one state found such deficiencies in about 6 percent of homes, whereas another state found them in about 54 percent of homes. We previously reported that confusion about the definition of actual harm contributed to inconsistency and understatement in state surveys. In addition, state surveyors continue to understate serious deficiencies, as shown by the larger number of serious deficiencies identified in federal comparative surveys than in state surveys of the same homes. Although federal comparative surveys since October 1998 show an overall decline in the proportion that identify serious deficiencies not identified by state surveys, data for the two most recent periods show an increase in such discrepancies, from 22 percent to 28 percent of comparative surveys. In the five large states we reviewed, federal surveyors concluded that the state surveyors had missed serious deficiencies in from 8 percent to 33 percent of comparative surveys — that is, these deficiencies existed and should have been identified at the time of the state survey. The federal surveyors' assessment is consistent with our July 2003 findings: a sample of deficiencies demonstrated considerable understatement of quality-of-care problems such as serious, avoidable pressure sores. The continuing evidence of inconsistency in survey results among states and understated deficiencies underscores the importance of initiatives to improve the consistency and rigor of nursing home surveys.

CMS has addressed many of the shortcomings we identified in nursing home survey and oversight activities, but several important initiatives have not yet been implemented, such as those intended to make state surveys more consistent across states and to reduce the understatement of deficiencies. Important steps CMS has taken include (1) revising the survey methodology, (2) issuing states additional guidance to strengthen complaint investigations, (3) implementing immediate sanctions for homes cited for repeat serious violations, and (4) strengthening oversight by conducting assessments of state survey activities. In addition, CMS has undertaken initiatives of its own. For example, it has made important information available to the public on nursing home quality through its Nursing Home Compare Web site and has contracted with independent quality organizations to work with nursing homes to improve quality. Although CMS has addressed many weaknesses in survey and oversight processes, other initiatives either have not effectively targeted the problems identified or have shortcomings that impair their effectiveness. For example,

CMS has not fully addressed issues with the accuracy and reliability of the data underlying consumer information published on its Web site.

CMS, states, and nursing homes face a number of key resource and workload challenges in their efforts to further improve nursing home quality and safety. CMS is moving to require older nursing homes to install sprinkler systems, a proven life-saving device, but implementation could be delayed because of concerns about the cost of the retrofit to these homes. CMS indicated that it plans to ask for public comment about the length of the phase-in period rather than proposing one itself. States are continuing to experience problems in hiring and retaining qualified surveyors, a factor that survey agency officials believe contributes to inconsistency and understatement in the citation of serious deficiencies. State survey agencies attributed high turnover and recruiting difficulties to the lack of competitive salaries for registered nurses (RN), who are a major component of states' surveyor workforce, and intense competition from hospitals and other providers because of the RN shortage. Increased nursing home oversight has strained both CMS and state survey agency resources, resulting in delays for some key initiatives. For example, CMS has undertaken time-consuming state survey agency performance reviews and significantly increased the number of federal comparative surveys performed. In addition, state survey agency workloads have grown as a result of initiatives that require the prompt investigation of complaints alleging resident harm and the need to conduct on-site revisits at nursing homes to ensure that serious problems actually have been corrected. However, the increased number of quality and safety initiatives has required CMS to establish priorities, with some initiatives taking precedence over others. For example, CMS attached a high priority to including quality indicator data on its public Web site and implemented this initiative promptly, while the revision of the survey process has encountered delays due to higher priorities. Continued attention and commitment to improving nursing home oversight are essential to maintaining the momentum built by CMS's accomplishments to date and thus better ensuring quality care and safety for nursing home residents.

QUESTIONS

1. Given the seriousness of elder abuse in care facilities and nursing homes, should more public resources be devoted to addressing this problem? How should combating the problem be financed?

2. Does the lack of consistency in state policy concerning institutional elder abuse call for a greater federal role in this area?

3. Does the federal government appear to be committed and capable of addressing elder abuse in nursing homes and similar facilities?

4. Noninstitutional Abuse

The National Committee for the Prevention of Elder Abuse and The National Adult Protective Services Association: Abuse of Adults Age 60+: The 2004 Survey of Adult Protective Services
February 2006
http://www.apsnetwork.org/Resources/docs/AbuseAdults60.pdf*

This report contains the results of a national survey on elder abuse conducted by the National Center on Elder Abuse (NCEA). Information presented here represents Fiscal Year (FY) 2003 data from Adult Protective Services (APS) in all fifty states, the District of Columbia, and Guam. The report primarily summarizes data concerning reports of abuse for individuals 60 years of age and older. The National Committee for the Prevention of Elder Abuse (NCPEA) and the National Adult Protective Services Association (NAPSA), partners of the Center, carried out the project. The University of Kentucky conducted the research for NCPEA.

The purpose of the *2004 Survey of Adult Protective Services* was to gather the most recent and accurate state-level APS data on elder abuse. The project was a follow-up to the 2000 report, *A Response to the Abuse of Vulnerable Adults: The 2000 Survey of State Adult Protective Services* and provides data, where comparable, to identify trends. The first part of this report compares the 2004 data concerning abuse of adults of all ages with the 2000 data to provide a context for the age 60+ specific information.

National Trends — Abuse of Vulnerable Adults of All Ages

- APS received a total of 565,747 reports of elder and vulnerable adult abuse for persons of all ages (50 states, plus Guam and the District of Columbia). This represents a 19.7% increase from the 2000 Survey (472,813 reports).

- APS investigated 461,135 total reports of elder and vulnerable adult abuse for persons of all ages (49 states). This represents a 16.3% increase from the 2000 Survey (396,398).

- APS substantiated 191,908 reports of elder and vulnerable adult abuse for victims of all ages (42 states). This represents a 15.6% increase from the 2000 Survey (166,019 substantiated reports).

- The average APS budget per state was $8,550,369, compared to an average of $7,084,358 reported in the 2000 Survey (42 states).

Statewide Reporting Numbers

- APS received a total of 253,426 reports on persons aged 60+ (32 states).

- APS investigated a total of 192,243 reports on persons aged 60+ (29 states).

- APS substantiated 88,455 reports on persons aged 60+ (24 states).

- APS received a total of 84,767 reports of self-neglect on persons aged 60+ (21 states).

- APS investigated a total of 82,007 reports of self-neglect on persons aged 60+ (20 states).

- APS substantiated 46,794 reports of self-neglect on persons aged 60+ (20 states).

- The most common sources of reports of abuse of adults 60+ were family members (17.0%), social services workers (10.6%), and friends and neighbors (8.0%).

Categories of Elder Abuse, Victims Aged 60+

- Self-neglect was the most common category of investigated reports (49,809 reports or 29.4%), followed by caregiver neglect (26.1%) and financial exploitation (18.5%).

- Self-neglect was the most common category of substantiated reports (26,752 reports or 39.3%), followed by caregiver neglect (21.6%) and financial exploitation (13.8%).

Substantiated Reports, Victims Aged 60+

- States reported that 65.7% of elder abuse victims were female (15 states).

- Of the victims aged 60+, 42.8% were 80 years of age and older (20 states).

- The majority of victims were Caucasian (77.1%) (13 states).

- The vast majority (89.3%) of elder abuse reports occurred in domestic settings (13 states).

Substantiated Reports, Alleged Perpetrators of Victims Aged 60+

- States reported that 52.7% of alleged perpetrators of abuse were female (11 states).

- Over three-fourths (75.1%) of alleged perpetrators were under the age of 60 (7 states).

- The most common relationships of victims to alleged perpetrators were adult child (32.6%) and other family member (21.5%) (11 states).

- Twenty-one states (40.4%) maintain an abuse registry or database of alleged perpetrators, while 31 (59.6%) do not.

Interventions and Outcomes, Victims Aged 60+

- Over half (53.2%) of cases were closed because the client was no longer in need of services or the risk of harm was reduced (8 states). Other reasons for closure were the death of the client, client entering a long-term care facility, client refusing further services, client moving out of the service area, unable to locate client, and client referred to law enforcement.

- Only four states, Colorado, Connecticut, Louisiana, and Massachusetts, and Guam provided information on outcomes of APS involvement.

QUESTIONS

1. What, if anything, about these statistics surprised you?

2. How accurate are these statistics likely to be? How much of a problem is noninstitutional elder abuse?

a. Physical, Sexual, and Emotional Abuse

BILLINGSLEA v. STATE
780 S.W.2d 271 (Tex. Crim. App. 1989)

DUNCAN, J.

* * *

Appellant, his wife, and son lived with Hazel Billingslea (also referred to as the decedent), appellant's 94 year old mother, in a small two story frame house in Dallas. Hazel Billingslea's home had been her son's residence since approximately 1964. Appellant's only sibling was his sister, Katherine Jefferson, a resident of New Mexico. Virginia Billingslea (the decedent's granddaughter), Katherine Jefferson's daughter, lived approximately fifteen blocks from her grandmother's Dallas' home. Virginia Billingslea was raised by Hazel Billingslea and had a close relationship with her. Accordingly, she kept in regular contact by telephone and by occasional visits to her grandmother's house.

Unspecified frailties of old age affecting the elder Mrs. Billingslea forced her to become bedridden in March, 1984. Granddaughter Virginia, unaware of her grandmother's condition, made several attempts to visit her during the ensuing weeks. On each occasion her uncle (appellant) "testily" informed her that her grandmother was "asleep." Undaunted, Virginia attempted to reach her grandmother by telephone, only to be threatened by her uncle on at least two occasions to "keep [her] goddamned motherfucking ass out of him and his mother's business or he would kill [her]."

After all attempts to visit her grandmother failed, Virginia contacted her mother (appellant's sister), Katherine Jefferson, in New Mexico. Mrs. Jefferson in turn contacted the Dallas Social Security Office and requested a formal inquiry into her mother's welfare.

Velma Mosley with the Adult Protective Services section of the Texas Department of Human Resources testified that she received a report from the Social Security Office on April 20, 1984, requesting that she check on the elder Mrs. Billingslea. A few days later, Ms. Mosley, accompanied by two Dallas police officers and a police social service employee, proceeded to Mrs. Billingslea's house.

They came upon the appellant in the front yard. After some discussion, he reluctantly allowed them to enter the premises. Upon entering, they were assailed by the strong, offensive odor of rotting flesh permeating the household. While one of the police officers remained downstairs with the appellant, who wanted to know "what these motherfuckers were doing in his house," the social worker and police officer made their way upstairs. Upon entering the bedroom, they found Hazel Billingslea lying in bed, moaning and asking for help. Ms. Mosley testified that the stench was so overwhelming that she was forced to cover her face. Ms. Mosley pulled back the sheets to examine Mrs. Billingslea. Nude from the waist down, Mrs. Billingslea appeared weak and in a great deal of pain.

Ms. Mosley discovered that part of Mrs. Billingslea's heel was eaten away by a large decubitus (bedsore). Other decubiti on her hip and back appeared to have eaten through to the bone. When Ms. Mosley attempted to raise Mrs. Billingslea from the bed to continue her physical examination, "she moaned so much till I didn't look any further." Mrs. Billingslea was immediately transported to Parkland Hospital in Dallas.

Dr. Frase, at that time Chief Medical Resident at Parkland Hospital, examined Mrs. Billingslea. He testified that she was severely cachectic, i.e., that she had suffered severe muscle loss. Her mental state was one of near total disorientation, and she had apparently been unable to feed herself for some time. In addition to the decubiti, second degree burns and blisters were found on her inner thighs, caused by lying in pools of her own urine. Maggots were festering in her open bedsores.

Dr. Frase testified that weeping bedsores as severe as those he found on Hazel Billingslea would have taken anywhere from four to six weeks to develop. He further testified that until her death Mrs. Billingslea required large dosages of narcotics to relieve her pain. In his opinion, the bedsores, burns, blisters, and loss of muscle resulted in serious bodily injury indicative of overall neglect of Mrs. Billingslea in the months prior to her death.

QUESTIONS

1. The facts in *Billingslea* seem unusual, but how unusual are they?

2. Must abuse rise to this level in order to be considered "abuse"?

b. Financial Abuse: Consumer Fraud Against the Elderly

Special Committee on Aging Hearing: Schemers, Scammers and Sweetheart Deals: Financial Predators and the Elderly
Opening Statement of Senator John Breaux, Chairman
May 20, 2002
http://www.preventelderabuse.org/new/breauxstate.html

Over the years, we in Congress have focused on different types of elder mistreatment including physical abuse, sexual abuse, emotional or psychological abuse, abandonment and neglect to merely name a few. Today we will focus on yet another form of elder abuse: the financial and material exploitation of our elderly. Elder abuse in general is difficult to quantify. There is a large disparity between the number of cases reported and those that go unreported. This disparity is referred to as "The Iceberg Theory" which is indicated on a chart I had prepared. According to the National Elder Abuse Incidence Study, only 16% of all elder abuse cases are actually reported. As you see, a large majority of these cases are not reported to authorities. The financial and material loss is obviously devastating, but as my second chart shows, that is also just the tip of the iceberg. Financial independence is shattered and long term psychological and emotional scars may never be overcome. There is even data to conclude that a financially abused elder has a higher risk of premature death.

Let me take a moment to define the issue of financial and material exploitation: it is the illegal or improper use of an elder's funds, property or assets. There have been a few attempts to quantify this crime. Most recently the National Elder Abuse Incidence Study, mandated by Congress, was completed in 1998. In this study, it was determined that 30% of all reported and substantiated elder abuse cases were financial exploitation while 25% were physical abuse. There have also been studies outside the US, all of which indicate that the predominant type of reported elder abuse (after neglect) is financial.

Today's hearing will focus on those in our society who exploit our vulnerable elder population — depleting their lifelong savings and exposing them to financial ruin, emotional despair and even death. The hearing will address several specific forms of financial exploitation that the current system has difficulty defining, let alone preventing. It is not uncommon for these actions to evade the criminal justice system. What our panelists will show is that there are many psychological pieces to this criminal puzzle such as diminished capacity, undue influence and the ability to consent. Seniors, like anyone, can be psychologically and intentionally manipulated for the purpose of taking their money. This is a tarnish on our Golden Years, the period of our lives during which we all hope to be able to enjoy the fruits of our lifelong labors. Today, we will hear a sampling of these cases involving family, home repairmen, and professional criminal groups such as Travelers and Rom Gypsies that target the elderly. On this issue, let me say up front that it is not our intent to condemn all people who consider themselves Travelers or Rom Gypsies, but to focus on those within these groups where illegal activities are the main fuel for their existence.

It has been estimated that 70% of our nation's wealth is held by those 50 years old and above. Over the next 10 years, there will be $10 trillion in assets invested by the elderly. Financial predators therefore target the elderly for the same reason that Jean Lafitte pirated ships and Jesse James robbed banks and trains — it's where the money is. Looking into the future, even more opportunities for fraud and exploitation await senior citizens in the new millennium.

A recent AARP survey revealed that 85% of individuals 60 years and older want to stay in their homes and live independently for as long as possible. We all have the right of self determination and to live as we choose, but when there are sharks in the waters, someone needs to pull those at risk to shore. As more and more of the Baby Boomers draw closer to senior citizen status, sons, daughters, grandchildren, and our society must exercise vigilance in protecting those who have protected us during our vulnerable years.

What we have found is that in most states, the protective system currently in place, although well intended, is fragmented at best. Public service professionals across our country unanimously agree that protection services, law enforcement and prosecutors lack the special skills, training, funding and legislative support to properly investigate and resolve increasingly complex cases of elder financial abuse. With the lack of comprehensive, ongoing, reliable studies regarding the extent and nature of elder financial abuse, there is little information to help us focus on designing specific services and remedies. This hearing will help to lift the veil from elder financial abuse and start us in the direction of creating a functional elder justice infrastructure.

Special Committee on Aging Hearing: Schemers, Scammers and Sweetheart Deals: Financial Predators and the Elderly Statement of Chayo Reyes, Los Angeles (CA) Police Department (Retired)
May 20, 2002
http://www.preventelderabuse.org/new/chayo.html

Mr. Chairman, members of the committee, my name is Chayo Reyes. I am a retired Detective from the Los Angeles Police Department and I developed the Department's first Elder Person's Estate Unit in 1987. I am also a co-founder of the Los Angeles County Financial Abuse Specialist Team and in 1993, I co-authored (with attorney Marc Hankin and former partner Dave Harned) California Senate Bill 1742 (enacted in January 2001). This law enables investigators to secure the remaining assets of a vulnerable elder or dependent adult during the course of a criminal investigation in order to prevent further losses. Since my retirement, I have remained active in this field as a consultant and educator and I am currently on the Board of Directors for the National Committee for the Prevention of Elder Abuse, here in Washington, D.C.

Ever since vulnerable elders and dependent adults have had assets, there have been individuals to financially exploit them. Our elders are the fastest growing segment of our society and they are also the financial backbone of our country's economy. They are living longer and saving more than ever before. But we as a society do not always recognize the threats to this vulnerable population. There are a number of circumstances that put an elderly person at risk: Physical and mental health issues, such as stroke, Alzheimer's, isolationism and other causes still exist in spite of our best efforts to protect our seniors.

Throughout my 15 years in working elder abuse cases, I have identified a common theme: The victims generally live alone, may be in poor health and in 95% of our cases suffer from diminished mental capacity. These conditions make them at risk to exploitation through undue influence or duress. They are easily swayed and are likely to place their entire estate in control of befriending suspects.

It wasn't until medical experts such as Doctor Margaret Singer of Berkeley, California shed light on the phenomenon of undue influence were we able to begin to understand how this all happens. Undue influence is when people use their role and influence to exploit the trust, dependency, and fear of others. They use this power to deceptively gain control over the decision making of the second person. Training from medical experts in the field of undue influence is paramount for investigators of elder abuse cases.

The most common suspects I've come across have been family members, in-home care providers, friends and neighbors, but anyone in a position of trust can exert undue influence over a vulnerable person. It can be fellow church members, attorneys, accountants, befriending strangers, ex-con caretakers, and predators, who specifically target the elderly. It is troubling to conclude that if there is an endless list of "silent" culprits there must also be an endless list of "silent" victims.

The suspects often isolate and/or relocate the victim in order to obtain complete control. The suspects then create what my former partner Dave Harned and I refer as a "civil mirage," by coercing the victims into signing powers of attorney, contracts, quitclaim deeds, wills, living trusts, adding their names onto the victim's bank accounts and obtaining numerous credit cards under the victim's name. In some cases, the suspects marry the vulnerable elder as another means of obtaining total control of their estate through "community property."

Once in so-called legal control of the estate, the suspects operate as though they have a license to steal. They withdraw the victim's life savings; obtain loans on the property, making it subject to foreclosure; and max out the credit cards. They may even file bankruptcy to conceal the theft.

Ultimately, the elder becomes a "double victim." First, by not having the benefit of their assets which were depleted by the suspect, and secondly, the victims are responsible for any accumulated debt and tax penalties.

Most people who discover or suspect these matters (to include law enforcement and prosecutors) often do not have the training or experience in gathering evidence to support the allegation. They too often assume that the documents show the suspect had "legal access" to the elder's estate. For these reasons, many reporting persons are automatically misinformed by authorities (social workers, law enforcement and prosecutors), that "it is a civil matter," when in fact they are "hidden and silent" crimes. It is imperative that anyone in the position of recognizing elder abuse or exploitation be given specific training so they can adequately protect our vulnerable population.

Due to the victims' age and poor health and the suspects' ability to quickly deplete the estate, timely preliminary investigations are extremely critical. Unlike other financial crime victims, these victims are not able to financially or emotionally recover. These cases may also cause physical harm and even death to the victims. As a result of being swindled, the victim may go into a depression and ultimately suffer from a condition know as "self-neglect." They start out as productive, self sufficient citizens and ultimately end up relying on government and/or family aid for the rest of their lives.

Our mission at LAPD was to network with multiple government and private organizations in order to maximize resources and utilize experts from different fields, in an effort to proactively put a halt to the exploitation and at the same time address the elders' long term needs to prevent them from falling victim again.

From 1987-1999, along with members of the Los Angeles County Area Agency on Aging "Financial Abuse Specialist Team" or "FAST," our unit prevented the loss of and/or recovered over $91,000,000 in victims' assets (*e.g.*, homes, vehicles and life savings). This figure only reflects LAPD cases, it does not include the millions of losses prevented or recovered, while networking with law enforcement agencies across the country. The LA FAST team was the first in the country and is coordinated by WISE Senior Services in Santa Monica, California.

With the growing elder/dependant adult population, the abuse of this vulnerable population will continue to be a growing problem and major concern for social workers, law enforcement, prosecutors, financial institutions and health care professionals.

There is a nationwide lack of training, expertise and resources to properly investigate, prosecute and litigate these cases. For example, most states lack legislation to address consent by victims who may be subject to undue influence or duress.

It is imperative that such matters involving victims suffering from dementia, subject to undue influence or duress be handled with the same attention, sensitivity, and resources given to juvenile and domestic violence crime victims. We must continue to take care of those who have taken care of us.

National Fraud Information Center
They Can't Hang Up: Five Steps to Help Seniors Targeted by Telemarketing Fraud
http://www.fraud.org/elderfraud/hangup.htm[*]

According to the National Consumers League's National Fraud Information Center, nearly a third of all telemarketing fraud victims are age 60 or older. Studies by AARP show that most older telemarketing fraud victims don't realize that the voice on the phone could belong to someone who is trying to steal their money.

Many consumers believe that salespeople are nice young men or women simply trying to make a living. They may be pushy or exaggerate the offer, but they're basically honest. While that's true for most telemarketers, there are some whose intentions are to rob people, using phones as their weapons. The FBI says that there are thousands of fraudulent telemarketing companies operating in the United States. There are also an increasing number of illegal telemarketers who target U.S. residents from locations in Canada and other countries.

---

[*] Reprinted by permission.

It's difficult for victims, especially seniors, to think of fraudulent telemarketers' actions as crimes, rather than hard sells. Many are even reluctant to admit that they have been cheated or robbed by illegal telemarketers.

The first step in helping older people who may be targets is to convince them that fraudulent telemarketers are hardened criminals who don't care about the pain they cause when they steal someone's life savings. Once seniors understand that illegal telemarketing is a serious crime — punishable by heavy fines and long prison sentences — they are more likely to hang up and report the fraud to law enforcement authorities. They can help catch the crooks and put them in jail — where they belong.

The second step in fighting telemarketing fraud against seniors is to understand why they are particularly vulnerable. It's a myth that victims are incompetent, lonely, or isolated. In fact, AARP research shows that many older victims are active people who are simply lured by false promises of great deals or ways to add to their "nest eggs." Fraudulent telemarketers take advantage of the fact that:

- It's difficult to tell whether someone is legitimate. Good salespeople are convincing, but so are crooks. They use many of the same sales tactics — being friendly, getting people excited, creating a sense of urgency;

- Seniors tend to be trusting. Since they have difficulty imagining that some telemarketers are criminals, they're more likely to give them the benefit of the doubt;

- It's easy to wear people down. Seniors are targeted relentlessly — some get more than 20 calls a day from scam artists. They may also receive dozens of mailings every week asking them to call about sweepstakes and other offers;

- We all want to believe. Who doesn't want to win a valuable prize, take a free trip, or strike it rich on an investment? People want to believe that it's their lucky day, and may react with anger or suspicion when others question their optimism; and,

- It's hard to hang up. Many seniors feel that it's impolite to hang up on people. Swindlers know how to take control of the conversation and are prepared to tell any lies necessary to keep potential victims on the phone.

The third step is helping older people recognize the "red flags" of fraud:

- A promise that you can win money, make money, or borrow money easily;

- A demand that you act immediately or else miss out on this great opportunity;

- A refusal to send you written information before you agree to buy or donate;

- An attempt to scare you into buying something;

- Insistence that you wire money or have a courier pick up your payment; and,

- A refusal to stop calling after you've asked not to be called again.

The common thread that runs through all telemarketing scams is the demand for payment upfront. Seniors need to know that:

- It's illegal for companies that operate contests or sweepstakes to ask you to pay to enter or claim your prize or even to suggest that your chances of winning will improve if you buy something;

- It's illegal for telemarketers to ask for a fee upfront to help you get a loan if they guarantee or strongly imply that the loans will be made;

- There is no reason to give your credit card number or bank account number to a telemarketer unless you are actually making a payment with that account; and,

- If you have to pay first before getting detailed information about the offer, it's probably a scam.

The fourth step is to recognize when older people have been victimized or may be in grave danger and know how to help them. Seniors may be in trouble if they:

- Receive lots of mail for contests, "free trips," prizes, and sweepstakes;

- Get frequent calls from strangers offering great deals or asking for charitable contributions;

- Make repeated and/or large payments to companies in other states or countries;

- Have difficulty buying groceries and paying utility and other bills;

- Subscribe to more magazines than anyone could normally read;

- Receive lots of cheap items such as costume jewelry, beauty products, water filters, and knick knacks that they bought to win something or received as prizes;

- Get calls from organizations offering to recover, for a fee, money they have lost to fraudulent telemarketers.

If you are trying to help an older person with a telemarketing fraud problem, don't be critical. It could happen to anyone — con artists are very good at what they do. Encourage them to:

- Report actual or attempted fraud to the National Fraud Information Center, 800-876-7060, M-F, 9 a.m. to 5 p.m., or at www.fraud.org. That information will be transmitted to law enforcement agencies;

- Change his or her phone number if con artists call repeatedly; and,

- Change his or her bank account or credit card numbers if they have fallen into the hands of thieves.

The fifth step in fighting telemarketing fraud is to inform older people about how to reduce the number of unwanted sales calls and mailings they receive and how to deal effectively with telemarketers.

- Avoid getting on sucker lists. Don't fill out contest entry forms at fairs or malls — they are a common source of "leads" for con artists. Ask companies you do business with not to share your personal information with other marketers.

- Know your "Do-Not-Call" rights. Under federal law, you can tell a telemarketer not to call you again. Ask your state attorney general's office or consumer affairs department if there is a state "Do-Not-Call" law and how it protects you.

- Know who you're dealing with. If it's an unfamiliar company or charity, check it out with your state or local consumer protection agency and the Better Business Bureau.

- Screen your calls. Use an answering machine, Caller ID, or other services that may be available from your phone company to help you determine who you want to talk to and who you want to avoid.

- Have a plan for speaking to telemarketers. Before you pick up the phone, know what questions you want to ask or what you want to say. Be polite, but firm. Hang up if someone refuses to answer your questions or you detect the "red flags" of fraud.

- Know that your phone number may be collected. When you call a company, your number can be displayed through Automatic Number Identification (ANI). If you have an account with the business, this enables the customer service representative to pull up your records and help you faster, but ANI can also be used for marketing purposes. Ask what information is being collected and tell the company if you don't want to be put on a marketing list.

[Other Strategies]: Better Business Bureau (BBB). Check the complaint records of companies. Call the BBB nearest to you to find out how to reach the BBB where the company is located or use the BBB locator at www.bbb.org/BBBComplaints/lookup.asp. Remove your name from telemarketing and mail lists of major companies (you'll still hear from them if you are current customer).

National Fraud Information Center. Get advice about telemarketing offers and report suspected fraud through this hotline operated M-F, 9 a.m. to 5 p.m., by the National Consumers League, 800-876-7060, www.fraud.org.

Securities and Exchange Commission. Get general advice and check the records of investment brokers and advisers, 800-732-0330 or www.sec.gov. Also check with your state securities regulator, listed in your phone book under state government or at the North American Securities Administrators Association Web site, www.nasaa.org. Check the records of national charities through [the Wise Giving Alliance] operated by the Better Business Bureau. Visit www.give.org or call 703-276-0100.

Your state or local consumer protection agency. Ask if you have a state "Do-Not-Call" law or other telemarketing rights and get help with telemarketing complaints.

QUESTION

Do you agree that the elderly are particularly vulnerable to consumer fraud? Why or why not?

c. Self-Neglect

320 Ill. Comp. Stat. 20/2 (i-5)

"Self-neglect" means a condition that is the result of an eligible adult's inability, due to physical or mental impairments, or both, or a diminished capacity, to perform essential self-care tasks that substantially threaten his or her own health, including: providing essential food, clothing, shelter, and health care; and obtaining goods and services necessary to maintain physical health, mental health, emotional well-being, and general safety.

Illinois Government News Network
Governor's Office Press Release
Governor Blagojevich signs legislation to help protect Illinois seniors from self-neglect
August 1, 2006
http://www100.state.il.us/PressReleases/
ShowPressRelease.cfm?SubjectID=3&RecNum=5124*

[A new Illinois] law is intended to help prevent cases of self-neglect by senior citizens by requiring the Illinois Department on Aging (IDoA) to respond to reports of self-neglect beginning January 1, 2007. "This new law helps us take care of senior citizens who can't take care of themselves," said Gov. Blagojevich. "It means that when a senior citizen has a hard time meeting their basic needs, we'll now be able to help them."

"Government has a responsibility to help those most deserving of our support — the poor, the sick, the young and, of course, the elderly," said Chicago Mayor Richard M. Daley. "For too many of our seniors, the golden years can be the lonely years. Without realizing it, they gradually lose the ability to take care of themselves, and they often reject help from friends and family members. The welfare of the elderly is not just a government responsibility. It's also an individual responsibility. Our time should never be so precious that we neglect the older people in our lives — our parents, grandparents and long-time acquaintances."

---

* Copyright © 2006. Reprinted with permission.

Under the new law, self-neglect is defined as a condition resulting from the inability to perform essential self-care tasks that threaten the person's health. This includes providing essential food, clothing, shelter, and health care, and obtaining goods and services needed to maintain physical health, mental health, emotional wellbeing and general safety.

The law will allow individuals to report cases of self-neglect to the Illinois Department on Aging's Elder Abuse Hotline and other approved elder abuse provider agencies regarding adults age 60 or older living alone, with family members or a caregiver, in a residential care facility or an unlicensed community-based facility.

The legislation, which becomes effective January 1, 2007:

- Requires provider agencies that receive reports of self-neglect to conduct face-to-face assessments that will help the State connect individuals with specific services, such as Meals on Wheels.

- Directs IDoA by January 1, 2008, to work with a newly created Elder Self-Neglect Sterring Committee to develop specific rules to respond to reports of self-neglect; protect the autonomy, rights, privacy, and privileges of seniors during investigations of possible self-neglect; collect all necessary data about cases of self-neglect, and when necessary work with law enforcement and provider agencies.

- Gives the staff of the Chicago Department on Aging access to reports of self-neglect and other alleged abuses, neglect and exploitation upon request.

QUESTIONS

1. Review the statistics reported in the 2004 APS Survey. How serious is the problem of self-neglect?

2. One commentator has observed: "If the individual has the right to decide whether to refuse medical care even though that refusal may result in death, there is surely a right to make less life-threatening choices regarding personal eating habits, dress, appearance, cleanliness, and other elements of one's lifestyle." Katheryn D. Katz, *Elder Abuse*, 18 J. FAM. L. 695, 720 (1979-80). Do you agree? Does this undercut the existence of self-neglect as a category of elder abuse?

B. FEDERAL RESPONSES TO ELDER ABUSE

1. The Older Americans Act of 1965 and Its Subsequent Amendments

U.S. Senate Special Committee on Aging
Developments in Aging: 1996, at 259-60
(Report No. 105-36, 105th Cong., 1st Sess., June 24, 1997)

The Older Americans Act (OAA), enacted in 1965, is the major vehicle for the organization and delivery of supportive and nutrition services to older persons. It was created during a time of rising societal concern for the needs of the poor. The OAA's enactment marked the beginning of a variety of programs specifically designed to meet the social and human needs of the elderly.

The OAA was one in a series of Federal initiatives that were part of President Johnson's Great Society programs. These legislative initiatives grew out of a concern for the large percentage of older Americans who were impoverished, and a belief that greater Federal involvement was needed beyond the existing health and income-transfer programs. Although older persons could receive services under other Federal programs, the OAA was the first major legislation to organize and deliver community-based social services exclusively to older persons.

* * *

When enacted in 1965, the OAA established a series of broad policy objectives designed to meet the needs of older persons. Although the OAA then lacked both legislative authority and adequate funding, it did establish a structure through which the Congress would later expand aging services.

* * *

The Act authorizes a wide array of service programs through a nationwide network of 57 State agencies on aging and 660 area agencies on aging (AAAs).

* * *

The Act establishes the Administration on Aging (AOA) within the Department of Health and Human Services (HHS) which administers all of the Act's programs except for the Senior Community Service Employment Program administered by the Department of Labor (DOL), and the commodity or cash-in-lieu of commodities portion of the nutrition program, administered by the U.S. Department of Agriculture (USDA).

* * *

The Act has been amended 13 times since the original legislation was enacted. Major amendments included the creation of the national nutrition program for the elderly in 1972 and the network of area agencies on aging in 1973. Other amendments established the long-term care ombudsman program and a separate grant program for older Native Americans in 1978, and a number of additional service programs under the State and area agency on aging program in 1987, including in-home services for the frail elderly, programs to prevent elder abuse, neglect and exploitation, and health promotion and disease prevention programs, among others. The most recent amendments in 1992 created a new Title VII to consolidate and expand certain programs that focus on protection of the rights of older persons (which under prior law were authorized under Title III).

During the 1970s, Congress significantly improved the OAA by broadening its scope of operations and establishing the foundation for a 'network' on aging under a Title III program umbrella. In 1973, the area agencies on aging were authorized. These agencies, along with the State Units on Aging (SUAs), provide the administrative structure for programs under the OAA. In addition to funding specific services, these entities act as advocates on behalf of older persons and help to develop a service system that will best meet older Americans' needs. As originally conceived by the Congress, this system was meant to encompass both services funded under the OAA, and services supported by other Federal, State, and local programs.

QUESTION

What effect did the 1973 amendments have on the original OAA?

2. "A Decade of Shame and Inaction": 1978-1987

Subcommittee on Health and Long-Term Care
House Select Committee on Aging
Elder Abuse: A Decade of Shame and Inaction, at 66-68
(Comm. Pub. No. 101-752, 101st Cong., 2d Sess., April 1990)

What follows is an analysis of the evolution of State and Federal policy in the recognition and prevention of elder abuse since that issue first received national attention in the late 70s.

* * *

The States have the primary responsibility for protecting the rights of all their citizens, young and old alike.

* * *

State advocates of Federal involvement in the area of protective services for elders suggest that one way to encourage States to make the [necessary] statutory and administrative changes would be to make Federal funding for elder abuse-related contingent on certain State level requirements. . . . The Prevention, Identification and Treatment of Elder Abuse Act (H.R. 7551), introduced by Reps. Mary Rose Oakar (D-Ohio) and Claude Pepper (D-Fla.) in the 96th Congress [1979-1980], used this method to encourage States to modify their elder abuse-related laws and procedures. Although this bill enjoyed wide bipartisan co-sponsorship and was supported by virtually all the States, it died in the 96th Congress before passage.

In subsequent Congresses, Reps. Oakar and Pepper introduced the measure again. H.R. 769 was referred in the 97th Congress to the House Education and Labor and Energy and Commerce Committees. By the end of the Congress it enjoyed the support of 84 cosponsors but did not pass. Again in the 98th Congress, the measure was again introduced as H.R. 3833. It too was referred to the Committees on Education and Labor and Energy and Commerce, but failed to pass the House. At the beginning of the 99th Congress, the 100th Congress, and the 101st Congress, H.R. 1674, H.R. 3899, and H.R. 220 were introduced respectively. All three failed to receive full consideration or House passage.

Aside from H.R. 1674, elder abuse prevention was the subject of legislation under two other bills enacted during the 98th Congress. The Child Abuse Amendments of 1984 (P.L. 98-457) contained authorization for support of demonstration grants to establish, maintain and expand programs to prevent incidents of family violence. . . . Regrettably, no appropriations were ever made available for these provisions.

* * *

The [other piece of legislation enacted during the 98th Congress was the] Older Americans Act Amendments of 1987.

QUESTION

Why was so little accomplished between 1978 and 1987?

3. The Older Americans Act Amendments of 1987

Subcommittee on Health and Long-Term Care
House Select Committee on Aging
Elder Abuse: A Decade of Shame and Inaction, at 68
(Comm. Pub. No. 101-752, 101st Cong., 2d Sess., April 1990)

The Older Americans Act Amendments of 1987 . . . required Area Agencies on Aging to assess the need for elder abuse prevention services and the extent to which the need was being met within each planning and service area. In addition, the law added a new "State plan on aging" requirement to govern the conduct of elder abuse prevention activities when the State Agency on Aging opted to provide such services. Under this provision, the State plan would have to assure that any area agency carrying out elder abuse prevention activities would conduct its program consistent with State law and be coordinated with existing State adult protection services activities. The program was to provide public education to identify and prevent abuse; receive reports on incidence of abuse; provide outreach, conferences and referrals to other sources of assistance; and refer complaints to law enforcement or public protective service agencies. . . . While $5 million was authorized to be spent in 1988, 1989 and 1990 under the Act for this new elder abuse program, as of this writing no money has been appropriated for that purpose.

Molly D. Velick
Mandatory Reporting Statutes:A Necessary Yet Underutilized Response to Elder Abuse
3 ELDER L.J. 165, 178-79 (1995)[*]

The 1990 report on elder abuse by the House Subcommittee on Health and Long-Term Care continually refers to government's "woefully inadequate" funding of [state-based] adult protective services. The report also notes that many states which passed mandatory reporting laws during the 1980s expected to receive federal funding for adult protective services. The states anticipated that eligibility for such funding would be based in part on the enactment of mandatory reporting requirements. The Elder Abuse and Prevention Act (House Bill 7551), a bill originally introduced in the Ninety-sixth Congress, promised funding for state adult protective services. When the bill failed to pass, however, states were hard pressed to actually carry out their new adult protective-services mandates. Congress did pass another piece of legislation aimed at helping the elderly, the Older Americans Act Amendments of 1987, but it did not appropriate any money to implement the Act until 1990.

Even then, Congress appropriated only a meager $3 million.

QUESTION

What were the 1987 amendments designed to do?

4. The Nursing Home Reform Act of 1987

In connection with the following excerpt, read the Nursing Home Residents' Bill of Rights (42 U.S.C. §1395i-3(c)) in the statutory supplement, especially subsection (1)(A)(ii) and subsection (6).

George S. Ingalls et al.
Elder Abuse Originating in the Institutional Setting
74 N.D. L. REV. 313, 316-17 (1998)[**]

[I]n order to combat the increase in nursing home abuse that came to light in the 1980s, Congress passed the Nursing Home Reform Act (included in the Omnibus Budget Reconciliation Act of 1987 [OBRA]).

---

[*] Copyright © 1995. Reprinted with permission. Copyright to the *Elder Law Journal* is held by the Board of Trustees of the University of Illinois.

[**] Copyright © 1998. Reprinted with permission.

This Act mandates that, for a facility to qualify for federal funding, "A skilled nursing facility must provide services to attain or maintain the highest practicable physical, mental, and psychological well-being of each resident in accordance with a written plan of care which" describes the resident's needs and how those needs will be met. This plan of care is to be prepared initially with the participation of the residents' families and is to be periodically reviewed and revised. "The resident has a right to a dignified existence, self determination, and communication with and access to persons and services inside and outside the facility." "The resident has the right to be free of interference, coercion, discrimination, and reprisal from the facility in exercising his or her rights." To achieve these goals, the law provides that a resident has certain rights that must be met by the nursing facility. The "facility must care for its residents in a manner and in an environment that promotes maintenance or enhancement of each resident's quality of life." "The facility must promote care for residents in a manner and in and environment that maintains or enhances each resident's dignity and respect in full recognition of his or her individuality."

OBRA 1987 includes a "Residents' Bill of Rights" which provides the basic requirements for the care of residents in skilled nursing facilities. This Bill of Rights is found in 42 U.S.C. § 1395i-3(c)-(h) and 42 C.F.R. § 483.10-483.15.

QUESTIONS

1. With respect to the topic of elder abuse, what rights does this legislation provide?

2. How effective is the legislation at guaranteeing these rights?

5. The Older Americans Act Amendments of 1992

Alison Barnes
The Policy and Politics of Community-Based Long-Term Care
19 Nova L. Rev. 487, 520 (1995)[*]

The 1992 amendments to the OAA . . . included a new provision, Title VII, authorizing programs for prevention of abuse and neglect and the provision of legal assistance. The administration of Title VII funds differs from [previous approaches under Title III] in that states can bypass administration by the network of federal administrative Area Agencies on Aging. States were also given permission to transfer funds between service and nutrition programs to maximize their ability to meet the needs of target groups.

Administration on Aging
Elder Rights and Resources
Preventing [Elder] Fraud & Abuse
http://www.aoa.gov/eldfam/Elder_Rights/Preventing_Fraud/
Preventing_Fraud.asp

The Administration on Aging (AoA) is dedicated to promoting consumer awareness, preventing elder victimization, and working to implement community partnerships to prevent Medicare and Medicaid fraud, error, and abuse. By informing and training senior volunteers, aging network personnel, and health care providers, AoA wants to make older Americans and their advocates better health care consumers.

The mission of AoA's Anti Fraud and Abuse Team is to serve as the agency's focal point for coordinating, implementing, monitoring, expanding, evaluating, and promoting efforts to provide consumer information and protection designed to detect, prevent and report error, fraud and abuse in the Medicare and Medicaid programs.

* * *

Senior Medicare Patrols

Since 1997, the U.S. Administration on Aging (AoA) has worked in partnership with the Department of Health and Human Services' Office of Inspector General, the Centers for Medicare and Medicaid Services (formerly the Health Care Financing Administration), the Department of Justice, community-based grantees, retired professionals, service and health care providers, AARP, and other interested individuals and organizations to address this serious national problem.

In the initial phase of this initiative, known as ORT, $23 was returned in improper payments, fines and settlements for every dollar spent on the effort.

Today, AoA provides grants to community-based agencies in nearly every state to train volunteers how to educate Medicare and Medicaid beneficiaries and their families how to protect their Medicare number as they would their credit card, how to take a more active role in protecting their health care programs, and how to detect and report potential instances of error, fraud, and abuse.

U.S. Senate Special Committee on Aging
Developments in Aging: 1996, at 261, 263
(Report No. 105-36, 105th Cong., 1st Sess., June 24, 1997)

Title III [of the Older Americans Act, as amended] authorizes grants to State and area agencies on aging to act as advocates on behalf of programs for the elderly and to coordinate programs for this group. This program supports 57 State agencies on aging, 660 area agencies on aging, and over 27,000 service provider organizations. This nationwide network of supportive, nutrition, and other social services programs receive most of the Act's total Federal funding (65 percent in fiscal year 1997).

* * *

Title VII [of the Older Americans Act, as amended] authorizes funds for activities that protect the rights of the vulnerable elderly. Programs authorized are — The Long-Term Care Ombudsman Program; programs to prevent elder abuse, neglect, and exploitation; elder rights and legal assistance, outreach, counseling, and assistance programs on insurance and public benefits. Title VII also authorizes an elder rights program for Native American elderly. Funds are distributed to State agencies on aging based on a formula which takes into account State population age 60 or over.

QUESTIONS

How does Title VII differ from Title III?

U.S. Senate Special Committee on Aging
Older Americans Act Amendments of 1999
S. Rep. No. 106-399 (2000)

* * *

Section 705. Prevention of elder abuse, neglect, and exploitation

Section 705 clarifies that exploitation includes financial exploitation; requires coordination of the elder abuse prevention program with State and local law enforcement systems and courts of competent jurisdiction; and requires training of caregivers regarding issues related to elder abuse prevention, among other things.

Section 705 adds a provision requiring the Secretary of DHHS to conduct a study of the nature and extent of financial exploitation of older individuals, in consultation with the Department of the Treasury and the Attorney General. The purpose of the study is to:

- Define and describe the scope of financial exploitation of older individuals;

- Provide an estimate of the number and type of financial transactions considered to be financial exploitation; and

- Examine the adequacy of current Federal and State legal protections to prevent financial exploitation.

The provision requires the Secretary to submit a report on the study to Congress, including recommendations to combat financial exploitation, no later than a year and a half after enactment of the bill.

Section 706. Assistance programs

Section 706 repeals chapter 5, outreach counseling, and assistance programs. It also simplifies provisions of chapter 4, State legal assistance development program.

Section 707. Native Americans programs

Section 707 authorizes for elder rights programs for Native Americans $5 million for FY2001, and such sums as may be necessary for FY2002-FY2005.

Summary of H.R. 6197,
Older Americans Act Amendments of 2006
(enacted as P.L. 109-365, 120 Stat. 2522, October 17, 2006)
http://thomas.loc.gov/cgi-bin/bdquery/z?d109:HR06197:
D&summ2=m& | TOM:/bss/d109query.html

Title I: General Provision —

(Sec. 101) Reauthorizes the Older Americans Act of 1965.

Revises the definition of "information and assistance service" to include such a service for older individuals at risk for institutional placement. Defines the term "elder justice" to mean effort to prevent, detect, treat, intervene in, and respond to elder abuse, neglect, and exploitation and to protect elders with diminished capacity while maximizing their autonomy.

Title II: Administration on Aging —

(Sec. 201) Authorizes the Assistant Secretary for Aging to designate within the Administration on Aging responsibility for elder abuse prevention and services. Assigns to the Assistant Secretary the duty of developing objectives, priorities, policy, and a plan for: (1) facilitating the implementation of an elder justice system in the United States; (2) supporting states' efforts in carrying out elder justice programs; (3) establishing federal guidelines and disseminating best practices for uniform data collection and reporting by states; (4) collecting and disseminating data relating to the abuse, neglect, and exploitation of older individuals (abuse); (5) establishing an information clearinghouse; (6) researching such abuse; (7) providing technical assistance to states and other entities; (8) conducting a study concerning the degree of abuse; and (9) promoting collaborative efforts and diminishing duplicative efforts in elder justice programs in all levels of government.

* * *

Title VII: Allotments for Vulnerable Elder Rights Protection Activities —

(Sec. 701) Authorizes appropriations for vulnerable elder rights protection activities.

(Sec. 702) Includes among grant requirements that states shall use grant funds to carry out activities to intervene and investigate elder abuse, neglect, and exploitation.

(Sec. 703) Requires the Assistant Secretary to establish a program for enabling entities to support multidisciplinary elder justice activities.

(Sec. 704) Authorizes the Assistant Secretary to make grants to states through a competitive process to promote the implementation of comprehensive elder justice systems.

(Sec. 705) Declares that vulnerable elder rights protection provisions of the Older Americans Act shall not be construed to interfere with the right of an older individual to practice religion through reliance on prayer alone for healing in a case in which such decision: (1) is contemporaneously expressed by the older individual when the individual is competent to make the decision; (2) is set forth prior to the occurrence of the illness or injury in a valid advance directive document; or (3) may be unambiguously deduced from the older individual's life history.

QUESTIONS

1. What was the justification for eliminating the outreach, counseling, and assistance provisions of Title VII?

2. How do the 2006 amendments to the OAA broaden the Administration on Aging's responsibility for or role in monitoring elder abuse? Is this involvement likely to have an impact on the incidence of abuse?

OVERALL QUESTIONS ON THE FEDERAL ROLE

1. How would you characterize the federal government's response to the problem of elder abuse?

2. Should the federal government's role in combating elder abuse be expanded even further? If so, how?

C. STATE RESPONSES TO ELDER ABUSE

1. Adult Protective Services — Background

The National Committee for the Prevention of Elder Abuse and The National Adult Protective Services Association: Abuse of Adults Age 60+: The 2004 Survey of Adult Protective Services
February 2006
http://www.apsnetwork.org/Resources/docs/AbuseAdults60.pdf

[Adult Protective Services] . . . is not a national program. Established under Title XX of the Social Security Act in 1975, it was a federally mandated program with little or no funding attached. Thus, APS programs developed in accordance with the needs and constructs of each state. While programs do have similarities, each is tailored to the laws and regulations of each state, and the ability of individual states to respond to survey questions are reflective of this fact. For example, there are only ten states that have specific statutory definitions for self-neglect (i.e., Alaska, Colorado, Louisiana, Maryland, New Hampshire, New York, Utah, Washington, Wisconsin and Wyoming.) In the remaining twenty-seven states that provide services for self-neglecting elders and/or vulnerable adults, self-neglect is included as part of another category in the statute.

* * *

According to a generic definition of APS developed by the National Association of Adult Protective Services, "Adult Protective Services (APS) are those services provided to older people and people with disabilities who are in danger of being mistreated or neglected, are unable to protect themselves, and have no one to assist them." In most states, APS programs are the first responders to reports of abuse, neglect, and exploitation of vulnerable adults.

Read the Florida Adult Protective Services statute set out in the Statutory Supplement.

National Association of Adult Protective Services Administrators: Report on Problems Facing States' Adult Protective Services and the Resources Needed to Resolve Them
January 2003
http://www.apsnetwork.org/Resources/docs/ProblemsFacingStates.pdf*

INTRODUCTION

* * *

Recent studies indicate that at least half a million vulnerable older people and people with disabilities are subjected to abuse, neglect and financial exploitation annually. Many experts believe that this figure represents only the "tip of the iceberg," suggesting that many cases of abuse go unrecognized or unreported.

Over the next twenty-five years, the number of Americans over the age of 65 will virtually double. The growth of this population is likely to significantly increase the number of potential abuse victims. The principal public source of response to reports of adult abuse, neglect and exploitation is Adult Protective Services (APS). These programs are empowered by states and local communities to accept and investigate reports of abuse, neglect and financial exploitation of older and disabled adults.

Adult Protective Services workers are frequently called upon to make critical, life changing decisions in complex situations. Many cases involve life and death medical problems, and complicated legal issues involving questions of capacity,

---

undue influence, guardianship, powers of attorney, and the rights of the victims to self determination vs. the duty of the state to protect its helpless citizens. Other situations may involve complicated financial matters, mental health concerns, problems of substance abuse, domestic violence and family dysfunction.

FINDINGS

Problems Facing State Adult Protective Services Programs

The forty-two states responding to this survey identified twelve problem areas of concern. Problems are ranked according to the percentage of states that provided responses in the following categories:

1. (57%) Insufficient funding at state and national levels

2. (43%) Staffing issues/problems

3. (24%) Lack of emergency/alternative placement options

4. (22%) Lack of public awareness of APS issues and programs

5. (19%) Insufficient community based supportive resources

6. (19%) Law enforcement/legal issues

7. (17%) APS is not priority of state legislatures — competition with child welfare programs

8. (15%) Lack of reliable national and state data

9. (15%) Internal problems in the state administration of the APS programs

10. (14%) Poor communication/collaboration with multiple agencies serving the same population, particularly with the developmental disabilities and mental health service systems

11. (10%) Persons ages 18-59 are not adequately covered under those APS programs that are directed to people age 60 and older

12. (5%) Guardianship issues/problems

Insufficient Funding

Over half of the reporting states (57%) indicated that insufficient funding for APS programs was a major problem. Significant issues were reported concerning the acknowledgement and support for APS programs at the state level, as well as overall state budget cutbacks. However, the lack of federal funding earmarked for APS was identified as a more serious obstacle to program operation. The limited amount of funds from the Older Americans Act to support APS programs was mentioned. For some states, the necessity of competing with child welfare services for reduced Social Services Block Grant funds as populations in need of APS services increase was also identified as problematic. While several states stated that they had received increases in state dollars for APS programs, most indicated that the concomitant increases in APS referrals reduced the effectiveness of the additional dollars.

Staffing Issues

Inadequate staffing for APS programs was most often mentioned in connection with funding issues. The inability to obtain and retain enough staff with expertise in APS to effectively operate existing programs was identified as a major problem by 43% of the respondents. Large caseloads and low wages resulted in high staff turnover in several states. States also mentioned that lack of funds prohibited them from providing the necessary training to develop staff expertise in APS. Two states related that staff carried caseloads of both APS clients and child abuse cases due to staff shortages in the departments.

Lack of Emergency Resources

A more specific and concrete problem identified by nearly one quarter (24%) of the respondents was the lack of emergency and alternative placement resources for a wide range of populations, including people with physical disabilities, older victims of domestic violence and abuse and people with mental health problems and developmental disabilities.

Lack of Public Awareness

Almost one quarter (22%) of the states surveyed indicated their frustrations with the lack of public awareness of APS issues and problems, feeling that the general public does not understand the phenomena of adult abuse or have knowledge about the programs designed to address abuse, exploitation and neglect of vulnerable adults. Additionally, states reported that this lack of awareness is also a problem with state legislatures (17%). Several states commented that efforts made to educate legislators regarding APS issues were futile in that legislators continued to view APS as a competitor with child welfare services. APS was not as a priority for legislative funding. In one state, legislators questioned the right of a state agency to intervene in domestic situations. Insufficient community resources for APS clients, waiting lists for Medicaid waiver programs and the lack of sufficient in-home supportive services were also mentioned as problems by nearly one fifth (19%) of respondents.

Problems with the Legal System

Problems with law enforcement (19%) were viewed as barriers to service delivery for APS clients and were manifested in such areas as: lack of training for law enforcement staff, inadequate criminal investigations, low rates of prosecution, and unwillingness of the courts to deal with APS issues. One state mentioned that no single agency had authority to investigate allegations of adult abuse, neglect and exploitation and that coordination among agencies was problematic. Another state mentioned that neglect and exploitation cases may sit in the prosecutor's office for six to nine months with no action. A lack of coordination and collaboration between APS agencies and law enforcement was mentioned by several states.

Lack of Reliable Data

While respondent states appear to be in varying stages of development regarding their information systems, about 15% mentioned the lack of reliable state and federal data as a major problem for APS agencies. Responses related to this issue included: the lack of good outcome data to evaluate programs and establish benchmarks as well as the need to track clients within the APS program and in other delivery systems such as mental health, developmental disabilities and the legal system.

Internal Administrative Issues

Overall internal administrative issues for APS programs at the state level were identified by six of the states, including the need for revisions to state statutes; confusion and stress caused by the restructuring of state agencies; reduction of staff training due to budget cuts; reduction of the APS workforce; the lack of priority status for APS within the state agency responsible for program operation and the lack of clear legislative mandates which delegate authority to specific state and local units.

Other Problems

Other problem areas identified by states included: poor communication and collaboration among the multiple agencies serving APS clients, particularly between APS programs and systems for people with mental illness and developmental disabilities (14%); legal definitions of abuse that focus APS services only on people age 60+ which results in the lack of adequate protective services for people ages 18 to 59 (10%); and guardianship issues (.05%). The two states that identified guardianship problems reported a lack of guardians, unequal distribution of guardians across the states and actual exploitation of APS clients perpetrated by guardians.

Resources Needed to Solve the Problems Identified

Respondent states indicated twelve resource areas which were needed to address the problems they identified. The percentage of states responding in each category are presented as follows.

1. (64%) Increased federal and state funding for APS

2. (38%) Improvement of training and best practice models

3. (26%) A national public awareness campaign

4. (26%) Improvement in relationships with other agencies serving APS clients, especially with systems for people with mental illness and developmental disabilities

5. (19%) A uniform automated data system

6. (17%) Changes in the role of the Federal government

7. (12%) Increase in trained staff who specialize in APS

8. (10%) Improvement in the role of the legal system regarding APS cases

9. (7%) Development of emergency shelters

10. (5%) Support for leadership role of NAAPSA

11. (5%) Expansion of supportive community based services

12. (2%) Emphasis on APS for at-risk adults over age 18, not just older
    people

Increased Funding

Predictably, the most frequent response to the question of resources needed
by APS programs was more funding (64%). Several states surveyed felt that the
federal government should increase its support for APS, as states are not assuming this responsibility. One state suggested that training be 100% federally
funded based on the elderly population in states. While most respondents did not
specify the source of increased dollars, one state reported that states should provide guaranteed funding for APS and another reported the need for the stabilization of Social Services Block Grant program. Funding is needed for salary
increases for APS staff, rate increases for providers, training, increased investigations, outreach, and public awareness efforts.

Four states reported a need for resources to bring experts in to provide technical assistance for the growing number of complex and difficult APS cases.

Better Staff Training

The second highest percentage of responses (38%) focused on increasing the
overall quality of APS service delivery through the improvement of staff training and developmet, particularly for APS staff. This category also included certain resources that address quality through best practice models, standards
and uniform policies and procedures. Most states responding in this category
stressed the importance of high quality, specialized on-going training for APS
staff that would include such areas as forensic interviewing and financial
exploitation; assistance with the development of training materials; cross training with other delivery systems; video conferencing; specific APS training institutes and the development of training packets which could be adapted by states
and local programs.

One state recommended the development of a basic core APS curriculum
that would include investigative techniques, documentation, assessment, care
planning and effective responses to client needs. An additional state mentioned
that resources should be available to bring national experts into states for
training, as most states have reduced or eliminated out-of-state travel. Another
state reported interest in "any kind of training." In addition to training, two
states expressed the hope that national standardized definitions be developed
which could be used to design state statutes and that best practice models from
other states should be available to be used in program planning.

An increase in trained staff with expertise in APS was proposed as a resource
by 12% of the states. Two states suggested that staff should be dedicated to APS
and not also serve as child abuse investigators. One state related that staff
reductions had necessitated using inexperienced and untrained workers for
APS cases, and spoke to the need for funding to hire dedicated APS staff.

Increased Public Awareness

Over one quarter (26%) of the states reported that increased public awareness
of adult abuse, neglect and exploitation could provide needed incentives for

public support of APS programs, particularly as populations in need increase. The primary focus of these responses was on the need for a national media campaign for both the general public and professionals to explain neglect, abuse and exploitation and what can be done about it, including the mechanisms for reporting incidences. The goal of such a campaign would be to facilitate acknowledgement of the problem by the wider public; this could provide incentives for state and local solutions. It was also suggested that such a campaign could raise community consciousness about adult abuse to the same level of outrage that people have about child abuse.

Improved Interagency Relationships

One fourth of the states surveyed identified the need for better relationships with agencies and programs that serve the same populations. Agencies that serve people with mental illness and developmental disabilities were most often mentioned in this regard. States reported an increase in referrals from these systems. One state suggested an emphasis on permanency planning and collaboration. It was suggested by three states that these relationships become more formalized through written protocols, procedures and memoranda of understanding between agencies for shared cases. Cross training and joint program evaluations were also suggested. States which advocated for the improvement of relationships with the legal system (10%) and its role in APS cases suggested the following: developing special units to prosecute related crimes, expanding the jurisdiction of the Medicaid fraud unit, and developing ways to increase the commitment of prosecutors to prosecute crimes against vulnerable adults.

Uniform Data

The development of a national automated data system which would collect uniform data from the states was identified by 19% of the surveyed states. Such a system could provide more effective management of APS programs through standardized information regarding advocacy, program development and management, evaluation, client tracking and case management.

Federal Leadership

A stronger role for the federal government was proposed by 17% of the respondents. Suggested roles for the federal government included the establishment of a federal agency or program with administrative responsibility for APS, which was defined by one state as a "federal home" for APS. This agency would collect annual data and provide over all administrative support and oversight to state APS programs. One respondent urged better coordination among the many federal agencies involved in APS issues.

Other Resources

The development of alternative placement options, particularly emergency shelters, was proposed by 7% of the states as well as the expansion of other community based resources for clients (5%). In-home community based services were most likely to be needed by older people and physically disabled clients while emergency shelters were identified as a need for people with mental illness and developmentally disabilities. A small percentage (2%) of the states indicated the need to emphasize that APS programs should be serving all vulnerable adults, ages 18 to 60+, with less focus on serving only older people.

A small percentage of states addressed the role of NAAPSA in the improvement of the APS system, and suggested such activities for the organization as: taking a lead role in developing training materials for the states; assisting states by conducting a national media blitz, developing ways to recognize people doing exceptional work in the field; continuing to lobby and testify at the national level, and providing technical assistance to the states.

DISCUSSION

In this survey, states reported frustration with just being able to maintain their APS programs. Referrals are increasing and cases are more complex, necessitating interventions that require specialized services, case management and a wide range of community resources. Additionally, populations served are expanding to include people with mental illness and developmental disabilities. Program operations are limited due to staff who are often under paid, poorly trained and carry large caseloads. Internal administrative conflicts, budget reductions and poor planning at the state level contribute to low staff morale and impose real barriers to maintaining and developing quality programs.

From a more global perspective, the major problem facing the APS delivery system is the lack of federal, state and local support. As evidenced by the frequency of responses in this area, states are very concerned that there is no federal agency with administrative responsibility for APS programs, and that states vary significantly in their support of APS as well. Related to the lack of support for APS is the fact that widespread public awareness campaigns need to be conducted to build public support for the service delivery programs. While the key manifestation of this lack of support is insufficient funding to do the job, ambiguities as to who is in charge compound this problem. Additionally, the lack of uniform standards, data collection systems, state statutes and legal definitions of the APS population present an unstructured framework for developing effective APS programming.

In spite of the multiple, complex and interrelated problems facing APS programs, states responding to this survey indicated a strong commitment to quality programming. Improved training and the distribution of best practice models and standards were prioritized in their responses. In addition, good data systems at state and federal levels to support such activities as program evaluation, new program development, research and client tracking among the various delivery systems were identified as key resources needed. Specialized, highly trained staff to respond to the complexity of issues presented by new groups of clients was also identified as needed to expand the scope of APS programs.

IMPLICATIONS FOR POLICY

As a system of care for the growing population of older people and people with disabilities, APS needs to be adequately funded by the federal government so that states can maintain, expand and improve the quality of their protective service programs. This funding needs to include dollars for services and for quality improvement in such areas as: the development of training modules, a uniform data system, standards and best practice modules and technical assistance for states. In addition to financial support for APS, the federal government needs to establish an administrative office for APS, which collects data, issues reports, provides oversight and coordinates national programs involved in APS issues. In addressing the increased numbers of adults ages 18 through 60+ who require APS services, states need to respond with administrative structures which provide services to all populations, are accountable to funding sources, are flexible, and have stability and creditability within the state system. As with the federal government, states should support APS programs both through funding and by expanding public awareness of APS issues and services.

In order to facilitate services for APS clients, states should formalize methods of coordination and collaboration among the various agencies involved in APS through memoranda of understanding, joint planning, data collection, cross training, and joint policies and procedures. Agencies that should be involved include law enforcement, prosecutors, the judicial system, mental health, developmental disabilities, substance abuse programs, Medicaid, regulatory agencies, area agencies on aging and long term care ombudsmen programs. Federal and/or foundation funds should to be available to support of NAAPSA for the development of training materials and the provision of technical assistance to states.

The need for protective services for older people and people with disabilities who are victims of abuse, exploitation and neglect continues to grow. Federal and state agencies must address this problem now through strong legislative initiatives which include sufficient funding to meet the protective needs of our most vulnerable citizens.

2. Mandatory Reporting; Liability for Failure to Report

Substance Abuse and Mental Health Services Administration Center for Substance Abuse Prevention
Prevention Pathways — Out of the Shadows: Uncovering Substance Use and Elder Abuse: Reporting Elder Abuse
http://pathwayscourses.samhsa.gov/elab/elab_5_pg5.htm

Regardless of variations in coverage and definition, most States have mandatory reporting procedures that require certain professionals to report suspected cases of elder abuse.

Mandatory reporting involves two categories:

* Those requiring all citizens to report

* Those requiring only certain categories of individuals to report

Health care professionals, long-term care facility personnel, and mental health professionals are almost uniformly required to report abuse. Some States have exempted certain professionals, such as clergy, physicians, lawyers, and therapists who work personally with the victims or perpetrators.

States differ in the type of abuse that triggers the reporting requirement. For example, in Missouri, the likelihood of suffering physical harm and the need for protective services force the reporting. Some States enable professionals to use their own judgment. Illinois specifies additional conditions on reporting. The person filing the report must believe the adult is unable to seek assistance for himself or herself, and the abuse/neglect or financial exploitation must have occurred with the previous 12 months. To date, 44 States have some form of mandatory reporting.

All States grant mandatory and voluntary reporters good faith immunity from civil and criminal liability. To be protected, a person must believe his or her report is based on the truth or what is reasonably true. Civil immunity, in most cases, protects the reporter from being sued for defamation or malicious prosecution. In States requiring mandatory reporting of elder abuse, failure to report is a misdemeanor of varying degrees.

QUESTIONS

1. Should the reporting of elder abuse be mandatory? Why or why not?

2. Should mandatory reporting laws include professionals such as lawyers and physicians? What ethical problems might such reporting laws raise?

3. If the reporting of elder abuse is mandatory, what sanctions, if any, should be administered to persons who fail to comply with the reporting requirements?

D. REMEDIES AGAINST ABUSERS

1. Overview

U.S. Department of Justice Office of Justice Programs
Annual Report Fiscal Year 2000
http://www.ojp.usdoj.gov/annualreport/chapter7.htm

* * *

Understanding and Preventing Victimization of Elders

In January 2000, the Bureau of Justice Statistics (BJS) released the report, Crimes against Persons Age 65 or Older, 1992-97. It found that people 65 and older are substantially less likely to be violent crime victims than are younger men and women. Each year from 1992 through 1997, there were 5 violent crimes per 1,000 U.S. residents 65 years old or older, less than a tenth the rate of 56 crimes per 1,000 of those age 12 through 64, according to the BJS National Crime Victimization Survey (NCVS). The only crime category that affected the elderly at about the same rate as most others (except those ages 12-24) was personal theft, which includes purse snatching and pocket picking. Although people 65 or older made up 15 percent of the population, they accounted for 7 percent of all victims of crimes measured in the survey.

OJP was an active participant in the Justice Department's Elder Justice Initiative. The primary objective of this initiative was to enhance enforcement, training, coordination, and awareness regarding the problems of elder abuse, fraud, and exploitation; create the infrastructure for broad-based collaboration at the national policy level, as well as at the state and grass roots levels; and to bridge the historical gap between those on the front lines, who see the problems first hand, and those charged with enforcing the law.

Building on these efforts, on October 30-31, 2000, the Justice Department — in partnership with the Department of Health and Human Services — convened a national symposium on preventing and responding to the victimization of older persons. The symposium, "Our Aging Population: Promoting Empowerment, Preventing Victimization, and Implementing Coordinated Interventions," showcased federal, state, and local programs designed to prevent older people from becoming victims of abuse, exploitation, fraud, and neglect. It also focused on improving the response of law enforcement and social service agencies when victimization does occur. Financial exploitation and consumer fraud, domestic/community abuse and neglect, and institutional abuse and neglect were the three primary issues addressed at the symposium.

The Blackfeet Nation received OVC funding in FY 2000 to continue its development of a coordinated response to crimes against the elderly by adapting the Triad program approach to Indian country. Triad is a joint effort of the American Association of Retired Persons, the International Association of Chiefs of Police, and the National Sheriffs' Association to build coordinated services for elderly victims of crime. Triad combines the efforts and resources of law enforcement, senior citizens and organizations that represent them, and victim assistance providers.

BJA continued to support a consortium of prevention, education, and prosecution projects working to thwart fraudulent telemarketers who prey on senior citizens. A major component of the project is the Telemarketing Fraud Training Task Force, a multiagency committee led by the National Association of Attorneys General. The Task Force includes the National District Attorneys Association through the American Prosecutors Research Institute, the National White Collar Crime Center, and the American Association of Retired Persons Foundation. The Task Force works to broaden criminal and civil enforcement efforts by increasing the numbers of state and local telemarketing prosecutions; coordinate statewide and local investigations and prosecutions; enhance technical and case preparation assistance for state and local prosecutors; and increase U.S.-Canada cooperation to reduce the cross-border flow of telemarketing fraud.

In addition, members of the Task Force provided training to five BJA-funded demonstration sites that have implemented innovative telemarketing prevention and enforcement programs. The programs are located in Los Angeles, California, Atlanta, Georgia, Hillsborough County (Tampa), Florida, Raleigh, North Carolina, and Montpelier, Vermont.

* * *

Martha L. Ridgway
Civil, Criminal, and Administration Remedies
in Cases of Abuse, Neglect, and Financial
Exploitation of the Elderly
Colorado Gerontological Society and Senior Answers and Services
http://www.senioranswers.org/Pages/elderabuse.htm[*]

* * *

There are three categories of legal remedies for the victim of elder abuse, neglect and financial exploitation: (1) criminal, (2) civil and (3) administrative. Although the focus of this paper is on civil and administrative remedies, criminal remedies will be discussed briefly.

A. Criminal Remedies

A criminal case is brought on behalf of the public at large ("the people") by the District Attorney or the Attorney General for violations of state criminal law, and by the U.S. Attorney for violations of federal law. The State . . . or the United States [is] the plaintiff in criminal cases and the perpetrator of abuse, neglect or financial exploitation is the defendant. The victim is not a party to the case, but rather is a witness. It is generally in the discretion of the District or U.S. Attorney to file a criminal case.

Prosecuting cases involving elder abuse, neglect and financial exploitation can be difficult: the victim is often a poor witness, whether from fear, confusion, diminished capacity, memory failure or frailty. Conversely, the defendant is often a better witness and can raise defenses such as the impairment of the elder's memory, claims that the elder made a gift, the elder entered into a contract, etc.

Colorado's Criminal Code contains a section entitled Wrongs to At-Risk Adults, C.R.S. § 18-6.5-101-106, which specifically targets abuse, neglect and exploitation cases.

Additionally, provisions in the Criminal Code provide stiffer sentences for defendants who commit crimes against an elderly person or a person with a disability. It is also a crime to violate a civil restraining order.

B. Civil Remedies

In a civil case, a victim of abuse, neglect or financial exploitation, or someone on his or her behalf such as a guardian or conservator, can sue the perpetrator directly for monetary damages. The victim is the plaintiff and the perpetrator is the defendant. As a part of a civil case, a victim can also sue for injunctive relief. An injunction is a court order which directs someone to perform a specific act or to refrain from performing a specific act.

Thus, for example, an elder could sue a perpetrator for money damages for injuries sustained from an assault and battery and, at the same time, ask the

---

[*] Reprinted by permission.

court to issue an injunction prohibiting the perpetrator from having any contact with the victim.

As with criminal cases, bringing a civil case can be difficult. For example, the elderly victim may be a poor witness, statutes of limitations may have expired before the elder seeks help, pursuing a lawsuit can be costly and there may be a long delay before a court date.

However, Colorado law provides for an earlier trial date when a party suffers from an illness or condition which raises a medical doubt of survival beyond one year or if the person is age 70 or older and can prove to the court that he has a meritorious claim and a substantial interest in the case.

Another civil remedy is a restraining order, which can be issued separately from and independent of a civil suit. A restraining order is a court order that restrains a person from taking certain actions.

A third civil remedy is to seek the appointment of a guardian and/or a conservator or other protective arrangement on behalf of an elder under the Colorado Probate Code.

1. Civil Suits

There are a number of legal theories under which a victim of elder abuse, neglect or financial exploitation can sue the perpetrator. The following is representative only and is not intended to be an exclusive list of legal theories.

1. Assault is the willful attempt or threat to inflict injury on a person, and any display of force that would cause the victim to fear or expect immediate bodily harm. An assault can be committed without actually touching, striking or harming the victim. An example is shaking a fist in the elder's face in a threatening manner.

2. Battery is the willful physical contact of a person which causes bodily injury or is offensive. This can include punching, hitting or rough handling.

3. Intentional infliction of emotional distress is engaging in conduct for the purpose of causing severe emotional distress on another person or knowing that certain conduct will have that result. An example is threatening to put an elder in the nursing home if he does not "behave."

4. False imprisonment is the intentional restriction of a victim's freedom of movement. This can include the use of physical restraints, removal of the elder's means of transportation (e.g., cane or wheelchair) or locking the elder in a room.

5. Duress is coercing a person to do something against his or her free will, such as forcing an elder to sign a check payable to the perpetrator.

6. Negligence is the failure to use the care that a reasonably prudent person would use under similar circumstances, which results in harm to the victim. An example is failure to administer medication in a timely manner.

7. Conversion is the civil equivalent to theft. Conversion means that a person takes control over the property of another with the intent to deprive the victim of the property, such as stealing money or personal property.

8. Fraud and deception is the making of a false representation of a material fact to another, when the person making the representation knows that the representation is false and knows that the victim will act on it, thereby causing damage to the victim. Examples include telephone scams, sweepstakes, requests to send money to "win."

9. Breach of fiduciary duty. A fiduciary is a person or entity who, as the result of a particular undertaking, has a duty to act primarily for the benefit of another in matters connected with the undertaking. This duty is often referred to as a fiduciary duty. An example of a fiduciary is a conservator or a stockbroker. When a person breaches a fiduciary duty, the victim incurs damages, such as loss of property or money. An example is self-dealing or using the elder's funds or property.

10. Unjust enrichment occurs when a person benefits unjustly, at the expense of another, and it is unfair for the defendant to retain the benefit. An example is an informal promise to provide care to an elder, being paid in advance, and the caregiver not providing the care.

11. Breach of contract. When a person enters into a contract with another, and fails to perform under the terms of the contract, the defendant has breached the contract. An example is a written agreement to provide care to an elder, being paid in advance, and the caregiver not providing the care.

12. Constructive trust. When a person acquires the property of another by abusing a confidential relationship that exists between the two people, the court can remedy this abuse by imposing a constructive trust on the property. This means that the defendant no longer owns the property, but that it is held for the benefit of the plaintiff. For example, an adult daughter convinces her elderly mother to deed the home to the daughter without paying the mother. If the mother sues the daughter, the court could hold the property in trust for the benefit of the mother.

13. Other legal remedies. Malpractice (medical, accountant, legal and other professionals), violations of securities laws, etc., are also available to the elderly plaintiff.

2. Restraining Orders

Under Colorado law, C.R.S. 14-4-102, in cases of domestic abuse, a temporary and permanent restraining order can be entered by a municipal, county or district court in order to prevent such abuse. The restraining order can prohibit a person from threatening, molesting, injuring or contacting the party seeking the restraining order. Unfortunately, this statute does not address psychological abuse.

Another provision of Colorado law, C.R.S. 13-6-107, addresses restraining orders to prevent emotional abuse of the elderly. Elderly is defined as age sixty years or more. A temporary or permanent restraining order to prevent emotional abuse of the elderly may include restraining a party from repeated acts which constitute verbal threats or assaults; from repeated acts which constitute verbal harassment; from repeated acts which result in the inappropriate use or the threat of inappropriate use of medications upon a person; from repeated acts which result in the inappropriate use of physical or chemical restraints; and from repeated acts which result in the misuse of power or authority granted to a person through a power of attorney or by a court in a guardianship or conservatorship proceeding which results in unreasonable confinement or restriction of the liberty of an elderly person.

As discussed above, violation of a restraining order constitutes a criminal offense. Additionally, a person who violates a restraining order can be held in contempt of court.

3. Guardianship, Conservatorship and Other Protective Arrangements

The Colorado Probate Code, C.R.S. 15-14-101 *et. seq.*, provides that an elder or someone on his or her behalf can petition the court to appoint a guardian and/or a conservator or to enter a protective order for the benefit of the elder. A guardian is a person or institution appointed by the court to make decisions concerning the person of someone who is incapacitated. For example, a guardian decides where the person will reside, what kind of medical treatment will be administered, etc. A conservator is a person or institution appointed by the court to manage the estate and affairs of a person who is unable to manage his or her property and affairs effectively. Instead of appointing a conservator, the court can issue a protective order, authorizing, directing or ratifying any transaction necessary or desirable to achieve any security, service or care arrangement meeting the foreseeable needs of the person in need of protection. An example of a protective arrangement is a court order permitting the sale of the elder's home. A probate court also has broad powers to order an accounting of all funds expended on behalf of the protected person.

C. Administrative Remedies

One of the most important administrative remedies available to a victim of elder abuse, neglect or financial exploitation is a law entitled Protective Services for Adults at Risk of Mistreatment or Self-Neglect Act. C.R.S. 26-3.1-201 *et. seq.* This law "urges" (but does not require) professionals and others who are in a position to detect abuse, neglect and financial exploitation of an elder to report to the county Department of Social Services or, during non-business hours, to law enforcement agencies, when they have "observed the mistreatment or self-neglect of an at-risk adult." The statute designates those who are "urged" to report in the following general categories: medical personnel (including hospital and nursing home personnel engaged in the admission of patients); mental health professionals; social workers; dentists; law enforcement officials; court appointed guardians and conservators; fire protection personnel; pharmacists; community centered board staff; financial institution personnel; state and local long-term care ombudsmen; and personnel, volunteers or consultants for any licensed care facility, agency, home or governing board.

Additionally, "any other person may report such known or suspected mistreatment or self-neglect of an at-risk adult." Once the Department has received a report, it is immediately required to "make a thorough investigation." A written report must be made within 48 hours. If it is determined that an at-risk adult is being mistreated or self-neglected, or is at risk thereof, the Department can immediately provide protective services if the adult consents. If the adult does not consent, the Department can file for the appointment of a guardian and/or a conservator for the adult. However, any protective services sought must constitute "the least restrictive intervention."

A victim of abuse, neglect or financial exploitation can also file a complaint against an entity or a person who is regulated by an administrative agency. For example, nursing homes must comply with the regulations of the Colorado Department of Health. Insurance companies are governed by the regulations of the Colorado Commissioner of Insurance. Stock brokerages must comply with the regulations of the Colorado Commissioner of Securities and the U.S. Securities and Exchange Commission. If the administrative agency determines that a potential violation of its regulations has occurred, it can conduct an investigation and take action against the wrongdoer.

State of Nevada Office of the Attorney General
Protocols Help Better Protect Nevada Seniors
http://ag.state.nv.us/ag press/1998/98-12.htm

Nevada's Elder Task Force kicked off its second year in January with the announcement of a historic agreement by government officials and law enforcement to implement protocols aimed at the enhancement of the investigation and prosecution of Elder Abuse Crimes in our state.

In September of 1996 the Attorney General's Office and the Division for Aging Services held meetings that brought together representatives from more than twenty different public and private agencies and organizations sharing an interest in preventing elder abuse. Those meetings resulted in the "Action Plan to Better Protect Nevada's Elderly." The Action Plan included the formation of a "Networking-Response Committee" to find ways to help improve the communication, coordination, and understanding of procedures among the various local and state agencies involved in responding to a report of elder abuse, neglect, exploitation and isolation.

The Elder Abuse Protocols are one of the projects of that committee. Adequate education of law enforcement was cited as one of the essential elements for preventing elder abuse in our state. The protocols assist patrol officers, investigators, detectives and prosecutors in their understanding of the older victim. They also address the laws and procedures involved with reporting and prosecuting crimes against the elderly and the resources available to assist the elderly victim.

Officers or investigators who respond to an initial complaint of elder abuse need to know that, in addition to his or her criminal investigation, the complaint should be reported to a licensing board or agency if the complaint involves a licensed professional or facility.

The protocols will also help law enforcement better realize which other agencies may need to conduct parallel investigations. For example, the Bureau of

Licensure and Certification has a duty to investigate complaints which occur in nursing homes and other licensed facilities and may impose administrative remedies, including monetary sanctions, as a result of its investigation. The Medicaid Fraud Control Unit within the Office of the Attorney General also investigates and criminally prosecutes patient abuse and neglect in facilities which receive Medicaid funds. Professionals, including nurses, licensed administrators of facilities, physicians, dentists and therapists are regulated by licensing boards which may investigate and impose disciplinary sanctions.

During a ceremonial signing last month, the Attorney General's Office and the Division for Aging Services were joined by the Clark County and Washoe County District Attorneys' Offices, Clark County Social Services, Las Vegas Metropolitan Police Department, the state Bureau of Licensure and Certification, the state Health Care Financing and Policy Unit and the state Department of Human Resources among others in signing the Protocols. The next step is to take the Protocols to law enforcement statewide for their review and approval.

Enhanced coordination and communication between law enforcement and non-law enforcement agencies, designated by state law to investigate reports of elder abuse, are also essential. In addition to the Elder Abuse Protocols, the Network-Response Committee has published a Guidebook for Mandatory Reporters of Elder Abuse. The guide helps to explain the roles and responsibilities of the agencies involved with reporting, investigating and prosecuting elder abuse, as well as agencies which may discipline or regulate a person or entity responsible for elder abuse, neglect, exploitation or isolation.

Other accomplishments in the year since the Action Plan was released include the distribution of 1200 copies of the video "Rx for Abuse." Starring Shirley Jones and Marty Ingels, the video is an important tool that helps medical professionals do their part to try and stop the mistreatment of Nevada's seniors. Funding for two additional Elder Abuse videos and materials to be produced in the coming year will help continue education and training for law enforcement.

The 1997 Nevada State Legislature enacted legislation proposed by the Plan including a bill that makes Nevada one of the first states in the country to recognize intentional isolation of the elderly as a serious crime and punish it accordingly. Another bill passed during the 1997 session doubled the amount of damages a victim of Elder Abuse can recover from the abuser. Assemblywoman Vivian Freeman and Assemblyman Jack Close proposed successful legislation which requires fingerprinting of long term care workers, and, a bill proposed by Assemblyman Mark Manendo increases the minimum penalty for criminal elder abuse and was amended to add morticians as mandatory elder abuse reporters and to authorize an elder abuse reporting hotline.

Betsy Kolkoski, Chief of Elder Rights for the Division for Aging Services, has announced that, over the next year, plans are in the works for the development of continuing education programs for prosecutors and other attorneys, additional legislation for the benefit of seniors, creation of a better tracking system of crimes against the elderly and a 15 county tour of rural Nevada to implement the public awareness campaign of the Action Plan.

* * *

QUESTIONS

1. Although the articles above concern Colorado and Nevada law, those states' laws are typical of those available in most jurisdictions (not all states provide all remedies discussed in the excerpts). Given the array of federal and state remedies available to address elder abuse, why does abuse continue to be a significant problem?

2. Most lawyers who consider themselves to be "elder law" specialists are not involved in tort-based litigation against nursing homes and similar facilities; such lawsuits are typically handled by so-called "personal injury" lawyers. Yet these suits can be extremely lucrative — damage awards in the millions of dollars are common. Why might this be?

2. Caregiver Liability Outside the Institutional Context

Joann Blair,
"Honor Thy Father and Thy Mother" — But For How Long?: Adult Children's Duty to Care for and Protect Elderly Parents
35 U. LOUISVILLE J. FAM. L. 765, 768 (1996-1997)[*]

In order to be criminally liable for a failure to act or for an omission, such as failing to care for an elderly parent, a corresponding legal duty to act must exist. A legal duty can be expressly provided for in a criminal statute itself, imposed by another statute, based upon a contract, or voluntarily assumed. Legal duties may also arise via special relationships such as parent and child, husband and wife, employer and employee, landlord and licensee, or a supervisory relationship in which one individual is responsible for supervising the conduct of another who is deemed physically dangerous. A person must have notice that a legal duty to take affirmative action exists before liability for violating that duty can attach.

PEOPLE v. HEITZMAN
886 P.2d 1229 (Cal. 1994)

LUCAS, Chief Justice.

Penal Code section 368, subdivision (a), is one component of a multi-faceted legislative response to the problem of elder abuse. The statute imposes felony criminal liability on

> [a]ny person who, under circumstances or conditions likely to produce great bodily harm or death, willfully causes or permits any elder or dependent adult, with knowledge that he or she is an elder or dependent adult, to suffer, or inflicts thereon unjustifiable physical pain or

---

[*] Copyright © 1997. Reprinted with permission.

mental suffering, or having the care or custody of any elder or dependent adult, willfully causes or permits the person or health of the elder or dependent adult to be injured, or willfully causes or permits the elder or dependent adult to be placed in a situation such that his or her person or health is endangered. . . .

In this case, we must decide whether the statute meets constitutional standards of certainty. As we shall explain, we conclude initially that, on its face, the broad statutory language at issue here fails to provide fair notice to those who may be subjected to criminal liability for "willfully . . . permit[ting]" an elder or dependent adult to suffer pain, and similarly fails to set forth a uniform standard under which police and prosecutors can consistently enforce the proscription against "willfully . . . permit[ting]" such suffering. Under these circumstances, section 368(a) would be unconstitutionally vague absent some judicial construction clarifying its uncertainties.

We conclude that the statute may properly be upheld by interpreting its imposition of criminal liability upon "[a]ny person who . . . permits . . . any elder or dependent adult . . . to suffer . . . unjustifiable pain or mental suffering" to apply only to a person who, under existing tort principles, has a duty to control the conduct of the individual who is directly causing or inflicting abuse on the elder or dependent adult. Because the evidence in this case does not indicate that defendant had the kind of "special relationship" with the individuals alleged to have directly abused the elder victim that would give rise to a duty on her part to control their conduct, she was improperly charged with a violation of section 368(a). We therefore reverse the judgment of the Court of Appeal.

I. FACTS

The egregious facts of this case paint a profoundly disturbing family portrait in which continued neglect of and apparent indifference to the basic needs of the family's most vulnerable member, an elderly dependent parent, led to a result of tragic proportion. Sixty-seven-year-old Robert Heitzman resided in the Huntington Beach home of his grown son, Richard Heitzman, Sr., along with another grown son, Jerry Heitzman, and Richard's three sons. On December 3, 1990, police were summoned to the house, where they discovered Robert dead in his bedroom. His body lay on a mattress that was rotted through from constant wetness, exposing the metal springs. The stench of urine and feces filled not only decedent's bedroom, but the entire house as well. His bathroom was filthy, and the bathtub contained fetid, green-colored water that appeared to have been there for some time.

Police learned that Jerry Heitzman was primarily responsible for his father's care, rendering caretaking services in exchange for room and board. Jerry admitted that he had withheld all food and liquids from his father for the three days preceding his death on December 3. Jerry explained that he was expecting company for dinner on Sunday, December 2, and did not want his father, who no longer had control over his bowels and bladder, to defecate or urinate because it would further cause the house to smell.

At the time of his death, decedent had large, decubitus ulcers, more commonly referred to as bed sores, covering one-sixth of his body. An autopsy revealed the existence of a yeast infection in his mouth, and showed that he suffered from congestive heart failure, bronchial pneumonia, and hepatitis. The forensic pathologist who performed the autopsy attributed decedent's death to septic shock due to the sores which, he opined, were caused by malnutrition, dehydration, and neglect.

Twenty years earlier, decedent had suffered a series of strokes that paralyzed the left side of his body. Defendant, 31-year-old Susan Valerie Heitzman, another of decedent's children, had previously lived in the home and had been her father's primary caregiver at that time. In return, defendant's brother Richard paid for her room and board. Richard supported the household by working two full-time jobs, and supplemented this income with decedent's monthly Social Security and pension checks.

One year prior to her father's death, defendant decided to move away from the home. After she moved out, however, she continued to spend time at the house visiting her boyfriend/nephew Richard, Jr. Since leaving to live on her own, she noticed that the entire house had become filthy. She was aware that a social worker had discussed with Jerry the need to take their father to a doctor. When she spoke to Jerry about it, he told her he had lost the doctor's telephone number the social worker had given him. She suggested to Jerry that he recontact the social worker. She also discussed with Richard, Jr., the need for taking her father to the doctor, but she never made the necessary arrangements.

In the last six weekends before her father died, defendant had routinely visited the household. She was last in her father's bedroom five weeks prior to his death, at which time she noticed the hole in the mattress and feces-soiled clothing lying on the floor. Another of decedent's daughters, Lisa, also visited the house that same day.

Two weeks prior to her father's death, defendant spent the entire weekend at the house. On Sunday afternoon, she saw her father sitting in the living room, and noticed that he looked weak and appeared disoriented. A week later, during Thanksgiving weekend, and several days prior to decedent's death, defendant again stayed at the house. Decedent's bedroom door remained closed throughout the weekend, and defendant did not see her father. On the day decedent died, defendant awoke mid-morning and left the house to return to her own apartment. Around one o'clock in the afternoon, Jerry discovered decedent dead in his bedroom.

In a two-count indictment, the Orange County District Attorney jointly charged Jerry and Richard, Sr., with involuntary manslaughter, and Jerry, Richard, Sr., and defendant with violating section 368(a). At the preliminary examination, the magistrate determined that, although defendant did not have care or custody of decedent as did her brothers, there was probable cause to believe she owed a duty of care to her father and that she had been grossly negligent in failing to carry out that duty. She was therefore held to answer along with her brothers for willfully permitting an elder to suffer unjustifiable physical pain and mental suffering.

On November 4, 1994, an information was filed in superior court charging defendant with a violation of section 368(a). Thereafter, she moved to set aside the information pursuant to section 995 on the basis that the evidence presented at the preliminary hearing failed to establish probable cause she had committed a crime. In relevant part, defendant argued that the evidence that she knew of her father's deteriorating condition did not create a duty for her to act to prevent the harm suffered by him. In its opposition to her motion, the prosecution contended that defendant's duty of care was established by section 368(a) itself, which imposes a duty on every person to not permit any elderly or dependent adult to suffer unjustifiable pain.

* * *

The superior court agreed with defendant that the statutory language at issue was unconstitutionally vague, . . . dismissed the case against her. The People appealed the court's order of dismissal, and the Court of Appeal reversed. . . . The court found that such a duty did exist, based on the special relationship between a parent and child codified in the financial support statutes, section 270c and Civil Code former sections 206 and 242, and thus rejected defendant's vagueness challenge.

* * *

II. DISCUSSION

A. Criminal Liability for a Failure to Act

* * *

Defendant here was charged under section 368(a) with willfully permitting her elder father to suffer the infliction of unjustifiable pain and mental suffering. It was thus her failure to act, i.e., her failure to prevent the infliction of abuse on her father, that created the potential for her criminal liability under the statute. Unlike the imposition of criminal penalties for certain positive acts, which is based on the statutory proscription of such conduct, when an individual's criminal liability is based on the failure to act, it is well established that he or she must first be under an existing legal duty to take positive action.

* * *

When a criminal statute does not set forth a legal duty to act by its express terms, liability for a failure to act must be premised on the existence of a duty found elsewhere. . . .

Whether the statute adequately denotes the class of persons who owe such a duty is the focus of the constitutional question presented here.

B. Vagueness

The Fourteenth Amendment to the United States Constitution and article I, section 7 of the California Constitution, each guarantee that no person shall be deprived of life, liberty, or property without due process of law. This constitutional command requires "a reasonable degree of certainty in legislation, especially in the criminal law. . . ."

* * *

For several reasons, we reject the People's contention that the statute itself imposes a blanket duty on everyone to prevent the abuse of any elder. The wide net cast by a statutory interpretation imposing such a duty on every person is apparent when we consider that it would extend the potential for criminal liability to, for example, a delivery person who, having entered a private home, notices an elder in a disheveled or disoriented state and purposefully fails to intervene.

Under general principles of tort law, civil liability is not imposed for the failure to assist or protect another, absent some legal or special relationship between the parties giving rise to a duty to act. In the absence of any indication, express or implied, that the Legislature meant to depart so dramatically from this principle, well established at the time section 368(a) was enacted, it would be unreasonable to interpret the statute as imposing a more serious form of liability, indeed, felony criminal liability, on every person who fails to prevent an elder from suffering abuse, absent some legal or special relationship between the parties.

* * *

[D]ecisions construing either section 368(a) or the felony child abuse statute on which it was modeled do not provide a clear definition of those under a duty to protect either elders or children, respectively. Under these circumstances, section 368(a) fails to provide adequate notice as to the class of persons who may be under an affirmative duty to prevent the infliction of abuse. Of equal, if not greater, constitutional significance, police and prosecutors may lack sufficient standards under which to determine who is to be charged with permitting such abuse.

* * *

Richard, Sr., and Jerry were not the only family members residing with decedent. Richard, Sr.'s three sons also lived in the home. One of these individuals, Richard, Jr., was defendant's boyfriend. For the last six weekends before her father's death, defendant had routinely been in the house visiting with Richard, Jr. Approximately one month before her father died, defendant discussed with Richard, Jr., the possibility of his helping her take decedent to the doctor. The record therefore would appear to support an inference that whatever defendant knew about her father's deteriorating condition, Richard, Jr., knew as well. Under the prosecutor's reading of the statutory language, the first part of section 368(a) would also appear to be applicable to decedent's grandson, Richard, Jr. He was, however, neither arrested nor charged.

Lisa, a fourth Heitzman sibling who, like defendant, did not reside in the same house as her father and brothers, had visited the home five weeks before decedent's death. She was present in the home when defendant entered their father's room for the last time and discovered the hole where the mattress had rotted through. The record also indicates that at one point Lisa contacted the Orange County Department of Social Services concerning her father's condition, but that the agency did not follow up on her call. It would thus appear that Lisa, like defendant, was well aware of decedent's situation. Unlike defendant, however, Lisa was neither arrested for nor charged with a violation of section 368(a).

* * *

We have determined that the portion of section 368(a) purporting to impose on any person the duty to prevent the infliction of pain or suffering on an elder fails to meet the constitutional requirement of certainty. Before declaring a statute void for vagueness, however, we have an obligation to determine whether its validity can be preserved by "giv[ing] specific content to terms that might otherwise be unconstitutionally vague."

* * *

The Restatement Second of Torts provides guidance as to both the nature and the scope of the special relationships that would give rise to a duty to prevent an individual from inflicting pain or suffering on an elder, pursuant to section 368(a). These special relationships are defined as those between (1) parent and minor child, (2) employer and employee, (3) landowner and licensee, and (4) "[o]ne who takes charge of a third person whom he knows or should know to be likely to cause bodily harm to others if not controlled."

* * *

From this it follows that one will be criminally liable for the abusive conduct of another only if he or she has the ability to control such conduct.

* * *

III. DISPOSITION

Based on their status as Robert Heitzman's caretakers, felony criminal liability was properly imposed on Richard, Sr., and Jerry pursuant to section 368(a) for the role they played in bringing about their father's demise.

* * *

Furthermore, given defendant's failure to intercede on her father's behalf under the egregious circumstances presented here, we can well understand the prosecution's decision to charge defendant under section 368(a). Because the People presented no evidence tending to show that defendant had a legal duty to control the conduct of either of her brothers, however, we reverse the judgment of the Court of Appeal with directions to reinstate the trial court's order dismissing the charges against defendant.

We emphasize that our disposition of this case in no way signifies our approval of defendant's failure to repel the threat to her father's well-being. The facts underlying this case are indeed troubling, and defendant's alleged indifference to the suffering of her father cannot be condoned. The desire to impose criminal liability on this defendant cannot be accomplished, however, at the expense of providing constitutionally required clarity to an otherwise vague statute.

The judgment of the Court of Appeal is reversed.

KENNARD, ARABIAN and GEORGE, JJ., concur.

BAXTER, Justice, dissenting.

I respectfully dissent. The majority essentially holds that even though defendant knew her aged and disabled father was living in her brothers' home under conditions that were painful, degrading, and ultimately fatal, she cannot be criminally prosecuted for her failure to act because she did not stand in a "special relationship" with either her father or her brothers under tort law.

* * *

Based on the preliminary hearing record in this case, there was ample evidence that defendant's failure to intervene in her father's behalf was criminally negligent, and thus violated section 368.

* * *

In brief, the preliminary hearing record indicates that defendant — formerly her father's caretaker — knew he was paralyzed, incontinent, and completely dependent upon others to feed, clean, and move him. For a period of at least six weeks before her father died, defendant repeatedly visited and spent the night in the home where her brothers and father lived. Defendant had actual knowledge during this time that her father required, but did not receive, medical attention; that his person and physical surroundings had become filthy from human waste and debris; that the mattress from which he could not move without assistance was damp and rotted through; and that he was confined alone in his room for long stretches of time.

Nevertheless, defendant did not take any steps to assist her father during this period. She did not attempt to obtain professional help (e.g., telephoning the doctor, social worker, or paramedics); to care for him while present in the home (e.g., feeding or cleaning him); or to discuss with other family members the possibility of making different care arrangements (e.g., hospitalization or professional caretaking assistance). The evidence further discloses that defendant's father died as a result of the deplorable conditions of which defendant was actually or presumably aware (septic shock from bed sores, malnutrition, and dehydration).

In light of the foregoing, I would affirm the judgment of the Court of Appeal insofar as it reversed the superior court's order sustaining defendant's demurrer and dismissing the case.

MOSK and WERDEGAR, JJ., concur.

QUESTIONS

1. With which do you agree: the majority opinion in *Heitzman*, or the dissent? Why?

2. To what extent should family members have a duty to care, physically or financially, for their elderly parents or relatives?

3. Penalty/Damages Enhancement

UNITED STATES v. CURLY
167 F.3d 316 (6th Cir. 1999)

CONTIE, CIRCUIT JUDGE. Defendant-appellant Raymond William Curly ("Curly") appeals the district court's decision to increase his offense level pursuant to U.S.S.G. § 3A1.1(b), the sentencing guidelines' vulnerable victim enhancement. We affirm the district court's imposition of the vulnerable victim enhancement for the following reasons.

I.

On October 3, 1996, the grand jury for the Western District of Tennessee returned a fifty-two count indictment charging Curly (a.k.a. Roy Drew) with: mail fraud (in violation of 18 U.S.C. § 1341); using a false, fictitious or assumed name for the purpose of committing mail fraud (in violation of 18 U.S.C. § 1342); wire fraud (in violation of 18 U.S.C. § 1343); and conspiracy to commit an offense against the United States (in violation of 18 U.S.C. § 371). In the indictment, the United States repeatedly noted that it was seeking an enhanced penalty pursuant to 18 U.S.C. § 2326, which provides for lengthy terms of imprisonment for persons convicted under sections 1341, 1342 and 1343 "in connection with the conduct of telemarketing," 18 U.S.C. § 2326, that "victimized ten or more persons over the age of 55 [or] targeted persons over the age of 55." *Id.*

Curly and Baker formed Memphis Music Corporation on or about December 5, 1990. Curly "was an officer, director, beneficial owner and true party in interest of Memphis Music Corporation." In that capacity, Curly "had responsibility for the direction, control, and management of said entity, including its sale of 'investments' in various ventures, including, but not limited to, stock offerings, franchise opportunities, and musical concert promotions to the public." According to the indictment, the conspirators sought to induce individuals to invest large sums of money in bogus investments related to the music industry.

5. It was a principle [*sic*] object of the conspiracy that the defendants would, by means of various false and fraudulent pretenses, representations, and promises, induce numerous individuals to each invest large sums of money in what were purported to be "investments" in various ventures, including, but not limited to, stock offerings, franchise opportunities, and musical concert promotions, thereby unlawfully enriching themselves.

6. It was a principle [*sic*] object of the conspiracy that the defendants would solicit, and direct the solicitation and acceptance of, orders and money from investors throughout the United States, in a scheme and artifice to promote the sale and execution of "investments" in various ventures, including, but not limited to, stock offerings, franchise opportunities, and musical concert promotions.

7. It was a principle [*sic*] object and purpose of the conspiracy to carry out and to execute the above-listed objects of the conspiracy for the ultimate personal gain, benefit, profit, advantage, and accommodation of the defendants.

On February 5, 1997, Curly was arraigned and entered not guilty pleas to all fifty-two counts in the indictment. On August 8, 1997, Curly changed his plea. Specifically, Curly pled guilty to all fifty-two counts of the indictment in exchange for the United States' promise that it would not seek an enhanced penalty under 18 U.S.C. § 2326. Though the United States agreed to an acceptance of responsibility reduction if Curly continued to cooperate with the government's investigation and prosecution, the United States reserved its right to recommend that Curly be sentenced at the high end of the sentencing guideline range.

On or about October 22, 1997, Curly's Presentence Investigation Report was filed in district court. In it, the probation officer recommended a 70-87 month term of imprisonment (adjusted offense level 20; criminal history category VI) and a two to three year term of supervised release. The probation officer also suggested that Curly make restitution to the victims of his crimes.

On November 10, 1997, Curly filed his objections to the Presentence Investigation Report. Specifically, Curly objected to the two-level vulnerable victim enhancement under U.S.S.G. § 3A1.1(b). The probation officer rejected Curly's objections.

On November 14, 1997, the district court sentenced Curly to concurrent 60-month terms of imprisonment (Counts 1 through 26), and concurrent 27-month terms of imprisonment (Counts 27 through 52), the concurrent terms to run consecutively. Accordingly, the district court sentenced Curly to 87 months' imprisonment, to be followed by a three-year term of supervised release, and ordered Curly to pay restitution in the amount of $1,121,811.80. Curly thereafter filed his timely notice of appeal. On appeal, Curly challenges the applicability of U.S.S.G. § 3A1.1(b)'s vulnerable victim enhancement.

II.

Standard of Review

"This court applies a clearly erroneous standard of review to the district court's factual findings, and, while giving due deference to the district court's application of the guidelines to those facts, it renders de novo review of the district court's legal conclusions." *United States v. Smith*, 39 F.3d 119, 122 (6th Cir. 1994).

The Applicability of U.S.S.G. § 3A1.1(b) to Curly's Criminal Conduct

On appeal, Curly asserts that the district court should have required the prosecution to establish that he intentionally selected or targeted victims due to an unusual vulnerability that he knew or should have known about. In response, the United States asserts that the district court properly applied the vulnerable victim enhancement provision simply by requiring proof that Curly knew or should have known of the victims' vulnerabilities.

Section 3A1.1(b) (as amended November 1, 1995) provides: "If the defendant knew or should have known that a victim of the offense was unusually vulnerable due to age, physical or mental condition, or that a victim was otherwise particularly susceptible to the criminal conduct, increase by 2 levels." United States

Sentencing Commission, Guidelines Manual, § 3A1.1(b) (Nov. 1997). Prior to November 1, 1995, the commentary following section 3A1.1 provided:

> This adjustment applies to offenses where an unusually vulnerable victim is made a target of criminal activity by the defendant. The adjustment would apply, for example, in a fraud case where the defendant marketed an ineffective cancer cure or in a robbery where the defendant selected a handicapped victim. But it would not apply in a case where the defendant sold fraudulent securities by mail to the general public and one of the victims happened to be senile. Similarly, for example, a bank teller is not an unusually vulnerable victim solely by virtue of the teller's position in a bank. U.S.S.G. § 3A1.1, comment. (Nov. 1994).

In an effort to resolve the inconsistent application of section 3A1.1(b), the United States Sentencing Commission deleted the "targeting" language from the commentary following section 3A1.1 on November 1, 1995. The revised commentary states that the vulnerable victim provision "applies to offenses involving an unusually vulnerable victim in which the defendant knows or should have known of the victim's unusual vulnerability." U.S.S.G. § 3A1.1, comment. (Nov. 1995). Accordingly, most courts eliminated the "targeting" element for sentencing enhancement purposes and simply require that the defendant knew of the victims' vulnerabilities. *See, e.g., United States v. Burgos*, 137 F.3d 841, 843 (5th Cir. 1998) (the applicability of section 3A1.1(b)'s vulnerable victim enhancement does not require proof of "targeting"). . . . Because section 3A1.1 no longer requires proof of "targeting" in light of the November 1, 1995 amendments to the sentencing guidelines, this court's 1994 decision requiring proof of "targeting" is no longer good law. *See United States v. Smith*, 39 F.3d at 124 ("We think that those courts that apply the victim vulnerability provision when evidence shows that the defendant targeted his victims because of an unusual vulnerability have captured the intended meaning of the guidelines.").

In this action, United States Postal Inspector Gregory Caouette testified that 22 of Curly's 24 victims were individuals in their late 70s and early 80s. Because many of the victims in this action made multiple investments with Curly over a period of years, Curly's claim that he did not know his victims' ages and vulnerabilities is suspect. Indeed, Curly's coconspirator, Kenneth Baker, previously victimized one of the elderly investors in an earlier fraudulent telemarketing scheme. By passing 18 U.S.C. § 2326, Congress recognized that older individuals are particularly susceptible to fraudulent telemarketing investment schemes like the one committed in this action by Raymond Curly.

The district court rejected Curly's arguments and imposed the vulnerable victim enhancement because of the victims' ages and vulnerabilities, and Curly's repeated efforts to compel the victims to invest their life savings in his bogus investment scheme. Because the district court properly imposed section 3A1.1(b)'s vulnerable victim enhancement provision, we reject Curly's assignment of error.

Accordingly, we AFFIRM the district court's sentencing determinations.

QUESTIONS

The penalty enhancement provisions of the Federal Sentencing Guidelines for "vulnerable" victims have been emulated in many states. In addition, as noted in the general readings, many states have enacted laws that increase penalties when the victim is elderly, or allow the recovery of double or treble damages. Are such laws "ageist" or overly paternalistic?

FURTHER READING. Alison Barnes et al., COUNSELING OLDER CLIENTS ch. 27 (1997); Winsor C. Schmidt Jr., GUARDIANSHIP: THE COURT OF LAST RESORT FOR THE ELDERLY AND DISABLED (1995); Peter J. Strauss & Nancy M. Lederman, THE ELDER LAW HANDBOOK ch. 13 (1996); Peter J. Strauss et al., AGING AND THE LAW, chs. 20, 21 (1996).

Chapter 8

HEALTH CARE

In this chapter, we examine a range of medical issues confronting the elderly. We begin, in Part A, with a brief overview of the health-care system in the United States. In Part B, we evaluate the mechanisms, both governmental and private, by which elderly persons can manage and pay for their medical needs.

A. THE U.S. HEALTH-CARE SYSTEM: AN OVERVIEW

BRIEF SUMMARIES OF MEDICARE & MEDICAID:
Title XVIII and Title XIX of The Social Security Act
as of November 1, 2005
http://new.cms.hhs.gov/MedicareProgramRatesStats/downloads/
MedicareMedicaidSummaries2005.pdf

Since early in this century, health care issues have continued to escalate in importance for our Nation. Beginning in 1915, various efforts to establish government health insurance programs have been initiated every few years. From the 1930s on, there was agreement on the real need for some form of health insurance to alleviate the unpredictable and uneven incidence of medical costs. The main health care issue at that time was whether health insurance should be privately or publicly financed.

Private health insurance coverage expanded rapidly during World War II, when fringe benefits were increased to compensate for government limits on direct wage increases. This trend continued after the war, in part due to the favorable tax treatment of providing compensation in the form of fringe benefits. Private health insurance (mostly group insurance financed through the employment relationship) was especially needed and wanted by middle-income people. Yet not everyone could obtain or afford private health insurance. Government involvement was sought. Various national health insurance plans, financed by payroll taxes, were proposed in Congress starting in the 1940s; however, none was ever brought to a vote.

In 1950, Congress acted to improve access to medical care for needy persons who were receiving public assistance. This permitted, for the first time, Federal participation in the financing of State payments to the providers of medical care for costs incurred by public assistance recipients. In 1960, the Kerr-Mills bill provided medical assistance for aged persons who were not so poor, yet still needed assistance with medical expenses. But a more comprehensive improvement in the provision of medical care, especially for the elderly, became a major congressional priority.

After consideration of various approaches, and after lengthy national debate, Congress passed legislation in 1965 establishing the Medicare and the Medicaid programs as Title XVIII and Title XIX of the Social Security Act. Medicare was established in response to the specific medical care needs of the elderly (and in 1973, the severely disabled and certain persons with kidney disease). (The recent Medicare Prescript Drug, Improvement, and Modernization Act (MMA) of 2003 (Public Law 108-173) introduced the most sweeping changes to the program since its enactment. The most significant change is that, beginning in 2006, the MMA establishes the new Medicare prescription drug benefit.) Medicaid was established in response to the widely perceived inadequacy of welfare medical care under public assistance.

Responsibility for administering the Medicare and Medicaid programs was entrusted to the Department of Health and Human Services (DHHS). In 1977, the Health Care Financing Administration (HCFA) was established under the Department of Health and Human Services to administer the Medicare and Medicaid programs, renamed in 2001 to the Centers for Medicare & Medicaid Services (CMS).

NATIONAL HEALTH CARE EXPENDITURES

Historical Overview

Health spending in the United States has brown rapidly over the past few decades. From $27 billion in 1960, it grew to $888 billion in 1993, increasing at an average rate of more than 11 percent annually. This strong growth boosted health care's role in the overall economy, with health expenditures rising from 5.1 percent to 13.4 percent of the gross domestic product (GDP) between 1960 and 1993.

Between 1993 and 1999, however, strong growth trends in health care spending subsided. Over this period health spending rose at a 5-percent average annual rate to reach $1.2 trillion in 1999. The share of GDP going to health care stabilized, with the 1999 share measured at 13.2 percent. This stabilization reflected the nexus of several factors: then movement of most workers insured for health care through employer-sponsored plans to lover-cost managed care; low general and medical-specific inflation; excess capacity among some health service provider, which boosted competition and drove down prices; and GDP growth that matched slow health spending growth.

Between 2000 and 2002, growth picked up again, increasing 7.0 percent in 2000, 8.9 percent in 2001, and 9.3 percent in 2002. Health spending as a share of GDP increased sharply from 13.3. percent in 2000 to 15.3 percent in 2003, as strong growth in health spending outpaced economy-wide growth. For the 296 million people residing in the United States, the average expenditure for health care in 2003 was $5,670 per person.

Health care is funded through a variety of private payers and public programs. Private funds include individuals' out-of-pocket expenditures, private health insurance, philanthropy and non-patient revenues (e.g., gift shops, parking lots, etc.), as well as health services that are provided in industrial settings. For the years 1974 through 1991, these private funds paid for 57 to 60 percent of all health care costs. By 1996, however, the private share of health expenditures had dropped to 54 percent of the country's total health care expenditures due primarily to the falling share of out-of-pocket spending, and remained relatively stable at 54-55 percent between 1996 and 2003. The share of health care provided by public spending increased correspondingly during the 1992-1996 period and stabilized during the period 1997-2003.

Public spending represents expenditures by Federal, State, and local governments. Of the publicly funded health care expenditures for our Nation, each of the following account for a small percentage of the total: the Department of Defense health care programs for military personnel; the Department of Veterans Affairs health programs; non-commercial medical research; payments for health care under Workers Compensation programs; health programs under State-only general assistance programs; and the construction of public medical facilities. Other activities which are also publicly funded include: maternal and child health services; school health programs; public health clinics; Indian health care services; migrant health care services; substance abuse and mental health activities; and medically-related vocational rehabilitation services. The largest shares of public health expenditures, however, are made by the programs run by CMS — Medicare, Medicaid, and the State Children's Health Insurance Program (SCHIP).

Together, Medicare, Medicaid, and SCHIP financed $557 billion in health care services in 2003 — one-third of the country's total health care bill and almost three-fourths of all public spending on health care. Since their enactment, both Medicare and Medicaid have been subject to numerous legislative and administrative changes designed to make improvements, with financial considerations, in the provision of health care services to our nation's aged, disabled and disadvantaged.

QUESTIONS

Do you agree that government involvement in the provision of health care is appropriate? Why or why not?

B. MANAGING AND PAYING FOR HEALTH CARE

1. Medicare

Social Security Board of Trustees,
A Summary of the 2006 Reports
May 2, 2006
http://www.ssa.gov/OACT/TRSUM/trsummary.html

The fundamentals of the financial status of Social Security and Medicare remain problematic under the intermediate economic and demographic assumptions. Social Security's current annual surpluses of tax income over expenditures will soon begin to decline, and will be followed by deficits that begin to grow rapidly toward the end of the next decade as the baby-boom generation retires. Expenditures of Medicare's Hospital Insurance (HI) Trust Fund that pays hospital benefits are projected to exceed taxes and other dedicated revenues in 2006, with annual cash flow deficits expected to continue and to grow rapidly after 2010 as baby boomers begin to retire. The projected growing deficits in both programs will exhaust HI trust fund reserves in 2018 and Social Security reserves in 2040, under current financing arrangements. In addition, the Medicare Supplementary Medical Insurance (SMI) Trust Fund that pays for physician services and the new prescription drug benefit will require substantial increases over time in both general revenue financing and beneficiary premium charges. As Social Security and HI reserves are drawn down and SMI general revenue financing requirements continue to grow, pressure on the Federal budget will intensify. We do not believe the currently projected long-run growth rates of Social Security or Medicare are sustainable under current financing arrangements.

* * *

Medicare

As we reported last year, Medicare's financial difficulties come sooner — and are much more severe — than those confronting Social Security. While both programs face demographic challenges, the impact is more severe for Medicare because health care costs increase at older ages. Moreover, underlying health care costs per enrollee are projected to rise faster than the wages per worker on which the payroll tax is paid and on which Social Security benefits are based. As a result, while Medicare's annual costs were 2.7 percent of GDP in 2005, or over 60 percent of Social Security's, they are now projected to surpass Social Security expenditures in a little more than 20 years and reach 11 percent of GDP in 2080.

The projected 75-year actuarial deficit in the HI Trust Fund is now 3.51 percent of taxable payroll, up from 3.09 percent in last year's report due primarily to greater costs in 2005 than expected, changes in managed care assumptions, advancing the projection period, and more recent data that suggests higher utilization of health services in the future. The fund again fails our test of short-range financial adequacy, as assets drop below the level of the next year's projected expenditures within 10 years — in 2012. The fund also continues to fail our long-range test of close actuarial balance by a wide margin. The projected date of HI Trust Fund exhaustion moves forward to 2018, from 2020 in last year's report, and projected HI tax income falls short of outlays in this and all future years. HI could be brought into actuarial balance over the next 75 years by an immediate 121 percent increase in program income, or an immediate 51 percent reduction in program outlays (or some combination of the two). As with Social Security, however, adjustments of far greater magnitude would be necessary to the extent changes are delayed or phased in gradually, or to make the program solvent on a sustainable basis over the next 75 years and beyond.

Part B of the SMI Trust Fund, which pays doctors' bills and other outpatient expenses, and the recent Part D, which pays for access to prescription drug coverage, are both projected to remain adequately financed into the indefinite future by operation of current law that automatically sets financing each year to meet next year's expected costs. Expected rapid cost increases, however, will result in rapidly growing general revenue financing needs — projected to rise from just under 1 percent of GDP today to almost 5.0 percent in 2080 — as well as substantial increases over time in beneficiary premium charges.

The Medicare Modernization Act of 2003 requires that the Medicare Report include a determination of whether the difference between total Medicare outlays and dedicated financing sources (such as premiums and payroll taxes) exceeds 45 percent of total outlays within the first seven years of the projection period (2006-2012 for the 2006 Report). The Act requires that an affirmative determination in two consecutive reports be treated as a funding warning for Medicare that would, in turn, require a Presidential proposal to respond to the warning and expedited Congressional consideration of such proposal. The 2006 Report projects that the difference will reach 45 percent in 2012, marking the first time a determination of "excess general revenue Medicare funding" has been made. A similar determination in next year's report would trigger the Medicare funding warning.

Conclusion

Though highly challenging, the financial difficulties facing Social Security and Medicare are not insurmountable. We must, however, take action to address them in a timely manner. The sooner these challenges are addressed, the more varied and less disruptive their solutions can be. With informed public discussion and creative thinking that relates the principles underlying these programs to the economic and demographic realities, and to the changing needs and preferences of working and retired households, Social Security and Medicare can continue to play a critical role in the lives of all Americans.

BRIEF SUMMARIES OF MEDICARE & MEDICAID:
Title XVIII and Title XIX of The Social Security Act
as of November 1, 2005

http://new.cms.hhs.gov/MedicareProgramRatesStats/downloads/
MedicareMedicaidSummaries2005.pdf

DATA SUMMARY

The Medicare program covers 95 percent of our nation's aged population, as well as many people who are on Social Security because of disability. In 2004, Part A covered about 41 million enrollees with benefit payments of $167.6 billion, and Part B covered about 39 million enrollees with benefit payments of $135.4 billion. Administrative costs in 2004 were under 1.8 percent of disbursements for Part A and under 2.1 percent of disbursements for Part B. Total disbursements for Medicare in 2004 were $308.9 billion.

* * *

PROGRAM FINANCING, BENEFICIARY LIABILITIES, & PAYMENTS TO PROVIDERS

All financial operations for Medicare are handled through two trust funds, one for Health Insurance (Part A) and one for Supplemental Medical Insurance (Parts B and D). These trust funds, which are special accounts in the U.S. Treasury, are credited with all receipts and charged with all expenditures for benefits and administrative costs. The trust funds cannot be used for any other purpose. Assets not needed for the payment of costs are invested in special Treasury securities. The following sections describe Medicare's financing provisions, beneficiary cost-sharing requirements, and the basis for determining Medicare reimbursements to health care providers.

Program Financing

The HI trust fund is financed primarily through a mandatory payroll tax. Almost all employees and self-employed workers in the United States work in employment covered by Part A and pay taxes to support the cost of benefits for aged and disabled beneficiaries. The Part A tax rate is 1.45 percent of earnings, to be paid by each employee and a matching amount by the employer for each employee, and 2.90 percent for self-employed persons. Beginning in 1994, this tax is paid on all covered wages and self-employment income without limit. (Prior to 1994, the tax applied only up to a specified maximum amount of earnings.) The Part A tax rate is specified in the Social Security Act and cannot be changed without legislation.

Part A also receives income from the following sources: (1) a portion of the income taxes levied on Social Security benefits paid to high-income beneficiaries; (2) premiums from certain persons who are not otherwise eligible and choose to enroll voluntarily; (3) reimbursements from the general fund of the U.S. Treasury for the cost of providing Part A coverage to certain aged persons who retired when Part A began and thus were unable to earn sufficient quarters of coverage (and those Federal retirees similarly unable to earn sufficient quarters of Medicare-qualified Federal employment); (4) interest earnings on its invested assets; and (5) other small miscellaneous income sources. The taxes paid each year are used mainly to pay benefits for current beneficiaries.

The SMI trust fund differs fundamentally from the HI trust fund with regard to the nature of its financing. As previously noted, SMI is now composed of two parts, Part B and Part D, each with its own separate account within the SMI trust fund. The nature of the financing for both parts of SMI is similar, in that both parts are primarily financed by beneficiary premiums and contributions from the general fund of the U.S. Treasury.

Part B is financed through premium payments ($93.50 per beneficiary per month in 2007) and contributions from the general fund of the U.S. Treasury. (Penalties for late enrollment may apply.) Beneficiary premiums are generally set at a level that covers 25 percent of the average expenditures for aged beneficiaries. Therefore, the contributions from the general fund of the U.S. Treasury are the largest source of Part B income.

Similarly, Part D [is] . . . financed primarily through premium payments and contributions from the general fund of the U S. Treasury, with general fund contributions accounting for the largest source of Part D income, since beneficiary premiums are to represent, on average, 25.5 percent of the cost of standard coverage. . . . The premiums and general fund contributions for Part D will be determined separately from those for Part B. (In 2004 and 2005, the general fund of the U.S. Treasury financed the transitional assistance benefit for low-income beneficiaries by providing funds to a Transitional Assistance account within the SMI trust fund. The proceeds were transferred to the Part D account at the conclusion of the temporary program.)

* * *

Beneficiary Payment Liabilities

Fee-for-service beneficiaries are responsible for charges not covered by the Medicare program and for various cost-sharing aspects of both Part A and Part B. These liabilities may be paid (1) by the Medicare beneficiary; (2) by a third party, such as an employer-sponsored retiree health plan or private "Medigap" insurance; or (3) by Medicaid, if the person is eligible. The term "Medigap" is used to mean private health insurance that pays, within limits, most of the health care service charges not covered by Parts A or B of Medicare. These policies, which must meet federally imposed standards, are offered by Blue Cross and Blue Shield and various commercial health insurance companies.

For beneficiaries enrolled in Medicare Advantage plans, the beneficiary's payment share is based on the cost-sharing structure of the specific plan selected by the beneficiary, since each plan has its own requirements. Most plans have lower deductibles and coinsurance than are required of fee-for-service beneficiaries. Such beneficiaries pay the monthly Part B premium and may, depending on the plan, pay an additional plan premium.

For hospital care covered under Part A, a fee-for-service beneficiary's payment share includes a one-time deductible amount at the beginning of each benefit period ($992 in 2007). This deductible covers the beneficiary's part of the first 60 days of each spell of inpatient hospital care. If continued inpatient care is needed beyond the 60 days, additional coinsurance payments ($248 per day in 2007) are required through the 90th day of a benefit period. Each Part A beneficiary also has a "lifetime reserve" of 60 additional hospital days that may be used when the covered days within a benefit period have been exhausted. Lifetime reserve days may be used only once, and coinsurance payments ($496 per day in 2007) are required.

For skilled nursing care covered under Part A, Medicare fully covers the first 20 days of skilled nursing facility care in a benefit period. But for days 21-100, a copayment ($124 per day in 2007) is required from the beneficiary. After 100 days of skilled care per benefit period, Medicare pays nothing for nursing facility care. Home health care has no deductible or coinsurance payment by the beneficiary. In any Part A service, the beneficiary is responsible for fees to cover the first 3 pints or units of non-replaced blood per calendar year. The beneficiary has the option of paying the fee or of having the blood replaced.

There are no premiums for most people covered by Part A. Eligibility is generally earned through the work experience of the beneficiary or of his or her spouse. However, most aged people who are otherwise ineligible for premium-free Part A coverage can enroll voluntarily by paying a monthly premium, if they also enroll in Part B. For people with fewer than 30 quarters of coverage as defined by the Social Security Administration (SSA), the 2007 Part A monthly premium rate is $410; for those with 30 to 39 quarters of coverage, the rate is reduced to $226. Voluntary coverage upon payment of the Part A premium, with or without enrolling in Part B, is also available to disabled individuals for whom cash benefits have ceased due to earnings in excess of those allowed for receiving cash benefits. (Penalties for late enrollment may apply.)

For Part B, the beneficiary's payment share includes the following: one annual deductible ($131 in 2007); the monthly premiums; the coinsurance payments for Part B services (usually 20 percent of the medically allowed charges); a deductible for blood; certain charges above the Medicare-allowed charge (for claims not on assignment); and payment for any services that are not covered by Medicare. For outpatient mental health treatment services, the beneficiary is liable for 50 percent of the approved charges.

ENTITLEMENT AND COVERAGE

* * *

It should be noted that some health care services are not provided under any part of Title XVIII. Non-covered services under Medicare include long term nursing care or custodial care, and certain other health care needs — such as dentures and dental care, eyeglasses, hearing aids, most prescription drugs, etc. These are not a part of the Medicare program unless they are a part of a private health plan under the Medicare Advantage program.

Provider Payments

For Part A, before 1983, payments to providers were made on a reasonable cost basis. Medicare payments for most inpatient hospital services are now made under a reimbursement mechanism known as the prospective payment system (PPS). Under PPS, a specific predetermined amount is paid for each inpatient hospital stay, based on each stay's diagnosis-related group (DRG) classification. In some cases the payment the hospital receives is less than the hospital's actual cost for providing the Part A-covered inpatient hospital services for the stay; in other cases it is more. The hospital absorbs the loss or makes a profit. Certain payment adjustments exist for extraordinarily costly inpatient hospital stays. Payments for skilled nursing care, home health care, inpatient rehabilitation, and long-term hospital care are made under separate prospective payment systems. Payments for psychiatric hospital care are currently reimbursed on a reasonable cost basis, but a prospective payment system is expected to be implemented in the near future, as required by the BBA.

For Part B, before 1992, physicians were paid on the basis of reasonable charge. This amount was initially defined as the lowest of (1) the physician's actual charge; (2) the physician's customary charge; or (3) the prevailing charge for similar services in that locality. Beginning January 1992, allowed charges were defined as the lesser of (1) the submitted charges, or (2) the amount determined by a fee schedule based on a relative value scale (RVS). Payments for DME and clinical laboratory services are also based on a fee schedule. Most hospital outpatient services are reimbursed on a prospective payment system, and home health care is reimbursed under the same prospective payment system as Part A.

If a doctor or supplier agrees to accept the Medicare-approved rate as payment in full ("takes assignment"), then payments provided must be considered as payments in full for that service. The provider may not request any added payments (beyond the initial annual deductible and coinsurance) from the beneficiary or insurer. If the provider does not take assignment, the beneficiary will be charged for the excess (which may be paid by Medigap insurance). Limits now exist on the excess that doctors or suppliers can charge. Physicians are "participating physicians" if they agree before the beginning of the year to accept assignment for all Medicare services they furnish during the year. Since Medicare beneficiaries may select their doctors, they have the option to choose those who participate.

Medicare payments to Medicare Advantage plans are based on a blend of local and national capitated rates, generally determined by the capitation payment methodology described in section 1853 of the Social Security Act. Actual payments to plans vary based on demographic characteristics of the enrolled population. New "risk adjusters" based on demographics and health status are currently being phased in to better match Medicare capitation payments to the expected costs of individual beneficiaries. As previously mentioned, the Medicare Advantage program will undergo changes beginning in 2006. Plan bids will be replacing the current payment structure for Medicare Advantage plans.

For Part D, in 2006 and later, PDPs (including the prescription drug portion of Medicare Advantage plans) will pay for most FDA-approved prescription drugs and biologicals under the benefit structure described in the previous section. Plans may set up formularies for their prescription drug coverage, subject to statutory standards.

* * *

Administration

The Department of Health and Human Services has the overall responsibility for administration of the Medicare program. Within the Department, responsibility for administering Medicare rests with CMS. SSA assists, however, by initially determining an individual's Medicare entitlement, by withholding Part B [and Part D] premiums . . . from the Social Security benefit checks of beneficiaries, and by maintaining Medicare data on the master beneficiary record, which is SSA's primary record of beneficiaries. The Internal Revenue Service in the Department of the Treasury collects the Part A payroll taxes from workers and their employers.

* * *

a. Traditional Fee-for-Service

OVERVIEW

Title XVIII of the Social Security Act, designated "Health Insurance for the Aged and Disabled," is commonly known as Medicare. As part of the Social Security Amendments of 1965, the Medicare legislation established a health insurance program for aged persons to complement the retirement, survivors and disability insurance benefits under Title II of the Social Security Act.

When first implemented in 1966, Medicare covered most persons age 65 and over. In 1973, the following groups also became eligible for Medicare benefits: persons entitled to Social Security or Railroad Retirement disability cash benefits for at least 24 months; persons with end-stage renal disease (ESRD) requiring continuing dialysis or kidney transplant; and certain otherwise non-covered aged persons who elect to pay a premium for Medicare coverage [$410 per month in 2007]. The Medicare, Medicaid, and SCHIP Benefits Improvement and Protection Act of 2000 (Public Law 106-554) allowed persons with Amyotrophic Lateral Sclerosis (Lou Gehrig's Disease) to waive the 24-month waiting period.

Medicare has traditionally consisted of two parts: Hospital Insurance (HI), also known as Part A, and Supplementary Medical insurance (SMI), also known as Part B. . . .

When Medicare began on July 1, 1966, approximately 19 million people enrolled. In 2005, over 42 million people are enrolled in one or both of Parts A and B of the Medicare program . . . .

ENTITLEMENT AND COVERAGE

Part A (HI) is generally provided automatically, and free of premiums, to persons age 65 and over who are entitled to Social Security or Railroad Retirement Board benefits, whether they have claimed these monthly cash benefits or not. Also, workers and their spouses with a sufficient period of Medicare-only coverage in Federal, State, or local government employment are eligible beginning at age 65. Similarly, individuals who have been entitled to Social Security or Railroad Retirement disability benefits for at least 24 months, and government employees with Medicare-only coverage who have been disabled for more than 29 months, are entitled to Part A benefits. . . . In 2004, Part A provided protection against the costs of hospital and specific other medical care to about 419 million people (35 million aged and 6 million disabled enrollees). Part A benefit payments totaled $167.6 billion in 2004.

* * *

Medicare and You
A handbook published for consumers by the Centers for Medicare and Medicaid Services

Medicare is a Health Insurance Program for:

- People 65 years of age and older;

- Certain younger people with disabilities;

- People with End-Stage Renal Disease (people with permanent kidney failure who need dialysis or a transplant).

* * *

What is the Original Medicare Plan?

The Original Medicare Plan is the traditional pay-per-visit arrangement. You can go to any doctor, hospital, or other health care provider who accepts Medicare. You must pay the deductible. Then Medicare pays its share, and you pay your share (coinsurance). The Original Medicare Plan has two parts: Part A (Hospital Insurance) and Part B (Medical Insurance). If you are in the Original Medicare Plan now, the way you receive your health care will not change unless you enroll in another Medicare health plan.

* * *

What is Part A (Hospital Insurance)?

Part A (Hospital Insurance) helps pay for care in hospitals and skilled nursing facilities, and for home health and hospice care. If you are eligible, Part A is premium free — that is, you don't pay a premium because you or your spouse paid Medicare taxes while you were working. Your Fiscal Intermediary can answer your questions on what Part A services Medicare will pay for and how much will be paid. You are eligible for premium-free Medicare Part A (Hospital Insurance) if:

- You are 65 or older. You are receiving or eligible for retirement benefits from Social Security or the Railroad Retirement Board, or

- You are under 65. You have received Social Security disability benefits for 24 months, or

- You are under 65. You have received Railroad Retirement disability benefits for the prescribed time and you meet the Social Security Act disability requirements, or

- You or your spouse had Medicare-covered government employment, or

- You are under 65 and have End-Stage Renal Disease.

If you don't qualify for premium-free Part A, and you are 65 or older, you may be able to buy it. (Contact Social Security Administration).

* * *

What is Part B (Medical Insurance)?

Part B (Medical Insurance) helps pay for doctors, outpatient hospital care and some other medical services that Part A doesn't cover, such as the services of physical and occupational therapists. Part B covers all doctor services that are medically necessary. Beneficiaries may receive these services anywhere (a doctor's office, clinic, nursing home, hospital, or at home). Your Medicare carrier can answer QUESTIONS about Part B services and coverage. You are automatically eligible for Part B if you are eligible for premium-free Part A. You are also eligible if you are a United States citizen or permanent resident age 65 or older. Part B cost $93.50 per month in 2007. Part B is voluntary. If you choose to have Part B, the monthly premium is deducted from your Social Security, Railroad Retirement, or Civil Service Retirement payment. Beneficiaries who do not receive any of the above payments are billed by Medicare every 3 months.

If you didn't take Part B when you were first eligible, you can sign-up during 2 enrollment periods:

General Enrollment Period: If you didn't take Part B, you can only sign up during the general enrollment period, January 1 through March 31 of each year. Your Part B coverage is effective July 1. Your monthly Part B premium may be higher. The Part B premium increases 10% for each 12-month period that you could have had Part B but did not take it.

Special Enrollment Period: If you didn't take Part B because you or your spouse currently work and have group health plan coverage through your current employer or union, you can sign up for Part B during the special enrollment period. Under the special enrollment period, you can sign up at any time you are covered under the group plan. In addition, if the employment or group health coverage ends, you have 8 months to sign up. The 8-month period starts the month after the employment ends or the group health coverage ends, whichever comes first. Generally, your monthly Part B premium is not increased when you sign up for Part B during the special enrollment period.

* * *

What Are Your Out-of-Pocket Costs?

The Original Medicare Plan pays for much of your health care, but not all of it. Your out-of-pocket costs for health care will include your monthly Part B premium [$93.50 per month in 2007]. In addition, when you get health care services, you will also have to pay deductibles [Part A annual deductible is $992, and Part B deductible is $131 in 2007] and coinsurance or copayments. Generally, you will pay for your outpatient prescription drugs. You also pay for routine physicals, custodial care, most dental care, dentures, routine foot care, or hearing aids. Physical therapy and occupational therapy services, except for those you get in hospital outpatient departments, are subject to annual limits. The Original Medicare Plan does pay for some preventive care, but not all of it.

Your Out-of-Pocket Costs May Depend On:

- Whether your doctor accepts assignment.

- How often you need health care.

- What type of health care you need.

QUESTIONS

1. Would you characterize the traditional fee-for-service Medicare program as an insurance program or a public benefits program?

2. What significant gaps in coverage can you identify?

b. Medicare Managed Care

BRIEF SUMMARIES OF MEDICARE & MEDICAID: Title XVIII and Title XIX of The Social Security Act as of November 1, 2005
http://new.cms.hhs.gov/MedicareProgramRatesStats/downloads/
MedicareMedicaid Summaries2005.pdf

OVERVIEW OF MEDICARE

* * *

Medicare has traditionally consisted of two parts: Hospital Insurance (HI), also known as Part A, and Supplementary Medical insurance (SMI), also known as Part B. A third part of Medicare, sometimes known as Part C, is the Medicare Advantage program, which was established as the Medicare+Choice program by the Balanced Budget Act of 1997 (Public Law. 105-33) and subsequently renamed and modified by the Medicare Prescription Drug, Improvement, and Modernization Act (MMA) of 2003 (Public Law 108-173). The Medicare advantage program expands beneficiaries' option for participation in private-sector health care plans.

* * *

When Medicare began on July 1, 1966, approximately 19 million people enrolled. In 2005, over 42 million people are enrolled in one or both of Parts A and B of the Medicare program, and about 5 million of them have chosen to participate in a Medicare Advantage plan.

ENTITLEMENT AND COVERAGE

* * *

Medicare Advantage (Part C) is an expanded set of options for the delivery of health care under Medicare. While all Medicare beneficiaries can receive their benefits through the original fee-for-service program, most beneficiaries enrolled in both Part A and Part B can choose to participate in a Medicare Advantage plan instead. Organizations that seek to contract as Medicare Advantage plans will have to meet specific organizational, financial, and other requirements. Following are the primary Medicare Advantage plans:

- Coordinated care plans, which includes health maintenance organizations (HMOs), provider-sponsored organizations (PSOs) preferred provider organizations (PPOs), and other certified coordinated care plans and entities that meet the standards set forth in the law.

- The private, unrestricted fee-for-service plans, which allow beneficiaries to select certain private providers. For those providers who agree to accept the plan's payment terms and conditions, this option does not place the providers at risk, nor vary payment rates based upon utilization.

These Medicare Advantage plans are required to provide the current Medicare benefit package, excluding hospice services. Plans may offer additional covered services and are required to do so (or return excess payments) if plan costs are lower than the Medicare payments received by the plan.

* * *

It should be noted that some health care services are not provided under any part of Title XVIII. Non-covered services under Medicare include long term nursing care or custodial care, and certain other health care needs — such as dentures and dental care, eyeglasses, hearing aids, most prescription drugs, etc. These are not a part of the Medicare program unless they are a part of a private health plan under the Medicare Advantage program.

QUESTIONS

1. What concerns might motivate someone to go outside the "Original" Medicare program?

2. What public policy concerns are implicated by the trend toward managed care?

2. Supplemental Health Insurance

a. "Medigap"

Kathy J. Greenlee
Medicare
KANSAS LONG-TERM CARE HANDBOOK 30-44
(KANSAS BAR ASS'N 2001)[*]

Medicare supplement insurance is designed to cover many, but not all, of the health care costs which are not paid by Medicare. Although Medicare is a federal program, Medicare supplement insurance is private health insurance and is regulated by the insurance department in each state. Medicare supplement insurance is called commonly referred to as "Medigap" insurance or Med-Sup" insurance. A specific definition of a Medicare supplement policy can be found at 42 U.S.C. § 1395ss(g)(1) . . .

* * *

The Omnibus Budget Reconciliation Act of 1990 defines ten standard Medicare supplement plans. Only these 10 plans may be sold in the United States. (42 U.S.C. § 1395ss(p)(2)) These plans are labeled with letters, A through J, and every company must use the same letter to label its plan. A company does not have to sell all 10 plans, but every Medicare supplement company must sell Plan A (basic Coverage). (42 U.S.C. § 1395ss(o)) The other none plans add different combinations of other benefits to Plan A's basic coverage. These benefits cannot be modified in any way. All 10 plans protect against catastrophic health care costs. The best plan for a particular individual depends on many factors, such as health care needs, type of benefits desired, and price.

* * *

All Medicare supplement policies must contain an identical set of basic benefits. (42 U.S.C. § 1395ss(o)) The plan which contains only these basic benefits is the first plan, Plan A. The following benefits are identical in all 10 plans:

1. Part A: Hospitalization (Per Benefit Period)

   - Days 61-90 Full coinsurance coverage.

   - Days 91-150: Full coinsurance coverage. These are known as "lifetime reserve days."

   - Beyond 150 days: 100% of all eligible Part A charges for 365 lifetime nonrenewable days.

   - First three pints of blood (Part A charges).

2. Part B: Medical Expenses (Per Calendar Year)

   - 20% Coinsurance after the [$131 in 2007] annual deductible.

---

[*] Copyright © 2001. Reprinted with permission.

- First three pints of blood (Part B charges).

3. Evaluating these Benefits. With just Basic Benefits, the insured person is protected against the costs of an extended hospital stay and physicians' services. However, deductibles, excess charges from non-participating physicians, and services not covered by Medicare are still the responsibility of the insured.

* * *

All Medicare supplement policies issued must be guaranteed renewable. This means that the company cannot cancel the policy, except for failure to pay premiums. (42 U.S.C. § 1395ss(q)(1))

* * *

A Medicare supplement policy is secondary to Medicare, which means it pays only after Medicare payments have been authorized. Most payments are tied solely to an eligible and approved Medicare charge. Commonly found exclusions are mental or emotional disorders, alcohol and drug addiction, cosmetic surgery, foot care, chiropractic or other care to correct spinal disorders, dental care, eyeglasses, hearing aids, eye exams, rest cures, custodial care, and routine physical exams.

* * *

Insurer must offer a six month open enrollment period to Medicare beneficiaries aged 65 and older. The six month period begins with the first month in which the beneficiary first enrolls in benefits under Medicare Part B. During this open enrollment period the insurance company must accept all individuals who apply. Insurers may apply waiting periods for pre-existing condition. For those persons who work past age 65 and delay enrolling in Medicare Part B, open enrollment starts when Part B coverage begins and continues for six months.

* * *

. . . Insurers that offer Medicare Supplement policies may accept new applications after the open enrollment period has expired. However, at that time, an insurer may reject an applicant based upon the applicant's health condition. As a person ages, they typically develop a more complicated health profile. A Medicare beneficiary is not required to purchase a Medicare supplement policy at the time they [sic] turn 65. If they wait, however, they run the risk of not being able to purchase a Medicare supplement policy in later years.

QUESTIONS

1. Why are Medigap policies limited in number and required to be standardized nationwide?

2. Why is the federal government so intimately involved in the regulation of acute care insurance products for the elderly, but not for other population groups and not for long-term health care insurance?

b. Medicare Prescription Drug Plans

BRIEF SUMMARIES OF MEDICARE & MEDICAID:
Title XVIII and Title XIX of The Social Security Act
as of November 1, 2005

http://new.cms.hhs.gov/MedicareProgramRatesStats/downloads/
MedicareMedicaid Summaries2005.pdf

OVERVIEW OF MEDICARE

* * *

The MMA also established a fourth part of Medicare: a new prescription drug benefit, also known as Part D, beginning in 2004. . . .

* * *

ENTITLEMENT AND COVERAGE

* * *

Beginning in 2006, Part D began providing subsidized access to prescription drug insurance coverage on a voluntary basis, upon payment of a premium, to individuals entitled to Part A or enrolled in Part B, with premium and cost-sharing subsidies for low-income enrollees. Beneficiaries may enroll in either a stand-along prescription drug plan (PDP) or an integrated Medicare Advantage plan that offers Part D coverage. . . .

Part D coverage includes most FDA-approved prescription drugs and biologicals. (The specific drugs currently covered in Parts A and B will remain covered there.) However, plans may set up formularies for their prescription drug coverage, subject to certain statutory standards. Part D coverage can consist of either standard coverage . . . or an alternative design that provides the same actuarial value (though the specific actuarial equivalence test leaves very little flexibility for plans to design alternative coverage). For an additional premium, plans may also offer supplemental coverage exceeding the value of basic coverage.

* * *

PROGRAM FINANCING, BENEFICIARY LIABILITIES,
AND PAYMENTS TO PROVIDERS

* * *

. . . for Part D, . . . general fund contributions will account for the largest source of income, since beneficiary premiums are to represent, on average, 25.5 percent of the cost of standard coverage. (As of this writing, it is estimated that the average standard premium for Part D will be $32.20 per beneficiary per month in 2006. The actual premium will vary according to the plan in which the beneficiary has enrolled. Penalties for late enrollment may apply. Certain low-income beneficiaries may pay a reduced or no premium.)

In addition to contributions from the general fund of the U.S. Treasury and beneficiary premiums, Part D will also receive payments from the States. With the availability of prescription drug coverage and low-income subsidies under Part D, Medicaid will not longer be primary payer for prescription drugs for Medicaid beneficiaries who also have Medicare, and States will be required to defray a portion of Part D expenditures for those beneficiaries.

* * *

For Part D, standard coverage is defined for 2006 as having a $250 deductible with 25 percent coinsurance (or other actuarially equivalent amounts) for drug costs above the deductible and below an initial coverage limit of $2,250. The beneficiary is then responsible for all costs until a $3,600 out-of-pocket limit is reached. [The so-called "doughnut hole." — Eds.] For higher costs, there is catastrophic coverage that requires enrollees to pay the greater of 5 percent coinsurance or a small copay ($2 for generic or preferred brands and $5 for any other drug). After 2006, these benefit parameters are indexed to the growth in per capita spending in Part D. Certain beneficiaries with low income and modest assets will be eligible for certain subsidies that reduce or eliminate their Part D cost-sharing requirements. In determining out-of-pocket costs, only those amounts actually paid by the enrollee or another individual (and not reimbursed through insurance) are counted. The exception to this provision is cost-sharing assistance from Medicare's low-income subsidies and from State Pharmacy Assistance programs. The monthly premiums required for Part D coverage are described in the previous section.

c. Long-Term Care Insurance

Most long-term care is provided by family members. But in situations where services must be purchased, the costs are paid largely out-of-pocket. Often people do not realize that Medicare covers only short-term nursing home care in a Medicare-certified nursing facility. The only type of care Medicare will pay for is "skilled" level of care (ongoing nursing or therapy care), even though most residents in a nursing home need only custodial level of care (periodic assistance with routine activities, such as bathing and dressing). Even when skilled care is needed, Medicare benefits go only to those people who have been hospitalized for three days prior to admission into the nursing home. In 1995, Medicare paid for only nine percent of national nursing home costs.

Medicare also pays for certain skilled care at home. Again, however, benefits are paid only under very stringent conditions that are very restrictive. For example, only about half of the home care agencies in this country are Medicare-certified. Also, Medicare reasons that if you need care every day then you should be cared for in a nursing home. So it only pays for intermittent care at home; yet you must be homebound.

A different program, Medicaid, pays for long-term care if individuals are poor. What often happens is that a person enters a nursing home, initially using personal funds to meet the cost. Then very quickly, their savings are exhausted, and their income is too low to meet the costs of care. When their economic situation falls below the means-tested eligibility levels for Medicaid, they can then apply for help from the government.

Each state is required to pay for nursing home care for individuals in their state who meet the Medicaid eligibility requirements. Currently Medicaid pays for approximately half of the nursing home expenses in the United States. The Medicaid program in many states also covers care at home, but states are not required to provide home care assistance through Medicaid. However, the home care eligibility requirements are sometimes more restrictive than the nursing home requirements. For this reason, Medicaid is not a major payer for care at home.

Since most of the persons needing long-term care receive that care at home, the major burden for care is left with family members, and typically when family can no longer provide the needed care at home the patient is moved to a nursing home to utilize Medicaid.

The federal Health Insurance Portability and Accountability Act (Act) became effective on January 1, 1997. This Act has for the first time established federal guidelines for long-term care insurance by offering limited tax incentives to policy holders that purchase "qualified plans." Plans are considered to be "qualified" if they meet specific consumer standards when purchased after January 1, 1997. Policies purchased before January 1, 1997 are grandfathered and are also considered to be "qualified."

This Act provides three limited tax incentives for individuals.

13. First it clarifies that any benefits from a "qualified" plan would not be subject to federal income taxes.

14. Second you can deduct any unreimbursed long-term care expenses along with any other unreimbursed medical expenses that are greater than 7.5% of your adjusted gross income.

15. Third you can deduct a portion of your long-term care premiums for a "qualified" plan, based upon your age, if you have unreimbursed medical expenses greater than 7.5% of your adjusted gross income.

The 2007 deductibility limits are: Age 40 or younger — $290; Age 41 to 50 — $550; Age 51 to 60 — $1,110; Age 61 to 70 — $2,950; and Age 71 or more — $3,680. Since very few individuals have unreimbursed medical expenses above 7.5% of their adjusted gross income, however, most people will not be able to use these tax incentives. In addition, the Act requires "qualified" long-term care insurance plans to meet many of the National Association of Insurance Commissioners consumer protection standards.

On February 8, 2006, President Bush signed "The Deficit Reduction Act of 2005" (DRA) into law [2005 PL 109-171 (S. 1932)], and § 6021 of the Act contains significant enhancements to incentives for the purchase of long-term care insurance. The long-term care insurance policy must be "qualified" pursuant to the Internal Revenue Code [I.R.C. §7702B(b)], and it must include most of the requirements of the long-term care insurance model Act as promulgated by the National Association of Insurance Commissioners (as adopted as of October

2000). The DRA requires that a Medicaid estate recovery claim will be offset — dollar-for-dollar — to the extent that qualified long-term care insurance benefits have offset Medicaid payments.

Aging Internet Information Notes: Long Term Care Insurance
http://www.aoa.gov/naic/longterminsurance.html

Public policy interest in long-term care insurance has steadily increased in response to the rising costs of in-home and institutional care. Currently two-thirds of all nursing home residents are supported through Medicaid with less than 3% of total nursing home expenditures paid by long term care insurance. With the increased costs of long term care in institutional, community and in-home settings, public policy analysts are concerned about how families will pay the costs of long term care without spending down assets to qualify for public assistance. Unfortunately many adults are unaware that the costs of personal support services and that long-term health care services are not covered by Medicare or other health insurance policies.

Agency for Health Care Research and Quality Health Care Costs and Financing
http://www.ahrq.gov/research/jan96/dept3.htm

Up to 23 percent of elderly Americans could be rejected for private long-term care insurance at age 65.

Private insurance is one strategy for financing the large and growing cost of long-term care. Currently, insurance premiums are based on individuals considered to be average risks, and medical underwriting is used to reject those insurers fear may represent above-average risks. Little is known, however, about how much this practice limits the potential for private insurance to cover nursing home care or how well underwriting criteria identify high-cost groups.

New research from the Agency for Health Care Policy and Research indicates that under current medical underwriting practices, between 12 percent and 23 percent of Americans would be rejected if they applied for this insurance at age 65. These figures rise to between 20 and 31 percent at age 75, according to the study by former AHCPR researchers Christopher M. Murtaugh, Ph.D., and Peter Kemper, Ph.D., and Brenda C. Spillman, Ph.D., of AHCPR's Center for Cost and Financing Studies. They arrived at these conclusions by simulating underwriting criteria using a nationally representative sample of elderly decedents.

Based on these criteria, the study simulates probable exclusion of persons who are current or recent nursing home residents, are unable to perform basic activities of daily living (ADLs), have cognitive disabilities such as Alzheimer's disease or other forms of dementia, or major illnesses such as cancer, cirrhosis of the liver, long-term diabetes, or chronic obstructive pulmonary disease.

Underwriters possibly also would exclude persons who are obese or heavy drinkers and those who have had a stroke or recent heart attack with complications.

These criteria successfully identify persons who represent poor financial risks to insurers, although the extent to which that is true depends on policy characteristics. For a "low option" policy lacking inflation protection and non-forfeiture benefits, all the simulated criteria identify groups with insurance benefits exceeding the premiums they paid into the policies. For example, the simulations suggest that insurance benefits for those who are cognitively impaired at age 65 would be more than seven times their expected premium collections, and benefits for those unable to perform ADLs at age 65 would be three times premium collections. Under a more generous policy with inflation protection and nonforfeiture, however, only those with cognitive impairment, limitations in ADLs, and those who had suffered stroke would have benefits exceeding premiums paid.

Based on the study results, the researchers suggest that policymakers may want to consider options such as high-risk insurance pools for those who are uninsurable. Insurers could offer higher premium policies to those believed to be higher risks or follow the life insurance practice of offering dividends when experience is more favorable than expected. Both of these options would allow insurers to gather more information about actual risks represented by those now considered poor risks.

QUESTIONS

1. Poll your extended family. Does anyone have long-term care insurance? Has anyone considered its purchase? What reasons did this person give for his or her choice?

2. What level of government involvement in the provision of long-term care services do you think is appropriate? Why?

3. Medicaid and Long-Term Care

BRIEF SUMMARIES OF MEDICARE & MEDICAID: Title XVIII and Title XIX of The Social Security Act as of November 1, 2005
http://new.cms.hhs.gov/MedicareProgramRatesStats/downloads/ MedicareMedicaidSummaries2005.pdf

OVERVIEW of MEDICAID

Title XIX of the Social Security Act is a Federal-State matching entitlement program that pays for medical assistance for certain vulnerable and needy individuals and families with low incomes and resources. This program, known as Medicaid, became law in 1965 as a jointly funded cooperative venture between the Federal and State governments (including the Territories and the District of Columbia) to assist States furnishing medical assistance to eligible needy persons. Medicaid is the largest source of funding for medical and health-related services for America's poorest people.

Within broad national guidelines established by Federal statutes, regulations and policies, each State: (1) establishes its own eligibility standards; (2) determines the type, amount, duration, and scope of services; (3) sets the rate of payment for services; and (4) administers its own program. Medicaid policies for eligibility, services, and payment are complex, and vary considerably even among similar-sized and/or adjacent States. Thus, a person who is eligible for Medicaid in one State might not be eligible in another State; and the services provided by one State may differ considerably in amount, duration, or scope from services provided in a similar or neighboring State. In addition, Medicaid eligibility and/or services within a State can change during the year.

* * *

MEDICAID SUMMARY AND TRENDS

* * *

Long term care is an important provision of Medicaid that will be increasingly utilized as our nation's population ages. The Medicaid program paid for over 40% of the total cost of care for persons using nursing facility or home health services in 2002. National data for 2002 show that Medicaid payments for nursing facility (excluding ICF/MRs) totaled $39.3 billion for more than 1.8 million beneficiaries of these services — an average expenditure of $22,245 per nursing home beneficiary. The national data also show that Medicaid payments for home health services totaled $3.9 billion for 1.1 million beneficiaries — an average expenditure of $3,685 per home health care beneficiary. With the percentage of our population who are elderly and/or disabled increasing faster than the younger groups, the need for long term care is expected to increase.

* * *

More than 51.6 million persons received health care service through the Medicaid program in FY 2002 (the last year for which beneficiary data are available). In FY 2004, total outlays for the Medicaid program (Federal and State) were $276.8 billion, including direct payment to providers of $197.6 billion, payments for various premiums (for HMOs, Medicare, etc.) of $51.8 billion, payments to disproportionate share hospitals of $12.9 billion, and administrative costs of $14.5 billion. . . . With no changes. . . , expenditures under Medicaid . . . are projected to reach $402 billion . . . by FY 2010.

* * *

a. Assistance for Low-Income Seniors

BRIEF SUMMARIES OF MEDICARE & MEDICAID:
Title XVIII and Title XIX of The Social Security Act
as of November 1, 2005
http://new.cms.hhs.gov/MedicareProgramRatesStats/downloads/
MedicareMedicaidSummaries2005.pdf

THE MEDICAID — MEDICARE RELATIONSHIP

Medicare beneficiaries who have low incomes and limited resources may also receive help from the Medicaid program. For persons who are eligible for full Medicaid coverage, the Medicare health care coverage is supplemented by services that are available under their State's Medicaid program, according to eligibility category. These additional services may include — for example — nursing facility care beyond the 100 day limit covered by Medicare, prescription drugs, eyeglasses, and hearing aids. For persons enrolled in both programs, any services that are covered by Medicare are paid for by the Medicare program before any payments are made by the Medicaid program, since Medicaid is always the "payer of last resort."

Certain other Medicare beneficiaries may receive help through their State Medicaid program. Qualified Medicare Beneficiaries (QMBs) and Specified Low-Income Medicare Beneficiaries (SLMBs) are the best known and the largest in numbers. QMBs are those Medicare beneficiaries who have resources at or below twice the standard allowed under the SSI program, and incomes at or below 100 percent of the FPL [$817 for an individual in 2006]. This also includes persons who are eligible for full Medicaid coverage. For QMBs, the State pays the HI and SMI premiums and the Medicare coinsurance and deductibles, subject to limits that States may impose on payment rates. SLMBs are Medicare beneficiaries with resources like the QMBs, yet with incomes that are higher — but still less than 120 percent of the FPL. For SLMBs, the Medicaid program only pays the SMI premiums.

* * *

The Centers for Medicare & Medicaid Services (CMS) estimates that Medicaid currently provides some level of supplemental health coverage for about 6.5 million Medicare beneficiaries.

Starting January 2006, a new Medicare prescription drug benefit is providing drug coverage for Medicare beneficiaries, including those who also receive coverage from Medicaid. In addition, individuals eligible for both Medicare and medicaid will receive the low-income subsidy for both the Medicare drug plan premium and assistance with cost sharing for prescriptions. Medicaid will no longer provide drug benefits for Medicare beneficiaries.

Since the Medicare drug benefit and low-income subsidy will replace a portion of State Medicaid expenditures for drugs, States will see a reduction in Medicaid expenditures. To offset this reduction, the Medicare Prescription Drug,

Improvement, and Modernization Act of 2003 (Public Law 108-173) requires each State to make a monthly payment to Medicare representing a percentage of the projected reduction. For 2006 this payment is 90 percent of the projected 2006 reduction in State spending. After 2006 the percentage decreases by 1-2/3 percent per year to 75 percent in 2014 and later.

* * *

Medicare and You
A handbook published for consumers by the
Centers for Medicare and Medicaid Services

Medicare Savings for Qualified Beneficiaries

Help in Paying Medicare Out-of-Pocket Expenses for Some Low-Income People

The Centers for Medicare and Medicaid Services (CMS), a Federal government agency that administers Medicare and Medicaid, and your State have developed programs that can help pay your Medicare out-of-pocket expenses. These programs help people who have limited resources and income to pay for some Medicare expenses. This could save you hundreds of dollars each year. If you qualify, you may not have to pay for your:

- Medicare premiums, and in some cases, deductibles, and coinsurance.

* * *

You may qualify . . . if:

1. You are entitled to Medicare Part A. If you do not have Part A or you are not sure, check your Medicare card or call the Social Security office on 1-800-772-1213 to find out how to get it.

2. Your financial resources, such as bank accounts, stocks, and bonds, are not more than $4,000 for one person or $6,000 for a couple. Some things — like the home you live in, one automobile, burial plots, home furnishings, personal jewelry, and life insurance — usually do not count as resources. (If the combined face value of the life insurance policy is less than $1,500, it is not counted.)

3. Your monthly income is at or below a certain level. Income includes Social Security benefits, pensions, and wages as well as interest payments and dividends on stocks and bonds you may own. The amount of help you can get depends upon your monthly income.

QUESTIONS

1. What fundamental differences can you identify between Medicare and Medicaid?

2. What barriers to access to Medicaid are apparent from your reading so far?

b. Nursing Facility Care

Molly Mead Wood
Medicaid Eligibility for Long-Term Care: The Basics
16 PREVENTIVE L. REP. 8 (Summer 1997)[*]

Seniors seeking assistance with the cost of long-term nursing facility care from Medicaid must meet the following four-part eligibility test:

MEDICAL NEED: Nursing home care, whether skilled, intermediate, or custodial, must be the appropriate level of care for the medical assistance applicant. Most states require applicants to complete a screening prior to, or soon after, nursing home admission. Practitioners should be alert to the range of in-home services which would postpone institutionalization.

* * *

THE INCOME TEST: Find out if your state has an income cap. For those states, a Medicaid applicant must receive less than the cap to be eligible for assistance. Unfortunately, the maximum cap for these applicants is 300% of the Supplemental Security Income level, which is [$1,872 per month — 300% of $623 in 2007], and some states are lower. It is implausible that anyone could pay his or her cost of care after other resources are exhausted with that level of income, and until October 1, 1993, this requirement produced harsh results.

Part of the Omnibus Budget Reconciliation Act of 1993, however, created a loophole. 42 U.S.C. § 1396p(d)(4)(B) codified the "Miller" trust, so named for the case that launched the legislation. *Miller v. Ibarra*, 746 F.Supp. 19 (D. Colo. 1990). These trusts are appropriate only in income cap states, must contain only the income of the Medicaid recipient, and must include a payback provision upon termination.

[In states without an income cap, i]f the Medicaid applicant's income is less than his/her private pay cost of care, the applicant meets the income test. Attribution of income follows the name on the check, that is, income is attributed to the spouse to whom payment is drawn. Jointly held income producing property is allocated pro rata.

THE RESOURCE TEST: A Medicaid recipient cannot retain over $2,000 in non-exempt resources.

Exempt resources include:

- A home of any value. An applicant generally is entitled to exempt the home even if there is no real expectation that he or she will be able to return.

- A car of any value;

- Household goods, family keepsakes, memorabilia;

- Life insurance with a death benefit of $1,500 or less;

---

[*] Copyright © 1997. Reprinted with permission.

- Real property, equipment or materials used in an income producing trade or business. (These exceptions help conserve the family farm or other small business); and

- Irrevocable burial plans.

All other resource are non-exempt, including, but not limited to:

- Cash assets;

- Cash value of life insurance policies of which the applicant or the applicant's spouse is the owner.

- Resource available to the applicant as the beneficiary of a grantor trust established before August 10, 1993 to the extent the trustee has discretion to invade principal for the benefit of the applicant. . . .

- For trusts created after August 10, 1993, assets of a Medicaid applicant conveyed to a trust (other than by Will) for the benefit of the individual or the individual's spouse are considered available, regardless of the purposes of the trust, if the trust is revocable, or, if irrevocable, the trustee has any discretion with respect to distributions of principal or income. . . .

- Fair market value of real estate other than the home.

Spousal Impoverishment

Division of assets modifies the resource test in the context of a well spouse remaining in the community. Here, the community spouse retains all the exempt property. All the non-exempt resources of the married couple are pooled, regardless of ownership, and a portion is set aside for the community spouse. The community spouse retains a minimum of $20,328 [2007] and a maximum of $101,640 [2007]. If the total non-exempt resources of the couple are greater than $40,656 [2007] and less than $203,280 [2007], the community spouse retains one-half of the couple's non-exempt resources.

After the institutionalized spouse has spent his half down to the protect $2,000 amount, he has met the resource test. Proper spend-down techniques include purchase of prepaid exempt burial plans for both marital partners, improvements and repairs to the exempt home, upgrade of the exempt family car, and, of course, payment of medical and other expenses for both marital partners.

Do not begin to spend down until after institutionalization! Because the allocation of resources takes place at the time the Medicaid applicant enters the nursing home, keeping the couple's total non-exempt resources as high as possible will generally make the community spouse's protected amount greater.

The community spouse of a Medicaid recipient is also potential eligible for a spousal income allowance — a sort of "division of income" in which her income can be supplemented to $1,650 [2007] from the income of the institutionalized spouse after the Medicaid applicant has become eligible.

* * *

[Eds. On February 8, 2006, President Bush signed the Deficit Reduction Omnibus Reconciliation Act of 2005 (S. 1932) into law. It amended 42 U.S.C. § 1396p(c) to enhance penalties applied to nursing home residents seeking Medicaid assistance who, within 5 years of applying for assistance, make gifts so as to reduce their assets. It purports to disqualify any applicant who makes a transfer of assets for less than adequate consideration within five years preceding eligibility. The length of the ineligibility penalty is calculated by dividing the amount of the gift by "the average monthly cost to a private patient of nursing facility services in the State (or, at the option of the State, in the community in which the individual is institutionalized) at the time of application." For example, a gift of $10,000 would produce a two-month penalty in a state where the average monthly private pay cost is $5,000. The penalty begins to run when the applicant would otherwise be eligible, that is, after the applicant has already exhausted his or her remaining resources.

To avoid undue hardship, a nursing facility in which the insitutionalized person is residing may seek a waiver of the penalty on behalf of the individual (with the individual's consent or the consent of the individual's lawful agent).] Transfers which may incur a penalty include:

- disclaimer of an inheritance or failure to exercise spousal election which diminishes the applicant's resources;

- a triggering event which makes a revocable trust irrevocable;

- addition of other owner(s) in joint tenancy or as remaindermen to real property; and

- uncompensated transfers by the community spouse after August 10, 1993, if resource eligibility is obtained under the spousal impoverishment provisions.

QUESTIONS

1. Why should people buy long-term care insurance if the Medicaid program will pay for their care?

2. Is it ethical for lawyers to explain how to transfer assets to become eligible for Medicaid? Why or why not?

ERIC HOLLOWAY, APPELLANT, v. RILEY'S OAK HILL MANOR, INC., APPELLEE

Court of Appeals of Arkansas, Division III.
No. CA 02-74.

Oct. 9, 2002. Appellee Riley's Oak Hill Manor, Inc. brought an action against appellant Eric Holloway and Hattie Holloway to collect a debt owed in connection with treatment received by Hattie, who is Eric's mother. After a bench trial, the trial court ruled that Riley's was entitled to judgment against both Eric Holloway and Hattie Holloway for breach of contract, as well as on the alternative theories of unjust enrichment and promissory estoppel. The trial court awarded $6,664.20, in addition to interest, court costs, and attorney's fees. For reversal, appellant argues that the evidence does not support the judgment. We affirm.

* * *

After suffering a broken hip, Hattie Holloway resided at Riley's nursing home from March 20, 1995, until July 1995. Judy Weiss worked for Riley's during that time, and she testified that the initial paperwork was not filled out prior to Ms. Holloway's admission. She stated that soon thereafter she spoke with Eric Holloway on the telephone about payment arrangements and advised him to consult the Arkansas Department of Human Services to apply for Medicaid. Because Mr. Holloway was unable to come to the nursing home during working hours, Ms. Weiss prepared the paperwork and left copies for him to sign on a weekend. Mr. Holloway signed two admission agreements in the capacity of "responsible party." Each agreement contained the following provision:

> The patient and/or responsible party agrees to pay a daily rate of ___ and the Nursing home will accept this agreement in full consideration for care and services rendered.

Ms. Weiss indicted that the forms contained blanks because the facility is unable to determine each resident's rate of pay without first being contacted by the Arkansas Department of Human Services. One of the admission agreements provided:

> If Medicaid is not secured, the sponsor hereby agrees to pay the private pay rate per classification of care. This classification is determined by the physician and the medical staff. If the care requirement increases it would normally be necessary to increase the daily rate and the sponsor hereby agrees to payment of the new rate.

Mr. Holloway was never able to obtain any Medicaid assistance with regard to services provided by Riley's. [Eds. The Court did not discuss why Holloway's mother, whose Social Security income appears to have been $346 per month (see below), was unable to obtain Medicaid assistance.]

A document with the heading "current month statement," and dated September 13, 1995, was admitted into evidence. The document provides:

Services for HOLLOWAY, HATTIE
Cust # 2653

Previous Month Balance	$7910.00
Payments Received	$1245.80
Balance Forward	$6664.20
Residence Service Charges 09/01/95-9/30/95	$0.00
Additional Charges Since 09/01/95	_____
Total Amount Due	$6664.20

Underneath the "Total Amount Due" are the following handwritten calculations:

April nursing care 28 days at $70.00 =	$1960.00
May nursing care 31 days at $70.00 =	$2170.00
June nursing care 30 days at $70.00 =	$2100.00
July nursing care 24 days at $70.00 =	$1680.00
Total charges	$7910.00
May social security check	($346.00)
June social security check	($346.00)
July social security check	($346.00)
August insurance reimbursement	($207.80)
	$6644.20

Also in the record are copies of several communications from Riley's to Mr. Holloway requesting payment of the outstanding bill.

Carolyn Ferguson, officer of asset services for the Area Agency on Aging, testified for the appellant. She stated that she received a telephone call from Mr. Holloway, and that he informed her that he owed six thousand dollars to the nursing home, but that he signed some papers without knowing what he was signing. According to Ms. Ferguson, Mr. Holloway told her that no one explained the forms to him, and she was shocked because when a person is admitted to a nursing home, "there is always someone there to explain." In her opinion, the social worker who handled the admission process was negligent because she gave no explanation as to important parts of the agreement, including rates.

Mr. Holloway testified that he signed the forms with the intent that his mother would be admitted to the nursing home. He stated that he did not know he was going to be made responsible for the bill, and thought that social security or SSI would cover it. Mr. Holloway maintained that, "My sole purpose for signing was for her to be admitted, but not for me to be responsible for any kind of bill whatsoever." He stated that he was first approached about paying the bill on July 14, 1995, when he was trying to get his mother moved from the facility. On rebuttal, a Riley's employee testified that a bill for $1635.87 was sent to Mr. Holloway on April 27, 1995.

Mr. Holloway argues that the trial court erred in granting a judgment in favor of Riley's. He submits that he never intended to make himself obligated for his mother's nursing home expenses. Because there was no "meeting of the minds" with regard to any agreement to that effect, Mr. Holloway argues that the judgment against him was erroneously entered.

* * *

The next case cited by Mr. Holloway is *St. John's Episcopal Hosp. v. McAdoo*, 405 N.Y.S.2d 935 (N.Y.Civ.Ct.1978). In that case, the defendant signed a contract that included an obligation to pay his estranged wife's hospital bill. However, the

New York Civil Court refused to enforce the contract because, when the defendant signed it, he was convinced his wife was near death and the heading of the contract bore the heading, "ASSIGNMENT OF INSURANCE BENEFITS." Although the provisions of the contract stated that the defendant would be responsible for charges not covered by insurance, the court ruled against the hospital, announcing: It is reasonable in this situation for defendant to have seen himself as powerless to do anything other than sign the form. A hospital emergency room is certainly not a place in which any but the strongest can be expected to exercise calm and dispassionate judgment. The law of contracts is not intended to use "superman" as its model. If the reasonable man standard is applied here, defendant's failure to read the document or to give it more than the most cursory attention is understandable.

* * *

Finally, Mr. Holloway cites *Rohrscheib v. Helena Hosp. Ass'n,* 12 Ark.App. 6, 670 S.W.2d 812 (1984). In that case, appellant's sister-in-law had incurred in excess of $4000.00 in medical bills, and appellant subsequently signed an admission sheet on the line marked, "Signature of Responsible Party." We reversed in favor of appellant because there was no promise on his part to pay the debt; although the admission sheet used the words "responsible party," it failed to provide what that party was responsible for. We further held that the contract was unenforceable for lack of consideration because the original debt had already been incurred, and "[t]he mere naked promise in writing to pay the existing debt of another without any consideration therefor is void." [Citation omitted.] We hold that this case is distinguishable from those cited by Mr. Holloway, and that the trial court did not clearly err in finding that Mr. Holloway breached an enforceable contract. Although not binding on this court, the reasoning employed in *St. John's Episcopal Hosp. v. McAdoo, supra,* is not applicable to the facts of the instant case because in that case the contract was signed under the trauma of an emergency medical crisis, whereas in this case no such emergency existed. Moreover, Mr. Holloway testified under oath in his deposition that, unlike Mr. McAdoo, he read the forms in detail and felt like he understood everything when he signed them. In the case at bar, the contract signed by Mr. Holloway clearly states in several different provisions that as a "responsible party" he is charged with making payments to Riley's to cover his mother's treatment. This contrasts with the facts of *Rohrscheib v. Helena Hosp. Ass'n, supra,* because the contract in that case failed to provide that the "responsible party" was responsible for any expenses. And while we further stated in that case that the contract was without sufficient consideration, such is not the case here because when Mr. Holloway signed the contract he was agreeing to be responsible for payment for future treatment of his mother, and not simply an existing debt. While a contract must be supported by consideration, the consideration does not have to flow directly to the person making the promise, but may move from the promisor to a third person.

* * *

We hold that the trial court committed no error in finding a breach of contract and in awarding the appellee $6664.20 on that basis. Thus, we need not address its decision that, even in the absence of a breach, the appellee is entitled to judgment on the theories of unjust enrichment and promissory estoppel. Affirmed.

QUESTION

Should adult children generally be liable for the nursing facility costs of their indigent parents?

c. Estate Recovery

MATTER OF ESTATE OF THOMPSON
586 N.W.2d 847 (N.D. 1998)

AFFIRMED.

SANDSTROM, Justice. Filed 12/22/98 by Clerk of Supreme Court.

Lyndon R. Thompson, personal representative of the estate of Victoria Jane Thompson (the personal representative), appealed an order granting the claim of the Department of Human Services (the department) against Victoria Thompson's estate for medical assistance provided to her spouse, Nathaniel M. Thompson. We conclude 42 U.S.C. § 1396p authorizes the department's claim and North Dakota's estate recovery statute was not applied retroactively. We affirm.

I.

Nathaniel Thompson received medical assistance benefits of $58,237.30 between January 1, 1991, and his death on December 20, 1992. His wife, Victoria Thompson, died on September 15, 1995, leaving an estate of $46,507.98. A copy of an application for informal probate and appointment of a personal representative was mailed to the department. [Section 50-24.1-07, N.D.C.C., requires a personal representative to forward to the department a copy of the petition or application commencing probate, heirship proceedings, or joint tenancy tax clearance proceedings.] Lyndon Thompson was appointed personal representative.

The department filed a claim against Victoria Thompson's estate for $58,237.30 in medical assistance provided to Nathaniel Thompson and $9,356.79 in interest. The personal representative filed a notice of disallowance of the claim. The department petitioned the trial court for allowance of the claim. The personal representative moved for summary judgment, arguing: "The state statute [N.D.C.C. § 50-24.1-07] would allow recovery from the estate of a spouse while the federal statute [42 U.S.C. § 1396p(b)(1) and (2)] would not." The department also moved for summary judgment. On January 8, 1998, the court denied the personal representative's motion for summary judgment and granted the department's motion for summary judgment and petition for allowance of its claim. The personal representative appealed. . . .

II.

The personal representative contends the trial court erred in construing 42 U.S.C. § 1396p(b)(1) to allow the department to recover medical assistance benefits provided to Nathaniel Thompson from the estate of his surviving spouse, arguing the plain meaning of the federal statute prohibits recovery of medical assistance benefits from the estate of a deceased recipient's surviving spouse.

Summary judgment is a procedure for the prompt and expeditious disposition of a controversy without trial if either party is entitled to judgment as a matter of law, if no dispute exists as to either the material facts or the inferences to be drawn from undisputed facts, or if resolving factual disputes would not alter the result. [Citation omitted]. . Interpretation of a statute is a question of law, which is fully reviewable by this Court. [Citation omitted].

The primary objective of statutory construction is to ascertain the Legislature's intent. [Citation omitted]. In ascertaining legislative intent, we look first at the words used in the statute, giving them their ordinary, plain-language meaning. [Citation omitted]. We construe statutes as a whole to give effect to each of its provisions, whenever fairly possible. [Citation omitted]. "If the language of a statute is clear and unambiguous, the legislative intent is presumed clear from the face of the statute." [Citation omitted]. If statutory language is ambiguous, we may resort to extrinsic aids to construe the statute. [Citation omitted]. For an ambiguous statute, "[w]here a public interest is affected, an interpretation is preferred which favors the public. A narrow construction should not be permitted to undermine the public policy sought to be served." . . .

When Nathaniel Thompson began receiving medical assistance benefits, N.D.C.C. § 50-24.1-07 provided, in part:

> On the death of any recipient of medical assistance who was sixty-five years of age or older when he received such assistance, the total amount of medical assistance paid on behalf of the decedent following his sixty-fifth birthday must be allowed as a preferred claim against the decedent's estate. . . . No claim must be paid during the lifetime of the decedent's surviving spouse. . . .

Effective August 1, 1995, N.D.C.C. § 50-24.1-07 was amended to provide in part:

1. On the death of any recipient of medical assistance who was *fifty*-five years of age or older when the recipient received *the* assistance, *and on the death of the spouse of such a deceased recipient,* the total amount of medical assistance paid on behalf of the *recipient* following the *recipient's fifty*-fifth birthday must be allowed as a preferred claim against the decedent's estate. . . .

2. No claim must be paid during the lifetime of the decedent's surviving spouse, if any. . . .

[Emphasis added.]

When Nathaniel Thompson died on November 20, 1992, 42 U.S.C. § 1396p(b) (1988) provided in part:

> *(b)* *Adjustment or recovery of medical assistance correctly paid under a State plan.* (1) No adjustment or recovery of any medical assistance correctly paid on behalf of an individual under the State plan may be made, except —
>
> . . . .
>
>> (B) in the case of any other individual who was 65 years of age or older when he received such assistance, from his estate.
>
> (2) Any adjustment or recovery under paragraph (1) may be made only after the death of the individual's surviving spouse, if any. . . .

Effective October 1, 1993, after Nathaniel Thompson's death, but before Victoria Thompson died on September 14, 1995, 42 U.S.C. § 1396p(b) (1994) was amended to provide in part:

> *(b)* *Adjustment or recovery of medical assistance correctly paid under a State plan.* (1) No adjustment or recovery of any medical assistance correctly paid on behalf of an individual under the State plan may be made, except *that the State shall seek adjustment or recovery of any medical assistance correctly paid on behalf of an individual under the State plan in the case of the following individuals:*
>
> . . . .
>
>> (B) In the case of *an* individual who was *55* years of age or older when *the individual* received such medical assistance, *the State shall seek adjustment or recovery* from *the individual's* estate. . . .
>
> . . . .
>
> (2) Any adjustment or recovery under paragraph (1) may be made only after the death of the individual's surviving spouse, if any. . . .
>
> . . . .
>
> *(4)* *For purposes of this subsection, the term "estate", with respect to a deceased individual —*
>
>> *(A)* *shall include all real and personal property and other assets included within the individual's estate, as defined for purposes of State probate law; and*
>
>> *(B)* *may include, at the option of the State . . . any other real and personal property and other assets in which the individual had any legal title or interest at the time of death (to the extent of such interest), including such assets conveyed to a survivor, heir, or assign of the deceased individual through joint tenancy, tenancy in common, survivorship, life estate, living trust, or other arrangement.*

[Emphasis added.]

The personal representative contends the plain meaning rule of statutory construction requires reversal because 42 U.S.C. § 1396p(b)(1) does not allow recovery of medical assistance benefits from the estate of a recipient's spouse. He argues:

> It contains a general blanket prohibition on the recovery and recoupment of correctly paid medical assistance benefits ("no . . . recovery . . . may be made"). *Id.* It then goes on to provide several exceptions to this general prohibition ("except that the State shall seek . . . recovery . . . in the case of the following individuals"). *Id.* The statute does *not* then allow recovery from the estate of the recipient's surviving spouse, but only from the estate of the recipient. *Id.*

However, the "plain meaning" of the very broad definition of the recipient's estate in 42 U.S.C. § 1396p(b)(4) must also be considered. That definition gives the State the option to include in the recipient's "estate" from which it may recover medical assistance benefits after the death of the recipient's surviving spouse any:

> real and personal property and other assets in which the individual had any legal title or interest at the time of death (to the extent of such interest), including such assets conveyed to a survivor, heir, or assign of the deceased individual through joint tenancy, tenancy in common, survivorship, life estate, living trust, or other arrangement.

That expansive definition is broad enough to encompass the department's claim against the estate of a deceased spouse of a deceased recipient of medical assistance benefits for the amount of medical assistance paid out, to the extent the recipient at the time of death had any title or interest in assets which were conveyed to his or her spouse "through joint tenancy, tenancy in common, survivorship, life estate, living trust, or other arrangement." [The personal representative has not contended Victoria Thompson's estate includes any assets not acquired from Nathaniel Thompson "through joint tenancy, tenancy in common, survivorship, life estate, living trust, or other arrangement."]

The court in *In re Estate of Craig*, 604 N.Y.S.2d 908, 911 (N.Y. Ct. App. 1993), has also construed the 1993 amendment to 42 U.S.C. § 1396p(b):

> The Omnibus Budget Reconciliation Act of 1993 (Pub.L. 103-66), signed into law on August 10, 1993, amended the estate recovery provisions of the Federal Medicaid law. This Act gives the States, at their option, the power to recover against a spouse's estate, but only against the recipient's assets that were conveyed through joint tenancy and other specified forms of survivorship.

The court in *In re Estate of Budney*, 541 N.W.2d 245 (Wis. Ct. App. 1995), ruled 42 U.S.C. § 1396p(b)(1) does not authorize recovery of medical assistance benefits paid on behalf of a recipient from the estate of a recipient's surviving spouse. However, the *Budney* court did not address the effect of the broad definition of "estate" in 42 U.S.C. § 1396p(b)(4), and we are not persuaded by the decision.

The personal representative contends use of extrinsic aids in interpreting the federal statute also warrants reversal. The relevant amendment to 42 U.S.C. § 1396p was contained in the Omnibus Budget Reconciliation Act of 1993. The personal representative observed in his brief, "The language that was ultimately passed into law is *not* the language that was originally proposed." Relying on "the original House version of the bill," which specifically provided for recovery of medical assistance benefits "from the estate of the surviving spouse," the personal representative argues: "It may be inferred, therefore, that Congress did *not* intend to allow recovery from the estate of the surviving spouse of a recipient of medical assistance." However, this Court has held "public policy is declared by the action of the legislature not by its failure to act." [Citation omitted].

Furthermore, consideration of the purpose of the estate recovery provisions also warrants rejection of the personal representative's construction. "Allowing states to recover from the estates of persons who previously received assistance furthers the broad purpose of providing for the medical care of the needy; the greater amount recovered by the state allows the state to have more funds to provide future services." *Belshe v. Hope*, 38 Cal. Rptr. 2d 917, 925 (Cal. Ct. App. 1995). That broad purpose is furthered more fully by allowing states to trace a recipient's assets and recover them from the estate of a recipient's surviving spouse. Also, Senate and conference committee reports reflect an intent to require states to attempt estate recoveries of medical benefits and to allow states a wide latitude in seeking estate recoveries:

Present Law

States have the option to recover the costs of all Medicaid expenditures from the estates of deceased Medicaid claimants who were at least 65 years old when they were eligible for Medicaid. . . . Current law does not specify a definition of estate.

Committee Proposal

Extends current law as a mandate on all states. Provides a minimum definition of estate as including all real and personal property and other assets included within estate as defined by state laws governing treatment of inheritance. Allows states to expand the definition of estate to include other real or personal property or other assets in which the individual had any legally cognizable title or interest at the time of death, including such assets conveyed to a survivor, heir, or assignee of the deceased individual through joint tenancy, survivorship, life estate, living trust or other arrangement.

Senate Report No. 103-36, 103d Cong., 1st Session (1993).

Medicaid Estate Recoveries (Section 13612). — Requires States to recover the costs of nursing facility and other long-term care services furnished to Medicaid beneficiaries from the estate of such beneficiaries. . . . At the option of the State, the estate against such recovery is sought may include any real or personal property or other assets in which the beneficiary had any legal title or interest at the time of death, including the home.

House Conference Committee Report No. 103-213, 103rd Cong., 1st Session (1993), reprinted in 3 U.S.C.C.A.N. 1523-1524 (1993). The 1993 amendments, and our interpretation of them, reflect the Congressional purpose to broaden states' estate recovery programs, as indicated in the history of amendments incorporated in the present Federal statute.

We conclude consideration of all the relevant statutory provisions, in light of the Congressional purpose to provide medical care for the needy, reveals a legislative intention to allow states to trace the assets of recipients of medical assistance and recover the benefits paid when the recipient's surviving spouse dies.[1]

III.

The personal representative contends, even if the 1993 version of the federal statute is construed to allow recovery from the estate of the surviving spouse, the department's claim in this case is not legally supportable. He argues:

> In 1992 even the state statute did not purport to allow recovery of medical assistance from the estate of the surviving spouse of a recipient of such benefits. Therefore, the Department is seeking to apply the post-1995 version of Section 50-24.1-07 to a claim which arose in 1992 (upon the payment of all benefits to Nathaniel Thompson). This is a classic example of an attempted, inappropriate retroactive application of a statute.

However, this Court has said "[a] statute is not retroactive because it draws upon antecedent facts for its operation or because part of the requisites of its action is drawn from time antecedent to its passing." [Citation omitted]. The obligation to repay the medical assistance benefits Nathaniel Thompson received arose when he received them:

> [T]he obligation to repay, if any, arises upon receipt of the benefits, i.e., prior to the decedent's death. Although the Department's ability to enforce the claim was tolled until Hooey's death, the obligation was incurred by Hooey during her lifetime.

In re Estate of Hooey, 521 N.W.2d 85, 87 (N.D. 1994). Thus, the obligation to repay arose before Nathaniel Thompson's death in 1992, although the department's right to recover the benefits paid was suspended until the death of his surviving spouse. We conclude the department's claim is not a retroactive application of the 1995 amendment to N.D.C.C. § 50-24.1-07.

IV.

The order is affirmed.

---

[1] Because the expansive federal definition of "estate" in 42 U.S.C. § 1396p(b)(4) extends only to assets in which the medical assistance benefits recipient "had any legal title or interest in at the time of death," it is a matter of little moment whether the department seeks to recover the benefits paid by filing a claim in the estate of the recipient after the death of the recipient's surviving spouse or by filing a claim in the surviving spouse's estate.

QUESTIONS

1. If Medicaid is a program for low-income people, why would the Congress require the States to recover benefits from the estates of recipients?

2. Do you agree with the public policy arguments underlying *Thompson*? Why or why not?

FURTHER READING. A. Kimberley Dayton, et al., ADVISING THE ELDERLY CLIENT, chs. 24-31 (2006); L. Frolik & Kaplan, ELDER LAW IN A NUTSHELL 4-6 (2003); Peter J. Strauss & Nancy M. Lederman, THE ELDER LAW HANDBOOK chs. 1-2, 5-10 (1996); Peter J. Strauss, et al., AGING AND THE LAW, chs. 14-17, 36 (1996).

Chapter 9

HOUSING

Many of us fear dependency — and for some the most punishing lack of independence occurs if we lose our ability to stay at home, where the heart is. This chapter will review the "continuum of care" response to this challenge, from the single family home to the nursing facility, and the legal issues which arise in consequence.

Lawrence A. Frolik
The Special Housing Needs of Older Persons: An Essay
26 STETSON L. REV. 647 (Winter 1996)[*]

When we think about the challenges that face older members of our society, we are likely to think of problems such as paying for medical care, mental capacity, economic insecurity, and end-of-life health care decisionmaking. One issue that does not often come to mind is housing. Yet, housing, where the older person lives, is one of the key determinants of the quality of life for older Americans. Along with good health and economic security, appropriate housing that meets the needs of the older resident is surely necessary if an older person is to have a comfortable and satisfying life. Housing that is adequate for old age, however, does not just happen. Older persons who are happy with their housing (at least within the limits of what they can afford) usually are not just lucky. Rather, they have housing they like because they, and those who advised

---

[*] Copyright © 1996. Reprinted with permission.

them, took stock of their needs, values and capabilities and selected a housing option that was right for them.

A. HOME OWNERSHIP AND "AGING IN PLACE"

The Taxpayer Relief Act of 1997 repealed the one-time $125,000 exclusion of income from the sale of a principal residence by taxpayers age 55 or over and replaced this provision with an exclusion of up to $250,000 (or $500,000, in the case of married taxpayers filing a joint return) of income realized on sale or exchange of a principal residence by taxpayer regardless of age.

To claim the exclusion, a taxpayer must meet the ownership and use tests. This means that during the 5-year period ending on the date of the sale, the taxpayer must have:

> Owned the home for at least 2 years (the ownership test), and

> Lived in the home as a principal residence for at least 2 years (the use test).

The exclusion is not a one-time exclusion, but is generally available no more frequently than once every two years. Exception: If you owned and lived in the property as your main home for less than 2 years, you can still claim an exclusion in some cases, but the maximum amount you can exclude will be reduced.

H.E.L.P., A Non-Profit Information Resource for Older Adults
Think Twice (or More) Before Giving Away Your Home
http://www.help4srs.org/money/yourhome.htm[*]

Many people, as they grow older, consider giving away their homes during their lifetimes. We call this "lifetime transfer" and contrast it with a transfer to heirs that becomes effective at death. When thinking about a lifetime transfer of their homes, people often consider things like avoiding probate, having someone else take responsibility for upkeep, helping a family member, or encouraging someone to live with them and provide care to them. Sometimes they believe that if they need nursing home care, [Medicaid] will take their homes from them.

Things to Consider

If you are thinking about making a lifetime transfer of your home, there are many things to consider first.

Loss of Control: If you transfer your home, you will lose control over it. You will have no say in whether it is sold, mortgaged or used for purposes you don't like. You may lose your right to live in your home or to rent it out.

---

[*] Reprinted by permission of H.E.L.P., a non-profit information resource helping people meet aging-related legal and care challenges, Torrance, California, (310) 533-1996 <http://www.help4srs.org>

Creditors: If you transfer your home, you may create problems if a creditor has a lien on it or if you file for bankruptcy. Also, the new owner of the home may have creditors who are able to make claims against the home.

Impact on SSI Benefits: If you receive SSI (Supplemental Security Income), transfer your home and continue to live there without paying rent, your SSI benefits will likely be reduced. Also, giving your home to someone who receives SSI and already owns a home will likely cause that person to lose SSI benefits.

QUESTIONS

1. What other legal issues weigh against a lifetime transfer of the home?

2. What alternatives could you offer a client who was considering transfer of the home to a family member in exchange for personal care?

ESTATE OF FURGASON v. DHSS
566 N.W.2d 169 (Wis. App. 1997)

The estates of Mildred and John Furgason appeal from a judgment affirming a decision of the Wisconsin Department of Health and Social Services (DHSS). DHSS concluded that the Furgasons were ineligible for medical assistance (MA) benefits because the farm that they placed in a revocable trust did not qualify as an exempt asset. We conclude that the farm held in trust was an exempt homestead, and therefore DHSS erred in denying the Furgasons MA benefits. Accordingly, we reverse.

BACKGROUND

John Fergason applied for and began to receive MA as a nursing home resident on March 12, 1990. On April 16, 1991, John and his wife, Mildred, transferred their farm into the Furgason Family Trust. Mildred continued to live on the farm until July 1995, when she entered the nursing home. Her application for MA benefits was denied on September 6, 1995. Furthermore, on September 6, 1995, the county notified John that his MA benefits would be discontinued effective October 1, 1995.

The basis for both the denial of Mildred's benefits and the termination of John's benefits was that each had excess assets. The asset that caused their ineligibility was the corpus of the trust. The farm was the only asset transferred to the trust. John and Mildred were the original settlors, trustees and primary beneficiaries of the trust, and the trust was fully revocable by either one of them.

On September 13, 1995, the Furgasons petitioned DHSS to review the county's determination. The DHSS hearing examiner upheld the county's decision, and on May 29, 1996, the circuit court affirmed DHSS's decision. The estates of Mildred and John were subsequently substituted as the proper parties because Mildred died on March 14, 1996 and John on March 17, 1996. The estates appeal.

* * *

Medical Assistance, also known as "Medicaid," is a joint state and federal program intended to provide medical services to the poor and needy. [Citation omitted.] To be eligible to receive MA benefits, an individual must meet strict income and asset limits. [Citation omitted.]

Because George and Mildred were over sixty-five years of age, they were eligible for MA benefits if they met the financial conditions of eligibility. MA applicants are ineligible for benefits if their non-exempt assets exceed a certain level. Both the Furgasons and the DHSS agree that revocable trusts are considered a resource available to the applicant in determining MA benefit eligibility. They disagree, however, as to whether the corpus of the trust — the Furgasons' farm — is exempt from consideration.

Section 49.47(4)(b)1, Stats., provides that an MA applicant is eligible for benefits "if the applicant's property does not exceed," among other things, "[a] home and the land used and operated in connection therewith if the home is used as the person's or his or her family's place of abode." Similarly, Wis. Adm. Code provides that "[a] home owned and lived in by an applicant or recipient is an exempt asset." A home is exempt as long as the applicant resides in it, or intends to return to it. [Citation omitted.]

DHSS argues that the farm is owned by the trust, not the Furgasons, and therefore the trust property does not qualify for this homestead exemption. The Furgasons argue that they have a sufficient ownership interest in the trust property to make the farm exempt from consideration.

The Furgasons were the settlors of the trust and its trustees and primary beneficiaries during their lifetimes. Section 701.05(1), Stats., provides that "[u]nless the creating instrument expressly limits the trustee to a lesser title or to a power, *the trustee takes all title of the settlor* ." (Emphasis added.) In addition, Section 701.05(2) provides that "[i]f a trustee of a private trust has title to the trust property, a beneficiary has an equitable interest, present or future, in the trust property." Furthermore, *Becker v. Becker* [Citation omitted.], states that "[w]hen a settlor creates a trust by declaration naming himself as sole trustee, no transfer of ownership occurs."

Accordingly, . . . the Furgasons continued to have an ownership interest in the farm as the trustees and beneficiaries of the trust. Because the Furgasons continued to own the farm, the farm was exempt under Section 49.47(4)(b)1, Stats., as long as either John or Mildred or both intended to return there. The State apparently concedes that such intent to return to the farm did exist. Therefore, DHSS erred in denying the Furgasons MA benefits.

DHSS argues that the Furgasons were ineligible for benefits because Section 49.45(23), Stats., 1991-92, and Section 49.454, Stats., which expressly govern the treatment of trusts under the MA program, take precedence over Section 701.05, Stats., a general trust law provision. In support of its argument, DHSS cites *City of Muskego v. Godec,* [citation omitted] which provides that "[w]hen we compare a general statute and a specific statute, the specific statute takes precedence."

We reject DHSS's argument because we do not see a conflict between the MA statutes and the general trust statutes. "The rule of statutory construction that favors the specific over the general statutory provision applies only where there is a conflict between the two provisions." [Citation omitted.] The MA statutes do not provide that anyone with access to revocable trust assets is ineligible for MA benefits. Rather, the statutes provide that the assets in a revocable trust are considered "available" to the MA applicant. Trust assets available to the applicant are still subject to the property exemptions of Section 49.47(4)(b), Stats. [Citation omitted.] The Furgasons have an ownership interest in the trust assets under Section 701.05, Stats., and therefore the farm is an exempt homestead under Section 49.47(4)(b)1. This result is not inconsistent with the MA statutes which provide that the trust assets are "available" to the Furgasons.

Finally, DHSS argues that by placing the farm in trust, the Furgasons are shielding their property from the lien and estate claim recovery remedies otherwise available to the government against an MA recipient's home. For example, Section 49.496(2), Stats., provides that DHSS may obtain a lien on an MA recipient's home "if the recipient resides in a nursing home and cannot reasonably be expected to be discharged from the nursing home and return home," and Section 49.496(3) provides that DHSS must file a claim against an MA recipient's estate for benefits paid while the recipient resided in a nursing home. Because the trust owns the farm and trust property may be passed to heirs outside of probate, DHSS argues that neither the lien recovery nor estate claim recovery remedies of Section 49.496 are available against the Furgasons' farm. DHSS contends that if we consider the farm as an exempt homestead, we would place the Furgasons at an advantage over other MA recipients who simply own their homes.

We do not see how DHSS's ability to recover benefits paid from the trust assets is relevant to whether the Furgasons may receive MA benefits in the first place. The statutes provide the eligibility requirements for MA benefits. The statutes also provide the situations in which a settlor's creditor may reach trust assets. If the legislature believes that it is inequitable to allow MA applicants to place their homes in revocable trusts and still receive MA benefits, it can change the statutes accordingly. But it is for the legislature, not this court, to make such a policy determination. [Citation omitted.] We cannot rewrite the statutes to meet DHSS's desired construction.

By the Court. — Judgment reversed.

QUESTIONS

1. If DHSS — the Medicaid administering agency — would allow a homestead exemption for Medicaid eligibility purposes, why did it object to the same exemption on the same property when the Furgasons transferred it to their trust?

2. Would you expect a different response from DHSS if the Furgasons had made a lifetime transfer of their home to their children? Different judgment by the Court?

IN RE ESTATE OF SEROVY
711 N.W.2d 290 (Iowa 2006)

Allan Serovy and Pearl Serovy, the son and daughter-in-law of Mary H. Serovy, deceased, appeal from an order of the probate court subjecting a joint-tenancy interest in real estate held by Mary at the time of her death to a claim of the Iowa Department of Human Services for the cost of medical assistance provided to Mary as a Medicaid recipient. Allan and Pearl are the surviving joint owners of the property. They urge that, to the extent Iowa Code section 249A.5(2) (2003) authorizes the ruling of the probate court, that statute is an unlawful impairment of the obligation of a contract between Mary and them, thus violating Article I, Section 10 of the Constitution of the United States and article I, section 21 of the Iowa Constitution. The district court rejected that contention, and so do we.

The property at issue was for many years Mary's home. It was located in Solon. Prior to the death of her husband Frank in 1966, she and Frank owned the property in joint tenancy. Following Frank's death, Mary owned the property in fee simple and continued to reside there. In the mid-1980s, Mary's health began to deteriorate. Her son, Allan, and daughter-in-law, Pearl, who lived on a farm located seven miles from Solon, found it necessary to visit Mary several times each day in order to assist her in caring for herself.

Mary hoped to remain in her home as long as possible, and to aid in accomplishing that wish, she entered into an agreement with Allan and Pearl whereby they, at their own expense, would build an addition on Mary's home in order to provide additional living space for themselves and their daughter, as well as for Mary. As part of the agreement, they would move into the home and provide Mary with care and assistance in her daily living. It was agreed that Mary would execute a warranty deed conveying her residence to herself, Allan, and Pearl, as joint tenants with right of survivorship.

Allan and Pearl did build an addition on Mary's house at their own expense, with Allan and his sons doing much of the labor. On March 14, 1988, after the improvements had been substantially completed, Mary executed the warranty deed transferring title to the property to herself, Allan, and Pearl as joint tenants. Allan, Pearl, and their daughter moved into Mary's home in 1989, at which time some of the remodeling was yet to be completed. Allan and Pearl cared for Mary in the family home until 1997, when Mary's condition required her relocation to a nursing home. She remained in the nursing home until her death on October 11, 1998, during which time she received medical-assistance benefits under Title XIX of the Social Security Act.

On November 30, 1998, Allan filed a petition for probate of Mary's will without present administration. On April 17, 2003, the Estate Recovery Program of Health Management Systems, an agent for the Iowa Department of Human Services, filed a claim in Mary's estate for reimbursement of $28,707.54 plus accruing interest, which was alleged to be the cost of medical assistance provided to Mary under Medicaid in 1997 and 1998. On April 21, 2003, Ben Chatman, an agent of the Estate Recovery Program, petitioned for probate of Mary's will with administration. That was granted. Chatman was appointed executor.

On December 11, 2003, a special executor was appointed to review the Medicaid-reimbursement claim presented by the Estate Recovery Program. The special executor filed a report recommending that the claim be allowed. On February 16, 2004, the executor filed a motion seeking an order granting him authority to sell Mary's home to satisfy the Medicaid-reimbursement claim and other obligations of the estate. Allan and Pearl filed a formal resistance to the executor's motion, raising the constitutional issues that they are urging on this appeal.

The probate court ruled that invoking Iowa Code section 249A.5(2) in order to subject Mary's joint-tenancy interest to payment of the Medicaid-reimbursement claim did not result in an impairment of the obligation of any contract between Mary and her son and daughter-in-law. The court concluded that the contract between those parties had been fully performed prior to the time that Iowa Code section 249A.5(2)(c) and (d) was enacted in 1994.

* * *

II. *Impact of Medicaid Recovery Legislation on Mary Serovy's Joint-Tenancy Interest.*

A. *The 1994 Medicaid recovery legislation.* The controversy now before the court has arisen as the result of an amendment to Iowa Code section 249A.5 in 1994, which expanded the category of assets that can be reached by the Iowa Department of Human Services to satisfy claims filed in decedents' estates for the cost of medical-assistance benefits provided to Medicaid recipients. That legislation contained the following provisions.

2. The provision of medical assistance to an individual who is fifty-five years of age or older, or who is a resident of a nursing facility, . . . who cannot reasonably be expected to be discharged and return to the individual's home, creates a debt due the department from the individual's estate for all medical assistance provided on the individual's behalf, upon the individual's death.

. . . .

c. For purposes of this section, the estate of a medical assistance recipient, surviving spouse, or surviving child includes any real property, personal property, or other asset in which the recipient, spouse, or child had any legal title or interest at the time of the recipient's, spouse's, or child's death, to the extent of such interests in jointly held property, retained life estates, and interests in trusts.

d. For purposes of collection of a debt created by this subsection, all assets included in the estate of a medical assistance recipient, surviving spouse, or surviving child pursuant to paragraph "c" are subject to probate.

1994 Iowa Acts ch. 1120, § 10 (amending Iowa Code § 249A.5).

We have previously considered the effect of this legislation in *In re Estate of Laughead*, 696 N.W.2d 312 (Iowa 2005), and *In re Barkema Trust*, 690 N.W.2d 50 (Iowa 2004). Our decision in *Laughead* permitted the recapture of the value of a life estate for satisfaction of a Medicaid-reimbursement claim subsequent to the death of the recipient. Our decision in *Barkema* allowed a Medicaid recipient's beneficial interest in a discretionary support trust to be subjected to a claim for the cost of Medicaid services, following the death of the recipient, although all interest in the trust was to pass to a named beneficiary upon the recipient's death.

In discussing the right to reach the assets in the discretionary-support trust in *Barkema*, we considered and discussed the situation of joint-tenancy property. As to such property, we observed:

> [B]esides interests in trusts, the Medicaid recovery statute includes jointly held property in the definition of "estate." Under property law, joint tenancy property passes by operation of law to the other joint tenant when one joint tenant dies. If "at the time of death" meant "at the moment of death," the jointly held property would already have passed to the decedent's joint tenant at the time when the decedent's "estate" is to be defined for purposes of the Medicaid recovery statute. This interpretation of "at the time of death" would render the legislature's inclusion of jointly held property in the definition of "estate" meaningless. *Id.* at 56.

Although the discussion of joint-tenancy property in the *Barkema* case was dictum, we are satisfied that it sets forth an accurate depiction of how the Medicaid recovery legislation affects joint-tenancy interests. The purpose of this legislation was to capture and make available for payment of Medicaid-reimbursement claims certain interests in property that are not ordinarily subject to the payment of a decedent's debts. Because other types of jointly held property, such as tenancy in common, have always been available for the payment of claims in probate, the legislature must have intended the reference to "jointly held property" in section 249A.5(2)(*c*) to embrace joint-tenancy interests.

B. *Whether the Medicaid recovery legislation impairs the obligation of a contract affecting Allan and Pearl's interest.* Allan and Pearl argue that the probate court erred in rejecting their constitutional challenge under the obligation-of-contract clauses of the federal and state constitutions. The federal constitutional provision on which they rely provides "[n]o State shall . . . pass any . . . Law impairing the Obligation of Contracts." U.S. Const. art. I, § 10. The Iowa constitutional provision they have invoked provides that "[n]o . . . law impairing the obligation of contracts shall ever be passed." Iowa Const. art. I, § 21.

In applying these constitutional provisions, we have recognized that the prohibition therein contained is not absolute and must yield to a reasonable exercise of the police power for the public good. *Adair Benevolent Soc'y v. State Ins. Div.*, 489 N.W.2d 1, 5 (Iowa 1992); *Amana Soc'y v. Colony Inn, Inc.*, 315 N.W.2d 101, 112 (Iowa 1982). In *Federal Land Bank of Omaha v. Arnold*, 426 N.W.2d 153 (Iowa 1988), we adopted a three-step analysis for dealing with constitutional claims alleging abrogation of the obligation of a contract. That analysis is:

(1) [I]f the state law operates as a substantial impairment of a contractual relationship,

(2) the state must have a significant and legitimate public purpose behind the regulation, which

(3) adjusts the contracting parties' rights and responsibilities based on reasonable conditions appropriate to the public purpose.

Arnold, 426 N.W.2d at 159. In deciding the constitutional challenge lodged by Allan and Pearl, the probate court went no further than the first step outlined above and concluded that the legislation has caused no impairment of a contractual relationship. We agree with that conclusion and uphold the ruling on that ground.

The probate court found that the contract between Mary on the one hand and Allan and Pearl on the other required no more of Mary than her creation of a property interest in which these three individuals owned the property that had been Mary's residence as joint tenants with right of survivorship. The probate court concluded that this obligation on Mary's part was satisfied upon the execution and delivery of a warranty deed establishing the respective property interests on which the parties had agreed. The probate court's interpretation of the agreement appears to us to be consistent with the evidence concerning the intention of the parties. We favor that interpretation of the contract on our de novo review and may affirm the probate court's ruling on that basis. Under that interpretation of the contract, the statute being challenged did not alter what was agreed to among the parties, it simply affected the subject matter of the agreement after it had been fully performed.

Allan and Pearl contend that the agreement was not simply to create a joint-tenancy interest in the property for each of the three joint tenants named in the deed, but also included a promise on Mary's part to have her joint interest in the property transferred to Allan and Pearl in fee simple upon her death without impairment or diminution. Even if we accept this interpretation of the agreement, that will not support a finding that the obligation of the parties' agreement has been impaired by the statute. If Mary had contracted to transfer her joint interest in the property to Allan and Pearl in fee simple without encumbrance, the Medicaid recovery legislation did not discharge that obligation. It simply made it impossible for her to perform the contract, but under circumstances in which the impossibility would not discharge the obligation. A promisor is not discharged from a contractual duty on the theory of impossibility if the promisor brought about the occurrence that has prevented performance. *Associated Grocers of Iowa Coop., Inc. v. West*, 297 N.W.2d 103, 108 (Iowa 1980).

The circumstances that prevented Mary from transferring the agreed exchange to Allan and Pearl upon her death were of her own making as a result of her applying for and receiving Medicaid benefits subsequent to the enactment of section 249A.5(2)(c) and (d). The situation is the same as if a judgment creditor had levied on and sold her joint interest in the property during her lifetime. Consequently, even if the agreement was as it has been urged to be by Allan and Pearl, they have a breach-of-contract claim against Mary, the unimpaired obligation of which survived her death, pursuant to Iowa Code section 611.20. *See Jackson Sawmill Co. v. United States*, 580 F.2d 302, 311-12 (8th Cir. 1978) (legislation diluting city's ability to retire revenue bonds resulted in city's breach of contract for acting pursuant to the legislation, but did not impair the obligation of contract in violation of the constitution).

* * *

IV. *The Extent of the Interest Subject to Administration in Probate.*

The probate court's order clearly identifies the interest that is subject to administration in probate pursuant to section 249A.5(2)(*d*) as Mary's one-third interest in the subject property. Notwithstanding that finding on the court's part, it proceeded to order the sale of the entire property with the provision that one-third of the proceeds after costs of sale were to be utilized for the payment of the medical-assistance claim under Medicaid and the costs of administering the estate. Although this disposition may have been prompted by the court's desire to accelerate a possible future order for partition among the joint owners of the property, we are convinced that it was beyond the power of the court to order the sale of Allan and Pearl's interests in the property at this stage.

It is axiomatic that a decedent's personal representative is only empowered to sell the decedent's interest in property owned at the time of death in order to satisfy claims. This rule has been expressed as follows: A decedent's personal representative's authority to sell real property extends only to the decedent's estate's interest in the property; a personal representative is not empowered to exercise dominion over property that was never owned by the decedent or the estate. Thus, if the decedent held title to the property as a tenant in common, only that interest may be sold. 31 Am. Jur. 2d *Executors & Administrators* § 739, at 498 (2002). Similarly, in *Green v. Gustafson*, 482 N.W.2d 842 (N.D. 1992), the court stated:

> We agree . . . that [the personal representative's] authority to sell the property extended only to Marvin's estate's interest therein, which consisted of Marvin's 1/3 interest and the 1/3 interest of George's heirs which was quieted in Marvin's estate in the action to quiet title. . . . It is axiomatic that the personal representative is not . . . empowered to exercise dominion over property which was never owned by either the decedent or the estate. *Green*, 482 N.W.2d at 846. We modify the district court's order so as to limit the property that may be sold by the personal representative to the one-third joint interest owned by Mary immediately prior to her death.

As an alternative to a sale of property to satisfy the Medicaid-reimbursement claim, the probate court established a buyout figure. In describing that figure in their argument on appeal, Allan and Pearl suggest that the figure was the amount of the Medicaid-reimbursement claim plus accumulated interest. In reading the probate court's order it appears to us that the figure was the court's valuation of Mary's one-third interest in the property immediately prior to her death. We are satisfied that any buyout figure that the Estate Recovery Program can be made to accept in lieu of a sale of the property must require payment of its claim plus all accumulated interest. Of course, the parties are free to negotiate an alternative buyout figure that would avoid the sale of Mary's interest in the property.

We have considered all issues presented and conclude that the orders of the probate court should be affirmed as modified in our opinion. Costs on appeal are assessed to Allan and Pearl.

AFFIRMED AS MODIFIED.

QUESTIONS

What alternatives could you offer a client who was considering transfer of the home to a family member in exchange for personal care?

Jean Reilly
Reverse Mortgages: Backing into the Future
5 ELDER L.J. 17 (Spring 1997)[*]

In 1995 there were 2.89 million households headed by persons sixty-five years of age or older. The median income of these seniors was $18,500, while the median value of their homes was $70,000. Thus, many seniors find themselves in the position of being house rich, but cash poor. They find it increasingly difficult to meet home maintenance expenses, energy costs, property taxes, insurance premiums, health care bills, and even subsistence needs. Yet, according to a survey by the American Association of Retired Persons, 86% of seniors indicated that they wanted to live in their homes for the rest of their lives. For those older homeowners faced with the dilemma of wanting to stay in their homes and yet not having enough income to meet their expenses, reverse mortgages may be the answer.

* * *

HUD
Top Ten Things To Know If You're Interested In A Reverse Mortgage
http://www.hud.gov/offices/hsg/sfh/hecm/rmtopten.cfm

Reverse Mortgages are becoming popular in America. The U.S. Department of Housing and Urban Development (HUD) created one of the first. HUD's Reverse Mortgage is a federally-insured private loan, and it's a safe plan that can give older Americans greater financial security. Many Seniors use it to supplement social security, meet unexpected medical expenses, make home improvements, and more. You can receive free information from AARP about Reverse Mortgages by calling 1-800-209-8085, toll-free.

Since your home is probably your largest single investment, it's smart to know more about reverse mortgages, and decide if one is right for you!

---

[*] Copyright © 1997. Reprinted with permission. Copyright to the *Elder Law Journal* is held by the Board of Trustees of the University of Illinois.

1. *What is a reverse mortgage?*

A reverse mortgage is a special type of home loan that lets a homeowner convert the equity in his or her home into cash. The equity built up over years of home mortgage payments can be paid to the homeowner: in a lump sum, in a stream of payments, or as a supplement to Social Security or other retirement funds. But unlike a traditional home equity loan or second mortgage, no repayment is required until the borrowers no longer use the home as their principal residence. HUD's reverse mortgage provides these benefits, and it is federally-insured as well.

2. *Can I qualify for a HUD reverse mortgage?*

To be eligible for a HUD reverse mortgage, HUD's Federal Housing Administration (FHA) requires that the borrower is a homeowner, 62 years of age or older; own your home outright, or have a low mortgage balance that can be paid off at the closing with proceeds from the reverse loan; and must live in the home. You are further required to receive consumer information from HUD-approved counseling sources prior to obtaining the loan. You can contact the Housing Counseling Clearinghouse on 1-800-569-4287 to obtain the name and telephone number of a HUD-approved counseling agency and a list of FHA approved lenders within your area.

3. *Can I apply if I didn't buy my present house with FHA mortgage insurance?*

Yes. While your property must meet FHA minimum standards, it doesn't matter if you didn't buy it with an FHA-insured mortgage. Your new HUD reverse mortgage will be a new FHA-insured mortgage loan.

4. *What types of homes are eligible?*

Your home must be a single family dwelling or a two-to-four unit property that you own and occupy. Townhouses, detached homes, units in condominiums and some manufactured homes are eligible. Condominiums must be FHA-approved. It is possible for condominiums to qualify under the Spot Loan program. The home must be in reasonable condition, and must meet HUD minimum property standards. In some cases, home repairs can be made after the closing of a reverse mortgage.

5. *What's the difference between a reverse mortgage and a bank home equity loan?*

With a traditional second mortgage, or a home equity line of credit, you must have sufficient income to qualify for the loan, and you are required to make monthly mortgage payments. A reverse mortgage works very differently. The reverse mortgage pays you, and it is available regardless of your current income. You don't make payments, because the loan is not due as long as the house is your principal residence. Like all homeowners, you still are required to pay your real estate taxes and other conventional payments like utilities, but with an FHA-insured HUD Reverse Mortgage, you cannot be foreclosed or forced to vacate your house because you "missed your mortgage payment."

6. Can the lender take my home away if I outlive the loan?

No! Nor is the loan due. You do not need to repay the loan as long as you or one of the borrowers continues to live in the house and keeps the taxes and insurance current. You can never owe more than your home's value.

7. Will I still have an estate that I can leave to my heirs?

When you sell your home or no longer use it for your primary residence, you or your estate will repay the cash you received from the reverse mortgage, plus interest and other fees, to the lender. The remaining equity in your home, if any, belongs to you or to your heirs. None of your other assets will be affected by HUD's reverse mortgage loan. This debt will never be passed along to the estate or heirs.

8. How much money can I get from my home?

The amount you can borrow depends on your age, the current interest rate, other loan fees and the appraised value of your home or FHA's mortgage limits for your are, whichever is less. Generally, the more valuable your home is, the older you are, the lower the interest, the more you can borrow.

9. Should I use an estate planning service to find a reverse mortgage? I've been contacted by a firm that will give me the name of a lender for a "small percentage" of the loan?

HUD does NOT recommend using an estate planning service, or any service that charges a fee just for referring a borrower to a lender! HUD provides this information without cost, and HUD-approved housing counseling agencies are available for free, or at minimal cost, to provide information, counseling, and free referral to a list of HUD-approved lenders. Before you agree to pay a fee for a simple referral, call 1-800-569-4287, toll-free, for the name and location of a HUD-approved housing counseling agency near you.

10. How do I receive my payments?

You have five options:

- Tenure — equal monthly payments as long as at least one borrower lives and continues to occupy the property as a principal residence.

- Term — equal monthly payments for a fixed period of months selected.

- Line of Credit — unscheduled payments or in installments, at times and in amounts of borrower's choosing until the line of credit is exhausted.

- Modified Tenure — combination of line of credit with monthly payments for as long as the borrower remains in the home.

- Modified Term — combination of line of credit with monthly payments for a fixed period of months selected by the borrower.

HUD

How HUD's Reverse Mortgage Program Works

http://www.hud.gov/offices/hsg/sfh/hecm/hecmabou.cfm

Homeowners 62 and older who have paid off their mortgages or have only small mortgage balances remaining are eligible to participate in HUD's reverse mortgage program. The program allows homeowners to borrow against the equity in their homes.

* * *

Unlike ordinary home equity loans, a HUD reverse mortgage does not require repayment as long as the borrower lives in the home. Lenders recover their principal, plus interest, when the home is sold. The remaining value of the home goes to the homeowner or to his or her survivors. If the sales proceeds are insufficient to pay the amount owed, HUD will pay the lender the amount of the shortfall. The Federal Housing Administration, which is part of HUD, collects an insurance premium from all borrowers to provide this coverage.

The size of reverse mortgage loans is determined by the borrower's age, the interest rate, and the home's value. The older a borrower, the larger the percentage of the home's value that can be borrowed.

For example, based on a loan with an interest rates of approximately 9 percent, and a home qualifying for $100,000, a 65-year-old could borrow up to 22 percent of the home's value; a 75-year-old could borrow up to 41 percent of the home's value; and, an 85-year-old could borrow up to 58 percent of the home's value. The percentages do not include closing costs because these charges can vary.

There are no asset or income limitations on borrowers receiving HUD's reverse mortgages.

There are also no limits on the value of homes qualifying for a HUD reverse mortgage. The value of the home will be determined by an independent appraisal. However, the amount that may be borrowed is capped by the maximum FHA mortgage limit for the area, which varies from $200,160 to $362,790 [2006]. For Alaska, Guam, Hawaii and the Virgin Islands, the FHA mortgage limits may be adjusted up to 150 percent of the ceiling depending on the area. The FHA limits usually increase each year. As a result, owners of higher-priced homes can't borrow any more than owners of homes valued at the FHA limit.

HUD's reverse mortgage program collects funds from insurance premiums charged to borrowers. Senior citizens are charged 2 percent of the home's value as an up-front payment plus one-half percent on the loan balance each year, which is paid out on a monthly basis for the life of the loan. These amounts are usually paid by the lender and charged to the borrower's principal balance.

QUESTIONS

1. Husband was born in January of 1928 and wife was born in February 1931. Their home's current value is $220,000 and they live in Wichita, KS. How

much could they extract from their home as a lump sum through a Home Equity Conversion Loan? Would the amount increase or decrease if the home was in Long Island, NY?

2. What barriers to wider use of reverse mortgages can you identify?

Jean Reilly
Reverse Mortgages: Backing into the Future
5 ELDER L.J. 17 (Spring 1997)[*]

I. Obstacles Impeding Acceptance of Reverse
Mortgages by Borrowers and Lenders

Litigation surrounding reverse mortgages and tales of predatory lending have made borrowers wary of this complex financial instrument. The growth of the reverse mortgage market has been further hindered by lenders' aversion to the perceived risks and delays inherent in these mortgages.

A. Litigation and "Predatory Lending"

Beginning in 1999 these have been a series of lawsuits by disappointed reverse mortgage borrowers who accuse lenders of defrauding them out of the equity in their home. The suits, all against private lenders, have generated bad press and have scared potential borrowers away from even the relatively safe government-backed reverse mortgages. *Barron's*, the well-respected financial publication, trumpeted in an article, "Reverse mortgages can be a nightmare. . . . Some retirees have seen their home equity completely wiped out in five years or less." The magazine further stated, without differentiating among reverse mortgage lenders, that reverse mortgages "can leave people shell-shocked, with little or no money to pay for expensive stays in nursing homes during their final years of life — or to pass on to their heirs." Similarly, the headline of a *Worth* article discussing charges that some reverse mortgage lenders "bilked millions of dollars from trusting senior citizens" gave potential borrowers the generic warning: "Beware Reverse-Mortgage Mania: Don't Let A Bad Deal Burn Up Your Home Equity." The legal profession also has warned of predatory lending, high interest rates, and unconscionable terms in reverse mortgage transactions. The result has been to make the public wary of reverse mortgages. This public distrust is best exemplified by a woman who wrote into the Newark *Star-Ledger's* Question and Answer Financial Column asking, "It is my belief that many senior citizens have obtained reverse mortgages without knowing the actual cost of such borrowing, because the mortgage lenders did not reveal those costs. Am I correct?" The answering columnist confirmed her perceptions: "These is little doubt that some unscrupulous lenders did not reveal the true cost of reverse mortgages to gullible seniors."

* * *

QUESTION

To what extent should senior citizens be shielded from the consequences of their own choices — foolish or otherwise?

FLORES ET AL. v. TRANSAMERICA HOMEFIRST, INC.
93 Cal. App. 4th 846,
113 Cal. Rptr. 2d 376 (Cal. Ct. App. 2001)

Plaintiffs Donald J. and Helen Flores, husband and wife, are senior citizens who obtained a reverse mortgage on their home from defendant Transamerica HomeFirst, Inc., (HomeFirst). After plaintiffs filed suit against HomeFirst for unfair business practices and other tortious conduct, HomeFirst petitioned to compel arbitration pursuant to arbitration clauses contained in the loan agreement and deed of trust signed by plaintiffs. The trial court denied the petition, finding the arbitration clauses to be unconscionable and unenforceable. Home-First appeals from that ruling, which we now affirm.

I. BACKGROUND FACTS

In February 1997, plaintiffs, then ages 80 and 76, executed a "Loan Agreement and Note" and a deed of trust in order to obtain a reverse mortgage on their home from HomeFirst. Under the reverse mortgage plan, plaintiffs received a lump sum plus monthly payments from HomeFirst until July 1999, when plaintiffs sold their home. In connection with the sale, plaintiffs received a final loan payoff demand from HomeFirst and were shocked to discover that they owed not only the $72,018 in principal they had borrowed plus interest on that principal but also another $75,000 in "contingent interest" which represented 50 percent of the market value appreciation over the two-year loan period. Plaintiffs paid the payoff demand under protest and then filed suit claiming unfair business practices, violations of the Consumer Legal Remedies Act (Civ. Code § 1750 et seq.), unconscionability, fraud, unlawful prepayment penalties, and bad faith. HomeFirst removed the action to federal court on the ground of federal preemption, but the federal court remanded the matter back to state court.

The loan agreement is 14 pages long, and an arbitration clause appears on page 11 in section 20. The first paragraph appears in bold face, enlarged type surrounded by a border:

> ARBITRATION. Any controversy or claim arising out of or relating to this Loan Agreement, the Security Instrument, or any other document relating to the Loan, the breach of any of them or the default under any of them, other than an action or proceeding to foreclose on the Property pursuant to the Security Instrument, will be settled by binding arbitration under the jurisdiction of the American Arbitration Association in accordance with its Commercial Arbitration Rules. The arbitration will be conducted in the County of San Francisco or the County of Los Angeles, whichever is closer to the Property Address, unless you and I agree on a different location. Judgment upon any award rendered by the

> arbitrator may be entered in any appropriate court. Such arbitration may not, however, without your consent, delay or adversely affect your ability to exercise any of the remedies available to you under this Loan Agreement or under the Security Instrument. Your pursuit of such remedies will not constitute a waiver by you of your rights to submit any controversy or claim to arbitration. No arbitration conducted hereunder shall be consolidated or combined with any other arbitration absent Lender's express written consent.

The second paragraph is not in bold face type and does not appear within a border:

> "Notwithstanding anything that may be contained in this Section to the contrary, this Section does not limit your right to foreclose against the Property (whether judicially or non-judicially by exercising your right of sale or otherwise), to exercise self-help remedies such as set-off, or to obtain injunctive relief for the appointment of a receiver from any appropriate court, whether before, during or after any arbitration."

Throughout these quoted provisions, the terms "you," "your," and "Lender" refer to HomeFirst. "I" refers to the borrower.

Based on these provisions, HomeFirst petitioned to compel arbitration. Plaintiffs opposed the petition on the ground that the underlying loan documents were unconscionable. The trial court ruled that the arbitration provisions within the loan documents were unconscionable pursuant to the then-newly filed decision of the Supreme Court in *Armendariz v. Foundation Health Psychcare Services, Inc.* (2000) 24 Cal. 4th 83, 99 Cal. Rptr. 2d 745, 6 P.3d 669 (*Armendariz*). HomeFirst moved for reconsideration on the ground that the parties had not been given an opportunity to brief the question whether justification exists for the lack of mutuality in the arbitration agreement. The trial court then granted reconsideration but ruled that HomeFirst had failed to demonstrate a justification, and the court again denied the petition to compel arbitration.

II. DISCUSSION

A written agreement to arbitrate is enforceable, "save upon such grounds as exist for the revocation of any contract." [Citation omitted.] As is true for any contract, an arbitration provision may be held unenforceable if it is unconscionable.

* * *

C. UNCONSCIONABILITY

In *A&M Produce Co. v. FMC Corp.* [citation omitted], the court outlined an analytic framework for determining whether a particular contractual provision is unconscionable, explaining that unconscionability has both a procedural and a substantive element. [Citation omitted.] The procedural element focuses on "oppression" or "surprise." [Citation omitted.] Oppression arises from an inequality of bargaining power that results in no real negotiation and an absence of meaningful choice. Surprise involves the extent to which the supposedly agreed-upon terms are hidden in a prolix printed form drafted by the party seeking to enforce them. [Citation omitted.] The substantive element has to do with the effects of the contractual terms and whether they are overly harsh or one-sided. [Citation omitted.]

Analysis of unconscionability begins with an inquiry into whether the contract was a contract of adhesion — i.e., a standardized contract, imposed upon the subscribing party without an opportunity to negotiate the terms. [Citation omitted.] A finding of a contract of adhesion is essentially a finding of procedural unconscionability. [Citation omitted.]

In the present case, the arbitration clauses contained in the loan agreement and deed of trust constituted a contract of adhesion. HomeFirst unquestionably had superior bargaining strength in that it presented its preprinted documents, cast in generic language, to plaintiffs for signature. Plaintiffs were offered no opportunity to negotiate. The "IMPORTANT INFORMATION FOR ALL BOR-ROWERS" which plaintiffs received indicated that in order to establish the reverse mortgage plaintiffs were required to sign the standardized loan documents. Plaintiffs were never informed that the documents, much less the arbitration provisions, were negotiable. Moreover, according to plaintiffs' son, HomeFirst's representative told plaintiffs that HomeFirst was the only company in California offering reverse mortgages, thereby indicating that plaintiffs had no real choice of alternate lenders. In sum, the undisputed facts indicate that the arbitration agreement was imposed upon plaintiffs on a "take it or leave it" basis. The arbitration agreement was a contract of adhesion and thereby procedurally unconscionable.

As already noted, substantive unconscionability focuses on the one-sidedness of the contract terms. In the context of an arbitration agreement, the agreement is unconscionable unless there is a "'modicum of bilaterality'" in the arbitration remedy. [Citation omitted.] "Although parties are free to contract for asymmetrical remedies and arbitration clauses of varying scope, . . . the doctrine of unconscionability limits the extent to which a stronger party may, through a contract of adhesion, impose the arbitration forum on the weaker party without accepting that forum for itself." [Citation omitted.]

Here, we agree with the trial court's conclusion that the arbitration provisions do not display a modicum of bilaterality. Under the loan agreement plaintiffs' principal obligation is to repay the sums advanced with interest. Plaintiffs' indebtedness is non-recourse, secured solely by the deed of trust. In the event of a breach by plaintiffs, HomeFirst's remedy is mandatory prepayment, and if plaintiffs do not repay the loan, then HomeFirst is allowed to sell the property. Pursuant to section 20 of the loan agreement and the deed of trust, while plaintiffs are required to arbitrate "[a]ny controversy" arising out of the loan agreement or deed of trust, HomeFirst is allowed to proceed by judicial or non-judicial foreclosure, by self-help remedies such as set-off, and by injunctive relief to obtain appointment of a receiver.

Moreover, the loan documents allow HomeFirst to proceed with foreclosure despite the pendency of disputes brought to arbitration. The arbitration clauses provide that arbitration "may not . . . without [HomeFirst's] consent, delay or adversely affect [HomeFirst's] ability to exercise any of the remedies available to [HomeFirst] under [the loan agreement or deed of trust]." And finally, we note that section 19 of the deed of trust declares that "[a]ll of [HomeFirst's] remedies under this Security Agreement are cumulative to any other right or remedy under this Security Instrument or the Loan Agreement, or *which is afforded by law or equity*, and may be exercised concurrently, independently, or successively." (Italics added.) Realistically, then, the mandatory arbitration provisions apply to claims of the borrower against HomeFirst but not vice-versa. We conclude that this unilateral obligation to arbitrate is so one-sided as to be substantively unconscionable.

D. JUSTIFICATION

In *Armendariz*, [citation omitted], the Supreme Court clarified that not all lack of mutuality in an adhesive arbitration agreement is invalid. Rather, quoting from *Stirlen*, [citation omitted] the court explained that "a contract can provide a 'margin of safety' that provides the party with superior bargaining strength a type of extra protection for which it has a legitimate commercial need without being unconscionable." Thus, if the stronger party has a justification "grounded in something other than the [stronger party's] desire to maximize its advantage based on the perceived superiority of the judicial forum," then the arbitration agreement would not be unconscionable. [Citation omitted.] Conversely, a one-sided arbitration agreement that imposes arbitration on the weaker party while providing a choice of forums for the stronger party is unfair and unconscionable "without at least some reasonable justification for such one-sidedness based on 'business realities.'" [Citation omitted.] However, unless the "business realities" that create the special need for such an advantage are explained in the contract itself, they must be factually established.

HomeFirst argued below and reiterates on appeal that business realities dictate that it be allowed to foreclose against the property as a legitimate commercial means of ensuring its security for the non-recourse loan. We are not persuaded.

As a practical matter, by reserving to itself the remedy of foreclosure, HomeFirst has assured the availability of the only remedy it is likely to need. In any event, foreclosure is not the only remedy reserved to HomeFirst from the scope of arbitration. Rather, HomeFirst is entitled to exercise any rights or remedies "afforded by law or equity" while plaintiffs are confined to arbitration for all purposes. Moreover, by the terms of the arbitration agreement, HomeFirst is allowed to proceed with its own remedies despite the pendency of any claims in arbitration. The clear implication is that HomeFirst has attempted to maximize its advantage by avoiding arbitration of its own claims. . . .

E. PREEMPTION UNDER FEDERAL ARBITRATION ACT

HomeFirst maintains that the Federal Arbitration Act (9 U.S.C. § 1 et seq.) (hereafter FAA) applies and precludes a determination under California law that the arbitration agreement is unenforceable. HomeFirst relies on the principle that the FAA preempts state laws that single out and thwart arbitration provisions. [Citation omitted.] The argument is unsound.

Section 2 of the FAA contains language virtually identical to that of section 1281.2 of the Code of Civil Procedure: a written agreement to arbitrate a controversy "shall be valid, irrevocable, and enforceable, save *upon such grounds as exist at law or in equity for the revocation of any contract.*" (9 U.S.C. § 2, italics added.) The United States Supreme Court has recognized that "generally applicable contract defenses, such as fraud, duress, or unconscionability, may be applied to invalidate arbitration agreements without contravening [Section] 2 [of the FAA]." [Citation omitted.] Thus, the California Supreme Court has concluded that the inquiry under the FAA is the same as under California law-i.e. whether there are reasons based on general contract principles for refusing to enforce an arbitration agreement. [Citation omitted.]

The Supreme Court has explained that arbitration is a favored method of resolving disputes only when it is voluntary. [Citation omitted.] The " 'strong public policy of this state in favor of resolving disputes by arbitration'" does not extend to an arbitration agreement permeated by unconscionability. [Citation omitted.] Rather, "an arbitration agreement is to be rescinded on the same grounds as other contracts or contract terms. In this respect, arbitration agreements are neither favored nor disfavored, but simply placed on an equal footing with other contracts." [Citation omitted.]

A preemption argument identical to HomeFirst's was rejected in *Stirlen*: "The FAA does not reflect a congressional intent to occupy the entire field of arbitration but preempts state regulation in this area only to the extent that it stands as an obstacle to the accomplishment and execution of the full purposes and objectives of Congress. [Citation omitted.] Judicial refusal to enforce an arbitration clause clearly unconscionable under a general contract law principle not at all hostile to arbitration presents no obstacle to the objective of the FAA or any other congressional purpose."

Armendariz agreed with the *Stirlen* court that enforcing a "modicum of bilaterality" in arbitration agreements does not single out arbitration for disfavor. While the form of unconscionability (e.g., one-sided choice of forums) may be peculiar to the context of arbitration, the application of ordinary principles of unconscionability does not disparage arbitration as a favored voluntary remedy. [Citation omitted.]

F. SEVERANCE

Civil Code section 1670.5 permits the court, upon finding a contract to be unconscionable, to refuse to enforce the contract or to "enforce the remainder of the contract without the unconscionable clause. . . ." HomeFirst contends that this court should sever the provisions which reserve from arbitration the remedies of foreclosure, set-off, and appointment of a receiver. And HomeFirst argues that such a severance would have no effect on the arbitrability of plaintiffs' claims here, as those claims do not implicate such remedies. We decline to do so.

In *Armendariz*, [citation omitted], the Supreme Court found no abuse of discretion in the trial court's refusal to sever the invalid arbitration provisions where the unilateral arbitration agreement was "permeated" with unconscionability: "[S]uch permeation is indicated by the fact that there is no single provision a court can strike or restrict in order to remove the unconscionable taint from the agreement. Rather, the court would have to, in effect, reform the contract . . . by augmenting it with additional terms." [Citation omitted.] Courts have no inherent powers to reform contracts; consequently, the court must void the entire arbitration agreement. [Citation omitted.]

In the present case, we are likewise faced with an arbitration agreement in which no single provision can be stricken to remove the unconscionable taint. As we have previously mentioned, the lack of bilaterality appears not only in the reservation of remedies specified in section 20 of the loan documents (foreclosure, set-off, appointment of receiver) but also in the provisions allowing HomeFirst to proceed with its remedies despite a claim pending in arbitration and giving HomeFirst all remedies "afforded by law and equity." HomeFirst has cited no precedent, and we are aware of none, in which a unilateral agreement to arbitrate was saved by severing the offending provisions.

Indeed, it strikes us as woefully unfair to plaintiffs to allow HomeFirst at this late date — after a dispute has arisen and after the reverse mortgage has terminated — to refute the unconscionable aspects of the arbitration agreement which HomeFirst itself drafted and from which HomeFirst stood to benefit over the life of the loan. "The overarching inquiry [under the doctrine of severance] is whether the interests of justice . . . would be furthered." [Citation omitted.] We do not believe justice would be served by an effort to save the arbitration agreement by removing post hoc offending provisions for which HomeFirst no longer has any use.

III. DISPOSITION

The order denying the petition to compel arbitration is affirmed.

* * *

Jean Reilly
Reverse Mortgages: Backing into the Future
5 ELDER L.J. 17 (Spring 1997)[*]

B. Lenders: "Headaches" and Hesitation

Financial institution managers, despite their constant search for additional sources of loan volume and their long-held interest in the potential benefits of leveraging the equity of elderly homeowners, have nevertheless been hesitant to enter the reverse mortgage market. . . . [F]inancial institutions are reluctant to offer reverse mortgages because of four perceived risks: value risk, reputation risk, tort risk, and demand risk.

With value risk, the concern is that the mortgage might accrue interest and principal that will eventually exceed the value of the house. Such fate befell Providential, the lender that was the defendant in the fraud and misrepresentation lawsuit [Citation omitted]. Providential got in trouble partly because it made loans at the top of the California real estate market, based on expectations that property prices would continue to appreciate at a 5% rate. Instead, California home prices declined at a 5% annual rate from 1988 to 1994. The result was that Providential's reverse mortgage portfolio, which was listed as having a carrying value of $51 million, received a $33 million write-down in 1994. The write-down cut the value of Providential reverse mortgage holdings by 65% and caused shares of stock in the company to plummet to $5 per share from a high of $16. Providential subsequently sold off all of its loans and liquidated itself. Capital Holding, Providential's closest competitor, also withdrew from the reverse mortgage market in 1993 because it did not believe it could make any money. . . .

With reputation risk, lenders are worried about how their image may be affected in the event of foreclosure due to default. . . .

Moral hazard describes the tendency of borrowers to act against the interests of lenders. For example, when it becomes apparent to an elderly person that she will have to vacate the home by the end of the year because she needs to enter a nursing home, she may cease maintaining the home. This is particularly likely to be true if all the equity in the house has been used up by the reverse mortgage. . . .

Tort risk involves the possibility of claims by the borrowers or their heirs and relatives that the borrower was deceived by the bank regarding the material terms of the reverse mortgage. . . .

Lenders also face an interest rate risk with reverse mortgages. In a rising rate environment, a fixed rate investor normally has the benefit of reinvesting cash flows into higher yielding investments. This benefit is not available to the reverse mortgage lender, however, because reverse mortgages do not result in any intermediate cash flows to the lender. A fixed rate, reverse mortgage lender is helplessly locked into a rising rate environment. Although an adjustable-rate reverse mortgage is certainly more attractive to the lender with regards to interest rate, it is not risk-free. In a rising rate environment, an adjustable-rate reverse mortgage accrues increasing amounts of interest. Thus, the lender faces risk from negative amortization; that is to say, the possibility increases that the accrued interest and principal will exceed the resale value of the home.

QUESTIONS

1. Under what circumstances would you recommend a reverse mortgage to your elder clients?

2. What barriers to wider use of reverse mortgages can you identify?

National Reverse Mortgage Lenders Association
Reverse Mortgage Volume Nearly Doubles From Last Year
October 27, 2006
http://www.nrmlaonline.org/rms/press.aspx?article_id=448

Fueled by rising home values, larger sales forces, and increased consumer acceptance, the number of federally insured reverse mortgages made in the U.S. in 2006 grew by 77 percent, according to the National Reverse Mortgage Lenders Association. During the most recent federal fiscal year, ending September 30, [2006] the Federal Housing Administration (an arm of the U.S. Department of Housing and Urban Development), insured 76,351 Home Equity Conversion Mortgages (HECMs) compared to 43,131 the prior year. "More seniors are recognizing that traditional retirements tools, such as IRAs, pensions, and 401(k)s are not providing sufficient income to help fund everyday living expenses and healthcare," said Peter Bell, President of NRMLA. "Thru proper education, more retirees are recognizing that the home they have lived in for so many years can now take care of them by using a reverse mortgage to access the equity accumulated over 20, 30, 40 years, to help them living more comfortably."

B. THE ELDERLY TENANT

1. Protection from Discrimination

National Resource and Policy Center on Housing and Long Term Care, USC Andrus Gerontology Center
Housing Highlights: What Are Your Rights
(January 13, 1998)[*]

WHY ARE THE RIGHTS OF TENANTS WITH DISABILITIES IMPORTANT TO OLDER PERSONS?

Many older people are unable to manage daily activities as well as they once did. They may have difficulty walking, seeing, hearing, taking care of personal or health needs or doing household chores. Landlords may refuse to rent to them, or ask them to move, simply because they need assistance with certain activities. These rejections or evictions of older people are illegal under the Fair Housing Amendments Act of 1988, and other federal and state laws.

WHAT IS THE FAIR HOUSING AMENDMENTS ACT?

The Fair Housing Amendments Act of 1988 is a federal statute that protects frail or disabled persons against discrimination in housing.

---

[*] Copyright © 1998. Reprinted with permission.

<u>What It Does:</u>

- Extends civil rights protection in the housing area to people with disabilities.

- Requires new construction of dwellings with four or more units to include features such as wheelchair accessibility, reinforced walls to accommodate later installation of grab bars.

- Requires landlords to treat people with disabilities just like they treat everyone else.

- Prohibits landlords from asking current tenants or people applying for housing questions about their age, health or ability to live independently, unless this information is necessary for a special program.

- Requires landlords to make reasonable accommodations in rules and procedures, and to allow reasonable modifications to the premises, at the request of tenants with disabilities.

<u>What It Does Not Do:</u>

- Does not apply to rental buildings which contain fewer than four units, where the owner also lives in the building.

- Does not require a landlord to rent to current users of illegal drugs.

- Does not require a landlord to rent to a person who is a threat to the safety or health of other tenants, or whose tenancy would result in substantial damage to property of others.

- Does not require a landlord to provide services to a tenant with disabilities, unless the housing program already includes services.

- Does not require a landlord to change the basic nature of the housing program.

<u>What Changes Can Be Made?</u>

REASONABLE ACCOMMODATIONS: Changes in rules or procedures which (1) are reasonable under the circumstances, and (2) give a disabled tenant equal opportunity to use and enjoy the residence. Examples include:

- waiving a no-pets rule for a tenant with a mental disability who is emotionally dependent on their pet.

- waive a no-guest rule for a tenant who needs a live-in aide.

- changing the due date for rent to allow a tenant time to deposit their disability check and avoid late charges.

- arranging to have a staff person pick up the trash from the apartment of a tenant who is ill and cannot carry the bag to the trash disposal.

- providing large print notices for a vision-impaired tenant.

REASONABLE MODIFICATIONS: Changes to the physical structure of the premises, which (1) are reasonable and (2) give a tenant with disabilities equal access to residence. A tenant has the right to make reasonable modification at his or her own expense, but may be required to restore the premises to the original condition upon moving out. The landlord must pay for the costs of modification to common areas of the building. Examples include:

- installing grab bars in the bathroom and replacing doorknobs with lever handles.

- widening doorways for wheelchair access.

- installing a ramp at the entrance to the building.

- replacing small floor numbers with large numbers which contrast with the wall so that tenants can read them more easily.

2. Rental Subsidies

National Resource Center on Supportive Housing and Home Modification
A project supported by The Archstone Foundation and The California Endowment, Headquartered at the University of Southern California's Ethel Percy Andrus Gerontology Center
http://www.homemods.org/library/index.shtml[*]

GOVERNMENT HOUSING ASSISTANCE AND THE ELDERLY

Government housing assistance is available to low-income elderly through several programs in the form of affordable housing or rental assistance. Most government housing assistance for the elderly is administered by local public housing authorities (PHAs). Other agencies include the local Department of Housing and Community Development, the respective State Housing Finance Agencies and the U.S. Department of Agriculture's (USDA) Rural Development Office. Funds from the U.S. Department of Housing and Urban Development (HUD) and USDA's Rural Housing Services also support some housing assistance programs. All government housing assistance for the elderly are over-subscribed, with waiting lists that vary in length. Government housing assistance available to low-income older persons include the following: the HOPE for Elderly Independence Program, the Housing Choice Voucher Program, Local Rental Assistance Programs, Public Housing, the Rural Housing Service Rental Assistance Program, and the Section 202 Supportive Housing for the Elderly Program.

IMPORTANCE OF GOVERNMENT HOUSING ASSISTANCE TO OLDER PERSONS

- Provides assistance to a majority of older renters who have excessive housing costs.

---

[*] Reprinted with permission.

- Provides low-income elderly with service-enriched options to live independently.

TYPES OF GOVERNMENT HOUSING ASSISTANCE

HOPE for Elderly Independence Program

Some PHAs administer the Homeownership and Opportunity for People Everywhere (HOPE) program which provides a combination of HUD Section 8 rental assistance with case management and supportive services to low-income elderly persons. The aim is to expand access to Section 8 rental assistance to the frail elderly tenant population and help them avoid nursing home placement or other restrictive settings when home and community-based options are appropriate. Contact the local PHA for availability and more information about the program. To locate the local PHA, refer to the blue pages of the local telephone directory or call HUD at (202) 708-1112. Eligibility: Elderly persons, aged 62 or older, who have difficulty performing at least three activities of daily living (e.g., eating, bathing, grooming, dressing) and home management activities (e.g., housekeeping, laundry, shopping or getting to and from one place to another).

Housing Choice Voucher/Section 8 Program

The Housing Choice Voucher (or "Section 8") program, administered locally by PHAs, provides very low-income families, the elderly, and persons with disability affordable, decent, and sanitary housing in the private market. Participants are free to find their own housing that meets the requirements of the program. Housing assistance is provided on behalf of the family or individual. To locate the local PHA, refer to the blue pages of the local telephone directory or call HUD at (202) 708-1112.

Eligibility: In general, the family's income may not exceed 50% of the median income for the county or metropolitan area in which the family chooses to live. This is determined by the PHA based on the total annual gross income and family size and is limited to U.S. citizens and specified categories of non-citizens. The local PHA can provide information about income limits for the area and family size.

Local Rental Assistance Programs

Local rental assistance may be available through the HOME Investment Partnership Program. Contact the local Community Housing and Development Office by referring to the blue pages of the local telephone directory.

Public Housing

Public housing provides affordable, decent, and safe rental housing for eligible low-income families, the elderly, and persons with disabilities. Tenants typically pay no more than 30 percent of their monthly income for rent. Local PHAs that receive funding from the federal government own and operate public housing complexes. For more information about public housing and income limits, visit www.hud.gov/phprog.cfm. To locate the local PHA, refer to the blue pages of the local telephone directory or call HUD at (202) 708-1112. Eligibility: Public housing is limited to low-income families and individuals. The local PHA determines the applicant's eligibility based on: 1) annual gross income; 2) status: elderly 62+, a person with a disability, or as a family; and, 3) U.S. citizenship or eligible immigration status. If eligible, the PHA will check references to ensure that applicant and family members will be good tenants.

Rural Housing Service (RHS) — Rental Assistance Program (Section 521)

For rural America, rent subsidies under the U.S. Department of Agriculture's RHS Rental Assistance Program (Section 521) ensure that elderly, disabled, and low-income residents of multi-family housing complexes financed by RHS are able to afford rent payments. With the help of the Rental Assistance Program, a qualified applicant pays no more than 30 percent of his or her income for housing. To determine eligibility or to apply, please contact the Rural Development State Office. The closest one can be found by calling Rural Housing Service National Office at (202) 720-4323.

Section 202 Supportive Housing for the Elderly Program

The Section 202 Program is provided by private, nonprofit housing and service-oriented organizations that have received capital advances from the government to finance the construction and rehabilitation of structures. These structures serve as supportive housing for very low-income elderly persons. The Section 202 program provides rent subsidies for the projects to help make them affordable. Supportive services provided under the Section 202 program include meals, transportation, and accommodations for residents with disabilities. Contact the local housing authority (see above). Eligibility: The program benefits low-income residents age 62 years or older.

SELECTION PREFERENCES

PHAs sometimes give preference to specific groups of individuals or families. This enables the PHAs to direct their limited housing resources to people with the greatest housing needs. Since the demand for housing assistance often exceeds the limited resources available to HUD and the local PHAs, long waiting periods are common. It is not uncommon for a PHA to close its waiting list when there are more people on the list than can be assisted in the near future.

Examples of local housing preferences for receiving assistance include:

- People experiencing high rent burden (rent is greater than 50% of income).

- Residents who live and/or work in the jurisdiction.

- The homeless or those living in substandard housing.

- Veterans and veterans' families.

- Victims of reprisals or hate crimes.

- Working families and those unable to work because of age or disability.

3. Legal Remedies

GREENE AVE. ASSOC. v. CARDWELL
191 Misc. 2d 775, 743 N.Y.S.2d 842 (N.Y. Misc. 2002)

This holdover proceeding was commenced by Petition and Notice of Petition each dated September 19, 2001, following a Thirty Day Notice of Termination of Tenancy dated June 28, 2001. Petitioner seeks to recover apartment E-15 at 80 Greene Avenue, as well as use and occupancy at the rate of $1,087.00 per month from January 1, 2001. A prior holdover proceeding, commenced on January 16, 2001, was dismissed by Hon. Oymin Chin on June 25, 2001, because Petitioner served a rent demand after the notice of termination.

The Petition alleges that Respondent Jessie Cardwell took possession of the premises pursuant to a lease dated February 14, 1992, and that her right to possession expired on August 31, 2001, the date specified in the Thirty Day Notice. Respondents Tiffany Ann Cardwell, John Doe and Jane Doe are alleged to be "undertenant(s)" of Jessie Cardwell.

The Thirty Day Notice states that Jessie Cardwell is "in material noncompliance of [her] tenancy," because she permitted Tiffany Ann Cardwell to occupy the premises without Petitioner's prior written approval, and failed to report a change in family composition, apartment occupants or income. The premises are said to be "contained in a housing project specifically set up for the elderly and which has a mortgage aided by government insurance," and the notice is given pursuant to provisions of the written lease and "HUD Rules and Regulations." Paragraphs 13, 15 and 16 of the lease, and a "house rider," are cited, as well as "paragraph 23B and the HUD regulation handbook 4350.3(4-18)."

In a Notice of Appearance, Answer and Counterclaim dated November 13, 2001, Respondent Jessie Cardwell denied the allegations of the Petition and asserted eight Affirmative Defenses and a Counterclaim. The answer alleges, among other things, that Tiffany Ann Cardwell is Jessie Cardwell's "lawfully adopted daughter," her "adopted minor daughter, who is also her granddaughter;" that Tiffany is permitted to occupy the premises pursuant to Real Property Law § 235-f; that "Petitioner, its employees and / or agents have had knowledge that the Respondent's lawfully adopted daughter had lived with Respondent for a number of years, yet took no action," thereby establishing laches, waiver and estoppel. The Counterclaim alleges that "this summary holdover proceeding constitutes frivolous conduct as defined by 22 NYCRR § 130-1.1" and "is a clear attempt to knowingly harass and maliciously injure Respondent, an illiterate and sickly senior citizen."

Ms. Cardwell moved for summary judgment dismissing the action, which was denied by Hon. Marcia J. Sikowitz in a Decision / Order dated March 15, 2002. Judge Sikowitz found "questions of fact regarding Tiffany Cardwell's residence, and what, if any, information the respondent furnished to the petitioner about her adopted daughter Tiffany . . . [and] whether or not the petitioner is correct that a fraud was perpetrated on the petitioner as defined by HUD Handbook 4350.3 Section 5-19b."

A trial was held before this Court on April 8 through April 11. Petitioner presented three witnesses: Al Weeks, a "field agent" employed by Petitioner; Eva Diaz, a "secretary" employed by AMS Realty Company, Petitioner's managing agent, working at the building at 80 Greene Ave.; and Jessica Fernandez-Prada, also employed by AMS, working at its office in Great Neck. Respondent Jessie Cardwell testified, and her daughter, Linda Wilson-Warner testified on her behalf. The parties submitted post-trial briefs containing their respective legal and factual contentions and arguments.

As described by Judge Sikowitz in her Decision/Order on the motion for summary judgment, the subject premises is a "HUD Section 202 senior citizen housing unit." Under the Section 202 Program, "direct loans are provided by HUD at below market rates to . . . not-for-profit and public entities that agree to provide housing and related facilities for elderly . . . families . . . Rent subsidies, mostly under the Section 8 Program, are provided for all units in the Program.". . . .

HUD regulations and "handbooks" govern various aspects of Section 8 tenancies, including terminations, establishing substantive and procedural requirements. Handbook 4350.3, titled "Occupancy Requirements of Subsidized Multifamily Housing Programs," is applicable to this proceeding. . . . The provisions of the Handbook are intended to be mandatory, and are so treated by New York courts. . . . The amount of the rent subsidy is determined by certification and annual recertification. *See, generally,* Handbook 4350.3, Chapters 3 and 5.

In the Thirty Day Notice, Petitioner cites Paragraphs 13, 15, and 16 of the lease and a "house rider." Paragraph 13 provides that the Tenant, designated previously as Jessie Cardwell, "shall use the premises only as a private dwelling for himself/herself and the individuals listed on the *Certification and Recertification of Tenant Eligibility.* The Tenant agrees to permit other individuals to reside in the unit only after obtaining the prior written approval of the landlord." (The provision was amended in 1995 to underline "after.")

Paragraph 15 states that: Every year around the first day of November, the Landlord will request the Tenant to report income and composition of the Tenant's household and to supply any other information required by HUD for the purpose of determining the Tenant's rent and assistance payment, if any. The Tenant agrees to provide accurate statements of this information and to do so by the date specified in the Landlord's request.

There is no question that at the time of applying for an apartment, and each year thereafter when presented with the Owner's Certification of Compliance with HUD's Tenant Eligibility and Rent Procedures, Mr. Cardwell signed the form, indicating that she was the only person in the household, with no dependents, foster children or attendants.

Paragraph 16 is titled "Reporting Changes Between Regularly Scheduled Recertifications," and, as amended at some point during the tenancy, requires the Tenant to advise the Landlord immediately if "[t]he household's income cumulatively increases by $40 or more a month." As will appear below, there was no evidence at trial of any increase in Ms. Cardwell's household income, and no other provision in Paragraph 16 appears in any way relevant to this case. The reference in the Thirty Day Notice to a "house rider" must mean the "House Rules" attached to the lease, which include "[n]o boarders." The Thirty Day Notice states that the termination is based upon "material noncompliance" with the lease; the Notice cites Paragraph 23 but not Paragraph 25. Under Paragraph 23(b)(1), the Landlord may terminate for "material noncompliance"; Paragraph 23(b), as amended, defines that term as including "one or more substantial violations of the lease," and the "failure of tenant to timely supply all requested information on income and composition or eligibility factors, of the tenant household . . . or to *knowingly* (*sic*) provide incomplete or inaccurate information" (emphasis added). Paragraph 25, as amended, states: "*Knowingly* giving the Landlord false information regarding income or other factors considered in determining Tenant's eligibility and rent is a material noncompliance with the lease subject to termination of tenancy" (emphasis added).

The Thirty Day Notice states that the termination is also based upon "the HUD regulation handbook 4350.3 (4-18)." The cited provision of the Handbook states that "[o]wners may evict tenants . . . for . . . material non-compliance with the lease." Paragraph 4-18(c)(1). The next section of the Handbook states that the "term material noncompliance with the lease includes . . . one or more substantial violations of the lease . . . [and] failure of the tenant to timely supply all required information on the income and composition, or eligibility factors, of the tenant household . . . or to knowingly provide incomplete or inaccurate information." Paragraph 4-19(1), (3). As is apparent, Paragraph 23 of the lease, as amended, tracks Paragraphs 4-18 and 4-19 of the Handbook.

The provision in the Handbook cited in the Thirty Day Notice, Paragraph 4-18, appears in Chapter 4, "Leasing, Deposits and Termination of Tenancy." Chapter 5, "Recertification, Interim Adjustments, and Termination of Tenancy," contains provisions dealing with "fraud," including Paragraph 5-19(b), cited by Judge Sikowitz in her decision on the motion for summary judgment. Although it is stated that "fraud" encompasses "[p]roviding false information . . . [in] material noncompliance with the lease," Paragraph 5- 19(c), and that "material noncompliance" by "knowingly" providing false information gives the landlord "authority to pursue eviction in cases of tenant fraud," Paragraph 5-20(b), the precise relationship between the provisions of Chapters 4 and 5 is not clear. The intention, however, seems to be that the provisions of Chapter 5 on "fraud" are used to determine whether the tenant has "knowingly" provided incomplete or inaccurate information for purposes of the termination provisions of Chapter 4. The Petitioner apparently shares this view, in that despite the citation to Chapter 4 in the Thirty Day Notice, it has argued "fraud" throughout the proceedings before this Court and on the motion for summary judgment. . . .

Evidence at Trial

Jessie Cardwell was 64 years old when she moved to 80 Greene Avenue in February 1992. She had been living in a third-floor walk-up, but, after heart surgery, needed an apartment in a building with an elevator. According to the Section 8 certifications, her entire income has come from Social Security and she has no other assets. As stressed by her counsel, the highest level of formal education she achieved was the third grade. She uses a wheelchair, but it is not clear that she is wheelchair-bound.

Tiffany was five years old in February 1992. Her mother, Jessie Cardwell's daughter, was ill and eventually died in 1999. Her father, who was not married to her mother, had apparently died before 1992. Jessie Cardwell adopted Tiffany in February 1993. She explained at trial that a social worker had told her that, if she did not adopt Tiffany, she would be taken from her. Petitioner's witnesses testified that they did not learn that Tiffany was Ms. Cardwell's adopted daughter until recently, and Ms. Cardwell did not contradict them.

Ms. Cardwell maintains that she told Eva Diaz when she applied for the apartment that Tiffany would be living with her, and that Ms. Diaz told her that Tiffany could be named as an occupant or not as Ms. Cardwell pleased. Ms. Cardwell testified that she told Ms. Diaz that, since Tiffany would not be remaining in the apartment if anything happened to Ms. Cardwell, she wouldn't list her. She remembers Ms. Diaz joking with Tiffany about whether Tiffany had a job. No mention was made of any other apartments or buildings in which Ms. Cardwell might live with Tiffany.

Eva Diaz's testimony is consistent with Ms. Cardwell's up to a point. She testified that she never told Ms. Cardwell that she didn't have to list Tiffany, but she also never told Ms. Cardwell directly that she did. Consistent with Ms. Cardwell's testimony, Ms. Diaz testified that it was up to Ms. Cardwell to list Tiffany or not, and up to the main office to follow up when Ms. Diaz supplied information (as she did) that the tenant's submission was inaccurate. But Ms. Diaz denies that Ms. Cardwell told her at the beginning that Tiffany would be living with her.

Ms. Cardwell and Ms. Diaz agree that, for the most part, all dealings between Petitioner or AMS Realty and Ms. Cardwell with respect to the lease and recertifications were between the two women. (The exceptions were the letters and more recent telephone conversations described below.) Ms. Cardwell testified that she told Ms. Diaz that she had difficulty reading and didn't understand the documents she was asked to sign. Ms. Diaz explained that she relied on Ms. Cardwell's daughter Linda to read and explain the documents to Ms. Cardwell as necessary. However, Ms. Cardwell testified that Linda was "seldom around," and Ms. Wilson-Warner testified that she never saw any of the papers that her mother signed indicating that Ms. Cardwell was the only occupant of the apartment. Ms. Wilson-Warner said that the first holdover proceeding provided the first notice to her that only her mother was listed as a tenant.

The documentary evidence establishes that, each year at the time for recertification, Ms. Cardwell signed a notarized statement that notified Petitioner through AMS Realty that she was the only person living in the household, and that, virtually from the day she moved in, employees of the managing agent had concluded that the information was incorrect. In forwarding recertification information and documents to AMS Realty's office, Ms. Diaz would attach notes reading: "This tenant . . . has kid in apt living with her since she came to live in here" (October 13, 1994); "has granddaughter living with her since she been here like a tenant" (October 20, 1994); "granddaughter living with her since

1992" (December 29, 1997). (Moreover, each of these notes stated that the child attended private school.) Even earlier, when Ms. Cardwell signed a window guard notice in July 1993, Ms. Diaz wrote on top "she has child and don't wants (*sic*) to mark none of them," referring to the sections of the form that would indicate whether or not a child under 10 years old was living in the apartment. Ms. Diaz confirmed in her testimony having written these notes and their import, and Ms. Fernandez-Prada confirmed in her testimony having received them.

Apparently in response to the information received from Ms. Diaz, AMS Realty would write to Ms. Cardwell. On October 21, 1994, Ms. Fernandez-Prada wrote: "The apartment is for yourself and your *immediate family* (i.e. spouse, children) *only*. We will not add the additional people on your Certification . . ." (emphasis in original). Similar letters were written by another AMS Realty employee, Donna Ramos, on October 16, 1996 and October 24, 2000, although these letters state: "The apartment is for yourself." On October 27, 1997, Ms. Ramos wrote: "We have reason to believe your granddaughter is living with you." And three years later: "We have been informed that you still have a Stephanie living with you."

Ms. Diaz testified that Ms. Cardwell always maintained that Tiffany was not living with her; but Ms. Diaz didn't believe her; Ms. Diaz knew Tiffany was living with Ms. Cardwell. (Indeed, Ms. Cardwell testified that, at Ms. Diaz's insistence, the window guards were installed because she had Tiffany.) Ms. Fernandez-Prada also testified that Ms. Cardwell maintained that Tiffany didn't live with her, but Ms. Fernandez-Prada only spoke to Ms. Cardwell once.

There is some documentary evidence that supports the testimony that Ms. Cardwell responded to any inquiry by maintaining that Tiffany did not live with her. There is a letter dated October 20, 1994, signed by Ms. Cardwell and notarized, that states: "I live in my apartment alone!" Ms. Cardwell acknowledges her signature, but could not provide any information concerning the circumstances of the letter, although she said that she didn't prepare it.

Also, Ms. Cardwell's daughter, Linda Wilson-Warner, wrote a letter on December 4, 2000 to Donna Ramos, stating that Tiffany lived with her and always had. At trial, Ms. Wilson-Warner acknowledged that the letter (and an enclosed school application) were false. She explained that the letter was written in panic, in an attempt to protect her mother, after receipt of the papers in the first holdover proceeding, and after a conversation with Ms. Ramos in which Ms. Ramos insisted that Ms. Cardwell would be evicted if Tiffany did not leave. Although certainly not to be commended, given its date the letter cannot provide support for any contention by Petitioner that it was prevented from learning the truth by any misrepresentation in the letter.

Petitioner's policies concerning occupancy of the apartments at 80 Greene Avenue are somewhat indefinite. Although all of Petitioner's witnesses testified that the project is maintained for senior citizens only, they all also testified that children of senior citizens have lived with their parents, and Mr. Weeks testified that at least sometimes the occupancy was with the Petitioner's approval. Mr. Weeks said that, although Petitioner "discourages" occupancy by the minor children of seniors, "exceptions" have been made on a case-by-case basis; he did not know, however, the considerations that were used to determine whether approval would be granted.

Mr. Weeks also acknowledged that, presented with a wheelchair-bound senior who wished her adopted daughter to live with her, it was "possible" that Petitioner would make an "exception" and approve the daughter's occupancy. He maintained, however, that Petitioner would not certify any additional occupant when the person's presence was not reported by the tenant.

Both Ms. Diaz and Ms. Fernandez-Prada testified that minor children have been certified to occupy premises at 80 Greene Avenue. One situation described by Ms. Fernandez-Prada is similar to this case; a granddaughter was certified when the grandmother was granted custody after the death of the child's mother. (They have apparently been placed on a wait-list for premises in another building owned by Petitioner.) Ms. Diaz also testified that, in at least two apartments, adult children are living with their parents, with the knowledge of the "main office."

Ms. Fernandez-Prada acknowledged that Tiffany's occupancy of Ms. Cardwell's apartment would not constitute overcrowding under HUD regulations and would not otherwise violate HUD restrictions on sharing a bedroom. She testified generally to the importance to seniors of avoiding the "nuisance" that might be created by minor children, but could not remember any complaint that had been made about Tiffany. Ms. Diaz testified to a complaint in 1993 about "all of the kids" who were then living at 80 Greene Avenue, but testified to nothing more recent or specifically about Tiffany (who would have been six years old at the time).

Occupancy Restrictions

As noted, the Thirty Day Notice stated that Ms. Cardwell was in "material noncompliance" with the lease in that she permitted Tiffany to occupy the premises without Petitioner's prior written permission. Also, the HUD Handbook permits termination of the tenancy for a "material noncompliance," defined to include "one or more substantial violations of the lease." *See* discussion above.

In its Post-Trial Memorandum of Law, Petitioner appears to rely exclusively on fraud as the basis for the termination, referring to no lease provisions but citing and quoting from the HUD Handbook on fraud. However, as one of two alleged consequences of the fraud, Petitioner states: "If the tenant had admitted to caring for a child in the premises she would not have been allowed to move in the premises." (The Post-Trial Memorandum contains neither paragraph nor page numbers to allow reference.) Therefore, even if Petitioner were deemed to have abandoned any argument based on the occupancy itself, as opposed to any alleged falsity concerning it, the legitimacy of an exclusion on that basis is clearly at issue. Whether viewed as an independent ground, or in its relationship with the alleged fraud, the occupancy restrictions in the lease on the facts here cannot support termination of the tenancy. Petitioner quotes Paragraph 2-4(a) from the Handbook: "For projects or parts of projects designed for the elderly, owners may restrict occupancy for elderly units to persons 62 years of age and older, *and* to families where the head of the household or spouse is 62 years of age or older" (emphasis added). Ignoring the conjunctive, Petitioner argues that HUD permitted exclusion of Ms. Cardwell if Tiffany would be living with her. There is more evidence than one "and," however, that Petitioner is incorrect.Thus, "[o]ccupancy of [Section 202] projects is limited to elderly individuals 62 years of age or older and families where the head of household or spouse is 62 years of age or older. . . ." Handbook Paragraph 2-4(b). Paragraph 2-9 prescribes eligibility requirements for Section 202 projects funded before October 1991 (which 80 Greene Avenue presumably is), and refers to the definition of "elderly family" that includes "[a] single person who is 62 years of age or older" and "[f]amilies of two or more persons one of whom is 62 years of age or older." Handbook Paragraph 2-9(c)(1), Exhibit 2-1.

Perhaps more importantly:

> If the head of a household or spouse is sixty-two years of age or older, and the family is denied admission to such elderly units . . . because of familial status, the failure to admit the family would constitute discrimination proscribed by the Fair Housing Act unless the housing in exempt from the applicability of the familial status provision . . . The Department will not designate its elderly programs or projects under Section[ ] 202 . . . for an exemption from the familial status provision, since HUD policy precludes families which otherwise qualify for elderly housing, from being denied admission to an elderly project based on familial status.

Handbook Paragraph 2-4(e). *See also* Fair Housing Act, 42 USC § 3602(k) [2002] *et seq.* For purposes of the Act, "familial status" is defined as "one or more individuals (who have not obtained the age of 18 years of age) being domiciled with . . . a parent or another person having legal custody of such individual or individuals." 42 USC § 3602(k).

* * *

Respondent also points to Paragraph 21 of the lease, in which the "Landlord agrees not to discriminate based upon . . . age, . . . or because there are children in the family." At trial, Ms. Fernandez-Prada attempted to discount the import of this provision by stating that Petitioner used the same form of lease for all of its buildings, including those that are not intended as senior housing. Nonetheless, the provision is part of the lease that governs this tenancy, and must be taken into account in determining whether there has been a "substantial violation" of the lease. "Classic lease construction is that if there are any ambiguities in lease interpretation, making two constructions possible, any such ambiguities are to be resolved in the tenant's favor . . . Moreover, the interpretation should be adopted that limits restrictions on the free use of the property." . . . There is no evidence that Tiffany's occupancy of Ms. Cardwell's apartment has caused Petitioner any actual harm. Specifically with respect to occupancy restrictions, anti-discrimination laws and Real Prop L § 235-f have led courts to conclude that there had been no "substantial violation" of the lease, in some cases even though the landlord was not informed. [Citations omitted.] In such a case involving "an individual, residing in demised accommodations for the principal purpose of rendering necessary health services to the tenant," Appellate Term stated: [W]e are mindful of a growing class of older persons in our midst who, afflicted by the ravages of time, suffer from debilitating and chronic illnesses. To consign these individuals, absent medical necessity and against their wishes to institutions in order to receive proper health care rather than seek such care at home at the peril of being evicted, violates our notion of justice.

Inaccurate Information / Fraud

The conclusion is inescapable that Tiffany's occupancy cannot in itself be the basis for termination of Ms. Cardwell's tenancy. Nor can it be said that Petitioner suffered from any related "fraud," in that "[i]f the tenant had admitted to caring for a child in the premises she would not have been allowed to move into the premises," since it is apparent that she could not have been refused on that ground.

The only other consequence of the "fraud" that Petitioner cites is that it "was denied the opportunity to question the income of the child. For example, testimony was adduced that the child was going to a private school. This would be considered income and might have decreased the subsidy." Petitioner's Post-Trial Memorandum of Law. Although the Court specifically requested that the parties address in their post-trial submissions whether and how Ms. Cardwell's subsidy would have been affected had Tiffany's presence been taken into account, Petitioner provides no explanation or authority for its contention. The reason may be that the factual predicate is weak, the only evidence on the issue being that Tiffany has been attending parochial school, coupled with the assertion that, generally, parochial schools charge tuition. On the other hand, Ms. Cardwell has made a showing that, because of an allowance for dependents, her "share of the rent would have been less had she been given proper credit for her adopted daughter in the annual recertification required by HUD."

There came a time, however, when the Ms. Cardwell must have become aware that Tiffany's presence in the apartment was an issue. ASM Realty's first letter, dated October 21, 1994, would not have been that event, as the letter suggested that, as a member of Ms. Cardwell's immediate family, Tiffany was a permitted occupant. That this letter may have been a form that ASM Realty used for all Section 8 tenants, as was the testimony, is irrelevant; it was the letter sent to Ms. Cardwell, and there is no reason to discount any effect that it may have had on her mind.

The subsequent letters dated October 16, 1996, October 27, 1997, and October 24, 2000 were unqualified: no one other than Ms. Cardwell was permitted to live in the apartment, and no one else would be added to the Section 8 certification. We cannot know for certain what Ms. Cardwell thought in response to these letters, because she did not testify to it. The absence of any consequence to the letters over a nine year period until the Fall of 2000 must have had some effect on her mind and conduct, particularly since she reasonably believed that Ms. Diaz and her employer knew the facts. The issue here is not deception or waiver — i.e. the state of mind of Petitioner's agents — but Ms. Cardwell's state of mind — i.e. whether she acted "knowingly," "deliberately," "intentionally."

Other conclusions are fairly inescapable. On at least one occasion, the October 20, 1994 letter, Ms. Cardwell stated categorically that she lived in the apartment alone; the information was inaccurate, she knew it was inaccurate, and it was apparently given in response to an inquiry about Tiffany's presence in the apartment. Ms. Cardwell acted from a determination that Tiffany not be taken from her and that they not lose their home. There no evidence to suggest that Petitioner ever said anything to Ms. Cardwell about income eligibility or the amount of her subsidy, or that Ms. Cardwell would have harbored any concern about "imputed income." Although Petitioner's witnesses maintained that, had they been told about Tiffany, they would have found other suitable premises for Ms. Cardwell and Tiffany, Ms. Cardwell testified without contradiction that no one ever gave her any such assurance. To the contrary, the only evidence, the ASM letters, threatened that Tiffany or Ms. Cardwell, or both, would have to leave, notwithstanding, as demonstrated above, that the threats were illegal.

In an unreported decision, *Starret City v. Hamilton,* N.Y.L.J., February 21, 1991 at p. 27 c. 6, the Appellate Term, Second Department, addressed a landlord's claim that a Section 8 tenant misrepresented the amount of her income when applying for the apartment. Evidently, tenant misrepresented her financial situation in the belief that the landlord discriminated against welfare recipients and that if she did not do so she would not be given an apartment. As a result of her misrepresentation, tenant received less of a federal rent subsidy than that to which she was actually entitled. *Id.*

The proceeding was for nonpayment, after the landlord terminated the rent subsidy, because of the tenant's fraud on her income certification, and raised her rent to fair market levels. HUD Handbook 4350.3 provided that a ground for termination of the federal subsidy was the deliberate submission by the tenant of "false information on any application . . . for the purpose of obtaining a higher assistance payment or lower rent . . ." *Id.* Appellate Term held that the Handbook did not allow termination of the subsidy.

Tenant's misstatements do not fall within this definition because they were not for the purpose of obtaining a higher assistance payment or lower rent and, in fact, resulted in her receiving a lower assistance payment and higher rent than that to which she was actually entitled. [Citation omitted] Here, although it appears that Ms. Cardwell too would have been entitled to a higher subsidy if she had accurately reported to the landlord, she is not charged with providing false information about income (at least not directly), and the applicable provisions of the Handbook do not define "fraud" in terms of the amount of the subsidy; to the contrary, the Handbook says that the "effect on a tenant's income eligibility for assistance" need not be considered. Handbook Paragraph 5-20(a). But, taking the cue from Appellate Term, this Court concludes that Ms. Cardwell did not submit inaccurate or incomplete information "in order to gain some advantage dishonestly," Handbook Paragraph 5-19(b), but rather to avoid an unlawful and discriminatory refusal by the landlord to recognize Tiffany as a permitted occupant of the premises.

Having failed to establish the tenant's "fraud" or her "material noncompliance" with the terms of her lease, Petitioner has not shown that it is entitled to possession of the premises, and the Petition is dismissed.

The counterclaim is also dismissed. Except for Appellate Term's unreported decision in *Starret City v. Hamilton, supra,* the Court is not aware of any case law on the use of fraud as the basis for terminating a Section 8 tenancy. Although the Court has found that Petitioner's position in this case is not supportable, it cannot be characterized as frivolous.

QUESTION

What "special" protections from termination of their tenancies do elderly residents of federally subsidized housing enjoy that are not extended to others?

WALTON v. UCC X. INC., ET AL.
282 Ga. App. 847 (Ga. Ct. App. 2006)

Administrator of tenant's estate brought wrongful death action against landlord after tenant was struck by automobile while crossing highway from temporary parking area of apartment complex. The trial court granted summary judgment in favor of landlord. Administrator appealed.

The Court of Appeals affirmed.

Wendall Walton, as the administrator of the estate of Wallace David Abernathy, sued UCC X, Inc. d/b/a Cedar Heights Apartments ("Cedar Heights") and Chastity L. Fincher for Abernathy's wrongful death. The trial court granted Cedar Heights' motion for summary judgment, and Walton appeals. We affirm for the reasons set forth below.

To prevail on a motion for summary judgment, the moving party must demonstrate that there is no genuine issue of material fact, and that the undisputed facts, viewed in a light most favorable to the party opposing the motion, warrant judgment as a matter of law. O.C.G.A. § 9-11-56(c); *Lau's Corp. v. Haskins*, 261 Ga. 491, 405 S.E.2d 474 (1991). Our review is de novo, and we view the evidence and all reasonable inferences drawn from it in the light most favorable to the nonmovant. *Supchak v. Pruitt*, 232 Ga. App. 680, 682(1), 503 S.E.2d 581 (1998).

So viewed, the evidence shows that Abernathy rented an apartment from Cedar Heights in March of 2001. Apartments at the complex were available for rent only to low income persons who were 62 years of age or older. The United States Department of Housing and Urban Development ("HUD") made rental assistance payments on behalf of the tenants. The apartments were not a nursing home, and the residents were self-sufficient.

On November 20, 2003, apartment manager Rachel Bobbitt-Redding notified residents that the parking lot was scheduled to be resurfaced. According to the notice, "[residents] will all have to park [their] vehicles across the street," beginning on the afternoon of November 24, 2003, and all day on November 25,

2003. On the evening of November 25, 2003, 82-year-old Abernathy parked his truck in a lot across the highway that ran in front of the entrance to the apartment complex, and he was struck and killed by a motorist's car as he attempted to cross the highway on foot. The lot on which Abernathy had been directed to park was owned by a third party, Roger Tillary, but neither Bobbitt-Redding or any other Cedar Heights' representative had sought Tillary's permission for apartment residents to park on his property.

1. Walton contends that the trial court erred in concluding that HUD regulations do not support a cause of action for negligence per se in this case. We do not agree.

Generally, a plaintiff may assert a claim of negligence per se arising from violations of federal or state statutes as long as (1) that plaintiff falls within the class of persons the statute was intended to protect; (2) the harm complained of was the same harm the statute was intended to guard against; and (3) the violation of the statute proximately caused the plaintiff's injury. The violation of a regulation, no less than that of a statute, can likewise establish that a defendant breached a duty owed to a plaintiff as a matter of law. (Footnotes omitted.)

The lease agreement between Cedar Heights and Abernathy shows that HUD provided Cedar Heights with financing under section 202 of the Housing Act of 1959 and rent subsidies under Section 8 of the Housing Act of 1937. *See* 12 U.S.C. § 1701q; 42 U.S.C. § 1437f. Walton contends, and Cedar Heights does not dispute, that certain federal regulations are therefore applicable to the apartments. 24 CFR § 5.703 provides that "HUD housing must be decent, safe, sanitary and in good repair. Owners . . . must maintain such housing in a manner that meets the physical condition standards set forth in this section in order to be considered decent, safe, sanitary and in good repair." *See also* 24 CFR § 891.180. These standards include, as relied upon by Walton, that "[t]he site must not be subject to material adverse conditions," 24 CFR § 5.703(a), and "[a]ll areas and components of the housing must be free of health and safety hazards." 24 CFR § 5.703(f).

Walton also points to the fact that applicable regulations require that "[t]he owner must maintain the unit in accordance with [Housing Quality Standards]." 24 CFR § 982.404. These "HQS" regulations include that "[t]he site and neighborhood must be reasonably free from . . . dangers to the health, safety, and general welfare of the occupants." 24 CFR § 982.401(l)(1). Further, "[t]he site and neighborhood may not be subject to serious adverse environmental conditions, natural or manmade, such as . . . excessive noise, vibration or vehicular traffic." 24 § CFR 982(l)(2). Finally, "[t]he dwelling unit must be able to be used and maintained without unauthorized use of other private properties." 24 CFR § 982.401(k).

We agree with the trial court that Walton's allegations do not afford a basis for Walton to show that Cedar Heights was negligent per se. Even if Abernathy was within the class of persons intended to be protected by the HUD regulations, the harm complained of is not the harm that the regulations were intended to guard against. Under the common law, an owner or occupier of land has no duty to protect against harms occurring on public roadways or premises owned by third parties, when the owner or occupier has not exercised any control over the roadway or premises. [Citations omitted.] We do not believe that the HUD regulations — the primary purpose of which was to set forth the requirements that property owners must meet to receive public subsidies — were intended to eviscerate this common law principle. Thus, we conclude that the HUD regulations were not intended to protect tenants against harms arising off the HUD-regulated premises. In the present case, it is undisputed that Abernathy was not harmed on premises owned, occupied, or controlled by Cedar Heights. Moreover, the only relevant on-site activity, which was the parking lot resurfacing, was not shown to constitute a dangerous or hazardous condition. Accordingly, Walton's allegations are insufficient to sustain a claim for negligence per se based upon the HUD regulations.

2. Walton further contends that evidence of Cedar Heights' violation of OCGA § 30-5-8(a)(1), which provides that "it shall be unlawful for any person to abuse, neglect, or exploit any disabled adult or elder person," was sufficient to support his claim of negligence per se. We disagree.

For purposes of OCGA § 30-5-8(a), an "elder person" is defined as "a person 65 years of age or older who is not a resident of a long-term care facility." OCGA § 30-5-3(7.1). Neglect requires "the absence or omission of essential services" to an elder person, and abuse includes "the willful deprivation of essential services" to an elder person. OCGA § 30-5-3(1), (10). "Essential services" are defined as "social, medical, psychiatric, or legal services necessary to safeguard the . . . elder person's rights and resources and to maintain the physical and mental well-being of such person. These services shall include . . . protection from health and safety hazards. . . ." OCGA § 30-5-3(8).

Walton contends that Cedar Heights deprived Abernathy of an "essential service" by taking away a safe means of ingress and egress to his apartment. Although Cedar Heights barred Abernathy for a temporary period from parking his car on the apartment property, we cannot conclude that continuous and uninterrupted parking privileges constitutes an essential service under OCGA § 30-5-8(a) such that its negligent or intentional deprivation constitutes a violation of OCGA § 30-5-8(a)(1). Parking, in and of itself, is not a "social, medical, psychiatric, or legal service[ ]," nor can we conclude that continuous parking access was "necessary to safeguard [Abernathy's] rights and resources and to maintain [his] physical and mental well-being." OCGA § 30-5-3(8). It follows that the trial court correctly concluded that Walton could not show that Cedar Heights was negligent per se on account of a violation of OCGA § 30-5-8(a).

[The Court held, further, that (3.) the landlord did not breach a common law duty to tenant; and (4.) the administrator did not have cause of action in tort arising from a breach of lease contract.] *Judgment affirmed.*

QUESTIONS

1. Does this case seem inconsistent with *Green Ave. v. Cardwell*? Why or why not?

2. What are the limits of the "special" consideration extended to elderly tenants?

C. HOUSING WITH SERVICES

Stephanie Edelstein, V. Gottlich,
D. Siemon & B. Vignery
Housing Rights of Group Home and Nursing
Facility Residents
29 CLEARINGHOUSE REV. 664 (October 1995)[*]

I. Introduction

Housing options for persons who are unable to live independently include a variety of supervised living programs, ranging from small board-and-care programs to continuing care facilities, nursing facilities, and, the most recent trend, assisted living. Residents may encounter discrimination in the form of zoning and land-use restrictions, licensing, or health and safety regulations. This article discusses the ways in which federal civil rights laws are being used to challenge this discrimination in the context of group house and nursing facilities.

A. Overview of Relevant Statutes

Section 504 of the Rehabilitation Act of 1973 prohibits discrimination on the basis of disability or perceived disability in any program or activity that receives federal financial assistance, including public and subsidized housing programs and nursing facilities that receive Medicare or Medicaid funding. Section 504 requires that such programs be accessible to and usable by persons who are "handicapped" or who have disabilities. (29 U.S.C. § 794, as amended.) The Fair Housing Amendments Act of 1988 (FHAA) prohibits discrimination in almost all housing activities or transactions, whether in the public or private sector; in the provision of services or facilities in connection with a dwelling; and in the application of zoning, land use, or health and safety regulations. (42 U.S.C. § 3601 *et seq.*) These laws are complemented by the Americans with Disabilities Act (ADA). (42 U.S.C. § 12101 *et seq.*; 28 C.F.R. pt. 36, app. B.) Although Title II (state and local programs) and III (public accommodations) of the ADA do not specifically cover housing (and indeed specifically exclude entities covered by the FHAA), they apply to nonhousing function of a facility, such as meeting rooms, meal sites, adult day care, or long-term care. Under all three statutes, discrimination includes a refusal to make reasonable accommodations (adjustments to rules or procedures) or modifications (changes in the physical premises) upon request.

The three statutes use virtually the same definition of "handicap" or "disability." Individuals are protected if they (1) have a physical or mental impair-

---

ment that substantially limits one or more major life activities, such as performing manual tasks, walking, seeing, hearing, speaking, or personal care; (2) have a record of having such an impairment, whether or not the impairment still exists; or (3) are regarded as having such an impairment, whether or not the perception is accurate.

While age alone does not equal disability, the symptoms and conditions of the aging process may cause an individual to meet these definition. The protections extend to persons who are "frail," described in the Older Americans Act as being 60 years of age or older and unable to perform without assistance (i.e., verbal reminder, physical cue, or supervision) at least two activities of daily living. (42 U.S.C. § 3002.) The protections also extend to persons who, due to a cognitive or other mental impairment, require substantial supervision because of behavior that poses a serious health or safety hazard to themselves or others.

1. Assisted Living

Administration on Aging
Housing Highlights — Assisted Living
http://www.aoa.gov/eldfam/Housing/Housing_Services/HH_
Assisted_Living.asp

Assisted living communities are designed for individuals who cannot function in an independent living environment, but do not need nursing care on a daily basis. Assisted living communities usually offer help with bathing, dressing, meals, and housekeeping.

What Are Assisted Living Residences?

Assisted living residences are:

1. housing environments which provide individualized health and personal care assistance in a home-like setting. The level of care available is between that provided in congregate housing (housing with meal service) and a skilled nursing facility. In these settings:

- residents are semi-independent physically or mentally, or frail persons who need frequent assistance;

- services offered include, personal care assistance, health care monitoring, limited health care services and/or the dispensing of medications;

- state licensing and regulation by state social welfare agencies is required.

2. important because they promote independence by meeting residents' supportive needs while preventing inappropriate institutionalization.

3. known by various other names. The most common are: personal care homes, sheltered housing, residential care, homes for adults, managed care, catered living, board and care, and domiciliary care.

Who Resides In Assisted Living Residences?

Assisted living housing is often deemed necessary when you have difficulty performing daily tasks and have no one to help you. Some indicators are:

- needing help preparing meals, bathing, dressing, toileting, or taking medication

- needing assistance with housekeeping chores or laundry

- requiring some health care assistance or monitoring

- needing transportation to doctors, shopping, and personal business

- feeling frequently confused or experiencing memory problems

* * *

Currently most assisted living facilities are privately operated. This means that the costs of care are not usually covered by publicly financed programs. The average fee, which includes meals and personal care assistance, ranges from $1,200 to $2,000 a month [or more]. Costs are often keyed to your level of impairment and service need.

In some states, rent or service subsidies are available. However, the typical reimbursement rate provided by Supplemental Security Income (SSI) is often too low to assist those with higher levels of impairment and service needs. Your local social security office and Medicaid Office can determine this.

2. Board and Care

http://www.aoa.gov/eldfam/Housing/Housing_Services/ Board_Care.asp

Board and care homes are smaller in scale than assisted living facilities. They provide a room, meals, and help with daily activities. Some states will allow some nursing services to be provided, but these homes are not medical facilities. These homes may be unlicensed, and even licensed homes are infrequently monitored by the state.

3. Continuing Care Retirement Communities (CCRC)

http://www.aoa.gov/eldfam/Housing/Housing_Services/ Board_Care.asp

Continuing Care Retirement Communities (CCRCs) are sometimes called life care communities. Entering one is usually a once-in-a-lifetime choice and that's the appeal. Many have large campuses that include separate housing for those who live very independently, assisted living facilities that offer more support, and nursing homes for those needing skilled nursing care. With all on the same grounds, people who are relatively active, as well as those who have serious physical and mental disabilities, all live nearby. Residents then move from one housing choice to another as their needs change.

While usually very expensive, many guarantee lifetime shelter and care with long-term contracts that detail the housing and care obligations of the CCRC as well as its costs.

Living Spaces — A wide variety of independent living units may be available: large and small apartments, cottages, cluster homes, or single-family homes. In addition to usual features, they may include grab bars, a monitored emergency call system and other safety features. Residents of these units are usually active, older people.

Assisted living units may be small studio or one-bedroom apartments with scaled down kitchens. These may have group dining areas and common areas for social and recreational activities. Residents typically need some assistance in daily living activities but also want some independence.

Nursing home accommodations are usually furnished one-room units for two or more persons with an attached bathroom. Residents require skilled nursing care (short term or long term) and may benefit from rehabilitative therapy to maintain or improve their abilities.

The Cost — The costs of living in a CCRC can be quite high and unaffordable to those with low or moderate incomes and assets. Most communities require an entrance fee and monthly payments. These fees can range from lows of $20,000 to highs of $400,000. Monthly payments can range from $200 to $2,500. In some places, residents own their living space, and in others the space is rented. In some communities, the entrance fee may be partially refundable. Frequently three different fee schedules may be available:

- Extensive contracts, which include unlimited long-term nursing care at little or no increase in the monthly fee.

- Modified contracts that include a specified amount of long-term nursing care. Beyond that specified time, you are responsible for payments.

- Fee-for-service contracts in which you pay full daily rates for long-term nursing care.

Entry Requirements — Some CCRCs are affiliated with a specific ethnic, religious, or fraternal order, and membership may be a requirement. The majority of CCRCs require potential residents to have a medical examination to assess their physical and mental status. Selected pre-existing conditions may cause a CCRC to refuse an applicant. Some CCRCs require residents to have both Medicare Part A and B. Naturally, residents must be able to meet the entrance fee and monthly payments.

D. NURSING FACILITIES

1. Nursing Home Residents' Rights

a. Nursing Home Reform Act of 1987

Margaret Farley
Adult Care Homes
KANSAS LONG-TERM CARE HANDBOOK 1-11
(KANSAS BAR ASS'N 2001)[*]

I. NURSING HOME REFORM ACT OF 1987 AND AMENDMENTS

This section concerns the federal and state laws which govern the specific type
of adult care home known as nursing homes. Most nursing homes participate
in the federal Medicare or Medicaid program and are therefore subject to the
Nursing Home Reform Act of 1987, its amendments (the NHRA), and certain
federal regulations. . . .

A. Overview of the Nursing Home Reform Act of 1987 and Amendments

1. Introduction

In 1995 about 1.5 million Americans spent some time in a nursing home.
Ninety (90) percent of these nursing home residents were 65 years of age or
older; over thirty-five (35) percent were age 85 or older. Most nursing homes are
freestanding, but can also be long-term care units in hospitals or continuing care
retirement communities. In 1995, about 96% of all nursing homes were Medic-
aid- or Medicare-certified, or both.

2. The Nursing Home Reform Act of 1987

The NHRA became law with the passage of the Omnibus Budget Reconciliation Act of 1987. Consequently, for many years the NHRA was more commonly known as OBRA87. Public pressure for significant federal nursing home
legislation grew out of nursing home scandals, state studies and Congressional
hearings on the quality of nursing home care in the 1970s and early 1980's. In
1984, the Tenth Circuit ruled in the landmark *Estate of Smith v. Heckler*, that
the Department of Health and Human Services (DHHS) had a legal duty to
assure quality care for Medicaid recipients in nursing homes but had failed in
that duty. The federal appeals court directed DHHS to implement systemic
changes to remedy the breach.

When the Reagan administration instead proposed regulations for survey
and enforcement systems in the early 1980s which many believed were too
weak, Congress objected and placed two moratoria on the regulations and
threatened a third. A compromise was reached between the executive and legislative branches by an agreement that the DHHS commission a comprehensive
study of nursing home issues.

In 1986, the Committee on Nursing Home Regulation of the Institute of Medicine (IoM) published the resulting study, "Improving the Quality of Care in Nursing Homes." The IoM report was comprehensive and largely critical of a system of regulations and enforcement which failed to protect nursing home residents from poor care and rights violations. A pivotal document with clear recommendations for improvement, it became a blueprint for legislative reform. In the following year the NHRA was passed with remarkable consensus from the industry and consumer advocates and contained many of the IoM recommendations.

B. Sources of the Federal Law

Medicare requirements for certified facilities are located at 42 U.S.C. § 1395i-3; Medicaid requirements are found at 42 U.S.C. § 1396r. The implementing regulations for both programs are found at 42 C.F.R. 483. Interpretive guidelines published by the Health Care Financing Administration (HCFA) assist federal surveyors in applying the federal regulations and are a good research aid in understanding how the regulations are applied. Such guidelines are not legally enforceable standing alone, but are highly influential.

C. Key Provisions of the NHRA

1. Medicare Skilled Nursing Facilities

The Medicare portion of the NHRA defines a Medicare facility and sets out the requirements for, and assuring quality of care in, skilled nursing facilities, as follows:

> A Medicare skilled nursing facility (SNF) is defined as an institution which is primarily engaged in providing skilled nursing care (direct supervision or direct care by an RN) and related services for residents who require medical or nursing care, or rehabilitation services for the treatment of injured, disabled, or sick persons, and which is not primarily for the care and treatment of mental diseases.

A typical stay in a SNF is about 20 days, but at least partial Medicare coverage can last up to 100 days. Common qualifying conditions are those which may benefit from short term physical and occupational or speech therapies, such as stroke, cardiac rehabilitation or fractured hip. Otherwise, persons admitted to SNFs must require at least daily skilled nursing care such as, e.g., intravenous antibiotic administration, assessment and stabilization of complex medical conditions, or wound care.

2. Medicaid Nursing Facilities

The statutory definition for Medicaid NFs follows:

> . . . an institution . . . which is primarily engaged in providing to residents (A) skilled nursing care and related services for residents who require medical or nursing care, (B) rehabilitation services for the rehabilitation of injured, disabled, or sick persons, or (C) on a regular basis, health-related care and services to individuals who because of their mental or physical condition require care and services (above the level

of room and board) which can be made available to them only through institutional facilities, and is not primarily for the care and treatment of mental disease.

Notice that, except for subsection C above, the definitions for Medicare and Medicaid facilities are the same. Medicaid nursing facilities provide general nursing home care, above the level of room and board, in addition to the skilled nursing and rehabilitative services. Before the NHRA there were two separate levels of care in Medicaid-certified nursing homes, intermediate and skilled. Some facilities still characterize the level of care they provide as intermediate, but Medicaid certification no longer provides for this distinction. All Medicaid facilities are held to the same statutory and regulatory standards, i.e., there is no lesser standard for Medicaid certified care simply because a facility purports to provide intermediate care.

As noted above, facilities may be both Medicare- and Medicaid-certified. By far the majority of nursing homes are Medicaid-certified. Reference will be made to NFs throughout; all of the rules which follow in this discussion apply equally to Medicare SNFs unless specifically noted otherwise. Where applicable, footnote citations will be made to both the Medicare and Medicaid sections of the Social Security Act. Finally, these laws and regulations create duties and responsibilities for the entire certified facility. Thus the law, with rare exception noted below, protects all residents in any certified facility. Persons who pay for their care entirely from their own private funds or insurance benefit from the laws the same as persons receiving Medicare or Medicaid assistance.

3. Required Nursing Facility Services

Requirements relating to the facilities' services set out standards for targeted outcomes, process and structure, to achieve the goals of quality of care, quality of life and protecting residents' rights. Specific areas include quality of life, care planning, resident assessment, ancillary services, training of nurse aides and physician services. The cornerstone provision of the NHRA requires nursing homes to "provide services to attain or maintain the highest practicable physical, mental, and psycho-social well-being of each resident." An NF must also "care for its residents in such a manner and in such an environment as will promote maintenance or enhancement of the quality of life of each resident." And, facilities must establish an internal quality assurance committee which meets at least quarterly.

The NHRA requires the development of a standardized, comprehensive resident assessment coordinated by an RN within the first two weeks of admission, updated quarterly and "promptly after a significant change in the resident's physical or mental condition." The assessment becomes a part of the resident's medical record and the basis for comprehensive care planning. Prior to the NHRA, each facility used its own assessment form; many were cursory. Baseline data to evaluate a resident's progress or decline was scarce and updates were even rarer. The NHRA standardized form currently known as the Minimum Data Set for Nursing Home Resident Assessment and Care Screening, or MDS, is now used in all certified nursing homes.

Certain services must be available for residents. These include nursing and rehabilitative services, under the cornerstone standard "to attain or maintain the highest practicable physical, mental, and psycho-social well-being of each resident." Also required are social, pharmaceutical, dietary, activities program, and routine and emergency dental services. Nursing facilities are required to comply fully with all applicable federal, state and local laws and regulations and with accepted professional standards and principles which apply to professionals providing services in such facilities.

Implementing the statutory requirement to "attain or maintain the highest practicable" condition of residents, the HCFA also specified outcome standards in major quality of care areas. Specific standards addressed in the regulations include but are not limited to the following:

- activities of daily living, including toileting, ambulation, dressing;
- vision and hearing;
- pressure sores (also known as decubitus ulcers);
- urinary incontinence;
- limb range of motion;
- mental and psychosocial functioning;
- naso-gastric tube feedings;
- prevention of accidents, including falls;
- nutritional status;
- hydration;
- respiratory care;
- care of prostheses;
- ostomy care; and
- proper medication.

The facility must carry out an appropriate plan of care based upon a comprehensive interdisciplinary assessment to prevent each resident's condition from deteriorating unnecessarily. Most residents in nursing facilities have more than one disease or condition. The statute and regulations aim to prevent decline due to poor nursing and rehabilitative care or neglect. For example, concerning pressure sores, the regulations provide:

> Based upon the comprehensive assessment of a resident, the facility must ensure that; (1) a resident who enters the facility without pressure sores does not develop pressure sores unless the individual's clinical condition demonstrates that they were unavoidable; and (2) a resident having pressure sores receives necessary treatment and services to promote healing, prevent infection and prevent new sores from developing.

Thus, the HCFA developed a straightforward statement of the expected outcome of proper professional care based upon a comprehensive assessment and care planning.

Minimal professional nursing services are required. An LPN or RN must be on duty 24 hours a day, and a supervisory RN must be on duty 8 hours a day, 7 days a week. Each nurse aide on duty must complete a training and competency evaluation program within 4 months of employment. Residents' medical care must be under the supervision of a physician, emergency medical care must be available and detailed clinical records must be kept on each resident. Physicians must provide basic medical oversight of the quality of medical and other care of all residents in the facility and at least one physician must be a member of the quality assurance committee.

4. Express Resident Rights

The NHRA sets out the following explicit rights for each resident. Again, all resident rights apply equally to Medicare- and Medicaid-certified facilities. Other rights are set out in other specific sections of the law and will be discussed elsewhere in this section, e.g., management of personal funds. The rights of adjudicated incompetent residents devolve to, and may be exercised by, their state-appointed guardians, or their legally designated agents. Upon admission to the nursing facility, residents or their legal agents must be given specific notice of the delineated rights. Such notice must include, for example, the facility's procedure for handling personal funds, and its policy for implementing residents' advance directives.

a. Free Choice

Each resident must have a personal attending physician, and each resident has a right to choose his or her physician. The difficulty is that many physicians frequently decline to follow the care of their patients once they move to a nursing home. A Medicaid-certified facility is required to make transportation available for necessary medical appointments, so some residents may continue to see their physician in the office, but that is not always feasible or recommended. In practice, if a resident does not have a physician, the facility will offer the services of the "house physician," usually the medical director, as the resident's attending physician.

Freedom of choice includes the right to advance, informed consent to all care and treatment, including advance informed consent to changes in care and treatment which may affect the resident's well-being and the right to participate in care planning, unless a resident is an adjudicated incompetent. Even if a person has been adjudicated incompetent, it may be advisable to attempt to ascertain the person's wishes to the extent possible.

b. Freedom from Restraints and Abuse

i. Background

Before the implementation of the NHRA, the use of inappropriate physical and chemical restraints on residents in nursing homes was widespread. For many years restraints were a well-established intervention to prevent accidents, i.e., to keep residents from falling and injuring themselves or others, or from eloping and to control behavioral symptoms. The use of restraints is now closely controlled through NHRA provisions. Probably the most dramatic effect of the NHRA was an overwhelming reduction of the use of physical and chemical restraints within the first few years of the implementation of the law. Across the nation by 1992 (the NHRA became effective in 1990) the use of physical restraints had declined by at least 25%. . . .

Medical and nursing literature now abounds with the benefits of eliminating the use of restraints, i.e., eliminating the common negative side effects of inappropriate physical and chemical restraints (depression, physical injuries, decreased mobility and socialization, decubitus ulcers, dehydration, inactivity, muscle and bone loss, weight loss and malnutrition, to name a few). Contemporary lawsuits against nursing homes have successfully argued the negligence of facility staff for applying physical restraints when residents are injured or strangled to death struggling to free themselves from, for example, a vest restraint. Even side rails can kill.

ii. Definition of Physical and Chemical Restraints

Physical restraints are "defined as any manual method or physical or mechanical device, material, or equipment attached or adjacent to the resident's body that the individual cannot remove easily which restricts freedom of movement or normal access to one's body." A chemical restraint is "a psycho-pharmacologic drug that is used for discipline or convenience and not required to treat medical symptoms." "Discipline" is punishing or penalizing a resident; "convenience" is a facility action to control resident behavior not in the best interest of the resident and with a lesser amount of facility effort.

According to the interpretive guidelines, physical restraints include, but are not limited to, leg restraints, arm restraints, hand mitts, soft ties or vests, and wheelchair lap trays. Certain other facility practices are considered physical restraints, such as using bed rails to keep a resident from getting out of bed (as opposed to enhancing mobility), tucking a sheet so tightly that a bed-bound resident cannot move or placing a resident in a chair that prevents rising. Orthotic devices used as restraints are expressly prohibited in the guidelines.

* * *

c. Privacy

A resident has the right to privacy in accommodations, medical treatment, written and telephone communications, visits and meetings of family and resident groups. Thus, the facility must furnish a telephone in a private area for the use of residents and a private meeting room for a resident or family group, if requested.

d. Confidentiality

All personal and clinical records must be kept confidential. Within 24 hours (excluding weekends and holidays) upon a written request, a resident or his legal agent must be given access to current clinical records. The facility must provide, at a reasonable rate, copies of resident's records within two working days of such a request by the resident or the resident's legal representative.

e. Accommodation of Needs

Facilities must reasonably accommodate residents' individual needs and preferences, except where the health or safety of the resident or other residents would be endangered. This is a quality of life issue and requires facilities to be more "resident-centered." Also, residents must receive notice before a facility changes his or her room or roommate. In itself, the latter is largely an empty right, as there is no time requirement for advance notice and no explicit right to oppose the transfer.

However, many residents are frail, become attached to their room or roommate, and may be at risk to decline in health with a room transfer. Opposition to the change of room can be rested upon the duty to accommodate the individual needs and preferences of the resident, or to help him or her "maintain the highest practicable physical, mental, or psycho-social well-being." Concerning the change of roommate, obviously the rights and preferences of both residents would need to be taken into consideration.

f. Grievances

Residents have the right to voice grievances about treatment or care. The facility must make prompt efforts to resolve those grievances. The law prohibits reprisal and discrimination against residents for voicing grievances. Enforcing this provision is difficult, at best. Very few citations in surveys for retaliation can be found. Frail residents in nursing homes are completely dependent upon their care-givers. They cannot always vote with their feet; another nursing home may not be available. Many residents do not speak out for fear of retaliation despite this paper protection.

Anecdotally, many family members acting as residents' legal representatives have reported that they are asked to leave after they voice a grievance "if they are not satisfied with the care." Most would consider this a form of retaliation; yet, it is a tactic commonly enlisted without reproach from regulators. If it works, the resident leaves of his or her own volition, and transfer and discharge rights are effectively nullified. *See* section III on transfer and discharge rights.

g. Participation Resident and Family Groups

Residents have the right to organize themselves and to meet privately in the nursing home with other residents. Families are frequently the chief advocates for residents, and NHRA granted them the same right. Commonly called resident and family councils, respectively, these groups have the right to submit complaints and recommendations for change to the administration. If a complaint is submitted in writing to the facility, the staff must consider it and respond, without necessarily making the recommended change, of course.

h. Participation in Other Activities

Nursing homes must allow residents to participate in social, religious and community activities that do not interfere with the rights of other residents in the facility.

* * *

j. Access and Visitation Rights

Before the NHRA, a resident's contact with persons outside the nursing home was largely controlled by whether facility staff would permit access to the resident. The NHRA reversed that order and explicitly rested the right of granting and denying access to outside visitors with the resident. The resident's right of association thus takes precedence over the property rights of the facility operator, as follows: An NF must allow the resident immediate access to his or her physician and family, and a representative of the state, including an ombudsman. Friends and other visitors, including the resident's attorney must be granted immediate access, subject to reasonable restrictions. Outside service providers must be granted "reasonable access" to the resident. All visitors, except the state authorities, are subject to the resident's right to decline their visit.

5. Protection Against Medicaid Discrimination

An NF must establish and maintain identical policies and practices concerning transfer and discharge and services, regardless of whether the resident is receiving Medicaid assistance or paying privately. A facility may not require prospective residents to waive their rights to Medicaid benefits. Nor may the facility require oral or written assurance that individuals are not eligible for or will not apply for Medicaid benefits.

However, many facilities require a financial statement from prospective residents, which effectively allows a facility to calculate the length of time a prospective resident will remain on private pay. If the time is too short, the facility simply denies the resident admission. HCFA has failed to enforce discrimination prohibitions with regard to financial screening, and it is freely exercised.

In addition, facilities cannot require a third party guarantee of payment to the facility as a condition of admission or continued stay in the facility. Before the NHRA facilities frequently obtained assurances from family members signing as the "responsible party," that they would guarantee payment of the resident's bill. Facilities would then hold family members accountable for unpaid bills. That practice is now illegal.

6. Protection of Resident Funds

A nursing facility, upon written authorization by the resident, must hold, safeguard and account for the resident's personal funds, but cannot require residents to deposit personal funds with the facility. Any amount held by the facility for the resident in excess of one hundred (100) dollars may be placed in an interest bearing account separate from the facility's operating account. Amounts less than one hundred dollars must be maintained in a petty cash fund or non-interest bearing account. Separate written accounts must be maintained and residents must be given "reasonable access" to such records. Medicaid residents must be notified when their accounts are within two hundred (200) dollars of the Supplemental Security Income resource limit for one person and of the consequences of reaching such an amount. A nursing facility must promptly convey a deceased resident's personal funds and final accounting to the administrator or executor of the resident's estate within thirty days.

Medicaid residents' personal funds may not be charged in excess of the Medicaid or Medicare reimbursement for nursing facility services covered by the Medicaid state plan or the Medicare per diem rate.

QUESTIONS

1. Would physical restraints be appropriate when a mentally impaired resident has a history of elopement? Chemical restraints? Why or why not?

2. What restrictions on a resident's ability to leave the facility "at will" would be appropriate under the NHRA?

b. Other Remedies

Stephanie Edelstein, V. Gottlich, D. Siemon & B. Vignery
Housing Rights of Group Home and Nursing Facility Residents
29 CLEARINGHOUSE REV. 664 (October 1995)[*]

Nursing Facilities as Entities Subject to Section 504 and the Americans with Disabilities Act

Nursing facilities must comply with federal laws that prohibit discrimination on the basis of disability. In fact, several common nursing facility practices, including admission and discharge, use of special care units, eligibility for activities and services, imposition of additional costs, and retaliation, may be redressable under the ADA (42 U.S.C. § 12101 *et seq.*) and Section 504 (29 U.S.C. § 794) in combination with or in lieu of other laws, such as the Nursing Home Reform Law. (42 U.S.C. §§ 1395r-i(3)(a), 1396r(a)-(h).)

All facilities that receive Medicaid and/or Medicare funds are subject to Section 504. Facilities run by state or local governments are subject to Title II of the ADA, regardless of whether they receive federal funding. Privately operated nursing facilities are subject to Title III of the ADA, which prohibits discrimination by public accommodations that fall within one of the 12 enumerated categories. (Health care providers and social service establishments.) Depending on their operating structure, nursing facilities controlled by religious organizations may not be covered under Title III of the ADA, since religious entities are specifically exempt from the statute. (29 U.S.C. § 12187.)

A nursing facility may not discriminate by (1) denying an individual the opportunity to participate in its services becaue of the person's disability; (2) segregating the person by providing services in a segregated setting; (3) applying

---

[*] Copyright © 1995. Reprinted with permission.

eligibility criteria that serve to screen out individuals or classes of persons with disabilities, in considering whether the ADA applies to a particular situation, it is important to keep in mind three questions: What is the service being denied? What is the nature of the discrimination? Against whom is the facility discriminating?

QUESTION

Given the difficulty of the task, that is, caring for a group of extremely frail people, many of whom have significant mental impairments, is it fair to apply the ADA and Section 504 of the Rehabilitation Act to nursing facilities?

WAGNER v. FAIR ACRES GERIATRIC CENTER
49 F.3d 1002 (3d Cir. 1994)

MANSMANN, Circuit Judge.

The general issue we address is whether Fair Acres Geriatric Center, a county-operated intermediate care nursing facility, violated Section 504 of the Rehabilitation Act of 1973, 29 U.S.C. § 794, when it denied admission to Margaret C. Wagner, a 65 year old woman afflicted with Alzheimer's disease. Although Fair Acres admits Alzheimer's patients, it denied admission to Mrs. Wagner because it determined that its facility and staff could not accommodate the behavioral manifestations of her disease.

The jury was asked to decide whether, despite her handicap of Alzheimer's disease, Mrs. Wagner was "otherwise qualified" for admission to Fair Acres within the meaning of section 504, including any reasonable accommodation Fair Acres was required to make. Following the jury verdict in favor of Mrs. Wagner, the district court granted Fair Acres' motion for judgment as a matter of law and conditionally granted its motion for a new trial.

We find that there was legally sufficient evidence to support the jury's verdict. Thus, we will vacate the district court's grant of judgment as a matter of law for Fair Acres. We are uncertain, however, that given the correct legal standards, the district court would have exercised its discretion in finding that the verdict was against the great weight of the evidence. Thus we will also vacate the district court's conditional grant of Fair Acres' motion for a new trial and remand for reconsideration of this motion.

I.

In 1988, at age 58, Margaret Wagner was diagnosed as suffering from Alzheimer's disease, a chronic degenerative neurological disorder that impairs intellectual functioning. Alzheimer's is associated with and has a devastating effect on intellectual functions including memory, recognition, comprehension and basic functional ability. As the disease progresses, basic skills are lost, such as the ability to feed, dress, groom or bathe oneself. Mrs. Wagner suffers from a particularly difficult, but not unique, form of Alzheimer's disease which is characterized by screaming, agitation and aggressive behavior. Initially, Mrs.

Wagner was cared for by her husband, assisted by his two adult daughters and by visiting nurses supplied through the County Office of Services to the Aging, who provided care approximately 27 hours a week. In the summer of 1992, however, Mrs. Wagner suffered a marked deterioration in cognitive functioning and behavior associated with her dementia.

As a result, her family could no longer satisfactorily care for her at home. On August 23, 1992, Mrs. Wagner was admitted to Dowden Nursing Home, a private facility located in Newton Square in Delaware County, Pennsylvania. On September 2, 1992, she was transferred from Dowden to the Wills Geriatric Psychiatry Program operated by Thomas Jefferson University Hospital, due to Mrs. Wagner's severe episodes of agitated behavior and confusion. On September 16, 1992, Wills made an initial referral for Mrs. Wagner to be admitted to Fair Acres Geriatric Center. Fair Acres is a 900-bed skilled intermediate nursing facility operated by the Delaware County Board of Institutional Management, licensed by the Pennsylvania Department of Health and certified under Titles 18 and 19 of the Social Security Act. Fair Acres receives county, state and federal funding, including Medicare and Medicaid funding. At least 98% of its patients are admitted under medical assistance.

Fair Acres' stated mission and goal is to provide care primarily for the geriatric community. Approximately 60% of its patients suffer from Alzheimer's disease or some other form of dementia. Although it has a staff-to-patient ratio of one to eight, it is not staffed or equipped to handle psychiatric residents. Accordingly, if an applicant for admission poses a threat of injury to himself or others, the application is rejected. An applicant's psychiatric history is reviewed to determine (1) if the applicant's primary diagnosis is medical, warranting nursing home placement and (2) if the applicant can be absorbed comfortably and appropriately into Fair Acres' geriatric population. *See* Fair Acres' admission's guidelines containing its "Psychiatric Policy." (A. 676).

On September 16, 1992, upon receiving Mrs. Wagner's application for admission, Fair Acres' Admissions Committee made an initial determination that Mrs. Wagner was not then suitable for admission, but placed her application on "hold" pending further information regarding her condition. The Committee met again on October 8, 1992 and designated Mrs. Wagner's application as "medically disapproved," acting on the recommendation of its psychiatric consultant, Dr. Satyendra Diwan, that Mrs. Wagner was not appropriate for admission due to the behavioral problems she was exhibiting at Wills.

Between Mrs. Wagner's second and third evaluations, Linda Hadfield, Fair Acres' admissions RN, visited Wills to speak with Mrs. Wagner's nurses and staff and to observe Mrs. Wagner firsthand. Mrs. Wagner was put on "hold" again after the third admissions committee meeting on October 29, 1992. Dr. Diwan's notes in the "comments" area of Mrs. Wagner's October 29th evaluation form indicated that Mrs. Wagner "needs more time" and was "not appropriate for Fair Acres." (A. 226-227).

On December 30, 1992, due to contradictions in the documentation from Wills that had been submitted to Fair Acres, Ms. Hadfield made a second visit to Wills and on January 6, 1993, Dr. Diwan evaluated Mrs. Wagner for a fourth time. After reviewing Wills' progress reports, Dr. Diwan noted that Mrs. Wagner was still agitated, confused and irritable as late as December 29, 1992, but recommended a further evaluation in six to eight weeks. Finally, on February 17, 1993, a fifth evaluation took place. Although Wills' hospital records indicated that Mrs. Wagner's behavioral problems had improved slightly, the records showed that she continued to experience episodes of combativeness, agitation and assaultiveness on a daily basis. Under "comments," Dr. Diwan noted that Mrs. Wagner was a "borderline case and will not fit into our milieu." (A. 232). Accordingly, Mrs. Wagner was again denied admission to Fair Acres.

On April 12, 1993, approximately two months after her last evaluation by Fair Acres, Mrs. Wagner was admitted to Easton Nursing Center. Easton Nursing Center is located approximately 85 miles from the home of Mrs. Wagner's husband and children. Because this represents a commute by car of one and one-half hours each way, the number of visits between Mrs. Wagner and her husband and children was severely curtailed. While Mrs. Wagner was at Wills, she was visited by her husband on a daily basis unless he was ill. Due to the fact that her husband has vision only in one eye, he was unable to make the trip to Easton independently. Consequently, while Mrs. Wagner was at Easton, her family was only able to visit her twice a week.

On May 21, 1993, Margaret Wagner, by her next friend George Wagner, filed a two count complaint in United States District Court for the Eastern District of Pennsylvania. Count One alleged that Fair Acres had discriminated against Mrs. Wagner on the basis of her handicap, the behavioral aspects of her dementia, in violation of section 504 of the Rehabilitation Act of 1973, 29 U.S.C. § 794, by refusing to admit her to its nursing facility. Mrs. Wagner sought a declaration that the acts of Fair Acres had violated her rights under section 504 of the Rehabilitation Act and sought injunctive relief enjoining Fair Acres from unlawfully excluding her from its facility and directing Fair Acres to admit Mrs. Wagner to its first available bed. She also sought damages and an award of attorney's fees and costs.

* * *

At trial, Mrs. Wagner introduced the testimony of three expert witnesses to support her claim that she was qualified for admission to Fair Acres in spite of the behavioral manifestations of her Alzheimer's disease. Dr. Gary L. Gottlieb, a geriatric psychiatrist and the director of the geriatric psychiatry program at the University of Pennsylvania School of Medicine, testified, based on his review of Mrs. Wagner's medical records, that as early as September, 1992, Mrs. Wagner was appropriate for the type of care provided by a nursing facility such as Fair Acres.

Dr. Edward Kim, Mrs. Wagner's treating physician at Wills, testified that Mrs. Wagner could have been accommodated by a nursing home around the third week of October. Finally, Mrs. Wagner introduced the testimony of Dr. Bijan Etemad, a psychiatrist at Easton Nursing Center (where Mrs. Wagner resided at the time of trial), that in his judgment, Mrs. Wagner was appropriate for nursing home care.

Fair Acres argued that Mrs. Wagner's "sustained combative and assaultive behavior distinguished her from Fair Acres' patients and prevented her from being qualified for admission" (Appellee's brief at 15), because its guidelines prohibited it from admitting psychiatric patients. Challenging Mrs. Wagner's expert witnesses' lack of consideration for her need for one-on-one supervision, Fair Acres contended that it is not equipped, due to its staff to patient ratio, to provide one-on-one supervision for prolonged periods of time. It further asserted that Dr. Kim's testimony was at odds with and often contradicted his own progress notes, which indicated that Mrs. Wagner was still exhibiting symptoms of agitation and combativeness at the time when he claimed she became suitable for transfer to a nursing facility.

On September 22, 1993, at the close of all the evidence, Fair Acres moved for judgment as a matter of law pursuant to Fed. R. Civ. P. 50. The court reserved its judgment on this motion and submitted the case to the jury on one issue — whether Margaret Wagner was "otherwise qualified" for admission into Fair Acres within the meaning of section 504. After deliberating, the jury returned a verdict in favor of Mrs. Wagner.

On October 5, 1993, Fair Acres renewed its motion for judgment as a matter of law, or in the alternative for a new trial pursuant to Fed. R. Civ. P. 50(b), asserting that Mrs. Wagner was not "otherwise qualified" within the meaning of section 504 because she did not meet all of Fair Acres requirements for admission. Fair Acres also contended, for the first time, that Mrs. Wagner had not been discriminated against "solely by reason of handicap."

On October 7, 1993, Mrs. Wagner filed a motion for a new trial limited to damages only. On February 15, 1994, the district court entered its order granting Fair Acres' motion for judgment as a matter of law and conditionally granting its motion for a new trial. The district court found that Mrs. Wagner was not an "otherwise qualified" handicapped individual who had been denied a benefit solely by reason of her handicap, because according to the court, she "sought admission to Fair Acres because of her handicap and not in spite of it." *Wagner v. Fair Acres Geriatric Center*, 859 F. Supp. 776, 782 (E.D. Pa. 1994). According to the court, the decision not to admit Mrs. Wagner was a medical treatment decision made by Fair Acres' medical and health care professionals, and medical treatment decisions are generally immune from scrutiny under section 504. Observing that Fair Acres admits patients suffering from Alzheimer's disease, the court also held that section 504, by its very terms, does not cover discrimination among similarly handicapped persons. Finally, the court concluded that Mrs. Wagner was not "otherwise qualified" for admission to Fair Acres based on the evidence introduced at trial, because "it was not the function of Fair Acres to provide psychiatric services for persons with disruptive psychotic disorders." *Wagner v. Fair Acres*, 859 F. Supp. at 783. Accordingly, the court concluded that Mrs. Wagner failed to establish a case for relief under section 504.

* * *

II.

Section 504 of the Rehabilitation Act of 1973, 29 U.S.C. § 4, prohibits a federally funded state program from discriminating against a handicapped individual solely by reason of his or her handicap. Section 504 of the Rehabilitation Act reads in pertinent part:

> No otherwise qualified handicapped individual in the United States, as defined in section 706(7) of this title shall, solely by reason of his handicap, be excluded from participation in, be denied the benefits of or be subjected to discrimination under any program or activity receiving Federal financial assistance. . . . 29 U.S.C. § 794.

A "handicapped individual" for purposes of the Act is defined as "any person who (i) has a physical or mental impairment which substantially limits one or more of such person's major life activities, (ii) has a record of such impairment, or (iii) is regarded as having such an impairment." 29 U.S.C. § 706(7)(B). In order to establish a violation of the Rehabilitation Act, a plaintiff must prove (1) that he is a "handicapped individual" under the Act, (2) that he is "otherwise qualified" for the position sought, (3) that he was excluded from the position sought "solely by reason of his handicap," and (4) that the program or activity in question receives federal financial assistance. *[Citations omitted.]* It is undisputed that Mrs. Wagner is a handicapped individual within the meaning of the Act and that Fair Acres is a recipient of federal assistance. Indeed, the only issue submitted to the jury was whether Mrs. Wagner was "otherwise qualified" for admission to Fair Acres.

In *Southeastern Community College v. Davis*, 442 U.S. 397 (1979), the Supreme Court held that an "otherwise qualified" handicapped individual is one who can meet all of a program's requirements in spite of his handicap. *Id.* at 406. Significantly, the Court indicated that an individual may be otherwise qualified in some instances even though he cannot meet all of a program's requirements. In *Strathie*, we observed that "this is the case when the refusal to modify an existing program would be unreasonable and thereby discriminatory." 716 F.2d at 230.

Further interpreting the Supreme Court's decision in *Davis*, we held in *Strathie* that two factors pertain to the reasonableness of a refusal to accommodate a handicapped individual. First, requiring accommodation is unreasonable if it would necessitate modification of the essential nature of the program. Second, requiring accommodation is unreasonable if it would place undue burdens, such as extensive costs, on the recipient of federal funds. *[Citations omitted.]* In *Easley*, we held, "It follows, of course, that if there is no factual basis in the record demonstrating that accommodating the individual would require a fundamental modification or an undue burden, then the handicapped person is otherwise qualified." *Id.* Thus, in looking at whether an individual is otherwise qualified, we must analyze whether the person would be otherwise qualified if reasonable accommodations are made for his/her handicap.

A.

The district court reviewed these same cases and concluded that Mrs. Wagner was not an otherwise qualified handicapped individual because Mrs. Wagner "sought admission to Fair Acres because of her handicap and not in spite of her handicap, and thus she is not an 'otherwise qualified' handicapped individual who has been denied a benefit solely by reason of handicap." The district court concluded:

> . . . [I]n the absence of the Alzheimer's disease, Mrs. Wagner would not need the nursing home care she sought at Fair Acres. Clearly she sought a benefit because of her handicap and not in spite of it. Unlike the plaintiff in *Nathanson* [*Nathanson v. Medical College of Pennsylvania*, 926 F.2d 1368 (3d Cir. 1991)] who sought admission to medical school in spite of her back problem, not because of it, and the plaintiff in *Strathie* who sought a school bus driver's license in spite of his deafness, not because of it, Mrs. Wagner sought admission to an institution capable of caring for Alzheimer's sufferers because she also suffers from Alzheimer's. 859 F. Supp. at 782-83.

We believe that in focusing on why Mrs. Wagner sought access to Fair Acres, the district court's analysis is misplaced. It is irrelevant why a plaintiff sought access to a program, service or institution; our concern, for purposes of section 504, is why a plaintiff is *denied* access to a program, service or institution. Obviously, everyone that applies for admission to a nursing home does so because of his or her disabilities. Indeed, no one would be able to meet a nursing home's admissions requirements in the absence of some handicapping condition necessitating nursing home care. Further, if the district court's analysis is taken to its logical extreme, no program, service or institution designed specifically to meet the needs of the handicapped would ever have to comply with section 504 because every applicant would seek access to the program or facility *because* of a handicap, not in spite of it. This result would contradict both the statutory and regulatory framework of section 504.

The legislative history of section 504 indicates that Congress clearly contemplated that section 504 would apply to nursing homes that receive federal funding. The Senate Committee Report that introduced the Rehabilitation Act stated, "[T]he bill further proclaims a policy of nondiscrimination against otherwise qualified individuals with respect to participation in or access to any program which is in receipt of federal financial assistance." S. Rep. No. 1135, 92 Cong., 2d Sess. 49. *See also* 118 Cong. Rec. 32294. The Report identified examples of the types of programs that section 504 was designed to cover: housing, transportation, education and health services. Since the primary purpose of the Rehabilitation Act as enacted in 1973 was to extend and expand the 53-year old federal-state vocational rehabilitation program, Congress initially defined the phrase "handicapped individual" in terms of employment and employability. However, because it was clearly the intent of Congress in adopting section 504, which Congress labeled "nondiscrimination in federal grants", the term "handicapped individual" was no longer to be narrowly limited to employment. As the Senate Report accompanying the 1974 amendments to the Rehabilitation Act elaborated: Section 7(6) of the Rehabilitation Act of 1973 defines "handicapped individual." That definition has proven to be troublesome in its application to provisions of the Act such as sections 503 and 504 because of its orientation toward employment and its relation to vocational rehabilitation services. It was clearly the intent of the Committee and of Congress in adopting section 503 (affirmative action) and section 504 (nondiscrimination) that the term "handicapped individual" in those sections was not to be narrowly limited to employment (in the case of section 504), nor to the individual's potential benefit from vocational rehabilitation services under Titles I and III (in the case of both sections 503 and 504) of the Act.

* * *

The Committee substitute adds a new definition of "handicapped individual" for the purposes of titles IV and V of the Act in order to embody this underlying intent.

Section 504 was enacted to prevent discrimination against all handicapped individuals, regardless of their need for, or ability to benefit from, vocational rehabilitation services, in relation to Federal assistance in employment, housing, transportation, education, *health services*, or any other Federally-aided programs. *Examples of handicapped individuals who may suffer discrimination in the receipt of Federally-assisted services but who may have been unintentionally excluded from the protection of section 504 by the references to enhanced employability in section 7(6) are as follows*: physically or mentally handicapped children who may be denied admission to Federally-supported school systems on the basis of their handicap; *handicapped persons who may be denied admission to Federally-assisted nursing homes on the basis of their handicap*; those persons whose handicap is so severe that employment is not feasible but who may be denied the benefits of a wide range of Federal programs; and those persons whose vocational rehabilitation is complete, but who may nevertheless be discriminated against in certain Federally-assisted activities. S. Rep. No. 1297, 93d Cong., 2d Sess., *reprinted in* [1974] U.S. Code Cong. & Ad. News 6376, 6388-89. (Emphasis added.)

We interpret this legislative history as indicating that Congress contemplated that section 504 would apply to nursing home admissions decisions. Thus, we conclude that Mrs. Wagner was not prevented from seeking the protection of section 504 even though she was motivated to make application to Fair Acres because of her disability. The district court erred, as a matter of law, in holding to the contrary.

B.

In addition to finding that Mrs. Wagner was not "otherwise qualified" on the ground that she sought admission to Fair Acres because of her handicap and not in spite of it, the district court also found that she was not otherwise qualified because Fair Acres' decision was a "medical treatment" decision. Citing *Bowen v. American Hosp. Ass'n*, 476 U.S. 610 (1986) and *United States v. University Hosp., State University of New York at Stony Brook*, 729 F.2d 144 (2d Cir. 1984), the district court concluded that "medical treatment decisions are generally immune from scrutiny under section 504." We disagree with the district court's characterization of this case.

In *Bowen* and *University Hospital*, the applicability of section 504 to the withholding of heroic medical treatment to profoundly handicapped infants was at issue. In *University Hospital*, the United States sought an order directing University Hospital to provide the Department of Health & Human Services with access to the medical records of a handicapped infant whose parents had refused to consent to corrective surgical procedures but, rather, had opted for conservative treatment of their infant's disabilities. The Court of Appeals for the Second Circuit held that the "otherwise qualified" criteria of Section 504 cannot be meaningfully applied to such medical treatment decisions. The court observed,

> . . . [w]here medical treatment is at issue, it is typically the handicap itself that gives rise to, or at least contributes to the need for services. . . . As a result, the phrase cannot be applied in the comparatively fluid context of medical treatment decisions without distorting its plain meaning. In common parlance, one would not ordinarily think of a newborn infant suffering from multiple birth defects as "otherwise qualified" to have corrective surgery performed. . . . If Congress intended section 504 to apply in this manner, it chose strange language indeed. . . . The legislative history, moreover, indicates that Congress never contemplated section 504 would apply to treatment decision of this nature. 729 F.2d at 156.

Similarly, the issue in *Bowen* was whether the Secretary of Health and Human Services had authority under the Rehabilitation Act to regulate medical treatment decisions concerning handicapped newborn infants. The Supreme Court, however, did not reach the issue of whether a medical treatment decision made on the basis of handicap is immune from scrutiny under section 504, because the Court held there was no evidence that the hospitals had denied treatment on the basis of handicap. Rather, treatment was denied because of the absence of parental consent. Accordingly, the Supreme Court concluded, "A hospital's withholding of treatment from a handicapped infant when no parental consent has been given cannot violate Section 504, for without the parent's consent the infant is neither 'otherwise qualified' for treatment nor has he been denied care solely by reason of his handicap." 476 U.S. at 610.

Unlike these medical treatment cases involving handicapped infants which necessitate complex assessments of the medical needs, benefits and risks of providing invasive medical care, the issue we confront here concerns the "essential nature" of the service that Fair Acres provides and involves an assessment of whether providing the skilled nursing care, which no one disputes Mrs. Wagner required, would alter the essential nature of Fair Acres' program or impose an undue burden in light of its program. *See, e.g., Easley by Easley v. Snider*, 36 F.3d at 305. A decision of this type, regarding whether an institution can provide certain services without a modification of the essential nature of its program or imposition of an undue burden, involves administrative decision-making and not medical judgment. For example, here Fair Acres must determine whether it is able to provide the requisite staff (*i.e.*, nurses and nurses aids to care for, *i.e.*, feed, bathe, and occupy Mrs. Wagner) as well as the appropriate physical accommodations without incurring extensive cost. These are decisions that administrators routinely make.

III.

Applying these legal principles, we now review the record to determine whether Mrs. Wagner presented legally sufficient evidence that she was "otherwise qualified" for admission to Fair Acres. . . . When reviewing the jury's finding that Mrs. Wagner was "otherwise qualified" for admission to Fair Acres, we give to her, as the verdict winner, the benefit of all logical inferences that could be drawn from the evidence presented, resolve all conflicts in the evidence in her favor and, in general, view the record in the light most favorable to her. *[Citations omitted.]*

A.

In support of her assertion that there was a legally sufficient basis for the jury's determination that she was an "otherwise qualified individual," Mrs. Wagner points to the testimony of her three expert witness. Dr. Gottlieb reviewed Mrs. Wagner's medical records of her psychiatric hospitalization at Wills from September 2, 1992 until April 12, 1993. Based upon his review of these records, it was his opinion that Mrs. Wagner's behavior was consistent with a large proportion of people suffering from Alzheimer's disease. (A. 43). Dr. Gottlieb testified that the largest proportion of people in nursing home settings have Alzheimer's disease and that Mrs. Wagner was appropriate or qualified for the services and type of intermediate care provided by Fair Acres Nursing home. Based on a reasonable degree of medical certainty, he believed it appropriate to transfer Mrs. Wagner back to a nursing home setting sometime between the end of September and the end of October of 1992. (A. 94).

Dr. Gottlieb also testified regarding the type of accommodations that Fair Acres would have to make in order to care for Mrs. Wagner. (A. 56). He testified that Mrs. Wagner's combative assaultive behavior occurred relatively infrequently, rarely more than once a day, and often it was predictable as to when this behavior would occur. (A. 79). Thus, he concluded that she would need one-to-one supervision infrequently. (A. 57).

Dr. Kim, Mrs. Wagner's treating psychiatrist at Wills testified that she did not require one-to-one supervision for extended periods of time and could be redirected easily. It was his opinion that about the third week of October, 1992, Mrs. Wagner could have been managed and accommodated by a nursing home. (A. 124). Indeed, on October 23, 1992, Dr. Kim had written a letter to the administrator of Fair Acres stating that should Mrs. Wagner experience a deterioration in her mental status requiring rehospitalization, he would be willing to readmit her to Wills for further treatment and stabilization. (A. 126).

Dr. Etemad, the staff psychiatrist at Easton Nursing facility, testified that Easton Nursing Home is a regular nursing home that has patients at different levels of functioning. Although Dr. Etemad did not review the Wills records, he reviewed a final summary by a psychiatrist who was sent to Easton Nursing Home when Mrs. Wagner was transferred. (A. 173). Dr. Etemad evaluated Mrs. Wagner on April 14, two days after her admission to Easton and again around May 18, 1992. He testified that he saw her one time after that, and then there were no more requests by the staff for him to see her. During the five months preceding trial that Mrs. Wagner spent at Easton, Dr. Etemad informed the court that it was not necessary for her to be referred to an inpatient psychiatric hospital and that Easton was able to accommodate her and meet her needs. (A. 167). In his judgment, she is most appropriately classified as a nursing home patient.

Fair Acres' defense consisted of Mrs. Wagner's medical records and progress notes from her hospitalization at Wills, and the testimony of various members of Fair Acres' admissions committee who evaluated Mrs. Wagner's application for admission. R.N. Mimi Huver-Delaney, the Admissions Director at Fair Acres since 1982, testified that up to February 19, 1993, Fair Acres would not have been staffed to handle the kind of treatment that Mrs. Wagner required. (A. 236). Admissions case worker Amy Thomas testified that Mrs. Wagner was not admitted to Fair Acres because they could not meet her needs.

Dr. Satyendra K. Diwan testified that, as a consultant to Fair Acres since 1981, he did not examine Mrs. Wagner personally but instead reviewed Mrs. Wagner's records with respect to her admission at Fair Acres. He is not board certified in either psychiatry or geriatric psychology. (A. 258). Dr. Diwan testified that he does not rely on any written criteria in order to evaluate whether someone is appropriate for admission. His own personal criterion is that the patient be symptom-free of agitation for a 3-4 week period. (A. 278-280). [The reasonableness of this requirement for admission was called into question by Mrs. Wagner's experts. Dr. Kim testified that, by and large, a three week period without any symptoms of agitation is uncommon in many Alzheimer's patients and that it would be fairly common that a patient would exhibit some form of agitation on a daily basis. (A. 125). Dr. Etemad testified that it was not reasonable medical practice to look for symptom free behavior, *i.e.*, no agitation for a 3-week period, as a precondition of admission to a nursing home. In his practice, he has never seen a patient who was totally asymptomatic before transfer to a nursing home. (A. 178).] Dr. Diwan testified that Mrs. Wagner was inappropriate for care at Fair Acres the five times he reviewed her, mainly because of her dangerousness towards herself and others. (A. 259). He was not aware that, prior to her last review, she was not ambulating as her physical condition had weakened, nor was he aware of the fact that she was spending approximately 80% of her day confined in a geri-chair. (A. 275).

Linda Hadfield, admissions coordinator at Fair Acres, testified that she visits almost every patient before admission to Fair Acres. (A. 298). She visited Mrs. Wagner on October 23, immediately prior to the third review. (A. 300). She discussed the techniques employed by Wills to calm Mrs. Wagner: they would put her in a quiet room, massage her feet, play soft music for her — techniques Fair Acres would not provide. (A. 301). On October 29th, the third meeting, Fair Acres put Mrs. Wagner on "for hold" status. (A. 302). Hadfield visited Wills again on December 30, between the third and fourth evaluation of Mrs. Wagner's application for admission. She observed that Wills was still using the quiet room and Inapsine to calm Mrs. Wagner. (A. 304). She testified that the nurse's notes did not always reflect what the psychiatric doctor wrote. (A. 304).

B.

Based upon its review of this evidence, the district court held that there was no legally sufficient basis for the jury's determination that Margaret Wagner was an "otherwise qualified" individual for purposes of section 504, because the court found that she did not meet Fair Acres' requirements for admission. The district court opined, "It was not the function of Fair Acres to provide psychiatric services for persons with disruptive psychotic disorders." Further, the court opined, "Nor is it a case of Fair Acres making a reasonable accommodation." 859 F. Supp. at 783. The district court's conclusions, in these regards, are erroneous. Because the district court arrived at these conclusions based upon the application of incorrect legal precepts, our review is plenary. *[Citations omitted.]*

IV.

The inquiry into whether an applicant is otherwise qualified necessarily involves a determination of whether the applicant could have gained access to the program if the recipient of funds had made reasonable accommodations. *Alexander v. Choate,* 469 U.S. 287, 301 (1985). In the unanimous decision in *Alexander*, the Supreme Court stated:

> *Davis* . . . struck a balance between the statutory rights of the handicapped to be integrated into society and the legitimate interests of federal grantees in preserving the integrity of their programs: while a grantee need not be required to make "fundamental" or "substantial" modifications to accommodate the handicapped, it may be required to make "reasonable"ones.

> The balance struck in *Davis* requires that an otherwise qualified individual must be provided with meaningful access to the benefit that the grantee offers. The benefit itself, of course, cannot be defined in a way that effectively denies otherwise qualified individuals the meaningful access to which they are entitled; to assure meaningful access, reasonable accommodations in the grantee's program or benefit may have to be made. *Alexander*, 469 U.S. at 300 (citation and footnotes omitted).

As the Court of Appeals for the Fifth Circuit observed in *Brennan v. Stewart*, 834 F.2d 1248 (5th Cir. 1988), "After *Alexander*, it is clear that the phrase 'otherwise qualified' has a paradoxical quality; on the one hand, it refers to a person who has the abilities or characteristics sought by the grantee; but on the other, it cannot refer only to those already capable of meeting *all* the requirements — or else no reasonable requirement could ever violate section 504, no matter how easy it would be to accommodate handicapped individuals who cannot fulfill it." 834 F.2d 1248 (5th Cir. 1988). We agree with the Court of Appeals for the Fifth Circuit: "The question after *Alexander* is the rather mushy one of whether some `reasonable accommodation' is available to satisfy the legitimate interests of both the grantee and the handicapped person." 834 F.2d at 1262.

In light of *Alexander* and our decision in *Strathie*, we are required to review the record to determine additionally if there was a factual basis in the record demonstrating that Fair Acres' refusal to accommodate Mrs. Wagner was unreasonable. *See Strathie*, 716 F.2d at 230 (a section 504 claim could be defeated "if there is a factual basis in the record reasonably demonstrating that accommodating the individual would require either a modification of the essential nature of the program or impose an undue burden on the recipient of federal funds.")

See also School Bd. of Nassau County, Fla. v. Arline, 480 U.S. 273 (1987) (determinations regarding whether plaintiffs are "otherwise qualified" will generally require an individualized inquiry and appropriate findings of fact). Here there was ample evidence that Mrs. Wagner's aggressive behaviors associated with her Alzheimer's disease clearly rendered her, as amicus curiae characterizes her, "a challenging and demanding patient." We find that this fact alone cannot justify her exclusion from a nursing home that receives federal funds. Otherwise nursing homes would be free to "pick and choose" among patients, accepting and admitting only the easiest patients to care for, leaving the more challenging and demanding patients with no place to turn for care. [Dr. Gottlieb testified at trial that currently approximately four million Americans have been diagnosed with Alzheimer's disease and it is estimated that this disease affects 11 percent of all Americans who are over the age of 65. Moreover, the number of Americans afflicted with Alzheimer's disease is expected to increase with the size of the burgeoning elderly population. (A. 36). Consequently, many people who suffer from Alzheimer's will be forced to seek nursing home placement. Because Mrs. Wagner's plight is typical of a growing number of others, the issue of whether Fair Acres was required, in keeping with section 504, to make reasonable accommodations to care for Mrs. Wagner should have been, but was not, addressed. . . .The Alzheimer's Disease and Related Disorders Association of Greater Philadelphia points out in its amicus brief that "Contrary to the commonly held belief that nursing homes are 'genteel rest homes for elderly people, the prevalence of psychiatric behavioral disorders in nursing homes has been estimated to range from 68 to 94 percent.'" *[Citations omitted.]*]

Indeed, the evidence introduced at trial confirmed that Mrs. Wagner was a difficult patient, one for whom the ravages of Alzheimer's disease were manifested in a myriad of extremely unpleasant ways — by mood swings, periods of combativeness, and outbursts of shouting. However, as Mrs. Wagner's expert witness, Dr. Gottlieb, pointed out, "the fact that she had agitated behavior does not contradict that she could be managed in a nursing home." (A. 83-84).

Our review of the record reveals that Fair Acres presented little or no evidence about the type of accommodations it would have needed to make in order to provide care for Mrs. Wagner. While Fair Acres made general allegations that it could not adequately care for Mrs. Wagner or meet her needs due to her aggressive behavior, it failed to offer any factual basis demonstrating that the admission of Mrs. Wagner to Fair Acres would have changed the essential nature of the facility as a nursing home or imposed an undue burden on the facility, economically or otherwise. Larry Rendin, the medical director at Fair Acres for the past fifteen years, testified that of the 900 patients at his facility, some 64 to 70% are afflicted with Alzheimer's or dementia-related disease, that is, organic brain syndrome of one type or another. Mr. Rendin agreed that some of the characteristics of the Alzheimer's patients at Fair Acres included screaming, yelling, confusion, agitation, combativeness and aggression on occasion and that "Fair Acres takes care of them and the staff is equipped to deal with that." (A. 95). He agreed that some patients require one-to-one care for certain periods of time, and many times Fair Acres has two or three staff members providing care to one patient. His facility is equipped to provide that level of care. (A. 97). Rendin also testified that between 20-25 times a year it is necessary to transfer a patient from Fair Acres to an in-patient psychiatric facility. (A. 98). Most are returned to Fair Acres after a few weeks and Fair Acres is then able to accommodate their needs. (A. 99). Thus the record reveals Fair Acres is clearly capable of providing and, in fact, has provided the kinds of services that Mrs. Wagner required, although she may have needed them on a more frequent basis.

Linda Hadfield, Fair Acres' admissions coordinator, discussed the techniques employed by Wills to calm Mrs. Wagner during her disturbances. These techniques included putting Mrs. Wagner in a "quiet room," massaging her feet, talking to her and playing soft music. Although Ms. Hadfield testified that Fair Acres did not provide these services, there was no evidence that these were calming techniques that Fair Acres could *not* provide, or that to do so would change the essential nature of Fair Acres as a nursing home into an acute psychiatric facility or impose an undue burden on Fair Acres.

Ms. Hadfield opined that Mrs. Wagner was also not suitable for admission to Fair Acres because she had been receiving injections of Inapsine at Wills, a drug that Fair Acres had not previously administered. Dr. Kim testified that he prescribed Inapsine for Mrs. Wagner while she was at Wills because Inapsine is a neuroleptic, or tranquilizing agent, which is very short acting and is available in vials and ampoules. It is administered by intramuscular injection. Notwithstanding the fact that Inapsine had not been administered at Fair Acres before, Dr. Gottlieb testified that Inapsine could be administered in a nursing home setting and that roughly 25 percent of the people in nursing homes receive supertrophic, sedating drugs on a daily basis. Dr. Gottlieb's testimony was further supported by Larry Rendin when he testified that many of the patients at Fair Acres are administered Haldol. (A. 107). Thus, based on this evidence, a jury could reasonably conclude that the accommodations Fair Acres would need to make to care for Mrs. Wagner were not unreasonable.

Fair Acres also contended that accommodating Mrs. Wagner would have created a health and safety risk to the staff and patients at Fair Acres. (A. 389). Dr. Diwan testified that "each time I concluded that she is not appropriate because mainly of her dangerousness towards others and herself." (A. 260). Our review reveals that Dr. Diwan's testimony was contradicted by the testimony of Mrs. Wagner's treating physician at Wills, Dr. Kim. Dr. Kim testified that he did not view Mrs. Wagner as creating a health or safety risk. With respect to the references in her chart that she was combative and assaultive, Dr. Kim testified that, "[W]e describe being combative or assaultive as any behavior that is resistive or aggressive. . . . But this is all [done by] someone who is essentially bedridden and can barely [*sic*] walk and is more or less slapping out like a child." (A. 129). Dr. Kim also testified on cross-examination that at the time of Mrs. Wagner's final evaluation in early February, she was spending 60-80% of her waking hours in a geri-chair, and that she needed 80% support by staff to remain upright. (A. 155). Thus, there was sufficient evidence presented from which a reasonable jury could conclude that Mrs. Wagner, at least by February, posed little threat to anyone's health or safety due to her extremely weakened physical condition.

Finally, by the later dates on which Mrs. Wagner was denied admission to Fair Acres, the jury could infer from the evidence that Mrs. Wagner would not have needed a quiet room or much of anything in the way of reasonable accommodation. For example, Dr. Kim testified that, "We noted that progressively she became more and more physically handicapped. She needed increasing assistance to walk, she needed to be spoon-fed, by the end of her stay, she became incontinent, needed to be in a diaper, and spent most of her days sitting in a chair staring off into space, occasionally making semi-coherent expressions, sometimes crying. But for the most part staring blankly off into space for a majority of that time." (A. 128).

Based on our review of the evidence, we find that a jury could have determined that at some point during the period from September 1992 to February 1993, Mrs. Wagner was "otherwise qualified" for admission to Fair Acres in accordance with section 504 because Fair Acres could have cared for her if it made reasonable accommodations. Thus, we must reverse the district court's order granting summary judgment as a matter of law.

* * *

A.

At the close of all the evidence, Fair Acres submitted the following instruction for inclusion in the court's points for charge:

> Administrators from Fair Acres Geriatric Center are entitled to some measure of judicial deference in this matter, by reason of their experience with and knowledge of the administrative procedures in question.

Defendants' proposed points of charge No. 6. Counsel for Mrs. Wagner objected to this point for charge because counsel did not believe the charge to be a correct statement of the law. The district court sustained Mrs. Wagner's objection and decided not to include this point in its charge to the jury. (A. 328). In ruling on the motion for a new trial, the district court found its refusal to give this charged constituted prejudicial error. We disagree.

We addressed the issue of the deference to be given the judgment of program administrators in cases arising under section 504 in our decision in *Strathie v. Dept. of Transp.*, 716 F.2d 227 (3d Cir. 1983). There we rejected the notion that broad judicial deference was required, and instead we observed,

> Notably absent from the Supreme Court's opinion in *Davis*, however, is any discussion of the scope of judicial review with regard to the reasonableness of a refusal to accommodate a handicapped individual. Program administrators surely are entitled to some measure of judicial deference in this matter, by reason of their experience in question. *On the other hand, broad judicial deference* resembling that associated with the "rational basis" test *would substantially undermine Congress' intent* in enacting section 504 that stereotypes or generalizations not deny handicapped individuals access to federally-funded programs. 716 F.2d at 231 (citations omitted) (emphasis added).

We then held that "the following standard effectively reconciles these competing considerations: a handicapped individual who cannot meet all of a program's requirements is not otherwise qualified if there is a factual basis in the record reasonably demonstrating that accommodating that individual would require either a modification of the essential nature of the program, or impose an undue burden on the recipient of federal funds." 716 F.2d at 231. We observed that the Court of Appeals for the Second Circuit has also applied this "factual basis" standard, although it did not designate it as such. *[Citations omitted.]*

In the present case, there was no factual basis demonstrating that accommodating Mrs. Wagner would require Fair Acres to modify the essential nature of its program, or impose an undue burden upon it. In the absence of such a factual basis, Fair Acres' request that the jury be instructed that Fair Acres administrators be accorded "some" deference cannot be justified. Accordingly, the district court's failure to give an instruction that Fair Acres administrators were entitled to some measure of deference by reason of their experience with and knowledge of the procedures in question, was not legal error. Clearly it would not then rise to the level of fundamental error.

Here the district court's instructions to the jury in this regard struck the appropriate balance between deference to program administrators and the anti-discrimination mandate of section 504. The district court informed the jury that while Fair Acres was required to make reasonable accommodations, it was not required to make fundamental or substantial modifications to its program. Additionally, the district court instructed the jury that it must consider the views and evaluation process of Fair Acres. The court instructed the jury that it "must take into account the evaluation made by the institution itself in the absence of a showing that its standards and its application of those standards serves no purpose other than to deny access to handicapped persons." (A. 385).

B.

* * *

We have reviewed the record for evidence that is legally sufficient to support the jury's verdict. We find that Mrs. Wagner presented sufficient evidence to preclude the district court's granting judgment against her as a matter of law. Given, however, the district court's application of incorrect legal standards regarding the applicability of section 504 to the facts in this case, we are uncertain as to whether the court would have granted a new trial under the appropriate legal standards. Consequently, we will vacate the court's order granting a new trial and remand to the district court for reconsideration of this motion.

QUESTIONS

1. Does the *Wagner* ruling mean that nursing facilities must take all comers? Could any nursing facility like Fair Acres exclude those with a primarily psychiatric diagnosis after *Wagner*?

2. Why doesn't Fair Acres' denial of admission to Mrs. Wagner fall under the "medical treatment decision" exception to section 504?

3. If Mrs. Wagner was your grandmother, would you fight for her admission even though Fair Acres didn't want her? Why or why not?

2. Involuntary Transfer and Discharge

Stacey Gunya
Adult Care Homes
KANSAS LONG-TERM CARE HANDBOOK 28-34
(KANSAS BAR ASS'N 2001)*

III. LONG-TERM CARE FACILITY TRANSFER AND DISCHARGE

. . . Long-term care facilities . . . are governed by a complex set of federal laws regarding involuntary transfer and discharge. These laws, as they relate to Medicare certified facilities, are found at 42 USC § 1395i-3, *et seq.* The laws relating to Medicaid certified facilities are found at 42 U.S.C. § 1396r, et seq. While the sources of law come from a Medicare section and a Medicaid section, it is important to remember that facilities must maintain identical policies and practices for residents regardless of source of payment.

The [Center for Medicare and Medicaid Services] has codified these statutes as requirements for states and long-term care facilities at 42 C.F.R. § 483. . . . This section discusses the federal laws regarding involuntary transfer and discharge, how to initiate an involuntary transfer and how to defend a proposed transfer.

A. Intra-Facility Transfer

An intra-facility transfer is a transfer within the physical plant of the long-term care facility. Often a transfer occurs when a resident's Medicare days have ended. The facility may seek to move the resident to a distinct part of the facility that is not certified for Medicare. Transfers may also occur when the resident's care needs change or to accommodate roommate preferences.

The nursing facility is obligated to provide notice of the intended intra-facility transfer. The notice must be given to the resident and the legal representative or family member. The regulations do not specify any other requirements of the notice.

A resident has a general right to refuse a transfer. Additionally, a resident has an absolute right to refuse a transfer to a distinct part of the facility that is not a skilled nursing facility. The skilled nursing facility is the portion of the long-term care facility that is certified for Medicare. It may be advisable to refuse a transfer from the Medicare section of the facility if the resident is particularly frail. Transfers of any kind may be particularly traumatic to very frail residents.

If the facility fails to honor the residents refusal to transfer, then the resident has several choices. All residents have a right to file a grievance with the facility.

---

* Copyright © 2001. Reprinted with permission.

* * *

B. Inter-Facility Transfer and Discharge

Transfer and discharge generally involve the desire by the long-term care facility to remove the resident permanently. An inter-facility transfer may involve transfer to a psychiatric facility for evaluation or transfer to a hospital for treatment. A transfer or discharge may also involve admission to a different long-term care facility. Federal and state laws establish the requirements for an involuntary discharge.

Nursing facilities are generally charged with the duty to "ensure safe and orderly transfer" of a resident in all situations. The facility is not relieved of this duty in the involuntary discharge situation. Nursing facilities need to take care that the resident is not discharged into an unsafe environment.

For example, a resident might come to the facility after having been abused and neglected by a family member. Unless the resident should prefer to return to that home, it would not be appropriate to discharge that resident back to his family. Instead, the facility may need to contact other community resources about other safe locations to discharge that resident.

1. Therapeutic Transfers

Nursing home residents are often transferred to the hospital for treatment and/or evaluation. In these situations the resident needs to be concerned about holding a bed in the facility. Nursing homes are required to have a bed hold policy. Federal regulations give particular protection to the Medicaid resident. The bed hold policy must allow for readmission of the resident to the first available semi-private room. Notice of the policy is to be made available to the resident and family prior to the transfer and at the time of transfer. . . . Additionally, private pay residents would have a contractual right to return to the bed they have paid for.

2. Involuntary Discharge (Eviction)

Involuntary discharge or eviction from a nursing facility is a serious matter. Frail and elderly residents are likely to suffer life threatening consequences from transfer trauma. Medicaid residents generally face difficulty in choosing a facility and will want to fight to stay in their facility. A facility seeking to discharge a resident involuntarily will want to follow the statutory requirements carefully. Failure to follow the statutory requirements may mean the facility would face citation and fines from [the state regulatory agency] and litigation from the resident.

a. Notice

The statutory requirements for notice of involuntary discharge are found at 42U.S.C. § 1395i-3(c)(2)(B), 42 U.S.C. § 1396r(c)(2)(B), and 42 C.F.R. 483.12(a). The facility is required to provide written notice to the resident and/or his legal representative. The reasons for the discharge must be recorded in the resident's clinical record. The notice must be given 30 days in advance of discharge unless:

- The safety of other residents is at issue;

- The facility ceases to operate;

- The resident's health has improved so that care is no longer needed;

- The resident has an urgent medical need; or

- The resident has not resided in the facility for at least 30 days.

Contents of the notice are also governed by statute. The notice must contain the following information.

- The grounds for discharge;

- The location of the intended discharge;

- The right to appeal the discharge; and

- The name, address and telephone number of the state Long-Term Care Ombudsman.

b. Grounds

A long-term care facility is limited on the grounds that may be used to discharge a resident involuntarily. Only five (5) reasons are recognized as permissible grounds for involuntary discharge. Statutes also state how these grounds must be substantiated. The five permissible grounds are:

1. The discharge is necessary to meet the resident's welfare and resident's welfare cannot be met by the facility. This must be documented in the resident's clinical record by the resident's physician.

2. The resident's health has improved sufficiently so that the resident no longer needs the services provided by the facility. This must also be documented in the clinical record by the resident's physician.

3. The safety of individuals in the facility is endangered. The safety threat must be documented in the clinical record.

4. The health of individuals in the facility is endangered by the resident. Again, the health threat must be documented in the clinical record by the resident's physician.

5. The resident has failed after reasonable notice to pay for the stay in the facility.

* * *

d. Defending an Involuntary Discharge

A resident who wishes to defend an involuntary discharge will want to involve as many agencies as possible. The advocate should request [a Medicaid agency administrative] hearing as well as an investigation by [other state regulatory agencies]. Also, the advocate should contact the state Long-Term Care Ombudsman for assistance in resolving the dispute. The advocate should require the long-term care facility to produce all the resident's medical and social service records.

Typically the [Medicaid agency administrative] hearing will not take place before the date of intended discharge of the resident. If the facility will not voluntarily agree to postpone the discharge until after the . . . hearing, then the advocate will want to take steps to restrain the facility from transferring the resident. [Generally, none of the regulatory state agencies] have the power to stop a facility from transferring a resident. In exigent circumstances, a petition for injunctive relief and motion for temporary restraining order should be filed with the district court. . . . For the court to issue the temporary restraining order and the injunction, the resident must establish:

1. The applicant is likely to prevail when the court finally disposes of the matter;

2. Without relief the applicant will suffer irreparable injury;

3. The grant of relief to the applicant will not substantially harm other parties to the proceedings; and

4. The threat to public health, safety, or welfare relied on by the agency is not sufficiently serious to justify the agency's action in the circumstances.

* * *

e. Special Situations

i. Involuntary Discharge for Behavior Problems

A common reason for involuntary discharge is that the resident's behavior has become objectionable to the facility. For example, a resident with dementia may become violent or develop other difficult to manage behaviors. The resident may have a habit that is dangerous, like smoking. In either case where the behavior or condition of the resident is at issue, it is important to look at the care plan. Each resident should have an individual care plan. When a problem arises, there should be a multi-disciplinary team approach to dealing with the problem. Also, facilities have promised as part of their Medicare and Medicaid certification that they have staff trained to provide care to a variety of resident conditions including dementia.

PRACTICE TIP: In defending a behavior-based discharge, the key is generally the physician. The opinion of the physician is required in three of the five specified grounds for involuntary discharge. The physician is almost always an employee of the nursing facility or may see most of the facility's residents. Because of the close relationship between the long-term care facility and the physician it may be difficult for the physician to take the side of the resident. The resident, however, is always free to choose his own physician. A change of treating physician, therefore, may be necessary to successfully defend the discharge.

Additionally, an advocate should keep in mind other sources of law that may extend protections to the resident. In other jurisdictions, judges have extended the protections of the Americans with Disabilities Act, Section 504 of the Rehabilitation Act of 1973 and the Fair Housing Amendment's Act of 1978 to residents of long-term care facilities. These acts prohibit discrimination in the provision of services and housing to persons who are disabled.

A hypothetical example may help explain how all these regulations work. Suppose that Ruth is a nursing home resident. She has dementia and low vision. She has begun to spit at staff when they approach her to care for her. The nursing facility has decided to discharge Ruth claiming that the spitting is a health risk for the staff and other residents. In order to support this ground for discharge the medical record would need to reflect that there is indeed a medical risk as documented by the treating physician. Also, the problem should be addressed in a care plan meeting. The medical record should show attempts by the facility to try to deal with the problem. And finally, if discharge cannot be supported the facility will need to find an appropriate location to transfer Ruth.

Ruth's advocates will want to make sure that the notice is technically correct and carefully review the supporting documentation for the discharge. Any mistake by the facility should be promptly reported to [the relevant regulatory agency]. Her advocates should also contact their [State] Long-Term Care Ombudsman for assistance resolving the dispute and contact Social and Rehabilitation Services about requesting an appeal. It is also important to contact the treating physician about whether Ruth's behavior cannot be ameliorated in some way.

If Ruth's advocates cannot persuade the nursing home to keep Ruth until the appeal is heard, they will want to go to district court to try to enjoin the facility from transferring her. They may also want to bring a separate cause of action against the facility for discriminating against her because of her disability. Such litigation can be exhausting and financially costly for all parties. Hopefully, a case like Ruth's would be resolved before it reaches the courts.

ii. Involuntary Discharge for Non-payment

Non-payment is not as simple as it may appear. Non-payment extends only to non-payment of "covered services." Each state defines what constitutes "covered services" in their Medicaid plan. Only non-payment of those services is considered grounds for discharge. Non-payment of a Medicare co-pay is not considered non-payment and is not grounds for discharge. If the resident's stay is paid by Medicaid it is not considered non-payment. The state reimbursement rate for Medicaid is considerably lower than the private pay rate. The long-term care provider, however, in its contract with the State . . . has agreed to accept Medicaid as full payment of the resident's long-term care nursing bill. Additionally, the submission of a Medicaid application is sufficient to avoid discharge for non-payment.

Finally, the long-term care facility should be sensitive to whether financial exploitation is the reason for non-payment. If a family member or other fiduciary is controlling the resident's finances, but not paying for the resident's care, this may be financial exploitation. Medicaid may be denied because of malfeasance by the fiduciary. For example, an attorney in fact may have transferred property into his own name or have persuaded the resident to do so. This may make the resident ineligible for Medicaid. It also is a breach of fiduciary duty, and should be reported to [the state regulatory agency] as financial exploitation.

Attempting to discharge a resident for non-payment, while not exploring the issue of financial exploitation may expose the facility to other liabilities. Long-term care facility administrators and staff are mandatory reporters of abuse, neglect, and exploitation. Failure to report abuse and exploitation may be charged as a class B misdemeanor. Financial exploitation should be reported to [the state regulatory agency]. The appointment of a guardian and/or conservator may be necessary to protect the resident.

C. Conclusion

Transfer or discharge of a resident from a long-term care facility is carefully regulated by the state and federal government. The long-term care facility should take care to follow the requirements during any transfer and discharge. Residents should remember that they are not powerless when confronted with an unwanted transfer or discharge. Federal and state laws give residents recourse in these situations. Residents may also look to various state agencies . . . for assistance in resolving their disputes with a long-term care facility.

QUESTIONS

1. Why should a facility be required to keep a resident whose unacceptable behavior cannot be controlled?

2. Why would a family insist on such a resident staying in a facility which apparently cannot meet his or her needs?

3. What solutions to the problem of Ruth's spitting can you think of short of involuntary discharge?

FURTHER READING. Lawrence A. Frolik, RESIDENTIAL OPTIONS FOR OLDER AND DISABLED CLIENTS (Warren, Gorham & Lamont Eds., 1996); Lawrence A. Frolik & Richard L. Kaplan, ELDER LAW IN A NUTSHELL (3d ed. 2003).

Chapter 10

ISSUES FOR GRANDPARENTS: KINSHIP CARE, CUSTODY AND VISITATION, AND RELATED MATTERS

Changes in population demographics and many other factors have resulted in a huge increase over the past three decades in the number of children living with and being raised by one or both grandparents. The U.S. Census Bureau estimates that 4.4 million children reside in households with at least one grandparent. This phenomenon has created enormous and unexpected financial and emotional burdens for many older Americans who find themselves to be "parents again." Many such grandparents live on small fixed incomes; the costs of rearing a child can, quite literally, impoverish elderly persons living a marginal existence. Although public and private benefits are often available to grandparents raising grandchildren, qualifying for such benefits may involve complex legal and administrative rules or require that the grandparents obtain some form of legally-sanctioned custody as a condition of qualifying for the benefits. Yet such requirements may conflict with intra-family decision-making or create tensions between a child's parents and grandparents.

This chapter is concerned with selected legal issues associated with grandparents' relationship with their grandchildren. Specifically, it addresses the forms of custody (both legal and de facto) that such a relationship may entail; "kinship caregiving" and the public and private resources that are available to assist grandparent-caregivers with the financial and emotional aspects of child-rearing; and the emergent concept of "grandparents' rights." The first section below provides statistical information that serves as a foundation for discussing these three substantive matters.

A. STATISTICS

U.S. Census Bureau,
American Community Survey 2004
Table: PCT8 Grandparents Living with Own
Grandchildren under 18 Years

http://factfinder.census.gov/home/saff/main.html?_lang=en&_ts=

Grandparents	Estimate	Lower Bound	Upper Bound
Number of grandparents living with own grandchildren under 18 years in household	5,675,375	5,581,586	5,769,164
Responsible for grandchildren Years responsible for grandchildren	2,374,694	2,322,983	2,426,405
Less than 1 year	531,984	506,547	557,421
1 or 2 years	536,072	508,999	563,145
3 or 4 years	383,420	361,938	404,902
5 or more years	923,218	895,216	951,220
Characteristics of grandparents responsible for own grandchildren under 18 years			
Female	62.8	62.1	63.5
Married	71.7	70.7	72.7
In labor force	58.9	58.1	59.7
In poverty	19.5	18.6	20.4

Percent of Grandparents Responsible for their
Grandchildren: 2005
Data Set: 2005 American Community Survey

http://factfinder.census.gov/servlet/GRTTable?_bm=
y&-_box_head_nbr=R1001&-ds_name=ACS_2005_EST_G00_
&-_lang=en&-format=US-30

Rank	State	Percent	Margin of Error
1	South Dakota	63.9	+/-8.8
2	Oklahoma	61.8	+/-3.4
3	Arkansas	61.3	+/-3.7
4	Mississippi	59.9	+/-3.1
5	Alabama	58.8	+/-2.8
6	Montana	56.2	+/-8.0
7	Wyoming	55.3	+/-9.0
8	Louisiana	55.2	+/-3.1
8	West Virginia	55.2	+/-4.8
10	North Dakota	55.0	+/-10.5
10	Tennessee	55.0	+/-3.0

12	New Mexico	54.1	+/-3.9
13	Kentucky	53.7	+/-3.4
14	Iowa	53.6	+/-5.3
15	South Carolina	52.4	+/-3.0
16	Alaska	52.1	+/-7.1
17	District of Columbia	52.0	+/-8.0
18	Idaho	51.9	+/-6.5
19	Indiana	49.8	+/-3.2
20	North Carolina	49.7	+/-2.9
21	Missouri	49.0	+/-3.2
22	Oregon	48.3	+/-3.7
23	Georgia	48.2	+/-2.2
23	Kansas	48.2	+/-5.1
25	Texas	47.8	+/-1.4
26	Colorado	47.3	+/-3.6
27	Ohio	46.5	+/-2.1
28	Nebraska	46.1	+/-5.1
29	Arizona	45.5	+/-3.1
29	Wisconsin	45.5	+/-3.5
31	Michigan	45.2	+/-2.3
32	Utah	43.7	+/-3.8
33	Florida	43.1	+/-1.9
	United States	42.8	+/-0.5
34	Virginia	42.6	+/-2.9
35	Nevada	41.8	+/-4.1
36	Illinois	41.5	+/-1.8
37	Minnesota	40.3	+/-4.0
38	Pennsylvania	39.3	+/-2.0
39	Delaware	38.8	+/-5.8
39	Washington	38.8	+/-3.2
41	Maine	38.7	+/-7.7
42	Maryland	37.5	+/-2.8
43	Vermont	34.1	+/-9.3
44	New Jersey	33.8	+/-2.9
45	New York	33.6	+/-1.8
46	Connecticut	32.3	+/-4.0
46	New Hampshire	32.3	+/-6.5
48	California	30.5	+/-1.0
49	Massachusetts	28.5	+/-2.9
50	Hawaii	26.6	+/-3.5
51	Rhode Island	24.2	+/-8.2
	Puerto Rico	50.3	+/-1.9

Source: U.S. Census Bureau, 2005 American Community Survey

Lynne M. Casper & Kenneth R. Bryson
Co-Resident Grandparents and Their Grandchildren: Grandparent-Maintained Families
Population Division Working Paper No. 26
Population Division, U.S. Bureau of the Census (March 1998)
http://www.census.gov/population/www/documentation/
twps0026/twps0026.html

* * *

Researchers, public policy makers and the media first began to notice the huge increases in grandparent-maintained households around 1990, prompting them to question why this was happening. A dramatic increase in analytical research occurred in the early to mid-1990s which focused on answering this question and examining the area of grandparent caregiving in general. Several reasons have been offered for the dramatic increases in grandparents raising and helping to raise their grandchildren. Increasing drug abuse among parents, teen pregnancy, divorce, the rapid rise of single parent households, mental and physical illnesses, AIDS, crime, child abuse and neglect, and incarceration are a few of the most common explanations offered.

At the same time that research on grandparents was on the rise, the media also began to focus attention on the growing number of children being raised by their grandparents. It wasn't long before federal lawmakers followed suit — both the Senate and the House of Representatives recognized the importance of this trend as constituting a pressing issue for public policy by holding Congressional hearings on the matter in 1992. The Senate hearings focused on the causes of the trend (U.S. Senate, Special Committee on Aging 1992), while the House hearings focused on the new roles and responsibilities of grandparents (U.S. House of Representatives, Select Committee on Aging 1992). Both hearings also focused on policy deficiencies in the areas of grandparent rights and their access to public assistance.

As more recent data since 1990 have shown, the trend continues to grow. Although progress has been made in understanding the causes of this trend and in documenting the various hardships these grandparents and grandchildren face, the use of univariate and bivariate methods and nonrepresentative samples has limited our understanding of the relative importance of the factors related to the well-being of grandparents and their grandchildren as well as the generalizability of the findings. In this paper, we use the 1997 March Current Population Survey data to document the number of grandparents who maintain households for their grandchildren and to show how these numbers have changed in the 1990s. We focus on describing five types of grandparent-maintained households — both grandparents, some parents present; both grandparents, no parents present; grandmother only, some parents present; grandmother only, no parents present; and grandfather only — and examine who these grandparents are, where they live, and how they fare economically. We also look at the characteristics of the grandchildren in these homes and use multivariate techniques to ascertain whether the type of family a grandchild lives in affects his/her economic well-being, insurance coverage, and receipt of public assistance.

* * *

Why Should Family Structure Matter?

Research has shown that one of the most important factors affecting economic well-being is family structure. Poverty and family income are family characteristics rather than individual characteristics. That is, people are defined as poor or non-poor based on the economic status of the family in which they live. Two factors are particularly important in determining a family's economic status: (1) the total income of the family and (2) the ratio of dependents to earners in the family (the dependency ratio). Marital status, the number of adult members in the family, their gender, ages and their labor force participation influence both of these components. Marital status, the number of adult members in the family, and their gender are all elements of family structure. Thus, if we want to study the economic well-being of grandchildren living in households maintained by their grandparents, it is imperative to include a measure of family structure.

* * *

In this research we improve and expand on previous research in a number of ways. We use nationally representative data to document the change in grandparent-maintained families by detailed type. We use more recent data (1997) than any other study to profile grandparents in all households maintained by grandparents presenting characteristics by gender and family type and expand upon the number and variety of characteristics presented in past research. We also look at grandchildren in each of the family types and compare their characteristics to children in households maintained by parents. Finally, we use multivariate techniques to determine which types of grandparent households make children the most vulnerable, as well as to sort out which other factors are important.

Data and Analytical Samples

The majority of the analysis in this paper is based on data from the March 1997 Current Population Survey (CPS) conducted by the U.S. Bureau of the Census for the Bureau of Labor Statistics. The March CPS is a nationally representative household survey of the civilian noninstitutionalized population of the United States based on a complex sample design. In 1997, 50,000 households were sampled in 754 sampling areas across the United States. The main purpose of the CPS is to collect labor force information to estimate the monthly national unemployment rate and other employment statistics.

The March supplement, administered each year since 1947, collects additional information on household and family composition, income sources and amounts, and other social and demographic information. Because relatively comparable data have been collected for over half of a century, the CPS is the best sample data for documenting changes in family type and living arrangements. In addition, the large sample allows for in-depth examination of relatively rare family types such as grandfather only families and grandmother only families, with no parents present.

In this paper, we examine the social and economic characteristics of grandparents who maintain households for their grandchildren and the grandchildren living with them. While the CPS doesn't permit us to look at the day to day activities of the grandparents and grandchildren, it does permit us to determine co-residence within the grandparent's home. We argue that providing a home is certainly one of the key components of caregiving and may be used as a proxy for the number of grandparents raising or helping to raise their grandchildren.

* * *

Based on the four elements of family type described above — marital status, the number of adult members in the family, their gender, and their relationship to the child — we define five family types for analysis: both grandparents, some parents present; both grandparents, no parents present; grandmother only, some parents present; grandmother only, no parents present; and grandfather only. To estimate the number of grandparents in each family type, we ascertain the gender, marital status and living arrangements of the grandparents in all family households in which a grandparent is the householder — maintains a household for at least one grandchild under 18. Three family household types emerge: married couple grandparent family households (both spouses present), grandmother only family households (no grandfather present), and grandfather family households (no grandmother present).

Descriptive Results

FAMILIES

In 1997, 6.7 percent of families with children under 18 were maintained by grandparents. Of these families, 34 percent were both grandparents, some parents present; 17 percent were both grandparents, no parents present; 29 percent were grandmother only, some parents present; 14 percent were grandmother only, no parents present; and 6 percent were grandfather only (Figure 2A) [not reproduced — Eds.]. Slightly over half of these grandparent-maintained families were maintained by both grandparents, 43 percent were maintained by grandmothers only and 6 percent were maintained by grandfathers only. About two-thirds of the families maintained by grandparents had parents present.

In the 1990s, the number of grandparent-maintained households increased 19 percent from 2,051,000 in 1990 to 2,444,000 in 1997. Each type of grandparent-grandchild family increased in size between 1990 and 1997. Grandfather only families grew by an astounding 39 percent. Families with the children's parents absent also grew rapidly: both grandparents, no parents present families grew by 31 percent and grandmother only, no parents present families grew by 27 percent. Families with children's parents present grew only 13 percent. This is consistent with other Census Bureau data which shows the most growth among children residing with their grandparents with neither parent present.

GRANDPARENTS

In 1997, there were 3.7 million grandparents maintaining households for their grandchildren, the majority of whom were grandmothers — 1.4 million grandfathers compared with 2.3 million grandmothers. When compared with grandmothers, grandfathers who maintain households for their grandchildren are more likely to be White. In general, grandfathers are more actively involved in the labor force and are less likely to be poor than grandmothers. For example, 66 percent of grandfathers are currently employed compared with 51 percent of grandmothers, and 55 percent of grandfathers were employed full time/full year in 1996 compared with only 37 percent of grandmothers. Grandmothers are also almost twice as likely as grandfathers to be poor (23 percent versus 12 percent). Grandfathers are also more likely to have accumulated capital; they are more likely to own their own homes (81 percent versus 69 percent).

Substantial differences exist among family types for both grandfathers and grandmothers. Among grandfathers, those with no spouse present are less likely to be employed or to have worked full time/full year in 1996, more likely to be renting a home, more likely to be Black, and more likely to be poor when compared to other grandfathers. Similarly, grandmothers in grandmother only, no parent present households are less likely to have graduated from high school, less likely to be employed or to have been employed full time/full year in 1996, more likely to rent their home, more likely to be Black, and more likely to be poor when compared to other grandmothers.

Among all family types, grandmothers maintaining households alone are much more likely than grandparents in other family types to face economic hardship. For example, the mean household income of grandmother only, no parents present households is only $19,750, compared with $61,632 for households with both grandparents and a parent or parents of the grandchildren present. Grandmothers maintaining households alone, with no spouse or parents present, are also much less likely than other grandparent householders to be in the labor force.

GRANDCHILDREN

In 1997, there were 3.9 million grandchildren living in households maintained by their grandparents — 32 percent in both grandparents, some parents present families; 15 percent in both grandparents, no parents present families; 29 percent in grandmother only, some parents present families; 17 percent in grandmother only, no parents present families; and 6 percent in grandfather only families.

Children living in homes maintained by their grandparents differ greatly from those living in households maintained by their parents. One striking difference is that children living with grandparents are more likely to live with caregivers who have not graduated from high school. One-third of grandchildren living in their grandparents' homes are in households where no grandparent has a high school diploma. In contrast, only one-eighth of the children in parent-headed households have parents who have not finished high school. When compared to children living in a home maintained by their parent(s), those living in a home maintained by their grandparent(s) are more likely: to be younger, to have a household head who is older and who did not work in 1996, to live in the South and in central cities, and to be poor.

Characteristics of grandchildren living in different types of grandparent-headed households also differ. Overall, half of the grandchildren living in their grandparents' homes are younger than 6. When a parent or parents of the grandchildren are present in grandparent-headed households, it is more likely that the grandchildren will be preschool age. When parents of the grandchildren are not present, it is more likely that the grandchildren will be older. Grandchildren living with grandmothers only, regardless of whether or not a parent is in the home, are much more likely than those in other family types to be Black, and to be living in the central city of a metropolitan area.

A grandchild living in a grandmother only, no parent family is relatively uncommon among grandchildren living in their grandparents' homes — only 669,000 of the 3,894,000 grandchildren live in families of this type. However, the profile of a grandchild living in this family type comes closest to the much sensationalized popular stereotype of grandparents who raise their grandchildren: a poor, undereducated, single, nonemployed, grandmother caring for a black grandchild in a central city.

But how are grandchildren living in different types of families faring? Grandchildren in grandmother only, no parents present families are substantially more likely to be poor and to be receiving public assistance than children in any other family type, but especially compared to those living in households maintained by their parents (Figure 3) [not reproduced — Eds.]. However, grandchildren in both grandparents, no parents present families are the most likely to be uninsured.

In the next section, we use multivariate techniques to establish if family type is still significantly related to poverty status, health insurance coverage, and receipt of public assistance when other socioeconomic and demographic variables are taken into account.

Multivariate Results

FAMILY INCOME BELOW POVERTY LEVEL

Family type does affect the probability that a grandchild will be in poverty. We find that in support of our hypotheses, grandchildren in grandmother only, no parents present families are more likely to be poor than those in both grandparents, some parents present families, even when controlling for the other factors in the model. The odds ratio indicates that these grandchildren are 5.6 times more likely to be poor than grandchildren in both grandparents, some parents present households. However, children in both grandparents, no parents present families and those in grandmother only, some parents present families are no more likely to be poor than those in both grandparents, some parents present families (the omitted category).

Several other factors are also significant in this model. . . . Grandchildren in households with three or more members under 18, or whose grandparents do not have a high school diploma are more likely to be poor than those with one child in the household and those whose grandparents are better educated. Grandchildren with at least one grandparent who worked during 1996, or whose grandparents are 55 or older are less likely to be poor than those whose grandparents were not employed or are younger than 45.

GRANDCHILDREN WITHOUT HEALTH INSURANCE

Family structure is also significant in predicting whether a grandchild had any health insurance in 1996. Grandchildren in both grandparents, no parents present families were much more likely to be uninsured for the entire year of 1996. Other things being equal, grandchildren in these families are 2.7 times more likely than those in both grandparents, some parents present families to have been uninsured. These results partially confirm our hypotheses in that the more adults there were in the family type, the less likely children were to be uninsured. But this is only true for both grandparent family types. Grandchildren in grandmother only families, regardless of the presence of parents, are no more or less likely to be uninsured when compared to both grandparents, some parents present families. The results of this model also support the findings in the bivariate analysis and indicate that even when controlling for the other factors, family structure matters.

Only two other factors are significant in predicting health insurance coverage in this model. Grandchildren in families with incomes 150 to 199% of the poverty level are more likely to be uninsured than are those in families with incomes 200% of the poverty level and over. Also, grandchildren in the South are less likely to be uninsured.

In contrast to what was expected, Black and Hispanic grandchildren were no more likely to have been uninsured in 1996 than were White children. Once poverty level and other factors are controlled for, Black and Hispanic children do not appear to be more disadvantaged than White grandchildren when it comes to being covered by health insurance.

RECEIPT OF PUBLIC ASSISTANCE

Family structure also works as we hypothesized in predicting grandchildren's receipt of public assistance. Net of the other factors in the model, grandchildren in grandmother only, no parents present families are more than twice as likely as grandchildren in both grandparents, some parents present families to have lived in a family that received assistance during 1996. However, grandchildren in both grandparent, some parent families and grandmother only, some parent families, were no more likely to be receiving assistance than those in both grandparents, some parents present families. These results also confirm the bivariate results shown in Figure 3 [not reproduced — Eds.], and suggest that the relationship between family structure and receipt of public assistance continues to exist even when other factors are taken into account.

As expected, other factors are also significant in predicting receipt of public assistance. The family income relative to poverty indicators are all significantly related to the likelihood that grandchildren received assistance in 1996. Grandchildren in poor and near-poor grandparent-headed families are more likely to receive assistance than those in more well-to-do grandparent-headed families, all else being equal.

Grandchildren who live in households with three or more children are more likely to have received assistance than those who live in households with only one child. All else being equal, grandchildren with older grandparents and those where at least one grandparent worked full time throughout 1996 are less likely to have received assistance, compared with those with younger grandparents and those with grandparents who were unemployed in 1996.

Our race results differ from those presented in other studies. Race and Hispanic origin do not significantly affect the likelihood that grandchildren have received assistance — minority grandchildren are no more likely than others to receive public assistance, net of the effects of family structure, income level relative to poverty, and other factors in the model.

Discussion

Our results indicate that children who live in grandparents' homes do not fare as well economically as those who live in their parents' homes. To a certain extent, this is to be expected since grandparents tend to be older than parents and therefore past their prime earning years. Yet, even within grandparents' homes some grandchildren fare better than others because different types of family structures afford different advantages. We hypothesized that grandchildren residing in grandmother only families without any parents would fare the worst. The results indicate that this is indeed the case: grandchildren residing in grandmother only, no parents present families are much more likely than grandchildren in any other family type to be in poverty. Furthermore, we expected that grandchildren in both grandparents, some parents present families would be doing the best. However, these grandchildren were no less likely to be in poverty than those in both grandparents, no parents present, and grandmother only, some parents present households.

These findings suggest that the family structure disadvantage for grandchildren does not stem solely from the marital status of the household heads, nor from the number of adult family members, nor even from the gender of the householder, but rather from a combination of the three. Grandmothers in grandmother only, no parents present families suffer the disadvantages associated with each of the three elements we used to define family structure — the marital status of the grandparents, their gender, and the presence of parents in the household. They suffer because they have no spouse or parents of their grandchildren in the household to help shoulder the burden of providing care and financial support. In addition, they suffer because of their low earnings and labor force participation relative to grandfathers — grandmother householders earn on average about $13,000 less a year and are 15 percentage points less likely to be employed than grandfather householders. It appears that only when these three detrimental factors of family structure are combined that grandchildren are more likely to be in poverty.

We found that grandchildren in both grandparents, no parents present families were much more likely than other grandchildren to be uninsured. Family structure in this case poses a different set of disadvantages because of its special relationship to the dependent variable. A primary source of insurance coverage for children is through their parents' employers. This type of coverage is more unlikely among grandchildren in this family type because they don't have parents residing with them. In addition, those grandparents who are employed may not be able to obtain coverage for their grandchildren under their employer-provided health insurance, forcing them to purchase an individual policy which may be prohibitively expensive. Moreover, relative to grandparents in other family types, grandparents in both grandparents, some parents present families may have incomes too high to qualify for public health insurance, but not high enough to enable them to purchase private health insurance for their grandchildren.

We expected that grandchildren in grandmother only, no parents present households would be the least likely to be insured, but this was not the case. These grandchildren may not be any more likely to be uninsured than those in the two types of parents present families because they are more likely to be poor and to qualify for MEDICAID. In fact, a higher percentage of grandchildren do receive MEDICAID in grandmother only, no parents present families (72 percent) compared with those in both grandparents, parents present and grandmother only, parents present families (45 percent and 55 percent respectively).

The fact that there are very few significant factors in this model and many plausible explanations for the family structure effect suggests that it may be necessary to use a multinomial logit model to look at MEDICAID, private insurance, and no insurance separately to adequately explain the effects of family structure.

Despite the fact that grandchildren in grandmother only, no parents present families are more likely to be poor, they are also more likely to be receiving some type of public assistance than grandchildren in other family types. This is what one might expect, given that in order to qualify for many benefits, families must be poor. This finding is encouraging in so much as public assistance does seem to go where it's most needed. It is important to note that family structure has an effect independent of the ratio of family income to poverty. This suggests that something about this particular family type makes these grandmothers more able to secure the benefits they need. Perhaps these grandmothers were single mothers who themselves received public assistance and therefore are better able to negotiate the system.

Although there were not enough cases to meaningfully include grandchildren living in grandfather only families in the multivariate analyses, the bivariate results regarding grandparents point to additional family structure differences. Grandfathers in grandfather only families are much more likely to be in poverty and much less likely to be active in the labor force than grandfathers in married-couple families. This underscores the fact that marital status, one of our defining elements of family structure, makes a difference among grandfathers as well.

It is interesting to note that race is only significant in the model predicting poverty. All else being equal, Black and Hispanic grandchildren are more likely than White grandchildren to be in poverty. However, they are no more likely to be uninsured or to be receiving assistance, once other factors such as income relative to poverty level are taken into account. This suggests that benefits are being distributed fairly — that is, according to need, rather than race. The fact that Black and Hispanic children are still more likely be poor even though they are equally as likely to have received benefits, may mean the benefits are not enough to raise them out of poverty, or that their coverage tends to be more sporadic than White grandchildren's coverage.

Conclusions

The data we present in this study indicate a great increase in the number of grandparent-maintained families since 1990. Our research has shown that the most disadvantaged grandparent-maintained families are growing the fastest: grandfather only families, and families with no parents present. These continued increases are particularly troublesome because the development of programs and policies to address the special needs of grandparents and their grandchildren has not kept pace.

We find that many grandparents and the grandchildren they are raising or are helping to raise are in dire economic straits. Family structure — the marital status of the grandparents, their gender, and the presence or absence of parents in the home — is related to the economic well-being of grandparent-maintained families. Overall, 27 percent of children living in homes maintained by their grandparents are in poverty. Almost two-thirds of children in grandmother only, no parents present families are in poverty. In contrast, 19 percent of children living in homes maintained by their parents are in poverty. In addition, the vast majority of grandparents who provide homes for their grandchildren are women, and grandmothers are more economically disadvantaged than grandfathers.

Grandparents and their grandchildren would benefit greatly if policies and programs intended to help traditional parent-child families in times of need could be uniformly extended to grandchildren. Moreover, many grandparents are still in the labor force and with the advent of welfare reform, many more could be required to get a job, especially those in families with no parents present. As more and more grandparents find themselves raising children, the need for employer-based or subsidized child care and family-friendly policies for grandparents and their families can be expected to grow.

QUESTIONS

1. Many states having the highest percentage of elderly also have the lowest percentage of children residing with a grandparent. What implications might this have for the development of state policy and funding issues relating to kinship care?

2. Recent cuts in state funding of public benefits have had a double effect on grandparents raising grandchildren. Given the statistics on poverty rates among grandparents caring for grandchildren, what could be the long term consequences of today's budget cuts on the lives of children in kinship care? On their caregivers?

B. CUSTODIAL ISSUES

Holly S. Kleiner, Jodie Hertzog & Dena B. Targ
Grandparents Acting as Parents
Purdue University Cooperative Extension Service
January 1998
http://www.uwex.edu/ces/gprg/article.html[*]

* * *

What are the types of grandparent caregivers?

One common way to categorize grandparent caregivers is to divide them into three types. First are the custodial grandparents. These grandparents have legal custody of their grandchildren; they provide daily care and decision making tasks. Typically, severe problems existed in the child's nuclear family. The focus of this type of caregiving is on the grandchild and providing them with a sense of security.

The second type of grandparent caregivers are the "living with" grandparents. These grandparents provide daily care for their grandchildren, but do not have legal custody. The child's parent may or may not live in the home. These grandparents focus on providing an economically and emotionally stable environment for the child, and often on helping the parent. Because the grandparent does not possess legal custody, he or she has no way of protecting the child from an unsuitable or dangerous parent.

"Day care" grandparents are the third type of grandparent caregivers. Their focus is on helping the child's parent and on fulfilling their own needs. These grandparents tend to be least affected by their caretaking role because the children return home at the end of the day. They function closest to the societal definition of "grandparent."

Another way to divide grandparent caregivers is that used by the Census Bureau. Households are divided into those in which neither parent is present, only the mother is present, only the father is present, or both parents are present.

* * *

What are the legal issues?

The legal issues that grandparents raising their grandchildren must cope with depend on the type of care they are providing — specifically, whether they are "custodial," "living with," or "day care" grandparents. Custodial grandparents either seek or are forced to enter into a legally recognized relationship with their grandchild. This is a serious step for the grandparent; it means that he or she will have both physical and legal rights and responsibilities for the child.

---

[*] Reprinted with permission.

Legally recognized relationships open to grandparents are adoption, guardianship, certification as a foster parent, and powers of attorney. If the grandparent chooses adoption, all rights and obligations of the child's parents are terminated. This is often a difficult decision. Unless their child is deceased, it means that the grandparent must admit that their child is an unfit parent. Guardianship may be either permanent or temporary. Certification as a foster parent qualifies the caregiver for financial benefits on a par with other foster parents. Powers of attorney allow grandparents only to make decisions regarding the grandchildren. They do not transfer legal custody. It is important for grandparents to understand the legal and financial implications of different types of formal and informal custody.

Grandparents who assume daily responsibilities for their grandchild but have no legal rights or duties face difficulties as well. Their living arrangements are often not recognized, and they are ineligible for state benefits. They may be viewed as "baby-sitting" their grandchildren. Because they have no rights, they must abide by the decisions of the child's parent. This may or may not be a difficult thing to do. Some grandparents are merely helping out the child's parents, and know the arrangement to be a temporary one. Others, though, worry about returning their grandchild to an abusive or neglectful environment; their lack of rights may be the impetus to seek legal custody. Seeking custody is a time consuming, expensive and emotionally draining process. The courts are supposed to base their decision on the "best interests of the child" rather than the interests of the grandparent. However, the rights of the grandparents often come after the rights of the natural parent.

In connection with the following excerpt, read Minnesota Stat. §§ 245A.035, 257B, 257C, 259, 260C, 260.751 to 260.781, 524.5-505, and 525.615-525.6197, set out in the supplement.

Minnesota Kinship Caregivers Association
First Steps: Getting Started Raising Relatives' Children (2003)
http://www.mkca.org/raising-jump.html[*]

Learning Legal Options

The legal options available to each kinship caregiver depends on the family's individual circumstances. The following list of options is meant as a guide to point people in the right direction. The counsel of a family law attorney experienced in kinship issues is critical.

Delegation of Parental Authority

The Delegation of Parental Authority (DOPA) gives the caregiver permission to take a child to medical appointments, enroll a child in school, and consult with doctors and teachers, etc. The parent can revoke the DOPA at any time; so, it

---

does not guarantee the child can stay with the relative caregiver. The DOPA must be in writing and notarized. It does not survive the death of a parent.

Under a Delegation of Parental Authority

- Caregivers may seek medical care for a child and enroll him or her in school.

- Parents retain all legal rights and responsibilities and can take the child back at any time.

- Relative caregivers are eligible to receive, on behalf of the child, Minnesota Family Investment Plan (MFIP) child-only payments.

- Parents remain financially responsible for the children.

- Relative caregivers' powers are limited to those stated by the parent in the DOPA.

Foster Care

When a child must be placed away from home, child protection must first look to relatives for placement. If there are no relatives, the child can be placed in a non-related foster home.

If a child is placed in a caregiver's home by child protection or by the juvenile court, the caregiver is considered a "foster parent," and is eligible for foster care benefits. The child is eligible for Medical Assistance and an array of services.

In foster care:

- The county has custody of the child.

- Relatives must meet licensing requirements.

- The county is responsible for the care and support of the child.

- Foster parents are responsible for the day-to-day care of the child.

- All major decisions are made by the county with juvenile court oversight.

- Parents may have the right to visit the child, but the county structures the visits.

- If the child cannot be returned to the parents, a plan for permanency, either permanent custody or adoption, is determined.

Legal Custody

Caregivers may file for legal and physical custody of children in family court. A court will grant custody to a caregiver or other person with ties to the child in certain circumstances, if it is determined to be in the best interest of the child.

An order of legal custody is the best way to ensure that the child will be safe with the caregivers. Under such an order:

- Custodians make the major decisions concerning the child and are responsible for the child's day-to-day care.

- Funds from MFIP are available for the child.

- Parents remain financially responsible for the child and may be ordered to pay child support.

- Parents' rights are not terminated.

- Parents may bring a motion to modify the court order. But in order to have custody returned to them, the parents must prove the children are in danger living with the grandparents. The exception to this is if the caregivers agree that custody should be returned to the parents.

Adoption

Adoption is an option for some grandparents. But, both parents must either be deceased or have had their parental rights terminated. Adoption is available in juvenile court.

If a child is adopted by a relative or other third party, the adoptive parent(s):

- Becomes the child's legal parent(s).

- Determines the type of relationship the child will have with the birth parents.

- Assumes legal responsibility for the care, custody, and support of the child.

A subsidized adoption may be possible, but only if the adoption was through child protection.

Guardianship of a Minor

When both parents are deceased, someone must become the children's guardian. A petition for guardianship is filed in probate court.

Guardians:

- Are appointed in probate court upon the death of the parents, or if the mother dies and the father is not legally recognized as the father.

- Have all of the powers and responsibility of a parent.

- On behalf of the child, may receive MFIP funds, if the child is eligible.

Standby Custody

A seriously ill parent can designate a standby custodian to care for the children if the parent is too sick to care for them or if the parent dies.

Designation of a standby custodian:

- Allows a parent to make future plans for the children without having to legally transfer decision-making power.

- Is signed by the parent, naming a future caregiver, to go into effect upon the occurrence of a "triggering event," such as illness or death.

- Can be filed with and heard by the court immediately or within 60 days of the triggering event.

- The petition can be withdrawn once the parent is able to resume care of the children, and it can be reinstated when the custodial parent again can no longer take care of the children.

QUESTIONS

1. What advantages and disadvantages might be associated with each of the above-described forms of custody in a grandparent-grandchild kinship caregiving situation? Consider this question again after reading the materials in Part C, below.

2. In what circumstances would a grandparent want to adopt a grandchild and thereby become the child's legal *parent*? Assuming that at least one parent is still living, how might such an arrangement stand to benefit the child — or would it ever?

C. FINANCIAL ASSISTANCE AND PUBLIC BENEFITS FOR KINSHIP CAREGIVERS

1. Generally

Rob Geen, Pamela Holcomb, Amy Jantz, Robin Koralek, Jake Leos-Urbel & Karin Malm
On Their Own Terms: Supporting Kinship Care Outside of TANF and Foster Care
Prepared for the Assistant Secretary for
Planning and Evaluation (ASPE)
U.S. Department of Health and Human Services (HHS)
September 2001
http://aspe.hhs.gov/hsp/kincare01/

Executive Summary

In 2000, 2.2 million children in the United States lived with a grandparent, aunt, sibling or some other relative — a living arrangement commonly referred to as "kinship care" — because their own parents were unavailable or unable to care for them. Kin often face significant challenges carrying out their caregiving role. They are typically caring for children who have experienced a traumatic separation from their parents, often as a result of abuse or neglect. At the same time, kinship caregivers tend to be older, have less education and lower incomes, report being in poorer health, and are more likely to be single than parent caregivers. The children in these families are also at a comparative disadvantage, scoring lower on measures of cognitive, physical, and psycho-social well-being than children in parent families.

Despite their vulnerability, kinship care families have historically received little attention from policy makers. To the extent that social welfare agencies have offered kinship families support, it has been largely in the form of foster care payments through the child welfare system or cash assistance grants through the welfare system's cash assistance program (*i.e.*, the Aid to Families with Dependent Children [AFDC] and, since 1996, the Temporary Assistance for Needy Families [TANF] program).

More recently, however, welfare and child welfare policy makers have expressed greater interest in developing programs and services that address various types of kinship families' needs. This has occurred, in large part, because kinship care families constitute a significant and growing share of both the foster care and TANF cash assistance caseloads. There is growing recognition that despite the fact that so many children are living in kinship care, kin caregivers have been largely overlooked when considering how policies can be designed to effectively support families.

In response to these developments, there appears to be an emerging trend on the part of states and localities to consider different strategies for meeting the needs of kin outside of traditional foster care or TANF programs. This report describes some of these efforts currently underway in a select number of states and localities. Through a variety of information sources, we identified 57 programs that could be considered "alternative" kinship care programs — defined here as initiatives specifically designed to meet the needs of kinship care families and that serve, at least in part, families referred by child welfare and/or TANF agencies. The majority — 34 of the 57 programs — are "subsidized guardianship" programs which provide on-going financial support to kin who take permanent legal custody of a related child who has been abused or neglected. Almost half of the alternative kinship care programs identified have been operating for three years or less, underscoring the fact that alternative kinship care programs are still a new and evolving phenomenon.

Our findings are based primarily on written materials and telephone discussions with program administrators and site visits to seven alternative kinship programs or initiatives conducted between September and December 2000. The site visits included focus groups with kinship caregivers and interviews with program staff from a variety of agencies involved in the design or implementation of these alternative kinship programs. Below we highlight key findings and policy implications.

Characteristics and Service Needs of Kinship Caregivers

Kinship families are diverse. A typical kinship care arrangement is commonly perceived as an elderly grandmother caring for a young, neglected child. Most caregivers are grandparents, but one-third are aunts, uncles, siblings, or other relatives. Moreover, while some grandmothers are elderly, many more are under age 60 and quite a few are in their 30s or 40s. In addition, kinship caregivers take care of children of all ages, from newborns to teenagers.

Kinship care families have both financial and support service needs.
The costs associated with bringing a new child into a caregiver's current living arrangement can be daunting, particularly for those whose incomes are fixed or limited and who may still be raising their own children. At the same time, the needs of kinship families are not merely financial. There are a range of services and supports that can make a positive difference for these families.

- *Financial Assistance.* Kinship caregivers often face tremendous financial burdens when they add a new member to their family. Many are poor; two in five kinship care children live in families with incomes below the federal poverty level. Moreover, many kinship caregivers are grandparents who are often retired with a fixed income. Kinship caregivers often do not receive assistance from a variety of income support programs for which they are eligible including TANF, food stamps, and Medicaid. Many kin do not know that they are eligible for these programs, while others report not wanting a hand out or contact with public agencies.

- *Information and Emotional Support.* Support groups offer caregivers a source of emotional support and practical information. Both kinship caregivers participating in the focus groups and program staff consider support groups a valuable and helpful service.

- *Mental Health Needs.* Administrators as well as the kinship caregivers themselves identified the importance of mental health services for many caregivers and their children but also noted that this type of service is typically not included or easily accessible.

- *Child/Respite Care.* Because a large share of caregivers work outside the home, they often need assistance in accessing and paying for child care. Many older caregivers voiced the need for respite time from the demanding role of caring for a child.

- *Legal Assistance.* Kin caregivers need affordable legal assistance in making decisions about securing custody of the child in their care. Many kinship caregivers who are eager to adopt or take guardianship of the children in their care reported significant barriers to completing the process. One of these barriers is financial. Caregivers noted that the legal fees for completing an adoption are at least $5,000, under the best case scenario in which the adoption is not contested.

Alternative Kinship Care Program Models and Services

A unique feature of alternative kinship programs is the diversity of administrative and program structures which are used to operate and deliver services. Alternative kinship care programs may be administered by public agencies — including administrative entities responsible for TANF, child welfare, and aging services — or by private, community-based agencies. In part, this diversity reflects differences in these programs' orientation and goals, target population, service focus, and funding sources.

Alternative kinship care programs are funded through a wide variety of federal, state, local, and private funding sources. Ten of the subsidized guardianship programs identified are funded through TANF while 14 rely on state funds and one relies on funds from the federal Social Services Block Grant. Of the 23 other programs identified, 4 receive TANF funds, 1 receives other federal funds, 13 receive state funds, 8 receive local funds, and 10 receive private financial support.

Alternative kinship care programs are diverse in the services they provide. Some alternative kinship programs primarily provide financial assistance, others focus on providing non-financial, supportive services, and still others provide a combination of financial and non-financial services. While programs vary, it appears that those serving primarily child-welfare involved kinship care families provide roughly the same amount of attention to the child and the caregiver, while the programs serving primarily kin outside of the child welfare system appear to be more focused on the caregiver. Few made any efforts to work with parents to address whatever issues made them unavailable to be their child's primary caregiver.

- *Financial Assistance.* For child welfare clients, alternative programs may provide financial assistance as an alternative to an adoption or foster care payment. These payments may be monthly payments to kin who agree to assume legal guardianship of children who were in state custody due to abuse or neglect (subsidized guardianship). Alternative programs can also provide monthly financial assistance (beyond TANF) for kin who act as foster parents, but who do not complete the traditional foster parent licensing process. States can and have used the flexibility afforded by TANF to fund both subsidized guardianships and alternatives to foster care payments.

  Several states are also providing additional financial assistance to kinship care families in the welfare system by providing supplemental payments beyond the child-only grant as well as a host of services targeted to kinship care families. In addition to monthly financial assistance, many alternative kinship care programs provide emergency financial assistance, or assistance in meeting basic needs through food or clothing banks.

- *Supportive Services.* Case management is an important component of many alternative kinship care programs. For families involved in the child welfare system, alternative programs can supplement the case management services provided by child protective services workers. For welfare clients, alternative programs can assess and help meet the needs of child-only grant recipients, even if employment is not the goal. Case management services provided by alternative programs often include periodic visits to the relative's home, on-going contact with clients if needs or circumstances warrant more intensive interaction, referrals to other programs and services as needed, and advocacy for clients in a variety of settings. Case management can be a particularly effective service for kin given the diversity of their needs and the fact that so many do not access the services for which they are eligible.

  In addition to case management, support groups for kin caregivers were identified by administrators and caregivers as a particularly needed and valued service. Other supportive services provided by alternative kinship programs include respite care, child care, education/mentoring programs, transportation, health care, and mental health or counseling services, resource and referral, legal information, and services for the children of the caregiver.

Lessons Learned about Designing and Implementing Alternative Programs

Program administrators identified several key lessons they learned during the early development of their programs.

- **Define the target population.** One of the first and most challenging steps in developing an alternative kinship care program is defining what segments of the kinship care population to serve. This decision will likely have far reaching implications for how the program will be administered, funded, and staffed. One decision to be made is whether to serve families involved with child welfare, those outside the system, or both. Within child welfare, policy makers must decide whether to target all kin caring for children in state custody, those who cannot or do not want to be licensed, or those in which the state does not take custody. Outside of child welfare, policy makers may consider targeting all kin, those who receive TANF child-only benefits, or those who themselves are low-income.

- **Do not underestimate the need for services**. In each of the sites visited, program administrators expressed surprise at the extent and diversity of the needs of kinship care families. As a result, some of the programs expanded very quickly, more quickly than anticipated. Program administrators spoke of the growing pains they experienced not having sufficient staff and adequate facilities. As programs grew, administrators noted that is was hard to monitor service delivery and in hindsight, would have liked to spend more time up front developing operations procedures and guidelines.

- **Get buy-in from the courts.** Each of the child welfare administered programs visited had some difficulty getting family court judges to fully understand and support the alternative kinship care program. Some program administrators suggested that they would have been wise to involve the courts earlier in the planning process so that the courts would understand the rationale and goals of the alternative programs.

- **Tap into the strengths of private community-based agencies**. Administrators noted many advantages to operating alternative kinship care programs through private, community-based organizations. The most cited reason was that public agencies, especially child welfare agencies, are not well regarded by kinship care families. In contrast, kinship caregivers noted that private agencies were often part of their community and were there to help them, even when they were under contract from the child welfare system. Administrators also noted that private agencies are not as hampered by administrative regulations and thus have more flexibility in staffing and service delivery. However, if an alternative program is designed primarily to provide financial assistance, administrators believe that the program is best operated by a public agency.

Policy Implications

Given the diverse needs and circumstances of kinship care families, many public and private agencies have a role in supporting this vulnerable population. Policy makers at both the federal and state level, from child welfare, welfare, aging, and other health and social services agencies, are increasingly recognizing that traditional public support programs have not been adequate or appropriate for meeting the needs of kinship care families. This study identified a variety of alternative strategies for policy makers to consider.

Child Welfare

Regardless of when and how states choose to use kinship caregivers, child welfare policy makers must understand that kinship care is a unique phenomenon that touches all parts of the child welfare system. At the front-end, policy makers have also argued that the existing framework for financing and supporting kinship care may unintentionally give caregivers incentives to enter the already over-burdened child welfare system. At the same time, many child welfare agencies are seeking strategies to use kin as a resource to prevent the removal of children from their parents' homes. For example, at least 25 states are implementing Family Group Decision Making models to involve extended family members in developing and carrying out service plans.

While experts and policy makers generally agree that children who cannot live with their parents can benefit from being cared for by relatives, there is still widespread debate as to when and how to use kin. If child welfare agencies are going to continue to use kin as foster parents they need to acknowledge their fundamental differences from non-kin and respond accordingly. For example, non-kin foster parents are already licensed when they first receive a child. In contrast, kin generally are not licensed as foster parents when they are thrust into their new caregiving role and thus are likely to have little or no knowledge about what their role is and how child welfare workers can assist them. Such differences suggest the need for alternative service delivery approaches for kin.

With the focus on permanency planning amplified by the Adoption and Safe Families Act, it is not surprising that many alternative kinship care programs focus on helping kin who want to make a permanent commitment to care for a related child. At the federal level, the policy debate has focused on whether the federal government should treat guardianship arrangements like adoption by allowing states to claim reimbursement under title IV-E for such arrangements. More than half the states have moved forward with subsidized guardianship programs and many receive federal funds (under title IV-E through waivers, TANF, or the Social Services Block Grant). Expanding title IV-E to provide an open-ended entitlement for subsidized guardianship could result in significant cost shifting.

TANF/Welfare

The upcoming reauthorization of TANF in late 2002 sets the stage for policy makers to assess key policies and provisions embodied in the current welfare reform legislation. Families receiving child-only grants, many of whom are relatives caring for children, comprised a significant share (29 percent in 1999) of the total TANF caseload. TANF agencies are just now beginning to consider how the flexibility of the TANF block grant could better serve kinship care families who have traditionally been served through the child welfare system or the TANF system. It can be used to fund additional payments and services for child-only cases or it can be used to fund alternative programs for kinship families involved in the child welfare system.

At the state level, policy makers may also want to consider two technical changes. The first would be to broaden the definition of "kin." Under AFDC, the federal government defined rather narrowly which relatives could receive child-only AFDC payments. Under TANF, states define "relative caregiver." Many kin are not eligible to receive TANF because they are not closely related, if related at all, to the children they care for, but could be eligible if states expanded their definition of "relative."

The second technical change would affect child support enforcement policy. Child support cooperation requirements may place kin caregivers caring for children not involved with the child welfare system in a difficult position. They may choose not to comply with requirements out of fear that the birth parents will take their children back if they were forced to pay child support. States may want to examine their good cause exemptions and make sure they can be applied under certain circumstances for TANF child-only cases.

Other Agencies

There are many other public agencies that may have a role in addressing the needs of kinship care families. As one of the few public agencies that come into contact with all school-aged children, schools can play an essential role in identifying kinship caregivers that may need assistance. In addition, older kinship caregivers may be more likely to access services from an aging office than a TANF or child welfare agency, because they feel that the aging offices were set up specifically to meet their needs. As such, aging offices can play an important role in bringing kin together and identifying supports to meet caregivers' needs.

Overall, a variety of agencies are responding to the complex demographic and social phenomenon of kinship care, trying to better serve this group of families who do not fit into traditional, social service programs. This project investigated new programs designed to meet these families' needs.

* * *

Study Purpose and Overview

While part of the solution to meeting the needs of kin may be better information and outreach on available programs and supports, many policy makers have found that existing public agency services and programs are not appropriate or sufficient for kin. As a result, numerous states and localities have begun to develop kin-specific programs. In June 2000, the Department of Health and Human Services (HHS), Office of the Assistant Secretary for Planning and Evaluation (ASPE) noted the proliferation of such programs and, since little was known about them, contracted with the Urban Institute to conduct a study of alternative kinship care programs established outside of TANF and foster care. This report documents the findings from this study and describes the variety of alternative approaches states and localities are taking to address the needs of kinship caregivers.

There are many programs nationwide that serve kinship caregivers and children, but not all are alternatives to TANF or foster care. For the purposes of this study, "alternative" kinship care programs are those specifically designed to meet the needs of kinship care families and that serve, at least in part, families referred by child welfare and/or TANF agencies.

Identifying existing alternative kinship care programs required several strategies. First, knowledgeable individuals around the country were asked to identify alternative kinship care programs of which they were aware. Second, Cornell University's Child Abuse Prevention Network Listserve asked its members to identify programs. Third, kinship care experts and organizations that work with kin or with state and local TANF and child welfare agencies offered information. Fourth, a review of the agendas of recent conferences sponsored by children's organizations identified presentations by or about alternative kinship care programs. Finally, the Brookdale Foundation, which for the past few years has provided seed money to state and local agencies interested in expanding services for kinship care families, provided a list of programs they support.

In all, 167 programs serving kinship care families were identified, and researchers contacted 107 programs which were thought to fit the definition of alternative kinship care. Identified programs were asked to provide brochures, authorizing legislation, and other publicly available information about current and planned activities. The information provided showed that 57 of these programs served families referred by either TANF or child welfare and could be considered alternative programs. Of these 57, 34 are subsidized guardianship programs, programs that provide on-going financial support to kin who take permanent legal custody of a related child who has been abused or neglected. Such programs are alternative in that they provide an option only to kin that is different from traditional foster care or adoption assistance. Program administrators offered some basic information about all 57 alternative kinship programs. Researchers selected seven programs for more in depth study:

- **A Second Chance, Inc.** (ASCI) in Pittsburgh, PA is the largest private non-profit kinship foster care agency in the United States with an ongoing caseload of over 700 children. ASCI serves primarily families that have been referred by the Allegheny County Department of Human Services after a child has been adjudicated as abused or neglected and placed with a relative caregiver. Following referral, ASCI is responsible for all child welfare services needed until children achieve permanency including ensuring that kinship caregivers complete all foster parent licensing requirements. A unique attribute of ASCI, and what makes their program "alternative," is that the agency recognizes that kinship care families need to be served differently than traditional foster families. A Second Chance, Inc. works with the entire "triad" — the birth parent, child, and kinship caregiver. ASCI looks at permanency planning from the outset through a kinship strength assessment and reunification staff work simultaneously with kinship care and birth families to resolve family issues that serve as impediments to reunification. Sixty percent of kinship care children return home within six months of placement.

- **Denver's Grandparents and Kinship Program**, operating within the TANF division of the Department of Human Services, provides a supplemental child-only TANF payment and other supports to relatives caring for their grandchildren or other relative kin. Program participants receive the financial supplement in addition to their TANF child-only payment as well as case management and other supportive services. With the additional supplement, the TANF child-only payment becomes similar in amount to the foster care monthly payment. The program provides case management services, depending upon a participant's needs. Relative caregiver support groups are an integral part of the program. Relatives caring for children involved with child welfare (and receiving TANF child-only payments) receive the financial supplement through the program; however, case management services continue to be provided through the child welfare division.

- **Florida's statewide Relative Caregiver Program** serves children being cared for by relatives who, without the caregivers, would otherwise be in foster care. The relative must have a juvenile court order placing the child in their home under protective supervision (in cases where reunification with birth parents is the goal), or under temporary custody cases (where the parents are unavailable, unable or unwilling to pursue reunification). The program has two primary components: the relative caregiver payment and case management services. Additionally, children are eligible for Medicaid and day care. Families in the program receive monthly financial payments from the TANF program and are monitored (at a minimum for six months) by the child welfare system. Currently, the financial payment is approximately 70 percent of the foster care rate. One of the major goals of the program is permanency for children, and long-term relative placement is a court disposition and a permanency option most of the families in this program choose. Families in the program continue to be eligible for the payment until the child is 18 years old. Relatives who assume legal guardianship of the children in their care also continue to be eligible for the relative caregiver payment.

- **The Kentucky Kinship Care Program**, administered by the Kentucky Cabinet for Children and Families (an umbrella agency responsible for both child welfare and TANF), provides kin caring for children who have been abused or neglected as an alternative to becoming licensed as a foster parent. Rather than the state taking custody of children and licensing kin as foster parents, in the Kinship Care Program, kin caregivers take temporary legal custody of adjudicated children and must agree to accept permanent legal custody of children if they cannot return to their parents. Kinship caregivers receive a payment of $300 per month per adjudicated child in their care (approximately 50 percent of the foster care rate) and this payment continues until the child is 18. Agency supervision under the Kinship Care program is less intensive than when children are in foster care — there is typically six months of caseworker supervision following placement. The kinship care program is entirely TANF funded with $8 million allocated for the program in 2000.

- **The Kentucky KinCare Project** is a statewide network of 29 kinship care support groups that resulted from a unique partnership between the state Office of Family Resource and Youth Service Centers (part of the Kentucky Cabinet for Children and Families), the Office of Aging, and the Cooperative Extension Service. The Resource Centers are located in public schools throughout the state and host the support group meetings and provide ongoing operational support. The public schools assist in identifying and recruiting kinship caregivers for the support groups. A statewide steering committee provides day-to-day guidance as well as a long-term vision and advocacy for expanding supports to grandparent caregivers. Representatives from the Office of Aging and the Cooperative Extensive Service serve on the steering committee and were responsible for the development of the first grandparent support groups in the state.

- **The Kinship Support Network (KSN)**, is a comprehensive program designed to fill in the gaps in public social services to relative caregivers and the children they are raising. KSN is administered by the Edgewood Center for Children and Families, a private non-profit organization in San Francisco, California. KSN serves both families that are, and are not, actively involved with the county child welfare agency, the Department of Human Services (DHS). Approximately half of the referrals to KSN come from DHS with the remainder coming from other community agencies or self-referrals. KSN offers case management which includes monthly visits by community workers, as well as support services that include support groups, respite and recreation, mental health assessment and support, and advocacy. All KSN services are voluntary and there are no eligibility requirements. KSN is funded by DHS as well as through private resources.

- **Oklahoma** does not have a specific alternative kinship care program, but has many ongoing initiatives that involve services to relative caregivers. The Aging Services Division of Oklahoma's Department of Human Services (DHS) has sponsored an annual conference on grandparents raising grandchildren each year since 1997. At the conference, representatives from various agencies provide information about the child welfare and welfare systems. The Aging Division raised foundation funding to support local support groups and has also published a grandparent handbook which provides information and key phone numbers for local resources. In addition, Aging Services provides money for respite care to families in which a grandparent, age 60 or older, is the primary caregiver of a child. Families who are income eligible receive up to a $400 voucher each quarter to purchase respite care services.

The seven selected programs illustrate different service delivery approaches. They also vary in size, geographic areas and demographic groups they serve, funding mechanisms, and administration. Summary information about all 57 alternative kinship care programs identified is included in Appendix A [omitted

— Eds.]. Appendix B [omitted — Eds.] includes summary profiles of the seven programs selected for in-depth study.

Erie County (New York) Department of Senior Services Excerpts from Healthcare & Health Insurance for Grandparents & Grandchildren
(July 2005 rev.)
http://www.erie.gov/depts/seniorservices/rac/healthcare.phtml

Health Insurance Coverage

Grandparent caregivers may find it difficult to find health insurance coverage for their grandchildren. Grandparents in the paid work force that have employer-provided group insurance still run into problems because employer provided group health insurance is generally unavailable for children in kinship care arrangements. Sometimes the policy does provide coverage even for legal custodians, so you will need to insist that the insurance company find out for sure what coverage you have.

* * *

Grandparents who are retired and on Medicare are either forced to buy an individual policy or to try and qualify their grandchild for State Medical Assistance. On the Internet you can find information at this New York State Health Department web site: http://www.health.state.ny.us/nysdoh/medicaid/main-medicaid.htm

a. Medicaid

In New York State, the medical assistance program is called Medicaid. It is a program funded by state and federal government that helps people who are receiving public assistance and/or have a low income pay for doctor and hospital bills and some medication. You may apply for Medicaid on your grandchild's behalf at the Social Service Office in the county where your grandchild resides. . . .

Make sure you apply and sign the application form as soon as you realize you need Medical Assistance because payment for medical expenses can only go back three months from the date of application.

1. Eligibility

Federal law requires states to provide Medical Assistance benefits to individuals who receive Family Assistance (formerly AFDC) grants or Supplemental Security Income (SSI) and children in foster care.

Note: Even if you have grandchildren in your care who, for any reason, are not eligible for Family Assistance or SSI, you should still apply for Medicaid on their behalf by going to your local Social Services Office.

2. Early and Periodic Screening, Diagnosis and Treatment Program (EPSDT)

EPSDT is the Early and Periodic Screening, Diagnosis and Treatment Program. It is a provision of the federal Medicaid program that provides financially needy children with preventive health care. Every child who is eligible for Medicaid is eligible for federally funded EPSDT services. EPSDT is a critical program for your grandchild because it provides many services that may not be available to adult Medicaid recipients.

When you see your doctor for an EPSDT exam (sometimes called a well-child visit or a check-up), your grandchild should receive the following health checks:

A complete physical exam

Eye and hearing tests

Lab tests, including levels, if needed

Immunizations, if needed

Dental assessment

Health education about issues of concern for you and your grandchild

Nutrition assessment

Developmental assessment

3. Medicaid Managed Care Plans

If your grandchild or you are granted Medicaid benefits, you may need to sign up for a Medicaid Managed Care program. . . . Under this program, you may need to select an HMO (Health Maintenance Organization) within 60 days; otherwise you and/or your grandchild will be assigned to one. "Exception" situations, where a child is cared for by the grandparent(s), are subject to a review of the case and its history by the Managed Care Unit; and when an "exemption" status is given, grandparents are not required to enroll the children in an HMO but have the option to do so if they wish. Be sure to read the information that the Department of Social Services sends you about the HMOs (Health Maintenance Organizations) serving Erie County Medicaid recipients. Then call the HMOs that look best for your grandchild or family. Ask them for more information about what you need to know. They can send you a list of doctors and pharmacies and give you details on the services they offer.

When choosing an HMO, consider the following:

Do my family's doctors belong to this HMO?

Does this HMO have doctors, clinics, hospitals, and pharmacies near my home?

Are there enough specialists to treat my family's health needs?

Does this HMO offer special services or "extras?" For example, will they pay for any health care items not prescribed by a doctor? Do they offer free parenting classes?

* * *

b. Child Health Plus

In addition to the Medicaid program, New York State also offers a low-cost health insurance plan for children under age 19 called Child Health Plus. It is a program available to New York State families who are not eligible for Medicaid or who have limited or no health insurance. Even if your family income is high, you can enroll your grand child in the program, although you will have to pay more for your coverage.

The fees for Child Health Plus are based on family size and income.

* * *

Medical Consent

Under New York State law, only parents, legal guardians, or custodians can give consent for the medical, dental, health and hospital care of a child under age 18. Generally, grandparents do not automatically have the legal right to consent to necessary medical care on behalf of a grandchild in their care. However, many medical providers let grandparents consent to care even though medical providers do not have a legal obligation to honor their consent. A statement from you, the parent, or from a social worker, which shows your relationship to your grandchild may help you get medical care for your grandchild. In addition, the New York State Legislature recently enacted policy allowing parents to legally authorize a care giver's consent to medical care, for up to one year. Such authorization must be in writing, and contain the name of the care giver, minor child, the parent's signature and date of signature. A parent lacks authority to sign such authorization if prohibited by court order. Further, if a court order exists directing both parents to agree on health decisions concerning the child, both parents must sign.

New York State law does allow grandparents and older sisters and brothers to consent to a young child's immunizations.

In case of an emergency, take your grandchild to the emergency room of a hospital. You do not need legal guardianship or custody of your grandchild to get emergency medical treatment for your grandchild. In an emergency, the doctor will decide whether the child needs immediate medical attention. If there is not time to get consent from the parent and the life and health of your grandchild would be in danger if the child does not get medical treatment, then the doctor can treat the child without the parents' permission.

If a grandparent is having difficulty obtaining medical care, legal guardianship or custody may be necessary.

Health Care Services

In addition to your grandchild's pediatrician or family physician, the Erie County Department of Health offers many low and no cost health services for children and adults residing in Erie County. . . [These services include community health centers, pediatric services, dental programs, teen wellness, and "Baby Think It Over".]

Services for Children with Disabilities

The Early Intervention Program is a statewide program that provides many different types of early intervention services to infants and toddlers with disabilities and their families. The mission of the Early Intervention Program is to identify and evaluate, as early as possible, those infants and toddlers whose healthy development is compromised and provide for appropriate intervention to improve child and family development.

Free services are provided to help your child grow and develop and to help you care for your child. These services include evaluation services (including hearing and vision screening); home visits; speech, physical and other therapies; child development groups; family counseling; and, sometimes, even help with transportation.

The Preschool Program for Children with Special Needs is a program designed to meet the educational needs of 3-5 year old children with significant delays in one or more functional areas related to:

- Cognitive skills

- Communication skills

- Adaptive skills

- Social-emotional skills

- Motor skills which adversely affect their ability to learn.

A preschool child with special needs may be eligible to receive services via their school district which may include: Speech, Occupational or Physical Therapy, and Special Education. A preschool child who has been found to have special needs will receive services at no cost to the family.

Tips for Raising Healthy Grandchildren

Immunizations

Immunizations are shots that protect children from many contagious diseases. It is important for your grandchildren to get their shots at the right times in order to prevent them from getting sick with fevers and rashes or diseases that can cause more serious problems such as brain damage, heart problems, crippling, deafness, and blindness. School districts and daycare centers require proof of immunizations before a child can be enrolled. Visit the Immunization Action Coalition web site for information on recommended immunizations for children and adults at http://www.immunize.org as well as the New York State Department of Health and Centers for Disease Control sites listed below. Since recommendations change from time to time, please check with your health care provider for the most up-to-date recommendations.

Because your health is also important, please review the recommended immunizations for adults. Information on immunizations for adults in Erie County may be found at the WNY Adult Immunization Coalition web site, http://immunizewny.org

Keeping a record of the immunizations you and your grandchildren have received is very helpful.

Federal Citizen Information Center
Consumer Focus: Grandparents Raising Grandchildren
Tax Tips
http://www.pueblo.gsa.gov/cfocus/cfgrandparents03/focus2.htm

Grandparents raising grandchildren may be eligible to pay lower taxes. If you are a grandparent who had income from work and can claim a "qualifying child," you may qualify for any or all of the following:

- Earned Income Tax Credit (EITC) can provide tax credits to working grandparents who are raising children, thereby reducing or eliminating federal income taxes. You must meet income requirements, which vary depending on how many grandchildren you are raising.

- The Child and Dependent Care Credit helps families who must pay for childcare in order to work or look for work. The amount of the credit depends on the number of children, family income, and the amount paid for care.

- The Child Tax Credit can also be claimed on your federal income tax. It reduces the federal income tax but, like the Child and Dependent Care Credit, does not provide refunds over the amount of income tax paid. Grandparents can be eligible for both the Earned Income Credit and the Child tax Credit and, in some instances, may be eligible for an Additional Child Tax Credit.

QUESTIONS

1. Many elder law practitioners evolve into the elder law specialty via an estate-planning practice. Would such a background prepare an attorney for the issues faced by an older client who is raising a grandchild?

2. As the readings above suggest, the benefits and support available to kinship caregivers is largely a function of state policy. Yet the states bear very unequal burdens in terms of the number and percentage of children living in a grandparent-headed or grandparent-supported household. Should the federal government assume a more prominent role in this area? Does the National Family Caregiver Support Act *(see infra)* adequately address the problems inherent in relying on states to fund and maintain kinship caregiver and related programs?

2. The National Family Caregiver Support Act

Read Title IIIE of the Older Americans Act (42 U.S.C. §§ 3030s to 3030s-2) in the statutory supplement.

U.S. Department of Health and Human Services
Administration on Aging
Snapshot: National Family Caregiver Support Program
(August 27, 2003)

http://www.aoa.gov/press/fact/pdf/ss_nfcsp.pdf

Families, not social service agencies, nursing homes or government programs, are the mainstay of long-term care (LTC) for older persons in the United States. In many cases, both the caregivers and care recipients are aging adults. More than 22.4 million U.S. households are serving in family caregiving roles for persons over the age of 50, and that number will increase rapidly as the population ages, and as medical science continues to extend life. One out of every four people is a caregiver for a family member or friend.

* * *

Grandparents Raising Grandchildren

According to the U.S. 2000 Census, 5.8 million grandparents live with grandchildren younger than 18. Among these grandparents, 2.4 million are "grandparent caregivers," defined by the U.S. Census as people who have primary responsibility for their grandchildren younger than 18. Among grandparent caregivers, 39% have cared for their grandchildren for 5 or more years.

National Family Caregiver Support Program

Administered by the Department of Health and Human Services' Administration on Aging, the National Family Caregiver Support Program (NFCSP) was established in November 2000 as a new component of the Older Americans Act. In FY 2003, the National Family Caregiver Support Program was funded at $155.2 million. Of that amount, $6.2 million is for the Native American Caregiver Support Program, established within the NFCSP to address the special needs of caregivers of Native American elders. Innovation Grants and Projects of National Significance were awarded to 39 national, state and local organizations to develop and test model caregiving approaches. These grants focus on systems development, service components, linkages to special populations and communities, testing new approaches and national projects that enhance the development of caregiver programs.

The NFCSP calls for all states, working in partnership with area agencies on aging and local community service providers to have five basic services available for family caregivers, including:

1. Information to caregivers about available services;

2. Assistance to caregivers in gaining access to supportive services;

3. Individual counseling, organization of support groups, and caregiving training to assist the caregivers in making decisions and solving problems related to their caregiver roles;

4. Respite care to enable caregivers to be temporarily relieved from their caregiver responsibilities; and

5. Supplemental services on a limited basis, to complement the care provided by caregivers.

Who is eligible?

Family caregivers of older adults (age 60 and older) and grandparents and relative caregivers (60 and older) of children not more than 18 years of age are eligible for NFCSP services.

Older Americans Act is Vital

Caregiver support is not provided in a vacuum. Many older people who receive assistance from family members also receive assistance from other OAA-funded home and community-based services such as meals, personal care and transportation. These services help lessen the burden on family caregivers.

A 2002 survey of caregivers shows that:

- 86% said OAA services allowed them to provide care longer than they would have been able to on their own

- 69% reported that the services helped a lot in their efforts to provide care

- 96% were very or somewhat satisfied with the OAA services

NFCSP in Action

The National Aging Services Network (which includes 56 State Units on Aging; 655 Area Agencies on Aging; 244 tribal organizations and about 30,000 local service providers) has:

- Reached out to over 3.8 million individuals with information about caregiver programs and services;

- Provided assistance in accessing services to approximately 436,000 caregivers — significantly exceeding the agency target of 250,000 caregivers;

- Served almost 180,000 caregivers with counseling and training services;

- Provided respite to over 70,000 caregivers;

- Provided supplemental services to over 50,000 caregivers

Native American and American Indian tribal organizations have seized the opportunity the NFCSP presents to develop systems of support that meet the unique needs of their family caregivers. Most tribes are in the development stages of their programs. A total of 119 tribes received their initial funding in 2002 and:

- At least 4,230 caregivers received one or more caregiver support services

- All programs are administering public awareness campaigns

- Respite service is provided by most programs (92%), including respite for grandparents

- 58% of the programs are providing caregiver training

- Caregiver conferences have been held by 28% of the programs

- 64% of the programs are conducting support groups or individual counseling

D. GRANDPARENT VISITATION AND RELATED "RIGHTS"

The so-called "grandparents rights" movement has become a powerful grassroots effort to secure visitation and related rights on behalf of grandparents. It is largely but not exclusively an offshoot of "men's rights" organizations and is populated by the parents of divorced or unwed fathers who seek access to grandchildren when the father has lost parental rights or has limited custody of his children. What should happen when a grandparent seeks visitation rights or custody of a child over one or both parents' objection?

TROXEL v. GRANVILLE
530 U.S. 57 (2000)

JUSTICE O'CONNOR announced the judgment of the Court and delivered an opinion, in which THE CHIEF JUSTICE, JUSTICE GINSBURG, and JUSTICE BREYER join.

Section 26.10.160(3) of the Revised Code of Washington permits "[a]ny person" to petition a superior court for visitation rights "at any time," and authorizes that court to grant such visitation rights whenever "visitation may serve the best interest of the child." Petitioners Jenifer and Gary Troxel petitioned a Washington Superior Court for the right to visit their grandchildren, Isabelle and Natalie Troxel. Respondent Tommie Granville, the mother of Isabelle and Natalie, opposed the petition. The case ultimately reached the Washington Supreme Court, which held that § 26.10.160(3) unconstitutionally interferes with the fundamental right of parents to rear their children.

I

Tommie Granville and Brad Troxel shared a relationship that ended in June 1991. The two never married, but they had two daughters, Isabelle and Natalie. Jenifer and Gary Troxel are Brad's parents, and thus the paternal grandparents of Isabelle and Natalie. After Tommie and Brad separated in 1991, Brad lived with his parents and regularly brought his daughters to his parents' home for weekend visitation. Brad committed suicide in May 1993. Although the Troxels at first continued to see Isabelle and Natalie on a regular basis after their son's death, Tommie Granville informed the Troxels in October 1993 that she wished to limit their visitation with her daughters to one short visit per month.

In December 1993, the Troxels commenced the present action by filing, in the Washington Superior Court for Skagit County, a petition to obtain visitation rights with Isabelle and Natalie. The Troxels filed their petition under two Washington statutes, WASH. REV. CODE §§ 26.09.240 and 26.10.160(3) (1994). Only the latter statute is at issue in this case. Section 26.10.160(3) provides: "Any person may petition the court for visitation rights at any time including, but not limited to, custody proceedings. The court may order visitation rights for any person when visitation may serve the best interest of the child whether or not there has been any change of circumstances." At trial, the Troxels requested two weekends of overnight visitation per month and two weeks of visitation each summer. Granville did not oppose visitation altogether, but instead asked the court to order one day of visitation per month with no overnight stay. In 1995, the Superior Court issued an oral ruling and entered a visitation decree ordering visitation one weekend per month, one week during the summer, and four hours on both of the petitioning grandparents' birthdays.

Granville appealed, during which time she married Kelly Wynn. Before addressing the merits of Granville's appeal, the Washington Court of Appeals remanded the case to the Superior Court for entry of written findings of fact and conclusions of law. On remand, the Superior Court found that visitation was in Isabelle and Natalie's best interests:

> The Petitioners [the Troxels] are part of a large, central, loving family, all located in this area, and the Petitioners can provide opportunities for the children in the areas of cousins and music. . . . The court took into consideration all factors regarding the best interest of the children and considered all the testimony before it. The children would be benefitted from spending quality time with the Petitioners, provided that that time is balanced with time with the childrens' [sic] nuclear family. The court finds that the childrens' [sic] best interests are served by spending time with their mother and stepfather's other six children.

Approximately nine months after the Superior Court entered its order on remand, Granville's husband formally adopted Isabelle and Natalie.

The Washington Court of Appeals reversed the lower court's visitation order and dismissed the Troxels' petition for visitation, holding that nonparents lack standing to seek visitation under § 26.10.160(3) unless a custody action is pending. In the Court of Appeals' view, that limitation on nonparental visitation actions was "consistent with the constitutional restrictions on state interference with parents' fundamental liberty interest in the care, custody, and management of their children." Having resolved the case on the statutory ground, however, the Court of Appeals did not expressly pass on Granville's constitutional challenge to the visitation statute.

The Washington Supreme Court granted the Troxels' petition for review and, after consolidating their case with two other visitation cases, affirmed. The court disagreed with the Court of Appeals' decision on the statutory issue and found that the plain language of § 26.10.160(3) gave the Troxels standing to seek visitation, irrespective of whether a custody action was pending. The Washington Supreme Court nevertheless agreed with the Court of Appeals' ultimate conclusion that the Troxels could not obtain visitation of Isabelle and Natalie pursuant to § 26.10.160(3). The court rested its decision on the Federal Constitution, holding that § 26.10.160(3) unconstitutionally infringes on the fundamental right of parents to rear their children. In the court's view, there were at least two problems with the nonparental visitation statute. First, according to the Washington Supreme Court, the Constitution permits a State to interfere with the right of parents to rear their children only to prevent harm or potential harm to a child. Section 26.10.160(3) fails that standard because it requires no threshold showing of harm. Second, by allowing "'any person' to petition for forced visitation of a child at 'any time' with the only requirement being that the visitation serve the best interest of the child," the Washington visitation statute sweeps too broadly. "It is not within the province of the state to make significant decisions concerning the custody of children merely because it could make a 'better' decision." The Washington Supreme Court held that "[p]arents have a right to limit visitation of their children with third persons," and that between parents and judges, "the parents should be the ones to choose whether to expose their children to certain people or ideas." Four justices dissented from the Washington Supreme Court's holding on the constitutionality of the statute.

We granted *certiorari*, 527 U.S. 1069 (1999), and now affirm the judgment.

II

The demographic changes of the past century make it difficult to speak of an average American family. The composition of families varies greatly from household to household. While many children may have two married parents and grandparents who visit regularly, many other children are raised in single-parent households. In 1996, children living with only one parent accounted for 28 percent of all children under age 18 in the United States. U.S. Dept. of Commerce, Bureau of Census, Current Population Reports, 1997 Population Profile of the United States 27 (1998). Understandably, in these single-parent households, persons outside the nuclear family are called upon with increasing frequency to assist in the everyday tasks of child rearing. In many cases, grandparents play an important role. For example, in 1998, approximately 4 million children — or 5.6 percent of all children under age 18 — lived in the household of their grandparents. U.S. Dept. of Commerce, Bureau of Census, Current Population Reports, Marital Status and Living Arrangements: March 1998 (Update), p. i (1998).

The nationwide enactment of nonparental visitation statutes is assuredly due, in some part, to the States' recognition of these changing realities of the American family. Because grandparents and other relatives undertake duties of a parental nature in many households, States have sought to ensure the welfare of the children therein by protecting the relationships those children form with such third parties. The States' nonparental visitation statutes are further supported by a recognition, which varies from State to State, that children should have the opportunity to benefit from relationships with statutorily specified persons — for example, their grandparents. The extension of statutory rights in this area to persons other than a child's parents, however, comes with an obvious cost. For example, the State's recognition of an independent third-party interest in a child can place a substantial burden on the traditional parent-child relationship. Contrary to JUSTICE STEVENS' accusation, our description of state nonparental visitation statutes in these terms, of course, is not meant to suggest that "children are so much chattel." Rather, our terminology is intended to highlight the fact that these statutes can present questions of constitutional import. In this case, we are presented with just such a question. Specifically, we are asked to decide whether § 26.10.160(3), as applied to Tommie Granville and her family, violates the Federal Constitution.

The Fourteenth Amendment provides that no State shall "deprive any person of life, liberty, or property, without due process of law." We have long recognized that the Amendment's Due Process Clause, like its Fifth Amendment counterpart, "guarantees more than fair process." *Washington v. Glucksberg*, 521 U.S. 702, 719 (1997). The Clause also includes a substantive component that "provides heightened protection against government interference with certain fundamental rights and liberty interests." *Id.* at 720; *see also Reno v. Flores*, 507 U.S. 292, 301-302 (1993).

The liberty interest at issue in this case — the interest of parents in the care, custody, and control of their children — is perhaps the oldest of the fundamental liberty interests recognized by this Court. More than 75 years ago, in *Meyer v. Nebraska*, 262 U.S. 390, 399, 401 (1923), we held that the "liberty" protected by the Due Process Clause includes the right of parents to "establish a home and bring up children" and "to control the education of their own." Two years later, in *Pierce v. Society of Sisters*, 268 U.S. 510, 534-535 (1925), we again held that the "liberty of parents and guardians" includes the right "to direct the upbringing and education of children under their control." We explained in *Pierce* that "[t]he child is not the mere creature of the State; those who nurture him and direct his destiny have the right, coupled with the high duty, to recognize and prepare him for additional obligations." *Id.* at 535. We returned to the subject in *Prince v. Massachusetts*, 321 U.S. 158 (1944), and again confirmed that there is a constitutional dimension to the right of parents to direct the upbringing of their children. "It is cardinal with us that the custody, care and nurture of the child reside first in the parents, whose primary function and freedom include preparation for obligations the state can neither supply nor hinder." *Id.* at 166.

In subsequent cases also, we have recognized the fundamental right of parents to make decisions concerning the care, custody, and control of their children. *See, e.g., Stanley v. Illinois*, 405 U.S. 645, 651 (1972) ("It is plain that the interest of a parent in the companionship, care, custody, and management of his or her children 'come[s] to this Court with a momentum for respect lacking when appeal is made to liberties which derive merely from shifting economic arrangements'" (citation omitted)); *Wisconsin v. Yoder*, 406 U.S. 205, 232 (1972) ("The history and culture of Western civilization reflect a strong tradition of parental concern for the nurture and upbringing of their children. This primary role of the parents in the upbringing of their children is now established beyond debate as an enduring American tradition"); *Quilloin v. Walcott*, 434 U.S. 246, 255 (1978) ("We have recognized on numerous occasions that the relationship between parent and child is constitutionally protected"); *Parham v. J.R.*, 442 U.S. 584, 602 (1979) ("Our jurisprudence historically has reflected Western civilization concepts of the family as a unit with broad parental authority over minor children. Our cases have consistently followed that course"); *Santosky v. Kramer*, 455 U.S. 745, 753 (1982) (discussing "[t]he fundamental liberty interest of natural parents in the care, custody, and management of their child"); *Glucksberg, supra,* at 720 ("In a long line of cases, we have held that, in addition to the specific freedoms protected by the Bill of Rights, the 'liberty' specially protected by the Due Process Clause includes the righ[t] . . . to direct the education and upbringing of one's children" (citing *Meyer* and *Pierce*)). In light of this extensive precedent, it cannot now be doubted that the Due Process Clause of the Fourteenth Amendment protects the fundamental right of parents to make decisions concerning the care, custody, and control of their children.

Section 26.10.160(3), as applied to Granville and her family in this case, unconstitutionally infringes on that fundamental parental right. The Washington nonparental visitation statute is breathtakingly broad. According to the statute's text, "[a]ny person may petition the court for visitation rights at any time," and the court may grant such visitation rights whenever "visitation may serve *the best interest of the child.*" § 26.10.160(3) (emphases added). That language effectively permits any third party seeking visitation to subject any decision by a parent concerning visitation of the parent's children to state-court review. Once the visitation petition has been filed in court and the matter is placed before a judge, a parent's decision that visitation would not be in the child's best interest is accorded no deference. Section 26.10.160(3) contains no requirement that a court accord the parent's decision any presumption of validity or any weight whatsoever. Instead, the Washington statute places the best-interest determination solely in the hands of the judge. Should the judge disagree with the parent's estimation of the child's best interests, the judge's view necessarily prevails. Thus, in practical effect, in the State of Washington a court can disregard and overturn any decision by a fit custodial parent concerning visitation whenever a third party affected by the decision files a visitation petition, based solely on the judge's determination of the child's best interests. The Washington Supreme Court had the opportunity to give § 26.10.160(3) a narrower reading, but it declined to do so. *See, e.g.,* 137 Wash. 2d at 5, 969 P.2d at 23 ("[The statute] allow[s] any person, at any time, to petition for visitation without regard to relationship to the child, without regard to changed circumstances, and without regard to harm"); *id.* at 20, 969 P.2d at 30 ("[The statute] allow[s] 'any person' to petition for forced visitation of a child at 'any time' with the only requirement being that the visitation serve the best interest of the child").

Turning to the facts of this case, the record reveals that the Superior Court's order was based on precisely the type of mere disagreement we have just described and nothing more. The Superior Court's order was not founded on any special factors that might justify the State's interference with Granville's fundamental right to make decisions concerning the rearing of her two daughters. To be sure, this case involves a visitation petition filed by grandparents soon after the death of their son — the father of Isabelle and Natalie — but the combination of several factors here compels our conclusion that § 26.10.160(3), as applied, exceeded the bounds of the Due Process Clause.

First, the Troxels did not allege, and no court has found, that Granville was an unfit parent. That aspect of the case is important, for there is a presumption that fit parents act in the best interests of their children. As this Court explained in *Parham*:

> [O]ur constitutional system long ago rejected any notion that a child is the mere creature of the State and, on the contrary, asserted that parents generally have the right, coupled with the high duty, to recognize and prepare [their children] for additional obligations. . . . The law's concept of the family rests on a presumption that parents possess what a child lacks in maturity, experience, and capacity for judgment required for making life's difficult decisions. More important, historically it has recognized that natural bonds of affection lead parents to act in the best interests of their children.

442 U.S. at 602.

Accordingly, so long as a parent adequately cares for his or her children (*i.e.*, is fit), there will normally be no reason for the State to inject itself into the private realm of the family to further question the ability of that parent to make the best decisions concerning the rearing of that parent's children.

The problem here is not that the Washington Superior Court intervened, but that when it did so, it gave no special weight at all to Granville's determination of her daughters' best interests. More importantly, it appears that the Superior Court applied exactly the opposite presumption. In reciting its oral ruling after the conclusion of closing arguments, the Superior Court judge explained:

> The burden is to show that it is in the best interest of the children to have some visitation and some quality time with their grandparents. I think in most situations a commonsensical approach [is that] it is normally in the best interest of the children to spend quality time with the grandparent, unless the grandparent, [sic] there are some issues or problems involved wherein the grandparents, their lifestyles are going to impact adversely upon the children. That certainly isn't the case here from what I can tell.

The judge's comments suggest that he presumed the grandparents' request should be granted unless the children would be "impact[ed] adversely." In effect, the judge placed on Granville, the fit custodial parent, the burden of disproving that visitation would be in the best interest of her daughters. The judge reiterated moments later: "I think [visitation with the Troxels] would be in the best interest of the children and I haven't been shown it is not in [the] best interest of the children."

The decisional framework employed by the Superior Court directly contravened the traditional presumption that a fit parent will act in the best interest of his or her child. In that respect, the court's presumption failed to provide any protection for Granville's fundamental constitutional right to make decisions concerning the rearing of her own daughters. *Cf.*, *e.g.*, CAL. FAM. CODE ANN. § 3104(e) (1994) (rebuttable presumption that grandparent visitation is not in child's best interest if parents agree that visitation rights should not be granted);

ME. REV. STAT. ANN., Tit. 19A, § 1803(3) (1998) (court may award grandparent visitation if in best interest of child and "would not significantly interfere with any parent-child relationship or with the parent's rightful authority over the child"); MINN. STAT. § 257.022(2)(a)(2) (1998) (court may award grandparent visitation if in best interest of child and "such visitation would not interfere with the parent-child relationship"); NEB. REV. STAT. § 43-1802(2) (1998) (court must find "by clear and convincing evidence" that grandparent visitation "will not adversely interfere with the parent-child relationship"); R.I. GEN. LAWS § 15-5-24.3(a)(2)(v) (Supp. 1999) (grandparent must rebut, by clear and convincing evidence, presumption that parent's decision to refuse grandparent visitation was reasonable); UTAH CODE ANN. § 30-5-2(2)(e) (1998) (same); *Hoff v. Berg*, 595 N.W.2d 285, 291-292 (N. D. 1999) (holding North Dakota grandparent visitation statute unconstitutional because State has no "compelling interest in presuming visitation rights of grandparents to an unmarried minor are in the child's best interests and forcing parents to accede to court-ordered grandparental visitation unless the parents are first able to prove such visitation is not in the best interests of their minor child"). In an ideal world, parents might always seek to cultivate the bonds between grandparents and their grandchildren. Needless to say, however, our world is far from perfect, and in it the decision whether such an intergenerational relationship would be beneficial in any specific case is for the parent to make in the first instance. And, if a fit parent's decision of the kind at issue here becomes subject to judicial review, the court must accord at least some special weight to the parent's own determination.

Finally, we note that there is no allegation that Granville ever sought to cut off visitation entirely. Rather, the present dispute originated when Granville informed the Troxels that she would prefer to restrict their visitation with Isabelle and Natalie to one short visit per month and special holidays. In the Superior Court proceedings Granville did not oppose visitation but instead asked that the duration of any visitation order be shorter than that requested by the Troxels. While the Troxels requested two weekends per month and two full weeks in the summer, Granville asked the Superior Court to order only one day of visitation per month (with no overnight stay) and participation in the Granville family's holiday celebrations. ("Right off the bat we'd like to say that our position is that grandparent visitation is in the best interest of the children. It is a matter of how much and how it is going to be structured") (opening statement by Granville's attorney). The Superior Court gave no weight to Granville's having assented to visitation even before the filing of any visitation petition or subsequent court intervention. The court instead rejected Granville's proposal and settled on a middle ground, ordering one weekend of visitation per month, one week in the summer, and time on both of the petitioning grandparents' birthdays. Significantly, many other States expressly provide by statute that courts may not award visitation unless a parent has denied (or unreasonably denied) visitation to the concerned third party. *See, e.g.,* MISS. CODE ANN. § 93-16-3(2)(a) (1994) (court must find that "the parent or custodian of the child unreasonably denied the grandparent visitation rights with the child"); ORE. REV. STAT. § 109.121(1)(a)(B) (1997) (court may award visitation if the "custodian of the child has denied the grandparent reasonable opportunity to visit the child"); R.I. GEN. LAWS § 15-5-24.3(a)(2)(iii)-(iv) (Supp. 1999) (court must find that parents prevented grandparent from visiting grandchild and that "there is no other way the petitioner is able to visit his or her grandchild without court intervention").

Considered together with the Superior Court's reasons for awarding visitation to the Troxels, the combination of these factors demonstrates that the visitation order in this case was an unconstitutional infringement on Granville's fundamental right to make decisions concerning the care, custody, and control of her two daughters. The Washington Superior Court failed to accord the determination of Granville, a fit custodial parent, any material weight. In fact, the Superior Court made only two formal findings in support of its visitation order. First, the Troxels "are part of a large, central, loving family, all located in this area, and the [Troxels] can provide opportunities for the children in the areas of cousins and music." Second, "[t]he children would be benefitted from spending quality time with the [Troxels], provided that that time is balanced with time with the childrens' [*sic*] nuclear family." These slender findings, in combination with the court's announced presumption in favor of grandparent visitation and its failure to accord significant weight to Granville's already having offered meaningful visitation to the Troxels, show that this case involves nothing more than a simple disagreement between the Washington Superior Court and Granville concerning her children's best interests. The Superior Court's announced reason for ordering one week of visitation in the summer demonstrates our conclusion well: "I look back on some personal experiences. . . . We always spen[t] as kids a week with one set of grandparents and another set of grandparents, [and] it happened to work out in our family that [it] turned out to be an enjoyable experience. Maybe that can, in this family, if that is how it works out." As we have explained, the Due Process Clause does not permit a State to infringe on the fundamental right of parents to make childrearing decisions simply because a state judge believes a "better" decision could be made. Neither the Washington nonparental visitation statute generally — which places no limits on either the persons who may petition for visitation or the circumstances in which such a petition may be granted — nor the Superior Court in this specific case required anything more. Accordingly, we hold that § 26.10.160(3), as applied in this case, is unconstitutional.

Because we rest our decision on the sweeping breadth of § 26.10.160(3) and the application of that broad, unlimited power in this case, we do not consider the primary constitutional question passed on by the Washington Supreme Court — whether the Due Process Clause requires all nonparental visitation statutes to include a showing of harm or potential harm to the child as a condition precedent to granting visitation. We do not, and need not, define today the precise scope of the parental due process right in the visitation context. In this respect, we agree with JUSTICE KENNEDY that the constitutionality of any standard for awarding visitation turns on the specific manner in which that standard is applied and that the constitutional protections in this area are best "elaborated with care." Because much state-court adjudication in this context occurs on a case-by-case basis, we would be hesitant to hold that specific nonparental visitation statutes violate the Due Process Clause as a per se matter.[1] *See, e.g.,*

---

[1] All 50 States have statutes that provide for grandparent visitation in some form. *See* ALA. CODE § 30-3-4.1 (1989); ALASKA STAT. ANN. § 25.20.065 (1998); ARIZ. REV. STAT. ANN. § 25-409 (1994); ARK. CODE ANN. § 9-13-103 (1998); CAL. FAM. CODE ANN. § 3104 (WEST 1994); COLO. REV. STAT. § 19-1-117

Fairbanks v. McCarter, 330 Md. 39, 49-50, 622 A.2d 121, 126-127 (1993) (interpreting best-interest standard in grandparent visitation statute normally to require court's consideration of certain factors); *Williams v. Williams*, 256 Va. 19, 501 S.E.2d 417, 418 (1998) (interpreting Virginia nonparental visitation statute to require finding of harm as condition precedent to awarding visitation).

JUSTICE STEVENS criticizes our reliance on what he characterizes as merely "a guess" about the Washington courts' interpretation of § 26.10.160(3). JUSTICE KENNEDY likewise states that "[m]ore specific guidance should await a case in which a State's highest court has considered all of the facts in the course of elaborating the protection afforded to parents by the laws of the State and by the Constitution itself." We respectfully disagree. There is no need to hypothesize about how the Washington courts might apply § 26.10.160(3) because the Washington Superior Court did apply the statute in this very case. Like the Washington Supreme Court, then, we are presented with an actual visitation order and the reasons why the Superior Court believed entry of the order was appropriate in this case. Faced with the Superior Court's application of § 26.10.160(3) to Granville and her family, the Washington Supreme Court chose not to give the statute a narrower construction. Rather, that court gave § 26.10.160(3) a literal and expansive interpretation. As we have explained, that broad construction plainly encompassed the Superior Court's application of the statute.

There is thus no reason to remand the case for further proceedings in the Washington Supreme Court. As JUSTICE KENNEDY recognizes, the burden of litigating a domestic relations proceeding can itself be "so disruptive of the parent-child relationship that the constitutional right of a custodial parent to make certain basic determinations for the child's welfare becomes implicated." In this case, the litigation costs incurred by Granville on her trip through the Washington court system and to this Court are without a doubt already substantial. As we have explained, it is apparent that the entry of the visitation order in this case violated the Constitution. We should say so now, without forcing the parties into additional litigation that would further burden Granville's parental right. We therefore hold that the application of

---

(1999); CONN. GEN. STAT. § 46B-59 (1995); DEL. CODE ANN., TIT. 10, § 1031(7) (1999); FLA. STAT. § 752.01 (1997); GA. CODE ANN. § 19-7-3 (1991); HAW. REV. STAT. § 571-46.3 (1999); IDAHO CODE § 32-719 (1999); ILL. COMP. STAT., CH. 750, § 5/607 (1998); IND. CODE § 31-17-5-1 (1999); IOWA CODE § 598.35 (1999); KAN. STAT. ANN. § 38-129 (1993); KY. REV. STAT. ANN. § 405.021 (BALDWIN 1990); LA. REV. STAT. ANN. § 9:344 (SUPP. 2000); LA. CIV. CODE ANN., ART. 136 (SUPP. 2000); ME. REV. STAT. ANN., TIT. 19A, § 1803 (1998); MD. FAM. LAW CODE ANN. § 9-102 (1999); MASS. GEN. LAWS § 119:39D (1996); MICH. COMP. LAWS ANN. § 722.27B (SUPP. 1999); MINN. STAT. § 257.022 (1998); MISS. CODE ANN. § 93-16-3 (1994); MO. REV. STAT. § 452.402 (SUPP. 1999); MONT. CODE ANN. § 40-9-102 (1997); NEB. REV. STAT. § 43-1802 (1998); NEV. REV. STAT. § 125C.050 (SUPP. 1999); N.H. REV. STAT. ANN. § 458:17-d (1992); N.J. STAT. ANN. § 9:2-7.1 (SUPP. 1999-2000); N.M. STAT. ANN. § 40-9-2 (1999); N.Y. DOM. REL. LAW § 72 (MCKINNEY 1999); N.C. GEN. STAT. §§ 50-13.2, 50-13.2A (1999); N.D. CENT. CODE § 14-09-05.1 (1997); OHIO REV. CODE ANN. §§ 3109.051, 3109.11 (SUPP. 1999); OKLA. STAT., TIT. 10, § 5 (SUPP. 1999); ORE. REV. STAT. § 109.121 (1997); 23 PA. CONS. STAT. §§ 5311-5313 (1991); R.I. GEN. LAWS §§ 15-5-24 TO 15-5-24.3 (SUPP. 1999); S.C. CODE ANN. § 20-7-420(33) (SUPP. 1999); S.D. CODIFIED LAWS § 25-4-52 (1999); TENN. CODE ANN. §§ 36-6-306, 36-6-307 (SUPP. 1999); TEX. FAM. CODE ANN. § 153.433 (SUPP. 2000); UTAH CODE ANN. § 30-5-2 (1998); VT. STAT. ANN., TIT. 15, §§ 1011-1013 (1989); VA. CODE ANN. § 20-124.2 (1995); W. VA. CODE §§ 48-2B-1 TO 48-2B-7 (1999); WIS. STAT. §§ 767.245, 880.155 (1993-1994); WYO. STAT. ANN. § 20-7-101 (1999).

§ 26.10.160(3) to Granville and her family violated her due process right to make decisions concerning the care, custody, and control of her daughters.

Accordingly, the judgment of the Washington Supreme Court is affirmed.

[JUSTICES SOUTER and THOMAS concurred in the result but believed that the Washington Supreme Court's second reason for invalidating its own state statute — that it sweeps too broadly in authorizing any person at any time to request (and a judge to award) visitation rights, subject only to the State's particular best-interests standard — was consistent with this Court's prior cases. Accordingly, they contended, it was unnecessary to address the issue upon which JUSTICE O'CONNOR's plurality opinion rested. JUSTICES STEVENS, REHNQUIST, and SCALIA each filed dissenting opinions.]

QUESTIONS

1. Does the *Troxel* opinion take adequate account of the important role that grandparents play in their grandchildren's lives? Especially in situations where a parent has died, don't grandparents represent the most direct connection to the lost parent?

2. Although *Troxel* concerned grandparent visitation "rights," its reach is considerably broader and can be expected significantly to affect other matters involving conflicts between parents and grandparents, include custody decisions involving kinship caregivers and grandparents' rights respecting termination of parental rights.

3. The *Troxel* decision provoked sentiments ranging from disappointment to outrage in the community of advocates for the older population generally and "grandparents' rights" activists in particular. It also spawned an enormous body of scholarly commentary and a flurry of legislative activity. For information concerning state law pertaining to grandparent visitation and related matters after *Troxel*, see the AARP Website, http://www.aarp.org/litigation/table.html.

DOTSON v. ROWE
957 S.W.2d 269 (1997)

EMBERTON, JUDGE. The appellants, Glenn and Maxine Dotson, are the grandparents of Donald Thomas Rowe and Angel Leigh Rowe. They appeal from an order overruling their motion to intervene and set aside a decree terminating the parental rights of their daughter, appellant, Tonya Marie Dotson Rowe Richards. Tonya appeals from an order overruling her motion to set aside or vacate the decree on the basis that she was not properly served with summons.

Tonya was married to appellee, Ralph Rowe, in 1989 and two children, Donald and Angel, were born of the marriage. The couple divorced in 1991 with custody awarded to Ralph, and in 1994, the grandparents were awarded visitation.

Later in 1994, Ralph filed a petition for termination of Tonya's parental rights. Service on her was by warning order attorney; however, the notice was received by Tonya's brother. On May 4, 1994, the court ordered termination of her parental rights. The Dotsons were not named as parties to the termination proceeding, and on June 24, 1994, they sought to intervene and set aside the termination decree citing the failure to be joined as parties or to be given notice of the proceeding. The court held that the grandparents had no right to visitation following the termination of the parent's rights and denied the motion. Tonya's motion to set aside the termination on the basis of a lack of personal jurisdiction was also denied.

Prior to the enactment of KY. REV. STAT. (KRS) 405.021(1), a grandparent had no legal right to visitation. In order to respond to the changing dynamics of the familial relationship in today's society, KRS 405.021 now provides for grandparent's visitation in divorce proceedings if it serves the best interest of the child. *King v. King*, Ky., 828 S.W.2d 630 (1992). Prior to the current version of KRS 405.201, effective July 1996, the termination of parental rights severed all ties to the parental unit, including the extended family. As stated in *Hicks v. Enlow*, Ky., 764 S.W.2d 68, 71 (1989):

> Termination of parental rights, as provided for by statute, whether voluntary or involuntary, once legally adjudicated severs all relationship of parent and child as if the same had never existed. The statutory reasons underlying the termination process relate to parental abandonment, neglect and abuse so substantial that the child must be legally cutoff from the parent. They justify a legal structure that provides finality and blocks every path to further litigation to reestablish a connection to parents whose rights have been terminated. Litigation by grandparents, by the family of such parents, would frustrate and circumvent the termination decree. The statutory language of severance required in the termination decree now expresses no exception, and none may be created by implying an exception from the grandparents' visitation statute.

In *Hicks*, the court expressed sympathy for the grandparents in such cases, but concluded it was bound by the terms of the termination statute:

> While we certainly sympathize with the feelings of the grandmother who has been cut off from visitation with her grandchild by involuntary termination of her son's parental rights, we recognize that the language of the termination statute completely severs the connection to the terminated parent and the connection through him to his family. The termination and adoption procedures are domestic relations considerations of overriding importance, and no exceptions for grandparents to the terms of the termination order required by statute should be implied where none are provided.

The consequences of denial of grandparent visitation after the parental rights of a parent have been terminated can be detrimental not only for the grandparent but, even more significantly, to the child who has already been denied the parental affection of one parent. The benefit of contact with the extended family was aptly recognized in *King, supra*:

> If a grandparent is physically, mentally and morally fit, then a grand-child will ordinarily benefit from contact with the grandparent. That grandparents and grandchildren normally have a special bond cannot be denied. Each benefits from contact with the other. The child can learn respect, a sense of responsibility and love. The grandparent can be invigorated by exposure to youth, can gain an insight into our changing society, and can avoid the loneliness which is so often a part of an aging parent's life.

The public policy reasons for permitting continuation of grandparent visitation following the termination of a parent's rights, prompted the amendment of KRS 405.021(1), which now states:

> The Circuit Court may grant reasonable visitation rights to either the paternal or maternal grandparents of a child and issue any necessary orders to enforce the decree if it determines that it is in the best interest of the child to do so. Once a grandparent has been granted visitation rights under this subsection, those rights shall not be adversely affected by termination of parental rights belonging to the grandparent's son or daughter, who is the father or mother of the child visited by the grandparent, unless the Circuit Court determines that it is in the best interest of the child to do so.

Clearly, the situation now before this court is one which the legislature intended the amendment to apply. Prior to the institution of the proceeding to terminate the parental rights of their daughter, the Dotsons were granted visitation rights pursuant to KRS 405.021. The facts suggest, that although termination of Tonya's rights was the direct relief sought, given the turbulent relationship between Ralph and the Dotsons, the termination of their visitation rights was not an unintended consequence. The intent of the legislature was to prevent a dispute between grandparents and parents from depriving the child of the love and affection of the grandparent.

The purpose of the amendment to KRS 405.021 was to change the existing law to which the courts, and undoubtedly litigants, had expressed displeasure. It was neither logical nor consistent with public policy to sever the child from an established grandparent relationship without first determining if such action was in the child's best interest. The statute is clearly remedial in nature. If it is in the child's best interest, it preserves grandparent visitation established prior to the termination proceeding. It is applicable to cases prior to July 1996, as well as those after the effective date of the amendment. *Peabody Coal Co. v. Gossett*, Ky., 819 S.W.2d 33, 36 (1991).

The termination of Tonya's parental rights did not terminate or adversely affect the visitation rights of the Dotsons. Absent a finding that it is in the best interest of the child that such rights be denied, the visitation rights granted pursuant to KRS 405.021 remain.

Tonya argues that she was improperly served with process. KRS 625.070 provides that, if possible, service in termination cases is by personal service; since the parent often cannot be located, however, it expressly provides for constructive service. KY. R. CIV. P. (CR) 4.05 provides that constructive service may be had on a party whose name or place of residence is unknown. CR 4.05(e). Tonya testified that she was not at her residence in Kentucky between January 1993, and October 1994, and the Dotsons were not aware of her location until October 1994. Constructive service on appellant was not only appropriate, but was the only means through which service could be made.

The order of the trial court is reversed in that it terminates the Dotsons' visitation rights. The order denying Tonya's motion to vacate or set aside the termination decree is affirmed.

QUESTIONS

1. Does *Dotson* survive *Troxel*?

2. Should grandparents have a right to notice of termination of parental rights? Of the adoption of a grandchild? What purpose would such a notice serve? Would a state statute requiring such notice conflict with *Troxel*'s fundamental premises? Would it reflect a sound public policy?

3. Re-read MINN. STAT. § 257C in the supplement. Is this statute consistent with *Troxel*?

Chapter 11

END OF LIFE ISSUES

As we age, our tendency as human beings is to begin thinking about death — what it means biologically and metaphysically, its inevitability, how it occurs. For an older person who has been diagnosed with a progressive or terminal disease, concerns about pain, the financial costs of a major illness, and religious issues may become a central focus of her thoughts and actions. The elder law attorney must, accordingly, be educated about the various ethical, legal, and medical issues that are associated with the concept and process of "death." This section considers three substantive areas that might be described as end-of-life issues: viatical settlements, the right to die, and anatomical donations.

A. SENIOR SETTLEMENTS

A viatical settlement, often called a "senior settlement" is in essence a contractual arrangement by which a person who is near death due to old age or a terminal illness can sell a life insurance policy for a portion of its face value, paid either in installments or as a lump sum. By "accelerating" death benefits in this manner, the owner of the life insurance policy can access financial resources that would not normally be available until after death. The elderly are often the target of senior settlement offers, either as a potential seller of a life insurance policy, or, more commonly, as an investor in a viatical settlement pool. Although the premise of the viatical settlement seems reasonable enough, the actual process of obtaining such a settlement, and the substance these contracts, may present legal and ethical concerns for the attorney and her client.

1. Introduction

Indiana Department of Insurance Consumer Services
Viatical Settlements: A Guide for People
with Terminal Illnesses
http://www.in.gov/idoi/consumer_services/viatical.html

If you have a terminal illness — or if you are caring for someone who is terminally ill — chances are you're giving a great deal of thought to time and money. You may be thinking about life insurance, too. It's in that context that you may hear the phrases accelerated benefits and viatical settlements.

Accelerated benefits sometimes are called "living benefits." They are the proceeds of life insurance policies that are paid by the insurer to policyholders before they die. Occasionally, these benefits are included in policies when they are sold, but usually, they are offered as riders or attachments to new or existing policies.

Viatical settlements involve the sale of a life insurance policy. If you have a terminal illness, you may consider selling your policy to a viatical settlement company for a lump sum cash payment. In a viatical settlement transaction, people with terminal illnesses assign their life insurance policies to viatical settlement companies in exchange for a percentage of the policy's face value. The viatical settlement company, in turn, may sell the policy to a third-party investor. The viatical settlement company or the investor becomes the beneficiary to the policy, pays the premiums, and collects the face value of the policy after the original policyholder dies.

The fact is that any decisions affecting life insurance benefits can have a profound financial and emotional impact on dependents, friends, and caregivers. Before you make any major changes regarding your policy, talk to someone whose advice and expertise you can count on — a lawyer, an accountant, or a good friend.

Investigate Your Options

Options exist for people with terminal illnesses when financial needs are critical. For example, you may consider a loan from the original beneficiary of your life insurance policy, accelerated benefits on your life insurance policy, or a viatical settlement.

Many life insurance policies in force nationwide now include an accelerated benefits provision. Companies offer anywhere from 25 to 100 percent of the death benefit as early payment, but policyholders can collect these payments only under very specific circumstances. The amount and the method of payment vary with the policy.

Indeed, if you own a life insurance policy, call your insurance agent or company to find out about your alternatives. Ask whether your life insurance policy allows for accelerated benefits or loans, and how much it will cost. Some insurers add accelerated benefits to life insurance policies for an additional premium, usually computed as a percentage of the base premium. Others offer the benefits at no extra premium, but charge the policyholder for the option if and when it is used. In most cases, the insurance company will reduce the benefits advanced to the policyholder before death to compensate for the interest it will lose on its early payout. There also may be a service charge.

In addition, you may consider selling your life insurance policy to a viatical settlement company, a private enterprise that offers a terminally ill person a percentage of the policy's face value. It is not considered an insurance company.

The viatical settlement company becomes the sole beneficiary of the policy in consideration for delivering a cash payment to the policyholder and paying the premiums. When the policyholder dies, the viatical settlement company collects the face value of the policy.

Viatical settlements are complex legal and financial transactions. They require time and attention from physicians, life insurance companies, lawyers, and accountants or financial planners. The entire transfer process can take up to four months to complete.

Eligibility for Viatical Settlements

Each viatical settlement company sets its own rules for determining which life insurance policies it will buy. For example, viatical settlement companies may want to know that:

- You've owned your policy for at least two years;

- Your policy has a reasonably large face value;

- You have a waiver from current or potential beneficiaries; and

- You are terminally ill. Usually, this means that death is expected to occur within two years.

Investors may insist that your policy be from a company that is large or well-known and one that will be able to pay the death benefit. If your life insurance policy was provided by your employer, investors also will want to know if it can be converted into an individual policy or otherwise be guaranteed to remain in force before it can be assigned. Finally, investors probably will ask you to release all your medical records to them.

Financial Implications

If you sell your policy to a viatical settlement company, you may owe federal capital gains tax on the difference between the payment you receive and the amount you've paid in premiums. You also may owe state tax, although several states, including California and New York, have made these settlements tax-free.

Collecting accelerated benefits or making a viatical settlement also may affect your eligibility for public assistance programs based on financial need, such as Medicaid. The federal government does not require policyholders either to choose accelerated benefits or to cash in their policies before qualifying for

Medicaid benefits. But, once the policyholder cashes in the policy and receives a payment, the money may be counted as income for Medicaid purposes and may affect eligibility.

Guidelines for Consumers

The daily physical and emotional demands of a terminal illness can be overwhelming, and financial burdens can seem insurmountable. If you are considering making a viatical settlement on your life insurance policy — or if you are helping someone with this decision — these consumer guidelines should help you avoid costly mistakes and make the choice that's right.

- Contact two or three viatical settlement companies to make sure offers are competitive, and be aware of prevailing discount rates. A viatical settlement company may pay 60 percent of the face value of a policy to a person whose life expectancy is two years or less, and 80 percent to someone whose life expectancy is six months or less.

- Check with your state insurance department to see if viatical settlement companies or brokers must be licensed. If so, check the status of the companies with whom you are considering doing business.

- Don't fall for high pressure tactics. You don't have to accept an offer, and you can change your mind. Some states require a 15-day cooling off period before any viatical settlement transaction is complete.

- Verify that the investor or the company has the money for your payout readily available. Large companies may have cash on hand; smaller ones may have uneven cash flows or may be "shopping" the policy to third parties.

- Ask the company to set up an escrow account with a reputable financial institution at the beginning of the transfer so you can be sure the funds are available to cover the offer.

- Insist on a timely payment. No more than a few months should elapse from the initial contact with the company to closing. Check with your state attorney general's office or department of insurance to see if there are complaints against the company before you do business.

- Ask the company about possible tax consequences and implications for public assistance benefits. Some states require viatical settlement companies to make these disclosures and tell you about other options that may be available from your life insurance company.

- Ask about privacy. Some companies may not protect a policyholder's privacy when they act as brokers for payouts from potential investors.

- Contact a lawyer to check on the possible probate and estate considerations. If you make a viatical settlement, there will be no life insurance benefits for the person you originally designated as beneficiary.

For More Information

Any decision that affects your life insurance benefits can affect the people who care for and about you. Before you make a decision, talk to someone you trust — a lawyer, an accountant, or a good friend. You also may want to contact [the National Association of Insurance Commissioners, your state department of insurance, or the Federal Trade Commission].

* * *

Jim Mechler
Annotated Bibliography: Viatical Settlements
(December 1996)
http://www.neln.org/bibs/mechler2.pdf*

vi-at-i-cal *adj.* [Lat. viaticusvia, road.] *Of or relating to travel,*
a road, or a way.

* * *

Viatical Settlements — History and Mechanics

For many years, the traditional use of a life insurance policy was to bestow financial benefits on a survivor. In most instances this beneficiary was the purchaser's spouse, children, or parent. With improved medical technology though, people have been allowed to live longer, but for a price. With the high costs of medical treatment, many people have needed money to pay for procedures. This is the [rationale for] a viatical settlement.

Under the conventional "whole life" policy, the insured can cash in the policy while living, but will only receive the cash value of the policy — usually much less than if the death benefits were paid out. Because this cash value payout often did not cover costly experimental procedures, it offered a poor solution to the problem. Largely in response to the AIDS epidemic of the 1980s, the insurance industry created viatical settlements and accelerated death benefits.

In a viatical settlement, the insured assigns the proceeds of [her] life insurance policy to an investor. The insured receives a cash settlement for less than the value of the death benefit. The cash settlement is computed based upon the life expectancy of the insured, with a higher percentage payout for those closer to death. In return, the investor pays the premiums and when the insured dies, receives the death benefit value of the policy. Like any investment, the investor is speculating upon the happening of an event. In this case, that event is the

---

death of the insured. If the insured dies before the date predicated by the investor, then the return on the policy will be greater than the payout.

. . . With the advent of recent drug therapies which have increased the life expectancy of AIDS patients, the viatical settlement industry has begun cultivating a new type of seller. This new market includes those who suffer from cancer, ALS, Alzheimer's, or any other disease or condition that has resulted in a terminal diagnosis. Each viatical settlement company sets its own rules regarding which life insurance policies it will buy. Some considerations that the viatical settlement company will take into consideration include:

- that the individual has owned the life insurance policy for 2 years.

- that the individual is terminal (defined as death expected within six months).

- that the insured has a waiver from the current beneficiary of the policy.

- that the policy has a "large" value.

- that the policy is issued from a "well-known" insurance company.

The insured will probably also be asked to release his/her medical records to the viatical settlement firm.

* * *

Accelerated Death Benefits

Accelerated Death Benefits provisions are of two varieties. The first variety, known as the "lien" model, leaves the underlying policy untouched. The insured is paid a percentage of the policy's death benefit, with the remaining percentage for the policy's beneficiaries. The remaining percentage is reduced by the amount of premium paid by the insurer until the insured's death.

The second model, the "proceeds" model, is similar to a viatical settlement. Death benefits for a beneficiary are not preserved, with the insured receiving a discounted percentage of the policy's death benefit. Usually accelerated death benefits are available only if the original policy provided for them. In addition, accelerated death benefits are more restrictive than viatical settlements. ADB's usually require a note from the insured's physician stating that the insured has less than twelve months to live. Viatical settlements do not usually require such a prognosis. Accelerated death benefits offer an alternative to viatical settlements that allow the insured, in some cases, to retain death benefits while still receiving a portion of the benefits in advance.

Legal Issues Pertaining to Viatical Settlements

For several years the principal legal issue surrounding viatical settlements was whether viatical settlements constituted a security transaction as defined by the Securities Act of 1933. The 1933 Act expressly exempts insurance contracts from the definition of a "security." But viatical settlements, though tied to the proceeds of insurance policies, probably cannot be described as insurance contracts.

In 1992, two viatical brokers were issued cease-and-desist orders by North Dakota's Securities Commissioner. The Commissioner charged that what the brokers were engaging in was an "unregistered sale of securities." The SEC soon began its own investigation.

The SEC's investigation led it to file suit against Life Partners, the largest viatical settlement company, in August of 1994. The SEC claimed that viatical settlements are security transactions and must be registered. Life Partners claimed that viatical settlements are not securities and are not required to be registered. A year later, the federal district court for the District of Columbia concluded that viatical settlements are subject to federal securities laws and issued a preliminary injunction against Life Partners.

The decision was appealed to the Court of Appeals for the District of Columbia. The D.C. Circuit reversed the decision of the District Court. In *SEC v. Life Partners, Inc.* [7 F.3d 536 (D.C. Cir. 1996), the Court held that viatical settlements are not securities within the Securities Act of 1933 because there is no "venture" associated with ownership of a fractional interest in an insurance contract from which the investor's profit depends entirely on the mortality of the insured. The Court also found that the post-purchase activities of the viatical settlement company are ministerial in nature and do not have a material impact on the profits of the investors.

A second legal issue concerning viatical settlements is their proper tax treatment. Generally, neither the states or the federal government tax life insurance proceeds after the insured has died. But on the federal level, no such benefit exists for pre-death life insurance proceeds received from a viatical settlement.

In a 1994 private letter ruling, the IRS stated that viatical settlements are taxable income. The IRS has not issued any rulings concerning the tax treatment of accelerated benefits. This issue was finally resolved with the passage of legislation in 1995 that specifically exempts both viatical settlements and accelerated death benefits from federal income tax.

QUESTIONS

1. Why might the elderly be special targets of the sellers and brokers of viatical settlement agreements?

2. Read 26 U.S.C. § 101(g) in the statutory supplement. Do you approve of the tax provisions that exempt viatical settlements and accelerated death benefits from the federal income tax?

2. Regulatory Issues

The relative lack of regulation of the viatical settlement/accelerated death benefit industry is aggravated by the fact that many companies operate over the Internet and thus can appeal directly to potential viators. One viator advocate has estimated that "tens of dozens" of these organizations hawk their wares online. It may be difficult for a terminally-ill consumer to make rational choices about what type of contract, and what provider, is in the viator's best interests. Find and visit the website of at least one for-profit viatical company or broker (and don't assume that because the company's uniform resource locator ends in ".org" that the company is a non-profit entity). Does the company provide sufficient information to allow a potential viator to make a decision informed by the considerations listed by the FTC, above? Does the risk of fraud or overreaching justify special regulation of viatical settlement transactions carried out in whole or part over the Internet?

Michigan Office of Financial and Insurance Services
Viatical Settlements: The Undisclosed Risks;
What Every Investor Must Know
http://www.michigan.gov/documents/cis_ofis_fispub_0562_25009_7.pdf

WARNING:

Do not invest in viatical settlements until you
have read the following information.

What is a Viatical Settlement?

Following is a brief, general, overview of how viatical settlement investments work.

A viatical settlement is an arrangement between the owner of an insurance policy (the *viator*) and a third party (the *provider*). The provider negotiates with the viator for the purchase of his/her life insurance policy or the beneficiary rights under that policy. The broker then solicits funds from investors. The funds are used to consummate the viator-provider purchase/sale agreement.

Viators are typically terminally ill persons expected to die within 24 to 36 months. The viator receives a percentage of the face value of his/her life insurance policy. The viator may use the money for whatever he/she desires; typically it is used to pay current medical expenses and fulfill last wishes.

Upon the viator's death the investor or group of investors collects the value of the policy less any deducted expenses involved in the investment. This money is then distributed to the individual investors based on each's percentage of investment.

The State's Role

To date Michigan has enacted legislation protecting the viator. Under the law the Michigan Insurance Commissioner is vested with the authority to oversee the viator-dealer end of the viatical settlement process. The investor-provider end of the viatical settlement investment falls under the purview of the Michigan Uniform Securities Act. Viatical settlement contracts are considered securities on the premise that the sale of fractional interests in a viatical settlement to investors is a securities transaction.

As a New Investment Vehicle

Viatical settlements are fairly new. They were first publicly discussed as an investment vehicle in the mid 1980s and have only been widely available to the general public for the last three years. While every investment carries with it the risk of loss due to fraud or otherwise, many investors who lose money to viatical settlement investments lose it because they were not given the full or correct information concerning its risks. Sometimes it is simply that the information was available but the investor did not ask. Regardless of the specific circumstances, there are several risks inherent in a viatical investment of which all investors should be aware. A well informed investor is a prepared investor.

Important Risks

Factors that should be considered before investing:

- Rates of return may be projected but cannot be guaranteed since advances in science and medicine may increase a viator's life beyond that which can be foreseen. So while a viatical company or salesperson might "guarantee" a particular rate of return on your investment, remember that the rate of return on an investment in viatical settlements cannot actually be calculated since the longer a viator lives, the lower the rate of return on your investment will be.

- No one can accurately predict the life expectancy of a viator. This is true not only because of possible breakthroughs in treatments and cures for AIDS and cancer but also because of many other variables such as: the experience of the medical personnel making the prediction; the nature of the viator's illness; and, if the viator has AIDS, the definition of AIDS used by the viatical company.

- Who will be responsible for paying the premiums. If the policy premiums are not paid the insurance company will cancel the policy. Many viatical companies collect enough money from investors to cover the costs of paying premiums for the life expectancy of the viator; however, it is important to address the issue of who pays the premiums when the viator outlives his/her life expectancy.

- Term insurance policies have unique risks. A term policy is a policy issued for a definite period of time. If the viator outlives that time period the insurance company will not pay the death benefit. If your investment is in a term policy you should be aware of who will be responsible for renewing the policy when the term expires.

- Group policies are also unique. A group insurance policy is one that covers a specific group of individuals such as the employees of an employer. These policies may be converted to an individual policy; however, many group policies contain restrictions for such a conversion. If the viator's policy was converted from a group policy, any restrictions may pose problems for investors. A typical example is that the group policy premiums may be lower than those of the converted individual policy.

- Most policies have a contestability clause. A contestability clause allows the insurance company to "contest" the policy if a claim for benefits is made within two years of the policy's effectiveness. Contesting the policy means that the insurance company believes there is legal justification to deny the claim for benefit payments. Legal justification may be that the viator's death was an act of suicide or murder by an interested party, or even that the viator was not completely honest when applying for the life insurance. The insurance company will not pay the benefits if the viator dies within the contestability period AND the insurance company believes it has such justification to cancel the policy.

- The policy may also be contested by family members. Keep in mind that some family members, when aware of the policy and its benefits, may challenge the validity of the viatical settlement in court. This could delay payment, thus reducing your rate of return.

- Viatical settlements may carry significant risks for older investors who may be looking forward to the funds for living or medical expenses of their own, since investors may be asked to pay additional premiums or wait for a return on their investment for a period of time beyond that originally expected.

- IRA tax benefits may not be available if IRA funds are invested in viatical settlements. Internal Revenue Code section 408(a)(3) requires that, "no part of trust [IRA] funds will be invested in life insurance contracts."

- The timing involved with IRAs may also cause problems. Because the IRS requires individuals to draw money from their IRA at 70½ years old, investors need to consider both their age and the viator's age and possible life span when investing. There will be substantial penalties by the IRS when you reach age 70½ if IRA money cannot be distributed because the viator is still alive.

- Viatical settlement investments are not liquid investments. A liquid investment is one that can be easily disposed of by either selling the investment interest to another investor in a secondary market or by cashing it in for value with the issuer. Be advised that there may not be a secondary market for viatical settlement investments, and further, there can be no guarantee of a payout of funds via the death benefit.

- Check promises and "guarantees" closely. The viatical company may provide a fidelity bond or a performance "guarantee" or other similar instrument with your purchase. This idea is to ensure that investors will still get paid if there is a problem with the payout of beneficiary proceeds from the insurance company. If such a "guarantee" is provided, ask for a copy of the instrument as well as a copy of the contract between the viatical company and the company issuing the instrument. Also, contact the appropriate state regulatory agency to determine if the company issuing the "guarantee" is legitimate; try to obtain the company's financial statements. These are important steps because:

- The contract between the viatical company and the issuer of the instrument may affect the guarantee to you; something the contract may expose.

- The company issuing the guarantee may not have the financial resources to make payments under the guarantee; something financial statements should indicate.

- The life insurance company may go out of business. While Michigan has an insurance guarantee fund that provides money for beneficiaries of insurance companies that go out of business, that fund is limited to $100,000 per life insurance policy. Also, the process of collecting from this source may be delayed for viatical investors. A delay will reduce the rate of return on your investment.

- There is an increased opportunity for fraud where the viator is unidentifiable. Always contact the insurance company to determine whether or not the viator actually exists.

Many insurance companies may limit the information available, but some will disclose whether or not they have issued a life insurance policy to that person.

- The policy may be sold to more than one party. There is always the risk that the viator has sold his policy to two different viatical settlement companies. While most legitimate viatical settlement companies will perform due diligence investigations to combat this, it is a possibility. Ask whatever questions you feel are necessary until you are comfortable with the answers.

QUESTION

Read the Viatical Settlements Model Act in the statutory supplement. Does this proposed model act resolve some of the problems associated with viatical settlements?

B. THE RIGHT TO DIE AND HEALTH CARE DECISION MAKING

1. Introduction: Constitutional Considerations

The law has long recognized the right of competent persons to refuse medical treatment. In *Cruzan v. Director, Missouri Dep't of Health*, 497 U.S. 261 (1990), the United States Supreme Court implicitly acknowledged that this right, and a corollary "right-to-die," are protected by the Fifth and Fourteenth Amendment due process clauses. In *Cruzan*, the Court upheld a state evidentiary rule requiring that, before nutrition and hydration may be withdrawn from a person in a persistent vegetative state, it must be demonstrated by "clear and convincing evidence" that such action is consistent with the patient's previously manifested wishes. In that case, the family of Nancy Cruzan, who was in a persistent vegetative state as a result of an automobile accident, asked hospital employees to terminate the artificial nutrition and hydration procedures after it had become apparent that Nancy Cruzan had no chance of regaining her mental faculties. The hospital employees refused to do so without court approval, and the state of Missouri intervened in behalf of Nancy to prevent withdrawal of the feeding tube.

The Court said in *Cruzan* that the Due Process Clause does not require that the state rely on the judgment of the family, the guardian, or "anyone but the patient herself" in making a medical decision of this nature. Unless clear and convincing evidence exists that the patient herself had expressed an interest not to be sustained in a persistent vegetative state, or that she had expressed a desire to have a surrogate make such a decision for her, the state may refuse to allow withdrawal of nutrition and hydration. "A State is entitled to guard against potential abuses" that can occur if family members do not protect a patient's best interests, and "may properly decline to make judgments about the 'quality' of life that a particular individual may enjoy, and [instead] simply assert an unqualified interest in the preservation of human life to be weighed against the . . . interests of the individual."

The *Cruzan* decision was a narrow one in the sense that it held only that Missouri's evidentiary requirement did not violate the due process clauses. The Court's opinion in *Cruzan*, however, assumes that a competent person has a constitutionally protected right to refuse lifesaving hydration and nutrition. More important, a majority of Justices declared in a separate opinion that such a liberty interest exists. Thus, the Court appears committed to the position that the right to refuse nutrition and hydration — or other life sustaining measures — is subsumed in the broader right to refuse medical treatment, and is a right of constitutional dimension. Although *Cruzan* involved a young person, the decision has had a profound impact on public policy and how lawyers help their older clients plan for death.

Sarah E. Ubel
Living Wills: An Annotated Bibliography (May 1998)*
http://www.neln.org/bibs/ubel.html

"Just as I choose a ship to sail in or a house to live in, so I choose a death for my passage from life."

— *Seneca (4 B.C.–65 A.D.)*

* * *

Definitions and Explanations

Agent: A health care proxy appointed through a Durable Power of Attorney for Health care.

Artificially Administered Nutrition and Hydration (Tube Feeding): This does not mean food and water taken by mouth — eating and drinking. Tube feeding means providing nutrients and fluids through tubes that are inserted into a person's stomach through the nose (nasogastric or NG tube) or surgically inserted into the stomach (gastrostomy) or, less frequently, into the small intestine (jejunostomy). As a rule, tube feeding decisions are not about intravenous (IV) administration of fluids, nutrients, and medications. See Total Parenteral Nutrition (TPN) and Intravenous Nutrition and Hydration (IV)

Autonomy: The principle that a person has the ethical, legal, and medical right of self-determination to consent or refuse to consent to medical treatment, based on the moral principle of respect for person.

Brain Death: Characteristics of brain death consist of:

(1) unreceptivity and unresponsiveness to externally applied stimuli and internal needs;

(2) no spontaneous movements or breathing;

(3) no reflex activity; and

(4) a flat electroencephalograph reading after 24 hour period of observation. The brain death determination is used when a person is on a respirator and the usual determination of death, that there is neither cardiac (heart) nor respiratory (breathing) activity, cannot be applied.

Cardiopulmonary Resuscitation (CPR): Restoring breathing or heartbeat after either cardiac or respiratory arrest. CPR methods range from basic mouth to mouth breathing and chest compression to more advanced methods such as administration of electric shock to the heart, drugs and other mechanical or chemical agents.

Death: The cessation of life; permanent cessations of vital functions and signs. Numerous states have enacted statutory definitions of death which include brain related criteria. For example, many states have adopted, sometimes with variations, the Uniform Determination of Death Act definition: "An individual who has sustained either 1) irreversible cessation of circulatory and respiratory function, or 2) irreversible cessation of all functions of the entire brain, including the brain stem, is dead. A determination must be made in accordance with accepted medical standards."

Do Not Intubate Order (DNI Order): This means that a tube should not be inserted in the throat for purpose of putting someone on a respirator to maintain breathing indefinitely. In an emergency, paramedics may insert a tube into the throat for the purpose of resuscitation — to attempt to establish breathing — and a decision must be made later to withdraw it.

Do Not Resuscitate Order (DNR Order): Resuscitation includes various means of attempting to restart or to strengthen weak and irregular heartbeat and breathing. Neither of these two functions, breathing or heartbeat, can continue unassisted for many minutes without the other . . . Many people have taken basic CPR courses and learned how to do mouth-to-mouth breathing and apply pressure to the chest. . . . Resuscitation may involve applying a bag, a type of mask, over the person's mouth to assist in breathing, or intubation, which means inserting a tube into the person's throat so that mechanically assisted breathing can be started. Intubation requires placing the person on a respirator, sometimes called a ventilator. Resuscitation may involve injecting drugs or applying electric shock, or both, and then transporting the person to a hospital emergency room. A DNR order directs medical personnel NOT to resuscitate using one or more of these methods. Also see: Do Not Intubate Order.

Durable Power of Attorney for Health Care: A means by which one person, the principal, can appoint, by a written document, a second person, the attorney in fact or agent, to make health care decisions when the principal is unable to do so.

Intravenous (IV) Nutrition and Hydration: IV administration is usually short-term, because most people's veins will not tolerate long term use. IVs are not usually used for nutritional purposes in nursing homes or home health care.

Life Sustaining Procedures: Such procedures which may be suspended on a court order or pursuant to a living will in case of, for example, a comatose and terminally ill individual, are medical procedures which utilize mechanical or other artificial means to sustain, restore, or supplant a vital function, which serve only or primarily to prolong the moment of death, and where, in the judgment of the attending and consulting physicians, as reflected in the patient's medical record, death is imminent if such procedures are not utilized.

Living Will: A document that governs the withholding or withdrawal of life-sustaining treatment from an individual in the event of an incurable or irreversible condition that will cause death within a relatively short time, invoked when such person is no longer able to make decisions regarding his or her medical treatment.

Medical Health Care Power of Attorney: An instrument in writing whereby one person, as principal, appoints another as his or her agent and confers authority to make medical decisions on behalf of the principal. The agent is attorney in fact and his or her power is revoked on death of the principal by operation of law or upon the revocation of the principal.

Natural Death: A death that occurs by the unassisted operation of natural causes.

Natural Death Acts: Such statutes authorize an adult to make a written directive instructing his or her physician to withhold life-sustaining procedures in the event of a terminal condition. In the directive, which is to be executed in a prescribed manner and made a part of the patient's medical records, the declarant directs that if he or she has been certified by two physicians as being afflicted with a terminal condition, he or she is to be permitted to die naturally. Such laws relieve from civil or criminal liability physicians who act in accordance with its provisions. . . .

No CPR Order: See Do Not Resuscitate Order.

Patient Self-Determination Act: A federal law, effective December 1991, that requires hospitals, nursing homes, home health and hospice care providers, and health maintenance organizations (HMOs) to ask persons admitted for care if they have an advance directive. If so, the directive must be placed in the person's medical record. These health providers must also provide information about state law on advance directives and about their own policies related to patients' rights to make medical decisions, and provide community education about advance directives. They cannot discriminate on the basis of whether a person has or does not have directive.

Persistent Vegetative State (PVS): A condition caused by disease or injury in which the upper portion of the brain has been destroyed. A person in a PVS has lost all conscious function but may still have sleep/wake cycles, and there can be involuntary, repetitive arm and leg movements. The lower part of the brain, the brainstem, still functions, so breathing and heartbeat continue.

Respirator: These machines, sometimes called ventilators, are devices that either assist or take over the exchange of air for people who, because of disease, injury, or death (brain only) cannot breathe for themselves. A person is connected to the respirator by a tube that enters the body either through the nose and mouth or through a surgical incision in the throat (tracheostomy).

Right to Die Laws: Cases and statutes that recognize in some instances the right of a dying person to decline extraordinary treatment to prolong life, or the right of the person's guardian to request such. . . .

Substituted Judgment: A term used when making medical decisions for another, based on the principle of autonomy. It means to decide as the person would have decided for himself or herself, if he or she were able to do so. By honoring an advance directive, the health care proxy is exercising substituted judgment and respecting the declarant's right of self-determination.

Terminal Condition / Illness: An illness or injury from which there is no hope of recovery and for which death is the expected result. A living will does not go into effect until a person is in a terminal condition, which is defined differently in the various state living will laws.

Total Parenteral Nutrition (TPN): This is a type of tube feeding or artificially administered nutrition and hydration. Tubes are inserted into a large vein in the chest or neck for longer-term use than an IV. TPN is rarely used in terminal care, because it is more expensive and requires more intensive nursing care than NG and gastrostomy feedings.

QUESTIONS

1. Why might a person choose to execute a DNR or DNI order?

2. Should health care providers be liable to an individual or her family members for failing to comply with a DNR order?

BUSH v. SCHIAVO

885 So. 2d 321 (Fla. 2004)

Pariente, C.J.

The narrow issue in this case requires this Court to decide the constitutionality of a law passed by the Legislature that directly affected Theresa Schiavo, who has been in a persistent vegetative state since 1990. This Court, after careful consideration of the arguments of the parties and amici, the constitutional issues raised, the precise wording of the challenged law, and the underlying procedural history of this case, concludes that the law violates the fundamental constitutional tenet of separation of powers and is therefore unconstitutional both on its face and as applied to Theresa Schiavo. Accordingly, we affirm the trial court's order declaring the law unconstitutional.

FACTS AND PROCEDURAL HISTORY

The resolution of the discrete separation of powers issue presented in this case does not turn on the facts of the underlying guardianship proceedings that resulted in the removal of Theresa's nutrition and hydration tube. The underlying litigation, which has pitted Theresa's husband, Michael Schiavo, against Theresa's parents, turned on whether the procedures sustaining Theresa's life should be discontinued. However, the procedural history is important because it provides the backdrop to the Legislature's enactment of the challenged law. We also detail the facts and procedural history in light of the Governor's assertion that chapter 2003-418, Laws of Florida (hereinafter sometimes referred to as "the Act"), was passed in order to protect the due process rights of Theresa and other individuals in her position.

As set forth in the Second District's first opinion in this case, which upheld the guardianship court's final order, Theresa Marie Schindler was born on December 3, 1963, and lived with or near her parents in Pennsylvania until she married Michael Schiavo on November 10, 1984. Michael and Theresa moved to Florida in 1986. They were happily married and both were employed. They had no children.

On February 25, 1990, their lives changed. Theresa, age 27, suffered a cardiac arrest as a result of a potassium imbalance. Michael called 911, and Theresa was rushed to the hospital. She never regained consciousness. Since 1990, Theresa has lived in nursing homes with constant care. She is fed and hydrated by tubes. The staff changes her diapers regularly. She has had numerous health problems, but none have been life threatening. *In re Guardianship of Schiavo*, 780 So. 2d 176, 177 (Fla. 2d DCA 2001) (*Schiavo I*).

For the first three years after this tragedy, Michael and Theresa's parents, Robert and Mary Schindler, enjoyed an amicable relationship. However, that relationship ended in 1993 and the parties literally stopped speaking to each other. In May of 1998, eight years after Theresa lost consciousness, Michael petitioned the guardianship court to authorize the termination of life-prolonging procedures. *See id.* By filing this petition, which the Schindlers opposed, Michael placed the difficult decision in the hands of the court.

After a trial, at which both Michael and the Schindlers presented evidence, the guardianship court issued an extensive written order authorizing the discontinuance of artificial life support. The trial court found by clear and convincing evidence that Theresa Schiavo was in a persistent vegetative state and that Theresa would elect to cease life-prolonging procedures if she were competent to make her own decision. This order was affirmed on direct appeal, *see Schiavo I*, 780 So. 2d at 177, and we denied review. *See In re Guardianship of Schiavo*, 789 So. 2d 348 (Fla. 2001).

The severity of Theresa's medical condition was explained by the Second District as follows:

> The evidence is overwhelming that Theresa is in a permanent or persistent vegetative state. It is important to understand that a persistent vegetative state is not simply a coma. She is not asleep. She has cycles of apparent wakefulness and apparent sleep without any cognition or awareness. As she breathes, she often makes moaning sounds. Theresa has severe contractors of her hands, elbows, knees, and feet. Over the span of this last decade, Theresa's brain has deteriorated because of the lack of oxygen it suffered at the time of the heart attack. By mid 1996, the CAT scans of her brain showed a severely abnormal structure. At this point, much of her cerebral cortex is simply gone and has been replaced by cerebral spinal fluid. Medicine cannot cure this condition. Unless an act of God, a true miracle, were to recreate her brain, Theresa will always remain in an unconscious, reflexive state, totally dependent upon others to feed her and care for her most private needs. She could remain in this state for many years.

Schiavo I, 780 So. 2d at 177. In affirming the trial court's order, the Second District concluded by stating:

> In the final analysis, the difficult question that faced the trial court was whether Theresa Marie Schindler Schiavo, not after a few weeks in a coma, but after ten years in a persistent vegetative state that has robbed her of most of her cerebrum and all but the most instinctive of neurological functions, with no hope of a medical cure but with sufficient money and strength of body to live indefinitely, would choose to continue the constant nursing care and the supporting tubes in hopes that a miracle would somehow recreate her missing brain tissue, or whether she would wish to permit a natural death process to take its course and for her family members and loved ones to be free to continue their lives. After due consideration, we conclude that the trial judge had clear and convincing evidence to answer this question as he did.

Schiavo I, 780 So. 2d at 180.

Although the guardianship court's final order authorizing the termination of life-prolonging procedures was affirmed on direct appeal, the litigation continued because the Schindlers began an attack on the final order. The Schindlers filed a motion for relief from judgment under Florida Rule of Civil Procedure 1.540(b)(2) and (3) in the guardianship court, alleging newly discovered evidence and intrinsic fraud. The Schindlers also filed a separate complaint in the civil division of the circuit court, challenging the final judgment of the guardianship court. *See In re Guardianship of Schiavo*, 792 So. 2d 551, 555-56 (Fla. 2d DCA 2001) (*Schiavo II*).

The trial court determined that the post-judgment motion was untimely and the Schindlers appealed. The Second District agreed that the guardianship court had appropriately denied the rule 1.540(b)(2) and (3) motion as untimely. *See Schiavo II*, 792 So. 2d at 558. The Second District also reversed an injunction entered in the case pending before the civil division of the circuit court. *See id.* at 562. However, the Second District determined that the Schindlers, as "interested parties," had standing to file either a motion for relief from judgment under Florida Rule of Civil Procedure 1.540(b)(5) or an independent action in the guardianship court to challenge the judgment on the ground that it is "no longer equitable for the trial court to enforce its earlier order." *Schiavo II*, 792 So. 2d at 560 (quotation marks omitted). Nonetheless, the Second District pointedly cautioned that any proceeding to challenge a final order on this basis is extraordinary and should not be filed merely to delay an order with which an interested party disagrees or to retry an adversary proceeding. The interested party must establish that new circumstances make it no longer equitable to enforce the earlier order. In this case, if the Schindlers believe a valid basis for relief from the order exists, they must plead and prove newly discovered evidence of such a substantial nature that it proves either (1) that Mrs. Schiavo would not have made the decision to withdraw life-prolonging procedures fourteen months earlier when the final order was entered, or (2) that Mrs. Schiavo would make a different decision at this time based on developments subsequent to the earlier court order. *Id.* at 554.

On remand, the Schindlers filed a timely motion for relief from judgment pursuant to Rule 1.540(b)(5). *See In re Guardianship of Schiavo*, 800 So. 2d 640, 642 (Fla. 2d DCA 2001) (*Schiavo III*). The trial court summarily denied the motion but the Second District reversed and remanded to the guardianship court for the purpose of conducting a limited evidentiary hearing:

> Of the four issues resolved in the original trial. . . , we conclude that the motion establishes a colorable entitlement only as to the fourth issue. As to that issue — whether there was clear and convincing evidence to support the determination that Mrs. Schiavo would choose to withdraw the life-prolonging procedures — the motion for relief from judgment alleges evidence of a new treatment that could dramatically improve Mrs. Schiavo's condition and allow her to have cognitive function to the level of speech. In our last opinion we stated that the Schindlers had "presented no medical evidence suggesting that any new treatment could restore to Mrs. Schiavo a level of function within the cerebral cortex that would allow her to understand her perceptions of sight and sound or to communicate or respond cognitively to those perceptions." *Schiavo II*, 792 So. 2d at 560. Although we have expressed some lay skepticism about the new affidavits, the Schindlers now have presented some evidence, in the form of the affidavit of Dr. [Fred] Webber, of such a potential new treatment. *Id.* at 645.

The Second District permitted the Schindlers to present evidence to establish by a preponderance of the evidence that the judgment was no longer equitable and specifically held:

> To meet this burden, they must establish that new treatment offers sufficient promise of increased cognitive function in Mrs. Schiavo's cerebral cortex-significantly improving the quality of Mrs. Schiavo's life-so that she herself would elect to undergo this treatment and would reverse the prior decision to withdraw life-prolonging procedures.

Id. The Second District required an additional set of medical examinations of Theresa and instructed that one of the physicians must be a new, independent physician selected either by the agreement of the parties or, if they could not agree, by the appointment of the guardianship court. *See id.* at 646.

After conducting a hearing for the purpose set forth in the Second District's decision, the guardianship court denied the Schindlers' motion for relief from judgment. *See In re Guardianship of Schiavo*, 851 So. 2d 182, 183 (Fla. 2d DCA 2003) (*Schiavo IV*). In reviewing the trial court's order, the Second District explained that it was "not reviewing a final judgment in this appellate proceeding. The final judgment was entered several years ago and has already been affirmed by this court." *Id.* at 185-86. However, the Second District carefully examined the record:

> Despite our decision that the appropriate standard of review is abuse of discretion, this court has closely examined all of the evidence in this record. We have repeatedly examined the videotapes, not merely watching short segments but carefully observing the tapes in their entirety. We have examined the brain scans with the eyes of educated laypersons and considered the explanations provided by the doctors in the transcripts. We have concluded that, if we were called upon to review the guardianship court's decision de novo, we would still affirm it.

Id. at 186. Finally, the Second District concluded its fourth opinion in the Schiavo case with the following observation:

> But in the end, this case is not about the aspirations that loving parents have for their children. It is about Theresa Schiavo's right to make her own decision, independent of her parents and independent of her husband. . . . It may be unfortunate that when families cannot agree, the best forum we can offer for this private, personal decision is a public courtroom and the best decision-maker we can provide is a judge with no prior knowledge of the ward, but the law currently provides no better solution that adequately protects the interests of promoting the value of life. We have previously affirmed the guardianship court's decision in this regard, and we now affirm the denial of a motion for relief from that judgment.

Id. at 186-87. We denied review, *see In re Guardianship of Schiavo*, 855 So. 2d 621 (Fla. 2003), and Theresa's nutrition and hydration tube was removed on October 15, 2003.

On October 21, 2003, the Legislature enacted chapter 2003-418, the Governor signed the Act into law, and the Governor issued executive order No. 03-201 to stay the continued withholding of nutrition and hydration from Theresa. The nutrition and hydration tube was reinserted pursuant to the Governor's executive order.

On the same day, Michael Schiavo brought the action for declaratory judgment in the circuit court. Relying on undisputed facts and legal argument, the circuit court entered a final summary judgment on May 6, 2004, in favor of Michael Schiavo, finding the Act unconstitutional both on its face and as applied to Theresa. Specifically, the circuit court found that chapter 2003-418 was unconstitutional on its face as an unlawful delegation of legislative authority and as a violation of the right to privacy, and unconstitutional as applied because it allowed the Governor to encroach upon the judicial power and to retroactively abolish Theresa's vested right to privacy.

ANALYSIS

We begin our discussion by emphasizing that our task in this case is to review the constitutionality of chapter 2003-418, not to reexamine the guardianship court's orders directing the removal of Theresa's nutrition and hydration tube, or to review the Second District's numerous decisions in the guardianship case. Although we recognize that the parties continue to dispute the findings made in the prior proceedings, these proceedings are relevant to our decision only to the extent that they occurred and resulted in a final judgment directing the withdrawal of life-prolonging procedures.

The language of chapter 2003-418 is clear. It states in full:

Section 1. (1) The Governor shall have the authority to issue a one-time stay to prevent the withholding of nutrition and hydration from a patient if, as of October 15, 2003:

(a) That patient has no written advance directive;

(b) The court has found that patient to be in a persistent vegetative state;

(c) That patient has had nutrition and hydration withheld; and

(d) A member of that patient's family has challenged the withholding of nutrition and hydration.

(2) The Governor's authority to issue the stay expires 15 days after the effective date of this act, and the expiration of the authority does not impact the validity or the effect of any stay issued pursuant to this act. The Governor may lift the stay authorized under this act at any time. A person may not be held civilly liable and is not subject to regulatory or disciplinary sanctions for taking any action to comply with a stay issued by the Governor pursuant to this act.

(3) Upon issuance of a stay, the chief judge of the circuit court shall appoint a guardian ad litem for the patient to make recommendations to the Governor and the court.

Section 2. This act shall take effect upon becoming a law.

Ch. 2003-418, LAWS OF FLA. Thus, chapter 2003-418 allowed the Governor to issue a stay to prevent the withholding of nutrition and hydration from a patient under the circumstances provided for in subsections (1)(a)-(d). Under the fifteen-day sunset provision, the Governor's authority to issue the stay expired on November 5, 2003. *See id.* The Governor's authority to lift the stay continues indefinitely.

SEPARATION OF POWERS

The cornerstone of American democracy known as separation of powers recognizes three separate branches of government — the executive, the legislative, and the judicial — each with its own powers and responsibilities. In Florida, the constitutional doctrine has been expressly codified in article II, section 3 of the Florida Constitution, which not only divides state government into three branches but also expressly prohibits one branch from exercising the powers of the other two branches:

Branches of Government. — The powers of the state government shall be divided into legislative, executive and judicial branches. No person belonging to one branch shall exercise any powers appertaining to either of the other branches unless expressly provided herein.

"This Court . . . has traditionally applied a strict separation of powers doctrine," *State v. Cotton*, 769 So. 2d 345, 353 (Fla. 2000), and has explained that this doctrine "encompasses two fundamental prohibitions. The first is that no branch may encroach upon the powers of another. The second is that no branch may delegate to another branch its constitutionally assigned power." *Chiles v. Children A, B, C, D, E & F*, 589 So. 2d 260, 264 (Fla. 1991) (citation omitted).

The circuit court found that chapter 2003-418 violates both of these prohibitions, and we address each separately below. Our standard of review is de novo. *See Major League Baseball v. Morsani*, 790 So. 2d 1071, 1074 (Fla. 2001) (stating that a trial court's ruling on a motion for summary judgment posing a pure question of law is subject to de novo review).

Encroachment on the Judicial Branch

We begin by addressing the argument that, as applied to Theresa Schiavo, the Act encroaches on the power and authority of the judicial branch. More than 140 years ago this Court explained the foundation of Florida's express separation of powers provision:

The framers of the Constitution of Florida, doubtless, had in mind the omnipotent power often exercised by the British Parliament, the exercise of judicial power by the Legislature in those States where there are no written Constitutions restraining them, when they wisely prohibited the exercise of such powers in our State.

That Convention was composed of men of the best legal minds in the country — men of experience and skilled in the law — who had witnessed the breaking down by unrestrained legislation all the security of property derived from contract, the divesting of vested rights by doing away the force of the law as decided, the overturning of solemn decisions of the Courts of the last resort, by, under the pretence of remedial acts, enacting for one or the other party litigants such provisions as would dictate to the judiciary their decision, and leaving everything which should be expounded by the judiciary to the variable and ever-changing mind of the popular branch of the Government. *Trustees Internal Improvement Fund v. Bailey*, 10 Fla. 238, 250 (1863). Similarly, the framers of the United States Constitution recognized the need to establish a judiciary independent of the legislative branch. Indeed, the desire to prevent Congress from using its power to interfere with the judgments of the courts was one of the primary motivations for the separation of powers established at this nation's founding:

> This sense of a sharp necessity to separate the legislative from the judicial power, prompted by the crescendo of legislative interference with private judgments of the courts, triumphed among the Framers of the new Federal Constitution. The Convention made the critical decision to establish a judicial department independent of the Legislative Branch. . . . Before and during the debates on ratification, Madison, Jefferson, and Hamilton each wrote of the factional disorders and disarray that the system of legislative equity had produced in the years before the framing; and each thought that the separation of the legislative from the judicial power in the new Constitution would cure them. Madison's Federalist No. 48, the famous description of the process by which "[t]he legislative department is every where extending the sphere of its activity, and drawing all power into its impetuous vortex," referred to the report of the Pennsylvania Council of Censors to show that in that State "cases belonging to the judiciary department [had been] frequently drawn within legislative cognizance and determination." Madison relied as well on Jefferson's Notes on the State of Virginia, which mentioned, as one example of the dangerous concentration of governmental powers into the hands of the legislature, that "the Legislature . . . in many instances decided rights which should have been left to judiciary controversy."

Plaut v. Spendthrift Farm, Inc., 514 U.S. 211, 221-22, 115 S. Ct. 1447, 131 L. Ed. 2d 328 (1995) (citations omitted).

Under the express separation of powers provision in our state constitution, "the judiciary is a coequal branch of the Florida government vested with the sole authority to exercise the judicial power," and "the legislature cannot, short of constitutional amendment, reallocate the balance of power expressly delineated in the constitution among the three coequal branches." *Children A, B, C, D, E & F*, 589 So. 2d at 268-69; *see also Office of State Attorney v. Parrotino*, 628 So. 2d 1097, 1099 (Fla. 1993) ("[T]he legislature cannot take actions that would undermine the independence of Florida's judicial . . . offices.").

As the United States Supreme Court has explained, the power of the judiciary is "not merely to rule on cases, but to decide them, subject to review only by superior courts" and "[h]aving achieved finality . . . a judicial decision becomes the last word of the judicial department with regard to a particular case or controversy." *Plaut*, 514 U.S. at 218-19, 227, 115 S. Ct. 1447. Moreover, "purely judicial acts . . . are not subject to review as to their accuracy by the Governor." *In re Advisory Opinion to the Governor*, 213 So. 2d 716, 720 (Fla. 1968); see also *Children A, B, C, D, E & F*, 589 So. 2d at 269 ("The judicial branch cannot be subject in any manner to oversight by the executive branch.").

In *Advisory Opinion*, the Governor asked the Court whether he had the "constitutional authority to review the judicial accuracy and propriety of [a judge] and to suspend him from office if it does not appear . . . that the Judge has exercised proper judicial discretion and wisdom." 213 So. 2d at 718. The Court agreed that the Governor had the authority to suspend a judge on the grounds of incompetency "if the physical or mental incompetency is established and determined within the Judicial Branch by a court of competent jurisdiction." *Id.* at 720. However, the Court held that the Governor did not have the power to "review the judicial discretion and wisdom of a . . . Judge while he is engaged in the judicial process." *Id.* The Court explained that article V of the Florida Constitution provides for appellate review for the benefit of litigants aggrieved by the decisions of the lower court, and that "[a]ppeal is the exclusive remedy." *Id.*

In this case, the undisputed facts show that the guardianship court authorized Michael to proceed with the discontinuance of Theresa's life support after the issue was fully litigated in a proceeding in which the Schindlers were afforded the opportunity to present evidence on all issues. This order as well as the order denying the Schindlers' motion for relief from judgment were affirmed on direct appeal. *See Schiavo I*, 780 So. 2d at 177; *Schiavo IV*, 851 So. 2d at 183.

The Schindlers sought review in this Court, which was denied. Thereafter, the tube was removed. Subsequently, pursuant to the Governor's executive order, the nutrition and hydration tube was reinserted. Thus, the Act, as applied in this case, resulted in an executive order that effectively reversed a properly rendered final judgment and thereby constituted an unconstitutional encroachment on the power that has been reserved for the independent judiciary. *Cf. Bailey*, 10 Fla. at 249-50 (noting that had the statute under review "directed a rehearing, the hearing of the case would necessarily carry with it the right to set aside the judgment of the Court, and there would be unquestionably an exercise of judicial power").

The Governor and amici assert that the Act does not reverse a final court order because an order to discontinue life-prolonging procedures may be challenged at any time prior to the death of the ward. In advancing this argument, the Governor and amici rely on the Second District's conclusion that as long as the ward is alive, an order discontinuing life-prolonging procedures "is subject to recall and is executory in nature." *Schiavo II*, 792 So. 2d at 559. However, the Second District did not hold that the guardianship court's order was not a final judgment but, rather, that the Schindlers, as interested parties, could file a motion for relief from judgment under Florida Rule of Civil Procedure 1.540(b)(5) if they sufficiently alleged that it is no longer equitable that the judgment have prospective application. *See id.* at 561. Rule 1.540(b) expressly states that a motion filed pursuant to its terms "does not affect the finality of a judgment." Further, the fact that a final judgment may be subject to recall under a rule of procedure, if certain circumstances can be proved, does not negate its finality. Unless and until the judgment is vacated by judicial order, it is "the last word of the judicial department with regard to a particular case or controversy." *Plaut*, 514 U.S. at 227, 115 S. Ct. 1447.

Under procedures enacted by the Legislature, effective both before the passage of the Act and after its fifteen-day effective period expired, circuit courts are charged with adjudicating issues regarding incompetent individuals. The trial courts of this State are called upon to make many of the most difficult decisions facing society. In proceedings under chapter 765, Florida Statutes (2003), these decisions literally affect the lives or deaths of patients. The trial courts also handle other weighty decisions affecting the welfare of children such as termination of parental rights and child custody. *See* § 61.13(2)(b)(1), FLA. STAT. (2003) ("The court shall determine all matters relating to custody of each minor child of the parties in accordance with the best interests of the child and in accordance with the Uniform Child Custody Jurisdiction and Enforcement Act."); § 39.801(2), FLA. STAT. (2003) ("The circuit court shall have exclusive original jurisdiction of a proceeding involving termination of parental rights."). When the prescribed procedures are followed according to our rules of court and the governing statutes, a final judgment is issued, and all post-judgment procedures are followed, it is without question an invasion of the authority of the judicial branch for the Legislature to pass a law that allows the executive branch to interfere with the final judicial determination in a case. That is precisely what occurred here and for that reason the Act is unconstitutional as applied to Theresa Schiavo.

Delegation of Legislative Authority

In addition to concluding that the Act is unconstitutional as applied in this case because it encroaches on the power of the judicial branch, we further conclude that the Act is unconstitutional on its face because it delegates legislative power to the Governor. The Legislature is permitted to transfer subordinate functions "to permit administration of legislative policy by an agency with the expertise and flexibility to deal with complex and fluid conditions." *Microtel, Inc. v. Fla. Public Serv. Comm'n*, 464 So. 2d 1189, 1191 (Fla. 1985). However, under article II, section 3 of the constitution the Legislature "may not delegate the power to enact a law or the right to exercise unrestricted discretion in applying the law." *Sims v. State*, 754 So. 2d 657, 668 (Fla. 2000). This prohibition, known as the nondelegation doctrine, requires that "fundamental and primary policy decisions . . . be made by members of the legislature who are elected to perform those tasks, and [that the] administration of legislative programs must be pursuant to some minimal standards and guidelines ascertainable by reference to the enactment establishing the program." *Askew v. Cross Key Waterways*, 372 So. 2d 913, 925 (Fla. 1978); *see also Avatar Dev. Corp. v. State*, 723 So. 2d 199, 202 (Fla. 1998) (citing *Askew* with approval). In other words, statutes granting power to the executive branch "must clearly announce adequate standards to guide . . . in the execution of the powers delegated. The statute must so clearly define the power delegated that the [executive] is precluded from acting through whim, showing favoritism, or exercising unbridled discretion." *Lewis v. Bank of Pasco County*, 346 So. 2d 53, 55-56 (Fla. 1976). The requirement that the Legislature provide sufficient guidelines also ensures the availability of meaningful judicial review:

> In the final analysis it is the courts, upon a challenge to the exercise or nonexercise of administrative action, which must determine whether the administrative agency has performed consistently with the mandate of the legislature. When legislation is so lacking in guidelines that neither the agency nor the courts can determine whether the agency is carrying out the intent of the legislature in its conduct, then, in fact, the agency becomes the lawgiver rather than the administrator of the law.

Askew, 372 So. 2d at 918-19.

We have recognized that the "specificity of the guidelines [set forth in the legislation] will depend on the complexity of the subject and the 'degree of difficulty involved in articulating finite standards.'" *Brown v. Apalachee Regional Planning Council*, 560 So. 2d 782, 784 (Fla. 1990) (quoting *Askew*, 372 So. 2d at 918). However, we have also made clear that "[e]ven where a general approach would be more practical than a detailed scheme of legislation, enactments may not be drafted in terms so general and unrestrictive that administrators are left without standards for the guidance of their official acts." *State Dep't of Citrus v. Griffin*, 239 So. 2d 577, 581 (Fla. 1970).

In both *Askew* and *Lewis*, this Court held that the respective statutes under review violated the nondelegation doctrine because they failed to provide the executive branch with adequate guidelines and criteria. In *Askew*, the Court invalidated a statute that directed the executive branch to designate certain areas of the state as areas of critical state concern but did not contain sufficient standards to allow "a reviewing court to ascertain whether the priorities recognized by the Administration Commission comport with the intent of the legislature." 372 So. 2d at 919. The statute in question enunciated the following criteria for the Division of State Planning to use in identifying a particular area as one of critical state concern:

   (a) An area containing, or having a significant impact upon, environmental, historical, natural, or archaeological resources of regional or statewide importance.

   (b) An area significantly affected by, or having a significant effect upon, an existing or proposed major public facility or other area of major public investment.

   (c) A proposed area of major development potential, which may include a proposed site of a new community, designated in a state land development plan.

Id. at 914-15 (quoting section 380.05(2), FLORIDA STATUTES (1975)). The Court concluded that the criteria for designation of an area of critical concern set forth in subsections (a) and (b) were defective because they gave the executive agency "the fundamental legislative task of determining which geographic areas and resources [were] in greatest need of protection." *Id.* at 919. With regard to subsection (a), this Court agreed with the district court that the deficiency resulted from the Legislature's failure to "establish or provide for establishing priorities or other means for identifying and choosing among the resources the Act is intended to preserve." *Id.* (quoting *Cross Key Waterways v. Askew*, 351 So. 2d 1062, 1069 (Fla. 1st DCA 1977)). Subsection (b) suffered a similar defect by expanding "the choice to include areas which in unstated ways affect or are affected by any 'major public facility' which is defined in Section 380.031(10), or any 'major public investment,' which is not." *Id.*

Lewis involved a statute that gave the state comptroller the unrestricted power to release banking records to the public that were otherwise considered confidential under the Public Records Act. *See* 346 So. 2d at 55. The statute at issue provided in pertinent part:

> Division records. All bank or trust company applications, investigation reports, examination reports, and related information, including any duly authorized copies in possession of any banking organization, foreign banking corporation, or any other person or agency, shall be confidential communications, other than such documents as are required by law to be published, and shall not be made public, unless with the consent of the department, pursuant to a court order, or in response to legislative subpoena as provided by law. *Lewis*, 346 So. 2d at 54 (quoting section 658.10, FLORIDA STATUTES (1975)) (alteration in original). This Court held that the law was "couched in vague and uncertain terms or is so broad in scope that . . . it must be held unconstitutional as attempting to grant to the . . . [comptroller] the power to say what the law shall be." 346 So. 2d at 56 (quoting *Sarasota County v. Barg*, 302 So. 2d 737, 742 (Fla. 1974)) (alterations in original).

In this case, the circuit court found that chapter 2003-418 contains no guidelines or standards that "would serve to limit the Governor from exercising completely unrestricted discretion in applying the law to" those who fall within its terms. The circuit court explained:

> The terms of the Act affirmatively confirm the discretionary power conferred upon the Governor. He is given the "authority to issue a one-time stay to prevent the withholding of nutrition and hydration from a patient" under certain circumstances but, he is not required to do so. Likewise, the act provides that the Governor "may lift the stay authorized under this act at any time. The Governor may revoke the stay upon a finding that a change in the condition of the patient warrants revocation." (Emphasis added). In both instances there is nothing to provide the Governor with any direction or guidelines for the exercise of this delegated authority. The Act does not suggest what constitutes "a change in condition of the patient" that could "warrant revocation." Even when such an undefined "change" occurs, the Governor is not compelled to act. The Act confers upon the Governor the unfettered discretion to determine what the terms of the Act mean and when, or if, he may act under it.

We agree with this analysis. In enacting chapter 2003-418, the Legislature failed to provide any standards by which the Governor should determine whether, in any given case, a stay should be issued and how long a stay should remain in effect. Further, the Legislature has failed to provide any criteria for lifting the stay. This absolute, unfettered discretion to decide whether to issue and then when to lift a stay makes the Governor's decision virtually unreviewable.

The Governor asserts that by enacting chapter 2003-418 the Legislature determined that he should be permitted to act as proxy for an incompetent patient in very narrow circumstances and, therefore, that his discretion is limited by the provisions of chapter 765. However, the Act does not refer to the provisions of chapter 765. Specifically, the Act does not amend section 765.401(1), FLORIDA STATUTES (2003), which sets forth an order of priority for determining who should act as proxy for an incapacitated patient who has no advance directive. Nor does the Act require that the Governor's decision be made in conformity with the requirement of section 765.401 that the proxy's decision be based on "the decision the proxy reasonably believes that patient would have made under the circumstances" or, if there is no indication of what the patient would have chosen, in the patient's best interests. § 765.401(2)-(3), FLA. STAT. (2003). Finally, the Act does not provide for review of the Governor's decision as proxy as required by section 765.105, FLORIDA STATUTES (2003). In short, there is no indication in the language of chapter 2003-418 that the Legislature intended the Governor's discretion to be limited in any way. Even if we were to read chapter 2003-418 *in pari materia* with chapter 765, as the Governor suggests, there is nothing in chapter 765 to guide the Governor's discretion in issuing a stay because chapter 765 does not contemplate that a proxy will have the type of open-ended power delegated to the Governor under the Act.

We also reject the Governor's argument that this legislation provides an additional layer of due process protection to those who are unable to communicate their wishes regarding end-of-life decisions. Parts I, II, III, and IV of chapter 765, enacted by the Legislature in 1992 and amended several times, provide detailed protections for those who are adjudicated incompetent, including that the proxy's decision be based on what the patient would have chosen under the circumstances or is in the patient's best interest, and be supported by competent, substantial evidence. *See* § 765.401(2)-(3). Chapter 765 also provides for judicial review if "[t]he patient's family, the health care facility, or the attending physician, or any other interested person who may reasonably be expected to be directly affected by the surrogate or proxy's decision . . . believes [that] [t]he surrogate or proxy's decision is not in accord with the patient's known desires or the provisions of this chapter." § 765.105(1), FLA. STAT. (2003).

In contrast to the protections set forth in chapter 765, chapter 2003-418's standardless, open-ended delegation of authority by the Legislature to the Governor provides no guarantee that the incompetent patient's right to withdraw life-prolonging procedures will in fact be honored. *See In re Guardianship of Browning*, 568 So. 2d 4, 12 (Fla. 1990) (reaffirming that an incompetent person has the same right to refuse medical treatment as a competent person). As noted above, the Act does not even require that the Governor consider the patient's wishes in deciding whether to issue a stay, and instead allows a unilateral decision by the Governor to stay the withholding of life-prolonging procedures without affording any procedural process to the patient.

Finally, we reject the Governor's argument that the Legislature's grant of authority to issue the stay under chapter 2003-418 is a valid exercise of the state's parens patriae power. Although unquestionably the Legislature may enact laws to protect those citizens who are incapable of protecting their own interests, *see, e.g., In re Byrne*, 402 So. 2d 383 (Fla. 1981), such laws must comply with the constitution. Chapter 2003-418 fails to do so.

Moreover, the argument that the Act broadly protects those who cannot protect themselves is belied by the case-specific criteria under which the Governor can exercise his discretion. The Act applies only if a court has found the individual to be in a persistent vegetative state and food and hydration have been ordered withdrawn. It does not authorize the Governor to intervene if a person in a persistent vegetative state is dependent upon another form of life support. Nor does the Act apply to a person who is not in a persistent vegetative state but a court finds, contrary to the wishes of another family member, that life support should be withdrawn. In theory, the Act could have applied during its fifteen-day window to more than one person, but it is undeniable that in fact the criteria fit only Theresa Schiavo.

In sum, although chapter 2003-418 applies to a limited class of people, it provides no criteria to guide the Governor's decision about whether to act. In addition, once the Governor has issued a stay as provided for in the Act, there are no criteria for the Governor to evaluate in deciding whether to lift the stay. Thus, chapter 2003-418 allows the Governor to act "through whim, show [] favoritism, or exercis[e] unbridled discretion," *Lewis*, 346 So. 2d at 56, and is therefore an unconstitutional delegation of legislative authority.

CONCLUSION

We recognize that the tragic circumstances underlying this case make it difficult to put emotions aside and focus solely on the legal issue presented. We are not insensitive to the struggle that all members of Theresa's family have endured since she fell unconscious in 1990. However, we are a nation of laws and we must govern our decisions by the rule of law and not by our own emotions. Our hearts can fully comprehend the grief so fully demonstrated by Theresa's family members on this record. But our hearts are not the law. What is in the Constitution always must prevail over emotion. Our oaths as judges require that this principle is our polestar, and it alone.

As the Second District noted in one of the multiple appeals in this case, we "are called upon to make a collective, objective decision concerning a question of law. Each of us, however, has our own family, our own loved ones, our own children. . . . But in the end, this case is not about the aspirations that loving parents have for their children." *Schiavo IV*, 851 So. 2d at 186. Rather, as our decision today makes clear, this case is about maintaining the integrity of a constitutional system of government with three independent and coequal branches, none of which can either encroach upon the powers of another branch or improperly delegate its own responsibilities.

The continuing vitality of our system of separation of powers precludes the other two branches from nullifying the judicial branch's final orders. If the Legislature with the assent of the Governor can do what was attempted here, the judicial branch would be subordinated to the final directive of the other branches. Also subordinated would be the rights of individuals, including the well established privacy right to self determination. *See Browning*, 568 So. 2d at 11-13. No court judgment could ever be considered truly final and no constitutional right truly secure, because the precedent of this case would hold to the contrary. Vested rights could be stripped away based on popular clamor. The essential core of what the Founding Fathers sought to change from their experience with English rule would be lost, especially their belief that our courts exist precisely to preserve the rights of individuals, even when doing so is contrary to popular will.

The trial court's decision regarding Theresa Schiavo was made in accordance with the procedures and protections set forth by the judicial branch and in accordance with the statutes passed by the Legislature in effect at that time. That decision is final and the Legislature's attempt to alter that final adjudication is unconstitutional as applied to Theresa Schiavo. Further, even if there had been no final judgment in this case, the Legislature provided the Governor constitutionally inadequate standards for the application of the legislative authority delegated in chapter 2003-418. Because chapter 2003-418 runs afoul of article II, section 3 of the Florida Constitution in both respects, we affirm the circuit court's final summary judgment.

It is so ordered.

WELLS, ANSTEAD, LEWIS, QUINCE, CANTERO and BELL, JJ., concur.

* * *

Bush v. Schiavo did not put an end to the controversy around surrounding whether Terri Schiavo had expressed her wishes concerning end-of-life matters. On March 21, 2005, the Congress of the United States entered the fray over Terri Schiavo, enacting the following bill.

Public Law 109-3
109th Congress, 1st Sess.
(March 21, 2005)

An Act for the relief of the parents of Theresa Marie Schiavo.

Be it enacted by the Senate and House of Representatives of the United States of America in Congress assembled,

SECTION 1. RELIEF OF THE PARENTS OF THERESA MARIE SCHIAVO.

The United States District Court for the Middle District of Florida shall have jurisdiction to hear, determine, and render judgment on a suit or claim by or on behalf of Theresa Marie Schiavo for the alleged violation of any right of Theresa Marie Schiavo under the Constitution or laws of the United States relating to the withholding or withdrawal of food, fluids, or medical treatment necessary to sustain her life.

SEC. 2. PROCEDURE.

Any parent of Theresa Marie Schiavo shall have standing to bring a suit under this Act. The suit may be brought against any other person who was a party to State court proceedings relating to the withholding or withdrawal of food, fluids, or medical treatment necessary to sustain the life of Theresa Marie Schiavo, or who may act pursuant to a State court order authorizing or directing the withholding or withdrawal of food, fluids, or medical treatment necessary to sustain her life. In such a suit, the District Court shall determine de novo any claim of a violation of any right of Theresa Marie Schiavo within the scope of this Act, notwithstanding any prior State court determination and regardless of whether such a claim has previously been raised, considered, or decided in State court proceedings. The District Court shall entertain and determine the suit without any delay or abstention in favor of State court proceedings, and regardless of whether remedies available in the State courts have been exhausted.

SEC. 3. RELIEF.

After a determination of the merits of a suit brought under this Act, the District Court shall issue such declaratory and injunctive relief as may be necessary to protect the rights of Theresa Marie Schiavo under the Constitution and laws of the United States relating to the withholding or withdrawal of food, fluids, or medical treatment necessary to sustain her life.

SEC. 4. TIME FOR FILING.

Notwithstanding any other time limitation, any suit or claim under this Act shall be timely if filed within 30 days after the date of enactment of this Act.

SEC. 5. NO CHANGE OF SUBSTANTIVE RIGHTS.

Nothing in this Act shall be construed to create substantive rights not otherwise secured by the Constitution and laws of the United States or of the several States.

SEC. 6. NO EFFECT ON ASSISTING SUICIDE.

Nothing in this Act shall be construed to confer additional jurisdiction on any court to consider any claim related —

(1) to assisting suicide, or

(2) a State law regarding assisting suicide.

SEC. 7. NO PRECEDENT FOR FUTURE LEGISLATION.

Nothing in this Act shall constitute a precedent with respect to future legislation, including the provision of private relief bills.

SEC. 8. NO AFFECT ON THE PATIENT SELF-DETERMINATION ACT OF 1990.

Nothing in this Act shall affect the rights of any person under the Patient Self-Determination Act of 1990.

SEC. 9. SENSE OF THE CONGRESS.

It is the Sense of Congress that the 109th Congress should consider policies regarding the status and legal rights of incapacitated individuals who are incapable of making decisions concerning the provision, withholding, or withdrawal of foods, fluid, or medical care.

Approved March 21, 2005.

* * *

NOTES AND QUESTIONS

1. The federal legislation set out above permitted a fresh round of expedited litigation in federal court, but in the end the state court's decision to permit withdrawal of Terri Schiavo's feeding tube was allowed to stand, and ten days after her feeding tube was withdrawn, Terri Schiavo died. Sixteen years elapsed between the time of the incident the precipitated her condition to her death. The battle over who would manage her end-of-life treatment lasted almost seven years.

2. An excellent account of the events surrounding Terri Schiavo's life and death, and their aftermath, is available at Abstract Appeal, The Terri Schiavo Information Page, http://abstractappeal.com/schiavo/infopage.html.

3. Should states or the federal government be primarily responsible for regulating in the area of end-of-life decision-making?

2. Statutory Considerations

Read the Patient Self-Determination Act of 1990, Pub. L. 101-408 § 4206(a)(2), in the statutory supplement (codified at 42 U.S.C. § 1395cc(f)(1)-(4)).

Michigan Department of Public Health
Bureau of Health Systems
Michigan Notice to Patients Required by the Patient Self Determination Act
(November 1991)

http://bhs.msu.edu/mnp.htm#Notice

YOUR RIGHTS TO MAKE MEDICAL TREATMENT DECISIONS

We are giving you this material to tell you about your right to make your own decisions about your medical treatment. As a competent adult, you have the right to accept or refuse any medical treatment. "Competent" means you have the ability to understand your medical condition and the medical treatments for it, to weigh the possible benefits and risks of each such treatment and then to decide whether you want to accept treatment or not.

WHO DECIDES WHAT TREATMENT I WILL GET?

As long as you are competent, you are the only person who can decide what medical treatment you want to accept or reject. You will be given information and advice about the pros and cons of different kinds of treatment and you can ask questions about your options. But only you can say "yes" or "no" to any treatment offered. You can say "no" even if the treatment you refuse might keep you alive longer and even if others want you to have it.

WHAT IF I'M IN NO CONDITION TO DECIDE?

If you become unable to make your own decisions about medical care, decisions will have to be made for you. If you haven't given prior instructions, no one will know what you would want. There may be difficult questions: for instance, would you refuse treatment if you were unconscious and not likely to wake up? Would you refuse treatment if you were going to die soon no matter what? Would you want to receive any treatment your care givers recommend? When your wishes are not known, your family or the courts may have to decide what to do.

WHAT CAN I DO NOW TO SEE THAT MY WISHES ARE HONORED IN THE FUTURE?

While you are competent, you can name someone to make medical treatment decisions for you should you ever be unable to make them for yourself. To be certain that the person you name has the legal right to make those decisions, you must fill out a form called either a durable power of attorney for health care or a Patient Advocate Designation. The person named in the form to make or carry out your decisions about treatment is called a Patient Advocate. You have the right to give your Patient Advocate, your care givers and your family and friends written or spoken instructions about what medical treatment you want and don't want to receive.

WHO CAN BE MY PATIENT ADVOCATE?

You can choose anyone to be your Patient Advocate as long as the person is at least 18 years old. You can pick a family member or a friend or any other person you trust, but you should make sure that person is willing to serve by signing an acceptance form. It's a good idea to name a backup choice, too, just in case the first person is unwilling or unable to act when the time comes.

WHERE CAN I GET A PATIENT ADVOCATE DESIGNATION FORM?

Many Michigan hospitals, health maintenance organizations, nursing homes, homes for the aged, hospices and home health care agencies make forms available to people free of charge. Many senior citizens' groups and church and civic groups do, too. You can also get a free form from various members of the Michigan legislature. Many lawyers also prepare Patient Advocate Designations for their clients. The forms aren't all alike. You should pick the one which suits your situation the best.

HOW DO I SIGN A PATIENT ADVOCATE DESIGNATION FORM SO THAT IT'S VALID?

All you have to do is fill in the name of the advocate and sign the form in front of two witnesses. But that's not as simple as it sounds, because under this law some people cannot be your witnesses. Your spouse, parents, grandchildren, children, and brothers or sisters, for example, cannot witness your signature. Neither can anyone else who could be your heir or who is named to receive something in your will, or who is an employee of a company that insures your life or health. Finally, the law disqualifies the person you name as your Patient Advocate, your doctors and all employees of the facility or agency providing health care to you from being a witness to your signature.

It is easier to make a Patient Advocate Designation before you become a patient or resident of a health care facility or agency. Friends or co-workers are often good people to ask to be witnesses, since they see you often and can, if necessary, swear that you acted voluntarily and were of sound mind when you made out the form.

DO I HAVE TO GIVE MY PATIENT ADVOCATE INSTRUCTIONS?

No. A Patient Advocate Designation can be used just to name your Patient Advocate, the person you want to make decisions for you. But written instructions are generally helpful to everybody involved. And, if you want your Patient Advocate to be able to refuse treatment and let you die, you have to say so specifically in the Patient Advocate Designation document itself. Any other instructions you have you can either write down or just tell your Patient Advocate. Either way, the Patient Advocate's job is to follow your instructions.

CAN I JUST GIVE INSTRUCTIONS AND NOT NAME A PATIENT ADVOCATE?

Yes, you can simply tell somebody, for example, your care giver or your family and close friends, what your wishes are. Better yet, you can write what is called a "Living Will," which is a written statement of your choices about medical treatment. Even though there is not yet a state Living Will law, courts and health care providers still find Living Wills valuable. Those taking care of you will pay more attention to what you have written about your treatment choices, whether in a Patient Advocate Designation or a Living Will, because they can be more confident they know what you would have wanted. Most doctors, hospitals and other health care providers will also pay attention to what you've said to others, especially your family, about medical treatment. But again, it's better for everyone involved if you write your wishes down.

DO I HAVE TO MAKE A DECISION NOW ABOUT MY FUTURE MEDICAL TREATMENT?

No. You don't have to fill out a Patient Advocate Designation or a Living Will and you don't have to tell anybody your wishes about medical treatment. You will still get the medical treatment you choose now, while you are competent. If you become unable to make decisions, but you've made sure that your family and friends know what you would want, they will be able to follow your wishes. Without instructions from you, your family or friends and care givers may still be able to agree how to proceed. If they don't, however, a court may have to name a guardian to make decisions for you.

IF I MAKE DECISIONS NOW, CAN I CHANGE MY MIND LATER?

Yes. You can give new instructions in writing or orally. You can also change your mind about naming a Patient Advocate at all and cancel a Patient Advocate Designation at any time.

You should review your Patient Advocate Designation or Living Will at least once a year to make sure it still accurately states how you want to be treated and/or names the person you want to make decisions for you.

WHAT ELSE SHOULD I THINK ABOUT?

Treatment decisions are difficult. We encourage you to think about them in advance and discuss them with your family, friends, advisors and care givers. You can and should ask your facility or agency about their treatment policies and procedures to be sure you understand them and how they work.

If you want more information about a Patient Advocate Designation or Living Wills, or sample forms, please ask your care givers for assistance. Many facilities and agencies have staff available who can answer your qustions. Additional materials may be available from your state representative or senator.

Washington State Department of
Social and Health Services
Aging and Adult Services Administration
Your Legal Right To Make Decisions About Health Care
and Your Legal Right to Make Decisions About Health
Care and Advance Directives in Washington State **(1999)**
http://www1.dshs.wa.gov/pdf/Publications/22-015.pdf

These materials were developed as a general guide and are not intended as legal advice.

The information in this brochure contains Washington State Law. DSHS Aging and Adult Services Administration convened the Task Force on the Patient Self-Determination Act to develop this brochure. The Task Force included advocates, lawyers, nursing home administrators, nursing home residents, and state employees.

The Patient Self-Determination Act

All adults receiving health care have certain rights. For example, you have a right to confidentiality of your personal and medical records and to know about and consent to the services and treatment you may receive. This booklet answers some questions related to a federal law called "The Patient Self Determination Act" (PSDA). This law says that certain health care providers must give each consumer information about the right to make choices about their health care. Each health care provider is required to give you information about making health care decisions in advance (advance directives) and information about your legal choices in making decisions about your health care under Washington State law.

Health care providers covered by the PSDA are:

- Hospitals
- Nursing homes
- Hospices
- Home health care
- Personal care programs
- Health maintenance organizations (HMOs)
- Residential Habilitation Centers
- Adult Family Homes
- Psychiatric hospitals or facilities
- Mental health providers
- Boarding Homes
- Other care facilities licensed in Washington State

This brochure can help you make decisions in advance of treatment. Because these are important matters, you may want to talk with family, close friends, clergy, your attorney, or your doctor before deciding if you want an advance directive.

Introduction

You have the right to make choices about your medical care. When you enter a long-term care facility (such as a nursing home, boarding home, or adult family home) or receive services, such as personal care services, you may face some tough, very important decisions. Other people may give you advice, but remember the decision is yours. No matter where you live, you still have the right to control your health care. No one — a doctor, nurse, or family member — can force you to accept treatment, services, or medicines, except in limited circumstances.

In this booklet, you will learn about:

- Your right to make decisions about your own medical care;
- Informed Consent;
- Advance Directives, including:
- Living Will (Health Care Directive)
- Durable Power of Attorney for Health Care
- Code/No Code or Do Not Resuscitate (DNR)
- Organ or tissue donation

What Is Informed Consent?

Informed consent is a process of communication between you and your health care provider and/or your doctor. It is your right to make decisions about what care or treatment is to be done to your body. You must be given oral or written information about what could happen to you if you accept or refuse the treatment your doctor or health care provider is suggesting. This information must include other possible forms of treatment and the possible complications and expected benefits involved in the treatment.

If you are asked to sign a form to consent or to document your refusal of medical treatment, make sure you clearly understand your choices before signing. You can refuse treatment and you can refuse to sign a document.

According to Washington State law, you have the right to tell your doctor that you do not want to be told of the risks and benefits of medical treatments.

Is informed consent necessary if I live in a long-term care facility?

Yes. It does not matter where you live or whether your stay is temporary or permanent. You have the right to control your care and medical treatment.

How will I know what treatment I want?

Your doctor and/or health care provider must tell you about your options when your doctor suggests a new treatment or a significant change in your treatment. The law requires that the following be explained to you:

- Your medical condition

- The purpose of the treatment

- Why you need the treatment

- What the treatment is expected to do for your condition

- What could or will happen if you choose not to have the treatment

- What could or will happen if you choose to have the treatment

- Other possible treatments you could choose and their risks and benefits

After you know all about the suggested treatment, you can decide (informed consent). Before making such a decision, you have the right to discuss the treatment with your family, a different doctor, a close friend, clergy, a family lawyer, or anyone else with whom you feel comfortable.

Does my health care provider have to tell me every time it wants to change my medical treatment?

Yes. Each time a physician/healthcare provider suggests new treatment, a different medication, surgery, or other medical procedure that may significantly impact your health care, you must be given the information to help you make an informed choice. You stay in control.

How do I tell my health care provider what I want?

You should tell your health care provider your decision after you have all the information to make a choice. You can put your decision in writing and ask that it go in your medical file. You also have the right to read your medical file to be sure your decisions are recorded.

Can I refuse medical treatment?

Yes. You have the right to decide not to accept medical treatment after you have been told the risks and benefits. You also have the right to decide that you do not want to be told of any potential risks of medical treatment.

Can I refuse to be tied into a chair or bed; can I refuse medication that makes me sleepy?

Yes. Devices such as poseybelts, seat belts, hand mitts, and bed rails are called physical restraints. Some medications which make you sleepy are called chemical restraints. Just like any other medical treatment, you may refuse the use of these devices. In many long-term care settings, restraints cannot be used at all. In some settings, restraints can only be used with your informed consent and under very limited circumstances.

What if I am unable to give consent for health care?

If a medical decision is necessary and you are unable to give consent for treatment, the following people (surrogates) can give consent or refuse consent for medical care on your behalf. The law identifies who will be your surrogate decision-maker by using the list below. The surrogate(s) must be considered in the specific order from the following list:

1. Your guardian with health care authority; if none then

2. Your agent under a Durable Power of Attorney for Health Care; if none then

3. Your spouse; if none then

4. Your adult children; if none then

5. Your parents; if none then

6. Your adult siblings; if none, a guardian may be necessary.

The listed order must be followed. The health care provider may not "jump" a group, add another category to the list (such as nieces), or not recognize the decision of an appropriate decision-maker. If there is more than one person in a group (for example, several adult children) they must all agree on the decision. If agreement can not be reached it may be necessary to ask the court to appoint a guardian.

The consenting group member(s) must try to do what you would want done. If they do not know, they must do what they think is in your best interest.

In an emergency, if you are unable to give informed consent and have not made an advance directive, and the treatment is life-saving, your consent to treatment is implied.

What if my health care provider and I disagree?

You can still make your health care decisions. If you are refusing to consent, you may continue to refuse, and the doctor/healthcare provider must follow your decision. The court might be in the best position to determine whether you have the capacity to choose.

What if I do not have a surrogate to make the necessary decision?

Washington State law requires each healthcare provider to have policies and procedures that explain what will be done if you are not capable of making a decision. The superior court is responsible for determining who should make health care decisions for you if you become mentally incapacitated and do not have access to assistance from a surrogate. You should ask to see the facility's policies.

What Is an Advance Directive?

Advance Directives are instructions (directive) written to a health care provider, before (in advance) the need for medical treatment. An Advance Directive anticipates that an illness or accident may happen in the future which would make it impossible to consent to medical treatment at the time it is needed. Some Advance Directives are specific to terminal illness or a permanent unconscious state. In Washington the following Advance Directives are common:

- Living Will (also known as a Health Care Directive);

- Durable Power of Attorney for Health Care;

- Code/No Code or Do Not Resuscitate (DNR);

- Anatomical Gifts

What Is a Living Will (or Health Care Directive)?

The information in this section contains the language and requirements of the Washington Natural Death Act as amended in 1992 by the state legislature.

The Living Will, also known as a Health Care Directive, is allowed under a law in Washington State called the Natural Death Act. This is a written document that enables you to tell your doctor what you do or do not want if you are diagnosed with a terminal condition or are permanently unconscious. You may choose not to prolong the process of dying from an incurable and irreversible condition.

You must sign and date your Living Will in the presence of two witnesses, who must also sign. These two witnesses may not be, at the time of signing, any of the following:

- Related to you by blood or marriage;

- Entitled to inherit your money or property if you die;

- People to whom you owe money;

- Your doctor or your doctor's employees;

- Employee of the health care facility where you are a patient or resident.

What if I change my mind?

You can change your Living Will (Health Care Directive) any time if you are mentally capable. If you are not mentally capable, you can cancel or revoke your Living Will any time, but you cannot change what you have written or make a new one.

You can cancel your Living Will (Health Care Directive) by:

- Destroying it or having someone else destroy it in your presence; or

- Signing and dating a written statement that you are canceling the Living Will; or

- Verbally telling your doctor, or instructing someone to tell your doctor, that you are canceling it.

You, or someone you have instructed, must tell your attending doctor before the cancellation is effective.

Are health care providers and/or my doctor still required to inform me of my choices if I have put what I want in my Living Will?

Yes. The informed consent process is required when any significant treatment is recommended.

Will my health care provider and/or my doctor honor my decisions?

You should ask them directly. Your health care provider must give you its written policies on how it will handle Advance Directives. Some health care providers may have policies against carrying out your wishes based on moral, religious, or ethical concerns.

Washington State law says that a doctor or health care provider who will not honor your Advance Directive must tell you and give you the choice of keeping the doctor or the facility as your health care provider. If you choose to stay with the doctor and/or facility, there must be a written plan attached to your health care directive explaining what the facility and doctor will do to make sure your Advance Directive will be honored. This may mean that if your health condition changes, the doctor/healthcare provider will make arrangements with another doctor and/or facility to carry out your wishes.

Since the Living Will law changed in 1992, is my old Living Will still valid?

Yes. As long as your Health Care Directive generally follows the state law, it can be used. You may want to review your old Living Will. The law was expanded and allows you to make advance decisions about artificially provided nourishment (food and water).

Can someone make me write an Advance Directive?

No. It is against the law for a health care provider, including residential homes, to require that you have an Advance Directive. You have the right to choose whether or not to sign an Advance Directive. No health care provider can require that you sign or have any kind of Advance Directive as a condition of admission to a facility or as a condition of receiving service.

Where should I keep my Living Will (Health Care Directive)?

You should make several copies of your completed document. Keep a copy in your papers and give copies to:

- Your power of attorney for health care (if you have one);
- Your doctor;
- Your health care provider; and
- A family member or trusted friend.

What is a Durable Power of Attorney for Health Care?

This is another type of Advance Directive in Washington State. The Durable Power of Attorney for Health Care (DPOAHC) is a document that you write stating who you want to make health care decisions for you if you are unable to make your own. You can also write what type of health care decisions you want made for you and what the decisions should be.

Why wouldn't I be able to make my own decisions about health care?

An accident or illness could make you temporarily unable to understand or talk about your medical treatment choices. Sometimes illness causes permanent loss of mental capacity and may limit your ability to understand the risks and benefits of suggested medical treatment. Mental illness can cause temporary loss of capacity.

What do I need to do to make a Durable Power of Attorney for Health Care?

You should think carefully about what is important to you. Talking with a close friend, family member, clergy, or your doctor may help you think through your future health care decisions.

You should decide what type of health care is important. You should think about what you would want and what you wouldn't want if medical treatment, surgery or medication is proposed.

You should decide when the Durable Power of Attorney for Health Care can be used. It is important to be specific. You can have a Durable Power of Attorney for Health Care go into effect right after you sign it, or you can have it go into effect only when (or if) you are unable to make your own decisions.

If you decide to use a Durable Power of Attorney for Health Care (which becomes effective only when you become incapacitated), you should think about who should decide whether you are incapacitated and under what circumstances. For example, "My incapacity will be decided by my treating physician and my cousin, Mary Smith. They must document their agreement and review my ability to make my own decisions on a regular basis."

You should think about whom you trust to make your medical decisions for you and you should talk about it with the person you choose. The person you choose is also called your "agent." Sometimes the person you choose is called your "attorney in fact," although the person does not have to be a lawyer.

The person you choose will be the person your health care provider will talk to when you need treatment or when it is time to implement your written directive(s) if you are incapacitated. This person will provide the informed consent for treatment or refuse treatment on your behalf. *See* Informed Consent.

You do not need witnesses for a Durable Power of Attorney for Health Care. However, witnesses can be important since they "witness" that you understand what you are signing.

You may want to have the Durable Power of Attorney for Health Care notarized because some health care providers require it be notarized. However, state law does not require this unless the document also includes powers for financial matters.

Can someone make me write a Durable Power of Attorney for Health Care?

No. It is against the law for a health care provider, including any residential home, to require that you have an advance directive. You have the choice to have one or not. No provider of health care can require that you sign or have a

Durable Power of Attorney for Health Care as a condition of being admitted to a facility or as a condition to receive services.

Where should I keep my Durable Power of Attorney?

You should keep a copy with your papers and give copies to:

- Your agent

- Your doctor

- Your health care provider

- Your family or trusted friend.

What if I want to cancel it?

You can cancel a Durable Power of Attorney for Health Care. This is called "revoking the power of attorney." Any person or health care provider who believes your old Power of Attorney document is still in effect should be informed. This can be done in writing or verbally, regardless of your capacity. However, you may only appoint a new agent if you are mentally capable.

If the Power of Attorney for Health Care was recorded with the county clerk, the document revoking the Power of Attorney for Health Care must also be recorded with the county clerk.

What if I disagree with my agent's decisions about my health care?

If you and your agent disagree, you still get to decide for yourself. If you are unable to work out the disagreement with your agent, you can revoke the Power of Attorney or you can change it to limit your agent's powers. If, however, a court of law has appointed a guardian to make health care decisions and you disagree, you must ask the court to review the guardian's decision. You can see an attorney for advice about going to court or you can request the court review the guardianship.

What if I fill out an Advance Directive in one state and receive health care in a different state?

The laws about honoring an Advance Directive from another state are unclear. Because an Advance Directive tells your wishes regarding medical care, it may be honored wherever you are, if it is made known. But if you spend much time in more than one state, you may wish to consider having your Advance Directive meet the laws of each state, as much as possible.

What happens in an emergency? If my breathing or heart stops, will CPR be used on me?

CPR means cardiopulmonary resuscitation. It is an emergency procedure used when your breathing and/or heart has stopped. CPR is a form of medical treatment; you decide if you want it or not. You should make your decision after considering your specific medical condition, your values, your doctor's opinion, and further information about the procedure.

Why wouldn't a person want CPR?

Sometimes CPR can cause other medical problems. If a person is frail, pressing on the chest can break ribs and puncture internal organs. Sometimes after a period of not breathing, the brain can be permanently damaged. Often, lung resuscitation results in the person being placed on a respirator.

What do "Code/No Code" and "Do not Resuscitate" (DNR) mean?

These terms are used by doctors to tell staff your decision about whether or not to use CPR. "Code" means use CPR. "No Code" and "Do Not Resuscitate" (DNR) mean do not use CPR. Your health care decision is a part of the plan for your care.

Do I have to sign a form?

No. You do not have to sign a form indicating your choice for the use of CPR. If you want to document your choice, a signed form known as Code/No Code or DNR form is sometimes used to state under what circumstance you would or would not want CPR. This is put in your medical file to be followed by all medical staff. Most nursing facilities and hospitals have policies that require CPR if your heart stops and you have not previously indicated what you want. Some residential facilities are required by state law to call 911. Facility staff will give your directive to medical emergency staff upon their arrival.

What Is Organ or Tissue Donation?

Washington State law allows, upon your death, for a gift of specific body parts (like your eyes).

This is called tissue donation. You may also donate your entire body for medical research purposes. You can make a written statement witnessed by two people that says what body parts you wish to donate for which purposes or check the back of your driver's license for easy instructions. You can also make this statement in your will.

If you have not made your wishes known, your relatives may be asked to make a decision at the time of your death.

* * *

This brochure is available in alternate format, as well as Russian and Spanish translation.

It is the policy of the Department of Social and Health Services (DSHS) that people shall not be discriminated against because of race, color, national origin, creed, religion, sex, age, or disability.

QUESTIONS

1. Is a national policy favoring execution of advance directives, living wills, or health care powers of attorney really justified? Are hospitals and other health care providers the best purveyors of information on such legal documents?

2. Imagine that a seventy-three year old woman arrives at the emergency room suffering from shortness of breath and chest pains. Immediately upon her admission, she is given the Michigan Notice to Patients reprinted above. What message might this convey to the patient, who is already distraught? Is there a better way to address the concerns implicit in the Patient Self-Determination Act?

3. Read the Uniform Health-Care Decisions Act in the statutory supplement. In what ways does this statute go beyond the requirements of the Patient Self-Determination Act?

California Probate Code § 4701. Statutory form
[for advance health care directive]

ADVANCE HEALTH CARE DIRECTIVE

Explanation

You have the right to give instructions about your own health care. You also have the right to name someone else to make health care decisions for you. This form lets you do either or both of these things. It also lets you express your wishes regarding donation of organs and the designation of your primary physician. If you use this form, you may complete or modify all or any part of it.

You are free to use a different form.

Part 1 of this form is a power of attorney for health care. Part 1 lets you name another individual as agent to make health care decisions for you if you become incapable of making your own decisions or if you want someone else to make those decisions for you now even though you are still capable. You may also name an alternate agent to act for you if your first choice is not willing, able, or reasonably available to make decisions for you. (Your agent may not be an operator or employee of a community care facility or a residential care facility where you are receiving care, or your supervising health care provider or employee of the health care institution where you are receiving care, unless your agent is related to you or is a coworker.) Unless the form you sign limits the authority of your agent, your agent may make all health care decisions for you. This form has a place for you to limit the authority of your agent. You need not limit the authority of your agent if you wish to rely on your agent for all health care decisions that may have to be made. If you choose not to limit the authority of your agent, your agent will have the right to:

(a) Consent or refuse consent to any care, treatment, service, or procedure to maintain, diagnose, or otherwise affect a physical or mental condition

(b) Select or discharge health care providers and institutions.

(c) Approve or disapprove diagnostic tests, surgical procedures, and programs of medication.

(d) Direct the provision, withholding, or withdrawal of artificial nutrition and hydration and all other forms of health care, including cardiopulmonary resuscitation.

(e) Make anatomical gifts, authorize an autopsy, and direct disposition of remains.

Part 2 of this form lets you give specific instructions about any aspect of your health care, whether or not you appoint an agent. Choices are provided for you to express your wishes regarding the provision, withholding, or withdrawal of treatment to keep you alive, as well as the provision of pain relief. Space is also provided for you to add to the choices you have made or for you to write out any additional wishes. If you are satisfied to allow your agent to determine what is best for you in making end-of-life decisions, you need not fill out Part 2 of this form.

Part 3 of this form lets you express an intention to donate your bodily organs and tissues following your death.

Part 4 of this form lets you designate a physician to have primary responsibility for your health care.

After completing this form, sign and date the form at the end. The form must be signed by two qualified witnesses or acknowledged before a notary public. Give a copy of the signed and completed form to your physician, to any other health care providers you may have, to any health care institution at which you are receiving care, and to any health care agents you have named. You should talk to the person you have named as agent to make sure that he or she understands your wishes and is willing to take the responsibility.

You have the right to revoke this advance health care directive or replace this form at any time.

PART 1

POWER OF ATTORNEY FOR HEALTH CARE

(1.1) DESIGNATION OF AGENT: I designate the following individual as my agent to make health care decisions for me:

_____

(name of individual you choose as agent)

_____

(address) (city) (state) (zip)

_____

(home phone) (work phone)

OPTIONAL: If I revoke my agent's authority or if my agent is not willing, able, or reasonably available to make a health care decision for me, I designate as my first alternate agent:

_____

(name of individual you choose as first alternate agent)

_____

(address) (city) (state) (zip)

_____

(home phone) (work phone)

OPTIONAL: If I revoke the authority of my agent and first alternate agent or if neither is willing, able, or reasonably available to make a health care decision for me, I designate as my second alternate agent:

_____

(name of individual you choose as second alternate agent)

_____

(address) (city) (state) (zip)

_____

(home phone) (work phone)

(1.2) AGENT'S AUTHORITY: My agent is authorized to make all health care decisions for me, including decisions to provide, withhold, or withdraw artificial nutrition and hydration and all other forms of health care to keep me alive, except as I state here:

_____

_____

_____

_____

(Add additional sheets if needed.)

(1.3) WHEN AGENT'S AUTHORITY BECOMES EFFECTIVE: My agent's authority becomes effective when my primary physician determines that I am unable to make my own health care decisions unless I mark the following box. If I mark this box [ ], my agent's authority to make health care decisions for me takes effect immediately.

(1.4) AGENT'S OBLIGATION: My agent shall make health care decisions for me in accordance with this power of attorney for health care, any instructions I give in Part 2 of this form, and my other wishes to the extent known to my agent. To the extent my wishes are unknown, my agent shall make health care decisions for me in accordance with what my agent determines to be in my best interest. In determining my best interest, my agent shall consider my personal values to the extent known to my agent.

(1.5) AGENT'S POSTDEATH AUTHORITY: My agent is authorized to make anatomical gifts, authorize an autopsy, and direct disposition of my remains, except as I state here or in Part 3 of this form:

_____

_____

_____

(Add additional sheets if needed.)

(1.6) NOMINATION OF CONSERVATOR: If a conservator of my person needs to be appointed for me by a court, I nominate the agent designated in this form. If that agent is not willing, able, or reasonably available to act as conservator, I nominate the alternate agents whom I have named, in the order designated.

PART 2

INSTRUCTIONS FOR HEALTH CARE

If you fill out this part of the form, you may strike any wording you do not want.

(2.1) END-OF-LIFE DECISIONS: I direct that my health care providers and others involved in my care provide, withhold, or withdraw treatment in accordance with the choice I have marked below:

[ ] (a) Choice Not To Prolong Life. I do not want my life to be prolonged if (1) I have an incurable and irreversible condition that will result in my death within a relatively short time, (2) I become unconscious and, to a reasonable degree of medical certainty, I will not regain consciousness, or (3) the likely risks and burdens of treatment would outweigh the expected benefits, OR

[ ] (b) Choice To Prolong Life. I want my life to be prolonged as long as possible within the limits of generally accepted health care standards.

(2.2) RELIEF FROM PAIN: Except as I state in the following space, I direct that treatment for alleviation of pain or discomfort be provided at all times, even if it hastens my death:

_____

_____

_____

(Add additional sheets if needed.)

(2.3) OTHER WISHES: (If you do not agree with any of the optional choices above and wish to write your own, or if you wish to add to the instructions you have given above, you may do so here.) I direct that:

_____

_____

_____

(Add additional sheets if needed.)

PART 3

DONATION OF ORGANS AT DEATH (OPTIONAL)

(3.1) Upon my death (mark applicable box):

[ ] (a) I give any needed organs, tissues, or parts, OR

[ ] (b) I give the following organs, tissues, or parts only.

_____

(c) My gift is for the following purposes (strike any of the following you do not want:

    (1) Transplant

    (2) Therapy

    (3) Research

    (4) Education

PART 4

PRIMARY PHYSICIAN (OPTIONAL)

(4.1) I designate the following physician as my primary physician:

_____

(name of physician)

_____

(address) (city) (state) (zip)

_____

(phone)

OPTIONAL: If the physician I have designated above is not willing, able, or reasonably available to act as my primary physician, I designate the following physician as my primary physician:

_____

(name of physician)

_____

(address) (city) (state) (zip)

_____

(phone)

PART 5

(5.1) EFFECT OF COPY: A copy of this form has the same effect as the original.

(5.2) SIGNATURE: Sign and date the form here:

_____   _____
(date)   (sign your name)

_____   _____
(address)   (print your name)

_____
(address) (city) (state) (zip)

(5.3) STATEMENT OF WITNESSES: I declare under penalty of perjury under the laws of California (1) that the individual who signed or acknowledged this advance health care directive is personally known to me, or that the individual's identity was proven to me by convincing evidence, (2) that the individual signed or acknowledged this advance directive in my presence, (3) that the individual appears to be of sound mind and under no duress, fraud, or undue influence, (4) that I am not a person appointed as agent by this advance directive, and (5) that I am not the individual's health care provider, an employee of the individual's health care provider, the operator of a community care facility, an employee of an operator of a community care facility, the operator of a residential care facility for the elderly, nor an employee of an operator of a residential care facility for the elderly.

First witness   Second witness

_____   _____
(print name)   (print name)

_____   _____
(address)   (address)

_____   _____
(city) (state) (zip)   (city) (state) (zip)

_____   _____
(signature of witness)   (signature of witness)

_____   _____
(date)   (date)

(5.4) ADDITIONAL STATEMENT OF WITNESSES: At least one of the above witnesses must also sign the following declaration:

I further declare under penalty of perjury under the laws of California that I am not related to the individual executing this advance health care directive by blood, marriage, or adoption, and to the best of my knowledge, I am not entitled to any part of the individual's estate upon his or her death under a will now existing or by operation of law.

_____   _____
(signature of witness)   (signature of witness)

PART 6

SPECIAL WITNESS REQUIREMENT

(6.1) The following statement is required only if you are a patient in a skilled nursing facility — a health care facility that provides the following basic services: skilled nursing care and supportive care to patients whose primary need is for availability of skilled nursing care on an extended basis. The patient advocate or ombudsman must sign the following statement:

STATEMENT OF PATIENT ADVOCATE OR OMBUDSMAN

I declare under penalty of perjury under the laws of California that I am a patient advocate or ombudsman as designated by the State Department of Aging and that I am serving as a witness as required by Section 4675 of the Probate Code.

_____   _____
(date)   (sign your name)

_____   _____
(address)   (print your name)

_____
(city) (state) (zip)

QUESTIONS

1. Is there a difference between a living will and an advance directive for health care? Why might a client prefer one to the other?

2. Compare the explanations of living wills, advance directives, and health care powers of attorney offered by the state of Michigan and by the state of Washington. Is the information they contain consistent? What might account for any differences?

3. Find a state statute (other than California Probate Code § 4701) that articulates the requirements for a valid living will or health care power of attorney in that state. How would a directive drafted pursuant to the statute differ from the California directive set out above? From the suggested form for a health care directive drafted pursuant to the provisions of the Uniform Health Care Directives Act?

4. What happens if a health care directive executed in one state does not comply precisely with the laws of a different state? Will the directive nonetheless be valid in he second state? Does the Uniform Health-Care Decisions Act adequately address this potential problem?

5. Are there any circumstances in which you would advise a client NOT to execute a health care power of attorney?

3. Surrogacy Statutes

755 Illinois Compiled Statutes 40/25(a)

When a patient lacks decisional capacity, the health care provider must make a reasonable inquiry as to the availability and authority of a health care agent under the Powers of Attorney for Health Care Law. When no health care agent is authorized and available, the health care provider must make a reasonable inquiry as to the availability of possible surrogates listed in items (1) through (4) of this subsection. For purposes of this Section, a reasonable inquiry includes, but is not limited to, identifying a member of the patient's family or other health care agent by examining the patient's personal effects or medical records. If a family member or other health care agent is identified, an attempt to contact that person by telephone must be made within 24 hours after a determination by the provider that the patient lacks decisional capacity. No person shall be liable for civil damages or subject to professional discipline based on a claim of violating a patient's right to confidentiality as a result of making a reasonable inquiry as to the availability of a patient's family member or health care agent, except for willful or wanton misconduct.

The surrogate decision makers, as identified by the attending physician, are then authorized to make decisions as follows: (i) for patients who lack decisional capacity and do not have a qualifying condition, medical treatment decisions may be made in accordance with subsection (b-5) of Section 20; and (ii) for patients who lack decisional capacity and have a qualifying condition, medical treatment decisions including whether to forgo life-sustaining treatment on behalf of the patient may be made without court order or judicial involvement in the following order of priority:

(1) the patient's guardian of the person;

(2) the patient's spouse;

(3) any adult son or daughter of the patient;

(4) either parent of the patient;

(5) any adult brother or sister of the patient;

(6) any adult grandchild of the patient;

(7) a close friend of the patient;

(8) the patient's guardian of the estate.

The health care provider shall have the right to rely on any of the above surrogates if the provider believes after reasonable inquiry that neither a health care agent under the Powers of Attorney for Health Care Law nor a surrogate of higher priority is available.

Where there are multiple surrogate decision makers at the same priority level in the hierarchy, it shall be the responsibility of those surrogates to make reasonable efforts to reach a consensus as to their decision on behalf of the patient regarding the forgoing of life-sustaining treatment. If 2 or more surrogates who are in the same category and have equal priority indicate to the attending physician that they disagree about the health care matter at issue, a majority of the available persons in that category (or the parent with custodial rights) shall control, unless the minority (or the parent without custodial rights) initiates guardianship proceedings. . . .

Richard S. Saver
Critical Care Research and Informed Consent
75 N.C. L. Rev. 205, 266 (1996)[*]

A troubling problem of increased use of surrogate consent mechanisms is the danger that surrogates will substitute their own interests for the patient's. As already noted, family members may have conflicts of interest when acting as surrogates. Equally problematic is that even when acting with the best of intention, surrogates may simply not be accurate predictors of what the patient wanted because of the inherent subjectivity of the factors and judgments involved. Relying upon intuitive, subjective decision-making by surrogate family members makes judicial reviewabiliity of such decisions nearly impossible and thus offers little protection to patients who do not have idealized "selfless, loving families" to rely upon. Studies indicate that surrogates, even close family members, often do not adequately understand the preferences of the patients for whom they are acting.

QUESTIONS

1.   What are surrogacy statutes designed to do?

2.   Compare the list of potential surrogates in the Illinois statute above with the list in Section 5 of the UHCDA. Are there ways in which either list in under- or over-inclusive?

4. Physician Assisted Suicide

Leslie Joan Harris
Semantics and Policy in Physician-Assisted Death:
Piercing the Verbal Veil
5 Elder L.J. 251, 251, 264-71 (1997)[**]

During the last twenty years, courts and legislatures have developed principles that allow individuals and their surrogates to refuse medical care, even when refusal will lead to death. This article traces these developments, from

---

[*] Copyright © 1996 by the North Carolina Law Review Association. Reprinted with permission.

[**] Copyright © 1997. Reprinted with permission. Copyright to the *Elder Law Journal* is held by the Board of Trustees of the University of Illinois.

early cases concerning withdrawal of respirators and decisions not to treat fatal illnesses through withdrawal or refusal of artificial nutrition and hydration to the current debate over physician-assisted death. Throughout these developments, those who believed that the law should allow refusal of care have characterized the issue as a matter of personal autonomy, while their opponents have called refusal of care "suicide" and denial of care "homicide." This article traces the rhetorical battle from the early cases through the most recent Supreme Court decisions on physician-assisted death, showing that the rhetoric predicts outcomes but does not explain them. The rhetoric reveals one important set of issues that are at stake in these decisions — who should choose among the varying definitions of respect for human life and the role that law should place in this debate. However, the language obscures other important issues that should be figured heavily in deciding whether to allow refusal of treatment, as well as physician-assisted death. These issues include how power should be distributed between doctors and their patients and how much of society's resources should be allocated to health care.

In *Vacco v. Quill* [117 S. Ct. 2293 (1997)] and *Washington v. Glucksberg* [117 S. Ct. 2258 (1997)] the Supreme Court reversed decisions from the Second and Ninth Circuits which held that the Constitution requires that terminally ill people be allowed to seek the assistance of physicians in ending their lives. In *Vacco* and *Glucksberg*, the Court found that legislation in the area of physician-assisted death does not violate equal protection or due process, leaving the continuing debate over physician-assisted death to the various state legislatures. Legislation to allow physician-assisted death has been introduced in more than fifteen states, though only Oregon has enacted this type of legislation. The Oregon statute survived an effort to repeal it by popular initiative in November 1997.[1]

* * *

---

[1] The state legislature referred the Death with Dignity Act back to the voters recommending that they repeal it. H.R. 2954, 69th Leg. (Or. 1997). The electorate rejected this request and upheld the act by a margin of nearly 60%-40%. Suicide Law Stands, Portland Oregonian, Nov. 4, 1997, A, at 1.

The Oregon Death with Dignity Act was successfully challenged in the federal district court on the basis that it denied them from protection against incompetent doctors and their own mental incapacity. Lee v. Oregon, 891 F. Supp. 1429 (D. Or. 1995). However, the Ninth Circuit reversed because the challengers lacked standing. Lee v. Oregon, 107 F.3d 1382 (9th Cir.), *cert. denied*, 118 S. Ct. 328 (1997). Although there has been discussion about the opponents of the act refiling with the plaintiff who does have standing, this had not occurred as of early November 1997.

In *Compassion in Dying v. Washington*, the Ninth Circuit, sitting en banc, sharply criticized the district court opinion in *Lee*. 79 F.3d at 838 n.139. On appeal, the Supreme Court commented, "*Lee*, of course, is not before us, any more than it was before the Court of Appeals below, and we offer no opinion as to the validity of the *Lee* courts' reasoning. In *Vacco v. Quill*, however, . . . we hold that New York's assisted-suicide ban does not violate the Equal Protection Clause." Glucksberg, 117 S. Ct. at 2262 n.7.

The constitutional challenge in *Lee* is quite different from those in *Glucksberg* and *Quill*. The Supreme Court's holding in those cases — that the Constitution does not require states to allow physician-assisted suicide — does not mean that legislation allowing and regulating physician-assisted suicide is unconstitutional.

B. "Killing" Versus "Letting Die" — Passive and Active Euthanasia, Acts, Omissions, and Causation

A variety of terms in ethical and legal discussions have been used to draw a line between "killing" and "letting die" and between "committing suicide" and "escaping from suffering."

1. Active Versus Passive Euthanasia

The ethical terms with the oldest and most elaborate lineage are "passive" and "active" euthanasia. The distinction is typically made in this way: "Passive euthanasia involves allowing a patient to die by removing her from artificial life support systems such as respirators and feeding tubes or simply discontinuing medical treatments necessary to sustain life. Active euthanasia, by contrast, involves positive steps to end the life of a patient, typically by lethal injection."

When Glanville Williams proposed in the late 1950s to allow doctors to end the lives of terminally ill, competent, suffering patients at their request, he used these terms. In 1975, near the time of the *Quinlan* decision, when the moral and legal acceptability of withdrawing respirators and other sorts of life support was still disputed, a famous ethical debate over the topic was carried out in terms of "active" versus "passive" euthanasia. James Rachels argued that the distinction is not morally sustainable, asking "what is the point of drawing out the suffering" of a person who will die anyway? In reply, Tom Beauchamp argued that the distinction is morally significant and should be maintained because of the slippery slope problem, that "active" killing may lead to programs to exterminate people regarded as socially undesirable. Because the term "euthanasia" has become associated with this slippery slope, those who support actions that allow patients to die have largely quit using the term, while opponents continue to use the term for exactly the same reason.

2. Acts Versus Omissions and Legal Causation

On the legal side, early proponents of allowing withdrawal of life support confronted the legal distinction between acts and omissions. In most American jurisdictions, criminal liability for "omissions" is more limited than for acts, because a person is not legally liable for failure to act unless that person has a legal duty to act, and the sources of legal duty are limited. Writing in 1967, George Fletcher argued that a doctor who turned off the ventilator of a person with no brain activity should be treated as having "omitted" to care for the patient rather than having affirmatively "acted" to kill the patient and that the doctor "permitted death to occur" rather than "caused death." In *Barber v. Superior Court*, a 1983 criminal prosecution of a doctor for turning off the respirator of a patient in a persistent vegetative state, the court reversed the conviction, accepting the argument that the doctor had omitted to act when he had no duty to do so.

In other cases courts relied on principles of legal causation to preclude criminal liability for withdrawing life support. For example, in 1985, in *In re Conroy*, one of the most important and famous cases concerning withdrawal of feeding tubes, the New Jersey court relied in part on a causation argument, saying that refusal of treatment is not suicide because the person's underlying medical condition was not self-inflicted and the person dies from nature "taking its course."

3. Criticisms of the Distinctions as Artificial

Although the distinction between "killing" and "letting die" seems clear with regard to the newest issue, physician-aided death, both supporters and opponents of the practice have denied that the distinction is morally significant. For example, Yale Kamisar, who opposed withdrawal of treatment as well as physician-assisted death, wrote:

> Many who support the "right to die" say they are strongly opposed to active euthanasia. I must say I do not find the arguments made by proponents of this distinction convincing. Least persuasive of all, I think, are the arguments that lifting the ban against active euthanasia would be "to embrace the assumption that one human being has the power of life over another" (the withholding or withdrawal of life-sustaining treatment embraces the same assumption) and that maintaining the prohibition against active euthanasia "prevents the grave potential for abuse inherent in any law that sanctions the taking of human life" (passive euthanasia, at the very least, presents the same potential for abuse).

> Indeed I venture to say that a law that sanctions the "taking of human life" indirectly or negatively rather than directly or positively contains much more potential for abuse. Because of the repugnance surrounding active euthanasia — because it is what might be called "straightforward" or "out in the open" euthanasia — I think it may be forcefully argued that it is less likely to be abused than other less readily identifiable forms of euthanasia.

Similarly, Tom Beauchamp, who originally championed the distinction between "killing" and "letting die," has more recently argued that the distinction is difficult to make and creates moral and conceptual confusion. He argues that the right to autonomy which justifies allowing patients to refuse treatment seems in principle to extend to a patient's request for physician-assisted death.

C. Intent to Die Versus Intent to Relieve or Escape Suffering

Although some definitions of "suicide" include all voluntary acts that result in the ending of one's life, the actor's intent has commonly been used to limit the scope of the term. In *Satz v. Perlmutter*, a 1978 Florida case involving the request of a competent man with amyotrophic lateral sclerosis (Lou Gehrig's disease) to turn off his respirator, the court denied that Abe Perlmutter wanted to commit suicide. The court said that Perlmutter wanted to live, but not with assistance. A Florida trial court recently made a similar distinction in *McIver v. Krischer*, stating that a man who made a request for physician-assisted death "is not suicidal, but merely wishes to end what is to be a painful and protracted dying period."

The cases involving withdrawal of tube-feeding evoked some of the most spirited discussion about what kind of intention counted as "suicidal" and, by implication, homicidal, because the patients involved were not at immediate risk of dying from their underlying disease or condition, but rather perished most directly from lack of nutrition and hydration. Yet most courts, like the court in *In re Conroy*, which involved termination of tube-feeding, said that patients who decline treatment are not suicidal, in part because they do not have the specific intent to die.

As this discussion shows, at each of the major steps in the development of the legal "right to die" — withdrawing or withholding lifesaving treatments such as respirators, and withdrawing artificial nutrition and hydration — the ethical and legal debate has used remarkably similar terminology. Opponents of legalization call actions "euthanasia," "killing," and "suicide." Proponents accept that such categories exist but deny that the action currently under scrutiny fits into the category, relying on the distinction between acts and omission and the principles of causation and intention.

Those who seek to extend the legal right to die avoid these terms because they connote illicit choices. This pattern of debate continues, as illustrated in the Supreme Court's recent decisions about physician-assisted death.

* * *

<h1 style="text-align:center">Statement of Thomas Reardon, M.D.
Chair, American Medical Association Board of Trustees
AMA Reaction to Oregon Decision to Allow
Physician-Assisted Suicide Law
(AMA Press Release, November 5, 1997)</h1>

The announcement today of the decision by the citizens of Oregon to let stand its "Physician-Assisted Suicide Law," is a serious blow to their health and safety. Further, it sets a dangerous precedent for other states considering similar initiatives that physician-assisted suicide is an acceptable option for patients in the last phase of life.

We all have rights at the end of life that preclude us from having to resort to physician-assisted suicide. Not only is it our duty to educate ourselves, our loved ones and the public regarding these existing rights, it is our obligation to ensure that these rights are honored.

The American Medical Association is committed to making sure that the wishes of individuals with terminal and advanced chronic illness are carried out with compassion, comfort and dignity. In June, 1997, the American Medical Association affirmed "The Elements of Quality Care at the End of Life," a set of eight principles that all patients should reasonably expect when faced with death.

As the beacon for protecting patients and the ethics of the medical profession, the AMA will continue its unyielding opposition to physician-assisted suicide. We will do everything in our power to see that this practice never becomes a generally-accepted option to quality patient care.

Hearing on Assisted Suicide in the United States, Before the Subcommittee on the Constitution of the House Committee on the Judiciary

104th Cong., 2d Sess. (April 29, 1996)
(Statement of Lonnie R. Bristow, M.D., President,
American Medical Association)

My name is Lonnie R. Bristow, MD. I practice internal medicine in San Pablo, California, and I also serve as President of the American Medical Association (AMA). On behalf of the AMA, I appreciate the opportunity to present our views on physician-assisted suicide to this Subcommittee.

For nearly 2,500 years, physicians have vowed to "give no deadly drug if asked for it, [nor] make a suggestion to this effect." What has changed, that there should be this attempt to make "assisted suicide" an accepted practice of medicine? Certainly the experience of physical pain has not changed over time. Yet the blessings of medical research and technology present their own new challenges, as our ability to delay or draw out the dying process alters our perceptions and needs.

Our efforts in this new paradigm must recognize the importance of care that relieves pain, supports family and relationships, enhances functioning, and respects spiritual needs. Calls for legalization of physician-assisted suicide point to a public perception that these needs are not being met by the current health care system. In addition, society has not met its responsibility to plan adequately for end-of-life care. It is this issue — how to provide quality care at the end of life — which the AMA believes should be our legitimate focus.

The AMA believes that physician-assisted suicide is unethical and fundamentally inconsistent with the pledge physicians make to devote themselves to healing and to life. Laws that sanction physician-assisted suicide undermine the foundation of the patient-physician relationship that is grounded in the patient's trust that the physician is working wholeheartedly for the patient's health and welfare. The multidisciplinary members of the New York State Task Force on Life and the Law concur in this belief, writing that "physician-assisted suicide and euthanasia violate values that are fundamental to the practice of medicine and the patient-physician relationship."

Yet physicians also have an ethical responsibility to relieve pain and to respect their patient's wishes regarding care, and it is when these duties converge at the bedside of a seriously or terminally ill patient that physicians are torn.

The AMA believes that these additional ethical duties require physicians to respond aggressively to the needs of the patients at the end of life with adequate pain control, emotional support, comfort care, respect for patient autonomy and good communications.

Further efforts are necessary to better educate physicians in the areas of pain management and effective end-of-life care. Patient education is the other essential component of an effective outreach to minimize the circumstances which might lead to a patient's request for physician-assisted suicide: inadequate social support; the perceived burden to family and friends; clinical depression; hopelessness; loss of self-esteem; and the fear of living with chronic, unrelieved pain.

ETHICAL CONSIDERATIONS

Physicians' Fundamental Obligation: The physician's primary obligation is to advocate for the individual patient. At the end of life, this means the physician must strive to understand the various existential, psychological, and physiological factors that play out over the course of terminal illness and must help the patient cope with each of them. Patients who are understandably apprehensive or afraid of their own mortality need support and comforting, not a prescription to help them avoid the issues of death. Patients who believe sudden and "controlled" death would protect them from the perceived indignities of prolonged deterioration and terminal illness must receive social support as well as the support of the profession to work through these issues. Providing assisted suicide would breach the ethical means of medicine to safeguard patients' dignity and independence.

Pain Management and the Doctrine of Double Effect: Many proponents of assisted suicide cite a fear of prolonged suffering and unmanageable pain as support for their position. For most patients, advancements in palliative care can adequately control pain through oral medications, nerve blocks or radiotherapy. We all recognize, however, that there are patients whose intractable pain cannot be relieved by treating the area, organ or system perceived as the source of the pain. For patients for whom pain cannot be controlled by other means, it is ethically permissible for physicians to administer sufficient levels of controlled substances to ease pain, even if the patient's risk of addiction or death is increased.

The failure of most states to expressly permit this practice has generated reluctance among physicians to prescribe adequate pain medication. Additional uncertainty is produced by the potential for legal action against the physician when controlled substances are prescribed in large amounts to treat patients with intractable pain. This uncertainty chills physicians' ability to effectively control their terminally ill patients' pain and suffering through the appropriate prescription and administration of opiates and other controlled substances. In this area, states such as California and Texas have developed clear legislative guidance that resolves these concerns for most physicians. The AMA is developing similarly structured model legislation for state medical societies to pursue with their state legislatures and medical licensing boards.

In some instances, administration of adequate pain medication will have the secondary effect of suppressing the respiration of the patient, thereby hastening death. This is commonly referred to as the "double effect." The distinction between this action and assisted suicide is crucial. The physician has an obligation to provide for the comfort of the patient. If there are no alternatives but to increase the risk of death in order to provide that comfort, the physician is ethically permitted to exercise that option. In this circumstance, the physician's clinical decision is guided by the intent to provide pain relief, rather than an intent to cause death. This distinguishes the ethical use of palliative care medications from the unethical application of medical skills to cause death.

Distinction Between Withholding or Withdrawing Treatment and Assisted Suicide: Some participants in the debate about assisted suicide see no meaningful distinction between withholding or withdrawing treatment and providing assistance in suicide. They argue that the results of each action are the same and therefore the acts themselves carry equal moral status. This argument largely ignores the distinction between act and omission in the circumstances of terminal care and does not address many of the principles that underlie the right of patients to refuse the continuation of medical care and the duty of physicians to exercise their best clinical judgment.

Specifically, proponents who voice this line of reasoning fail to recognize the crucial difference between a patient's right to refuse unwanted medical treatment and any proposed right to receive medical intervention which would cause death. Withholding or withdrawing treatment allows death to proceed naturally, with the underlying disease being the cause of death. Assisted suicide, on the other hand, requires action to cause death, independent from the disease process.

The "Slippery Slope": Physician-assisted suicide raises troubling and insurmountable "slippery slope" problems. Despite attempts by some, it is difficult to imagine adequate safeguards which could effectively guarantee that patients' decisions to request assisted suicide were unambivalent, informed and free of coercion.

A policy allowing assisted suicide could also result in the victimization of poor and disenfranchised populations who may have greater financial burdens and social burdens which could be "relieved" by hastening death. As reported two years ago by the New York State Task Force on Life and the Law (composed of bioethicists, lawyers, clergy and state health officials), "[a]ssisted suicide and euthanasia will be practiced through the prism of social inequality and prejudice that characterizes the delivery of services in all segments of society, including health care."

Recent studies documenting reasons for patient requests for physician-assisted suicide speak to our "slippery slope"concerns. Patients were rarely suffering intractable pain. Rather, they cited fears of losing control, being a burden, being dependent on others for personal care and loss of dignity often associated with end-stage disease.

The Case of the Netherlands: While euthanasia and assisted suicide are not legal in the Netherlands, comprehensive guidelines have been established which allow physicians to avoid prosecution for the practice. Despite this environment, Dutch physicians have become uneasy about their active role in euthanasia, prompting the Royal Dutch Medical Association to revise its recommendations on the practice.

Findings of more than 1,000 cases of involuntary euthanasia in the Netherlands should raise hackles in the United States, particularly given the stark societal differences between the two countries. Health coverage is universal in the Netherlands, the prevalence of long-term patient-physician relationships is greater and social supports are more comprehensive. The inequities in the American healthcare system, where the majority of patients who request physician-assisted suicide cite financial burden as a motive, make the practice of physician-assisted suicide all the more unjustifiable. No other country in the world, including the Netherlands, has legalized assisted suicide or euthanasia. This is one movement in which the United States should not be a "leader."

EDUCATING PHYSICIANS AND PATIENTS

At its last meeting in December of 1995, the AMA House of Delegates adopted recommendations from a report issued by its Task Force on Quality Care at the End of Life. The report identified issues involved with care of the dying, including the need to develop a definition of "futility," provision of optimal palliative care, legislation ensuring access to hospice benefits, and the importance of advance care planning as a part of standard medical care. Based on the report's recommendations, the AMA is coordinating its current efforts and developing a comprehensive physician and patient education outreach campaign regarding quality of care at the end of life.

The AMA is uniquely capable of educating physicians and other caregivers, legislators, jurists, and the general public as to end of life care issues. Recognizing the profession's desire to structure discussions of end-of-life care and maintain an active and improved role in the care of dying patients, the AMA is currently designing a comprehensive physician education outreach to instruct physicians in conducting advance care planning and managing palliative care with their patients. In fostering such communication, the AMA is particularly concerned with enabling physicians to support patient autonomy, providing patients with sufficient background and support to make informed decisions regarding their end-of-life treatment.

* * *

Through continued educational efforts, physicians are committed to demonstrating their enduring commitment to providing the best patient care during every stage of life. Furthermore, provided the tools to facilitate improved terminal care, physicians can readily answer many of the arguments of assisted suicide's proponents.

MEDICARE AND MEDICAID COVERAGE

A significant portion of end-of-life care is provided under Medicare and Medicaid, with estimates showing that Medicare and Medicaid beneficiaries account for 65% of all deaths that occur each year in the United States. Based on the patient populations served by these two programs — the elderly, the disabled, the poor, and the bulk of the nation's nursing home patients — this is not surprising. While these programs have supported the establishment and expansion of the hospice benefit, end-of-life care for most Medicare and Medicaid patients is provided in hospitals. Under Medicare, hospital coverage is provided through the prospective pricing system based on the appropriate Diagnosis Related Group (DRG) payment amount. HCFA has announced that it is working with the Milbank Memorial Fund to explore the possibility of establishing a DRG for hospital inpatient care services related to palliative care for "final" illnesses. Consistent with this direction, AMA is asking the Current Procedural Terminology (CPT) Editorial Panel to consider the potential for development of CPT codes to identify physician services for palliative care.

* * *

CONCLUSION

The movement for legally sanctioning physician-assisted suicide is a sign of society's failure to address the complex issues raised at the end of life. It is not a victory for personal rights. We are equipped with the tools to effectively manage end-of-life pain and to offer terminally ill patients dignity and to add value to their remaining time. As the voice of the medical profession, the AMA offers its capability to coordinate multidisciplinary discourse on end-of-life issues, for it is essential to coordinate medical educators, patients, advocacy organizations, allied health professionals and the counseling and pastoral professions to reach a comprehensive solution to these challenging issues. Our response should be a better informed medical profession and public, working together to preserve fundamental human values at the end of life.

Oregon Department of Human Services
Physician-Assisted Suicide
Death with Dignity
Annual Report 2006
http://www.dhs.state.or.us/publichealth/chs/pas/ar-index.cfm

Summary

Physician-assisted suicide (PAS) has been legal in Oregon since November 1997, when Oregon voters approved the Death with Dignity Act (DWDA) for the second time. The Department of Human Services (DHS) is legally required to collect information regarding compliance with the Act and make the information available on a yearly basis. In this eighth annual report, we characterize the 38 Oregonians who died in 2005 following ingestion of medications prescribed under provisions of the Act, and look at whether the numbers and characteristics of these patients differ from those who used PAS in prior years. Patients choosing PAS were identified through mandated physician and pharmacy reporting. Our information comes from these reports, physician interviews and death certificates. We also compare the demographic characteristics of patients participating during 1998-2005 with other Oregonians who died of the same underlying causes.

In 2005, 39 physicians wrote a total of 64 prescriptions for lethal doses of medication. In 1998, 24 prescriptions were written, followed by 33 in 1999, 39 in 2000, 44 in 2001, 58 in 2002, 68 in 2003, and 60 in 2004. Thirty-two of the 2005 prescription recipients died after ingesting the medication. Of the 32 recipients who did not ingest the prescribed medication in 2005, 15 died from their illnesses, and 17 were alive on December 31, 2005. In addition, six patients who received prescriptions during 2004 died in 2005 as a result of ingesting the prescribed medication, giving a total of 38 PAS deaths during 2005. One 2004 prescription recipient, who ingested the prescribed medication in 2005, became unconscious 25 minutes after ingestion, then regained consciousness 65 hours later. This person did not obtain a subsequent prescription and died 14 days later of the underlying illness (17 days after ingesting the medication).

After an initial increase in PAS use during the first five years the Act was in effect, the number of Oregonians who use PAS remained relatively stable since 2002. In 1998, 16 Oregonians used PAS, followed by 27 in 1999, 27 in 2000, 21 in 2001, 38 in 2002, 42 in 2003, and 37 in 2004. The ratio of PAS deaths to total deaths trended upward during 1998-2003, peaking at 13.6 in 2003 and has since remained stable. In 1998 there were 5.5 PAS deaths per every 10,000 total deaths, followed by 9.2 in 1999, 9.1 in 2000, 7.1 in 2001, 12.2 in 2002, 13.6 in 2003, 12.3 in 2004, and an estimated 12/10,000 in 2005.

Compared to all Oregon decedents in 2005, PAS participants were more likely to have malignant neoplasms (84% vs. 24%), to be younger (median age 70 vs. 78 years), and to have more formal education (37% vs. 15% had at least a baccalaureate degree). During the past eight years, the 246 patients who took lethal medications differed in several ways from the 74,967 Oregonians dying from the same underlying diseases. Rates of participation in PAS decreased with age, although over 65% of PAS users were age 65 or older. Rates of participation were higher among those who were divorced or never married, those with more years of formal education, and those with amyotrophic lateral sclerosis, HIV/AIDS, or malignant neoplasms. . .

Physicians indicated that patient requests for lethal medications stemmed from multiple concerns, with eight in 10 patients having at least three concerns. The most frequently mentioned end-of-life concerns during 2005 were: a decreasing ability to participate in activities that made life enjoyable, loss of dignity, and loss of autonomy.

Complications were reported for three patients during 2005; two involved regurgitation, and, as noted above, one patient regained consciousness after ingesting the prescribed medication. None involved seizures. Fifty percent of patients became unconscious within five minutes of ingestion of the lethal medication and the same percentage died within 26 minutes of ingestion. The range of time from ingestion to death was from five minutes to 9.5 hours. Emergency Medical Services were called for one patient in order to pronounce death.

The number of terminally ill patients using PAS has remained small, with about 1 in 800 deaths among Oregonians in 2005 resulting from physician-assisted suicide.

Introduction

This eighth annual report presents data on participation in Oregon's Death with Dignity Act (DWDA), which legalizes physician-assisted suicide (PAS) for terminally ill Oregon residents. This report summarizes the information collected from physician reports, interviews, and death certificates.

History

The Oregon Death with Dignity Act was a citizen's initiative first passed by Oregon voters in November 1994 with 51% in favor. Implementation was delayed by a legal injunction, but after proceedings that included a petition denied by the United States Supreme Court, the Ninth Circuit Court of Appeals lifted the injunction on October 27, 1997. In November 1997, a measure asking Oregon voters to repeal the Death with Dignity Act was placed on the general election ballot (Measure 51, authorized by Oregon House Bill 2954). Voters rejected this measure by a margin of 60% to 40%, retaining the Death with Dignity Act. After voters reaffirmed the DWDA in 1997, Oregon became the only state allowing legal physician-assisted suicide.

Although physician-assisted suicide has been legal in Oregon for eight years, it remains highly controversial. On November 6, 2001, U.S. Attorney General John Ashcroft issued a new interpretation of the Controlled Substances Act, which would prohibit doctors from prescribing controlled substances for use in physician-assisted suicide. To date, all the medications prescribed under the Act have been barbiturates, which are controlled substances and, therefore, would be prohibited by this ruling for use in PAS. In response to a lawsuit filed by the State of Oregon on November 20, 2001, a U.S. district court issued a temporary restraining order against Ashcroft's ruling pending a new hearing. On April 17, 2002, U.S. District Court Judge Robert Jones upheld the Death with Dignity Act. On September 23, 2002, Attorney General Ashcroft filed an appeal, asking the Ninth U.S. Circuit Court of Appeals to overturn the District Court's ruling. The appeal was denied on May 26, 2004 by a three-judge panel. On July 13, 2004, Ashcroft filed an appeal requesting that the Court rehear his previous motion with an 11-judge panel; on August 13, 2004, the Court declined to rehear the case. On November 9, 2004, Ashcroft asked the U.S. Supreme Court to review the Ninth Circuit's decision. On October 5, 2005, the Supreme Court heard arguments in the case, and on January 17, 2006 it affirmed the lower court's decision [*Gonzalez v. Oregon*, 546 U.S. 243 (2006)]. At this time, Oregon's Death with Dignity Act remains in effect.

Requirements

The Death with Dignity Act allows terminally ill Oregon residents to obtain and use prescriptions from their physicians for self-administered, lethal medications. Under the Act, ending one's life in accordance with the law does not constitute suicide. However, we use "physician-assisted suicide" because that terminology is used in medical literature to describe ending life through the voluntary self-administration of lethal medications prescribed by a physician for that purpose. The Death with Dignity Act legalizes PAS, but specifically prohibits euthanasia, where a physician or other person directly administers a medication to end another's life.

To request a prescription for lethal medications, the Death with Dignity Act requires that a patient must be

- An adult (18 years of age or older),

- A resident of Oregon,

- Capable (defined as able to make and communicate health care decisions), and

- Diagnosed with a terminal illness that will lead to death within six months.

Patients meeting these requirements are eligible to request a prescription for lethal medication from a licensed Oregon physician. To receive a prescription for lethal medication, the following steps must be fulfilled:

- The patient must make two oral requests to his or her physician, separated by at least 15 days.

- The patient must provide a written request to his or her physician, signed in the presence of two witnesses.

- The prescribing physician and a consulting physician must confirm the diagnosis and prognosis.

- The prescribing physician and a consulting physician must determine whether the patient is capable.

- If either physician believes the patient's judgment is impaired by a psychiatric or psychological disorder, the patient must be referred for a psychological examination.

- The prescribing physician must inform the patient of feasible alternatives to assisted suicide, including comfort care, hospice care, and pain control.

- The prescribing physician must request, but may not require, the patient to notify his or her next-of-kin of the prescription request.

To comply with the law, physicians must report to the Department of Human Services (DHS) all prescriptions for lethal medications. Reporting is not required if patients begin the request process but never receive a prescription. In 1999, the Oregon legislature added a requirement that pharmacists must be informed of the prescribed medication's intended use. Physicians and patients who adhere to the requirements of the Act are protected from criminal prosecution, and the choice of legal physician assisted suicide cannot affect the status of a patient's health or life insurance policies. Physicians, pharmacists, and health care systems are under no obligation to participate in the Death with Dignity Act.

The Oregon Revised Statutes specify that action taken in accordance with the Death with Dignity Act does not constitute suicide, mercy killing or homicide under the law.

Methods

The Reporting System

DHS is required by the Act to develop and maintain a reporting system for monitoring and collecting information on PAS. To fulfill this mandate, DHS uses a system involving physician and pharmacist compliance reports, death certificate reviews, and follow-up interviews.

When a prescription for lethal medication is written, the physician must submit to DHS information that documents compliance with the law. We review all physician reports and contact physicians regarding missing or discrepant data. DHS Vital Records files are searched periodically for death certificates that correspond to physician reports. These death certificates allow us to confirm patients' deaths, and provide patient demographic data (e.g., age, place of residence, educational attainment).

In addition, using our authority to conduct special studies of morbidity and mortality, DHS conducts telephone interviews with prescribing physicians after receipt of the patients' death certificates. Each physician is asked to confirm whether the patient took the lethal medications. If the patient took the medications, we ask for information that was not available from previous physician reports or death certificates — including insurance status and enrollment in hospice. We ask why the patient requested a prescription, specifically exploring concerns about the financial impact of the illness, loss of autonomy, decreasing ability to participate in activities that make life enjoyable, being a burden, loss of control of bodily functions, uncontrollable pain, and loss of dignity. We collect information on the time from ingestion to unconsciousness and death, and ask about any adverse reactions. Because physicians are not legally required to be present when a patient ingests the medication, not all have information about what happened when the patient ingested the medication. If the prescribing physician was not present, we accept information they have based on discussions with family members, friends or other health professionals who attended the patients' deaths. We also accept information directly from these individuals. We do not interview or collect any information from patients prior to their death. In lieu of the telephone interview, physicians have the option of printing the questionnaire from our website, completing it at their convenience, and mailing the document to us. Reporting forms and the physician questionnaire are available at: http://www.oregon.gov/DHS/ph/pas/pasforms.shtml

Data Analysis

We classified patients by year of participation based on when they ingested the legally-prescribed lethal medication. Using demographic information from 1997-2004 Oregon death certificates (the most recent years for which complete data are available), we compared patients who used legal PAS with other Oregonians who died from the same diseases. Demographic- and disease-specific PAS rates were computed using the number of deaths from the same causes as the denominator. The overall PAS rates by year were computed using the total number of resident deaths. Annual rates were calculated using numerator and denominator data from the same year, except for 2005 where the number of resident deaths from 2004 was used as the denominator. SPSS, release 12 and PEPI, version 4.0 were used in data analysis. Statistical significance was determined using Fisher's exact test, the chi-square test, the chi-square for trend test, and the Mann-Whitney test.

Results

Both the number of prescriptions written and the number of Oregonians using PAS vary annually but have been relatively stable since 2002. In 2005, 39 physicians wrote 64 prescriptions for lethal doses of medication. In 1998, 24 prescriptions were written, followed by 33 in 1999, 39 in 2000, 44 in 2001, 58 in 2002, 68 in 2003, and 60 in 2004.

Thirty-two of the 2005 prescription recipients died after ingesting the medication. Of the 32 recipients who did not ingest the prescribed medication in 2005, 15 died from their illnesses, and 17 were alive on December 31, 2005. In addition, six patients who received prescriptions during 2004 died in 2005 as a result of ingesting their medication, giving a total of 38 PAS deaths during 2005.

In 1998, 16 Oregonians used PAS, followed by 27 in 1999, 27 in 2000, 21 in 2001, 38 in 2002, 42 in 2003, and 37 in 2004. Ratios of PAS deaths to total deaths have shown a similar trend: in 1998 there were 5.5 PAS deaths for every 10,000 total deaths, followed by 9.2 in 1999, 9.1 in 2000, 7.0 in 2001, 12.2 in 2002, 13.6 in 2003, 12.3, in 2004, and an estimated 12/10,000 in 2005.

The percentage of patients referred to a specialist for psychological evaluation beyond that done by a hospice team has declined, falling from 31% in 1998 to 5% in 2005.

Patient Characteristics

There were no statistically significant differences between Oregonians who used PAS in 2005 and those from prior years.

Although year-to-year variations occur, certain demographic patterns have become evident over the past eight years. Males and females have been equally likely to take advantage of the DWDA. Divorced and never-married persons were more likely to use PAS than married and widowed residents. A higher level of education has been strongly associated with the use of PAS; Oregonians with a baccalaureate degree or higher were 7.9 times more likely to use PAS than those without a high school diploma. Conversely, several groups have emerged as being less likely to use PAS. These include people age 85 or older, people who did not graduate from high school, people who are married or widowed, and Oregon residents living east of the Cascade Range.

Patients with certain terminal illnesses were more likely to use PAS. The ratio of DWDA deaths to all deaths resulting from the same underlying illness was highest for three conditions: amyotrophic lateral sclerosis (ALS) (269.5 per 10,000), HIV/AIDS (218.3), and malignant neoplasms (39.9). Among the causes associated with at least five deaths, the lowest rate (8.7) was for patients with chronic lower respiratory diseases (CLRD), such as emphysema.

During 2005, 36 patients died at home, and two died at assisted living facilities. All individuals had some form of health insurance (Table 4). As in previous years, most (92%) of the patients who used PAS in 2005 were enrolled in hospice care. The median length of the patient-physician relationship was 8 weeks.

Physician Characteristics

The prescribing physicians of patients who used PAS during 2005 had been in practice a median of 26 years (range 3-55). Their medical specialties included:

family medicine (62%), oncology (23%), internal medicine (10%), and other (5%). Family medicine physicians represent 15% of all physicians in Oregon, oncologists 0.9%, and internists 16%.

Seventy-four percent of the physicians who wrote prescriptions for lethal medication during 2005 wrote a single prescription. Of the 39 physicians who wrote prescriptions in 2005, 29 wrote one prescription, three wrote two prescriptions, three wrote three prescriptions, three wrote four prescriptions, and one wrote eight prescriptions.

During the first three years after the legalization of PAS, physicians were present at the patient's ingestion of lethal medication half or more of the time. During 2005, the prescribing physician was present 23% of the time.

It is the policy of DHS to report cases to the Oregon Board of Medical Examiners when required forms have not been completed correctly or have not been received in a timely fashion. During 2005, four cases were referred to the Oregon Board of Medical Examiners, one involving witnessing of signatures and three others for failure to file required documentation in a timely manner.

One case, in which a patient awakened after ingesting the prescribed medication, was referred to the Board of Pharmacy.

Lethal Medication

During 1998-2004, secobarbital was the lethal medication prescribed for 101 of the 208 patients (49%). During 2005, as during previous years, all lethal medications prescribed under the provisions of the DWDA were barbiturates. In 2005, 34 patients (89%) used pentobarbital and 4 patients (11%) used secobarbital. Since the DWDA was implemented, 56% of the PAS patients used pentobarbital, 43% used secobarbital, and 2% used other medications. (Three used secobarbital/amobarbital, and one used secobarbital and morphine).

Complications

During 2005, physicians reported that three patients experienced complications: two patients vomited some of the medication, one of whom died 15 minutes after ingestion and the other 90 minutes after ingestion. The former had been vomiting on a daily basis for the week and a half prior to ingestion. One patient became unconscious 25 minutes after ingestion, then regained consciousness 65 hours later. This person did not obtain a subsequent prescription, and died 14 days later of the underlying illness (17 days after ingesting the medication).

None of the patients experienced seizures. Emergency medical services were called to document one death. In no case was EMS called for medical intervention.

End-of-Life Concerns

Providers were asked if, based on discussions with patients, any of seven end-of-life concerns might have contributed to the patients' requests for lethal medication. In nearly all cases, physicians reported multiple concerns contributing to the request. The most frequently reported concerns included a decreasing ability to participate in activities that make life enjoyable (89%), loss of dignity (89%), and losing autonomy (79%).

Comments

Since 2002, both the number of prescriptions written for physician-assisted suicide and the number of terminally ill patients taking lethal medication have remained relatively stable with about 1 in 800 deaths among Oregonians in 2005 resulting from physician-assisted suicide. A large population study of dying Oregonians published in 2004 found that 17% considered PAS seriously enough to have discussed the matter with their family and that about 2% of patients formally requested PAS. Of the 1,384 decedents for whom information was gathered, one had received a prescription for lethal medication and did not take it. No unreported cases of PAS were identified.

Overall, smaller numbers of patients appear to use PAS in Oregon compared to the Netherlands. However, as detailed in previous reports, our numbers are based on a reporting system for terminally ill patients who legally receive prescriptions for lethal medications, and do not include patients and physicians who may act outside the provisions of the DWDA.

Over the last eight years, the rate of PAS among patients with ALS in Oregon has been substantially higher than among patients with other illnesses. This finding is consistent with other studies. In the Netherlands, where both PAS and euthanasia are openly practiced, one in five ALS patients died as a result of PAS or euthanasia. A study of Oregon and Washington ALS patients found that one-third of these patients discussed wanting PAS in the last month of life. Though numbers are small, and results must be interpreted with caution, Oregon HIV/AIDS patients are also more likely to use PAS.

Physicians have consistently reported that concerns about loss of autonomy, loss of dignity, and decreased ability to participate in activities that make life enjoyable as important motivating factors in patient requests for lethal medication across all eight years. Interviews with family members during 1999 corroborated physician reports. These findings were supported by a study of hospice nurses and social workers caring for PAS patients in Oregon. While it may be common for patients with a terminal illness to consider PAS, a request for PAS can be an opportunity for a medical provider to explore with patients their fears and wishes around end-of-life care, and to make patients aware of other options. Often once the provider has addressed a patient's concerns, he or she may choose not to pursue PAS.

QUESTIONS

1. When, if ever, would it be appropriate for an attorney to advise a client to seek assistance in actively terminating her own life?

2. Could an attorney ethically withdraw from representing a client who wished to assert a statutory right to physician-assisted suicide?

3. Should the American Bar Association, like the American Medical Association, adopt an "official" position on physician-assisted suicide?

4. Does the Oregon Department of Human Services Report set out above suggest that physician-assisted suicide laws create excessive risk of "erroneous" PAS decisions?

5. Palliative and Hospice Care

The World Health Organization defines palliative care as

> the active total care of patients whose disease is not responsive to curative treatment. Control of pain, of other symptoms, and of psychological, social, and spiritual problems is paramount. The goal of palliative care is achievement of the best possible quality of life for patients and their families. Many aspects of palliative care are also applicable earlier in the course of the illness for patients with chronic diseases. Palliative care affirms life and regards dying as a normal process; neither hastens nor postpones death; provides relief from pain and other distressing symptoms; integrates the psychological and spiritual aspects of patient care; offers a support system to help patients live as actively as possible until death; and offers a support system to help the family cope during the patient's illness and in their own bereavement.

Last Acts
A Means to a Better End: A Report on Dying in America
(Press Release, November 18, 2002)[*]

America does only a mediocre job of caring for its most seriously ill and dying patients, according to the nation's first state-by-state "report card" on end-of-life care released today. Last Acts, the nation's largest coalition working for better care and caring near the end of life, issued today's report, grading all 50 states and the District of Columbia on eight key elements of end-of-life care. Most states earned C's, D's and even E's on the majority of the criteria.

Corroborating these data, Last Acts also today released a national survey showing that a significant number of Americans, including those who have recently lost a loved one, are dissatisfied with the way the country's health care system provides care to the dying. The survey found that 93 percent of Americans believe improving end-of-life care is important.

The "report card" — Means to a Better End: A Report on Dying in America Today — evaluates the availability and use of key services. It is the product of more than a year's study by Last Acts, a Robert Wood Johnson Foundation funded campaign whose honorary chair is former First Lady Rosalynn Carter. Last Acts comprises more than 1,000 Partner organizations, including the American Medical Association, the American Nurses Association, the American Hospital Association, AARP and NAACP. An interactive special report on Means to a Better End, including research findings, is available on The Robert Wood Johnson Foundation Web site, http://www.rwjf.org/special/betterend.

---

[*] Copyright © 2002. Reprinted with permission.

"Changing the way America cares for the dying amounts to no less than a major social change," said Dr. Steven Schroeder, president of The Robert Wood Johnson Foundation, the nation's largest philanthropy devoted exclusively to health and health care. "As this report points out, although we have begun making progress on many fronts, today we find ourselves at a crossroads. We need the dedicated support of policymakers and health care leaders to put us on the path to establishing end-of-life care once and for all as an integral part of American medicine."

In the report, each state receives letter grades on each of eight key elements of palliative care. Palliative care, including hospice care, is widely recognized as the best approach for the seriously ill and dying. It relieves pain and other physical symptoms while supporting patients and families emotionally and spiritually and respecting their cultural traditions.

The report was compiled using the most recent data available, which were reviewed by national experts in end-of-life care.

Overall findings are:

- State Advance Directive Policies: Some states' laws include confusing language or create bureaucratic hurdles that make it difficult for citizens to express their preferences or to designate appropriate surrogate decision-makers.

- Location of Death: Although research shows that 70 percent of Americans would prefer to be at home with loved ones in their final days, only about 25 percent die at home. Where people die — in a hospital, a nursing home, hospice or at home — depends on the state or community where they live and the health care resources available there. Research has shown that these factors outweigh patient preferences.

- Rate of Hospice Use: Hospice care is a "gold standard" for end-of-life care. However, hospice is not widely used in most states. Furthermore, the average length of stay in hospice has dropped to well below the 60 days considered necessary for people to get maximum benefit. In fact, dying patients commonly have the support of hospice care for less than a week.

- Hospital End-of-Life Care Services: Though the number of organized palliative care programs in hospitals is increasing, such programs are not yet the norm. Nor do a sufficient number of hospitals offer pain management programs and hospice services.

- Care in Intensive Care Units at the End of Life: Nationwide, 28 percent of Medicare patients who die are treated in ICUs in their last six months of life. The rate varies widely, even within individual states. Patients in ICUs typically are subjected to heavy use of technology. This may be at the expense of attention to comfort or against expressed treatment preferences — often expressed as "I don't want to die hooked up to machines."

- Persistent Pain among Nursing Home Residents: Nearly half of the 1.6 million Americans living in nursing homes have persistent pain that is not noticed and not adequately treated.

- State Pain Management Policies: All states have laws addressing the use of controlled substances. Some are effective, but others create formidable barriers to good pain management.

- Numbers of Physicians and Nurses Certified in Palliative Care: Palliative care training for the nation's physicians and nurses lags far behind the needs of the aging U.S. population. This is true for medical and nursing students, as well as for the hundreds of thousands of professionals already in practice.

"Dying patients and their families today suffer more than they should," said Judith R. Peres, deputy director of Last Acts and the leader of the report's research team. "We still have a long way to go to improve health care and policy for this segment of the American population."

Peres noted that the Last Acts report offers a broad-brush statistical portrait of care for the dying across America, not a detailed analysis of each end-of-life care program in every state. "We know most states can cite examples of excellent care and progress being made to improve care," she said. "For example, over the past five years, we have seen an increase in the number of schools and textbooks teaching end-of-life care to medical and nursing students. State and local coalitions have developed innovative programs to improve care such as those making it easier for people to write advance directives. And more professional groups are getting involved in end-of-life care, including clergy, social workers and pharmacists."

"Fortunately we have examples of good end of life care. These examples take us part-way to understanding what is needed to fix the problem. To complete the journey, we recommend certain improvements," she said.

The Last Acts report recommends the following:

- Federal Policy: Medicare must be reformed to meet the needs of seriously ill and dying people. Benefits, coverage and payments must be altered to allow for seamless patient-centered care for those facing progressive, serious and terminal illnesses.

- State Policy: In many states, people will suffer needless pain until state lawmakers change the rules that affect doctors' ability to prescribe needed medications.

- Health Care Leaders: Physicians, nurses and other health care professionals must be specially trained in palliative care, and hospitals and nursing homes should have programs to deliver this care effectively. Research and data collection priorities must be established and funded.

- Families: Citizens need to understand more about end-of-life care choices and join coalitions working to expand the choices in their communities. Before placing a loved one in a nursing home or hospital, families should ask if the institution has a palliative care program — and if not, the family should find an institution that does.

Opinion Poll Shows Desire for Improved Care

Along with the national report card, Last Acts simultaneously released a public opinion poll today showing that the majority of Americans are critical of the care dying people in this country receive. Results also showed that most Americans believe improving care is important.

The survey found that six in 10 Americans give our current health care system a rating of only fair or lower, including a quarter who rate it as poor. Only one in 10 gives the system a rating of very good or excellent.

The poll, conducted by Lake Snell Perry & Associates surveyed 1,002 adults between August 30 and September 1, 2002. Three-quarters of those surveyed reported having lost a loved one — such as a family member or close friend — recently (in the past five years). People who had suffered these recent losses and people who had not were equally critical of the health care system's care for the dying, with 59 percent and 56 percent, respectively, giving a rating of only fair or worse.

Three-quarters of those surveyed rated the health care system fair or lower on assuring that families' savings are not depleted by end-of-life care. Almost half (47 percent) gave a rating of poor. Those who had had a loved one die recently were more likely to give a poor rating on this item than those who had not (49 percent vs. 40 percent).

When asked to rate the health care system for its ability to provide emotional support for the dying and their families, 46 percent of the respondents said the system does an only fair or poor job. Four in 10 believe the system is doing a good, very good, or excellent job in this area. Those who had suffered a loss recently were again more likely to give a poor rating than those who had not.

National Institute on Aging and National Cancer Institute Exploring the Role of Cancer Centers for Integrating Aging and Cancer Research (June 2001) Workshop Report, Working Group 6
Palliative Care, End-of-Life Care, and Pain Relief
http://www.nia.nih.gov/ResearchInformation/ConferencesAnd
Meetings/WorkshopReport/WorkingGroupReports/WorkingGroup6.htm

Introduction

Research on treatment- or cancer-related distress has not targeted older cancer patients as a group, even though persons aged 65 years and older experience most of the cancer burden. As a result, knowledge about measures of pain and other types of symptom control and palliative care in older cancer patients is limited. Moreover, palliative care in most adult age groups in the United States has not reached its full potential; attention to this issue is critically important, as 20 percent of the American population will be aged 65 years and older in less than three decades (by 2030). Accelerated strides in cancer therapy have tended to blur the distinction between hope for a cure and recognition that cancer is a terminal illness. In fact, cancer is often considered a chronic disease. However, recent advances in cancer treatment still require aggressive symptom management as well as psychological, social, and spiritual support throughout all phases of cancer diagnosis and treatment in all age groups. Supportive and palliative care is essential for managing the complications of cancer and its treatment at any stage of the disease. In addition, the psychosocial care of patients and families and care of the dying must be addressed.

Two key national studies have evaluated these issues. The first, a National Cancer Policy Board (NCPB) study, responded to the 1997 Institute of Medicine (IOM) report, Approaching Death: Improving Care at the End of Life, which discussed a range of end-of-life issues. This report received national attention and is now regarded as a milestone in palliative care. Opportunely, the NCPB report Improving Palliative Care for Cancer: Summary and Recommendations was issued by the IOM the week after the NIA/NCI cancer centers workshop. Two cancer center workshop participants, Dr. Kathleen M. Foley, the speaker for Working Group 6, and Dr. Charles S. Cleeland, a participant in Working Group 6, contributed to the NCPB report, which is an excellent resource for all initiatives generated from the priorities of Working Group 6.

Following the lead of the NCPB, Working Group 6 adopted the World Health Organization definition of palliative care as "the active total care of patients whose disease is not responsive to curative treatment." Control of pain; other symptoms; and psychological, social, and spiritual problems are of paramount importance in palliative care, whose goal is to achieve the best quality of life for patients and their families.

In her introductory remarks at the NIA/NCI cancer centers workshop, Dr. Foley indicated that the term palliative care was formerly associated with patients who were clearly near the end of life. In Dr. Foley's view, more comprehensive definitions of palliative care should address the multidimensional aspects — interpersonal, physical, psychological, social, and spiritual — of patients and their families. The primary objective of palliative care is to enhance the quality and meaning of life and death.

Research Questions

1. How can quality cancer care and treatment, including pain management, that provides comfort and reflects patient and family preferences be ensured for older individuals with cancer?

2. What are the available resources/difficulties in the current system for the specific needs of older patients and their caregivers during cancer care?

The lessons learned from palliative care in the older population can apply to all patients. The research priorities of Working Group 6 represent broad-based, epidemiologic studies and translational health services research. The outcomes of the proposed research may improve tolerance of therapy and supportive care and increase participation of the elderly in clinical trials.

Cancer Center Role

The NCPB report's summary and recommendations include a special focus on the contribution that cancer centers, in particular, could make to palliative care research. According to the NCPB, "NCI-designated cancer centers should play a central role as agents of national policy in advancing palliative care research and clinical practice, with initiatives that address many of the barriers identified in this report."

The activities recommended for cancer centers in palliative research include the following examples:

- Formally testing and evaluating new and existing practice guidelines for palliative and end-of-life care, such as pain relief and control of other symptoms;

- Incorporating the best palliative care, pain relief, and depression and fatigue management into NCI-sponsored clinical trials;

- Pilot testing quality indicators for end-of-life care at the patient and institutional level; and

- Developing innovations in the delivery of palliative and end-of-life care, including collaborating with local hospice organizations.

Research Priorities

1. Organize descriptive work that is relevant to older cancer patients in a well-thought-out manner.

- Outcomes should be correlated with the application of guidelines to comorbidity, treatment-related toxicities, and survival outcomes.

- Available methodologies for such evaluations need to be identified.

2. Develop and test service delivery models to provide palliative care to the elderly in a variety of contexts that include acute care, home care, and nursing homes.

- Prospective evaluations of older cancer patients should be implemented in these different settings.

- Parameters to be examined are cost of care, including the amount of cost shifted to the family (such as time off from work and the resulting loss in wages), and ways to make the models of care cost-effective.

- Prospective evaluations should address symptom control and end-of-life care over the continuum of care, as opposed to the traditional "cure versus care" approach.

- Caregivers and their activities should be evaluated to determine who they are, their locations with respect to the elderly patients for whom they care, their availability to provide care, and their own well-being.

- Special needs and resources, such as mental health, dental health, nutrition, cataracts, and hearing aids, should be addressed in these models.

- Principles of care that have research support should be applied to all age groups.

3. Test and facilitate the use of evidence-based guidelines for pain relief and symptom control. Examine drug selection, pharmacokinetics, effects of drugs on surgery, and drug-drug interactions as they relate to agents for comorbidities, chemotherapy, and palliative care medications.

- The focus should be on factors that influence decision making and outcomes, such as the ability of patients with comorbidities to understand and tolerate therapies. Physical symptoms need to be distinguished from overlapping psychological problems, such as confusion and depression.

- Access to care needs to be improved for underserved groups, including minority patients, patients whose primary language is not English, patients with limited financial resources, and patients who live far away from physicians or centers.

- Best practices for symptom control in the elderly must be determined.

- Generic guidelines for problems specific to the elderly (e.g., age-related comorbid conditions; limited functional reserve) should be examined.

Research Barriers

- Research in some areas requires descriptive studies before testing interventions. Although descriptive information is greatly needed, it is not usually highly regarded in the academic community.

- Few researchers are trained in geriatrics and palliative care.

- More health care providers in palliative care for the elderly are needed, including medical residents, hospice staff, nurse practitioners, physician assistants, and social workers. Working Group 6 also strongly recommended developing and implementing health professional training programs in palliative care for the elderly.

- The reimbursement and duration of hospice care is limited by current payment systems, which also severely limit options for palliative care, such as radiation therapy, in hospice settings.

Mechanisms

- More experts in palliative care need to participate in research, and this should be encouraged by developing incentives for investigators to design new protocols. This would demonstrate the importance of care for elderly cancer patients and of investigators' participation in research on such care.

- A Specialized Program of Research Excellence (SPORE) in symptom management and palliative care should be implemented.

- Professional education should be provided in cooperative groups and cancer center settings.

- Palliative care should be included in core grant shared resources.

- Existing Web-based resources should be used to disseminate information and assess existing data from Surveillance, Epidemiology, and End Results (SEER).

- Collaborations are needed within geriatric medicine and other pertinent specialties.

- Multidisciplinary approaches to treating elderly patients with cancer are needed to compare the new approaches with traditional models, such as Project Enable (Educate, Nurture, Advise, Before Life Ends).

- A network should be formed with the academic community to conduct research on aging and create links among NIH institutes — such as NIA; the National Heart, Lung, and Blood Institute; the National Institute of Diabetes and Digestive and Kidney Diseases; and the National Institute of Nursing Research — to focus on Alzheimer's disease, heart and lung disease, neurology, arthritis and pain, cancer, and nursing.

- A network should be formed among government agencies, such as the Centers for Medicare and Medicaid Services and the Health Resources and Services Administration, academic/regional cancer centers, and the NIH institutes to implement research findings more rapidly in cancer patients.

- Mechanisms are needed to ease navigation through the system by older cancer patients who require the support of nurses, social workers, and nutritionists. The relative costs of navigating this complex system should be assessed, and a more simple and cost-effective system of health care should be designed.

- A network should be formed with legislative bodies to inform them of findings that can be acted upon rapidly.

C. ANATOMICAL DONATIONS

For many reasons, a client may wish to ensure that, upon her death, organs or tissue are donated to individuals in need or the medical profession. Indeed, in some circumstances, organ and tissue donations may be made by living persons. Although the tendency may be to think that an older person's anatomical gift may be less "useful" than that of a younger person, this is not necessarily the case. Statistics compiled by the United Network for Organ Sharing show that in 1997, persons age 50 and older accounted for 28% of all organ donations by non-living donors, up from 11.6% in 1988, and 17.3% of all living-donor donations, up from 12.8% in 1988. Moreover, future anatomical gifts can be made as part of the larger process of planning for death, an activity in which older persons and their attorneys regularly engage. Finally, older persons are often *in need of* organ or tissue donations. A number of ethical issues, both theoretical and pragmatic, arise in connection with anatomical gift-giving. Anticipating these problems, federal and state statutes extensively regulate the area of organ and tissue donation. In this section, we look at some of these statutes and selected legal questions that are associated with their interpretation.

1. Introduction

Organ Procurement and Transplantation Network Data, National Data
http://www.optn.org[*]

Organs by Age — Current U.S. Waiting List
Based on OPTN data as of February 16, 2007

	All Ages	1 Year	1-5	6-10	11-17	18-34	35-49	50-64	65+
All Organs	94,692	116	492	427	913	10,010	26,892	42,200	13,661
Kidney	70174	4	115	142	476	8,117	21,038	29,250	11,047
Liver	16,992	75	254	180	236	837	3,385	9,962	2,066
Pancreas	1,746	16	36	0	9	275	993	410	7
Kidney / Pancreas	2,400	1	0	0	2	417	1392	580	8
Heart	2,839	33	75	59	75	289	569	1,354	385
Lung	2,844	0	9	33	111	418	707	1,359	207
Heart / Lung	132	0	3	6	10	45	42	26	0
Intestine	236	27	104	15	23	19	25	20	3

Deceased Donors Recovered in the U.S. by Donor Age
Based on OPTN data as of February 16, 2007

	To Date	2006	2005	2004	2003	2002	2001	2000	1999	1998
All Ages	106,307	7,386	7,593	7,150	6,457	6,190	6,080	5,985	5,824	5,793
1 Year	1,770	105	100	100	90	88	87	100	78	78
1-5 Years	3,926	204	190	201	166	187	208	196	201	235
6-10 Years	2,916	101	98	136	108	142	178	149	162	163
11-17 Years	10,901	478	511	542	522	518	516	564	531	587
18-34 Years	30,774	1,890	1,960	1,820	1,677	1,702	1,582	1,507	1,464	1,537
35-49 Years	26,757	1,982	1,975	1,879	1,716	1,609	1,598	1,594	1,586	1,504
50-64 Years	21,966	1,892	1,971	1,780	1,605	1,407	1,388	1,397	1,269	1,184
65 +	7,236	730	785	692	572	534	522	475	520	486
Unknown	61	4	3	0	1	3	1	3	13	19

---

[*] Copyright © 2007. United Network for Organ Sharing. Reprinted with permission.

U.S Department of Health and Human Services
Organ Donation:
The Secretary's Organ Donation Initiative
www.organdonor.gov.

Delivering on a promise he made on his first day on the job, Secretary Thompson announced his "Gift of Life Donation Initiative" on April 17, 2001.

Fifteen Americans die each day while waiting for an organ to become available. More than 75,000 men, women, and children now wait for a transplant to replace a failing kidney, heart, liver, lung or pancreas. Every 16 minutes, another person joins the waiting list.

Thousands more wait for tissue transplants, desperately need marrow to stay alive, and require blood transfusions. The facts are just astounding! Someone dies every 96 minutes because there aren't enough organs to go around. Sixty percent of the U.S. population is eligible to donate blood; however, only five percent do. And, only 25 to 35 percent of those who need a marrow transplant will find a match among their family members.

The 5 kick-off elements include:

1. *"Workplace Partnership for Life."* This feature of the Secretary's initiative involves a collaboration with companies and employee groups of all sizes to make information on donation available to employees. Employers and employee groups will be encouraged to develop their own campaigns. . . .

2. *Model Donor Card.* The Secretary unveiled a new model donor card that includes provisions for designating whether all organs and tissues may be donated, as well as lines for signatures by two witnesses. Witnesses ideally should be family members or others who are most likely to be contacted in the case of an emergency to help ensure that the donor's wishes will be carried out. An informal survey performed with the help of the American Bar Association confirmed that the card is compatible with state law in 50 states and the District of Columbia.

3. *National Forum on Donor Registries.* To help ensure that families and hospitals know an individual's wishes, HHS plans to look at mechanisms, including donor registries, to assure that an individual's intent to donate is clearly communicated. The Secretary has requested that HHS' Office of Inspector General conduct a study of existing registries that have been established by 16 states. The Health Resources and Services Administration (HRSA) will organize a national forum on the potential of registries, the options available and guidelines for registry development.

4. *National Gift of Life Medal.* The Secretary will support efforts to create a national Gift of Life medal presented to families to honor their donors.

5. *Driver's Education Curriculum.* HHS will create a model curriculum for drivers' education classes, and will encourage state and local education systems to require this curriculum. This initiative is based on a similar program implemented in Wisconsin.

Future Elements:

HHS will launch additional elements under the initiative, including review of potential federal responsibilities for monitoring the long-term safety and effectiveness of living donation (in which a kidney or part of a liver or lung are transplanted from a living donor to a recipient). In recent years, living donation has been the fastest growing source of transplanted organs, and Secretary Thompson believes HHS should do its part to ensure the safety and effectiveness of such procedures, for donor and transplant patients alike.

HHS also plans to work with other federal agencies and state governments to promote donor awareness efforts, and examine other possible steps for ensuring that individual's wishes to donate are recorded and carried out.

Ongoing Elements for Creating a Donation Friendly America:

While medical advances now enable more than 22,000 Americans per year to receive organ transplants that save or enhance their lives, not enough organs are available to help everyone in need. As a result, about 5,500 people die in the U.S. each year — about 15 every day — while waiting for a donated kidney, liver, heart, lung, or other organ. Today, more than 76,000 people are on the national organ transplant waiting list.

In recent years, progress has been made in creating awareness of the need for organ and tissue donation. Most Americans indicate they support organ donation. Nonetheless, only abut 50 percent of families asked to donate a loved one's organs agree to do so. Moreover, thousands of opportunities to donate are missed each year, either because families do not know what their loved ones wanted, or because potential donors are not identified for organ procurement organizations and their families are never asked.

The Department of Health and Human Services is committed to creating a donation friendly America. Focusing on known barriers to donation, HHS will take action to achieve substantial increases in donation and transplantation.

Ongoing Partnerships for a Donation Friendly America:

The essential role of families in consenting to donation is a key message of the initiative. Even when a donor card, driver's license, will, or living will is available to indicate the donor's wishes, next-of-kin will be asked to provide consent before donation can occur. HHS has teamed up with the Coalition on Donation, whose members include national and local organizations, to deliver a consistent, unified message on the importance of family discussion. With the Advertising Council, the Coalition on Donation has implemented a multi-year, national public awareness campaign. Materials developed for partners of the initiative feature the Coalition's message, "DONATE LIFE."

National advertising and public awareness campaigns help to communicate consistent messages about organ and tissue donation, but individuals and families also need to learn about the importance of donation from people and organizations they trust. HHS is building strong partnerships with health care, community, educational, religious, minority, professional, and ther organizations to ensure that Americans are given the opportunity to choose donation.

Health Care Community: The American Medical Association and the American Academy of Family Physicians are partnering with HHS to encourage physicians to make donation materials available in their offices and to discuss donation with patients. Already, one state medical society (the Texas Medical Association) is taking on organ donation as one of its major issues. Physicians in Texas are encouraged to offer educational materials in their offices and to express support for organ donation to patients who ask. The American Red Cross will, through its nationwide community network, expand upon its current public awareness and education activities to increase organ and tissue donation. The American Nurses Association will educate its members and provide materials. The American Association of Health Plans will encourage plans to provide members with educational materials. The National Medical Association will help educate minority medical professionals, especially through HHS' MOT-TEP program (see below.) The American Association of Neurological Surgeons and the Congress of Neurological Surgeons are also partners in the initiative.

Law Associations: The American Bar Association is partnering with HHS to encourage attorneys to discuss donation with their clients during estate planning. The ABA's Real Property, Probate, and Trust Section will distribute materials, stimulate continuing legal education programs, and encourage state and local bar associations to adopt resolutions similar to the ABA's 1992 resolution that urges attorneys to get involved in donor education efforts.

Educational Organizations: The Center for Study of the Freshman Experience and Students in Transition is teaming up with HHS to provide donor information to new college and university students in orientation packets and programs. In addition, HHS' Health Resources and Services Administration (HRSA) is funding a demonstration project with the American College Health Association, a national organization with more than 900 member institutions, to implement and test the effectiveness of college campus campaigns to increase donation. The project is modeled after a successful HRSA-sponsored pilot project at the University of Rhode Island. Finally, under a HRSA grant, TransWeb University has developed a new interactive electronic program to educate school-age children about organ donation and transplantation available at the Web site http://www.transweb.org/journey.

Religious Organizations: The Congress of National Black Churches, representing 65,000 congregations, is partnering with HHS in a national project to educate its members about organ, tissue, and bone marrow donation. The Union of American Hebrew Congregations, with support from HRSA, developed a program guide on organ donation and transplantation which it distributed to its 850 member congregations. In addition, the Presbyterian Church USA, the General Conference of the Seventh-Day Adventist Church, the Interfaith Conference of Metropolitan Washington, and other faith organizations were asked by HHS to urge congregations across the nation to consider donation during the annual National Donor Sabbath. The next National Donor Sabbath is planned for November 9-11, 2001.

Donor and Recipient Groups: The National Kidney Foundation's Donor Family Council and HHS have teamed up to create a new Web site at http://www.kidney.org/donor to provide information and bereavement support for donor families. In addition, HRSA, the Donor Family Council, and other national donor, recipient, and transplant organizations are sponsoring the seventh annual Donor Recognition Ceremony in July 2001 in Washington, D.C.

The National Minority Organ/Tissue Transplant Education Program (MOT-TEP): A collaborative effort between NIH's Office of Research on Minority Health and the National Institute of Diabetes and Digestive and Kidney Diseases, is the first national program specifically designed to empower minority communities to become involved in education activities to increase the number of minority donors and transplant recipients. More minority organ donors are needed to increase the chances that a well-matched organ will be available to minorities waiting for transplants. Now in 15 sites across the country, MOT-TEP's target audience represents the African American, Hispanic/Latino, Native American, Asian, Pacific Islander, and Alaskan Native populations. MOTTEP also includes a health promotion and disease prevention component, to reduce the incidence of conditions such as diabetes and hypertension that can lead to organ failure.

Business Organizations: The U.S. Chamber of Commerce and the Washington Business Group on Health, representing many large and small businesses and organizations, will help their members conduct employee organ and tissue donation education campaigns. The Home Depot will also conduct educational activities for employees.

State Organizations: HHS is working with the National Governors' Association, the National Conference of State Legislatures, the Council of State Governments and the Association of State and Territorial Health Officials to disseminate information about model programs and legislation and to encourage state activities to increase donation.

Media: The James Redford Institute for Transplant Awareness will reach out to national media organizations, especially using its films to build public awareness of the need for organ donation.

In addition, with assistance from the Office of Personnel Management, HHS is collaborating with other federal agencies to encourage federal employees to become donors, to share their decision with family members, and to serve as a model for the nation. For example, the Department of Defense, which has taken a progressive approach by routinely asking patients in its health care system to consider donation, is stepping up its efforts to encourage donation by making materials available in its treatment facilities and by improving the education of its providers on effective communication with patients and their families. In addition, the Office of Personnel Management included a full-page ad on donation in the Guide to Federal Employees Health Benefits Plans which was distributed to all federal employees. HHS is providing brochures, posters, ID badge stickers and other materials to Federal agencies to share with their employees.

Learning More About What Works to Improve Donation and Transplantation

On April 17th, HRSA announced the availability of $3 million in new grant funds to continue to support demonstrations of innovative approaches for increasing donation.

HHS agencies including HRSA, the National Institutes of Health, and the Health Care Financing Administration will conduct activities to identify the best approaches to increasing donation and priorities for future research.

National Women's Health Information Center
U.S. Department of Health and Human Services
Office of Women's Health
Organ Donation and Transplantation
http://www.4woman.gov/faq/organ_donation.htm

What is organ donation and transplantation?

Organs or tissues from one person (the donor) are put into another person's body (the recipient). People of all ages and backgrounds should consider themselves likely donors. What is the status of organ donation and transplantation in the United States?

The number of people needing a transplant continues to rise faster than the number of donors. About 3,700 transplant candidates are added to the national waiting list each month. Each day, about 77 people receive organ transplants. However, 18 people die each day waiting for transplants that can't take place because of the shortage of donated organs. There are now more than 94,000 people on the waiting list. Experts suggest that each of us could save or help as *many as 50 people by being an organ and tissue donor.*

Who can be an organ donor?

There are no age limits on who can donate. Newborns as well as senior citizens have been organ donors. If you are under age 18, you must have a parent's or guardian's consent. If you are 18 years or older, you can show you want to be an organ and tissue donor by signing a donor card. You can download and print an organ donor card at www.organdonor.gov/newdonorcard.pdf. Carry the card in your wallet. In some states, you can state your intent to be an organ donor on your driver's license. Even if you sign a donor card and/or state your intent on your driver's license, make sure your family knows your wishes. Your family may be asked to sign a consent form in order for your donation to occur. You may also want to tell your family health care provider, lawyer, and your religious leader that you would like to be a donor.

What organs and tissues can I donate?

- Kidney
- Heart
- Liver
- Lung
- Pancreas
- Intestines

- Cornea

- Skin

- Bone

- Bone marrow

Does the donor's family have to pay for the cost of organ donation?

No. The donor's family neither pays for, nor receives payment for organ and tissue donation. The transplant recipient's health insurance policy, Medicare, or Medicaid usually covers the cost of transplant.

If I am a donor, will that affect the quality of my medical care?

No. Many people think that if they agree to donate their organs, the doctor or the emergency room staff won't work as hard to save their life. This is not true. The transplant team is completely separate from the medical staff working to save your life. The transplant team does not become involved with you until doctors have determined that all possible efforts to save your life have failed.

Does organ donation disfigure your body?

No. Donation does not change the appearance of the body. Organs are removed surgically in a routine operation. It does not interfere with having a funeral, including open casket services.

Can I be an organ or tissue donor and also donate my body to medical science?

No. Total body donation is an option, but not if you choose to be an organ or tissue donor. If you wish to donate your entire body, you should contact the facility of your choice to make arrangements. Medical schools, research facilities, and other agencies need to study bodies to gain greater understanding of diseases in humans. This research is vital to saving and improving lives.

Can non-resident aliens donate and receive organs?

Non-resident aliens can both donate and receive organs in the United States.

Why should minorities be concerned about organ donation?

The need for transplants is high among minorities, particularly African Americans.

1. Some diseases of the kidney, heart, lung, pancreas, and liver that can lead to organ failure are found more frequently in minority women.

2. The rate of organ donation from minority women does not keep pace with the number needing transplants. Although minority women donate, in part, to their share of the population, their need for transplants is greater.

3. Matching donor organs to likely recipients requires genetic similarity. In most cases, people are more similar to people of their own race than to people of other races.

4. Minority women may have to wait longer for matched organs and therefore may be sicker at the time of transplant or die waiting. With more donated organs from this group, finding a match will be quicker and the waiting time will be cut, and more lives will be saved.

Who manages the distribution of organs?

The United Network for Organ Sharing (UNOS) maintains the Organ Procurement and Transplantation Network (OPTN). Through the UNOS Organ Center, organ donors are matched to waiting recipients 24 hours a day, 365 days a year.

What is the process for receiving an organ for transplantation?

1. If you need an organ transplant, your doctor will help you get on the national waiting list.

2. To get on the list, you need to visit a transplant hospital. Every transplant hospital in the United States is a member of UNOS. You can use the UNOS directory at www.unos.org/members/search.asp to find a transplant hospital.

3. A doctor will examine you and decide if you meet the criteria to be put on the list. You also can get on the waiting list at more than one transplant hospital. Each hospital has its own criteria for listing patients. If you meet their criteria, they will add you to the list.

4. The hardest part of this process is waiting. There is no way to know how long you will wait to receive a donor organ.

5. Your name will be added to a pool of names. When an organ donor becomes available, all the patients in the pool are compared to that donor. Factors such as blood and tissue type, size of the organ, medical urgency of the patient's illness, time already spent on the waiting list, and distance between donor and recipient are considered.

The organ is offered first to the candidate who is the best match. The organ is distributed locally first, and if no match is found, it is offered regionally and then nationally until a recipient is found.

2. The Uniform Anatomical Gift Act

Read the Revised Uniform Anatomical Gift Act in the statutory supplement. The 1968 version of this Act was adopted in every state; the 1987 version (which is reproduced in the supplement) in about half the states. In 2006, the National Conference of Commissioners on Uniform State Laws promulgated the 2006 Revised Uniform Anatomical Gift Act which is set out in the statutory supplement. As February 2007, no state had yet adopted the revised Act, although it had been introduced in several jurisdictions' legislative sessions.

QUESTIONS

1. What problems of interpretation does the language of the 1987 UAGA suggest?

2. Does the UAGA create an unacceptable risk of overreaching by potential beneficiaries of an anatomical gift?

3. One reason for the severe organ shortage in the U.S. is due to misconceptions about how organs are allocated and the effect of donation on the appearance of the body after death. What role should the elder law attorney play in attempting to correct these and similar notions?

a. Counseling the Client

UNIFORM DONOR CARD OF

_____

Print or type name of donor

In the hope that I may help others, I hereby make the anatomical gift, if medically acceptable, to take affect uopn my death.

The words and marks below indicate my desires.

I give   (a) _____ any needed organs or parts

          (b) _____ only the following organs or parts.

_____

Specify the organ(s) or part(s)

For the purposes of transplantation, therapy, medical research or education.

         (c) _____ my body for anatomical study if needed

Limitations or special wishes if any

_____

Fold

Signed by the donor and the following two witnesses in the presence of each other:

_____

Signature of donor   Date of Birth of Donor

_____

Date Signed   City & State

_____

Witness   Witness

QUESTIONS

1. What considerations are likely to be relevant to a client's decisions concerning after-death organ donation?

2. How proactive should the attorney be in encouraging organ donation by her clients as part end-of-life planning process?

b. Problems of Interpretation

Daniel G. Jardine
Comment: Liability Issues Arising out of Hospitals' and Organ Procurement Organizations' Rejection of Valid Anatomical Gifts: The Truth and Consequences
1990 WIS. L. REV. 1655, 1657-58[*]

Surprising as it may seem, despite the UAGA's unequivocal declaration that a decedent's written directive makes the donation of his organs a valid gift effective upon death, and that persons who accept such gifts in good faith are insulated from civil and criminal liability, the gifts are almost always rejected by attending physicians, hospitals and organ procurement organizations (OPOs). Though contrary to the clear language of the UAGA and the presumed intent of the state legislatures that have adopted it, healthcare officials will not accept organs donated by a decedent unless they obtain "consent" from the next of kin. However, it is clear that "consent" is a misnomer. In the eyes of the law, health care officials actually first reject the gift of the decedent, then look to the next of kin to make an anatomical gift (which is allowed by the UAGA when there is no indication of contrary intention by the decedent).

QUESTIONS

Why would potential beneficiaries or medical professionals reject a facially valid anatomical gift? Is this consistent with, for example, the medical profession's self-described duty to "do no harm"?

ALCOR LIFE EXTENSION
FOUNDATION, INC. v. MITCHELL
9 CAL. RPTR. 2d 572 (Cal. App. 1992)

JUDGES: Opinion by GATES, Acting P. J., with NOTT, J., and MANELLA, J., concurring

Appealing from the judgment entered in favor of Alcor Life Extension Foundation, Inc. (Alcor), and two of its members, the Department of Health Services,

---

[*] Copyright © 1977 by The Board of Regents of the University of Wisconsin System. Reprinted by permission of the *Wisconsin Law Review*.

its Office of the State Registrar and their respective heads (referred to collectively as DHS unless otherwise indicated), seek a determination from this court "that death certificates and disposition permits cannot be issued for bodies of persons who have designated Alcor as a donee pursuant to the Uniform Anatomical Gift Act [Health and Safety Code section 7150 *et seq.*] and have directed Alcor to store their bodies in cryonic suspension."

As set forth in Alcor's first amended complaint, "Cryonic suspension (also known as cryogenic suspension) is a process by which the legally dead but biologically viable body of a person who has been ill or injured is preserved at low temperatures until such time as medical science may be capable of reviving the person and implementing effective cure or treatment of the illness or injury. Since 1964, the practice of cryonic suspension has become widespread, with organizations formed in major cities to provide cryonic suspension for their members. The first reported cryonically suspended person has been maintained in that state since 1967."

The question here tendered is peculiarly unique and extremely narrow in scope and, hopefully, our affirmance of the challenged judgment will completely preclude this particular issue from arising again in the future. That is to say, we merely examine the propriety of the trial court's decision concerning DHS's recent actions which have resulted in the denial of death certificates (Health & Saf. Code, § 10375) and disposition permits (Health & Saf. Code, § 10376) to Alcor members who have been placed in cryonic suspension. Neither side contends these individuals are not legally dead (Health & Saf. Code, § 7180) and otherwise entitled to death certificates. Their conflict relates solely to the obtainment of disposition permits.

The trial court has expressed no opinion on the validity of cryonics or the manner in which it should be regulated, nor do we. The initial determination of such issues, at least in the absence of any conflict, is clearly an administrative or legislative function.

Even DHS, despite its determined efforts to render Alcor's operations illegal, asserts "this case is not an attempt to prohibit cryonic suspension activity." In fact, until questioned by us, in both its opening and closing briefs, DHS expressed a willingness to grant Alcor all necessary documentation if it would but utilize subterfuge to disguise its actual structure and the true nature of its operations. By way of example, although subsequently recanted, DHS in its reply brief had stated: "The Department has encouraged Alcor to obtain a license as a cemetery or mausoleum or appoint another entity, such as a research institute, hospital, or physician, as the donee under the U.A.G.A. so that Alcor's members can have their bodies or body parts cryonically suspended legitimately. However, Alcor has refused to do so."

Turning to the specific contention at hand, section 10375 of the Health and Safety Code provides: "No person shall dispose of human remains unless (a) there has been obtained and filed with a local registrar a death certificate, as provided in chapter 5 (commencing with Section 10200) of this division [division 9, Vital Statistics], and (b) there has been obtained from a local registrar a permit for disposition."

Appellant Office of the State Registrar is charged with executing the state's vital statistic statutes (Health & Saf. Code, § 10000 *et seq.*), including those pertaining to disposition permits. (Health & Saf. Code, § 10375 et seq.) It also has supervisory power over local registrars to insure uniform compliance with the requirements of vital statistics laws. (Health & Saf. Code, § 10026.)

Health and Safety Code section 10376 identifies three permissible methods of treating human remains for the purpose of the disposition permit: interment in a cemetery; cremation; and burial at sea. Viewed merely semantically, under the Health and Safety Code's circular definitions (*see* Health & Saf. Code, §§ 7003, 7005, 7009, 7012, 7015) Alcor might possibly be said to be operating a mausoleum. However, such statutory language was aptly characterized in *Cemetery Board v. Telophase Society of America* (1978) 87 Cal.App.3d 847, 855 [151 Cal. Rptr. 248], as "virtually nonsensical," and neither party, albeit for different reasons, now wishes Alcor to be so considered.

DHS has also recognized "scientific use," a disposition associated with the Uniform Anatomical Gift Act as an additional means of legally dealing with human remains. An anatomical gift of all or part of an individual's body may be made to the following donees:

   (1) A hospital, physician, surgeon, or procurement organization, for transplantation, therapy, medical or dental education, research, or advancement of medical or dental science.

   (2) An accredited medical or dental school, college, or university for education, research, or advancement of medical or dental science.

   (3) A designated individual for transplantation or therapy needed by that individual." (Health & Saf. Code, § 7153, subd. (a).)

For a number of years Alcor was apparently permitted to operate under that act. However, in March 1988, the Chief of the Office of the State Registrar, David W. Mitchell, in a letter making explicit reference to Alcor, advised the Riverside County Coroner that burial permits may not be issued for cryonic suspension. Mitchell further admonished that state law provides for "storage" of a dead body only if it is used "for scientific purposes or qualifies as a gift under the Anatomical Gift Act" and pointed out that disposing of a dead body anywhere in the city or county, except within a cemetery, is a misdemeanor.

Three months later, in response to an inquiry from the Riverside County Department of Health, Mitchell stated if Alcor was storing bodies or body parts in its facility, it would be "guilty of a misdemeanor" and "should be reported to the local District Attorney for investigation and prosecution as appropriate."

Shortly thereafter, DHS, through its Office of the State Registrar and pursuant to its supervisory authority over local registrars, issued a "Handbook for Local Registrars of Birth and Death" which instructed local registrars that disposition of human remains by cryonic suspension does not constitute "scientific use" within the meaning of the Uniform Anatomical Gift Act. The 1990 version of this book, the most recent one available at the time the instant summary judgment motion was heard, similarly specified: "The holding of human bodies in cryonic suspension does not constitute the operation of a cemetery, nor does arranging to have one's body so placed meet the scientific use requirements of the Uniform Anatomical Gift Act."

The authority cited for this statement was 63 Ops. Atty. Gen. 879 (1980). In its representation of DHS on this appeal, the Attorney General still purports to rely upon that opinion despite making suggestions which are totally inconsistent with the views it expressed there. Of course, such an opinion, even when correct, a debatable proposition here, would not be binding on this court. (*California Assn. of Psychology Providers v. Rank* (1990) 51 Cal. 3d 1, 17 [270 Cal.Rptr. 796, 793 P.2d 2].)

DHS now advises that it subsequently has altered its posture, concluding "it does not have the authority to determine whether or not cryogenic suspension of dead bodies or body parts constitutes valid science research and that such question should appropriately be decided by the Legislature." However, this shift in position does not aid Alcor since DHS refuses to recognize Alcor as a "procurement organization" for purposes of the Uniform Anatomical Gift Act, the donee category into which Alcor might possibly fit.

A procurement organization is defined as "a person licensed, accredited, or approved under the laws of any state or by the State Department of Health Services for procurement, distribution, or storage of human bodies or parts." (Health & Saf. Code, § 7150.1, subd. (j).)

DHS points out that Alcor has not been "licensed, accredited or approved" to function as a procurement organization, though obviously Alcor could not possibly have done so since DHS has not established any procedure or mechanism which would permit Alcor or any other organization even to make application therefor. DHS then announces its intention to await "further guidance from the Legislature prior to even considering Alcor as a possible procurement organization." It argues that Health and Safety Code section 7150.1 is merely a definitional provision.

Understandably, the trial court declined to accept this "catch-22" approach which exposes Alcor to potential criminal liability. Therefore, it "permanently enjoined and . . . ordered [DHS] to desist from prohibiting, instructing or directing against, or otherwise interfering with, the registration of deaths or the issuance of disposition permits for the bodies of persons who have designated Alcor as a donee pursuant to the Uniform Anatomical Gift Act (Health and Safety Code § 7150 *et seq.*) and who have directed that Alcor place their bodies in cryonic suspension, provided that . . . in the event and at such time as [DHS] implements an otherwise lawful licensing and registration system for procurement organizations pursuant to the Uniform Anatomical Gift Act, plaintiff Alcor will be subject to lawful and reasonable licensing and registration requirements."

Under the circumstances, particularly in the absence of any evidence that Alcor's operations pose an actual threat to the public health, we agree with the injunctive relief ordered by the trial court. We need not determine whether each of the court's individual findings was correct. It is enough that we agree DHS's sudden and unexplained about-face with respect to Alcor's status as a donee under the Uniform Anatomical Gift Act cannot be premised upon Alcor's failure to secure a license as a procurement organization when DHS has failed to establish a mechanism for obtaining such a license. Such conduct is, at the very least, inconsistent with DHS's basic duty to administer and enforce the statutes pertaining to the registration of death certificates and issuance of disposition permits.

In that regard, DHS frankly acknowledges that its "Office of the State Registrar [is] charged with the duty . . . of registering births, deaths, marriages, etc." but declares it is "at [a] loss as to how to register the status" of cryonically suspended persons without first receiving "specific guidance from the Legislature." However, like the trial court, we take a more sanguine view of appellants' abilities. In any event, if, in carrying out the trial court's mandate DHS proceeds in a fashion contrary to that envisioned by the Legislature because of the lack of statutory guidance, that body will no doubt take corrective action.

DHS also poses a number of what it characterizes as "serious questions," e.g.: "Should cryonically suspended people be considered 'dead' or should a separate category of 'suspended' people be created? How should such people be registered in official records? . . . What happens to the estate and the assets of the 'decedent' after the decedent is put in cryonic suspension? . . . What would happen to such estate and assets if and when cryonic suspension is successful and the decedent is restored to life? Whose identity is the person to assume or be assigned and what of the record of the person's death? Alcor also stores body parts, such as human heads and hands. In such cases, whose identity will the suspended heads and hands assume upon their restoration; the identity of the original owner of the body part or the identity of the new body to which the body part will be attached?"

These are, of course, but a few of the presently imaginable conundrums which could arise should Alcor at some future time actually succeed in reviving the currently dead. Nonetheless, we are confident that those persons who will then head our various branches of government will be far wiser than we and entirely capable of resolving such dilemmatic issues without our assistance.

The judgment is affirmed.

NOTT, J., and MANELLA, J., concurred.

QUESTIONS

1. How vulnerable is the senior population to the activities of organizations such as Alcor? In this regard, see Lawrence Donegan, *Frozen in Memory*, THE OBSERVER (July 14, 2002), http://observer.guardian.co.uk/focus/story/0,6903, 754898,00.html (concerning baseball great Ted Williams).

2. How might an attorney, without patronizing her client, "protect" the client from unscrupulous offers of "immortality"?

RAHMAN v. THE MAYO CLINIC

578 N.W.2d 802 (Minn. App. 1998)

SHORT, Judge

Marilyn Rahman brought suit against The Mayo Clinic after discovering it had retained her deceased son's pelvic block. On appeal from a grant of summary judgment in favor of the Clinic, Rahman argues the trial court erred in granting summary judgment under the Uniform Anatomical Gift Act's (UAGA) good faith immunity provision, MINN. STAT. § 525.9221(c) (1996).

FACTS

On March 17, 1994, Christopher Rahman (the decedent) was admitted to Saint Mary's Hospital, as the result of a self-inflicted gunshot wound to the head. The decedent was placed in the intensive care unit, where he was treated by Dr. Marc Goldman (treating physician), the chief resident associate of the Clinic's neurosurgery department. The following day, the treating physician determined the decedent's neurologic condition was "very poor" and concluded the gunshot wound would prove fatal. The treating physician informed the decedent's mother, Marilyn Rahman (Rahman), of his prognosis and that she had a right to make a donation of organs and tissue pursuant to the Uniform Anatomical Gift Act (UAGA), MINN. STAT. § 525.9214(a) (1996). Elizabeth Gayner, an employee of Life Source, a tissue and organ procurement agency, also spoke with Rahman at the Clinic to explain organ and tissue donation.

That same day, the decedent was declared brain-dead. Rahman again spoke with the treating physician and agreed to make a donation of organs and tissue. Rahman and the treating physician completed part of the organ donation permission form, which stated:

> Permission is granted for organ or tissue donation for transplantation, research or education purposes (subject to restrictions indicated below)
> Yes   No
>
> Restrictions:

The treating physician checked the "yes" box, wrote "none" on the restrictions line, and signed the form and placed it back into the decedent's medical charts. Rahman told the treating physician that she did not want a postmortem examination.

Subsequently, Rahman had a second conversation with Gayner. Rahman told Gayner that the decedent's organs were not to be used for medical research or education. Based on this conversation, Gayner wrote "no research" above the restriction area and added the phrase "heart, heart for valve, lungs, liver, pancreas, [k]idneys, long bones of lower extremities" to the restrictions line on the original organ donation permission form. Gayner failed to write "no education purposes" on the form. The treating physician was not present during Gayner's second conversation with Rahman, was unaware of Rahman's intentions to impose restrictions, and did not see the revised permission form.

After some of the decedent's organs were harvested for transplant purposes, the body was taken to an autopsy suite. Despite Rahman's objections, the coroner ordered an autopsy pursuant to MINN. STAT. § 390.11, subd. 2 (1996), due to the violent nature of the decedent's death. An autopsy was performed by a Clinic pathologist and pathology resident. As a standard part of the autopsy procedure, the decedent's pelvic block, which consists of the prostate, seminal vesicles, urinary bladder, and rectum, was removed and examined. The pathologist, who had read a copy of the revised organ donation permission form prior to performing the autopsy, decided to retain the pelvic block for educational use in the Mayo Medical School. The pelvic block, which would eventually be mounted in Plexiglass for use in the medical school, was placed into a container with fixative fluid for preservation and kept in a locked storage room, known as the "museum," at the Clinic.

Shortly thereafter, Rahman brought an unrelated suit against the decedent's life insurance carrier regarding death benefits. This suit was settled. During a review of her attorney's files, Rahman read that the decedent's urinary bladder, prostate, and seminal vesicles had been "preserved with [his] pelvic block for [the] museum." Rahman retained new counsel, who contacted the Clinic and discussed Rahman's concerns. The Clinic informed Rahman's counsel the pelvic block had not yet been used for research or educational purposes, and sought further instructions. Rahman commenced this lawsuit against the Clinic, Mayo Foundation, Mayo Group Practices, Mayo Foundation for Medical Education and Research, and Mayo Medical Services, Ltd. (collectively "the Clinic"), alleging it: (1) violated the UAGA, MINN. STAT. § 525.9212 (1996); (2) intentionally, recklessly, or negligently removed, withheld, mutilated, or operated upon the decedent's body; and (3) intentionally or unintentionally caused Rahman emotional distress.

ISSUE

Did Rahman present any evidence to defeat the Clinic's claim it acted in good faith under the UAGA?

ANALYSIS

On appeal from a grant of summary judgment, we must determine whether any genuine issues of material fact exist and whether the trial court erred in applying the law. MINN. R. CIV. P. 56.03; *State by Cooper v. French*, 460 N.W.2d 2, 4 (Minn. 1990). While we view the evidence in the light most favorable to the nonmoving party, the nonmovant must produce specific facts to create an issue for trial. We need not defer to the trial court's decision on purely legal issues.

Minnesota has adopted, without substantial modification, the UAGA. *See* MINN. STAT. §§ 525.921-.9224 (1996) (providing method of making anatomical gifts). The UAGA establishes a statutory scheme which outlines the means of effecting an anatomical gift, the classes of individuals entitled to effect such a gift, and the circumstances under which such a gift must be deemed null and void. The UAGA was enacted in response to the need for more family donations of organs and to the medical profession's uncertainty about whose consent was necessary for donations. *Perry v. Saint Francis Hosp. & Med. Ctr.*, 886 F. Supp. 1551, 1557 (D. Kan. 1995); *see* Unif. Anatomical Gift Act (1968) Prefatory Note,

8A U.L.A. 64-65 (1993) (recognizing need for comprehensive act addressing organ donation and concluding UAGA, wherever enacted, will eliminate uncertainty and protect all parties); *see also* Gloria J. Banks, *Legal and Ethical Safeguards: Protection of Society's Most Vulnerable Participants in a Commercialized Organ Transplantation System,* 21 AM. J.L. & MED. 45, 67 (1995) (stating UAGA amended in 1987 to better address issues, such as concern over providing "encouraged volunteerism" system with teeth needed to increase supply of transplantable organs); E. Blythe Stason, *The Uniform Anatomical Gift Act,* 23 BUS. LAW 919, 921-24 (1968) (recognizing legal uncertainties of organ donation laws during pre-UAGA era as providing major basis for adoption of model act).

In furtherance of its goals, the UAGA provides, in pertinent part:

> (a) If, at or near the time of death of a patient, there is no documentation in the medical record that the patient has made or refused to make an anatomical gift, the hospital administrator or a representative designated by the administrator shall discuss with the patient or a relative of the patient the option to make or refuse to make an anatomical gift and may request the making of an anatomical gift pursuant to section 525.9211 or 525.9212. The request must be made with reasonable discretion and sensitivity to the circumstances of the family. * * * An entry must be made in the medical record of the patient, stating the name of the individual making the request, and the name, response, and relationship to the patient of the person to whom the request was made.

MINN. STAT. § 525.9214 (a). The UAGA further provides:

> An anatomical gift by a person authorized * * * must be made by (i) a document of gift signed by the person, or (ii) the person's telegraphic, recorded telephonic, or other recorded message, or other form of communication from the person that is contemporaneously reduced to writing and signed by the recipient.

MINN. STAT. § 525.9212(c).

The Clinic moved for summary judgment arguing: (1) it had permission to retain the decedent's pelvic block for educational purposes, and in the alternative; (2) it was immune from liability under the UAGA's good faith immunity provision. In granting the Clinic's motion, the trial court concluded Rahman "failed to provide *any* evidence that the [Clinic] acted in deliberate contravention of [Rahman's] wishes." (Emphasis in original.) We are asked whether the Clinic's actions fall within the UAGA's good faith immunity provision.

The UAGA insulates individuals involved in the organ procurement process from civil and criminal liability, so long as they act in good faith. *See* MINN. STAT. § 525.9221(c) (providing hospital or person, acting in accordance with UAGA or with applicable anatomical gift law of another state or foreign country or attempting in good faith to do so, is not liable for that act in civil action or criminal proceeding). That statute provides immunity from suit, not simply a defense to liability. Whether actions constitute good faith is a question of law, properly resolved on summary judgment.

Neither the Minnesota legislature nor Minnesota courts have defined good faith in the context of the UAGA. However, other jurisdictions consistently define this statutory good faith requirement as activity involving an "honest belief, the absence of malice, and the absence of design to defraud or to seek an unconscionable advantage." In keeping with the UAGA's goal of providing uniformity among states, we adopt that definition of good faith. *See Perry*, 886 F. Supp. at 1558 (adopting same general definition of good faith in order to assure uniformity in enforcement and interpretation of UAGA among different states).

Both the treating physician and Gayner discussed organ donation with Rahman. Both completed parts of the organ donation permission form under Rahman's direction. With Gayner, Rahman expressed her desire that the decedent's organs not be used for medical research or education. Thus, the question of the Clinic's immunity turns on whether Rahman's instructions to Gayner are sufficient to negate the Clinic's claim that it acted out of an honest belief, and in the absence of fraud or design to seek an unconscionable advantage.[2] *See, e.g., Lyon*, 843 F. Supp. at 534 (concluding issue of hospital's good faith turns on whether everyone at hospital relied on signed form or whether hospital arranged for enucleation despite fact someone in authority knew family did not consent).

The undisputed facts are critical to our analysis. Despite Rahman's instruction that the decedent's organs not be used for medical research or education, Gayner only wrote "no research" on the permission form, and "heart, heart for valves, lungs, liver, pancreas, kidneys, long bones of lower extremities" on the restrictions line. Therefore, the revised organ donation permission form did not prevent the use of organs for educational purposes. The Clinic's pathologist read that form and decided to retain the pelvic block for educational use at the Mayo Clinic School. However, after learning Rahman's true intentions, the Clinic immediately attempted to correct the error.

Viewing the evidence in the light most favorable to Rahman, we conclude Rahman's conversation with Gayner is insufficient to negate the Clinic's claim that it acted in good faith because the Clinic pathologist relied on a facially valid organ donation permission form and, unaware of Rahman's actual wishes, acted out of an honest belief that retention of the decedent's pelvic block was in accordance with those wishes. *See Perry*, 886 F. Supp. at 1559 (concluding court can find as matter of law that hospital's actions were taken in good faith even when person in authority had actual notice of contrary indications); *see also Nicoletta*, 519 N.Y.S.2d at 931 (concluding Eye Bank entitled to good faith immunity when agent acted in justified reliance on written permission form that complied with requirements of UAGA and plaintiff failed to present any evidence Eye Bank had actual notice of any opposition to gift); *see, e.g., Lyon*, 843

---

[2] Rahman alleges Gayner was a designee of the clinic because she: (1) spoke with Rahman; (2) completed organ donation forms; and (3) oversaw the organ donation process. *See* MINN. STAT. § 525.9214(a) (providing hospital administrator or representative designated by administrator shall discuss wiht patient or relative option to make or refuse to make anatomical gift). Due to the posture of this case, we must assume Gayner is a designee of the Clinic.

F. Supp. at 535-36 (concluding hospital entitled to good faith immunity despite one doctor's knowledge of plaintiffs' contrary intentions where hospital employees relied on organ donation form and were unaware of plaintiffs' wishes).

Rahman also argues the good faith immunity provision of the UAGA is inapplicable because the Clinic removed the decedent's pelvic block during an autopsy, after the organ donation process was complete. *See* MINN. STAT. § 525.9221(c) (providing good faith immunity only to individuals acting in accordance with UAGA). However, the UAGA does not require organs to be harvested before an autopsy is performed; the statute specifically permits harvesting any time after death, and prior to embalming. *See* MINN. STAT. § 525.9217(a) (providing donee, upon death of donor and before embalming, shall cause body part donated to be removed without unnecessary mutilation); *see also* MINN. STAT. § 525.9213(a) (providing coroner or medical examiner may release and permit removal of body part within official's custody for transplantation or therapy under certain circumstances). Here, the Clinic's actions were taken pursuant to the UAGA. The Clinic's organ donation permission form, which places no time restrictions on the organ donation process, accompanied the decedent's body to the autopsy suite. The organ donation permission form was relied on by the pathologist, who decided to retain the decedent's pelvic block for educational purposes. Moreover, Rahman's lawsuit is based on her belief that, in retaining the decedent's pelvic block, the Clinic exceeded its authority under the UAGA. Under these circumstances, the UAGA, not the autopsy statute, is controlling. Thus, we conclude the Clinic's retention of the pelvic block after an autopsy does not prevent application of the UAGA's good faith immunity provision.

Rahman finally argues the Clinic may not use its own ambiguous forms to justify exceeding a patient's consent. However, the revised organ donation permission form unambiguously permits retention of organs for educational purposes. Even assuming an ambiguity existed, it would be insufficient to overcome the Clinic's claim of good faith immunity unless Rahman demonstrated the Clinic failed to act out of an honest belief that its actions were in accordance with Rahman's wishes. *See, e.g., Perry*, 886 F. Supp. at 1559-60 (concluding hospital not entitled to summary judgment based on good faith immunity where there was evidence of conscious or intentional wrongdoing carried out for dishonest purposes or furtive design).

DECISION

Rahman failed to allege any facts that demonstrate the Clinic acted dishonestly, maliciously, fraudulently, or unconscionably. There are no genuine issues of material fact to preclude summary judgment in favor of the Clinic.

Affirmed.

JACOBSEN v. MARIN GENERAL HOSPITAL
963 F. Supp. 866 (N.D. Cal. 1997),
aff'd, 192 F.3d 881 (9th Cir. 1999)

PATEL, District Judge.

MEMORANDUM AND ORDER

Plaintiffs Karen and Hardy Jacobsen (collectively, "plaintiffs") brought this action against defendants Marin General Hospital ("Hospital"), California Transplant Donor Network, Inc. ("Network") and Marin County Coroner's Office ("Coroner") alleging various claims under California law arising from the harvesting of organs from the body of their son Martin Jacobsen ("Martin"). This case is before the court pursuant to the court's diversity jurisdiction. 28 U.S.C. § 1332. Now before the court are separate motions to dismiss submitted by all three defendants in this action.

Having considered the parties' arguments and submissions and for the reasons stated below, the court now issues the following memorandum and order.

Background

Plaintiffs are citizens and residents of the Kingdom of Denmark and the parents of Martin Jacobsen, also a Danish citizen. Martin was visiting the United States as a tourist when he was found unconscious and suffering from head trauma in the early morning hours of October 4, 1995 on Northbound 101, south of the Waldo Tunnel in Sausalito, California. The parties do not know how this occurred. Martin was taken to defendant Hospital and admitted at 4:05 a.m. on October 4. At this time, Dr. Morris, the attending physician, presumed he was homeless and indicated that no identification had been made. At 8:25 a.m., defendant Network contacted defendant Coroner requesting organ donation; Coroner denied this request. At 9:00 a.m. on October 4, a search began for Martin's next of kin or other persons authorized to make an anatomical gift.

At 9:30 a.m. on October 4, photos were taken by the Marin County Sheriff's Office ("Sheriff") and the Coroner, where a blue card stating "Jacobsen, M" and "10/4/95" was displayed with the body. At 12:25 p.m., another request for organ donation was made, but Dr. Morris indicated that Martin was not brain dead at that time. At 2:00 p.m., Network called the Sheriff who revealed that the patient had been identified by the FBI as Martin Jacobsen from New York City.

The following day, on October 5, 1995 at 9:00 a.m., Network spoke with the Sheriff who stated that he felt "9/10" sure that the patient was Martin Jacobsen. At 9:40 a.m., Dr. Ramirez made a clinical determination of brain death. At 3:00 p.m., another determination of brain death was made by Dr. Nisam who stated in his report that the patient was being maintained pending identification of next of kin and that an extensive forty hour search by the Sheriff, Coroner, and FBI to find any family member or identification of the patient had been unsuccessful. His report also indicated that the body was "officially released" to Network for organ donation.

On October 6, 1995 around 9:00 a.m., the Sheriff reported to Network that they were unable to locate the identification of "this John Doe." At 10:13 a.m., Network requested authorization from Coroner to recover the organs of "John Doe." Coroner consented. Martin's kidney, liver, pancreas and heart were removed and the harvesting was completed at 2:16 a.m. on October 7, 1995.

Neither Martin nor plaintiffs would have consented to the maintenance of Martin's body or the removal of his organs for the purposes of making an anatomical gift. Plaintiffs filed their original complaint on October 4, 1996 and an amended complaint on January 22, 1997. Defendants Hospital, Network and Coroner subsequently filed separate motions to dismiss pursuant to Federal Rule of Civil Procedure 12(b)(6).

LEGAL STANDARD

A motion to dismiss for failure to state a claim will be denied unless it appears that the plaintiff can prove no set of facts which would entitle him or her to relief. All material allegations in the complaint will be taken as true and construed in the light most favorable to the plaintiff. Although the court is generally confined to consideration of the allegations in the pleadings, when the complaint is accompanied by attached documents, such documents are deemed part of the complaint and may be considered in evaluating the merits of a Rule 12(b)(6) motion.

DISCUSSION

Plaintiffs' various claims are rooted in the sequence of events culminating in the harvesting of Martin's organs in October 1995. They argue that defendants mutilated his body by maintaining it for harvesting, which was done without their consent. In their first amended complaint, plaintiffs bring the following six separate causes of action against all three defendants: (1) negligent search; (2) negligence in procuring injury-producing conduct of another; (3) intentional mutilation of a corpse and infliction of emotional distress; (4) negligent mutilation of a corpse and infliction of emotional distress; (5) joint enterprise liability; and (6) violation of equal protection under the fourteenth amendment.

In response, defendants argue that they were complying with the provisions of the Uniform Anatomical Gift Act, adopted by the California legislature in 1988, when they maintained Martin's body and harvested organs from it. Accordingly, they argue that plaintiffs do not state any claims in their first amended complaint for which relief may be granted.

I. The Uniform Anatomical Gift Act

Although all fifty states have adopted the Uniform Anatomical Gift Act (the "Gift Act") in some form, there is very little case law interpreting its provisions. *See Kelly-Nevils v. Detroit Receiving Hospital*, 207 Mich. App. 410, 526 N.W.2d 15, 17 (Mich. App. 1994). The Gift Act is intended to "make uniform the law with respect to [organ donation] among states enacting it" and is codified in California in the Health and Safety Code. Cal. Health & Safety Code § 7156.5. The Gift Act provides that several classes of people may authorize an anatomical gift: the decedent's (1) attorney-in-fact with power of attorney; (2) spouse; (3) adult son/daughter; (4) either parent; (5) adult brother/sister; (6) grandparent; or (7) guardian/conservator (collectively "next of kin"). *Id.* § 7151(a). If the next of kin, as defined in section 7151(a), cannot be located to provide consent, the coroner or hospital, whichever entity has custody of the body at the time the consent is given, may authorize the anatomical gift so long as several criteria are met, including a reasonable "search" for persons listed in section 7151(a).[3] *Id.* §§ 7151.5(a)-(b).

II. Equal Protection Claim

In their sixth claim, plaintiffs allege that while implementing the provisions of the Gift Act pertaining to the search for next of kin, defendant Coroner discriminated against plaintiffs because of their alien status. They assert that as foreign nationals, they were discriminated against because they were:

> more likely to have a relative of theirs have his or her organs harvested without consent to the detriment of the relatives' right to custody and possession of a decedent. In conducting a search for next of kin, the class of aliens are thus treated differently from the class of non-aliens.

[Complaint at 82.]

In their opposition papers, plaintiffs concede that their constitutional claim for violation of their fourteenth amendment rights implicates only defendant Coroner, not defendants Hospital and Network. In response to this claim, defendant Coroner argues that plaintiffs have not properly pleaded an equal protection claim because they do not allege any claim under 42 U.S.C. section 1983 as required in this Circuit. Coroner is correct. The Ninth Circuit has clearly stated that "a litigant complaining of a violation of a constitutional right must utilize 42 U.S.C. § 1983." *Azul-Pacifico, Inc. v. City of Los Angeles*, 973 F.2d 704, 705 (9th Cir. 1992), *cert. denied,* 506 U.S. 1081, 122 L. Ed. 2d 357, 113 S. Ct. 1049 (1993). Plaintiffs have not done this and therefore have not properly stated a claim for equal protection in their amended complaint.

Although plaintiffs could readily cure this defect if given leave to amend, the claim is so fundamentally futile that leave could not cure its substantive defects. As Coroner argues, plaintiffs lack standing to bring an equal protection claim because the clause applies only to persons within the territorial jurisdiction of the United States. In this case, plaintiffs were in Denmark when the events underlying their complaint took place.

The Fourteenth Amendment explicitly states "nor shall any state deprive any person of life, liberty, or property without due process of law; nor deny to any person within its jurisdiction the equal protection of the laws." U.S. Const. amend. XIV. In interpreting this language, the Supreme Court has stated that the provisions of the Fourteenth Amendment "are universal in their application, to all persons within the territorial jurisdiction, without regard to any differences of race, of color, or of nationality." *Plyler v. Doe*, 457 U.S. 202, 212, 72 L. Ed. 2d 786, 102 S. Ct. 2382 (1982). Here, it is undisputed that plaintiffs were not in United States territory when the events giving rise to their complaint

---

[3] As Danish citizens, plaintiffs allege that in Denmark, no organs are harvested without the consent of the decedent's next of kin and if no next of kin can be found, Danish law does not permit harvesting in the manner described in the Gift Act.

occurred. Accordingly, plaintiffs have no standing to invoke the protections of the Fourteenth Amendment and their equal protection claim against defendant Coroner must be dismissed.

III. Remaining State Law Claims

Having dismissed the only federal claim in plaintiffs' complaint, the court now considers plaintiffs' remaining state law claims under the court's diversity jurisdiction.

A. Claims Against Coroner

Defendant Coroner argues that plaintiffs' failure to file a claim under the California Tort Claims Act bars all of plaintiffs' state law claims against them. Under the California Tort Claims Act, a plaintiff seeking money damages from local public entities is required to file a claim against such entities not later than six months after the accrual of the action causing personal injury. Cal. Gov't Code §§ 905, 905.2, 910, 911.2. The Ninth Circuit has found that "failure to comply with state imposed procedural conditions to sue the State bars the maintenance of a cause of action based upon these pendent State claims." *Ortega v. O'Connor*, 764 F.2d 703, 707 (9th Cir. 1985), *rev'd in part on other grounds*, 480 U.S. 709 (1987).

At oral argument, plaintiffs admitted that they had not filed a claim as required under the Tort Claims Act. Plaintiffs offer no excuse for this non-compliance. Instead, they argue that the Tort Claims Act is inapplicable to them because it only applies where a federal court maintains supplemental jurisdiction over state claims, whereas here, the court maintains original jurisdiction over plaintiffs' state law claims under its diversity jurisdiction. In support of this contention, plaintiffs apparently rely on the fact that *Ortega* specifically discussed the Tort Claims Act in the context of pendent state claims.[4] *Id.* at 707. If true, plaintiffs' proposition would eviscerate state law requirements whenever parties filed their claims in federal court under diversity. Certainly, plaintiffs' misperception is incorrect. Because plaintiffs failed to file a claim with the State Board of Control pursuant to the California Tort Claims Act, plaintiffs are barred from bringing any claims against Coroner in this action.

The court will now consider the substance of plaintiffs' remaining claims against all of the defendants, including Coroner, assuming arguendo that plaintiffs could bring a claim against Coroner.

B. Negligent Search Claim

Plaintiffs argue that the defendants acted negligently in searching for persons authorized to provide consent for an anatomical gift. The Gift Act authorizes a

---

[4] Plaintiffs also argue that the state law requirement that parties exhaust administrative remedies under the California Tort Claims Act only applies to pendent claims, and not to those claims before the court under supplemental jurisdiction. Plaintiffs apparently perceive a substantive distinction between "pendent" and "supplemental" jurisdiction. This misperception is presumably derived from *Ortega*, which describes"pendent" state law claims. *Ortega*, 764, F.2d at 707. Plaintiffs are mistaken. In federal court, the change from "pendent" to "supplemental" jurisdiction over state law claims is procedural, rather than substantive, in nature. Congress would certainly be surprised to find that by making this procedural change, they had eviscerated state sovereign immunity.

coroner, medical examiner, hospital, or local public health official to release and permit removal of a body part where that institution has custody of a body and after a "reasonable effort has been made to locate and inform" next of kin of their option to make, or object to, an anatomical gift. Cal. Health & Safety Code §§ 7151.5(a)-(c). The court must determine whether the actions taken to locate plaintiffs, as described in the complaint, were reasonable under the requirements of the Gift Act.

Neither the parties nor the court has identified California cases interpreting what constitutes a "reasonable" search for next of kin under the Gift Act. Nevertheless, the Gift Act itself provides the court with some guidance. Where a coroner has custody of a body, the Gift Act states that "a reasonable effort [to locate next of kin] shall be deemed to have been made when a search for the persons has been underway for at least 12 hours." *Id.* § 7151.5(a)(2). Similarly, where a hospital has custody of a person who is still alive but expected to die, a reasonable search "may be initiated in anticipation of death, but . . . the determination [to release a body for an anatomical gift] may not be made until the search has been underway for at least 12 hours." *Id.* § 7151.5(b). This search

> shall include a check of local police missing persons records, examination of personal effects, and the questioning of any persons visiting the decedent before his or her death or in the hospital, accompanying the decedent's body, or reporting the death, in order to obtain information that might lead to the location of [next of kin].

Id. These provisions suggest that when the legislature adopted the Gift Act, the legislature considered and accepted that some searches for next of kin would be unsuccessful, and that where the next of kin could not be located in twelve hours, other institutions would be empowered to release a body in order to fulfill the underlying purposes of the Gift Act. In adopting the Gift Act, the California legislature likely recognized that "time is usually of the essence in securing donated organs at the time of the donor's death." *Lyon v. United States*, 843 F. Supp. 531, 536 (D. Minn. 1994).

By adopting a twelve hour search period and stating that a reasonable search "shall be deemed to have been made" once this amount of time has passed, it is clear that the California legislature contemplated (1) a relatively short period of time in which to conduct a search for next of kin and (2) the possibility that such a search might be unsuccessful. Therefore, the court must consider what actions could have reasonably been taken in a twelve hour period to determine whether a reasonable search for plaintiffs was conducted.

In plaintiffs' complaint, they state that a search for next of kin began at 9:00 a.m. on October 4 and continued until October 6 between 9:00 and 10:13 a.m., when Coroner released the body for harvesting. Martin had no identification on his person when he was found and brought to the hospital. As alleged in the complaint, the search for plaintiffs lasted about forty-eight hours, but was ultimately unsuccessful. The complaint discloses that the Sheriff was notified and involved in the search efforts, that five hours after the search had begun the FBI identified the body as belonging to Martin Jacobsen from New York City, and that a doctor's report described an extensive forty hour search conducted by the Sheriff, the Coroner and the FBI.

Plaintiffs argue that defendants search was negligent because they should have known he was from Denmark when they found a ring inscribed with Danish writing on Martin's finger and a Danish poem in his pocket. These facts do not establish that the search was unreasonable. It is quite possible that the hospital and police did not know that the language was Danish. Moreover, even if they could identify the language, these items alone do not immediately suggest nor create the inference that Martin was a Danish citizen.[5] Accordingly, the search for plaintiffs was not negligent simply because defendants did not assume, on the basis of these items, that Martin was from Denmark.

Plaintiffs also argue that the search was negligent because the Sheriff knew that Martin was a tourist and that based on this information, they should have checked the records of the Immigration and Naturalization Service ("INS") during their search for next of kin. The fact that the INS records were not checked during the search does not establish that it was unreasonable. The court notes that a person's status as a tourist in the San Francisco area does not immediately suggest that the person is from a foreign country. Many tourists from all over the United States and the world visit this area. Accordingly, the Sheriff's failure to check INS records upon discovering that Martin was a tourist provides little to support plaintiffs' negligent search claim.

Plaintiffs' description of the search suggests that all reasonable acts were taken to locate plaintiffs and obtain their consent prior to releasing Martin's body for harvesting. The complaint describes a search lasting over forty hours and involving the efforts of the Marin County Sheriff as well as the FBI; such a search is "reasonable" as contemplated by the legislature in adopting the Gift Act. Before Martin's body was released, defendants Hospital and Coroner complied with the Gift Act's provisions and conducted a reasonable, although ultimately unsuccessful, search to locate plaintiffs and obtain their consent.[6] Accordingly, the court finds that plaintiffs have failed to state a claim for negligent search against defendants Hospital and Coroner.

As for defendant Network, under the provisions of the Gift Act, Network had no legal duty to search for Martin's next of kin or obtain their consent for an anatomical gift. *See* Cal. Health & Safety Code § 7151.5 (placing this duty on

---

[5] For example, a person may enjoy reading French poems so much that she keeps a copy of her favorite poem in her wallet. It is absurd to think that the mere fact she has a French poem in her wallet suggests that she is a citizen or resident of France. Similarly, here, the Sheriff and the Hospital had no reason to think that simply because Martin carried a Danish poem and other items inscribed in Danish, that he was a Danish citizen from Denmark.

[6] The court notes that defendant Hospital had no legal duty under the provisions of the Gift Act to conduct a search for plaintiffs because defendant Coroner was the entity that ultimately gave the final consent and release of the body for harvesting. *See* Cal. Health & Safety Code § 7151.5. However, the Gift Act contemplates that a hospital might be required to conduct a reasonable search where it has custody of a body prior to its release. *Id.* § 7151.5(b). Here, plaintiffs' complaint clearly states that defendant Coroner released the body; accordingly, only defendant Coroner had a duty to search for next of kin prior to releasing the body. Defendants make much of this statutory distinction in their papers. However, this point is immaterial in light of the court's finding that the search for plaintiffs was reasonable under the provisions of the Gift Act.

other entities including coroners and hospitals). Plaintiffs urge the court to impose this duty on Network based on unspecified "common law" duties for which plaintiffs have provided no authority. The court has found no California cases supporting plaintiffs' position and declines the opportunity to create such a duty here. Accordingly, the court finds that plaintiffs have not stated a claim against Network for negligent search.

C. Remaining State Law Claims

Plaintiffs' remaining claims for negligence in procuring injury-producing injury, joint enterprise and negligent and intentional infliction of emotional distress are based on plaintiffs' allegation that defendants mutilated Martin's body by maintaining it prior to harvesting and actually harvesting organs from it. Plaintiffs' contend that all three defendants acted in concert to mutilate the body of their son and obtain organs for transplantation, thereby causing them injury.

Defendants' behavior, as described in plaintiffs' complaint, is consistent with the provisions of the Gift Act. As discussed above, defendants' search for Martin's next of kin complied with the provisions of the Gift Act and constituted a reasonable search. Defendants also acted in compliance with other sections of the Gift Act. For example, hospitals are required to "cooperate in the implementation of the anatomical gift or release and removal of a part." Cal. Health & Safety Code § 7152.5(d). The Gift Act also states that "each hospital in this state, after consultation with other hospitals and procurement organizations, shall establish agreements or affiliations for coordination of procurement and use of human bodies and parts." Id. § 7154.5. When identifying potential organ and tissue donors, hospitals must comply with laws requiring that the coroner be notified of all reportable deaths. Id. § 7184(a) (referenced in section 7152.5 of the Gift Act). Prior to harvesting, a donor must be determined to be dead pursuant to the Uniform Determination of Death Act (the "Death Act"). Id. §§ 7180-82. Death is "determined by determining that the individual has suffered an irreversible cessation of all functions of the entire brain, including the brain stem" and "there shall be an independent confirmation of death by another physician" before harvesting can take place. Id. § 7182. Furthermore, hospitals may contact organ and tissue procurement organizations when a potential donor is identified and ask them to assist in locating the potential donor's next of kin as required under section 7151 of the Gift Act. Id. § 71849(c) (referenced in section 7152.5 of the Gift Act).

These provisions suggest that defendants acted in compliance with the Gift Act when they maintained Martin's body and harvested organs from it. Defendants were required, under the provisions of the Gift Act, to cooperate with one another to maintain the body and its organs for transplantation purposes. In accordance with the Gift Act and the Death Act, defendants maintained Martin's body and did not release it for harvesting until after there had been a determination of brain death that was confirmed by another physician. Plaintiffs have not alleged any facts showing that defendants violated the provisions of the Gift Act or acted contrary to the purposes for which it was enacted by the California legislature. Defendants' efforts to comply with the provisions of the Gift Act may not serve as a basis for tort liability. Therefore, plaintiffs can prove no set of facts entitling them to relief on any of their remaining claims. *Conley*, 355 U.S. at 45-56. Accordingly, plaintiffs' remaining state claims against all three defendants must be dismissed.

Conclusion

For the foregoing reasons, defendants Coroner, Hospital and Network's motions to dismiss are granted and all claims in plaintiffs' first amended complaint are dismissed with prejudice.

IT IS SO ORDERED.

QUESTIONS

1. Does the result in *Rahman* encourage or discourage organ donation?

2. Should the standard of liability for misinterpreting the scope of an anatomical gift be different than the standard articulated in these two cases?

3. In a world that is growing increasingly smaller due to technological advances, how might international organizations work together to avoid the situation that occurred in *Jacobsen*?

3. The National Organ Transplant Act

Read the National Organ Transplant Act in the statutory supplement.

QUESTIONS

1. Why should the federal government prohibit the sale of organs?

2. Does the National Organ Transplant Act reflect an appropriate balancing of the various interests affected by the shortage of organs for transplant?

a. Allocation of Donated Organs

Read 42 C.F.R. 121.1 et seq. (2006) in the statutory supplement.

U.S. Department of Health and Human Services
Advisory Committee on Organ Transplantation
Recommendations to the Secretary
http://www.organdonor.gov/research/acotrecs.htm

Following more than a year of deliberations and meetings, Secretary Tommy G. Thompson's Advisory Committee on Organ Transplantation (ACOT) met on November 18-19, 2002, in Arlington, Virginia, and unanimously agreed upon a series of consensus recommendations with respect to a number of serious organ donation and transplantation issues, affecting all recipients as well as both deceased and living donors.

The first day of that meeting was devoted by the Committee to responding to Secretary Thompson's specific request to them that they look into several concerns he had with respect to the process of live organ donation and transplantation — particularly regarding the kidney, liver and lung — so as to ensure that the donation and transplantation process would be as safe and effective as possible, for both the living organ donor and the recipient of the donor's organ.

ACOT believes that the implementation of these first seven recommendations will ensure the protection of potential living donors and simultaneously enhance the effectiveness of living donation and transplantation.

Recommendation 1: That the following ethical principles and informed consent standards be implemented for all living donors.

The Secretary's first request was that ACOT consider the desirability of national disclosure standards. ACOT responded by recommending a series of ethical principles and elements of informed consent that should be implemented for all living donors.

ACOT agrees upon a set of Ethical Principles of Consent to Being a Live Organ Donor, which includes the view that the person who gives consent to becoming a live organ donor must be:

- competent (possessing decision making capacity)
- willing to donate
- free from coercion
- medically and psychosocially suitable
- fully informed of the risks and benefits as a donor and
- fully informed of the risks, benefits, and alternative treatment available to the recipient.

Two related ethical principles that ACOT endorses are:

- Equipoise; i.e., the benefits to both the donor and the recipient must outweigh the risks associated with the donation and transplantation of the live donor organ; and
- A clear statement that the potential donor's participation must be completely voluntary, and may be withdrawn at any time.

ACOT recommends that each institution develop an informed consent document that would be understandable to all potential donors. Such a document should be accessible to people at all educational levels, and appropriate for the potential donor's level of education. Apart from the need to employ specifically defined medical terms, the document should in most circumstances be written for readers with no higher than an 8th or 9th grade level of education. If the potential donor does not speak English, there should be an independent interpreter to facilitate understanding in the patient's language. Where appropriate, translations of such a document and accompanying materials should be made available.

ACOT further recommends that the following Standards of Disclosure: Elements of Informed Consent be incorporated in the informed consent document given to the potential live organ donor, with specific descriptions that would ensure the donor's awareness of:

- the purpose of the donation

- the evaluation process — including interviews, examinations, laboratory tests, and other procedures — and the possibility that the potential donor may be found ineligible to donate

- the donation surgical procedure

- the alternative procedures or courses of treatment for potential donor and recipient

- any procedures which are or may be considered to be experimental

- the immediate recovery period and the anticipated post-operative course of care

- the foreseeable risks or discomforts to the potential donor

- the potential psychological effects resulting from the process of donation

- the reported national experience, transplant center and surgeon-specific statistics of donor outcomes, including the possibility that the donor may subsequently experience organ failure and/or disability or death

- the foreseeable risks, discomforts, and survival benefit to the potential recipient

- the reported national experience and transplant center statistics of recipient outcomes, including failure of the donated organ and the possibility of recipient death

- the fact that the potential donor's participation is voluntary, and may be withdrawn at any time

- the fact that the potential donor may derive a medical benefit by having a previously undetected health problem diagnosed as a result of the evaluation process

- the fact that the potential donor undertakes risk and derives no medical benefit from the operative procedure of donation

- the fact that unforeseen future risks or medical uncertainties may not be identifiable at the time of donation

- the fact that the potential donor may be reimbursed for the personal expenses of travel, housing, and lost wages related to donation

- the prohibition against the donor otherwise receiving any valuable consideration (including monetary or material gain) for agreeing to be a donor

- the fact that the donor's existing health and disability insurance may not cover the potential long-term costs and medical and psychological consequences of donation

- the fact that the donor's act of donation may adversely affect the donor's future eligibility for health, disability, or life insurance

- additional informational resources relating to live organ donation (possibly through the establishment of a separate resources center, as separately recommended)

- the fact that Government approved agencies and contractors will be able to obtain information regarding the donor's health for life and

- the principles of confidentiality, clarifying that:

- communication between the donor and the transplant center will remain confidential;

- a decision by the potential donor not to proceed with the donation will only be disclosed with the consent of the potential donor;

- the transplant center will share the donor's identity and other medical information with entities involved in the procurement and transplantation of organs, as well as registries that are legally charged to follow donor outcomes; and

- confidentiality of all patient information will be maintained in accord with applicable laws and regulations.

ACOT also prepared two specific informed consent documents that embody these principles and elements. The first relates to the potential donor's initial consent for evaluation as a possible donor, Living Liver Donor Initial Consent for Evaluation (appendix 1) [Omitted — Eds.]. The second deals with the potential donor's informed consent for surgery, Living Liver Donor Informed Consent for Surgery (appendix 2) [Omitted — Eds.].

ACOT recognizes that institutions operating in different states across the nation may have different laws and needs that will affect the precise wording of the informed consent document(s) they will use. For that reason, these consent documents are submitted as examples and possible models only. Note as well that, although the specific examples are for living liver donation, ACOT is recommending such forms for all potential living organ donors.

Moreover, ACOT does not believe that these or any forms are a substitute for in-person communication between physicians and other involved professionals and the potential donor. These forms should be viewed instead as only the written evidence of discussions leading to informed consent based upon full disclosure.

Recommendation 2: That each institution that performs living donor transplantation provide an independent donor advocate to ensure that the informed consent standards and ethical principles described above are applied to the practice of all live organ donor transplantation.

The Secretary's second request was that ACOT consider the desirability of an independent donor advocate (or advocacy team) to represent and advise the donor so as to ensure that the previously described elements and ethical principles are applied to the practice of all live donor transplantation.

ACOT agrees with this principle and herein provides detailed recommendations as to how such an independent donor advocate should be established, as well as the role and qualifications of such an advocate.

ACOT recommends that each transplant center identify and provide to each potential donor an independent and trained patient advocate whose primary obligation would be to help donors understand the process, the procedure and risks and benefits of live organ donation; and to protect and promote the interests and well being of the donor.

ACOT recognizes that there is an acknowledged limitation of objectivity and independence, given the realities of the processes that take place within a transplant center among medical colleagues who regularly interact professionally; a modern, practicing physician does not work in a vacuum and cannot perform in a way that is wholly apart from other institutional staff. Moreover, the donor advocate should not be totally independent of events affecting the recipient, as there must be interaction of the advocate with the transplant surgeon of the recipient team. However, the concept of preserving a separate care physician for the donor is underscored as the reason to retain the word independent in the identity of the advocate.

Recommendation 3: That a database of health outcomes for all live donors be established and funded through and under the auspices of the U.S. Department of Health and Human Services.

The Secretary's third request was that ACOT consider the desirability of establishing a living organ donor registry. ACOT concurs with the Secretary's suggestion and recommends that a database of health outcomes of all live donors be established and further recommends that the registry or database should build upon existing smaller databases, but believes that a comprehensive national database will be necessary to answer the Secretary's desire that all potential organ donors be fully informed and aware of the likely consequences of their decisions.

The Secretary asked ACOT where such a database should be established and ACOT believes that only the Department of Health and Human Services has the authority and resources to establish such a registry. There are valid competing arguments as to what component of DHHS should have primary responsibility for funding and managing such a registry, and ACOT therefore offers no consensus suggestion on this question, but ACOT stands ready to assist the Department in further deliberations on this question.

ACOT further stands ready to assist the Secretary in suggesting information or data elements (and the time periods for the collection of such data) that should be included in such a registry, but it was felt that further discussions within the Department, and with the OPTN, as well as with the SRTR, would be necessary, given ACOT's understanding that the substantial cost implications in establishing and maintaining such a registry must be fully explored.

In order to guide Departmental deliberations on those questions, ACOT responds to the Secretary's request for its opinion on how the information collected should be used. ACOT believes that the primary purpose of such a registry should be to enable the medical community to define accurately the donor risks and benefits of live organ transplantation so as to give potential donors an accurate risk assessment.

Recommendation 4: That serious consideration be given to the establishment of a separate resource center for living donors and their families.

ACOT recommends advancing the information and resources available to living donors and their families through the implementation of detailed consent forms, the creation of independent donor advocates and the establishment of a living donor registry. To similar effect, ACOT recommends the establishment of a separate office, a resource center, for potential living donors, those who choose to donate, as well as their families. The primary function of such a resource center would be to ensure that each potential donor receives a complete and current set of information about living organ donation.

An existing model for such a resource center is in place at the OPTN, which has both a person to contact for information, and a web site with information specific to the needs of transplant candidates and recipients. The resource center could either be located under the aegis of the OPTN or the living donor registry. Such a distinct resource center would have the benefit of being clearly distinguished as separate and apart from the transplant team and hospital. Until such time as such an independent resource center is established, ACOT recommends that transplant centers should give consideration to providing such a resource center on their own, again with the purpose of ensuring that each potential donor receives a complete and current set of information about living organ donation.

Recommendation 5: That the present preference in OPTN allocation policy — given to prior living organ donors who subsequently need a kidney — be extended so that any living organ donor would be given preference as a candidate for any organ transplant, should one become needed.

This recommendation states that there should be a preference accorded to the living organ donor. The point value or other means of assigning such a preference is left to the OPTN.

Recommendation 6: That the requirements for HLA typing of liver transplant recipients and/or living liver donors should be deleted.

This testing may, however, be appropriate for some donors and recipients and in such cases should be compensated by Medicaid, Medicare or private insurers as appropriate, when specifically ordered, as for all other appropriate laboratory tests.

Recommendation 7: That a process be established that would verify the qualifications of a center to perform living donor liver or lung transplantation.

ACOT believes that a process needs to be established that would verify the qualifications of a center to perform living donor liver or lung transplantation. ACOT believes that the process for performing living kidney transplantation is sufficiently mature and established that no further verification processes are required. ACOT believes that, owing to the relative newness of the procedures, as well as the inherent intricacies of the operations, that centers performing and seeking to perform living donor liver and living donor lung transplantation each require further review and verification within the medical community.

The purpose of such a verification process would be to give patients an increased level of confidence in the institutions performing such operations, and to provide a guide for centers seeking to enter this field.

Although the Secretary's recent letters to the Committee have focused on living donation, his overall charge to the Committee has been much broader, and ACOT has responded to that charge by promulgating an additional series of recommendations not specific to living donation.

The second day of the ACOT meeting was devoted by the Committee to issues affecting equitable access to transplantation, and those relating to deceased or cadaveric donors.

ACOT believes that the implementation of the following two recommendations, which relate to access to transplantation, will especially benefit minority populations.

Recommendation 8: That specific methods be employed to increase the education and awareness of patients at dialysis centers as to transplant options available to them.

Available information indicates that too many patients at dialysis centers are unaware of the transplant options available to them. Too many of these patients are members of minority groups. Given the cost of sustained dialysis treatment, both to patients and to the Centers for Medicare and Medicaid Services, as compared to the cost of transplantation, this would also be cost-effective as well as life-saving.

In order to assure the accuracy of this assessment, ACOT recommends that procedural methodologies be developed to evaluate dialysis patient access and referral for organ transplant, as well as an accurate cost/benefit analysis, using existing data and/or new sources of data.

ACOT further recommends that, as soon as possible, a health education program be implemented, and/or that an educational coordinator be placed on site at individual dialysis centers so as to provide patients with adequate education about transplant options available to them. This would be a reinforcement of the implementation of existing regulations stipulating that dialysis patients be educated and evaluated by personnel from the transplant center concerning this therapeutic option.

Recommendation 9: That research be conducted into the causes of existing disparities in organ transplant rates and outcomes, with the goal of eliminating those disparities.

The fact of such disparities, particularly with regard to kidney transplantation rates, appears to be undisputed, and data developed by the SRTR for ACOT highlights this issue. HRSA, NIH and other DHHS agencies are presently committed to research aimed at ending such disparities with respect to health care delivery in other areas, and research should be undertaken to establish whether any separate reasons may exist for such disparities within the transplantation area, and, if so, how they may be eliminated.

ACOT believes that the implementation of the following nine recommendations, which primarily relate to increasing the supply of deceased donor organs, will ultimately, and in some cases very quickly, mean many more additional organs becoming available to potential recipients.

Recommendation 10: That legislative strategies be adopted that will encourage medical examiners and coroners not to withhold life-saving organs and tissues from qualified organ procurement organizations.

Studies indicate that coroners and medical examiners across the United States are not uniform in their approach to making organs available to organ procurement organizations, and that many unnecessarily withhold from retrieval organs that could be used for transplantation. Indeed, it is estimated that if all states followed the example of Texas, which has enacted a law containing a provision similar to the one below, then 700-1,000 additional organs would be made additionally available each year.

The Secretary is specifically encouraged to use his good standing with the National Governor's Association, the National Association of State Legislatures, the Uniform Commissioners of State Laws, and/or with individual states to seek the following change:

To amend the Uniform Anatomical Gift Act (UAGA) to add a new subsection at the end of section 4, as follows:

(d) If the medical examiner is considering withholding one or more organs or tissues of a potential donor for any reason, the medical examiner shall be present during the removal of the organs or tissue. In such case, the medical examiner may request a biopsy of those organs or tissue, or deny their removal. If the medical examiner denies removal of any organ or tissue, the medical examiner shall explain in writing the reasons for the denial and shall provide the explanation to the qualified organ procurement organization.

In the alternative, the Secretary is asked to encourage individual states to adopt state laws to the same or similar effect.

Recommendation 11: That the secretary of HHS, in concert with the Secretary of Education, should recommend to states that organ and tissue donation be included in core curriculum standards for public education as well as in the curricula of professional schools, including schools of education, schools of medicine, schools of nursing, schools of law, schools of public health, schools of social work, and pharmacy schools.

The Secretary of HHS, in collaboration with the Secretary of Education, should identify relevant core curriculum standards, and survey those courses and curricula that presently include education as to organ and tissue donation, with a view to promoting a model standard that can be broadly employed in public education. This would, at a minimum, include all high schools.

In addition, hospitals should establish ongoing basic introductory (new hire) programs, focused on organ and tissue donation that would be similar to CPR certification and recertification, and might in fact be accommodated within the same new hire program.

Efforts should also be made to ensure that organ and tissue donation be a part of the professional educational curricula at all professional schools related to health. Law schools are included because of the relevance of such issues to courses in elder law, estate planning, and health law.

Recommendation 12: That in order to ensure best practices, organ procurement organizations and the OPTN be encouraged to develop, evaluate, and support the implementation of improved management protocols of potential donors.

This recommendation builds upon those made at previous conferences held by various transplantation related organizations, as well as work performed under contract to the Department. A novel and improved standard of titrated care for heart and lung donors has been established and ACOT believes that it should be more generally implemented. It is known as the Critical Pathway for the Organ Donor (appendix 3) [Omitted — Eds.]. Similar improved standards of management and care should be developed to optimize the potential recovery of other organs.

Recommendation 13: That in order to ensure best practices at hospitals and organ procurement organizations, the following measure should be added to the CMS conditions of participation: each hospital with more than 100 beds should identify an advocate for organ and tissue donation from within the hospital clinical staff.

Such a designated advocate for organ and tissue donation would be responsible for assuring that the facility is in compliance with the Conditions of Participation as well as any other policies that pertain to organ and tissue donation. In addition, this designated advocate's responsibilities would include assuring that efforts are made to promote donation in the local community. (Given varying hospital management structures, such an advocate may not always be a member of the clinical staff; what is essential, however, is that the advocate have the institutional authority to effect change.)

Recommendation 14: That in order to ensure best practices at hospitals and organ procurement organizations, the following measure should be added to the CMS conditions of participation: Each hospital should establish, in conjunction with its OPO, policies and procedures to manage and maximize organ retrieval from donors without a heartbeat.

Such donation is often referred to as donation after cardiac death, and such donors are variously referred to as donors without a heartbeat or non-heart-beating donors. These policies and procedures will need to be developed in collaboration with the OPTN, the transplant centers and AOPO.

Recommendation 15: That the following measure be added to the CMS conditions of participation: Hospitals shall notify organ procurement organizations prior to the withdrawal of life support to a patient, so as to determine that patient's potential for organ donation. If it is determined that the patient is a potential donor, the OPO shall reimburse the hospital for appropriate costs related to maintaining that patient as a potential donor.

Recommendation 16: That the regulatory framework provided by CMS for transplant center and Organ Procurement Organization certification should be based on principles of continuous quality improvement. Subsequent failure to meet performance standards established under such principles should trigger quality improvement processes under the supervision of HRSA.

The relevant committee of the OPTN is encouraged to develop baseline measures/principles to guide the process of continuous quality improvement, a part of which process is the development of baseline measures. The quality improvement process envisioned by ACOT might resemble one that is presently utilized in some hospitals/facilities, and known as FOCUS-PDCA (appendix 4) [Omitted — Eds.].

Recommendation 17: That all hospitals, particularly those with more than 100 beds, be strongly encouraged by CMS and AHRQ to implement policies such that the failure to identify a potential organ donor and/or refer such a potential donor to the organ procurement organization in a timely manner be considered a serious medical error. Such events should be investigated and reviewed by hospitals in a manner similar to that for other major adverse healthcare events.

This measure could be added to the sort of physician profile which most facilities currently employ. (See example physician profile (appendix 5) [Omitted — Eds.]. ACOT expects that this Recommendation will have its greatest impact at those hospitals with trauma centers, as well as those with residency programs and/or academic affiliations.

Recommendation 18: That the Joint Commission on Accreditation of Healthcare Organizations (JCAHO) strengthen its accreditation provisions regarding organ donation, including consideration of treating as a sentinel event the failure of hospitals to identify a potential donor and/or refer a donor to the relevant Organ Procurement Organization in a timely manner. Similar review should be considered by the National Committee on Quality Assurance (NCQA).

JCAHO presently defines and identifies a sentinel event as: An unexpected occurrence involving death or serious physical or psychological injury, or the risk thereof. Serious injury specifically includes loss of limb or function. The phrase, "or the risk thereof" includes any process variation for which a recurrence would carry a significant chance of a serious adverse outcome. Such events are called "sentinel" because they signal the need for immediate investigation and response.

Failing to identify or refer a potential donor in a timely manner carries the serious risk of that donor's organs not being made available to a potential recipient. Given the shortage of organs and the fact of so many potential recipients dying while awaiting the possibility of transplantation, such a failure would appear to fall within the JCAHO definition of a sentinel event.

Monitoring hospitals for compliance with organ donation standards should become an integral part of the JCAHO hospital survey process. In addition to examination of the standard, the hospital JCAHO survey should include the OPO referral records which are submitted back to the hospital, as well as the supporting documentation of corrective measures or follow-up. There should be a compliance benchmark set (e.g., 90-100%), with anything below that benchmark requiring a gap analysis.

QUESTIONS

1. Does the federal regulatory scheme for regulating organ transplants adequately protect the interests of senior citizens as donors *and* as donees?

2. What role should the elder law attorney play respecting living donor organ donations by older clients?

3. To what extent might a person's religious or moral beliefs affect her views on organ donation? *See* http://www.giftoflife.on.ca/page.cfm?id=7D37BE22-0BC5-4F8D-AA9A-5F3BAA6BDF5F.

b. Problems of Interpretation

WHEAT v. MASS
994 F.2d 273 (5th Cir. 1993)

DUHE, Circuit Judge.

BACKGROUND

In November 1989, Margaret Gordon underwent tests by Dr. Joseph Mass at Our Lady of the Lake Regional Medical Center (OLOL) after she complained to him of abdominal pain. After the tests revealed severe liver disfunction, Mrs. Gordon was admitted to OLOL and was treated there by Drs. Joseph Mass, John Hoppe, and William Anderson. Mrs. Gordon's condition deteriorated, and she was transferred to Ochsner Hospital (Ochsner) in New Orleans to undergo evaluation by Dr. Luis Balart for a possible liver transplant.

At Ochsner, Mrs. Gordon's condition stabilized temporarily until December 10, when Ochsner physicians determined that she needed a liver transplant. Because Mrs. Gordon's medical insurance did not cover transplants, her family was contacted by Ochsner's social worker on December 11 and informed that a $175,000 down payment must be raised for the transplant. At the social worker's suggestion, Mrs. Gordon's family contacted the Louisiana state government for assistance and was subsequently informed on December 13 that funding for the transplant may be available from the state. Mrs. Gordon was immediately placed on the national transplant waiting list, but before an organ match was made, she passed away at 10:00 p.m. that night. In December 1990, Appellants sued Drs. Mass, Hoppe, OLOL, Ochsner, and Drs. Balart and Head, alleging that they discriminated against Mrs. Gordon on the basis of age, sex, and poverty while providing her medical services, in violation of the Civil Rights Act, Title VII, the U.S. Constitution, and the Louisiana Constitution. The district court dismissed the complaint, upon Appellees' motions, for failure to state a claim. The court also denied Appellants' motion to amend the petition. Appellants appeal both the dismissal and the district court's refusal to allow an amendment to the complaint.

DISCUSSION

I. Dismissal of Complaint.

A. Standard of Review.

Dismissal cannot be upheld unless it appears beyond doubt that Appellants would not be entitled to recover under any set of facts that could be proved in support of their claims.

B. Alleged causes of action.

Appellants' 42 U.S.C. § 1983 claim states that "Ochsner and its doctors, as well as proposed defendant state officials," are state actors who violated Mrs. Gordon's civil rights under the equal protection clause of the Fourteenth Amendment. Ochsner is not a state actor, and cannot be considered as such solely because it receives medicare and medicaid funds and is subject to state regulation. *Daigle v. Opelousas Health Care, Inc.*, 774 F.2d 1344, 1349 (5th Cir. 1985). Because no state action was involved, this claim was properly dismissed.

Appellants next argue that Ochsner violated Mrs. Gordon's equal protection rights under the Fifth Amendment by discriminating against her on the basis of sex. A Fifth Amendment claim is cognizable only against a federal government actor, and Appellants argue that Ochsner is such an actor by virtue of its membership in the United Network for Organ Sharing (UNOS).[7] Ochsner's receipt of federal funds by virtue of its participation in UNOS does not make Ochsner a federal actor. *See Wahba v. New York University*, 492 F.2d 96, 102 (2d Cir. 1974), *cert. denied*, 419 U.S. 874, 95 S. Ct. 135, 42 L. Ed. 2d 113 (1974) (private university's administration of public health service grants pursuant to statute does not make the university a federal actor); *Greenya v. George Wash-*

---

[7] The United Network for Organ Sharing has an exclusive contract with the Department of Health and Human Services to serve as the national organ procurement and transplant network under the National Organ Transplant Act of 1984, 42 U.S.C. § 273.

ington University, 167 U.S. App. D.C. 379, 512 F.2d 556, 559-60, (D.C. Cir. 1975), *cert. denied,* 423 U.S. 995, 96 S. Ct. 422, 46 L. Ed. 2d 369 (1975) (university's receipt of federal funding and exemption from taxation does not make university a government actor for purposes of a Fifth Amendment claim); *Fidelity Financial Corp. v. Federal Home Loan Bank of San Francisco,* 792 F.2d 1432, 1435 (9th Cir. 1986), *cert. denied,* 479 U.S. 1064, 107 S. Ct. 949, 93 L. Ed. 2d 998 (1987) (extensive and detailed regulation does not render business a government actor). Furthermore, Appellants have failed to allege any facts demonstrating that Mrs. Gordon was discriminated against on the basis of her sex. This claim was properly dismissed.

Third, Appellants argue that "Louisiana finances liver transplants with Medicaid funds on an arbitrary and political rather than reasonable and equitable basis" in violation of 42 U.S.C. § 1396b(i), which provides that states must distribute organ transplant funds equally to similarly situated individuals. This claim only applies to Ochsner, because Ochsner is the only Appellee that performs liver transplants or is involved in Louisiana's funding of transplants. We held in *Stewart v. Bernstein,* 769 F.2d 1088, 1092-94 (5th Cir. 1985), that the Medicaid Act does not furnish substantive rights enforceable in civil suits between private parties. The court's power to enforce this statute is limited to adjudication of whether a state properly administers federal medicaid funds, and therefore this claim against Ochsner was properly dismissed.

Fourth, Appellants argue that a cause of action exists under the Age Discrimination Act, 42 U.S.C. § 6101, which prohibits discrimination on the basis of age in federally assisted programs. Appellants argue that the organ transplant program is a federally assisted program because it is heavily subsidized and funded with federal Medicare and Medicaid funds. Again, this claim can only be asserted against Ochsner as Ochsner is the only Appellee involved in organ transplants. This Court has not considered whether a private cause of action exists under the Age Discrimination Act, nor has the Court considered whether such an action may be brought by a Plaintiff's survivors; we need not address these issues now. Appellants have made no showing whatsoever that Ochsner discriminated against Mrs. Gordon on the basis of her age, and for that reason the claim was properly dismissed.

Appellants next argue that Ochsner violated Title IX of the Education Amendment of 1972, 20 U.S.C. § 1681 which prohibits sexual discrimination in education programs receiving federal funding. Appellants argue that Ochsner is within the purview of Title IX because it has educational programs and receives federal funds through medicare and medicaid. Appellants then state that Ochsner discriminated against Mrs. Gordon on the basis of sex in violation of Title IX. This claim was properly dismissed because Appellants have made no showing that Mrs. Gordon's gender was a factor in her not receiving a liver transplant, or in any other decision involving her medical care.

Finally, Appellants argue that they are entitled to show that UNOS and its members such as Ochsner maintain a monopoly on organ transplants and create market harm by restricting the availability of such services and charging prohibitively high prices in violation of the Sherman Anti-Trust Act, 15 U.S.C. §§ 1, 2. Appellants have failed to state a claim under § 1 of the Sherman Act because they have failed to allege any effect on interstate commerce, and have failed to show Ochsner's requisite market power or intent to monopolize the market. Appellants have also failed to state a claim under § 2 of the Sherman Act because they have not shown an agreement between two or more economic entities, a specific intent to monopolize, or any overt act in furtherance of the conspiracy. These claims are frivolous, and were properly dismissed.

* * *

Conclusion

For the foregoing reasons, the district court's dismissal of Appellants' complaint and refusal to allow an amendment are AFFIRMED.

QUESTION

Are there any grounds upon which to challenge the national organ allocation system?

4. Defining Death

Read the Uniform Determination of Death Act in the statutory supplement. The Act has been adopted, with some modifications, in every state and the District of Columbia.

David DeGrazia
Biology, Consciousness, and the Definition of Death:
Report from the Institute for Philosophy and Public Policy
(Winter 1998)
http://www.puaf.umd.edu/ippp/winter98/biology_consciousness.htm[*]

When does a human life end? This question used to be answered quite easily. According to the traditional standard, which has only recently been questioned, a human being is dead when her heart and lungs have irreversibly ceased to function. In some cases, permanent loss of consciousness may precede cardiopulmonary failure. But the interval between these two events has typically been a matter of hours or days, and the traditional standard regards only the latter event as definitive. Today, however, the development of mechanical respirators, electronic pacemakers, and other medical technologies has created the possibility of a greater temporal separation between various system failures — a patient may lose consciousness a decade or more before his heart and lungs fail, for example. Meanwhile, interest in the availability of transplantable

---

organs has provided an incentive not to delay unnecessarily in determining that a person has died. (Current law, it need hardly be said, embraces the so-called "dead-donor rule": organs necessary for life may not be procured before donors are dead, since the removal of such organs would otherwise cause death — that is, kill the donors — violating laws against homicide.)

Two landmark reports helped to generate a movement away from exclusive reliance on the traditional standard: the 1968 report of the Harvard Medical School Ad Hoc Committee and a 1981 presidential commission report, *Defining Death*. This second document included what became the Uniform Determination of Death Act (UDDA). Today all fifty states and the District of Columbia follow the UDDA in recognizing whole-brain death — irreversible cessation of all functions of the entire brain — as a legal standard of death. The UDDA doesn't jettison the cardiopulmonary standard, however. Instead, it holds that death occurs whenever either standard (whichever applies first) is met. One important consequence of this change is that an individual can be legally dead even if her cardiopulmonary system continues to function. If a patient's entire brain is nonfunctioning, so that breathing and heartbeat are maintained only by artificial life-supports, that patient meets the whole-brain standard of death.

Some philosophers and scientists have argued that the whole-brain standard does not go far enough. Several leading authors on the subject have advocated a *higher-brain standard*, according to which death is the irreversible cessation of the capacity for consciousness. This standard is often met prior to whole-brain death, which includes death of the brainstem — that part of the brain which allows spontaneous respiration and heartbeat but is insufficient for consciousness. Thus, a patient in a permanent coma or permanent vegetative state (PVS) meets the higher-brain, but not the whole-brain, standard of death. Should society embrace the higher-brain standard? Should laws be changed so that permanently unconscious patients can legally be declared dead? This essay offers both conceptual and pragmatic grounds for rejecting such a change. However, it will also argue that the linkage between definitions of death and policies regarding life-supports and organ procurement is less strict than some observers might suppose. In other words, a rejection of the higher-brain standard does not imply an endorsement of policies that would prolong life at any cost.

QUESTIONS

1. Do you believe the typical layperson understands "death" to mean the condition described in the UDDA?

2. How might an attorney help a client to articulate her understanding of "death"? Might the word "death" have different meanings for a person depending on whether, for example, the issue is when to withdraw life support on the one hand, and when organs may be harvested on the other?

FURTHER READING. Peter J. Strauss & Nancy M. Lederman, THE ELDER LAW HANDBOOK ch. 10 (1996); Peter J. Strauss et al., AGING AND THE LAW, ch. 36 (1996); Melvin I. Urofsky & Philip E. Urofsky, THE RIGHT TO DIE: A TWO-VOLUME ANTHOLOGY OF SCHOLARLY ARTICLES (1996).